RICHARD **GROSS**

THEMES, ISSUES AND DEBATES
IN PSYCHOLOGY

RICHARD GROSS

THEMES, ISSUES AND DEBATES
IN PSYCHOLOGY
THIRD EDITION

HODDER
EDUCATION
PART OF HACHETTE UK

Orders: please contact Bookpoint Ltd, 130 Milton Park, Abingdon, Oxon OX14 4SB.
Telephone: (44) 01235 827720. Fax: (44) 01235 400454.
Lines are open from 9.00–5.00, Monday to Saturday, with a 24-hour message answering service.
You can also order through our website www.hoddereducation.co.uk.

British Library Cataloguing in Publication Data
A catalogue record for this title is available from the British Library.

ISBN: 978 0340 97587 9

First Published 2009
Impression number   10 9 8 7 6 5 4 3 2 1
Year   2012 2011 2010 2009

Hachette UK's policy is to use papers that are natural, renewable and recyclable products and made from wood grown in sustainable forests. The logging and manufacturing processes are expected to conform to the environmental regulations of the country of origin.

Cover illustration © Antar Daval/Illustration Works/Getty Images
Typeset by Servis Filmsetting Ltd, Stockport, Cheshire.

Printed in Malta for Hodder Education, an Hachette UK Company, 338 Euston Road, London NW1 3BH

DEDICATION

To Jan, who gives meaning to the madness.

CONTENTS

PICTURE CREDITS

The author and publishers would like to thank the following for permission to reproduce material in this book:

Figure 1.4 Adrian Arbib/CORBIS; Figure 2.1 Bettmann/CORBIS; Figure 2.2 AP/PA Photos; Figure 3.4a Andrew Brookes/CORBIS; Figure 3.4b Phil Schermeister/CORBIS; Figure 3.6 Oxford Scientific Films/ Photolibrary.com; Figure 3.7 Cengage Learning/Nelson Education; Figure 4.2 Permission of Philip Zimbardo, Inc.; Figure 4.2b Ronnie Kaufman/CORBIS; Figure 5.2 Wadsworth, a part of Cengage Learning, Inc. Reproduced with permission. www.cengage.com/permissions; Figure 5.6 Wellcome Photo Library; Figure 5.9 akg-images; Figure 6.1a Wellesley College Archives; Figure 6.1b Archives for the History of American Psychology, University of Akron; Figure 6.2 CARL DE SOUZA/AFP/Getty Images; Figure 6.3 The Creation of Adam and Eve from a Book of Hours (vellum), Brailes, William de (fl.c.1230)/Musée Marmottan, Paris, France, Giraudon/The Bridgeman Art Library; Figure 6.6 Courtesy of Cowan Kemsley Taylor, Art Director: Max Clemens & Copywriter: Alan Moseley; Figure 7.5 Mary Evans Picture Library; Figure 8.1 Geray Sweeney/ CORBIS; Figure 8.3 1993 Wadsworth, a part of Cengage Learning, Inc. Reproduced by permission. www. cengage.com/permissions; Figure 8.4 Thomas Hartwell/CORBIS; Figure 9.3 Mary Evans Picture Library; Figure 10.2 Science Museum Library/ Science and Society Picture Library; Figure 11.2 akg-images; Figure 11.3 John Springer Collection/CORBIS; Figure 11.5 akg-images; Figure 12.1 Museum Boijmans Van Beuningen © ADAGP, Paris and DACS, London 2008; Figure 12.2 Tate, London 2008 © ADAGP, Paris and DACS, London 2008; Figure 12.3 Laura Dwight/CORBIS; Figure 13.1 Mary Evans Picture Library 2008; Figure 13.3 Jeremy Walker/Science Photo Library; Figure 14.7 akg-images

Every effort has been made to obtain necessary permission with reference to copyright material. The publishers apologise if inadvertently any sources remain unacknowledged and will be glad to make the necessary arrangements at the earliest opportunity.

INTRODUCTION

Themes, Issues and Debates in Psychology was originally published in 1995, with a second edition appearing in 2003. Five years on, the basic themes, issues and debates discussed in those first two editions seem to have remained essentially the same. Very few books that I am aware of adopt a thematic approach as opposed to the traditional topic-based approach; the former allows the author (and reader) to draw from several areas of psychology (such as social, cognitive, individual differences, developmental and physiological), as well as the more philosophical, theoretical and critical aspects of the discipline. This is relevant to both the synoptic element of A2 specifications and undergraduate courses.

This edition removes two chapters from the previous edition: one on attribution and one on attachment and separation through the life cycle. I felt, with hindsight, that these weren't sufficiently deserving of the description 'theme, issue or debate' (despite being extremely relevant and interesting topics). The major addition is a chapter on positive psychology, one of the most recent areas of research to have appeared in psychology; its concern with some of the fundamental questions we ask about ourselves seems to justify its inclusion as a genuine theme and/or issue and/or debate.

Other changes include the updating, rewording and reorganizing of existing material; this is limited in some chapters but quite extensive in others. For example, there are expanded sections on certain aspects of ethics, consciousness and free will. The fairly full end-of-chapter summaries, web addresses and recommended further reading are all retained, as are the boxes and figures within the text.

In my 30-plus years of teaching psychology on a variety of courses, and giving talks at student and teacher conferences, I have come to regard the traditional carving-up of the discipline into distinct sections/topics/ areas as artificial – almost a distortion of what psychology 'really is'. This has led me to favour the thematic approach: if we can find links and connections between topics and areas of research that are 'officially' separate and distinct, then the mass of material that students always complain about (with good reason) may seem less daunting. Equally important, since ethical, methodological, and gender- and culture-related issues are always relevant when 'evaluating' 'discussing' or 'critically considering' any area of research, thinking about these issues should help students write better essays, seminar papers and practical reports.

In adopting a thematic approach, I am assuming that my reader has at least some degree of familiarity with the concepts, ideas, theories and research studies used to illustrate a particular theme, issue or debate (although sometimes I have chosen to describe these in some detail). For this reason, Themes, Issues and Debates is meant to complement other textbooks, which you will need to provide the basic material in sufficient detail. The topic-based approach of most textbooks and the thematic approach of this one can sit side-by-side quite happily at various points in your course. Themes, Issues and Debates isn't designed to be used after you have absorbed all the information from the main textbook(s), but rather as a way of synthesizing and integrating, as well as revising, (some of) that information as you go along.

ACKNOWLEDGEMENTS

I would like to thank Lynn Brown (again) for her highly efficient copy-editing of the manuscript, and Kevin Doherty for his expert proof-reading. Any remaining errors are, as ever, mine. Thanks too to Stephanie Matthews for her very efficient management of the whole project. Special thanks to Alex Linley and Todd Kashdan for their feedback on an early draft of the positive psychology chapter, as well as their generous and invaluable provision of research articles; between them they helped me to find my way along a road I'd not previously travelled. I'd also like to thank Hugh Coolican for his very useful comments and suggestions regarding the new edition.

CHAPTER 1

THE PERSON AS PSYCHOLOGIST

INTRODUCTION

As an alternative to the customary definition of psychology as the scientific study of behaviour and mental processes, I would like to propose that a more useful way of thinking about the discipline of psychology is to see it as part of the sum total of what people do. Like other scientific disciplines, *psychology is a human activity*, albeit a rather special one, as we will see.

Similarly, psychologists (also like other scientists) are, first and foremost, people – they are people long before they become psychologists, and being a psychologist is only a part of their total activity as a person. It follows from this that to properly understand what psychology is, and how it has changed during its history, as well as its achievements and limitations, we need to understand (among other things) *psychologists as people*.

However (you are probably saying to yourself), this is precisely what psychologists do – how can we understand psychologists as people before we have looked at what psychologists say about people (as people)? We seem to be facing a conundrum: are psychologists in some sense studying themselves? Exactly! One of the things that makes psychology unique as a scientific activity is that the investigator and the subject matter are, in all essential details, *the same*. Instead of having physicists studying gravity or light (which are definitely not human), or astronomers studying the stars and solar system (which are also definitely not human), we have a small number of human beings (psychologists) studying a much larger number of human beings (people) – but apart from these labels, there is no difference (that is, they are all 'people').

If that is so, surely we could learn something about psychologists as people by turning things around and looking at *people as psychologists*. In other words, if we want to understand psychologists as people before we can properly appreciate what they do as scientists, why not begin by looking for ways in which *we are all scientists*, as part of our everyday social activity? This way of looking at 'ordinary' people (non-psychologists or lay people) is one that psychologists themselves have found useful. Two research areas in which this model of ordinary people is made quite explicit are (i) that part of social psychology concerned with how we form impressions of other people's personality and how we explain the causes of their (and our own) behaviour (*person/social perception*), and (ii) that part of individual differences concerned with personality – specifically, Kelly's *personal construct theory*.

THE LAY PERSON AS PSYCHOLOGIST: PEOPLE AS EVERYDAY SCIENTISTS

According to Gahagan (1984):

> *It has at times been observed that had the physical sciences not been developed to their contemporary level the world would be a very different place, one in which we would have very*

little control over communications, disease, food production, and so forth. If, however, psychology as a scientific activity had not emerged, less difference between the contemporary world and the past would be detectable.

This is not meant as a criticism of psychology, but rather as a way of drawing attention to the fundamental point that:

. . . human beings have the capacity to reflect on their own behaviour and reflect on its causes; the human being is essentially a psychologist and always has been.

(Gahagan, 1984)

To the extent that we, as ordinary people, can already do the kinds of things that psychologists, as scientists, are trying to do (that is, reflect on the causes of behaviour), we are bound to be less affected than we are by other sciences which, by definition, are the domain of people with special training and expertise. This is not to say, however, that the science of Psychology (with a capital 'P') has no influence on human psychology (with a small 'p'). Indeed, Richards (2002) and others argue that Psychology can actually change its subject matter (psychology) unlike any other scientific discipline (see Chapter 10). These two claims – that people are already psychologists and that Psychology changes people's psychology – are not, however, contradictory; rather, they are two sides of the same coin.

The examples Gahagan gives of how science has changed the world are all *applications* of scientific knowledge (technological aspects of science). Equivalent 'technologies' can be found within psychology. Clinical psychology, for example, is aimed at helping people to change their behaviour when this is considered to be 'abnormal' in some way (see Chapters 7 and 9). However, the kinds of changes that Richards is talking about are not applications of psychological theory and research. Psychology has the potential for influencing how we 'do' psychology in our everyday lives – that is, the way we think about ourselves and others, the kinds of explanations we provide of behaviour, the theories we construct about 'what makes people tick'.

Gahagan claims that 'the infant science of psychology . . . has as yet had little effect on the existing heritage of lay people's psychology'. This is because of what we have said about people already being psychologists. She is also implying, however, that, given time, lay people's psychology (or common-sense psychology) will change. Richards (and others) believe that this has already happened (see Chapter 10).

COMMON-SENSE PSYCHOLOGY: LOOKING FOR HIDDEN CAUSES OF BEHAVIOUR

Fritz Heider, a European who emigrated to the USA, was greatly influenced by Gestalt psychology (see Gross, 2005). He wanted to apply this theory of object perception to the perception of people (*social or person perception*). The publication of his book *The Psychology of Interpersonal Relations* (1958) marked a new era in social psychology (Leyens and Codol, 1988). For Heider, the starting point for studying how people understand their social world is 'ordinary' people:

● How do people usually think about and infer meaning from what goes on around them?
● How do they make sense of their own and other people's behaviour?

These questions relate to what Heider called *common-sense psychology*. He saw the 'ordinary' person (the 'person in the street') as a naïve scientist, linking observable behaviour to unobservable causes (much as the professional scientist does):

The causal structure of the environment, both as the scientist describes it and as the naïve person apprehends it, is such that we are usually in contact only with what may be called the offshoots or manifestations of underlying core processes or core structures . . . Man is usually not content simply to register the observables that surround him . . . The underlying causes of events, especially the motives of other persons, are invariances of the environment that are relevant to him; they give meaning to what he experiences and it is these meanings that are recorded in his life space and are precipitated as the reality of the environment to which he then reacts.

(Heider, 1958)

So, a fundamental feature of common-sense psychology is the belief that underlying people's overt behaviour are causes, and it is these causes, rather than the observable behaviour itself, that provide the meaning of what people do. Such basic assumptions about behaviour need to be shared by members of a culture, for without them social interaction would be chaotic. Indeed, common-sense psychology can be thought of as part of the belief system that forms part of the culture as a whole, and that distinguishes one culture from another. According to Bennett (1993):

What interested him [Heider] was the fact that within our culture we all subscribe to essentially the same version of everyday psychology – for example, that human behaviour often reflects inner determinants such as abilities, wants, emotions, personalities, etc., rather than, say, witchcraft or the spirit forces of our ancestors . . . Of course, it is important that we do subscribe to a common psychology, since doing this provides an orientating context in which we can understand, and be understood by, others. Imagine a world in which your version of everyday psychology was fundamentally at odds with that of your friends – without a shared 'code' for making sense of behaviour, social life would hardly be possible . . .

Of course, common-sense psychology (at least that shared by members of western cultures) does not involve the belief that internal, unobservable causes are the *only* causes of behaviour. In fact, Heider identified two basic potential sources or causes of behaviour, namely *personal* or *dispositional* (internal) and *situational* or *environmental* (external). This distinction lies at the heart of *attribution theory*, which deals with the general principles that govern how the social perceiver selects and uses information to arrive at causal explanations (Fiske and Taylor, 1991). In other words, one of the major 'tasks' we all face in our daily interactions with others is deciding whether their behaviour can be explained in terms of internal causes (such as abilities, emotions, personality, motivation and attitudes) or external causes (such as the behaviour of other people, the demands of the situation, and aspects of the physical environment). This decision is the *attribution process* and it is what theories of attribution try to explain.

Understanding which set of factors should be used to interpret another person's behaviour will make the perceiver's world more predictable and give him/her greater control over it. Heider's basic insights provided the blueprint for the theories of attribution that followed (Hewstone and Antaki, 1988: see Gross, 2005).

According to Antaki (1984), attribution theory promises to:

. . . uncover the way in which we, as ordinary men and women, act as scientists in tracking down the causes of behaviour; it promises to treat ordinary people, in fact, as if they were psychologists.

So, if we are all already psychologists, it is not surprising that the science of Psychology should have had as little impact as Gahagan, for one, thinks it has. There already exists a body of 'knowledge' (a set of beliefs and assumptions) that we all use for interpreting and predicting people's behaviour (common-sense or *folk* psychology). This is part of our culture and so is highly resistant to change and is deeply ingrained in our everyday social interactions.

However, are there psychological theories that have proved so powerful that they have become absorbed by the culture and so have become part of common-sense psychology? By becoming absorbed into the culture, they may have become detached from the identity of the psychologist(s) responsible for them, becoming part of what we take for granted about human beings. Popular beliefs, such as 'gay men, as children, have had too close a relationship with their mother', 'the child's early years are critical' and 'boys need a father' can all be traced, more or less directly (and more or less accurately), to Freud's psychoanalytic theory. It is not the (objective) truth or otherwise of these claims that matters here but the impact they have had on the thinking and experience of ordinary people (see Chapters 10 and 14).

There is no doubting the tremendous impact Freud has had, both on Psychology and psychology. According to Clift (1984):

> He [Freud] has provided us with a set of ideas and concepts which, both in literature and everyday conversation, have helped us to formulate questions about ourselves, our inner experience and our social conditioning. He helped to explode the myth of 'rational Man' and has brought us face to face with our irrational selves, a new image of ourselves at least as valid as any other major image-of-man that Social Science has offered and perhaps as challenging and disturbing as any it is ever likely to offer.

Similarly, Thomas (1990) argues that:

> Sigmund Freud is probably the most famous of all psychologists . . . His ideas and development of them by other people have influenced our conception of morality, family life and childhood and thus perhaps the structure of our society. And they have changed our attitudes to mental illness. Freudian assumptions are now part of the fabric of literature and the arts.

The conceptual tools of the everyday psychologist

In making sense of human action, the everyday ('amateur') psychologist draws upon a considerable range of constructs and conceptual 'tools', which fall into two broad categories:

1 *psychological* (or *mentalistic*) – these are properties of the individual (desires, emotions, personality and other internal sources)
2 *social* – these are properties of the group(s) and society we belong to (rules, norms, roles and other external sources).

Everyday mentalistic psychology

According to Wellman (1990), two vital constructs lie at the heart of everyday thinking about action: desire and belief. What people do results from their believing that certain actions will bring about ends they desire. Almost every time we ask someone why they did something, we will be trying to find out about their desire or belief – or both.

In everyday psychology, these are accepted as the causes of what we do: 'Beliefs and desires provide . . . the internal mental causes for overt actions' (Wellman, 1990). However, the everyday psychologist also has some idea ('theory') about what causes desires and beliefs. Specifically, beliefs arise from perception, while desires result from basic emotions and physiological causes. Also, action is seen as producing certain reactions, typically *emotional* ones. Other people's emotions provide important cues about how to behave towards them (for example, try to comfort them, or steer clear of them), as well as insights into the strengths of their desires and beliefs.

Although emotion is clearly a basic construct of everyday psychology, it's not all there is in the lay person's conceptual 'tool bag'. Other key 'tools' – and perhaps the most important of all – are *thinking* and *intention*.

● *Thinking* is an active process, in which the mind is engaged in a variety of directive processes, such as attention, interpretation, and storing information and recalling it. This means that beliefs, for example,

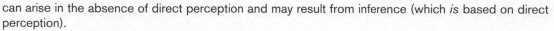

can arise in the absence of direct perception and may result from inference (which *is* based on direct perception).

● *Intentions* mediate between desire and action. They 'function to actualize (some but not all) desires', that is, they translate our wants into strategic courses of action that will help us to satisfy those wants. This translation involves planning and other cognitive activity and information processing.

However, everyday psychology also involves trying to understand recurrent patterns of behaviour (as opposed to one-off, specific acts). For this purpose, we commonly identify personality traits to explain and predict people's behaviour, and once we have, we are in a better position to predict all kinds of desires and beliefs the person might have. Particular actions can now be seen in a broader, more coherent, psychological context.

Everyday social psychology

This is usually more implicit than the mentalistic counterpart, and Wellman has much less to say about it. As most social psychologists would agree, action is to a considerable degree constrained by forces outside the individual, such as norms and conventions (see Chapter 4). According to Wegner and Vallacher (1977, in Bennett, 1993), people are 'implicit situation theorists' who subscribe to 'a set of expectations concerning the rules of behaviour in various settings'. Expectations also apply to the behaviours of people occupying particular *social roles* in particular situations. Everyday social psychology also includes our understanding of *event episodes*, which are *scripted* episodes – 'a predetermined stereotyped sequence of actions' (Schank and Abelson, 1977) – such as eating at a restaurant. Wellman's account of everyday psychology is summarized in Figure 1.1.

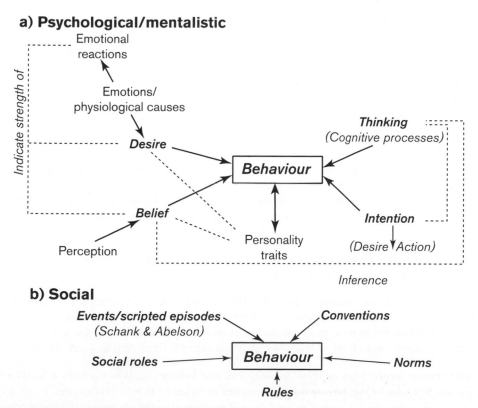

Figure 1.1 A schematized summary of Wellman's (1990) everyday psychology

Implicit and explicit theories: some similarities between formal and informal psychology

Ordinary people's assumption that behaviour is caused by either internal or external factors, combined with the attribution process, is part of the way in which we form impressions of others. Only if we attribute internal causes can we take the behaviour to indicate what the person is like; external causes, by definition, refer to influences on behaviour distinct from the actor him/herself. However, there is much more involved in forming impressions of others than simply attributing causes. As Gahagan (1984) says:

> When we form impressions of others we are making guesses or inferences based both on whatever selection of data, derived from our observations of them, is at hand and the theories that we already have about them. The study of person perception is the study of how the lay person uses theory and data in understanding other people.

Forming impressions

The kinds of theories the lay person uses when forming impressions of others are referred to as *intuitive theories* (see, for example, Nisbett and Ross, 1980) or *implicit personality theories* (IPTs). The most extensively investigated (and, arguably, the most important) examples are *stereotypes* and the related process of *stereotyping*, which Oakes *et al.* (1994) define as 'the process of ascribing characteristics to people on the basis of their group memberships'.

BOX 1.1 AN EXAMPLE OF STEREOTYPING

We observe a man wearing a grey, pinstripe suit and carrying a copy of the *Financial Times* and a briefcase (the data), label him as a 'businessman', and then infer that, like other businessmen, he votes Conservative (the theory). We already have an implicit theory of businessmen, a generalized belief about the characteristics shared by this particular group of human beings. So, when we observe a member of this group, without knowing anything at all about him as an individual, we immediately 'know' what he's like. The very limited data are supplemented by the theory, which then allows us to predict what this complete stranger is likely to think and believe, what his values are, and so on. (Here, 'voting Conservative' is shorthand for a long list of values, attitudes and beliefs, and so constitutes a stereotype in its own right.)

Being able to make such predictions based on such limited information gives us a sense of being in control, even if they are not actually put to the test (or even if they are not confirmed if they are). As a kind of *person schema*, stereotypes illustrate the general cognitive tendency to store knowledge and experience in the form of simplified, generalized representations. (Imagine what it would be like if we had to store details of each individual chair, cat or person we encounter!) As Atkinson *et al.* (1990) say:

> Without schemata and schematic processing, we would simply be overwhelmed by the information that inundates us. We would be very poor information processors.

The importance of schemas (or schemata) and other IPTs lies not in their accuracy but in their capacity for making the world a more manageable place in which to live. If psychologists are to understand human behaviour, they must look not at how good people are at explaining and predicting the world (especially the world of human behaviour) but rather at *how they go about doing it*. According to Asch (1952):

> We act and choose on the basis of what we see, feel, and believe . . . When we are mistaken about things, we act in terms of our erroneous notions, not in terms of things as they are. To understand human action it is therefore essential to understand the conscious mode in which things appear to us.

An early advocate of the view that it is essential to understand people's constructions of the world was Schutz (1932, in Bennett, 1993), a sociologist, according to whom:

> All our knowledge . . . in common-sense as in scientific thinking, involves constructions . . . strictly speaking, there are no such things as facts, pure and simple. All facts are from the outset facts selected from a universal context by the activities of our minds . . . This does not mean that, in daily life or in science, we are unable to grasp the reality of the world. It just means that we grasp merely certain aspects of it, namely those which are relevant to us.

This highlights the 'conceptually driven' nature of our everyday understanding; it is guided not by the intrinsic properties of the world, but by our prior ideas and beliefs about it. The data provided by the external environment are still relevant (as the example of the businessman illustrates), but these are 'filtered' through our schemas and implicit theories, so that we are incapable of seeing things 'as they really are' (see Chapters 10 and 14).

What does this mean for science?

If we accept this constructionist argument, then it is not surprising that people disagree about 'the way the world is' in their everyday dealings with each other. When applied to science, the constructionist viewpoint raises some very important – and awkward – questions regarding the nature of scientific activity and the status of scientific knowledge.

The *positivist* view of science maintains that the distinguishing characteristic of science is its *objectivity*. The scientist, equipped with appropriate empirical methods, has access to the world 'as it really is', which assumes that the observations, measurements, experiments and so on s/he performs are unbiased, and that data can be collected without any kind of preconception or expectation influencing their collection.

However, by analogy with the lay person's use of theory and data to understand other people, the scientist (including the scientific psychologist) also collects data through the 'lens' of theory; there is simply no way of avoiding it. According to Popper (1972), observation is always pre-structured and directed, and this is as true of physics as it is of psychology. Similarly, Deese (1972) argues that, despite the reliance of science on observation, data play a more modest role than is usually believed. The function of empirical observation is not to find out what causes what, or how things work in some ultimate sense, but simply to provide justification for some particular way of looking at the world. In other words, observation justifies (or not) a theory the scientist already holds (just as the everyday psychologist already has stereotypes of particular social groups), and theories determine what kinds of data are collected in the first place.

The interdependence between theory and data is shown in Deese's belief that (i) theory in the absence of data is not science, and (ii) data alone do not make a science. Both theory and data are necessary for science, and so-called facts do not exist independently of a theoretical interpretation of the data:

> *Fact = Data + Theory*

Are intuitive/implicit theories real theories?

Wellman (1990) identifies three essential features of a theory:

1 *coherence* – the different concepts that make up the theory should be interconnected, making it impossible to consider a single concept in isolation; in other words, the meaning of any given concept is determined by its role in the theory as a whole
2 *ontological distinctions* – it 'carves up' phenomena into different kinds of entities and processes, making fundamental distinctions between different classes of things
3 *causal explanatory framework* – it accounts for the phenomena it deals with by identifying their causes.

Wellman believes that in terms of these three criteria, everyday psychology can reasonably be considered to constitute a theory.

Implicit and explicit theories: some differences between formal and informal psychology

Even if we agree with Wellman that the everyday psychologist's implicit theories share certain features with scientific theories, it is difficult to deny that the scope of implicit theories is nothing like as broad as that of scientific/academic psychology (Bennett, 1993). There are other important differences as well.

The meaning of 'implicit' and 'explicit'

The lay person may be only dimly aware, or completely unaware, of the reasoning s/he has followed when making inferences about others, and this reasoning may change from situation to situation. They draw on their theories in an unselfconscious way. This is part of what 'implicit' conveys.

By definition, the scientist must be able to show how his/her theory was developed and hypotheses derived. They use their theories *as theories*. So, while lay people might use constructs about what causes people to act as they do (the *attribution process*), a scientific psychologist produces constructs about constructs – that is, an explanation of everyday explanation (a 'second level' explanation, such as *theories of attribution*). This is what 'explicit' conveys.

Applying scientific method

Scientists are obliged to follow scientific method, a set of rules governing the use of theory. These include *falsifiability* – being able to show that the theory is false, rather than merely finding data to support it (i.e. *verification*; see Popper, 1959). Everyday psychologists, of course, are not obliged to follow the rules of scientific method and tend to look for evidence that supports their position.

The purpose of psychological theories

The psychologist as scientist is trying to construct scientific laws of human behaviour and cognitive processes (or, at least, establish general principles), often for their own sake. The lay person, however, is using theories as 'guidelines for their everyday transactions with others' (Gahagan, 1991). For example, whereas you or I might avoid someone who looks very aggressive or whom we believe to be short-tempered, the psychologist studying aggression may be interested in finding out what cues people use to judge others as aggressive, or why some people are actually more aggressive than others. In other words, the lay person's intuitive/implicit theories serve a *practical/pragmatic* purpose. They:

> . . . guide his daily behaviour, and make the behaviour of others appear more intelligible and predictable than it would otherwise. We have to make sense of others' behaviour in order to act at all ourselves.
>
> (Gahagan, 1984)

Berger and Luckmann (1966) talk about 'recipe knowledge', knowledge that gets results, as the primary purpose of lay theories. Scientists, though, are interested in '*truth*' (rather than usefulness); they want to construct as full an account as possible of the structures, processes and contents associated with a particular phenomenon.

The relationship between formal and informal psychology

Professionals and ordinary people have in common the task of trying to understand other people's motives and their personalities. The professional 'spies' on the lay person as s/he undertakes the task of 'being' a psychologist. Since 'person perception' is the term given by professional psychologists to the study of the lay person as psychologist, this represents the convergence of professional and lay, formal and informal psychology (Gahagan, 1991).

According to Harré *et al*. (1985):

> *The task of scientific psychology consists of making the implicit psychologies of everyday life explicit, and then, in the light of that understanding, applying the techniques of theory-guided empirical research to develop, refine, and extend that body of knowledge and practices.*

Harré *et al*. cite Freud's theory of dreams as an obvious extension of our common-sense or folk beliefs about the source of dream contents. Common sense forms 'part of the literature' – that is, a proper part of the body of knowledge available in the science of psychology. Agreeing with Heider, Harré *et al*. say that common sense is the platform from which the enterprise of psychology must start.

MAN-THE-SCIENTIST: KELLY'S PSYCHOLOGY OF PERSONAL CONSTRUCTS

Three years before the publication of Heider's book in which he proposed the notions of common-sense psychology and the naïve scientist, George Kelly published a book called *A Theory of Personality: The Psychology of Personal Constructs* (1955).

According to Kelly, not only are scientists human but humans can also be thought of as scientists. *Personal construct theory* (PCT) is a theory about the personal theories of each one of us, and one of its distinctive features is that it applies as much to Kelly himself (as the originator of the theory) as to everyone else. If science is first and foremost a human activity, a form of behaviour, then any valid psychological theory must be able to account for that activity or behaviour; this, of course, includes the construction of psychological theories (in the case of scientific psychology). PCT can do this quite easily (not true of most psychological theories) and so is said to display *reflexivity*.

According to Weiner (1992):

> *It is puzzling that while psychologists try to explain the behaviour of their clients, or people in general, the theories they have formulated cannot account for their own scientific activity.*

However:

> *Kelly's theory . . . can explain scientific endeavours, for Kelly considered the average person an intuitive scientist, having the goal of predicting and understanding behaviour. To accomplish this aim, the naive person formulates hypotheses about the world and the self, collects data that confirm or disconfirm these hypotheses, and then alters personal theories to account for the new data. Hence, the average person operates in the same manner as the professional scientist, although the professional scientist may be more accurate and more self-conscious in their attempts to achieve cognitive clarity and understanding.*
>
> *(Weiner, 1992)*

Our hypotheses about the world take the form of *constructs*. These represent our attempt to interpret events (including the behaviour of ourselves and others) and they are put to the test every time we act. Kelly was originally trained in physics and mathematics, and he worked for a time as an engineer. Not surprisingly, perhaps, he chose the model of *man-the-scientist*. He wondered why it was that only those with university degrees should be privileged to feel the excitement and reap the rewards of scientific activity (Fransella, 1980):

When we speak of man-the-scientist we are speaking of all mankind and not merely a particular class of men who have publicly attained the stature of 'scientists'. We are speaking of all mankind in its scientist-like aspects.

(Kelly, 1955)

This model of human beings not only seems intuitively valid (people really are as the model describes them), but it has quite fundamental implications for how we make sense of (construe) what is going on in psychological research and how it needs to be conducted if anything meaningful is to come out of it. In Kelly's own words:

It is customary to say that the scientist's ultimate aim is to predict and control. This is a summary statement that psychologists frequently like to quote in characterizing their own aspirations. Yet, curiously enough, psychologists rarely credit the human subjects in their experiments with having similar aspirations. It is as though the psychologist were saying to himself, 'I, being a psychologist, and therefore a scientist, am performing this experiment in order to improve the prediction and control of certain human phenomena; but my subject, being merely a human organism, is obviously propelled by inexorable drives welling up within him, or else he is in gluttonous pursuit of sustenance and shelter.'

In other words, in their role as scientists, psychologists perceive people as something less than whole persons, certainly as something very different from themselves. People are 'reduced' to the status of subject, implying that the psychologist is in control and dictates what will happen in the experimental situation, while the other merely responds to events in a passive and unthinking way. Not only is the term dehumanizing (Heather, 1976; see also Chapter 9), but there is a fundamental methodological issue involved.

Another psychologist who (implicitly) regards people as intuitive scientists is Orne (1962), who introduced the term *demand characteristics* to refer to all the cues that convey to the 'subject' the experimental hypothesis (and, hence, represent important influences on his/her behaviour).The mere fact that experimental psychologists do all they can to conceal from their subjects the true purpose of an experiment (and thus prevent them from, consciously or unconsciously, complying with it) suggests that the former believe that the latter, like themselves, 'search for meaning in their environment, formulate hypotheses, and act on the basis of these belief systems' (Weiner, 1992). If ordinary people did not engage in essentially the same kind of intellectual activities as scientists, it would not be necessary to use the often elaborate controls and deceptions that are an almost inevitable feature of traditional experimental research (see Chapter 10).

How, though, can people be both 'subjects' (very different from the psychologist) and, at the same time, capable of figuring out (or at least puzzling about) what is going on in the mind of the psychologist (much as the psychologist is doing in his/her role as scientist)? Using Kelly's concept of constructs, 'we might see the subject as one who is desperately trying to construe the construction processes of the psychologist' (Fransella, 1980). From this perspective, the term 'subject' is inappropriate: not only are ordinary people scientists, but psychologists can only hope to understand and predict others' behaviour to the extent they are aware of the constructs those others place upon events. Some behaviour might appear extraordinary to the observer but be totally meaningful in the context of the actor's own world view. As Fransella (1980) says: 'To understand the behaviour of others, we have to know what construct predictions are being put to the test.'

As a consequence of the 'human-as-scientist' model, the psychologist and the client ('subject') are now equal partners; the former is no longer of higher status and 'in charge' (Weiner, 1992). According to Bannister and Fransella (1980):

Construct theory sees each man as trying to make sense out of himself and his world. It sees psychology as a meta-discipline, an attempt to make sense out of the ways in which men make sense out of their worlds. This not only puts the psychologist in the same interpretive business as his so-called subject – it makes them partners in the business, for on no other basis can one man understand another.

If 'subject' reduces the person to something less than a whole person, for PCT the person is the irreducible unit:

Traditional psychology is not, in the main, about persons. By making the person the central subject matter of psychology, construct theory changes the boundaries and the content of the existing science.

(Bannister and Fransella, 1980)

Research within a PCT framework would look very different from its conventional, 'mainstream' form. It would be about 'the process whereby people come to make sense of things' and would involve working *with* and *not on* subjects. The researcher's constructions would be made explicit and the results obtained:

. . . will be seen as less important, in the end, than the whole progress of the research itself – which, after all, represents one version of the process it is investigating. The crucial question, about any research project, would then be how far, as a process, it illuminated our understanding of the whole human endeavour to make sense of our lives, and how fruitful it proved in suggesting new explanatory ventures.

(Salmon, 1978, in Bannister and Fransella, 1980)

These views regarding the nature of psychological research are echoed in feminist psychology (see Chapter 6) and in collaborative/new paradigm research (see Chapter 10).

HOMO PSYCHOLOGICUS: HUMAN BEINGS AS NATURAL PSYCHOLOGISTS

According to Humphrey (1986):

The minds of human beings are part of nature. We should ask: What are minds for? Why have they evolved in this way rather than another? Why have they evolved at all, instead of remaining quite unchanged?

Language, creativity and self-awareness are unique to human beings (although many would challenge this; see, for example, Gross, 2005) and human societies are infinitely richer, more stable and more psychologically demanding than anything that exists elsewhere in nature. Nowhere on earth, though, can human beings survive outside society. Consequently, nowhere on earth can we survive without a deep sensitivity to, and understanding of, our fellow creatures. Humphrey asks:

Did people . . . then evolve to be psychologists by nature? Is that what makes our families and commitments work? Has that been the prime mover behind the evolution of our brains and our intelligence? If so, it would mean that almost all the earlier theories of human evolution had got it upside down. Fifteen years ago, nothing in the textbooks about evolution referred to man's need to do psychology: the talk was all of tool-making, spear-throwing and fire-lighting – practical rather than social intelligence.

It has been argued that the mark of the first man-like ape was the ability to walk on his hind legs, to eat and digest a wide range of grassland food, and to relate his fingers to his thumb. However, according to Humphrey, as important as these were:

Not fingers to thumb, but person to person. The real mark of a man-like ape would have been his ability to manipulate and relate himself – in human ways – to the other apes around him.

Humphrey argues that there is sufficient archaeological evidence to suggest that by two million years ago the fundamental pattern of human social living had already been established. While the Kalahari bushmen may be biologically modern, in many respects their lifestyle has not changed in the last million years. By observing them, we can still see just how far the success of a hunter-gatherer community depends on the psychological skills of its individual members. Their social system works, but only because they, like all human beings,

. . . are . . . supremely good at understanding one another. They come of a long, long line of natural psychologists whose brains and minds have been slowly shaped by evolution . . . Small wonder human beings have evolved to be such remarkable psychological survivors, when for the last six million years their heavy task has been to read the minds of other human beings.

Figure 1.2 Self-awareness/consciousness and the ability to understand and predict the behaviour and responses of others may be the essential characteristics of human beings which make them distinctive from all other species

But how do we do it? Essentially, as intelligent social beings we use knowledge of our own thoughts and feelings (through 'introspection': see Chapter 10) as a guide for understanding how others are likely to think and feel and, therefore, behave. Humphrey goes even further and claims that we are conscious (that is, we have self-awareness) *because* this is so useful to us in this process of understanding others and thus having a successful social existence. Consciousness is a biological adaptation, which has evolved to enable us to perform this introspective psychology.

Consistent with Humphrey's discussion of the evolution of human beings as nature's psychologists (*phylogenesis*) is the recent interest among developmental psychologists in how an understanding of other people's minds develops in the individual child (*ontogenesis*). This capacity appears, on average, between the ages of three and four, and is called the child's 'theory of mind' (see Gross, 2005, 2008). Humphrey's theory of consciousness is discussed further in Chapter 12.

CONCLUSION

To begin a book on psychology by looking at people as psychologists seems, in many ways, the only logical way to start. Since most of us are, by definition, neither professional psychologists nor any other kind of 'literal' scientist, the person-as-psychologist is a metaphor: let's 'pretend' that everyone is a psychologist/scientist and see where that takes us in understanding ourselves.

Compared with other metaphors (such as people-as-information-processors: see Chapter 14), it feels intuitively 'right'. After all, science, including psychology, is done by people, scientists are people, and, as far as we know, science is a uniquely human behaviour. By contrast, information-processing machines are designed *by* people, and it seems odd to liken people to something they have designed. At the same time, this makes us unique among such machines, because we design machines as part of our scientific activity. We are organisms that 'do science', which also makes us unique within the biological world.

SUMMARY

○ Psychology is part of the sum total of what people do, a (rather special) human activity.

○ One of the things that makes psychology unique as a science is that the investigator and the subject matter are, essentially, the same.

○ A useful way of trying to understand 'ordinary' (lay) people is to regard them as psychologists/scientists, as in person perception. Ordinary people can already do the kinds of things that psychologists as scientists are trying to do (such as reflecting on the causes of behaviour).

○ Heider was interested in common-sense (or folk) psychology, i.e. how the lay person acts as a naïve scientist, by linking observable behaviour to unobservable causes. The causes of behaviour are what give meaning to what people do.

○ Social life requires that members of a particular culture share the same basic version of everyday psychology.

○ Heider distinguished between personal or dispositional (internal) and situational or environmental (external) causes, which is the central feature of attribution theory. Assigning internal or external causes to behaviour is called the attribution process.

○ Influential psychological theories, notably Freud's psychoanalytic theory, may become part of our taken-for-granted beliefs about the causes of behaviour.

○ According to Wellman, desire, belief, thinking and intention are key constructs involved in everyday mentalistic psychology.

○ Everyday social psychology refers to social norms, rules and conventions, and social roles, and also includes understanding of event/scripted episodes.

○ The lay person's theories are called intuitive/implicit personality theories, an important example being stereotypes (and the related process of stereotyping). Stereotypes are a kind of person schema.

○ Schemas and other implicit theories make the world more manageable, through making it more predictable; this is more important than their accuracy.

○ Many sociologists, psychologists and philosophers of science argue that our knowledge of the world is constructed by us; this challenges the positivist view of science, according to which science is objective.

○ Scientific observation is always pre-structured and directed; data are always collected in the light of a particular theory, and 'facts' do not exist independently of theory.

○ Scientists, but not everyday psychologists, are obliged to follow the rules of scientific method, including falsification (as opposed to mere verification); the former are also obliged to make them explicit.

○ Psychologists as scientists are trying to construct laws of behaviour/psychological processes as an end in itself, while the lay person's theories serve a practical/pragmatic purpose ('recipe knowledge').

○ According to Kelly's personal construct theory (PCT), people can be thought of as intuitive scientists (man-the-scientist), who use their personal constructs to make predictions about, and to explain, behaviour. To understand other people's behaviour, we must know what constructs they are putting to the test.

- In the experimental situation, subjects formulate hypotheses about the experimental hypothesis being tested; this relates to Orne's demand characteristics.

- In traditional psychology, the experimenter is of higher status and 'in charge', while within a PCT framework, research is a cooperative venture between 'equals'; the process of research is much more important than the results obtained.

- According to Humphrey, human beings have evolved as natural psychologists (*homo psychologicus*). What makes us distinctive as a species is our ability to read the minds of other human beings.

- Consciousness is a biological adaptation that has evolved to enable us to perform introspective psychology.

USEFUL WEBSITES

http://www.apa.org/
http://www.bps.org.uk
http://www.as.wvu.edu/~sbb/comm221/chapters/attrib.htm

RECOMMENDED READING

Bannister, D. and Fransella, F. (1980) *Inquiring Man* (2nd edn). Harmondsworth: Penguin.

Gross, R. (2008) *Key Studies in Psychology* (5th edn). London: Hodder Education. (Chapters 7 and 14.)

Heider, F. (1958) *The Psychology of Interpersonal Relations.* New York: Wiley.

Humphrey, N. (1986) *The Inner Eye.* London: Vintage. (Especially Chapter 2.)

Kelly, G.A. (1955) *A Theory of Personality: The Psychology of Personal Constructs.* New York: Norton.

Ross, L. and Nisbett, R.E. (1991) *The Person and the Situation: Perspectives of Social Psychology.* New York: McGraw-Hill. (Especially Chapter 3.)

Weiner, B. (1992) *Human Motivation: Metaphors, Theories and Research.* Newbury Park, CA: Sage. (Especially Chapters 6 and 7.)

CHAPTER 2

POSITIVE PSYCHOLOGY

WHAT IS POSITIVE PSYCHOLOGY?

In a word, positive psychology (PP) is about 'happiness' (Seligman, 2003). Seligman uses 'happiness' and 'well-being' interchangeably as '. . . soft, overarching terms to describe the goals of the whole positive psychology enterprise . . .' and points out that these words are sometimes used to refer to feelings (such as ecstasy and comfort) and sometimes to positive activities devoid of feelings (such as absorption and engagement).

PP can be defined as the scientific study of the positive aspects of human subjective experience, of positive individual traits, and of positive institutions. As such, it promises to:

> . . . *improve the quality of life and also to prevent the various pathologies that arise when life is barren and meaningless . . .*
>
> *(Seligman and Csikszentmihalyi, 2000)*

PP can be understood as a reaction against the almost exclusive emphasis by psychology on the negative side of human experience and behaviour, namely, mental illness. Seligman (2003) believes that for the second half of the twentieth century, psychology was largely dominated by this single topic. While psychologists can now measure with some precision such previously 'fuzzy' concepts as depression and alcoholism – and despite the fact that we know a fair amount about how these problems develop across the lifespan and about

---

BOX 2.1 SOME DEFINITIONS OF PP

- What is positive psychology? It is nothing more than the scientific study of ordinary human strengths and virtues. Positive psychology revisits 'the average person', with an interest in finding out what works, what is right, and what is improving . . . positive psychology is simply psychology. (Sheldon and King, 2001)
- Positive psychology is the study of the conditions and processes that contribute to the flourishing or optimal functioning of people, groups and institutions. (Gable and Haidt, 2005)
- Positive psychology is about scientifically informed perspectives on what makes life worth living. It focuses on aspects of the human condition that lead to happiness, fulfilment and flourishing. (*The Journal of Positive Psychology*, 2005, in Linley *et al.*, 2006)
- Positive psychology is the scientific study of optimal human functioning . . . it aims to redress the imbalance in psychological research and practice by calling attention to the positive aspects of human functioning and experience, and integrating them with our understanding of the negative aspects of human functioning and experience.

(Linley et al., *2006)*

their genetics, biochemistry and psychological causes, and, most significantly, how to relieve them – Seligman believes that this progress has come at a high cost:

> . . . *Relieving the states that make life miserable has relegated building the states that make life worth living to a distant back seat.*

It is interesting to note that today, when happiness seems to be the point both of life and government reports, depression is everywhere. The World Health Organization (WHO) predicts that by 2010 depression will have become the single largest public health problem after heart disease (Appignanesi, 2008).

A BRIEF HISTORY OF PP

PP as we know it can be traced back to Seligman's 1998 presidential address to the American Psychological Association (Seligman, 1999). He realized that psychology had largely neglected two of its three pre-Second World War aims, namely, (i) helping all people to lead more productive and fulfilling lives, and (ii) identifying and nurturing talent and giftedness. Following the end of the war, with the establishment of the US Veterans Administration (in 1946) and the US National Institute of Mental Health (in 1947), the third aim, curing mental illness, became the focus of psychology, as noted above. Psychology became a healing discipline, based on a disease model and illness ideology (Linley *et al.*, 2006).

The origins of PP

As with any movement, within psychology or any other discipline – scientific or non-scientific – PP did not suddenly appear out of nowhere. While it may be convenient to date PP from 1998/1999 (just as the 'birth' of psychology itself is taken to be 1879: see Chapter 10), it clearly did not 'begin' then. In fact, according to Linley *et al.* (2006):

> . . . *positive psychology has always been with us, but as a holistic and integrated body of knowledge, it has passed unrecognized and uncelebrated, and one of the major achievements of the positive psychology movement to date has been to consolidate, lift up, and celebrate what we do know about what makes life worth living . . .*

Research into what we now call PP has gone on for decades. In broad terms, PP has common interests with aspects of humanistic psychology, in particular the latter's emphasis on the fully functioning person (Rogers, 1951) and the study of healthy individuals (Maslow, 1968: see Chapter 14). More than 50 years ago, Maslow stated:

> *The science of psychology has been far more successful on the negative than on the positive side. It has revealed to us much about man's shortcomings, his illness, his sins, but little about his potentialities, his virtues, his achievable aspirations, or his full psychological height. It is as if psychology has voluntarily restricted itself to only half its rightful jurisdiction, and that, the darker, meaner half.*
>
> *(Maslow, 1954)*

Maslow even talked specifically about a positive psychology, that is, a more exclusive focus on people at the extremely positive ends of the distribution, rather than what is understood today by PP. Nevertheless, in a broad sense, there is a strong convergence between the interests of humanistic psychology and modern PP (Linley, 2008a).

PP, humanistic psychology and the medical model

Seligman *et al.* (2005) acknowledge that PP has built on the earlier work of Rogers and Maslow. This is quite a significant step, given the often contentious relationship between PP and humanistic psychology (Joseph and Linley, 2006). However, although it is true that Rogers and Maslow had visions similar to those of positive psychologists in terms of wanting to understand the full range of human experience – from negative to positive – their vision was more than just this. Rogers and Maslow were also vigorous critics of the medical model as applied to psychology, and it was their alternative view of human nature that made their positive psychology also a humanistic psychology (Joseph and Linley, 2006).

Rogers and Maslow recognized that psychology's adoption and application of the medical model to psychological problems might serve to help people in one sense, but that it also served to alienate and damage people in another. The medical model (then and now) pervades the way in which western culture views psychological issues; as such, it was implicitly taken for granted without being properly challenged. This made it difficult to recognize its potentially damaging effects.

Some positive psychologists are similarly critical of the medical model, but PP as a movement largely continues to operate within the medical model and so condones the 'medicalization' of human experience. For example, Seligman *et al.* (2005) suggest that:

> *positive interventions can supplement traditional interventions that relieve suffering and may someday be the practical legacy of positive psychology.*

According to Joseph and Linley (2006), this statement disguises the full vision of an applied PP. Some positive psychologists have previously rejected the *categorical approach* that is current within clinical psychology. (This is based on the psychiatric classification and diagnosis of psychopathology or psychological disorders, involving the application of a label, such as 'schizophrenia' or 'obsessive-compulsive disorder'. See Chapter 7.) Instead, these critics have argued for the *dimensional approach*, according to which psychopathology may be best understood as varying along a continuum of human functioning (Maddux, 2002; Maddux *et al.*, 2004). (We should perhaps note that favouring the dimensional approach does not on its own make you a positive psychologist. In fact, it has been suggested elsewhere that the categorical and dimensional approaches mirror the important difference between psychiatry and psychology respectively: Bentall, 2003; Lilienfeld, 1998; Marzillier, 2004; Pilgrim, 2000. Again, see Chapter 7.)

When a dimensional model is adopted, the person's experience is viewed as *unitary,* with positive and negative experiences being opposite ends of a continuum, rather than as falling into distinct categories. As Joseph and Linley (2006) point out, within a dimensional model:

> *. . . any intervention that serves to decrease the negative also serves to increase the positive, and any intervention that increases the positive also decreases the negative by definition.*

The humanistic psychologists were proposing a view of human functioning as an *alternative* to the medical model; this was based on the assumption that people are intrinsically motivated towards development, growth and socially constructive behaviour but that the social environment can thwart this intrinsic motivation, causing distress, suffering and psychopathology (see Chapter 14). This means that therapy is always concerned *simultaneously* with the relief of suffering and the promotion of well-being. These are not two separate and distinct tasks but one single task.

So, if PP is seen only as a supplement (as Seligman *et al.* suggest), then this represents a limited view in which PP may serve only as an 'extra' for those already capable and well functioning, rather than as a useful guide for people wherever they are on the continuum of functioning. In other words, PP should stand *in opposition* to the medical model with its impetus towards the medicalization of human experience. If positive psychologists do not make their opposition explicit, there is a danger of PP being incorporated into the medical model (Joseph and Linley, 2006).

The deficit model and the need for the strengths perspective

Another way of referring to the medical model is the deficit model, according to which psychological problems are equated with biological problems within the individual, rather than being influenced by a wider social context. (This is a form of *reductionism*: see Chapters 10 and 12, and Gross, 2005.) This illness ideology dictates that psychological problems require medical intervention. As well as being the dominant model within clinical psychology:

> . . . *This negativity bias, for which substantial empirical evidence has been provided, also pervaded empirical psychology throughout the second half of the twentieth century, with social and cognitive psychologists, for example, more typically focused on errors, biases, illusions and delusions – the negative poles of their areas of inquiry – rather than more positive constructs.*
>
> (Linley, 2008b)

In this context of the deficit model, the strengths perspective was proposed as an alternative fundamental assumption for the PP approach. Rather than focusing on what is broken, the strengths perspective focuses on what works, on what is improving, strong and effective. It works from the counter assumption that:

> . . . *growth can best ensue from working on what is already effective to make it even better, that the biggest improvements come from taking something that is 'average' and making it 'superb', rather than taking it from 'bad' to 'not bad'. Understood in this way, the strengths perspective is ultimately a mindset shift, a change in philosophy and assumptions, which then subsequently leads to new ways of framing old questions, and to new questions that have not been previously considered.*
>
> (Linley, 2008b)

One source of the strengths perspective in PP is the strengths revolution described by Buckingham and Clifton (in Linley), which argued for shifting the focus from what is wrong with people to what is right with them, and understanding the strengths that people possess which enable them to deliver their best performances and be functioning at their optimal level. Other roots and influences include:

- de Shazer's solution-focused therapy (which, as the name indicates, focuses on the solution rather than the problem)
- Tedeschi and Calhoun's concept of post-traumatic growth as a label for the experience of positive outcomes following trauma, in contrast to the dominant focus of post-traumatic stress disorder (see below).

As Linley notes, what all these (and many other) cases have in common is the challenge to the predominant emphasis on pathology, problem, dysfunction and disease.

THE CONCEPT OF HAPPINESS

What does happiness mean?

Philosophers have debated the definition of happiness for thousands of years without reaching a consensus. For Aristotle, the realization of one's potential was a critical ingredient (cf. the humanistic psychologists), while for Bentham, happiness consisted of the presence of pleasure and the absence of pain (cf. Skinner's concepts of reinforcement and punishment: see Chapter 14).

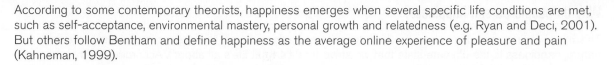

According to some contemporary theorists, happiness emerges when several specific life conditions are met, such as self-acceptance, environmental mastery, personal growth and relatedness (e.g. Ryan and Deci, 2001). But others follow Bentham and define happiness as the average online experience of pleasure and pain (Kahneman, 1999).

Like Seligman (2003: see above), Oishi *et al.* (2007) use the term happiness interchangeably with subjective well-being, or the subjective evaluation of one's life. This relatively stable feeling of contentment or satisfaction with one's life represents the highest level of a hierarchy of happiness. At the next level there are four components: pleasant emotions, unpleasant emotions, life satisfaction and domain satisfaction. Each of these can be further subdivided into specific aspects of life experiences (such as love, worry, meaning and health). Below these in the hierarchy is the conscious experience of happiness.

Are there different types of happiness?

According to Kashdan *et al.* (in press), in recent years researchers into subjective well-being (SWB) have distinguished between *eudaimonic happiness* (e.g. meaning and purpose; taking part in activities that allow for the actualization of one's skills, talents and potential) and *hedonic happiness* (e.g. high frequencies of positive affect, low frequencies of negative affect, and evaluating life as satisfying). Unfortunately, this distinction (originally made by Aristotle in the 4th century BCE) does not necessarily translate well to science. Among the problems of drawing a sharp line between 'types of happiness' is the fact that eudaimonia is not well defined and lacks consistent measurement. Eudaimonic and hedonic happiness also appear to overlap conceptually, and may represent psychological mechanisms that operate together.

Kashdan *et al.* discuss the problems and costs involved in distinguishing between two types of happiness and provide detailed recommendations for a research programme on SWB that has greater scientific precision. At the end of the article, they observe that when Aristotle originally drew the distinction between eudaimonia and hedonism, he rejected the pursuit of pleasure as such, suggesting that human beings ought to listen to a higher calling of a life of virtue. Yet he also claimed that eudaimonia was the most pleasant of human experiences. Years of research on the psychology of SWB have demonstrated that often human beings are happiest when they are engaged in meaningful pursuits and virtuous activities. While the *source* of happiness may well be important:

> . . . *to date no evidence suggests that the why of happiness leads to a qualitatively different form of well-being. Rather, the Good Life as it has been studied in psychology would appear to be not simply a happy life, but a happier life* . . .

> *(Kashdan* et al.*)*

They go on to point out that, in the larger debate about the importance of happiness to the Good Life, scholars often refer to Nozick's (1974) classic *thought experiment*: the experience machine. Would anyone want to be hooked up to a machine that would allow the person to experience the illusion of perpetual joy? The answer, of course, is 'no', and this is often used to demonstrate that 'authentic experience trumps happiness'.

> . . . *But hedonic experience is embedded in daily life and real experience. Perhaps we thought experimenters cannot escape the notion that, although we might be happy in the machine, we would be happier engaged in real life.*

> *(Kashdan* et al.*)*

Why do people pursue happiness?

This might at first seem like a question that doesn't need asking. Surely the answer is obvious: by its very nature, happiness is the ultimate state that we strive for ('it's what life's all about'). According to Aristotle, happiness is the ultimate goal of life: we choose it for its own sake and not for any other reason. All other goals and aspirations (money, health, reputation, friendship and so on) are instrumental goals pursued in order to meet the ultimate goal of happiness.

However, there are more practical reasons why people pursue happiness. For example, happiness is believed to reflect the extent to which one's life is going well (Sumner, 1996). Being happy implies success, whereas not being happy implies failure (King and Napa, 1998). Not surprisingly, evidence exists which shows that many Americans strive for happiness and even feel pressure to be happy (cited by Oishi *et al.*, 2007).

If there is some kind of equation made – at least, within western cultures – between happiness and success, one potential consequence of this pressure to be happy/to succeed is the very opposite of happiness.

BOX 2.2 DOES SUCCESS NECESSARILY MAKE US HAPPIER?

- In two recent books (*Affluenza* (2007) and *The Selfish Capitalist* (2008)), James explores his belief that the English-speaking world has become more dysfunctional the richer its people become and the harder they work.
- In *Britain on the Couch* (1997), he pointed out that a 25-year-old American is 3–10 times more likely to be depressed today than in 1950. *Affluenza* was his attempt to explain why things have become so much worse. James travelled around the world looking at the levels of emotional distress (depression, anxiety, substance abuse and personality disorders) and discovered a direct correlation between this and 'Selfish Capitalism' – the system that operates in most English-speaking countries.
- *The Selfish Capitalist* offers the scientific evidence behind his theory. (Of course, we must remember that correlation does not imply cause; it is possible that high levels of emotional distress are responsible for the increasing dominance of the 'free market' and the 'cult of the individual', seen in both the USA and the UK since the 1970s.) In societies where citizens are encouraged to gain the best exam results, earn the most money, and be thinner and more beautiful than everybody else, people are more unhappy. For James, these social and cultural pressures are unquestionably the cause of this unhappiness.

Is happier always better?

Oishi *et al.* (2007) also pose the question, 'Is happier always better?' Emotions probably evolved to solve specific problems that our ancestors faced in their everyday lives (e.g. Damasio, 1994; Darwin, 1872; Frijda, 1988) – for example, fear can help us avoid danger and prepare for stressful situations, anxiety can motivate us to work harder and perform better, and guilt and shame can motivate us to avoid moral transgressions. Indeed, although negative affect is unpleasant and is often avoided, individuals who do not experience *any* often suffer negative consequences (such as psychopaths/sociopaths: see Chapter 14 and Gross, 2005).

Based on consistent findings from their analysis of a very large cross-sectional study (involving over 118,000 people in 96 countries and regions around the world), an intense data-collection project with college students, and four large longitudinal studies, Oishi *et al.* concluded that the optimal level of happiness varies across domains and contexts. In the case of voluntary work and relationships, the optimal level is the highest level of happiness possible. But in the case of income and education, a moderate (but still high) level is the optimal one.

This *does not* mean that it is bad to be very happy, or that it is desirable to be unhappy. Although very happy people tend to be worse off than the moderately happy in certain domains, they still tend to report more successful functioning than those individuals at the midpoint of the distribution, and they are usually better off than those at the lowest ends.

Does success make us happy or does happiness lead to success?

According to Lyubomirski *et al.* (2005), research on well-being consistently reveals that the characteristics and resources valued by society (such as fulfilling marriage and relationships, a high income, superior work performance, physical and mental health, community involvement and a long life) all correlate with reports of high levels of happiness. This has led most researchers to infer that success makes people happy. However, Lyubomirski *et al.* propose that as well as success leading to happiness, positive affect (PA) produces success.

In a meta-analytic study of three kinds of evidence – cross-sectional, longitudinal and experimental – Lyubomirski *et al.* found that happiness is associated with and *precedes* several successful outcomes, as well as behaviours and cognitions that parallel success (such as sociability, optimism, energy, originality and altruism). In addition, the evidence suggests that PA – the hallmark of well-being – may be the cause of many of the desirable characteristics, resources and successes that are correlated with happiness:

> . . . *It appears that happiness, rooted in personality and in past successes, leads to approach behaviours that often lead to further success. At the same time, happy people are able to react with negative emotions when it is appropriate to do so.*
>
> *(Lyubomirski* et al., *2005)*

Is positive affect necessarily good for your health?

Self-help books, popular magazines and Sunday newspaper supplements have suggested for years that PA can improve people's health. However, this hypothesis has been relatively ignored by researchers – for example, there are over 20 times more studies on depression and health than there are on happiness and health (Pressman and Cohen, 2005).

In a review of the literature examining the relationship between measures of PA and markers of physical health status, Pressman and Cohen defined PA as:

> . . . *the feelings that reflect a level of pleasurable engagement with the environment . . . such as happiness, joy, excitement, enthusiasm, and contentment.*

They also make an important distinction between more stable disposition-like PA (*trait* PA) and relatively short-term bouts of positive emotions (*state* PA).

Evidence suggests that there is an association between trait PA and lower morbidity (i.e. reduced chances of dying) and between both state and trait PA and decreased symptoms and pain. Trait PA is also associated with increased longevity among older people living in the community. Experimentally inducing intense bouts of activated state PA triggers short-term increases in physiological arousal and associated (potentially harmful) effects on immune, cardiovascular and pulmonary function. However, naturally occurring state PA is not usually arousing in this way, is less intense, and is often associated with health-protective responses (Pressman and Cohen, 2005).

Too much of a good thing?

Fully functioning individuals are often described as those who have loving relationships and contribute to society through work, family, voluntary work and political involvement (e.g. Peterson and Seligman, 2004; Ryan and Deci, 2001). Given that no specific level of happiness is associated with all of these positive outcomes, there is no single level of happiness that is optimal for every individual and every activity. Important mediating variables include the individual's value priorities, personality dispositions and culture. Also, as we saw above, past success increases the likelihood of future success (Lyubomirski *et al.,* 2005).

According to Oishi *et al.* (2007), happiness has become a major life goal around the world. But there are dangers involved in searching for ultra-happiness. Because of the need to adapt, and because happiness is partly influenced by people's temperaments, obtaining continuous very high levels of happiness could require risky behaviours such as thrill-seeking activities and drug-taking. Seeking very high levels of positive affect might also stimulate novelty-seeking, in which the individual continually looks for new partners and activities in order to maintain those high levels. This search for constant, intense happiness is likely to lead to instability in a person's life (see Box 2.2). Oishi *et al.* conclude by saying:

> *. . . our findings suggest that extremely high levels of happiness might not be a desirable goal, and that there is more to psychological well-being than high levels of happiness. It is up to psychologists to educate lay people about optimal levels of happiness and the levels of happiness that are realistic . . .*

Is happiness a valid concept?

Happiness became the subject of empirical research in the 1960s, and over 3000 studies are listed in the World Database of Happiness (Veenhoven, 2003). The research has been reviewed by Diener (1999) and Argyle (2002).

Veenhoven believes that criticisms of the concept of happiness are misguided:

(i) *Happiness can be defined:* happiness is currently conceived as 'the overall appreciation of one's life as a whole'. This regards it as an outcome of life, distinct from preconditions for a good life (such as a liveable environment and good-life abilities). This way of defining happiness differs from current notions of 'quality of life', which combine anything good.

(ii) *Happiness can be measured:* happiness is a conscious state of mind; hence, it can be measured by simply asking people about it. It is an overall judgement, so it can be measured by single questions. Thus, happiness can be assessed in large-scale surveys. Several standard questions have been shown to be quite valid and fairly reliable (Diener, 1995, in Veenhoven, 2003). Degree and duration of happiness are combined in assessment of 'happy life-years' (Veenhoven, 1996, in Veenhoven, 2003).

(iii) *Enduring happiness is possible:* though some things called happiness are fleeting (such as luck and ecstasy), happiness in this sense is not. Follow-up after 12 months shows stability rates of about 0.65.

(iv) *Happiness of a great number is possible:* although unhappiness prevails in some parts of the present-day world, most people in most countries are happy. In 2000, only 4 per cent of the British ticked 'not at all satisfied' on a Eurobarometer survey question about global satisfaction with the life that one leads (European Commission, 2000, in Veenhoven, 2003). Time-sampling studies on daily affect show predominantly good mood.

(v) *Greater happiness is possible:* at the *macro* level, happiness depends heavily on societal qualities such as wealth, justice and freedom. Social policy can improve these conditions. At the *meso* level, happiness depends on institutional qualities, such as autonomy at work or in care institutions. Organizational reform can improve such situations. At the *micro* level, happiness depends on personal capabilities, such as efficacy, independence and social skills. Education and therapy can improve these capabilities.

(vi) *Happiness does not deprave:* follow-up studies on consequences of happiness have shown positive effects on moral behaviour: happiness fosters altruism and sociability. There is also evidence that happiness promotes activity and initiative, with no negative effects on creativity. Last but not least, happy people live longer (Veenhoven, 1988, in Veenhoven, 2003).

(vii) *Happiness is a good outcome criterion:* quality of life (QoL) is typically measured by the presence of conditions considered to be good for people; happiness, on the other hand, indicates how well people *actually* flourish. Current QoL measures are scores of very different things that cannot be meaningfully added, while happiness provides an obvious overall appraisal of life. While current QoL measures treat external conditions and inner capabilities separately, happiness reflects the apparent 'fit' between the two. This makes happiness the best available outcome criterion (Veenhoven, 2000, 2002, in Veenhoven, 2003). Veenhoven (2003) concludes by stating:

> *All in all, the criterion of happiness has value and should be used more in assessing outcomes of social policies and psychological therapies.*

WHY DO WE NEED POSITIVE PSYCHOLOGY?

This question is partially answered by the dominance of the emphasis on mental illness described above. Despite the undoubted prevalence of psychological disorders, this emphasis blinds us to people's mental health, that is, all those qualities and abilities that we aspire to and which parents and teachers (among others) try to develop in their children/adolescents. Positive psychology is an attempt to redress the balance.

There is a second, and arguably even more important, motive. Seligman (2003) maintains that if there is any doctrine which positive psychology seeks to overthrow, it is what he calls the 'rotten-to-the-core' (RTTC) view, which pervades western thought. According to this view:

> *. . . virtue and happiness are inauthentic, epiphenomenal, parasitic upon or reducible to the negative traits and states . . .*

What does he mean? We could 'translate' this as:

Figure 2.1 Temptation in the Garden of Eden

Positive human qualities (including happiness/ well-being) are not real or genuine, they are mere by-products of, feed on, and can be explained in terms of, negative traits and states (such as selfishness, jealousy, and hatred).

Seligman gives some examples which make his statement a little clearer. The earliest form of this RTTC view is the theological doctrine of original sin. The sin of Adam and Eve (eating fruit from the forbidden tree of knowledge – of good and evil) is thought to have passed down the male line – transmitted in the semen, according to St Augustine. So, every child is condemned, even before birth, to inherit the sin of a remote ancestor, and the central doctrine of Christianity is that of 'atonement' for this 'original sin' (Dawkins, 2006).

Seligman describes (aspects of) Freud's psychoanalytic theory as 'dragging' the RTTC view into the twentieth century. For Freud, all of civilization is just an elaborate defence against basic conflicts over infantile sexuality and aggression. So, Bill Gates's competitiveness is really a desire to outdo his father, and Princess Diana's crusade against land mines was really a sublimation of her murderous hate for Prince Charles and the other royals.

In other words, the *true* motive(s) for (apparently) pro-social behaviour are always *negative*. This is consistent with *universal egoism*, according to which everything we do, no matter how noble and beneficial to others, is really directed towards the ultimate goal of self-benefit. We are fundamentally – and thoroughly – selfish, and altruism (help performed for the benefit of others with no expectation of personal gain) is an impossibility (Dovidio, 1995). This has been, and still is, the dominant ethos in social science, including psychology. Similarly, *sociobiologists* consider acts of *apparent* altruism to be acts of selfishness in disguise (for example, Dawkins's (1976) *selfish gene* theory: see Gross, 2005).

Against this, those who advocate the *empathy–altruism hypothesis* (e.g. Batson, 1991), while not denying that much of what we do (including what we do for others) is egoistic, also claim that there is more than just egoism: under certain circumstances, we are capable of a qualitatively different form of motivation, whose ultimate goal is to *benefit others* (see Gross, 2005).

Despite its acceptance in the religious and secular worlds, there is not a shred of evidence that forces us to believe that virtue is derived from negative motives (Seligman, 2003). On the contrary, Seligman believes that:

> . . . *evolution has favoured both sorts of traits, and any number of adaptive roles in the world have selected for morality, cooperation, altruism, and goodness, just as any number have also selected for murder, theft, self-seeking, and terrorism* . . .

He advocates the *dual aspect theory*, according to which strengths and virtues are just as basic to human nature as the negative traits.

IS POSITIVE PSYCHOLOGY REALLY THAT NEW? GIVING PSYCHOLOGY AWAY

In Miller's 1969 presidential address to the American Psychological Association (entitled 'Psychology as a means of promoting human welfare'), he set out the role he believes psychology should play in society, namely, 'a means of promoting human welfare'. This can and should be achieved by 'giving psychology away': encouraging non-psychologists ('ordinary people') to practise psychology, to be their own psychologists, helping them to do better what they already do through familiarizing them with (scientific) psychological knowledge. Psychology should not be the 'property' of the scientific/professional experts: psychological principles and techniques can usefully be applied by everyone. As Miller says:

> *The techniques involved are not some esoteric branch of witchcraft that must be reserved for those with PhD degrees in psychology. When the ideas are made sufficiently concrete and explicit, the scientific foundations of psychology can be grasped by sixth-grade [12-year-old] children.*

This represents a 'policy document' or blueprint for what psychology *ought* to be doing, a prescription for its social function. In the context of mainstream psychology, which claims to be *value-free* (part and parcel of the 'objectivity' of science: see Chapter 10), Miller is explicitly advocating certain values. Although the presidential address (both in the USA and the UK) has traditionally been an opportunity for taking stock of the discipline of psychology and trying to move it forward, Miller's advocacy of 'giving psychology away' and promoting human welfare ('happiness'?) was quite a radical thing to be doing in the 1960s.

According to Murphy *et al.* (1984), Miller's address captures the turmoil that psychology was experiencing during the late 1960s. It continues to be cited and many psychologists have endorsed his sentiments, including Shotter (1975) and Kay in his 1972 presidential address to the British Psychological Society. More recently, Rappaport and Stewart (1997) have discussed Miller's call to 'give psychology away' in the context of *critical psychology.*

Murphy *et al.* believe that Miller seems to have drawn attention to two particular issues which had been raised by the radical critics of psychology in the late 1960s, namely (i) the accusation that psychology has created a dehumanizing image of human beings, and (ii) the accusation that psychology has ignored the real-world setting within which human beings live their lives.

(i) This is related to the notion of behavioural *control*, which Miller discusses at length. What makes it dehumanizing is that people are capable of *self*-control, controlling their own behaviour, so that imposing a behavioural technology of control removes a basic human freedom, as well as conveying the impression that people are machine-like. This is discussed in detail by Heather (1976).

(ii) Miller advocates that we must start with what people themselves believe their problems to be. This is reminiscent of Joynson's (1974) attack on the behaviourists for looking at people as objects, from the outside, while ignoring their experience and rejecting the validity of their attempts to explain their own behaviour (see Chapters 11 and 14). Radical psychologists would regard any attempt to study people as objects as both ethically and scientifically unsound, since people can and do choose how to act: any theory or system which ignores this feature of human beings must be presenting only a partial or inaccurate account (see Chapters 9 and 11).

As important as these issues are, when discussing 'giving psychology away' Miller seems to be talking mainly about helping people solve their personal – and professional – problems, and so is advocating a problem-centred approach. But doesn't the promotion of human welfare mean more than this? Surely it also involves a much more positive approach, whereby people can realize their potential as human beings (although this will be much harder to achieve when the person faces problems, especially those relating to basic survival needs: see Chapters 7 and 14). Indeed, positive growth may occur *because of* (rather than despite) such problems, that is, through the process of trying to overcome problems and hardships – this is something that some positive psychologists have investigated (see Delle Fave and Massimini, 2003, and Linley and Joseph, 2003, below).

A great deal of psychotherapy is aimed at changing individuals' perception of themselves and increasing their self-understanding. It also aims at increasing autonomy or independence (Lindley, 1987, in Fairbairn, 1987), that is, *taking control of one's own life*. To the extent that taking control of one's own life is itself an essential part of human flourishing (Lindley, 1987), much psychotherapy would seem to be based on respect for individuals as persons. This principle is central to the positive evaluation of any changes brought about by psychologists, helping others to make responsible decisions about their lives, because taking responsibility for one's own life is at least part of what it is to function fully as a person (Fairbairn, 1987).

Hawks (1981, in Fairbairn and Fairbairn, 1987) believes that prevention rather than cure should be a primary aim of psychology, enabling people to cope by themselves, without professional help. But there is more to happiness than 'mere coping', isn't there?

WHAT MAKES LIFE WORTH LIVING?

According to Seligman and Csikszentmihalyi (2000), as we entered the new millennium:

> . . . the social and behavioural sciences can play an enormously important role. They can articulate a vision of the good life that is empirically sound while being understandable and attractive. They can show what actions lead to well being, to positive individuals, and to thriving communities. Psychology should be able to help document what kind of families result in children who flourish, what work settings support the greatest satisfaction among workers, what policies result in the strongest civic engagement, and how our lives can be most worth living.

But what does make life worth living? Psychology has helped us understand how people survive and endure under conditions of adversity. But we know very little about how normal individuals flourish under more benign conditions. As we noted earlier, since the Second World War, psychology has become a science largely concerned with healing. It focuses on repairing damage within a disease model of human functioning (the medical model: see Chapter 7). However:

> . . . this almost exclusive attention to pathology neglects the fulfilled individual and the thriving community. The aim of positive psychology is to begin to catalyze a change in the focus of psychology from preoccupation only with repairing the worst things in life to also building positive qualities.

And again:

> . . . psychology is not just the study of pathology, weakness, and damage; it is also the study of strength and virtue. Treatment is not just fixing what is broken; it is nurturing what is best. Psychology is not just a branch of medicine concerned with illness or health; it is much larger. It is about work, education, insight, love, growth, and play . . . it tries to adapt what is best in the scientific method to the unique problems that human behaviour presents to those who wish to understand it in all its complexity.

At the *subjective level,* positive psychology is about valued subjective experience: well-being, contentment and satisfaction (past), hope and optimism (future), and flow and happiness (present). At the *individual level*, it is about positive individual traits – the capacity for love and vocation, courage, interpersonal skills, aesthetic sensibility, perseverance, forgiveness, originality, future-mindedness, spirituality, high talent and wisdom (Seligman and Csikszentmihalyi).

Seligman (2003) proposes a terminology that might form the basis of a scientifically viable positive psychology. He distinguishes three desirable lives: the *pleasant* life, the *good* life and the *meaningful* life. These are described in Box 2.3.

The importance of a balanced time perspective

According to Boniwell and Zimbardo (2003), one key to learning how to live a fulfilling life is discovering how to achieve a balanced time perspective (TP): 'the ability to switch one's temporal focus according to the demands of the current behavioural setting' (Zimbardo and Boyd, 1999, in Boniwell and Zimbardo).

One's TP refers to the subjective conception of focusing on various temporal (time-related) categories or time frames when making decisions and taking action. It is one of the most powerful influences on almost all aspects of human behaviour, in particular affecting our quality of life.

Measuring TP and individual differences

The Zimbardo Time Perspective Inventory (ZTPI) is a single integrated scale for measuring TP – it is reliable, valid and easy to use. Underlying the ZTPI are five main factors: past-negative, past-positive, present-hedonistic, present-fatalistic and future. Past TP is associated with focus on family, tradition and history. A past-negative TP is associated with focusing on personal experiences that were aversive or noxious, while the past-positive TP reflects a warm, pleasurable, often sentimental and nostalgic view of one's past, with an emphasis on maintaining relationships with family and friends.

The present-hedonistic TP is associated with the enjoyment of present momentary activities and with little concern over the consequences of behaviour. A person with a predominantly present-hedonistic TP is essentially a biological creature, determined by stimuli, situational emotions and spontaneity, oriented towards sensation- and pleasure-seeking. By contrast, the present-fatalistic TP is associated with hopelessness and inflexible beliefs that outside forces control one's life (cf. Rotter's (1966) high external locus of control).

BOX 2.3 THE THREE DESIRABLE LIVES OF POSITIVE PSYCHOLOGY (SELIGMAN, 2003)

- **The pleasant life:** *happiness and well-being are the desired outcomes of positive psychology.* Positive emotions are divided into three kinds: (a) those directed towards the *past* (e.g. satisfaction, contentment, pride, serenity), (b) those directed towards the *future* (e.g. optimism, hope, confidence, trust, faith), and (c) those directed towards the *present*. In turn, positive emotions relating to (c) divide into two crucially different categories: the pleasures and the gratifications (see below). The pleasures also fall into two categories: (i) The pleasures comprise bodily pleasures (momentary positive emotions that come through the senses, such as delicious tastes and smells, sexual feelings, moving your body well, delightful sights and sounds). We use words such as scrumptiousness, warmth and orgasm to describe such pleasures. (ii) The higher pleasures are also momentary, but they are triggered by events that are more complicated and more learned than sensory ones and are defined by the feelings they bring about: ecstasy, rapture, thrill, bliss, gladness, mirth, glee, fun, ebullience, comfort, amusement, relaxation and so on. All pleasures are at rock bottom subjective, and they can be measured in a consistent and reliable way. The pleasant life is *a life that successfully pursues the positive emotions about the present, past and future.*
- **The good life:** unlike the pleasures, the *gratifications* are not feelings but activities we like doing – for example, reading, rock-climbing, dancing, good conversation, volleyball or playing bridge. These absorb and engage us fully, blocking self-consciousness and felt emotion (except in retrospect – 'Wow, that was fun!'), and they create *flow* (a state in which time stops and we feel completely at home). The gratifications cannot be obtained or permanently increased without developing the *strengths* and *virtues*. So, happiness is not just about obtaining pleasant, momentary subjective states. Our strengths and virtues are the natural routes to gratification and the gratifications are the routes to the good life: *using your strengths and virtues to obtain abundant gratification in the main realms of life.*
- **The meaningful life:** happiness comes by many routes. Our life task is to deploy our strengths and virtues in the major realms of living: work, love, parenting. A 'happy' individual need not experience all or even most of the positive emotions and gratifications. A meaningful life adds one more component to the good life: *it is the use of your strengths and virtues in the service of something much larger than you are.*

A person with a future TP is concerned with working for future goals and rewards, often at the expense of present enjoyment. A future-oriented individual lives in abstraction, suppressing the reality of the present for the imagined reality of an ideal future world.

The TP construct is predictive of a wide range of behaviours. For example, a present TP has been found to relate to risky driving and other forms of risk-taking (Zimbardo *et al.*, 1997, in Boniwell and Zimbardo), as well as substance abuse (drugs and alcohol) (Keough *et al.*, 1999, in Boniwell and Zimbardo). Unemployed people living in shelters who have a future TP are more likely to use their time constructively to seek jobs, while those with present TP tend to engage in non-instrumental activities or to waste time watching TV (Epel *et al.*, 1999, in Boniwell and Zimbardo).

The dangers of western TPs

Although each of the TP factors has some value, an excessive orientation towards any one perspective can become dysfunctional. For example, western ways of life have become predominantly goal- and future-oriented. Time-saving technological devices help to increase productivity and efficiency, but they fail to free up actual time to enjoy oneself (Zimbardo, 2002, in Boniwell and Zimbardo). The concept of 'time famine' refers to the lack of time and people's difficulty in finding an optimal balance in their use of time. For example, the dilution of boundaries between work and home has resulted in the future-oriented TP associated with work being increasingly applied to our leisure time as well. Another example involves emails – do they save us time or do we spend time sending more of them, both necessary and unnecessary?

There are costs and sacrifices associated with valuing achievement-oriented 'workaholic' traits over life enjoyment and social interaction. It seems that we are prepared to sacrifice friends, church, family, recreation, hobbies, even household chores (Myers, 2000, in Boniwell and Zimbardo). As Boniwell and Zimbardo say:

> . . . *The danger here is the risk of undermining the rituals and narratives essential to a sense of family, community and nation.*

Too much time and wasting time

However, an abundance of time does not necessarily make for a more fulfilling life. Retired and unemployed people often suffer from depression, and many people do not find their leisure time rewarding. Csikszentmihalyi (1992, in Boniwell and Zimbardo) suggests that a majority of leisure time is wasted in passive entertainment, such as watching TV, and is not enjoyed by the participants. TV viewing is associated with boredom, low levels of concentration and potency, lack of clear thinking, and lack of flow.

The need for balance

Do such examples reflect a lack of balance in our TP and the inability to be flexible in shifting from one TP to another? For example, immersion in future- and achievement-oriented perspectives of work may make it difficult to return to a present-oriented 'here-and-now' TP for relaxation. The only way to 'switch off' becomes to enter the atemporal, mindless experience of passive TV watching.

Boniwell and Zimbardo propose a 'balanced TP' as a more positive alternative to living life as a slave to a particular temporal bias. People with a balanced TP are capable of operating within a temporal mode appropriate to the situation they find themselves in. So, when with friends and relatives, or engaged in some other leisure activity, they immerse themselves fully, not worrying or feeling guilty about work. Similarly, when working and studying, they concentrate fully on this, wearing their more appropriate future TP hat.

Based on research with exceptionally happy people (cited in Boniwell and Zimbardo), functioning within past-positive and present-hedonistic modes enhances your chances of developing happy personal relationships, a key factor in your overall sense of well-being. On the other hand, a future TP is correlated with higher socio-economic status, which is moderately associated with well-being (Diener, 2000).

> . . . *Laughing when it's time to laugh, working when it's time to work, playing when it's time to play, listening to grandma's old stories, connecting with your friends, valuing desire and passion, and taking fuller control of your life; these should be some of the benefits of learning to achieve a balanced time perspective. They are possible keys to unlocking personal happiness and finding more meaning in life despite the relentless, indifferent movement of life's time clock. The value of a balanced time perspective is that it suggests new approaches to psychological interventions while offering yet another answer to the question 'What is a good life?'.*
>
> (Boniwell and Zimbardo, 2003)

SOME OTHER MAJOR TOPICS WITHIN POSITIVE PSYCHOLOGY

The reference above to Seligman and Csikszentmihalyi (2000) is their editors' introduction to the millennial issue of *American Psychologist*. This was devoted exclusively to positive psychology and comprised 16 articles by leading figures in the field, including one or two already well known from their contribution to other areas of psychology (such as David Buss and evolutionary psychology, and Paul Baltes and developmental psychology).

In their introductory article, Seligman and Csikszentmihalyi identify three main topics that run through the 16 articles: (i) positive experience, (ii) positive personality and (iii) positive community and institutions. They summarize the theory and research relating to each of these topics under four headings, and we shall do the same below. We should note that there is considerable overlap between (i) and (ii), since happiness, for example, can be seen as *state-like* (what accounts for moments of happiness) or *trait-like* (what distinguishes happy individuals).

POSITIVE PERSONAL TRAITS

Subjective well-being

Subjective well-being refers to what we think and how we feel about our lives, that is, the cognitive and affective conclusions we reach when we evaluate our existence (Diener, 2000). In practice, SWB is a more scientific-sounding term for what we usually mean by happiness (and note that Seligman, 2003, explicitly equates the two terms: see above). Even though SWB research relies primarily on rather global self-ratings which could be criticized on various methodological grounds, its findings are plausible and coherent.

Diener's account begins with a review of the temperamental and personality correlates of SWB, and the demographic characteristics of groups high on SWB. His review of the extensive cross-cultural research suggests some interesting links between macro-social conditions and happiness (see above). A central issue is how a person's goals and values mediate between external events and the quality of experience. It has become almost a truism within psychology that it is not what happens to us that determines how we feel or respond (here, how happy we are), but how we *interpret* what happens.

Happiness

Myers's (2000) discussion of empirical evidence on happiness is informed by a belief that traditional values must contain important elements of truth if they are to survive across generations. This makes him more attuned than most to issues that are not very fashionable in the field, such as the often-found association between religious faith and happiness. The two other candidates for promoting happiness that Myers considers are economic growth and income (where there is only a weak association once a minimum threshold of affluence is passed) and close interpersonal relationships (where there is a strong association).

Although the evidence is based on correlational data from survey studies of self-reported happiness, the robustness of the findings which have been replicated across time and different cultures suggests that it should be taken seriously by anyone interested in understanding the factors that contribute to a positive quality of life. (See the discussion of happiness above.)

Optimism

Optimism represents one dispositional trait that appears to mediate between external events and a person's interpretation of them. It refers to both 'little optimism' (e.g. 'I will find a convenient parking space this evening') and 'big optimism' (e.g. 'Our nation is on the verge of something great'). Peterson (2000) believes that optimism comprises cognitive, emotional and motivational components. People high on optimism tend to have better moods, to be more persevering and successful, and to experience better physical health.

How does optimism work? How can it be increased? When does it begin to distort reality? These are some of the questions Peterson addresses. Like the other contributors, Peterson is aware that complex psychological issues cannot be understood in isolation from the social and cultural context in which they are embedded (see below). Hence, such questions as 'How does an overly pessimistic culture affect the well-being of its members?' and conversely 'Does an overly optimistic culture lead to shallow materialism?'

Self-determination

Ryan and Deci (2000) discuss self-determination theory, which investigates three related human needs: for competence, belongingness and autonomy. When these needs are satisfied, personal well-being and social development are optimized; people in this condition are intrinsically motivated, able to fulfil their potentialities and search for progressively greater challenges. Especially important is the ability to maintain autonomy even under external pressures that seem to prevent it.

These three related needs overlap with those that appear in Maslow's (1954) *hierarchy of needs*. Maslow is one of the influential humanistic psychologists, who introduced this approach as a 'third force' within psychology (the other two being behaviourism and psychoanalytic theory: see Chapter 14). Fulfilling one's potentialities (what Maslow, and Rogers, 1951, call self-actualization) appears at the peak of the hierarchy. Ryan and Deci's discussion shows that the promises of humanistic psychology can generate a vital programme of empirical research (Seligman and Csikszentmihalyi, 2000).

Taking a more historical and philosophical approach, Schwartz (2000) expresses concern about the emphasis placed on autonomy in our culture. This emphasis produces a kind of psychological tyranny – an 'excess of freedom' that may lead to dissatisfaction and depression. Particularly problematical is the cherished belief in free will (see Chapter 11): the burden of responsibility for autonomous choices often becomes too heavy, leading to insecurity and regrets. For most people in the world, individual choice is neither expected nor desired. Cultural constraints are necessary for leading a meaningful and satisfying life. Although Ryan and Deci's self-determination theory takes relatedness into account as one of the three components of personal fulfilment, Schwartz's argument highlights even further the benefits of relying on cultural norms and values.

Other examples of what might be thought of as positive personal traits (or virtues) include wisdom, mature defences and exceptional performance (creativity and talent). Seligman and Csikszentmihalyi discuss these under the heading of 'fostering excellence' (see below). One that is not discussed in the 16 articles selected by Seligman and Csikszentmihalyi is *gratitude*.

Gratitude

Wood *et al.* (2007) quote Cicero (106–43BC), according to whom:

Figure 2.2 The terrorist attacks of 9/11

Gratitude is not only the greatest of the virtues, but the parent of all of the others.

With some cultural variations, gratitude seems to be experienced in countries around the world (Naito *et al.,* 2005), and many people have reported increased gratitude and appreciation of life following the terrorist attacks of 9/11 (Peterson and Seligman, 2003, in Wood *et al.*).

Gratitude is also a central tenet of the world's major religions. Yet, until very recently, psychologists have largely ignored gratitude as a topic for research.

Gratitude can be thought of as an affect ('moral' or prosocial), a behaviour or a personality trait. Specifically, it acts as (i) a barometer, drawing attention to help received, (ii) a moral motivator, encouraging a prosocial response to help, and (iii) a moral reinforcer, where the expression of gratitude makes the helper more likely to offer help in the future (McCullough *et al.,* 2001).

Most recent research has focused on gratitude as a personality trait. Several studies now suggest that people who feel more gratitude (more often and more intensely, and towards a wider range of people and events) are much more likely to have higher levels of happiness and lower levels of depression and stress (e.g. McCullough *et al.,* 2004).

However, many personality traits are related to levels of mental health, so what makes gratitude unique? Wood *et al.* provide two major answers:

● Gratitude seems to have one of the strongest links with mental health of any personality variable. Park *et al.* (2004, in Wood *et al.*) found that gratitude was more strongly related to life satisfaction than 21 out of 23 other traits; the correlation of 0.43 suggests that about 18.5 per cent of individual differences in people's happiness could be predicted by the amount of gratitude they feel.
● Gratitude may be uniquely important in social relationships. The 'moral' effects of emotional gratitude are likely to be as important in maintaining individual relationships as they are in maintaining a smooth-running society. People who feel more gratitude in life are more likely to notice when they have been helped, to respond appropriately and to return the help at some point in the future. The original helper is then more likely to help again, causing an upward spiral of helping and mutual support. This suggests that grateful people are likely to have better social relationships, which involve greater closeness and reciprocal social support.

Early indications suggest that *gratitude interventions* may have considerable applications to coaching and psychotherapy. Seligman *et al.* (2005) randomly assigned people to one of six therapeutic intervention conditions. The biggest short-term effects were seen for the 'gratitude visit', where participants wrote and delivered a letter to someone who had helped them substantially at some point in their lives. On average, people's happiness scores rose by 10 per cent and their depression scores also fell significantly. Compared with a placebo condition, these effects lasted up to a month longer.

In Seligman *et al.*'s study, the longest-lasting treatment effects also involved gratitude. Participants were asked to make a list every day for a week of three good things about their lives ('counting your blessings') and had increased levels of happiness each time they were tested; the largest benefits were seen six months after treatment. This remarkable finding may have been produced by people choosing to continue with the exercise long after the intervention ended.

These findings suggest that increasing people's levels of gratitude actually increases well-being. But could it be that people who are 'naturally' grateful see the social world through 'rose-coloured glasses', interpreting help they receive as more valuable, costly and altruistic, with strong implications for the quality of their social relationships? Wood *et al.* (2007) believe that research will show no clear direction of causality between gratitude, well-being and social relationships. Rather, there is probably an interactive upward spiral, whereby being grateful leads to greater success, which in turn leads to gratitude, perpetuating the cycle.

Implications of positive personal traits for mental and physical health

As we saw earlier in the chapter, one of the arguments for positive psychology is that since the 1950s psychology has become increasingly focused on mental illness; as a result, psychology has developed a distorted view of what normal – and exceptional – human experience is like. So, how does mental health look when seen from the perspective of positive psychology?

Mature defences

According to the psychiatrist George Vaillant (2000), it is impossible to describe positive psychological processes without taking a lifespan, or at least a longitudinal approach; a truly positive psychological adaptation should unfold over a lifetime. Relying on the results of three large samples of adults studied over several decades, Vaillant summarizes the contributions of *mature defences* – altruism, sublimation, suppression, humour and anticipation – to a successful and joyful life. Even though he still uses the pathocentric term 'defences', his view of mature functioning, which takes full account of the importance of creative, proactive solutions, is a departure from the 'victimology' which has been one of the legacies of the psychoanalytic approach (see Chapter 14; Seligman and Csikszentmihalyi, 2000).

Optimism again

A widely held assumption is that it is healthy to be rigorously objective ('realistic') about one's situation; to paint a rosier picture than the facts warrant (delusional beliefs) is often seen as a sign of pathology (cf. Peterson, 2000, Schwartz, 2000 and Vaillant, 2000). However, Taylor *et al.* (2000) argue that unrealistically optimistic beliefs about the future can protect us from illness. The results of several studies with patients suffering from life-threatening diseases, such as AIDS, suggest that those who remain optimistic show symptoms later and survive longer than those who confront reality more objectively.

Taylor *et al.* believe that the positive effects of optimism are mediated mainly at a cognitive level. An optimistic patient is more likely to practise habits that enhance health and to enlist social support. But it is also possible that positive affective states have a direct physiological effect that slows down the course of illness (see Gross, 2005).

Positive affect has positive effects

In their review of the impact of a broad range of emotions on physical health, Salovey *et al.* (2000) conclude that, because of the pathological bias of most research in this field, a great deal more is known about how negative emotions promote illness than about how positive emotions promote health. However, as the two types of emotion are generally inversely related, substituting positive for negative can have preventive and therapeutic effects. Salovey *et al.* consider research which shows the direct effects of emotion on physiology and the immune system, and indirect effects through marshalling psychological and social resources, as well as motivating health-promoting behaviours.

Fostering excellence

If we wish to improve the human condition, it is not enough to help those who suffer. The majority of 'normal' people also need example and advice for reaching a richer and more fulfilling existence. This is why psychologists such as William James Jung, Allport and Maslow were interested in exploring spiritual ecstasy, play, creativity and peak experiences. When these interests were eclipsed by medicalization and 'physics-envy', psychology neglected an essential portion of its agenda. Positive psychologists try to focus on the tail of the normal distribution that includes the most positive human experiences (Seligman and Csikszentmihalyi, 2000).

Wisdom

Wisdom is one of the most prized traits in all cultures – and always has been. Although the first President of the APA, G. Stanley Hall, tried to develop a model of wisdom in ageing as long ago as 1922, the topic has not been popular since.

According to Baltes and Kunzmann (2003):

> . . . *At the core of this concept [of wisdom] is the notion of the perfect, quasi-utopian integration of knowledge and character, of mind and virtue.*

Because it is considered an ideal endpoint of human development, the original impetus for the psychological study of wisdom evolved in the context of lifespan psychology and the study of ageing. The search for positive human functioning has been a hallmark of developmental psychology since its beginning: (i) in Piaget's (e.g. 1950) theory of cognitive development, formal operational thought is seen as the optimal form of human intelligence; and (ii) in Erikson's (e.g. 1950) psychosocial theory of development, wisdom is the human virtue (or quality of strength) associated with maturity (ego integrity) in adulthood (50s and over: see Chapter 14 and Gross, 2005).

At the most general level, Baltes and Kunzmann define wisdom as:

> . . . *expert knowledge and judgement about important, difficult, and uncertain questions associated with the meaning and conduct of life. Wisdom-related knowledge deals with matters of utmost personal and social significance.*

They assess wisdom by presenting people with difficult hypothetical situations, such as, 'Imagine that someone gets a call from a good friend who says that s/he cannot go on any more and wants to commit suicide'. These are poorly defined problems, with many possible solutions; therefore, high-quality responses require exceptional intellectual and social-emotional abilities. Participants give 'think-aloud' responses, and trained raters evaluate them in terms of five criteria. The major findings are described in Box 2.4.

BOX 2.4 WHO IS WISE? (BALTES AND KUNZMANN, 2003)

- True to the spirit of wisdom as representing excellence of utopian quality, *high levels of wisdom-related knowledge are rare.* Many adults are on the way to wisdom, but very few actually attain it.
- The period of *late adolescence and early adulthood is the primary age window for wisdom-related knowledge to emerge.* In the older-than-young-adulthood samples, there were no further changes in the average level of wisdom compared with those found in early adulthood.
- For wisdom-related knowledge and judgement to develop further, either beyond the level achieved in early adulthood or in the course of one's lifetime, *factors other than age become critical.* These relate to psychological, social, professional and historical domains. Not surprisingly, therefore, older adults are (perhaps disproportionately) among the top performers in wisdom-related knowledge. But getting older is not enough.
- During adulthood, *higher predictive value is offered by personality-related factors,* such as openness to experience, generativity (Erikson's term for concern with others beyond the immediate family, such as future generations and the nature of the world in which those future generations will live), creativity or a judicial cognitive style (a preference for comparing, evaluating and judging information). In addition, specific life experiences (such as being trained and practising in a field concerned with difficult life problems), having wisdom-enhancing mentors, or having been exposed to and overcome certain personal or social circumstances all contribute to higher levels of wisdom-related knowledge.
- People possess larger amounts of wisdom-related knowledge than is evident in the standard assessment procedure. For example, people express a significantly higher level if guided by memory cueing or internal dialogues with significant others.

Further, people higher in wisdom-related knowledge show a preference for values that consider the welfare of others and report engaging themselves in the interest of others, including strategies of negotiation in conflict resolution. According to Baltes and Kunzmann (2003):

. . . Its [wisdom's] very foundation lies in the orchestration of mind and virtue towards the personal and public good.

Evolutionary perspectives

To some people, evolutionary approaches are distasteful because they deny the importance of learning and self-determination (see Chapters 11 and 14). But this need not be the case. Both Buss (2000) and Massimini and Delle Fave (2000) provide uplifting examples of how a psychology based on evolutionary principles can be applied to the improvement of the human condition (Seligman and Csikszentmihalyi, 2000).

Buss focuses on three reasons why positive states are so elusive:

1 Because our current environment is so different from the ancestral environment to which our body and mind have been adapted, we are often misfit in modern surroundings.
2 Evolved distress mechanisms are often functional; for example, jealousy alerts us to make sure of the fidelity of our spouse (especially important for males: see Gross and Rolls, in press).
3 Selection tends to be competitive and to involve zero-sum outcomes.

These represent major obstacles to well-being. One of the major differences between ancestral and current environments is the paradoxical change in our relationship to others: although we live surrounded by many more people than our ancestors did, we are intimate with fewer individuals, thus experiencing greater loneliness and alienation.

While Buss bases his arguments solely on biological evolution, Massimini and Delle Fave venture into the less explored region of psychological and cultural evolution. In a sense, they begin where Buss leaves off: by looking analytically at the effects of changes in the ancestral environment, and specifically at how the production of *memes* affect and are affected by human consciousness. See Box 2.5.

BOX 2.5 MEMES: CULTURAL GENES

- The term 'memes' was coined by Dawkins (1976) to provide an example of a replicator other than the gene; in other words, a mene is a cultural replicator.
- They are ideas, skills, habits, stories or any kind of information that is copied from person to person. They include written and spoken words, rules like driving on the left (or right) and habits like eating with chopsticks (or a knife and fork), as well as songs, dances, clothes fashions and technologies (including computers and other storage devices) (Blackmore, 2003).
- Although the theory of memes is highly controversial and has been criticized by biologists, sociologists, anthropologists and philosophers, it potentially provides a completely new way of understanding the evolution of consciousness (Blackmore, 2003).

Massimini and Delle Fave begin with the assumption that living systems are self-organizing and oriented towards increasing complexity. Thus individuals are the authors of their own evolution, continuously involved in the selection of the memes that will define their own individuality; when added to the memes selected by others, they shape the future of the culture.

Unlike biological evolution, psychological selection is not motivated solely by the pressures of adaptation and survival, but also by the need to reproduce optimal experiences. Whenever possible, we choose behaviours that make us feel fully alive, competent and creative. Massimini and Delle Fave conclude by providing instances, drawn from their own experiences, of cross-cultural interventions where psychology has been applied to remedy traumatic social conditions created by runaway modernization.

CONCLUSIONS: TURNING NEGATIVES INTO POSITIVES

Disability and personal growth

According to Delle Fave and Massimini (2003), quality of life depends not only on health conditions but also on personality and style of interaction with the environment. Sick people often report positive consequences of illness, such as improved relationships, positive personality changes, and even a better quality of life (Albrecht and Devlieger, 1999; Sodergren and Hyland, 2000, both in Delle Fave and Massimini).

Delle Fave (2001) and Delle Fave and Maletto (1992) (both in Delle Fave and Massimini, 2003) administered the Flow Questionnaire (Csikszentmihalyi and Csikszentmihalyi, 1988, in Delle Fave and Massimini) to a sample of 56 people with congenital disabilities (blindness and motor impairments). All but one of them reported *optimal experience* in their lives; it was mostly associated with work, study and the use of media. Jobs and learning were occasions for enjoyment, intrinsic reward and skill development, as well as opportunities for participation in the productive life.

The same questionnaire was given to 45 people who became blind, paraplegic or tetraplegic during adolescence or adulthood (Delle Fave, 1966, Delle Fave and Maletto, 1992, both in Delle Fave and Massimini). They had to face dramatic changes, often being deprived of activities previously associated with optimal experiences. Nevertheless, 41 participants acknowledged optimal experience in their present life. Blind people mostly associated it with media (reading in Braille, listening to radio and TV) and work, paraplegic and tetraplegic people with sport (such as basketball and table tennis), work and physiotherapy. Many of the skills and activities linked to optimal experience were acquired/discovered following their spinal injury or becoming blind.

Delle Fave and Massimini (2003) conclude by saying:

> . . . *physical impairments, rather than preventing development, can help individuals discover new opportunities for optimal experience and can foster personal growth. . . rehabilitation programmes . . . should focus on the activities subjectively associated with optimal experiences in order to exploit the behavioural flexibility and resource potential of disabled people, promoting their development and their active contribution to culture.*

Trauma and personal growth

According to Linley and Joseph (2003), various philosophies, literatures and religions throughout history have claimed that personal gain can be found in suffering. Although there is considerable evidence for post-traumatic stress disorder (PTSD) in survivors of various traumatic events (e.g. Joseph *et al.*, 1997, in Linley and Joseph), there is also a growing body of empirical evidence that trauma can provide the impetus for personal and social transformation. Why is it that some people are able to grow and thrive as a result of traumatic experience, achieving a higher level of functioning and self-actualization than they enjoyed before the trauma?

Calhoun and Tedeschi (1999, in Linley and Joseph) found that 30–90 per cent of people who experience some form of traumatic event report at least some positive changes following the trauma (the figure varies according to the type of event and other factors). These positive changes can underpin a whole new way of living that embraces the central tenets of positive psychology (Linley, 2000, in Linley and Joseph). People may:

● change their life philosophy, learning to appreciate each day to the full (i.e. positive subjective experience) and renegotiating what really matters in the full realization that their life is finite (Tedeschi *et al.,* 1998, in Linley and Joseph)

- believe themselves to be wiser or act more altruistically in the service of others (i.e. positive personal characteristics) and have a greater sense of personal resilience and strength, perhaps combined with greater acceptance of their vulnerabilities and limitations
- dedicate their energies to social renewal or political activism (i.e. positive institutions and communities), or
- report that their relationships are enhanced in some way, such as valuing their friends and family more (i.e. positive social relationships).

Psychotherapy and counselling

It appears that people who report more growth in the aftermath of trauma go on to show better long-term adjustment. It follows that trying to facilitate growth is a legitimate therapeutic goal (Linley and Joseph, 2002, in Linley and Joseph, 2003). This cannot be achieved through simple generalization from what we know about the treatment of PTSD (such as cognitive behaviour therapy (CBT)). Linley and Joseph (2003) believe that more client-centred, experiential and existential psychotherapies are likely to be of value in bringing about post-traumatic growth.

In existential therapy, the therapist–client relationship is the central concern. It aims to:

> . . . clarify and elaborate the . . . [client's] way of being-in-the-world, by using the therapeutic context as a microcosmic indication of the client's relationship to the world . . . This is what makes the existential perspective a positive approach – it seeks to examine and illuminate what is there, rather than correct what is lacking.

> (Bretherton and Ørner, 2003)

By stepping back from their own prejudices and stereotypes, existential therapists can identify clients' possibilities as well as their limitations, their strengths as well as their weaknesses (van Durzen-Smith, 1988, in Bretherton and Orner), rather than being attuned principally to the signs and symptoms of psychological disorder. This dual concern with possibility and limitation:

> . . . provides a framework within which the practice of positive psychology can recognize human potential without succumbing to an unrealistic optimism . . .

> (Bretherton and Ørner, 2003)

The existential approach is neither pessimistic nor optimistic, but can be profoundly *hopeful* – meaning can be found even in the face of the unchangeable givens of life, such as pain, guilt, and death (Frankl, 1969). By facing up to the questions posed by human suffering, existential psychotherapy lends itself to the understanding of people confronting the extreme challenges of life, such as HIV (Milton, 1997, in Bretherton and Orner) or terminal cancer (Jacobsen *et al.*, 2000, in Bretherton and Orner).

According to Bretherton and Orner, the existential approach is positive psychotherapy 'in disguise', given its recognition of human potential coupled with an awareness of the irreversible difficulties of the human condition.

SUMMARY

O Positive psychology (PP) is about happiness or (subjective) well-being (SWB) and can be defined as the scientific study of the positive aspects of human subjective experience.

O PP can be understood as a reaction against psychology's predominant emphasis on mental illness since the 1950s. Curing mental illness became psychology's preoccupation following the Second World War.

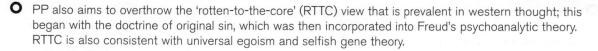

- PP also aims to overthrow the 'rotten-to-the-core' (RTTC) view that is prevalent in western thought; this began with the doctrine of original sin, which was then incorporated into Freud's psychoanalytic theory. RTTC is also consistent with universal egoism and selfish gene theory.

- The 'official' beginning of PP can be traced to Seligman's acknowledgement that psychology had largely neglected its aims to (i) help people lead more productive lives and (ii) identify and nurture talent and giftedness.

- The roots of PP lie in the humanistic psychology of Maslow and Rogers. As well as advocating the study of the full range of human experience, they vigorously attacked the medical model as applied to psychology.

- Those positive psychologists who are critical of the medical model reject the categorical approach current within clinical psychology ('borrowed' from psychiatric classification and diagnosis) and advocate the dimensional approach. The latter sees people's experience as unitary, whereby therapy is always aimed at the relief of suffering and the promotion of well-being.

- PP should stand in opposition to the medical model, which medicalizes human experience. Otherwise, PP might become incorporated into the medical model.

- The medical model is also known as the deficit model, whose negativity bias has been applied more widely by social and cognitive psychologists to 'normal' behaviour. As an alternative fundamental assumption for PP, the strengths perspective focuses on what works, what is improving, strong and effective.

- Influences on the strengths perspective include the strengths revolution (Buckingham and Clifton), solution-focused therapy (de Shazer) and the concept of post-traumatic growth (Tedeschi and Calhoun).

- Recently, researchers into SWB have taken up Aristotle's distinction between eudaimonic and hedonic happiness, but this has proved both methodologically and conceptually difficult. While the source of happiness may well be important, it does not appear to affect the experience of well-being.

- In western culture, happiness is often equated with success. Evidence indicates that social and cultural pressure to have more money, be more beautiful and so on make people more unhappy (depressed, anxious and so on).

- The optimal level of happiness appears to vary across domains and contexts – there is no single level that is optimal for every individual and activity. But very happy people tend to report more successful functioning than those of average happiness.

- As well as success (such as fulfilling relationships, high income, superior physical and mental health) making people happy, evidence suggests that positive affect (PA) produces success.

- The search for constant, intense happiness is likely to lead to instability in a person's life.

- Miller's advocacy of 'giving psychology away' and promoting human welfare has much in common with the aims of PP. While his approach is problem-centred, some positive psychologists have investigated how overcoming disability, trauma and suffering can be used to enhance personal growth.

- Client-centred, experiential and existential psychotherapies (as opposed to treatments such as cognitive behaviour therapy used to treat post-traumatic stress disorder) are likely to be of value in bringing about post-traumatic growth.

○ In trying to specify 'what makes life worth living', Seligman describes the pleasant life (happiness and well-being), the good life (favourite activities) and the meaningful life (using our strengths and virtues in work, love and parenting).

○ Another key to learning how to live a fulfilling life is discovering how to achieve a balanced time perspective (TP).

○ Positive personal traits that are correlated with SWB include (apart from happiness) optimism, self-determination, gratitude, mature defences, positive affect and wisdom.

○ From a biological evolutionary perspective, obstacles to well-being stem from differences between our current and ancestral environment. In terms of cultural evolution, individuals select the memes that will define their individuality; whenever possible, we choose behaviours that make us feel fully alive, competent and creative.

USEFUL WEBSITES

www.positivepsychology.org
www.personalitystrengths.com
www.eur.nl/fsw/research/happiness
www.cappeu.org

RECOMMENDED READING

Linley, P.A. (2008) *Average to A+: Realising Strengths in Yourself and Others.* Coventry: Capp Press.

Linley, P.A., Joseph, S., Harrington, S. and Wood, A.M. (2006) Positive psychology: past, present, and (possible) future. *The Journal of Positive Psychology, 1*(1), 3–16.

Oishi, S., Diener, E. and Lucas, R.E. (2007) The optimum level of well-being: can people be too happy? *Perspectives on Psychological Science, 2,* 346–60.

The Psychologist, 16(3) (2003) This is a special issue containing a number of articles on positive psychology.

Seligman, M.E.P. and Csikszentmihalyi, M. (2000) Positive psychology: an introduction. *American Psychologist, 55,* 5–14. (This is a special issue containing 16 articles on various aspects of positive psychology.)

CHAPTER 3

THE IDIOGRAPHIC AND NOMOTHETIC APPROACHES TO THE STUDY OF BEHAVIOUR

PSYCHOLOGY: THE STUDY OF INDIVIDUALS OR THE STUDY OF PEOPLE?

Of all the methods traditionally used by psychologists to study human beings, the *case study* is the one most often criticized for being unscientific (or the least scientific). The reason usually given is that, since only one 'case' is being studied, it is not possible to *generalize* the results. In other words, we cannot base our theories of what people are like on the study of individuals.

According to the same argument, the experiment is the most powerful method of research, partly because it *does* allow us to generalize (notwithstanding the criticisms of artificiality and so on). This is possible only because the characteristics of *particular* subjects/participants, being controlled through the use of experimental design, are *irrelevant*: it is *group averages* that are statistically analysed and that the investigator is interested in, as opposed to *individual performance*.

Consequently, if psychologists want to find out about people, the last thing they should do is study . . . people! This might seem like an absurd conclusion to draw, but is it also an inevitable one?

A number of points need to be made here.

- Imagine a chemist refusing to generalize the results of an investigation on the grounds that the particular sample of the chemical used was not typical or representative. However bizarre that may sound, it is the equivalent of the situation with regard to the psychological case study.
- It follows that human beings are different from chemicals (and other aspects of the physical world) in at least one major respect, namely they are not all identical or interchangeable but display great variability and variety.
- Different psychologists have interpreted (and studied) the nature and extent of this variability and variety in different ways. A convenient way of identifying these different approaches is to quote Kluckhohn and Murray (1953):

> *Every man is in certain respects like all other men, like some other men, and like no other men.*

How we are *all alike* is a way of referring to *general psychology*, the study of basic psychological processes, with the emphasis very much on the *process* (such as memory, perception and learning). It is almost as if the process occurs in some disembodied way, with the memorizer, perceiver or learner being almost irrelevant, or at least unnecessary, for an understanding of the process under investigation. This is part of what goes on in the name of psychology, so it must be to do with the study of people, mustn't it?

The nomothetic approach

Ways in which we are like *some* other human beings is the subject matter of *individual differences*. While this approach acknowledges that humans are definitely not like chemicals, it also claims that there is only a limited, relatively small number of ways in which people differ from each other, sometimes referred to as *group norms*. Examples include personality, intelligence, age, gender, and ethnic and cultural background.

This way of studying people is called the *nomothetic approach* (from the Greek *nomos*, meaning 'law'). If psychologists can establish the ways in which we are like *some* others, then they can also tell us how we are *different* from others – these are two sides of the same coin. In either case, people are *compared* with each other, and this is usually done using *psychometric tests* ('mental measurement'). The results of these tests are then analysed using a statistical technique called *factor analysis*, which is used to identify the basic factors or dimensions that constitute personality, intelligence, etc. Once these have been identified, the basis for comparing people with each other has been established. Factor-analytic theories of intelligence include Spearman's two-factor theory (1904, 1927), Burt's (1949, 1955) and Vernon's (1950) hierarchical model, Thurstone's primary mental abilities (1938), and Guilford's structure of intellect (1959). Eysenck (1953, 1965) and Cattell (1965) are probably the best-known factor-analytic personality theorists.

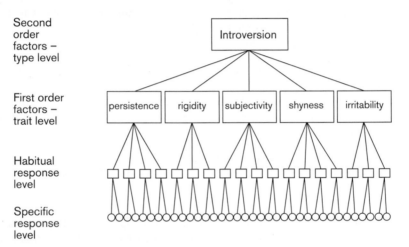

Figure 3.1 Eysenck's hierarchical model of personality in relation to the introversion dimension (After Eysenck, H.J. (1953), *The Structure of Human Personality*. London, Methuen)

According to Jones and Elcock (2001):

> *An important effect of the use of such statistical methods [factor analysis] on scores from groups of subjects was to create an idealized 'average' person. Psychology was to become the scientific investigation of such hypothesized average 'individuals', rather than investigating individuals themselves.*

The idiographic approach

Ways in which we are *unlike anyone else* is the subject matter of those psychologists who adopt an *idiographic approach* (from the Greek *idios*, meaning 'own' or 'private'). This is the study of *individual norms*, of people as unique individuals. Gordon Allport (1937, 1961) is arguably the main advocate of an idiographic approach. The humanistic personality theories of Maslow (1954, 1968) and Rogers (1951, 1961) and Kelly's (1955) personal construct (PC) theory also represent this approach and embody many of its basic principles and assumptions (see Chapters 1 and 14).

Some questions for consideration

1 Are the nomothetic and idiographic approaches mutually exclusive – that is, do we have to choose between them? Are there any theories of personality that embody both approaches?
2 Does it make sense to talk about a totally unique person, someone whose personality has nothing in common with that of any other?
3 Must we agree with Allport (1937) that, since all science is nomothetic, and since psychology should be concerned with the study of individuals, therefore psychology cannot be a science?
4 Have we found a solution to the riddle concerning the study of people (that psychologists, in order to learn about people, should not study people)? If we distinguish between *people as individuals* and *people as groups*, then perhaps we have; we need to be clear whether our aim is to find out about this *particular* person, or how this person *compares with others*. The *idiographic* approach takes the *individual* as its basic unit of analysis, while for the *nomothetic* approach it is *groups* of individuals. In the former, the data obtained represent a sample of the individual's total set ('population') of emotions, cognitions, personality traits and so on, while in the latter, the obtained data represent a specified trait or behaviour as measured in a sample of individuals drawn from some larger population of individuals. It is the difference between a *population of many* (nomothetic) and a *population of one* (idiographic) (see Figure 3.2).

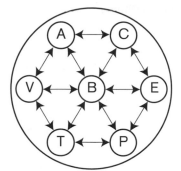

a) Basic unit of study = the individual

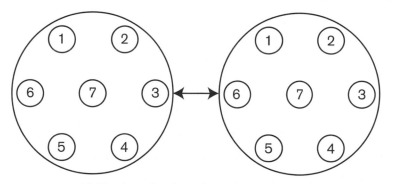

b) Basic unit of study = the group

Figure 3.2 Differences in the kind of generalization involved in the (a) idiographic and (b) nomothetic approaches. In the idiographic approach, data collected represent samples from an individual's total population of characteristics (A, attitudes; B, behaviour; C, cognition; E, emotion; P, physiological make-up; T, traits; V, values) and the norms that operate are individual norms (generalizing *within* the individual).

In the nomothetic approach, data collected represent either (i) samples from the total population of the characteristic in question (e.g. How do high E (extroversion) scorers compare with low E scorers on some task?) or (ii) samples from the total population of performance on some task with individual differences held constant. In both cases, this gives group norms (generalizing *across or between* individuals).

41

If the answers to the first question (1) are 'no' and 'yes' respectively, and if the answer to the second (2) is 'no', then we should regard the process of studying individuals as individuals as being inseparable from the process of comparing individuals with each other. By the same token, if the answer to the third question (3) is 'no', then we should be willing to accept that generalizing from the individual case, as well as generalizing about the same individual, are legitimate scientific activities: the nomothetic and idiographic approaches are compatible with each other.

HISTORICAL BACKGROUND

The idiographic/nomothetic distinction is related to another distinction made, independently, by two nineteenth-century German philosophers, Dilthey and Windelband, between two kinds of science:

- the *Naturwissenschaften* (natural sciences), such as physics and chemistry, aim to establish general laws, allowing predictions based on statements about cause-and-effect relationships
- the *Geisteswissenschaften* ('moral sciences'), such as philosophy, the humanities, history, biography and literary criticism, and 'social science', involve *Verstehen*, an intuitive, empathic understanding (see Figure 3.3).

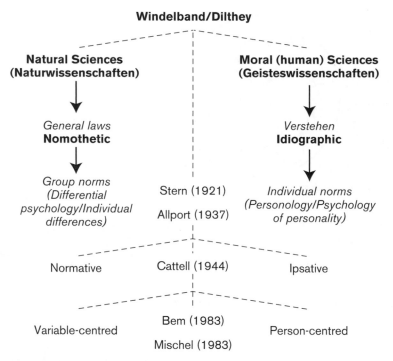

Figure 3.3 The nomothetic–idiographic distinction and its relationship to other, corresponding distinctions

The natural sciences are concerned with the natural world, and so quite appropriately *explain* it in terms of 'natural laws' ('laws of nature') and analyse it into elements. But the moral or human sciences require an *understanding* of human mental activity (i.e. consciousness), stressing the inner unity of individual life and the person as an articulated whole (Valentine, 1992). Rather than treating the individual case as incidental to the discovery of general laws, the social sciences focus primarily on the particular (whether this be a person, historical event or literary work). Windelband, together with another German, Rickert, went on to argue that all the disciplines concerned with 'man and his works' should not – and by their very nature cannot – generalize, but must devote themselves to the understanding of each particular case (Holt, 1967).

Corresponding to the distinction between the natural and human sciences is that between a *variable-centred* and *person-centred* approach (Bem, 1983; Mischel, 1983), and a *normative* ('compared with others') and *ipsative* ('compared with the self') approach (Cattell, 1944) respectively (see Figure 3.3).

According to Holt (1967), there are a number of false beliefs, still widely held, about the nomothetic/idiographic distinction. He points out that (i) these are false beliefs as held by those of an idiographic persuasion, and (ii) a distinction is commonly made between *personology* (the psychology of personality) and *differential psychology* (the psychology of individual differences). These correspond to the idiographic and nomothetic approaches respectively.

Figure 3.4 The nomothetic and idiographic distinction is related to the distinction made in the nineteenth century between *Naturwissenschaften* (natural sciences) and *Geisteswissenschaften* (moral sciences), which can be recognized as the distinction between the scientist in the laboratory and the philosopher in his/her armchair

The goal of personology is understanding, while that of nomothetic science is prediction and control

According to Holt (1967), all the highly developed sciences aim at prediction and control *through* understanding, and these goals cannot be separated. He argues that:

Most scientists, as contrasted with technologists, are themselves more motivated by the need to figure things out, to develop good theories and workable models that make nature intelligible, and less concerned with the ultimate payoff, the applied benefits of prediction and control that understanding makes possible . . .

Holt believes that many psychologists, based on this misconception of natural science as totally rigorous, objective and machine-like, try to emulate this nomothetic approach. It is *because of*, rather than despite, the 'intrinsically difficult and ambiguity-ridden' nature of psychology that this view of natural science is so appealing, especially to behaviourist psychologists (see Chapters 10 and 14). But at the 'opposite extreme' lies *Verstehen* (see above), an attempt to know something from the inside, by non-intellectual means, as directly as possible, through trying to gain an empathic feeling for it. This is non-explanatory, 'a subjective effect properly aimed at by artists, not scientists' (Holt, 1967).

But even accepting Holt's argument regarding the importance of understanding in natural science, and the important difference between 'scientific' and 'non-scientific' understanding, isn't this only half the story? Does it necessarily follow that prediction and control are appropriate aims for psychology (as they clearly are for physics and chemistry, along with explanation/understanding)?

George Miller (1969) for one believes that control is inappropriate, at least in the sense of one person (the experimenter/investigator/therapist) assuming a powerful, directing role in relation to another (subject/patient) (see Chapter 9). Critics of mainstream psychology (especially Skinner's *radical behaviourism*: see Chapter 14) see the attempt to apply principles and methods derived from the laboratory study of rats and pigeons to human behaviour as the ultimate kind of mechanistic, dehumanizing approach (e.g. Heather, 1976; Shotter, 1975).

Not only is *understanding* the appropriate aim for psychology (as opposed to control), but Miller argues that *self-understanding* is what psychology should be striving to provide people with. This is what he means by 'giving psychology away' (see Chapter 2). Attempts to realize these aims are perhaps best seen in psychotherapy, much of which attempts to change individuals' self-perception and increase their self-understanding (*insight*). It also aims at increasing *autonomy* (Lindley, 1987, in Fairbairn, 1987). Taking control of one's own life is a very different form of control compared with its meaning in the natural sciences.

The proper methods of personology are intuition and empathy, which have no place in natural science

Holt (1967) rejects this claim by pointing out that all scientists make use of intuition and empathy as part of the most exciting and creative phase of their work, namely when deciding what to study, what variables to control, what empirical strategies to use, and when making discoveries within the structure of empirical data. To the extent that such processes are inevitably involved in science, which is, first and foremost, a human activity, no science can be thought of as wholly objective (see Chapters 1 and 10). The failure to recognize the role of these processes, and the belief in the 'objective truth' produced by the use of the 'scientific method', can result in theories and explanations that can work to the detriment of certain individuals and social groups (as in the 'race and IQ debate': see Chapter 9).

While 'hard science' may appear softer when the role of intuition is acknowledged, it is also nomothetic psychology that has been most guilty of the 'crimes' of racism, ethnocentrism and sexism (see Chapters 6 and 8).

The concepts of personology must be individualized, not generalized as are the concepts of natural science

General laws are not possible in personology because its subject matter is unique individuals that have no place in natural science

These two beliefs are dealt with together, because they lie at the very heart of the nomothetic/idiographic debate. They relate to two fundamental questions:

- Does it make sense to talk about a wholly unique individual?
- What is the relationship between individual cases and general laws/principles in scientific practice?

The wholly unique individual

Allport (1961) distinguished between three types of personal traits or dispositions: *cardinal*, *central* and *secondary*. Briefly, *cardinal traits* refer to a particular, all-pervading disposition (for example, greed, ambition or lust) that dictates and directs almost all of an individual's behaviour. In practice, these are very rare. *Central traits* are the basic building blocks that make up the core of the personality and constitute the individual's characteristic ways of dealing with the world (such as honest, loving, happy-go-lucky). A surprisingly small number of these is usually sufficient to capture the essence of a person. *Secondary traits* are less consistent and influential than central traits, and refer to tastes, preferences and so on, that may change quite quickly and do not define 'the person' as central traits do.

These *individual traits* are peculiar (idiosyncratic) to each person, in at least three senses.

1 A trait that is central for one person may be only secondary for another, and irrelevant for a third. What makes a trait central or secondary is not what it *is* but how often and how strongly it influences the person's behaviour (Carver and Scheier, 1992).
2 Some traits are possessed by only one person; indeed, there may be as many separate traits as there are people.

3 Even if two different people are given (for convenience) the same descriptive label (for example, 'aggressive'), it may not *mean* the same for the individuals concerned, and to that extent it *isn't* the same trait.

For Allport, since personality dispositions reflect the subtle shadings that distinguish a particular individual from all others, they must often be described at length (for example, 'little Susan has a peculiar anxious helpfulness all her own') instead of by a single label ('helpful'). What all this means is that it is very difficult to compare people:

> *Suppose you wish to select a roommate or a wife or a husband, or simply to pick out a suitable birthday gift for your mother. Your knowledge of mankind in general will not help you very much . . . [Any given individual] is a unique creation of the forces of nature. There was never a person just like him and there will never be again . . . To develop a science of personality we must accept this fact.*
>
> *(Allport, 1961)*

While the idiographic approach contends that people are not comparable (everyone is, in effect, on a 'different scale'), comparing people in terms of a specified number of traits or dimensions (in order to determine individual differences) is precisely what the nomothetic approach involves. According to this view, traits have the same *psychological meaning* for everyone, so that people differ only in the extent to which the trait is present. For example, everyone is more or less introverted, which means that everyone will score somewhere on the introversion–extroversion scale: the difference between individuals is one of *degree* only (a *quantitative difference*). By contrast, the idiographic approach sees differences between people as *qualitative* (a difference in kind).

Allport himself recognized that people *can* be compared with each other, but in terms of *common traits* (basic *modes of adjustment* applicable to *all* members of a particular cultural, ethnic or linguistic group). They are what is measured by personality scales, tests or ratings, but at best they can provide only a rough approximation to any particular personality. For example, many individuals are predominantly outgoing or shy, yet:

> *. . . there are endless varieties of dominators, leaders, aggressors, followers, yielders, and timid souls . . . When we designate Tom and Ted both as aggressive, we do not mean that their aggression is identical in kind. Common speech is a poor guide to psychological subtleties.*
>
> *(Allport, 1961)*

According to Holt (1967), to describe an individual trait we either have to create a new word (neologism) for each unique trait, or we use a unique configuration of already existing words. While the former would make ordinary communication, let alone science, impossible, the latter is a concealed form of nomothesis, a 'fallacious attempt to capture something ineffably individual by a complex net of general concepts' (Allport, 1937, in Holt, 1967).

What does 'unique' actually mean?

Disagreement between Allport and those of a nomothetic persuasion is not so much to do with whether or not they believe in the idea of uniqueness, but rather *how uniqueness is defined*. Eysenck, for example, sees uniqueness as reflecting a unique combination of levels on trait dimensions, with the dimensions themselves being the same for all:

> *To the scientist, the unique individual is simply the point of intersection of a number of quantitative variables.*
>
> *(Eysenck, 1953)*

As we have seen, this is a definition of uniqueness in terms of *common* traits. But, for Allport, this is a contradiction in terms, since only individual traits capture the individuality of individuals. He objects to Eysenck's claim by asking:

> *What does this statement mean? It means that the scientist is not interested in the mutual interdependence of part-systems within the whole system of personality . . . [and] is not interested in the manner in which your introversion interacts with your other traits, with your values, and with your life plans. The scientist, according to this view, then, isn't interested in the personality system at all, but only in the common dimensions. The person is left as a mere 'point of intersection' with no internal structure, coherence or animation . . .*
>
> *(Allport, 1961)*

Agreeing with Holt, Brody (1988, in Eysenck, 1994) argues that:

> *If the trait applies only to one person, then it cannot be described in terms that apply to more than one person. This would require one to invent a new language to describe each person or, perhaps, to develop the skills of a poet to describe an individual.*

According to Krahé (1992), the idiographic claim that there are unique traits that apply to only one individual is undoubtedly false, if taken literally. Traits are defined as differential constructs referring to a person's position on a trait dimension relative to others. But at the other extreme, Krahé believes that the traditional (nomothetic) view of traits as explanatory constructs that apply to everyone is equally misguided.

Holt believes that the nomothetic/idiographic distinction is based on a *false dichotomy*. All descriptions involve some degree of generalization, so that when we describe an individual case, there is always (at least implicitly) a comparison being made with other instances of the category or class to which the individual belongs. To describe *this* person, we must already have (and be applying) our concept of 'a person'. If our concept of a person includes their uniqueness, this at least is something that everyone has in common and is perfectly consistent with Eysenck's (nomothetic) concept of uniqueness. Indeed, could we even recognize a person who was totally unlike any other, in any respect, *as* a person?

The relationship between individual cases and general principles

When Windelband distinguished between *Naturwissenschaften* and *Geisteswissenschaften* in 1894, the mechanistic science of the time operated on the principle that science does not deal with individual cases. The individual case is not lawful, since laws were seen as empirical regularities; an average is the only fact and all deviations from it are merely errors (Holt, 1967). Since it is not possible to generalize from a single case, and since the aim of science is to formulate general laws and principles, the study of single cases is not a valid part of scientific practice.

But is this a valid view of science as it is practised today? Are there different senses in which generalization can take place? Given the false dichotomy between the nomothetic and idiographic approaches, how should we understand the relationship between individual cases and general laws or principles?

Finding the general in the particular

Holt (1967) acknowledges that, while we cannot carry out the complete scientific process by the study of one individual,

> *. . . in certain of the disciplines concerned with man, from anatomy to sensory psychology, it has usually been assumed that the phenomena being studied are so universal that they can be located for study in any single person . . .*

However, no matter how intensively prolonged, objective and well controlled the study of a single case may be, we can never be sure to what extent the findings will apply to other people. Unless and until the investigation is repeated with an adequate sample, we cannot know how 'typical' the single case actually is. This is the logic behind the study by psychologists of groups of people, so that personality and other individual differences do not 'get in the way' of the key individual variable under investigation. But while the reasons behind this practice may be clear, are they necessarily valid?

The objections from an idiographic theorist like Allport should now be obvious, but a nomothetic theorist such as Eysenck will also object, although for very different reasons. Precisely because he emphasizes the basic dimensions of personality, in terms of which every person can be compared, he believes that any investigation that attempts to exclude them or render them irrelevant (through rigorous use of experimental design) is inadequate. For example:

- main experimental effects apply only to *averages* (*means*), preventing predictions about individual cases
- any theories or explanations based on such studies may have only very limited validity – that is, they may not generalize to samples with particular scores on important personality dimensions
- failure to take individual differences into account may result in main experimental effects being swamped or obscured.

Eysenck (1966) sees the dimensional approach (or typologies, see above) as a compromise between (i) the false extremes of the experimentalist, who seeks to establish general functional relationships (the nomothetic approach), where personality differences are largely excluded, and (ii) the idiographic personality theorist, who 'embraces the concept of the individual so whole-heartedly that it leaves no room for scientific generalization, laws, or even predictability of conduct' (Eysenck, 1966, in Valentine, 1992).

Single-subject designs are OK

The distinction between single-case and group studies may be another false dichotomy. An individual case can be, and often is, the subject of scientific investigation. Where data from individual subjects are seen as reliable and representative, single-subject designs are considered acceptable (Valentine, 1992).

From the idiographic perspective, the very notion of an individual being 'representative' is contentious (because it implies the opposite of unique). But the fact that the study of individual cases goes on at all within 'mainstream', nomothetic psychology indicates that the study of individuals may not, in and of itself, be incompatible with the aim of psychological science to generalize about behaviour.

Indeed, for Thorngate (1986, in Hilliard, 1993), the study of averages is often ill-suited to providing information about what people 'in general' do, since it typically cancels out systematic patterns in individual persons. (This is similar to Eysenck's criticisms of experimental psychology above.) Rather than searching for nomothetic laws based on averaged data, the discovery of these individual patterns requires a strategy in which the uniqueness of individuals is preserved. As Thorngate says:

> *To find out what people do in general, we must first discover what each person does in particular, then determine what, if anything, these particulars have in common . . . Nomothetic laws lie at the intersection of idiographic laws; the former can be discovered only after we find the latter.*

In other words, the generality of the findings would not be determined through group aggregates (finding the average for a large number of individuals) but by replication on a case-by-case basis. Thorngate is arguing that the two approaches are complementary and interdependent. According to Hilliard (1993):

> *Although single-case methodology has been identified with an exclusive idiographic focus in the minds of many, this identification is simply not warranted. Most single-case research clearly involves*

determining the generality across subjects of the relationships uncovered at the individual, or idiographic, level . . .

Hilliard gives as a prime example of such methodology Skinner's use of single-case research to study the principles of operant conditioning (see Box 3.1).

BOX 3.1 SKINNER'S SINGLE-SUBJECT EXPERIMENTAL DESIGN

Skinner typically studied the behaviour of *one subject* at a time. 'Experimental' denotes that only one variable is manipulated at a time. This allowed him to uncover causal (functional) relationships. Behaviourist researchers wish to detect principles that have generality – that is, cover a large number of cases and situations. The goal of research is not to discover idiosyncratic information about the particular situation being studied but general principles that allow accurate prediction and control in a wide variety of situations.

Part of Skinner's rationale for using individual organisms was that *groups do not behave* – only individuals do. Therefore, it makes more sense to study single organisms. Although general principles may apply to a group, the specifics of these principles may vary between organisms.

As we noted earlier, unlike psychology, the natural/physical sciences do not face the problem of the individuality of the entities under study. An appropriate research design in behavioural science must account for individual differences in a way that still produces general principles. Skinner argued that the single-subject design achieves this goal. Derived measures such as group averages are artificial contrivances that obscure important information about actual behaviour. The extent to which principles generally hold is discovered through replications with other single subjects.

One feature of such research is the fact that the individual rat or pigeon acts as its own control, since its behaviour is measured before, during and after the reinforcement contingencies are applied.

(Based on O'Donohue and Ferguson, 2001)

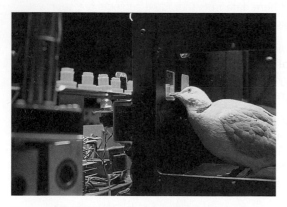

Figure 3.5 The individual pigeon acts as its own control in the Skinner box and represents single-case research

Sometimes, single cases may be all that is available to the investigator, as in neuropsychology, where patients who suffer brain injury and disease are patients first and subjects/participants second. While they may be intensely interesting in themselves, they are usually studied for what they can tell us about the *normal* functioning of the brain and nervous system. Unless an adequate baseline for comparison is provided, such as the patient's performance before the illness/injury, or scores from the normal population on standardized tests, the results are scientifically uninterpretable. Without replication, it is difficult to know whether the results are generalizable: such data are insufficient to establish general laws. However, even if the study of individual cases does not allow the testing of hypotheses, it may at least help to *formulate* them (Valentine, 1992).

Generalizing within the individual

The results from studies of individuals may also offer the potential for generalizing to other attributes or behavioural characteristics *of the individual being studied*. We noted earlier that idiographic research is aimed at generalizing within the individual, while nomothetic research seeks to generalize across individuals.

According to Krahé (1992), there is no inherent conflict between these aims – they are *complementary*, rather than mutually exclusive, research strategies:

> *Nomothetic procedures are important for investigating individual differences and differences in performance among groups of subjects, but provide no information on processes within individuals. Idiographic approaches, on the other hand, provide information about processes within individuals, but provide no information on individual differences or on the generality of findings across individuals. Thus, each procedure has its advantages and limitations, and neither is a substitute for the other.*
>
> *(Epstein, 1983, in Krahé, 1992)*

Logically, there is no reason to equate 'generalization' with the study of 'groups', although that is exactly what the nomothetic approach does. Allport was interested in the study of *individual norms* (as distinct from *group norms*), but both involve 'going beyond' the data that have actually been collected and making predictions about future 'performance'. This can either be the future performance of other individuals not included in the sample studied (group norms/nomothetic approach) or the future performance of the same individual (individual norms/idiographic approach).

According to Hilliard (1993), there has been a recent widespread resurgence of interest in single-case designs within psychotherapy research. Various terms are used for such designs, including: single case, N of 1, case study, small N, idiographic, intensive, discovery-oriented, intrasubject and time-series. These can be confusing, and single-case research is best viewed as a sub-class of intrasubject research, in which the focus is on the unfolding, over time, of variables within individual cases.

Consistent with this revival is the view that it is perfectly possible to apply systematic, reliable, quantitative or experimental methods to the study of individual cases. For example, factor analysis can be applied to individual as well as to group data (Krahé, 1992). Not only is this a scientifically valid approach, but there has been a proliferation of quantitative and experimental studies of the single case (Runyan, 1983, in Krahé, 1992).

RECONCILING THE NOMOTHETIC AND IDIOGRAPHIC APPROACHES

From the preceding discussion, it seems that psychologists are increasingly coming to believe that the two approaches, far from being opposed and mutually exclusive, are in fact complementary and interdependent. As Krahé (1992) puts it:

> *Thus, there seems to be a growing consensus that it is possible, in principle, for idiographic and nomothetic approaches to join forces so as to contribute to a more comprehensive analysis of the issues of personality psychology . . .*

Even Allport himself did not reject the nomothetic approach out of hand. Despite his insistence on the importance of the idiographic approach, Allport did not adopt an *exclusively* qualitative approach to research. Rather, he recommended that we should study individuals by using as many and varied means as possible (Ashworth, 2003). For example, when discussing the nature of psychology as a science, he says that:

> *Science aims to achieve powers of understanding, prediction and control above the level of unaided common sense. From this point of view it becomes apparent that only by taking adequate account of the individual's total pattern of life can we achieve the aims of science. Knowledge of general laws . . . quantitative assessments and correlational procedures are all helpful: but with this conceptual (nomothetic) knowledge must be blended a shrewd diagnosis of trends within an individual . . . Unless such idiographic (particular) knowledge is fused with nomothetic (universal)*

knowledge, we shall not achieve the aims of science, however closely we imitate the methods of the natural and mathematical sciences.

(Allport, 1960)

Also related to the aims of science, Jaccard and Dittus (1990, in Krahé, 1992) argue that a strictly idiographic approach *is not* directly opposed to the identification and development of universal laws of human behaviour. The idiographic researcher, like the nomothetic, is interested in *explaining* behaviour, and to do this both seek a general theoretical framework that specifies the constructs that should be focused upon and the types of relationship expected among these concepts. The essential difference between them is that one applies the framework to a single person, while the other applies it to people in general. They share the same scientific aim.

Both Allport and Windelband made it very clear that one and the same issue can, in principle, be considered either from an idiographic or nomothetic perspective, depending on the nature of the question under investigation (Krahé, 1992). According to Epstein (1983, in Krahé, 1992), the two approaches 'do not present different solutions to the same problem but solutions to different problems'. Lamiell's (1981, 1982, 1987) idiothetic approach is an attempt to integrate the aims of both approaches.

Idiographic methods, old and new

We began the chapter by pointing out the limitations (as judged from a nomothetic point of view) of the case study. A standard criticism of Freud's psychoanalytic theory is that he relied on the case study for the collection of his 'data'. But we have also seen that this method is central to neuropsychology. Perhaps it isn't the case study method itself that is of limited scientific value, but rather the use researchers make of it, the data that are obtained, and the resulting theories and hypotheses.

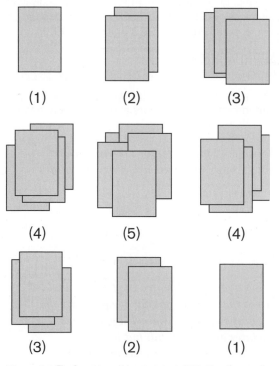

(1)   (2)   (3)

(4)   (5)   (4)

(3)   (2)   (1)

Figure 3.6 The Q-sort is used to assess an individual's self-concept

A more specific idiographic method is the Q-sort, originally devised and developed by Butler and Haigh (1954) and Stephenson (1953), but best known as it was used by Carl Rogers for assessing an individual's self-concept, especially in the context of psychotherapy (see Chapter 14). The basic procedure involves giving people a large set of cards containing self-evaluative statements (such as 'I am intelligent', 'I often feel guilty', 'I am ambitious'), phrases or single words. The person is asked to sort the cards into piles, one pile containing statements that are 'most like you', another that are 'least like you', and other piles representing gradations in between these two extremes. While each of the two 'extreme' piles may comprise only a single card, those in between are allowed to have more, with those in the middle having the most.

The technique forces the sorter to decide what s/he is like by comparing qualities with each other, while in (nomothetic) rating scales, each response is separate and unrelated to the others (all the descriptions apply equally well). This is impossible in the Q-sort (Carver and Scheier, 1992).

This same basic technique can be used to assess 'The kind of person I am (now)', 'The kind of person I used to be' (allowing an assessment of changes in the self-image over time) and 'The kind of person I would like to be' (a measure of the person's ideal self). Comparing self-image and ideal-self can be used as a measure of the progress of therapy, since the greater the similarity between the two, the greater the degree of *congruence*, one of the goals of Rogers's client-centred therapy. The Q-sort is repeated several times during the course of therapy.

The repertory grid technique (or 'rep grid') was used by Kelly to investigate a person's system of constructs – the individual's unique set of concepts and perceptions through which the world, both social and physical, is interpreted and predicted (see Box 3.2 and Chapter 1).

BOX 3.2 KELLY'S REPERTORY GRID TECHNIQUE

While there are different forms of the test, the basic method involves:

1 writing a list of the most important people in your life (*elements*)
2 choosing three of these elements
3 deciding how two of these are alike and different from the third; the resulting description is a *construct*, expressed in a *bipolar way* (e.g. affectionate–not affectionate)
4 applying the construct to all the other elements
5 repeating steps 2, 3 and 4 until either the person has produced all the constructs s/he can, or until a sufficient number has been produced as judged by the investigator.

All this information can be collated in the form of a *grid*, hence the name. The grid can be factor-analysed, in order to reveal any overlap between the person's constructs. Although the rep grid is primarily an idiographic technique, it can be used nomothetically. For example, Bannister and Fransella's *Grid Test of Thought Disorder* (1966, 1967) is designed for use with thought-disordered schizophrenics. It contains standardized elements and constructs (these are supplied by the investigator), and the test has been standardized on large numbers of similar patients, allowing individual scores to be compared with group norms.

Like the Q-sort, the rep grid has been used to study how patients participating in group psychotherapy change their perception of each other (and themselves) during the period of therapy. The group members and themselves are the elements, and constructs are supplied (Fransella, 1970). The method has been used extensively by Fransella (1972) with people being treated for severe stuttering.

As with the Q-sort and the rep grid, there is no single, definitive way of conducting *interpretative phenomenological analysis* (IPA). The aim of IPA is to explore in detail how (small numbers of) participants make sense of their personal and social world; the main currency of an IPA study is the *meanings* which particular experiences, events and states hold for participants (Smith and Osborn, 2003). The approach is phenomenological in that it attempts to explore personal experience and is concerned with an individual's personal perception or account of an object or event – as opposed to trying to define the object or event objectively. For example, in a study of nurses' perceptions of 'care and caring' (Bassett, 2002), it was the meaning of these abstract concepts that was the focus of study (see Gross, 2008).

CONCLUSIONS: A NEW WAY OF LOOKING AT THE RESEARCH PROCESS

Regardless of the details of particular new methodologies, the major implication of the resurgence of interest in the idiographic approach is a new conception of the relationship between the investigator and the person 'under investigation' (Krahé, 1992).

The traditional (nomothetic) perception of the process of psychological inquiry involves a clear-cut division of roles, whereby the investigator formulates hypotheses, produces operational definitions and selects appropriate measuring instruments, while the 'subject' delivers valid data by dutifully completing the measuring instruments. Interaction between the two is limited to (i) instructions, and (ii) debriefing. From the idiographic perspective, this role division is neither appropriate nor fruitful: it makes little use of the competence of the individual as an expert on his/her own personality.

Some investigators have explicitly advocated that the person whose personality is being studied should play a more active and cooperative role in the research process. For example, Hermans and Bonarius (1991, in Krahé, 1992) use the term co-investigator (compare this with Kelly's personal construct theory, in which the client is likened to a PhD student, with the therapist his/her supervisor; see Chapters 1 and 11). Collaborative and new paradigm research are becoming increasingly influential (see Chapter 10).

IPA illustrates this shift very well. According to Smith and Osborn (2003), IPA emphasizes that the research exercise is a dynamic process, in which the researcher is actively trying to get close to the participant's personal world (an 'insider's perspective': Conrad, 1987, in Smith and Osborn). But this cannot be achieved completely or directly. IPA involves a two-stage interpretation process: the participants are trying to make sense of their world, and the researcher is trying to make sense of the participants' efforts to make sense of their world.

The very use of the term participant, instead of 'subject' (e.g. British Psychological Society, 1990, 1993, 2000), reflects a change in the thinking of psychologists about the research process, especially its ethical features. Not only is the term 'subject' degrading and dehumanizing (e.g. Heather, 1976), but if a person is not studied as a unique individual (individual norms) but only in order to establish group norms, then s/he is not being treated fully as a person (see Chapter 9).

This, of course, is an ethical criticism of the nomothetic approach to research from an idiographic perspective. But just as there has been considerable reconciliation in recent years between the methodologies of the two approaches, so there is the promise that this reconciliation will make the study of human personality a more meaningful, and a more ethically acceptable, enterprise.

SUMMARY

O Human beings are not all identical or interchangeable, but display great variability and variety.

O The ways in which we are like some other people is the concern of individual differences, which is concerned with group norms, such as personality, intelligence, age, gender, ethnic and cultural background.

O The study of individual differences involves a nomothetic approach, according to which people are compared in terms of a limited number of factors or dimensions, established by factor analysis. Examples include the personality theories of Eysenck and Cattell.

O The ways in which we are unlike anyone else are the concern of the idiographic approach, which studies individual norms. Examples include Allport's trait theory, Maslow and Rogers's humanistic personality theories and Kelly's personal construct theory.

O The idiographic and nomothetic approaches are related to the *Geisteswissenschaften* ('moral sciences') and the *Naturwissenschaften* (natural sciences) respectively. The latter are concerned with establishing general laws that enable predictions to be made about the natural world, while the former involve *Verstehen*, which focuses on individual cases and does not permit generalization.

O Holt argues that the three goals of prediction and control (differential psychology/individual differences) and understanding (personology/psychology of personality) cannot be separated.

O There is much debate as to whether prediction and control are appropriate aims for psychology, and self-understanding may be more appropriate than understanding (best seen in psychotherapy).

O Intuition and empathy are not unique to personology but play a part in all scientific work, making science less than wholly objective.

O Allport distinguished between three kinds of individual traits (cardinal, central and secondary). Because these are idiosyncratic, it is impossible to use them to compare people; however, they can be compared in terms of common traits.

O The idiographic approach sees differences between people as qualitative, while the nomothetic approach sees them as merely quantitative.

O Uniqueness can be defined in different ways. Eysenck sees uniqueness as reflecting a unique combination of levels on trait dimensions (which are the same for everybody).

O Eysenck criticizes the (extreme nomothetic) attempt to eliminate individual differences from experimental studies, in order to establish general functional relationships, as well as the (extreme idiographic) emphasis on the individual that prevents generalization, laws, or even the prediction of behaviour.

O Single-case versus group studies is a false dichotomy; individual cases are often used in psychological research, indicating that the study of individuals may not be incompatible with making generalizations about behaviour.

O Most single-case research involves determining the generality across subjects of the relationships uncovered at the individual level, such as in Skinner's study of operant conditioning.

O Sometimes, single cases may be all that is available to the investigator, as in neuropsychology. But an adequate baseline must be provided if data from such single cases are to be scientifically useful.

O Allport advocated the use of both idiographic and nomothetic methods/knowledge in the pursuit of science's aim to achieve powers of understanding, prediction and control above the level of unaided common sense.

O The Q-sort is an idiographic method, best known as used by Rogers for assessing an individual's self-concept in the context of psychotherapy.

O Kelly's repertory grid technique (or 'rep grid') is used to identify a person's unique set of constructs. It can be used nomothetically, as with thought-disordered schizophrenics, patients in psychotherapy and people being treated for severe stuttering.

O Interpretative phenomenological analysis (IPA) is a qualitative research method that illustrates a new view of the relationship between the investigator and the person being studied ('the subject'). The latter is now regarded as much more of a co-investigator/collaborator/colleague in the research process.

USEFUL WEBSITES

http://www.nevada.edu/~russ/hurlburt-knapp-2006.pdf
http://www.aare.edu.au/93pap/rochl93265.txt

RECOMMENDED READING

Allport, G.W. (1962) The general and the unique in psychological science. *Journal of Personality, 30,* 405–22.

Holt, R.R. (1967) Individuality and generalization in the psychology of personality. In R.S. Lazarus and E.M. Opton (eds) *Personality.* Harmondsworth: Penguin. (This is a revised version of the original article, which appeared in the *Journal of Personality, 30,* 377–494.)

Krahé, B. (1992) *Personality and Social Psychology: Towards a Synthesis.* London: Sage. (Especially Chapters 6, 7 and 9.)

CHAPTER 4

TRAITS AND SITUATIONS AS CAUSES OF BEHAVIOUR

COMMON-SENSE VIEWS OF PERSONALITY

Part of 'common sense' psychology (the lay person's everyday understanding of behaviour; see Chapter 1) is the belief that people behave in a largely *consistent*, and hence predictable, way. As a general rule, if you ask someone to predict another person's behaviour, the response will depend on how well (or otherwise) s/he knows (or feels they know) the other person: complete strangers are (almost) impossible to predict, while with close relatives and friends it is much easier. Why?

Part of what we mean by saying we know somebody well is to be able to identify the traits and characteristics which comprise that person's personality. In turn, we take these traits to be relatively permanent features, which, collectively, make someone the person s/he is. Logically, it follows that people will behave consistently, and predictably, on different occasions and in different situations. Since personality is constant, behaviour will also be consistent:

Personality traits → *Consistency of behaviour* → *Predictability of behaviour*

As Krahé (1992) puts it:

Our experience with other people – as well as with ourselves – tells us that there is a certain regularity, consistency and uniqueness in the behaviours, thoughts and feelings of a person which define his or her personality.

But is this all there is to it? Even in terms of our common-sense psychology, aren't things more complex than the picture presented so far?

Surely they are, since another feature of our common-sense psychology is the view of people as being less than 100 per cent predictable. Indeed, we might regard someone who was so predictable as somehow being robot-like, more of an automaton than a person. We expect people to be different at different times, to show changes in mood, thought and behaviour, within certain limits. And what sets those limits? To some degree they are set by our general concept of a person ('people are not robots', etc.), but also by our familiarity with particular individuals (which relates to what we said above about what it means to say we know someone well). Our knowledge of (or, perhaps more accurately, our belief about) another's personality is based on interactions with that person and observations of his/her behaviour over a large number of occasions, in a variety of situations. So, we will have witnessed the variations in their behaviour, as well as the regularities, with the latter being used to draw our inferences about 'the kind of person' s/he is.

CONSISTENCY OF BEHAVIOUR AND PSYCHOLOGICAL ABNORMALITY

If part of our concept of a person is the element of unpredictability/inconsistency, then anyone who shows excessive consistency may, to that extent, be judged as displaying abnormal behaviour (see above). Indeed, the behaviour of individuals whom clinicians tend to work with may be highly predictable on the basis of some underlying trait or disposition. Clinical problems may, in fact, be associated with a rigidity or inflexibility to changing conditions (Wachtel, 1977). But at the other extreme, people who 'shift with the wind' may also be subject to emotional disorder, such as overdependence on the environment as a guide to behaviour:

> To be totally at the mercy of one's surroundings, like a rudderless ship, would seem to pose as many problems as being insensitive to varying environmental demands.
>
> (Phares, 1979, in Davison and Neale, 1994)

So, we could suggest that a criterion of psychological normality is a balance between consistent behaviour (usually taken to reflect the influence of personality traits) and inconsistent behaviour (usually taken to reflect the influence of situational factors).

PERSONALITY AND SOCIAL PSYCHOLOGY

Traditionally, it is personality psychologists who have been committed to the view that individuals can be characterized by enduring qualities that distinguish them from others and that make their behaviour highly consistent and predictable across a range of situations (high *intra-individual consistency*). By contrast, social psychologists have emphasized the impact on individuals of social situations, which can account for *high inter-individual consistency*. Since social psychologists are less interested in individual differences and more interested in the social influences on behaviour, they tend to stress how different people behave in *similar* ways in particular situations.

These two kinds of consistency relate to weak and strong situations respectively (Mischel, 1977):

- *weak situations* allow people to express their personal qualities easily – that is, they 'leave room' for individual differences (such situations are fairly 'open-ended')
- *strong situations* force behaviour into specific channels, making individual differences largely irrelevant – that is, most people behave in the same way in that (kind of) situation (such situations are highly structured).

Some of the most famous (and controversial) studies in the whole of social psychology, if not psychology as a whole, involve strong situations: Asch's studies of conformity, Milgram's studies of obedience, and Zimbardo's

Figure 4.1 Zimbardo's prison simulation experiment showed that it is the prison environment which makes inmates and guards behave as they do and not their predispositions or character traits, whereas at a party everyone is free to behave as they please: the environment is open or weak

study of a simulated or 'mock' prison (see Box 4.1). While there is evidence of individual differences in all three studies, what they have in common is their focus on the power of social situations to make individuals behave in similar ways (to create *inter-individual consistency*).

BOX 4.1 THE PRISON SIMULATION EXPERIMENT (HANEY *ET AL.*, 1973)

This study investigated why prisons induce destructive, dehumanizing and pathological behaviour in both staff and inmates. The conventional, widely held view is that prison guards are 'sadistic, uneducated and insensitive', while prisoners, by definition, are antisocial. It is these personal qualities of the people who populate prisons that make them the kinds of institutions they are (the *dispositional hypothesis*). What the prison experiment aimed to do was to *reject* the dispositional hypothesis in favour of a *situational explanation*: it is the physical, social and psychological conditions of prisons that are to blame, *not* the people in them.

Haney *et al.* believed they had found convincing evidence in support of the situational explanation, based largely on the abnormal reactions of both prisoners and guards; they were all volunteers, selected for their non-criminal, non-sadistic, psychologically well-adjusted personalities, and were randomly allocated to their respective roles. In this way, the characteristics of the participants were controlled, leaving only the prison environment to account for the pathological reactions that developed.

Like Milgram's obedience experiments before it, the prison study provoked considerable criticism, both from other psychologists and from the general public (see Chapter 9). However, Zimbardo (1973) believes that this was caused only in part by ethical concerns:

> *. . . another part of their [experiments like those of Milgram and Zimbardo] power lies precisely in their demonstration of how strong situational determinants are in shaping behaviour.*

What such dramatic studies demonstrate is that predicting the behaviour of individuals based on personal dispositions has its limits, set by the demands of strong situations. Equally strong, although far less dramatic, are all kinds of everyday situations in which the norms or rules of behaviour are very clearly defined and widely accepted (at least by those familiar with the culture), thus making *conformity* the 'easy' thing to do, and making the expression of personal qualities almost irrelevant. Personality psychologists do not deny the role of situational factors, and social psychologists acknowledge the part played by individual differences. There has also been some convergence between them in recent years. However, there is still a great divergence between them, social psychology still being very strongly biased towards *situationist* models of explanation and personality psychology still favouring *dispositionism* (Krahé, 1992).

SOME KEY ISSUES IN THE STUDY OF PERSONALITY

Consistency

As we have already seen, central to the concept of personality is the consistency and predictability of behaviour. What is commonly referred to as the *consistency controversy* was sparked in 1968, when Walter Mischel declared that, based on his review of a wide range of personality domains, there was very little support for intra-individual consistency. He argued that the average correlation between different behavioural measures designed to tap the same personality trait was typically between 0.1 and 0.2, often lower. He also claimed that correlations between (i) scores on personality scales designed to measure a given trait, and (ii) behaviour in any particular situation meant to tap that trait, rarely exceed 0.2 to 0.3. Hardly any studies produced correlations (either between individual pairs of behavioural measures or between personality scale scores and individual behavioural measures) exceeding the 0.3 'barrier'.

This effectively undermined the whole concept of a personality trait, since the possession of traits is what (according to personality theorists) accounts for consistency and predictability. According to Mischel, if you remove the usefulness of the trait concept, you are left with only situational influences to account for the inconsistency of individual behaviour. In other words, the same person behaves differently in different situations because different situations require different behaviour, are associated with different kinds of reinforcement, and so on. So, from this (rather extreme) situationist perspective, intra-individual inconsistency is exactly what you would expect!

Interactionism

While Mischel's attack on the concept of consistency produced a severe crisis of confidence in the field of personality (Krahé, 1992), Mischel came in for criticism of his own, largely in terms of the methodological flaws in many of the studies he reviewed in reaching his conclusions. These criticisms helped him to modify his views, so that he moved away from situationism and towards an *interactionist* perspective. Essentially, this sees behaviour as a joint function of both the person and the situation:

$$Behaviour = Person \times Situation$$

According to Ross and Nisbett (1991), Mischel *never did* argue that the absence of behavioural consistency across situations proves there are no measurable or predictable individual differences. On the contrary, he stressed that individuals might show responses that are very consistent within the same situation (i.e. *specific* responses to *specific* situations might be very stable over time, such as a child's tendency to copy from an answer book during a general knowledge test when apparently not being watched, as in Hartshorne and May's 1930 study of honesty/dishonesty). Indeed, *stability coefficients* (correlations between two measures of the same behaviour on different occasions) often exceed 0.4. However, he did believe that strong individual differences between people are limited to these very specific responses and situations, while the 'consistency debate' seemed to be about broad, cross-situational traits (such as 'honesty').

The 'formula' above for interactionism is also relevant to another major debate within social psychology, namely attribution theory, specifically the actor–observer effect (AOE) and the fundamental attribution error (FAE; see Chapter 8 and Gross, 2005). This mirrors the current debate within the field of personality.

The AOE (Jones and Nisbett, 1971) refers to the lay person's bias towards explaining other people's behaviour in terms of dispositional or internal causes – this, in fact, is the FAE (Ross, 1977) – and his/her own behaviour in terms of situational or external causes. By describing these as biases – the 'error' in the FAE is itself rather inaccurate (Fiske and Taylor, 1991) – we are implying that an unbiased, logical, objective analysis of social behaviour will always show that both the personal dispositions of the actor and features of the situation contribute to what the actor does, albeit in different ways and to varying degrees and in varying proportions. This can be seen in terms of weak and strong situations: dispositional factors play a much greater role in the former compared with the latter, but even here not everyone behaves in an identical way (see above).

The meanings of 'interactionism'

Interactionism seems to be the only logical, as well as empirically reasonable, view to take (as opposed to extreme dispositionism or extreme situationism). But are there different kinds of interactionism, or at least different ways of thinking about what an interaction between the person and the situation might mean?

According to Carver and Scheier (1992), there are four main ways in which the term has been used. One of these relates to the distinction between weak/strong situations, which we discussed earlier. A second relates to the 'formula' we considered above; this is probably the most common understanding of the term and is associated with the research of psychologists such as Endler and Magnusson (1976), Pervin (1985), and

Snyder and Ickes (1985). It is tied to the ANOVA (analysis-of-variance) understanding of how two (or more) variables (or classes of variables) influence an outcome. When a situation and a trait are examined in the same study, three systematic sources of influence on behaviour result:

1 Sometimes, variations in the situation have an overall (and fairly predictable) effect (corresponding to *strong* situations and *high* inter-individual consistency).
2 Sometimes, variations on a trait dimension have an overall effect (corresponding to *weak* situations and *low* inter-individual consistency).
3 Sometimes, variations in the situation affect different people in different ways. This may be *instead of* the first two sources of influence, or *in addition to* them. Either way, it is the interaction between person and situation that produces weak overall effects (or correlations) for both trait and situation. While the traditional dispositional view of behaviour (as held by personality theorists) sees the trait as being the crucial factor (for example, the tendency to dominate others), interactionists argue that the expression of this tendency will inevitably be influenced by situational factors. For example, authoritarian personalities bully less powerful or less important people, but are submissive to more powerful or more important people (Argyle, 1983).

A typical study aimed at testing the trait and interactionist models involves observing, or asking for reports of, the behaviour of a number of individuals in a number of situations, and calculating how much of the variation can be explained by person factors, how much by situation factors, and how much by interaction between them. The general pattern of results that emerges from this kind of study, involving a variety of populations, traits and situations, is very clear: situations are at least as important as persons, and person × situation interactions are *more* important than either (Argyle, 1983; Bowers, 1973). While it is now recognized that this kind of research cannot determine whether personality or situation is more important, the results nevertheless clearly favour the interactionist position (Argyle, 1983).

The third of Carver and Scheier's definitions describes how one of the limitations of the ANOVA approach to studying interaction effects is that it is largely laboratory-based, with people put into identical situations. While this might be very convenient for the investigators, it may not be ecologically valid – that is, it may not reflect what goes on outside the laboratory situation, where people exercise considerable choice over which situations or environments they expose themselves to. Because the choices people make depend partly on personality differences, the choosing of situations represents a kind of interaction that is very different from what is involved in the ANOVA model.

In their fourth definition, Carver and Scheier cite evidence that people differ in the kinds of responses they evoke in others, that introverts and extroverts tend to steer conversations in different directions, and that people manipulate one another, using charm, coercion, 'the silent treatment', and other tactics. All these effects of people serve to change the situation, so that the situation is different for different individuals involved. This reciprocal influence between persons and situations is another way of looking at person–situation interaction (Carver and Scheier, 1992).

A study by Ware and John (1995, in Pennington, 2003) illustrates two or more of the different senses of interactionism described above. They measured the punctuality of students at Berkeley University in the USA turning up for lectures over several days. The lectures took place at either 8am or 5pm. Two weeks before their punctuality was monitored (earliness–lateness), the students were given a questionnaire which (among other things) assessed their conscientiousness. Students were divided into high and low conscientiousness. The results are shown in Figure 4.2.

As Figure 4.2 shows, overall, high-conscientiousness students were more punctual than low-conscientious-ness students. But *both* groups were less punctual for the early lecture than for the late lecture. This suggests that the late lecture represents a 'strong' situation (it was more of a 'leveller'), while the early lecture was 'weak', allowing greater scope for individual differences to influence behaviour. These correspond to 'low-response freedom' and 'high-response freedom' respectively (Wright and Mischel, 1988).

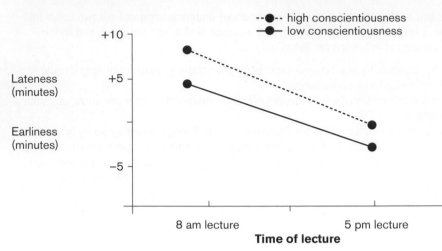

Figure 4.2 Punctuality of high- and low-conscientiousness students at an early and late lecture (adapted from Ware and John, 1995). Taken from D. Pennington (2003) *Essential Personality*, London: Arnold

The psychological situation

Although other actors are an important part of any situation, individual differences between actors, as we have seen, also contribute to how a particular situation is experienced by the various participants. In other words, not only are personality differences essential for any understanding of people's behaviour in particular situations but there is a very real sense in which *the situation is defined in terms of the individuals involved*.

Trying to define the situation in an objective way, independently of the actors involved, has only limited value. A critical determinant of behaviour is the 'psychological situation' – that is, the psychological meaning of a situation for the individual (how it is perceived). This represents a crucial factor in predicting behaviour and accounting for regularities in behaviour across situations (Krahé, 1992).

The trait dimension

Reference to the 'psychological situation' suggests at least a partial explanation of the lack of behavioural consistency claimed by Mischel. If people fail to show consistent behaviour across situations, couldn't this be because those situations might not all have the same meaning for the individuals concerned (which they 'should' have – and need to have – according to the researchers who define those situations in an objective way)? Only if the perceptions of actors and those of researchers coincide can there be any possibility of finding consistency.

A solution to this problem was proposed by Bem and Allen (1974). They basically conceded Mischel's claim about low consistency when a random sample of people responds to some fixed set of trait-relevant situations. But they argued that a rather more restricted trait theory might still be valid, namely the view that at least some traits can be appropriately applied to at least some people. That is, instead of claiming that everyone is more or less equally consistent and predictable according to whichever traits one chooses to measure, Bem and Allen argued that most people are probably consistent on some behavioural dimensions but not others, and people will differ regarding which traits are consistent for them and which are not.

The traditional trait approach (the target of Mischel's attack) adopts a nomothetic approach, assuming that every person can be meaningfully assigned a score on every personality dimension. Bem and Allen, on the other hand, were advocating an idiographic approach, focusing on the unique aspects of a given individual's personality configuration (Ross and Nisbett, 1991; see Chapter 3). To do this, one must first identify the particular traits that 'apply' for the individual in question (or, alternatively, identify particular individuals for whom the trait of interest is truly applicable) – that is,

> *. . . one must conduct one's search for behavioural consistency recognizing that only a subset of trait dimensions usefully characterizes any given individual, and that only a subset of individuals can be characterized in terms of any given trait dimension.*
>
> *(Ross and Nisbett, 1991)*

What made Bem and Allen's theoretical approach different was the assumption that consistency will be shown only by people striving to meet personal standards, trying to convey a consistent impression to others or actively monitoring their behaviour in an attempt to achieve consistency, and that it will be manifested only in the particular situations perceived as relevant by those individuals. However, what Bem and Allen advocated, and what they actually did, were not the same thing. What they did is described in Box 4.2.

BOX 4.2 BEM AND ALLEN'S (1974) STUDY OF TRAIT CONSISTENCY

Bem and Allen stipulated two specific traits, *friendliness* and *conscientiousness*, then classified all the available actors as high or low in consistency on these traits (based on self-ratings and ratings by peers and parents). This is essentially a nomothetic approach. The idiographic alternative, which is what they originally advocated, would have involved deriving trait dimensions and situations relevant to those dimensions from the participants themselves.

As far as both traits are concerned, the high-consistency individuals' peer ratings, parent ratings and self-ratings correlated highly with each other (the average correlation coefficient being 0.61 for friendliness and 0.48 for conscientiousness) and (although less highly) with the relevant behavioural measures (the average for friendliness being 0.47 and for conscientiousness 0.36). In all cases, coefficients for the low-consistency individuals were lower.

Regarding correlations between the relevant behavioural measures, (i) for *friendliness*, the high-consistency individuals scored 0.73, compared with 0.30 for the low-consistency individuals (clearly in line with predictions). However, (ii) for *conscientiousness*, the results were −0.04 and −0.19 respectively (clearly not what they expected or hoped to find).

Moderator variables

Carver and Scheier (1992) point out that attempts to replicate Bem and Allen's results have met with very mixed fortunes. However, their view of consistency represents an important *moderator variable,* which links personal dispositions and actual behaviour, and can account for the very low levels of consistency found in earlier studies (and on which Mischel based his attack on the trait approach).

Another such moderator variable is self-monitoring (Snyder, 1987). High self-monitors are expected to show low cross-situational consistency, since these individuals adapt their behaviour to suit the demands of the situation, while low self-monitors are expected to show high cross-situational consistency, since they tend to 'be themselves' regardless of the demands of the situation. If people can validly be classified as high or low self-monitors, this means that some people are less or more consistent in general than others.

Aggregated observations

Bem and Allen were trying to defend the trait concept against Mischel's attack. Another response has been to argue that, instead of measuring *single* instances of behaviour and calculating the correlations between these (individual) instances, we should take the *average* of several different individual measures ('items') and calculate the correlations between these *aggregated observations*. The main advocate of this view is Epstein (e.g. 1979), who argues that only by taking an average can we obtain a reliable or accurate measurement of a disposition. Only by doing this will random or extraneous factors partially cancel each other out: individual behaviours, like single items on a test of any kind, are highly unreliable and are likely to reflect the influence of several systematic and random factors other than the underlying personality disposition under investigation. This is a purely statistical argument, one that Mischel himself had made in 1968 (Ross and Nisbett, 1991).

According to the Spearman-Brown 'prophecy formula', championed by Epstein, if we took 25 measures of, say, extroversion for each individual, found the mean, then correlated this mean with that for a different set of 25 measures, we would obtain a correlation of 0.83. If we did the same for a mere nine measures, we would still obtain a correlation of 0.63.

Not surprisingly, Epstein's argument was greeted enthusiastically by personality test researchers. It seemed to explain why standarized pencil-and-paper self-reports, and peer ratings generally, produce high levels of stability over time and at least moderate levels of inter-rater agreement; these kinds of assessment are likely to be the product of many observations, made on different occasions, in a variety of situations (Ross and Nisbett, 1991).

Long-term consistency

One very important implication of Epstein's argument is that to measure consistency in the *short term* (based on one or two observations made close together in time) misses the point. The widely held definition of a personality trait is that it is a latent tendency or disposition that plays a causal role in determining both specific patterns of individual behaviour and individual differences in people's reactions to a given situation. Gordon Allport (1937), one of the pioneers of personality research and a major trait theorist, argued that a person with a particular disposition will behave in a particular way only if s/he meets with situations that *actualize* that disposition (allow it to be expressed).

Not only does this represent a form of interactionism, it implies that if we observe a person on just one or two occasions, we won't have given particular traits 'enough of a chance' to manifest themselves; it is only in the long term that intra-individual consistency can be meaningfully measured. Short-term inconsistency, but long-term consistency, is exactly what is predicted by trait theories of personality.

The constructionist approach

Another strand in the complex fabric of the 'trait debate' is to shift the focus away from the actor and onto the observer. Instead of traits denoting dispositional qualities of the individual, they are conceptualized as cognitive categories used by the perceiver to interpret an individual's behaviour across different situations. Therefore, consistency is construed by the perceiver, as much as manifested by the actor: judgements of an individual's personality depend as much on the interpretative activity of the perceiver as on the observed behaviour itself (Krahé, 1992).

While not rejecting the trait concept, the constructionist view maintains that personality does not have an objective reality independent of the observer, or of the cultural and historical context in which both the actor and observer are located. According to Hampson (1988), the process of personality construction is seen as a form of communication through which the actor, observer and the self-observer ideally arrive at a shared impression about the actor:

> *In this sense, personality should not be located within persons, but between and among persons.*

In relation to our role of self-observer, *self-monitoring* is a key process (see above). Also, the constructionist approach has led to a revival of research on *social desirability scales*, which may be measuring two distinct qualities: self-deception and impression management (Deary and Matthews, 1993).

An alternative constructionist reinterpretation of the trait concept is even more radical. This challenges the very notion of 'the individual' itself.

> **BOX 4.3** DECONSTRUCTING THE SELF
>
> Mainstream psychology as a whole, and personality theory in particular, takes the idea of the *individual* as its point of departure. The 'self' is a construct used in cognitive, psychoanalytic, social and humanistic theories, and all more or less share a view of the self as separate, self-contained, independent, consistent, unitary and private (Wetherell and Maybin, 1996). This view corresponds with our everyday/common-sense view, which seems to be the only view our culture permits (McGhee, 2001).
>
> However, some *social constructionists* (including Wetherell and Maybin) and *critical psychologists*, influenced by anthropology and sociology, have challenged this view (see Chapters 6 and 14). They criticize the psychological focus on the individual for ignoring how society shapes people in various ways (e.g. Shotter and Gergen, 1989). Role theory is used to highlight the impact of social expectations and situations on the self, which must be 'managed' in order to fulfil social norms and obligations (Goffman, 1971). Such an analysis implies a self that is flexible and dynamic, adopting and discarding 'multiple roles' as the situation demands – that is, a *fragmented* rather than a *unitary* self.
>
> For social constructionists, the self is *emergent* (not reducible to a lower biological or cognitive level), *contextual* (constructed in and for different situations and circumstances), *discursive* (constructed through language), *multiple* (has variable rather than unitary forms), *relational* (constructed through interaction with others), and *distributed* (participates in many roles, relationships and representations simultaneously). This more fluid, socially constructed self makes it difficult to answer questions such as 'What are the main underlying, stable differences between individual personalities?' (McGhee, 2001). This is not because there is insufficient empirical evidence with which to answer it, but because it is the wrong kind of question to ask.
>
> Some social constructionists, especially those critical psychologists influenced by Foucault (see Chapter 14), argue that the very sense of 'individual' is an illusion created by language and perpetuated by a society that has a vested interest in encouraging us to take responsibility for ourselves ('subjectivity'). According to Gough and McFadden (2001), one criticism of the concept of self predominant in western culture is that:
>
> > *the Western capitalist spotlight on individuals rather than societies facilitates a politics where individuals are blamed for problems which might otherwise be conceived in terms of social factors.*
>
> Gough and McFadden give the example of the murder of the black teenager Stephen Lawrence in 1993 and the subsequent bungled police inquiry. This sparked a debate about *institutionalized racism*, as opposed to the racial prejudice of a few extreme minds.

Personality factors

Finally, let's return to 'the beginning of the story', so to speak. According to Krahé (1992), despite its troubled history 'the trait concept presents itself in remarkably good shape at the beginning of the '90s'. Since the 1980s, there has been a vast amount of research involving a search for a small but comprehensive number of basic trait dimensions that can account for the structure of personality and individual differences. The results suggest that personality can be adequately described by five broad constructs, commonly referred to as the 'Big Five', namely: *Neuroticism* (N), *Extroversion* (E), *Openness* (O), *Agreeableness* (A) and *Conscientiousness* (C) (McCrae and Costa, 1989). The first two are almost identical to these dimensions as used in Eysenck's personality theory.

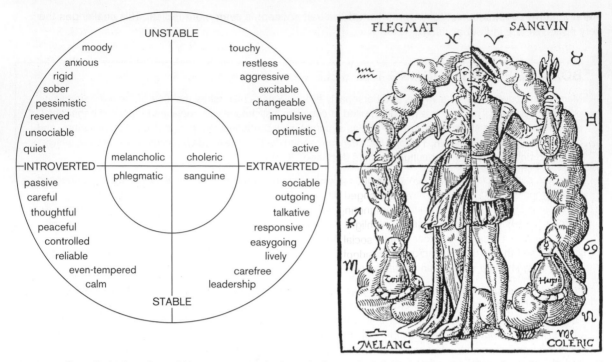

Figure 4.3 Personality has been dissected into component parts for thousands of years; what is interesting is how these ideas relate to the modern concept of personality traits, as shown by Eysenck's dimensions of personality (From Eysenck, 1965)

While different versions of the 'Big Five' have been proposed, the five-factor model has provided a unified framework for trait research (Costa and McCrae, 1993). However, this approach faces some of the same basic problems as more traditional theories, notably those of Eysenck and Cattell, and this stems from the fact that they all rest upon the use of the statistical technique of *factor analysis* (FA).

One of the sources of debate and disagreement between, say, Eysenck and Cattell has been to do with the 'best' method of FA to use, which in turn determines the number of factors (or basic trait dimensions) to be extracted from the mass of data derived from self-reports, observer ratings and so on. There is much more general agreement now among personality psychologists than there used to be about the number of factors that should be sought (i.e. five). But there remains the fundamental problem of the meaning of the factors that are extracted (Kline, 1993; Krahé, 1992):

> *The labelling of factor solutions is a largely intuitive process whereby the investigator typically inspects the items with high loadings on a given factor and then chooses a label that, in his or her view, contains the gist of the total range of items making up the factor. Thus, it is not surprising that different studies have arrived at different qualitative interpretations of their obtained five factor solutions . . .*
>
> *(Krahé, 1992)*

Ultimately, personality factors, however many or few, must be identified from their correlations with *external criteria* (Kline, 1993).

Finally, Bentall (1993), a clinical psychologist, asks whether personality theory has anything to offer in the context of helping or understanding people with psychological problems. He argues that the 'Big Five' seem to suffer from many of the disadvantages of traditional diagnostic approaches in psychopathology, for the following reasons:

- While these personality dimensions are described as 'natural' categories, the labels used to designate them seem to reflect the value systems of the researchers. For example, the anxious (neurotic), introverted, reserved person 'stands condemned as a lesser human being. Should any liberal society tolerate this way of classifying individuals?'. The use of assessment techniques derived from the 'Big Five' model in job selection, for example, raises serious ethical and political questions.
- While the 'consistency debate' has focused almost exclusively on 'normal' behaviour, as far as problem behaviour is concerned, it is often the *inconsistencies* that are most striking, such as the breakdown in normal functioning following some major life event (see Chapter 7).

CONCLUSIONS

Surely, for a theory of personality to even begin to be adequate, it must apply to both the consistencies *and* inconsistencies, the short *and* the long term, the predictable *and* the unpredictable features of behaviour. It must also be able to explain both normal and abnormal behaviour, as well as the emotional, cognitive, social and interpersonal components of behaviour, all within the cultural and historical context in which a person's personality is perceived and judged. Carver and Scheier (1992) sum things up like this:

> *Today's view isn't a picture in which traits exert a constant influence on behaviour . . . Rather, trait differences sometimes matter a lot and sometimes don't matter at all. People also display traits by choosing situations, not just by reacting to situations forced on them. This dynamic approach to understanding the role of traits in the constantly varying social environment recognizes complexities in behaviour that formerly were ignored. As a result, this picture is widely seen as a distinct improvement over simpler conceptions of the effects of traits.*

SUMMARY

- Part of our common-sense understanding of behaviour is the belief that people behave in fairly consistent, and hence predictable, ways, across a range of situations (high intra-individual consistency). This is attributed to their personality, which refers to the relatively permanent features of a person's make-up.

- Another common-sense belief is that people are not completely predictable; they are changeable, within certain limits, those limits being set by (a) our general concept of a person, and (b) our familiarity with particular individuals.

- Both excessive predictability/consistency and excessive unpredictability/inconsistency may be indicators of psychological abnormality.

- Personality psychologists have tended to stress high intra-individual consistency, while social psychologists have stressed the impact of social situations, accounting for high inter-individual consistency. These relate to weak and strong situations respectively.

- Many famous (and controversial) studies in social psychology involve strong situations, such as the prison simulation experiment. Such studies show that the validity of predicting the behaviour of individuals on the basis of personal dispositions is limited by the demands of strong situations.

- Despite recent convergence between personality psychology and social psychology, the former still strongly favours dispositionism and the latter situationism.

- Mischel sparked the consistency controversy by claiming that there was very little evidence of intra-individual consistency. This undermined the whole concept of a personality trait and introduced a situationist perspective into personality psychology, which predicts intra-individual inconsistency.

○ Criticisms of Mischel led him towards an interactionist perspective, which sees behaviour as a joint function of both the person and the situation. However, there are different forms of interaction.

○ The general pattern of results found in studies aimed at testing the trait and interactionist models is that situations are at least as important as persons, and person–situation interactions are more important than either.

○ In real life, people choose the situations to which they expose themselves. This represents a kind of interaction. Also, people change the situation by virtue of their personality and the responses they evoke in others, which represents another form of interaction.

○ Rather than trying to define situations independently of the actors involved, it is the psychological situation that is the crucial influence on behaviour.

○ Bem and Allen proposed a restricted trait theory, according to which most people are probably consistent on some behavioural dimensions but not others. People will differ regarding which traits are consistent for them and which aren't, depending on the personal relevance of different traits.

○ Empirical support for Bem and Allen is mixed, but their view of consistency represents an important moderator variable, another example being self-monitoring.

○ We should take the average of several individual observations and calculate correlations for these aggregated measures. We also need to recognize that intra-individual consistency is a long-term phenomenon.

○ Consistency is also viewed as construed by the perceiver, as much as manifested by the actor. This constructionist approach maintains that personality does not exist objectively but is a form of communication.

○ Social constructionists also challenge the concept of the individual and the self as traditionally understood. They propose both theoretical and political reasons for not seeing people as separate, self-contained, unitary and private.

○ Although the 'Big Five' personality trait dimensions/factors have provided a framework for trait research, there remains the fundamental problem of the meaning of the factors extracted by the use of factor analysis (FA).

○ The value of personality theory in relation to people with psychological problems has been questioned – in particular the 'Big Five', which seem to reflect the value systems of the researchers and overemphasize consistency relative to inconsistency.

USEFUL WEBSITES

http://muskingum.edu/~psychology/psycweb/history/milgram.htm
http://www.ship.edu/~cgboeree/perscontents.html
http://www.prisonexp.org/
http://en.wikipedia.org/wiki/Walter_Mischel

RECOMMENDED READING

Krahé, B. (1992) *Personality and Social Psychology: Towards a Synthesis.* London: Sage. (Especially Chapters 1–5 and 8.)

Mischel, W. (1968) *Personality and Assessment.* New York: Wiley.

Mischel, W. (1977) The interaction of personality and situation. In D. Magnusson and N.S. Endler (eds) *Personality at the Crossroads: Current Issues in Interactional Psychology.* Hillsdale, NJ: Lawrence Erlbaum.

CHAPTER 5

HEREDITY AND ENVIRONMENT

FRAMING THE QUESTIONS

The debate about the roles of heredity and environment (or *nature* and *nurture*) is one of the most enduring, as well as one of the most heated and controversial, both inside and outside psychology. Whether in a religious, philosophical, political or scientific context, the debate is concerned with some of the most fundamental questions that human beings (at least those from western cultures) ask about themselves: 'How do we come to be the way we are?', 'What makes us develop in the way we do?'

I have deliberately expressed these questions in a very general, abstract way, in order to highlight an ambiguity involved: are they concerned with the human species as a whole, relative to other species, or are they concerned with individual differences between human beings, i.e. individuals relative to each other? In a broad, general sense, the nature–nurture debate involves both types, or levels, of question. For example, 'Is language an innate (inborn) ability that is unique to the human species?' and 'Is it a "natural" (biologically given) ability that will appear, under "normal" environmental conditions, in people with normal brains?' represent the first (species) level. Clearly, if language is a species-specific ability, then the focus of theory and research will be on the nature of that ability, exactly what it is that is innate or biologically 'given', how the brain is specialized for language, and so on. Chomsky's (1965, 1968) Language Acquisition Device (LAD) is perhaps the prime example within modern psychology of such an approach. A related example is Pinker's (1994) view of language as an instinct (see the discussion of evolutionary psychology in Chapter 14).

Similar questions have been asked about perception and aggression. In the case of aggression, both types of question have been posed: 'Are human beings the naturally most aggressive species on the planet?' represents the same level as the first question regarding language, while 'Why are some people more aggressive than others?' represents the other level, the one that focuses on individual differences. According to Plomin (1994), it is in the latter sense (i.e. individual differences) that the nature–nurture debate takes place.

However, there is another, equally important, distinction that needs to be made between the kinds of questions that are asked relating to heredity and environment. In order to appreciate this distinction we need to take a brief look at the philosophical roots of the nature–nurture debate.

NATIVISM, EMPIRICISM AND INTERACTIONISM

As the word implies, *nativism* refers to the philosophical theory that sees nature (i.e. heredity) as determining certain abilities and capacities, rather than learning and experience. A well-known nativist, whose impact on psychology has been enormous, was the French philosopher, René Descartes (1596–1650). At the opposite philosophical extreme is *empiricism,* associated mainly with seventeenth-century British philosophers, in

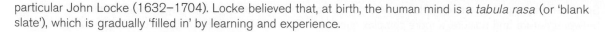

particular John Locke (1632–1704). Locke believed that, at birth, the human mind is a *tabula rasa* (or 'blank slate'), which is gradually 'filled in' by learning and experience.

At risk of some oversimplification, these two doctrines represent polar opposites – that is, they take the view that it is either nature (nativism) or nurture (empiricism) that accounts for human abilities: they are either innate or learnt.

Most present-day psychologists (and biologists) would reject such an extreme either/or approach to such a complex issue, mainly on the grounds that the two theories are attempts to answer the wrong question: to ask 'Is it nature or nurture?' is to ask an oversimplified question that will inevitably produce an oversimplified answer. Also, Descartes and Locke were asking the question at the level of 'the whole species' and not at the level of individual differences.

According to Dunbar (2008), the nature–nurture debate ground to a standstill in biology as long ago as the 1960s:

> . . . biologists began to realize that the question ['Is it nature or nurture?'] was actually meaningless: everything is the product of the interaction between both nature and nurture . . .

However, despite these two observations, nativism and empiricism have had a considerable impact on psychology – particularly, but by no means exclusively, in the early days of the discipline. The *Gestalt* psychologists (notably Wertheimer, Kohler and Koffka, during the 1920s and 1930s) believed that the basic principles of perceptual organization are innate, with perceptual experience having very little, if any, influence. One of the American pioneers of child psychology, Arnold Gesell (1925), introduced into psychology the concept of *maturation*. This refers to genetically programmed sequential patterns of change (Bee, 1989), according to which all babies and children will pass through the same series of changes, in the same order, and at more or less the same rate. A third, and more recent, example of a nativist theory is Chomsky's *LAD* (see above).

Empiricism has had its impact within psychology in many different forms. An early and extremely influential theory is behaviourism, whose American founder, John Watson (1878–1958), leaves the reader in no doubt as to the behaviourist position regarding the nature–nurture debate when he declares:

> *Give me a dozen healthy infants, well-formed, and my own specified world to bring them up in and I'll guarantee to take any one at random and train him to become any type of specialist I might select – a doctor, lawyer, artist, merchant-chief and, yes, even into beggar-man and thief, regardless of his talents, penchants, abilities, vocations and race of his ancestors.*
>
> (*Watson, 1925/26, in Soyland, 1994*)

He also claimed that 'there is no such thing as an inheritance of capacity, talent, temperament, mental constitution and character', and again:

> *The behaviourists believe that there is nothing from within to develop. If you start with the right number of fingers and toes, eyes, and a few elementary movements that are present at birth, you do not need anything else in the way of raw material to make a man, be that man genius, a cultured gentleman, a rowdy or a thug.*
>
> (*Watson, 1928, in Plomin, 1994*)

This extreme form of empiricism (or *environmentalism*) was perpetuated in the behaviour analysis work of B.F. Skinner (1904–90; see Chapter 14).

So, if extreme nativism and empiricism, whether in the form of philosophical or psychological theories, choose between nature and nurture, a more complex question to ask is, 'How much?' This, of course, presupposes that both nature and nurture are involved, a view that, as we noted above, most psychologists would subscribe to.

In turn, the 'How much?' question is linked, almost inevitably, to the 'individual differences' form of the debate. For Francis Galton (a cousin of Charles Darwin), the issue was clearly about the relative importance of heredity and environment, and he left us in no doubt as to which he considered the more important:

> There is no escape from the conclusion that nature prevails enormously over nurture when the differences in nurture do not exceed what is commonly to be found among persons of the same rank in the same country.
>
> (Galton, 1883, in Plomin, 1994)

Finally, even though 'How much?' represents an improvement on the rather crude, oversimplified 'Which one?', it is still concerned with trying to *quantify* the contributions of genetic and environmental factors. This has been the main focus of *behavioural* (or quantitative) *genetics*, which attempts to establish the extent to which individual differences (such as intelligence or personality) are due to differences in people's genetic make-up (i.e. *heritability estimates*). The methods used in behavioural genetics include twin studies, adoption studies and other studies of *family resemblance*. One reason for the emphasis on 'How much?' is the availability of these methods, which make it relatively straightforward to establish heritability estimates. We shall discuss behaviour genetics (and the related *molecular genetics*) in more detail later in the chapter.

A much more difficult third question about the nature–nurture relationship, which follows logically from the second, is 'How do they interact?' (Anastasi, 1958; Plomin, 1994). This is concerned with qualitative issues – that is, the ways in which heredity and environment influence each other. Much of the rest of this chapter will be concerned with some of the different attempts to understand this interaction, many of which also derive from behaviour genetics research. For now, we can agree with Plomin (1994) that for most behavioural scientists, it is probably inconceivable that there is no interaction between them.

THE NATURE OF 'NATURE'

Within *genetics* (the science of heredity), 'nature' refers to what is typically thought of as inheritance. This denotes (differences in) genetic material (chromosomes and genes), which are transmitted from generation to generation (i.e. from parents to offspring). The 'father' of genetics, Gregor Mendel, an Austrian monk, explained the difference between smooth and wrinkled seeds in garden peas in terms of different genes (1865). Similarly, in modern human genetics, the focus is on genetic differences among individuals. 'Nature' in this context *does not* refer to the nature of the human species, what we all have in common genetically with other human beings (and indeed with other primates), but rather to genetically produced differences among individuals within the (human) species. This was certainly how the term 'nature' was used by Galton, who coined the phrase *nature–nurture* in 1883 as used in the scientific arena (Plomin, 1994).

Genetics and evolution

The raw material of evolution is *genetic variability*: individuals with genes that help them to survive changing environmental conditions will be more likely to produce offspring (who also possess those genes), while those individuals lacking such genes won't. In this way, new species develop, and species-specific characteristics (including behaviours) are those that have enabled the species to evolve and survive.

However, the links between such species-typical evolution and genetic sources of individual differences are much looser than is often assumed (Plomin, 1994). Plomin cites the examples of sociobiology (e.g. Wilson, 1975), evolutionary psychology (e.g. Buss, 1991, in Plomin, 1993), and developmental psychology (e.g. Harper, 1992, in Plomin, 1993), all of which are mainly concerned with differences between species, although attempts have been made to incorporate individual differences (e.g. by Dawkins, 1983). It is easy to make the mistake of assuming that evolution implies genetic variation within a species, and vice versa. Taking the example of language again, if acquisition of language is a human species-specific behaviour, hardwired by evolution to occur if the minimal environment encountered by our species during development is present (most importantly, other language users), then we can say that we are natural language users. However, this does not imply that differences among individual language users in their language ability are also genetic in origin – such differences could be entirely due to environmental factors (Plomin, 1994).

> *The causes of average differences between species aren't necessarily related to the causes of individual differences within groups. Moreover, characteristics that have been subject to strong directional selection will not show genetic variability because strong selection exhausts genetic variability. In other words, when genetic variability is found among individuals within our species for a particular trait, it is likely that the trait was not important evolutionarily, at least in terms of directional selection . . .*
>
> *(Plomin, 1994)*

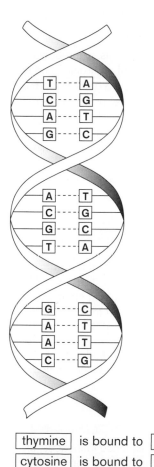

| thymine | is bound to | adenine |
| cytosine | is bound to | guanine |

Figure 5.1 The structure of a DNA molecule represented schematically. This shows its double-stranded coiled structure and the complementary binding of nucleotide bases, guanine to cytosine and adenine to thymine (From Pinel, 1993)

HEREDITY: CHROMOSOMES, GENES AND DNA

Now that we have established what nature *isn't*, let's take a closer look at what it *is*; clearly this is important if we are to try to understand the relationship between nature and nurture.

The basic units of hereditary transmission are genes. Genes are large molecules of deoxyribonucleic acid (DNA), extremely complex chemical chains, comprising a ladder-like, double-helix structure (discovered by Watson and Crick in 1953: see Figure 5.1). Genes occur in pairs, and are situated on the chromosomes, which are found within the nuclei of living cells. The normal human being inherits 23 pairs of chromosomes, one member of each pair from each parent. These consist of 22 pairs of autosomal chromosomes (the same in males and females) and two sex chromosomes (pair 23), which comprise two Xs in the case of females, and an X and a Y in males (see Figure 5.4).

The steps of the gene's double helix (or spiral staircase: Plomin, 1994) consist of four nucleotide bases (adenine, thymine, cytosine and guanine), which can occur in any order on one side of the double helix, while the other side is fixed, such that adenine always pairs with thymine, and cytosine always pairs with guanine. Taking just one member of each of the 23 pairs of chromosomes, the human *genome* (the total complement of genes) comprises more than 3 billion nucleotide base pairs (Plomin, 1994). Genes can range in size from fewer than 100 base pairs to several million. Two major functions of genes are *self-duplication* and *protein synthesis*.

Self-duplication

DNA copies itself by 'unzipping' in the middle of the spiral staircase, with each half forming its complement. In other words, when a cell divides, all the genetic information (chromosomes and genes) contained within the cell nucleus is reproduced, so that the 'offspring'

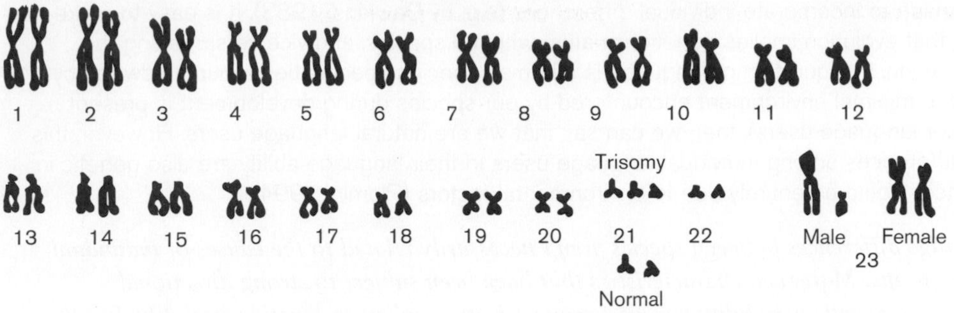

Figure 5.2 A sample karyotype. The 21st chromosome has one too many chromosomes, a common problem. This is called a 'trisomy'. The 23rd chromosome pair is shown with both male and female versions. In a normal karyotype, only one such pair would be found (From RUCH. *TI-PSYCHOLOGY: THE PERSONAL SCIENCE*, 1E. © 1984 Wadsworth, a part of Cengage Learning, Inc. Reproduced by permission. www.cengage.com/permissions)

cells are identical to the 'parent' cells. This process is called *mitosis* and applies only to *non-gonadal* (non-reproductive) cells (such as skin, blood and muscle cells).

The reproductive or germ cells (ova in females and sperm in males) duplicate through meiosis, whereby each cell contains only half the individual's chromosomes and genes (haploid); which member of a chromosome pair goes to any particular cell seems to be determined randomly. The resulting germ cells (called gametes in their mature state), therefore, contain 23 chromosomes, one of which will be either an X (female) or a Y (male). When a sperm fertilizes an ovum, the two sets of chromosomes combine to form a new individual with a full set of 46 chromosomes: if both parents contribute an X chromosome, it will be female, while if the father contributes a Y (remember, the mother only has Xs) it will be male. It is the father, therefore, who determines the baby's sex (see Figure 5.3 overleaf).

Protein synthesis

The 'genetic code' was cracked in the 1960s. Essentially, DNA controls the production of RNA (ribonucleic acid) within the cell nucleus. This 'messenger' RNA moves outside the nucleus, into the surrounding cytoplasm, where it is converted by ribosomes into sequences of amino acids, which are the building blocks of proteins and enzymes. Genes that code for proteins and enzymes are called *structural genes*, and they represent the foundation of classical genetics (Plomin, 1994). The first single-gene disorders discovered in the human species involved metabolic disorders caused by mutations (spontaneous changes) in structural genes. A much-cited example is phenylketonuria (PKU), which is discussed below in relation to gene–environment interaction.

However, most genes are regulator genes: they code for products that bind with DNA itself, and serve to regulate other genes. Unlike the structural genes, which are 'deaf' to the environment, the regulator genes communicate closely with the environment and change in response to it (Plomin, 1994).

THE NATURE OF NURTURE: WHAT IS THE ENVIRONMENT?

When the term 'environment' is used in a psychological context, we normally think of all those influences, or potential sources of influence, that lie outside the individual's body, in the form of other people, opportunities for intellectual stimulation and social interaction, as well as the physical circumstances of the individual's life ('environs' = 'surroundings').

For most babies and young children, the immediate family is the environmental context in which their development takes place, although the nature of this immediate environment is itself coloured and shaped by the wider social and cultural setting in which the family exists. In other words, we normally view the environment as:

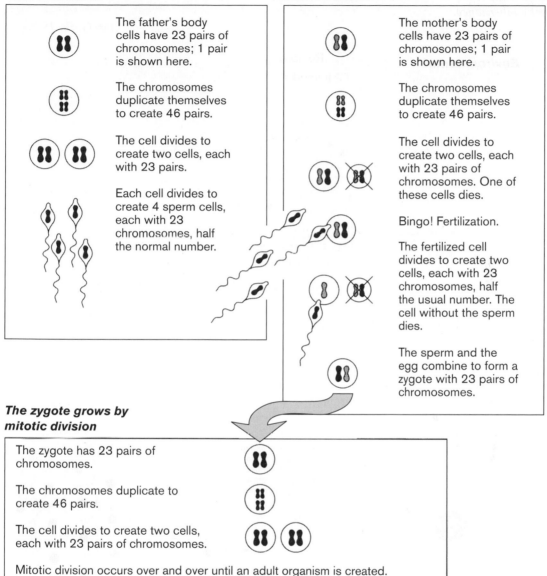

Figure 5.3 Mitotic and meiotic cell division (from Pinel, 1993)

- *external* to the individual
- *post-natal* (i.e. something that becomes important after birth)
- a way of referring to a whole set of (potential) influences that impinge on a *passive individual, shaped by* his/her environment, without in any way shaping or contributing to that environment (see Figure 5.4).

On all three counts, this view seems to be mistaken. Regarding the first two points, while the nature–nurture debate is normally conducted at the level of the immediate family and the society and culture within which it is embedded:

. . . opportunities for gene–environment interaction arise long before the birth process . . . [and] individual differences in environmental conditions have a modifying influence upon the expression of genetic inheritance.

(McGurk, 1975)

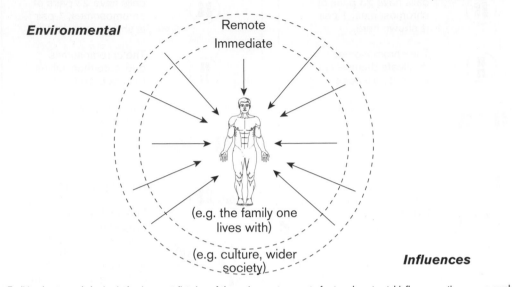

Figure 5.4 Traditional, extreme behaviourist/environmentalist view of the environment as a set of external, post-natal influences acting upon a purely passive individual

For example, with repeated mitosis, any one cell has a specific location within a cluster of other cells, but that location is forever changing as the cell's environment (the total number of cells in the cluster) continues to grow. At an even more micro level, the cell nucleus (which contains the genetic material) has as its environment the cytoplasm of the cell (see Figure 5.5).

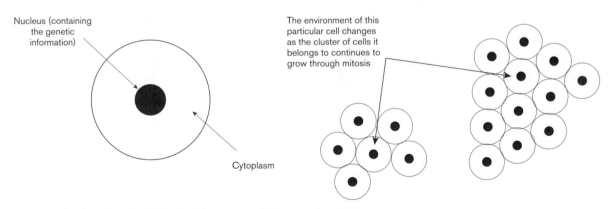

Figure 5.5 For the nucleus of an individual cell, the environment is the surrounding cytoplasm

Similarly, Rose (2005) claims that 'the environment' is as much a myth as is 'the gene' (see below). Environments exist at multiple levels. For an individual piece of DNA, 'the environment' is all the rest of the DNA in the genome, plus the cellular metabolic system that surrounds it, proteins, enzymes, ions, water, and so on. For a cell in a multicellular organism, the environment, constant or not, is the internal milieu in which it is embedded or adjacent cells, signalling molecules, bloodstream and extracellular fluids.

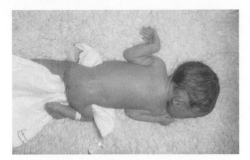

Figure 5.6 Alcohol consumption during pregnancy can result in foetal alcohol syndrome; the baby may be intellectually impaired, hyperactive and suffer from a very short span of attention. Physical abnormalities can also be present, such as a relatively small head, a short nose and low nasal bridge

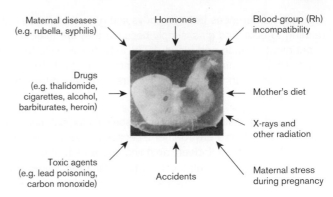

Figure 5.7 The pre-natal, biological environment

Strictly speaking, 'heredity' refers only to the particular set of chromosomes and genes that combine at the moment of fertilization; anything that occurs from that moment on is environmental (Kirby and Radford, 1976; Rose, 2005). This, of course, includes all the influences acting on the developing embryo (as the 'baby' is called during the first eight weeks of pregnancy, thereafter the 'foetus'), such as hormones, drugs taken by the mother, accidents, mother's diet, and so on. From a psychological perspective, the importance of this pre-natal, biological environment, relates to the damaging effects it can have on the unborn child's brain development. For example, of commonly taken (and legal) drugs, alcohol is the most harmful. It is toxic to brain cells during the first ten weeks of pregnancy, and foetal alcohol syndrome refers to intellectual impairment, hyperactivity and attention difficulties associated with very high levels of alcohol consumption during pregnancy (Rutter and Rutter, 1992).

The view of the environment as impinging on a passive individual applies to the *social* (and *cultural*) environment (as opposed to the biological), as well as the *physical*. This, as we have seen, is the level at which the nature–nurture debate normally takes place. If it is inaccurate to see the individual as at the mercy of the environment (as Watson, for one, would have us believe), then we need to ask, 'In what ways does the individual influence/contribute to his/her environment?'

Watson's extreme brand of environmentalism sees 'the environment' as existing largely independently of the individual, a passive receptacle for environmental influences. As we saw earlier, it relates to the 'Which one?' question regarding the nature–nurture debate. An alternative view of what the environment is, relevant to the 'How?' question (which, remember, assumes that both heredity and environment contribute to the development of individual differences), is to see people as making their own environments (Scarr, 1992). This runs counter to what most parents believe about the impact they have on their children, as well as what mainstream developmental psychology teaches. Scarr argues that:

> . . . *each child constructs a reality from the opportunities afforded by the rearing environment, and* . . . *the constructed reality does have considerable influence on variations among children and differences in their adult outcomes.*

Eliciting a response

One way in which people influence/contribute to their environments is through evoking or eliciting certain responses from other people. This may be due either to their behaviour or to particular biological characteristics. An example of the latter is gender. If people have stereotyped views and expectations regarding differences between boys and girls, then these are likely to be expressed through different ways of relating to boys and girls, simply because they *are* male or female. This is demonstrated in the 'baby X' experiments (Smith and Lloyd, 1978, in Rutter and Rutter, 1992). Toddlers were dressed in unisex snowsuits and then given names to indicate gender, half the time in line with their actual gender, half the time not. When adults played with the toddlers, they treated them differently according to what they believed the toddler's gender to be.

What this demonstrates is that a person's biological make-up (or, at least, others' perception of it) becomes part of that person's environment, because other people's reactions to our biological make-up is part of our (social) environment. Indeed, anything about us that may form the basis for others' stereotyped perceptions and reactions towards us (such as physical attractiveness, ethnic, racial or national background, or any physical disability) is as much a part of our environment as it is part of our biological make-up.

However, these examples all relate to static aspects of our make-up. What about more dynamic aspects, such as temperament and behaviour?

For example, children with a very sunny, easy-going and cheerful disposition are more likely to elicit friendly interactions with others than children perceived as miserable or 'difficult'; some children are simply 'easier to love' (Rutter and Rutter, 1992). Research has shown that aggressive boys not only behave more aggressively but also elicit more hostile behaviour in other boys. Their actions help to create a vicious cycle of negative interactions: when aggressive behaviour meets with a hostile response, this makes it more likely that further aggression will occur, and so on (Rutter and Rutter, 1992).

To the extent that all these characteristics are, to some degree, influenced by genetic factors, all the above examples illustrate gene–environment correlations (Rutter and Rutter, 1992; Scarr, 1992): aggressive children tend to experience aggressive environments because they tend to evoke aggressive responses in others. This illustrates reactive gene–environment correlations, while the 'static' examples of gender and physical appearance illustrate passive gene–environment correlations (Plomin *et al.*, 1977). Looking at the environment in this way helps to explain why different individuals have different experiences.

Shared and non-shared psychosocial environments

When the environment is being discussed as a set of (potential) influences that impinges on the individual, it is often 'broken down' into factors such as overcrowding, poverty, social class or socioeconomic status (SES) (which is correlated with the first two, as well as with other indicators), family break-up, marital discord, and so on. In studies of, say, intelligence or aggression, children are often compared with each other in terms of these environmental factors, which are then correlated with the behaviour or ability. So, for example, it may be concluded that children from low-SES backgrounds are more likely to behave in antisocial ways and to be labelled as juvenile delinquents.

When families are compared in this way, it is assumed that children from the same family will all be similarly and equally affected by those environmental factors (shared environment). However, for most characteristics, most children within the same family are not very similar – in fact, they are often extremely varied in personality, abilities and psychological disorders. This observation is most striking when two adopted children are brought up in the same family: 'they're usually very little more alike than any two people chosen at random from the general population' (Rutter and Rutter, 1992; Plomin, 1996).

This substantial within-family variation is exactly what we would expect to find if non-shared influences are the crucial ones: differences between children in the same family will be associated systematically with differences between their experiences. One of the few major studies of this relationship is Dunn and Plomin's (1990) *Separate Lives*. In that book, they argue that family-wide influences (such as SES and marital discord) cannot influence behavioural development unless their impact is experienced differently by each child.

A more specific way of trying to account for these findings is by distinguishing between relative and absolute differences between children in how they are treated. Dunn and Plomin found that the ways in which parents respond differently to their different children (relative differences) are likely to be much more influential than the overall characteristics of the family (absolute differences). For example, it may matter very little whether children are brought up in a home that is less loving or more punitive than average, whereas it may matter considerably that one child receives less affection or more punishment than his/her brother or sister.

These findings imply 'that the unit of environmental transmission is not the family, but rather micro-environments within families' (Plomin and Thompson, 1987). Consistent with these findings is the view that, provided children are brought up in good-enough, supportive, non-deprived/abusive/neglectful environments, the particular family in which they are raised makes very little difference to their personality and intellectual development. Most families provide sufficiently supportive environments for children's individual genetic differences to develop (Scarr, 1992). This could account for:

- temperamental differences between children
- why parents treat different offspring differently (the relative differences)
- differences in the experiences of different children.

BOX 5.1 ARE SHARED ENVIRONMENTS REALLY THAT UNIMPORTANT?

According to Scarr (1992), assuming a 'normal' environment, genes will express their potential. Environmental variations within the normal range are functionally equivalent. So, provided the environment is 'normal', environmental changes (such as extra stimulation as provided by early enrichment programmes: see Gross, 2005) will have no effect. Only if the environment is outside the 'average expectable environment' will such change significantly alter behavioural outcomes.

Dunn and Plomin's findings are only preliminary, but they represent a very important explanation of how the experiences of different individuals might differ; and to the extent that people's experiences differ, their environments are different.

Scarr's theory implies that children could be reassigned to and raised by different families, without significantly affecting how they turn out. For example, differences in *parenting style* make little difference, provided the parents are 'good enough'. But Scarr does not specify what she means by 'good-enough' parenting, and according to Baumrind (1993):

> *All nonabusive environments above the poverty line are not equally facilitative of healthy development.*

Scarr accepted that her theory depends on children experiencing a broad range of environments, but she excluded individuals with disadvantaged circumstances and restricted life choices (Slee and Shute, 2003). For Baumrind (1993), such 'excluded' individuals are in fact the norm worldwide: the *absence* of disadvantage *is not* the same as having a rich environment. Also, what is 'normal' or 'expectable' in one culture is totally unacceptable in another (see Chapter 8).

The constructionist view

What Dunn and Plomin's findings show is that it is futile trying to define the environment *independently* of the person experiencing it, since every person's experience is different. An extreme behaviourist approach would see the structure of experience as given in the environment, which provides stimuli that impinge and shape the individual regardless of who they are. According to *constructionist* views, however, people shape their own experiences: we do not merely respond differently to our environments (which implies a fairly passive role), we

actively create our own experiences. Cross-cultural psychology is based on the assumption that no sociocultural environment exists separately from the meaning that human participants give it (Shweder, 1990). Nothing real 'just is': realities are the product of how things get represented, embedded, implemented and reacted to (Scarr, 1992; see Chapters 8 and 14). The same applies to individual differences within the same culture. According to Scarr:

> *Different people, at different developmental stages, interpret and act upon their environments in different ways that create different experiences for each person. In this view, human experience is a construction of reality, not a property of a physical world that imparts the same experience to everyone who encounters it.*

This constructionist view relates to what Plomin *et al.* (1977) call *active gene–environment interactions*.

Facilitativeness

A further way of trying to answer the 'How?' question is to consider the idea of *vulnerability* or *susceptibility* to environmental influence; this represents an important kind of gene–environment interaction (Rutter and Rutter, 1992).

According to Horowitz (1987, 1990) a highly facilitative environment is one in which the child has loving and responsive parents, and is provided with a rich array of stimulation. When different levels of facilitativeness are combined with a child's initial vulnerabilities or susceptibilities, there is an interaction effect. For example, a resilient child (one with many protective factors and few vulnerabilities) may do quite well in a poor environment; equally, a vulnerable child may do quite well in a highly facilitative environment. Only the vulnerable child in a poor environment will do really poorly.

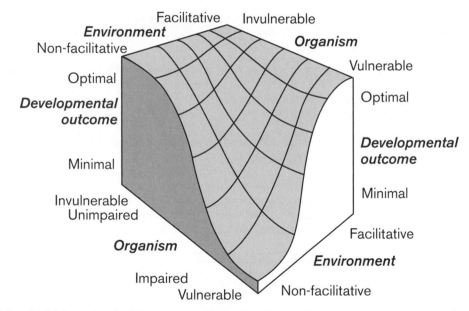

Figure 5.8 Horowitz's model of the interaction of a child's environment with protective factors and vulnerabilities. The surface of the curve illustrates the level of a developmental stage, such as IQ or social skills. According to this model, if a low-birthweight child is reared in a poor environment, then it is likely that that child will do less well than other children reared with a different combination of vulnerabilities and environment.

This interactionist view is demonstrated in a 30-year, longitudinal study, which took place on the Hawaiian island of Kauai (see Box 5.2 overleaf).

Some provisional conclusions regarding the gene–environment relationship

Although we are not free to choose the womb we are conceived in or the school we go to, it is clearly *not* our genes that determine these things (Dobzhansky and Penrose, 1955, cited in Plomin, 1994). However, as we have seen, the environment comprises more than such *macro* environments: we *are* free to choose and create the *micro* environments that form the bulk of our immediate, ongoing experience. As Plomin (1994) says:

> *Socially as well as cognitively, children select, modify, and even create their experiences. Children select environments that are rewarding or at least comfortable, niche-picking. Children modify their environments by setting the background tone for interactions, by initiating behaviour, and by altering the impact of environments . . . Children can make their own environments. That is, they can create environments compatible with their own propensities, niche-building . . .*

BOX 5.2 WERNER'S 'CHILDREN OF THE GARDEN ISLAND' (1989)

Starting in 1955, Werner and her colleagues studied all the children born on the Hawaiian island of Kauai – the Garden Island – in a given period (nearly 700 of them), following them up when they were 1, 2, 10, 18 and 31/32 years old.

Werner became interested in a number of 'high-risk' or 'vulnerable' children. Despite exposure to four or more of the following:

- reproductive stress (either difficulties during pregnancy and/or during labour and delivery)
- discordant and impoverished home lives (including divorce, uneducated, alcoholic or mentally disturbed parents)

before the age of two, these children went on to develop healthy personalities, stable careers and strong interpersonal relationships. There were two main kinds of protective factor that contributed to their resilience: *constitutional* and *environmental*.

Constitutional factors
These included temperamental characteristics that elicited positive responses from family and strangers, such as a fairly high activity level, a low degree of excitability and distress, and a high degree of sociability. They were typically described, as infants, as 'active', 'affectionate', 'cuddly', 'easy-going' and 'even-tempered', with no eating or sleeping habits that caused distress to their carers.

Environmental factors
Their families had four or fewer children, with two or more years between the child being studied and the next child. In spite of poverty, family discord or parental mental illness, they had established a close attachment to at least one carer (grandparent, older sibling, aunt or uncle, or a regular babysitter). They also found a great deal of emotional support from outside the family, were popular with their classmates and had at least one close friend. School became a home away from home, a refuge from a disordered household.

Of the 72 children classified as resilient, 62 were studied after reaching their 30s. As a group, they seemed to be coping well with the demands of adult life, three-quarters had received some college education, and nearly all had full-time jobs and were satisfied with their work. Werner (1989) concluded that:

> *As long as the balance between stressful life events and protective factors is favourable, successful adaptation is possible. When stressful events outweigh the protective factors, however, even the most resilient child can have problems.*

These findings challenge the traditional assumption that there is a simple and direct link between early experiences and later development (Werner, 1989).

BEHAVIOUR GENETICS: GOING BEYOND THE NATURE–NURTURE DEBATE

Much of what we have said above about gene–environment correlations and interactions (which relate to the 'How?' question) derives from the work of behaviour geneticists, such as Scarr and Plomin. But Pike and Plomin (1999) define behaviour genetics (BG) as exploring 'the origins of individual differences . . . in complex behaviours' and, more specifically, as attempting to quantify how much of the variability for any given trait (such as intelligence, schizophrenia or aggressiveness) can be attributed to:

● *heritability* (a statistical measure of the proportion of individual differences within a population attributable to genes)
● *shared environments*, and
● *non-shared environments*.

So, BG addresses both the 'How?' and the 'How much?' questions.

According to Jones (1993), most modern geneticists regard the 'Which one?' question as largely meaningless and the 'How much?' question as dull. The reason for this is that:

> *Nearly all inherited characteristics more complicated than a single change in DNA involve gene and environment acting together. It is impossible to sort them into convenient compartments. An attribute such as intelligence is often seen as a cake which can be sliced into so much 'gene' and so much 'environment'. In fact, the two are so closely blended that trying to separate them is more like trying to unbake the cake . . .*

Plomin (2001) agrees with Jones that the nature–nurture debate has largely faded – but for different reasons. Plomin argues that during the 1980s and 1990s, psychologists became much more accepting of genetic influence (the controversy between 'geneticists' and 'environmentalists' having been at its fiercest); BG research became much more 'mainstream'. But as well as demonstrating what behaviour geneticists had always believed – 'the ubiquitous importance of genetics throughout psychology' – BG research demonstrated that individual differences in complex psychological traits are due at least as much to environmental influences as they are to genetics. In fact, Plomin maintains that BG research 'provides the strongest available evidence for the importance of environmental factors'.

While this may seem paradoxical, we have seen how the concepts of gene–environment correlation and interaction try to explain environmental influences in terms of genetic factors. So, there is still a sense in which genes are 'primary', but Plomin's way of tying them into the environment, rather than looking at them in isolation, satisfies most psychologists' need to put 'the environment' into the equation. As Claridge and Davis (2003) put it:

> *The balanced view is that behaviour genetics is as much about determining environmental, as genetic, effects; though it is naturally the latter that mostly interests . . . [behaviour geneticists].*

Ironically, Plomin also believes that in some areas, especially psychopathology, the pendulum representing the accepted view may be swinging too far from environmental to genetic determinism.

Molecular genetics: going back to nature

A relatively recent new direction taken by researchers trying to explain individual differences biologically involves the attempt to identify (some of the) *specific genes* that are responsible. This is the aim of *molecular genetics* (MG). Some of this research is directed at psychological disorders, such as schizophrenia and autism. For example, an international research team led by Rutter and Monaco has identified a region of chromosome 7 that may be linked with vulnerability to autism (International Molecular Genetic Study of Autism Consortium, 1998). According to Plomin and Rutter (1998):

Finding specific genes that contribute to vulnerability to autism and other behaviour disorders and dimensions will provide the strongest evidence for genetic influence and will make it easier to explore the developmental interplay between nature and nurture.

Claims to have discovered the gene(s) for complex behavioural traits (what Rose, 1997, calls *reduction as ideology*) are currently widespread, both in popular writing and in scientific publications – but these are very misleading. According to Claridge and Davis (2003):

Genes code for very precise, literally microscopic, bits of biological material (proteins) that are both physically and conceptually very distant from the complex behavioural and psychological characteristics which they are supposed to – and perhaps in some sense do – influence. But it is unlikely that there are genes, or sets of genes, 'for' impulsivity, the preference for gay relationships, religiosity, anxiety, or even serious mental disorders, such as schizophrenia. The route from genes to behaviour is likely to be much more tortuous than that and, for any particular characteristic, to involve a multitude of genes and interactions among them – as well as an interplay between genes and environmental factors . . .

Claridge and Davis identify the rationale behind molecular genetic research as the belief that *phenotypic characteristics* (such as observable behaviour) can be found to be associated with a particular sequence of DNA at a given locus on a particular chromosome. But a DNA sequence can show variability (*polymorphisms*), and it is this variation that can be expressed phenotypically as a certain behaviour. Similarly, a single gene can have several different effects (*pleiotropic expression*), and the particular effect it produces depends on other genes (*contingent expression*). According to Rose (2001), the more we learn about pleiotropic and contingent expression:

. . . the more the assumption that the expression is simply an additive one becomes implausible. Gene expression changes depend both on the internal environment (including the other genes present in the organism), and the external one in which the organism develops . . .

BG as a whole is based on what Rose sees as the naïve belief that complex human psychological characteristics and behaviours can be quantified (see Chapters 3 and 10) and their origins partitioned into dichotomous 'genetic' and 'environmental' components. Underlying this belief is the assumption that the two factors are almost entirely *additive*, with little interaction between them. As Rose (2005) puts it:

. . . The very concept of unpicking genes and environment misspeaks the nature of developmental processes. The developing foetus, and the unique human which it is to become, is always both 100 per cent a product of its DNA and 100 per cent a product of the environment of that DNA – and that includes not just the cellular and maternal environment but the social environment in which the pregnant mother is located . . . there is no genetic 'program' present within the fertilized ovum, to be isolated from the context in which it is expressed . . .

The problem with phenotypes: what is schizophrenia?

While identifying the connections between genes and phenotype is relatively straightforward for recognizable, easily definable 'big effects' (such as well-known diseases), this is much more difficult for the kinds of phenotypes found in psychological research (such as personality and intelligence). This is partly because the core features that need explaining may not be all that obvious or agreed, and partly because, even if they are, they do not represent such huge differences between people that these will be discoverable above the 'noise' in the system (Claridge and Davis, 2003).

It is widely accepted that twin and other family resemblance studies show the contribution of genetic influences in schizophrenia (Gottesman, 1991), even in the absence of specific genes. Claridge and Davis claim that this is one of the few factual certainties about schizophrenia. But by the same token (and echoing Plomin: see above), they also claim that it is equally certain that environmental factors must also be important. So far, so good.

However, they cite studies that have produced some rather intriguing and puzzling findings. The same sets of monozygotic (MZ), or identical, twins were assessed for schizophrenia twice, once according to Schneider's (1959) first rank symptoms (passivity experiences and thought disturbances, auditory hallucinations and primary delusions) and on a separate occasion using broader criteria. In the latter case, the heritability estimate was 50 per cent, while using the first rank symptoms it was zero! This suggests, of course, that when we ask about the heritability of schizophrenia, our answer should be couched in 'well, it depends what you mean by . . .' terms. In other words, defining – and diagnosing – schizophrenia is more complex and less straightforward than for physical diseases.

Again, different studies have produced heritability estimates ranging from zero to 90 per cent. According to Claridge and Davis (2003):

> *Is it possible that the value of 50 per cent now generally quoted is merely some average of a range of heritabilities for entirely different psychotic disorders, different variants of schizophrenia, or just illnesses of different severity?*

One notable development in genetics research on schizophrenia is the realization that clinical diagnosis is a very blunt, inaccurate phenotype for exploring heritability (Claridge and Davis, 2003). Instead, we should substitute or look for the genetics of intermediate phenotypes (or *endophenotypes*: Gottesman, 1991). These are measures that do not at first glance seem to have much to do with psychotic symptomatology. Instead, it is assumed that they tap more basic, but quite narrow, behaviours that might underlie the clinical state. A widely cited example is smooth pursuit eye movement (SPEM). It has been found that a proportion of schizophrenic patients show abnormal ability to follow, effectively, a swinging pendulum. It doesn't follow, of course, that everyone who shows this inability is likely to be schizophrenic!

DRAWING SOME CONCLUSIONS: APPLICATIONS AND ETHICAL ISSUES

Watson, the co-discoverer of the double-helix structure of DNA and the former head of the Human Genome Project (the massive international attempt to identify every single human gene), claimed that 'we used to think that our fate was in our stars. Now we know, in large part, that our fate is in our genes' (in Horgan, 1993).

According to Koshland, an eminent biologist and editor of the influential journal *Science* (the journal of the American Association for the Advancement of Science), the nature–nurture debate is 'basically over', since scientists have shown that genes influence many aspects of human behaviour. He also claims (in Horgan, 1993) that genetic research may help to eliminate society's most intractable problems, including drug abuse, homelessness and violent crime. Horgan believes this illustrates that 'Eugenics is back in fashion'.

Figure 5.9 These young German men from 1934 demonstrate the stereotype of the Nazi ideal of fitness and health

The term eugenics (from the Greek for 'good birth') was coined by Galton in 1883, and it embodied the idea that human society could be improved through 'better breeding'. Beginning in the 1920s, the American Eugenics Society sponsored 'Fitter

Families Contests' at state fairs; just as cows and sheep were judged, so were people. Eugenicists helped to persuade more than 20 states to authorize the sterilization of men and women in prisons and psychiatric hospitals, and they also urged the federal government to restrict immigration of 'undesirable' races. Intelligence tests, which had been developed for the selection of soldiers during the First World War, were then used to justify the exclusion of certain nationalities, including those from eastern Europe, from entry into America during the 1920s and 1930s. It was, of course, precisely these groups that suffered at the hands of the Nazis, who took eugenics to its horrifying extreme, by exterminating six million Jews and other 'undesirables' in the gas chambers (see Gould, 1981; Gross, 2008).

X Chromosome   **Xq28 (Shared region)**

Figure 5.10 The Xq28 region of the X chromosome (From LeVay and Hamer, 1994)

Research into the genetics of homosexuality also raises some quite fundamental social and political issues, which go beyond homosexuality itself (see Box 5.3).

BOX 5.3 IS HOMOSEXUALITY GENETICALLY DETERMINED?

LeVay and Hamer (1994) discuss research that claims to have identified a segment of the X chromosome likely to be the site of the genes responsible for 'swaying', if not 'determining', sexual orientation. This research is a *linkage study* based on the finding that genes that are close together on a chromosome are almost always inherited together. So, if there is a gene that influences sexual orientation, it should be 'linked' to a nearby DNA marker (segments of DNA that indicate locations on a chromosome) that tends to travel along with it in a 'family'. Out of 40 pairs of gay brothers, 33 showed the same marker, located at the tip of the long arm of the X chromosome, in a region known as Xq28.

According to LeVay and Hamer:

> *The most straightforward interpretation of the finding is that chromosome region Xq28 contains a gene that influences male sexual orientation. The study provides the strongest evidence to date that human sexuality is influenced by heredity because it directly examines the genetic information [in] the DNA . . .*

However, LeVay and Hamer recognize that these are only initial findings and that, as well as the need for replication, the gene itself has not yet been isolated. Xq28 is about 4 million base pairs in length; although this represents less than 0.2 per cent of the total human genome, it is still long enough to contain several hundred genes. Searching for 'gay genes' is like looking for the proverbial 'needle in a haystack' (LeVay and Hamer, 1994).

As we have already noted, genes in themselves specify proteins, *not* behavioural or psychological phenomena. Although we know virtually nothing about how complex psychological phenomena are embodied in the brain, it is conceivable that particular DNA sequences might somehow cause the brain to be wired specifically for homosexual orientation. However, Byrne (1994) warns that:

> *. . . we should also be asking ourselves why we as a society are so emotionally invested in this research . . . Perhaps the answer to the most salient questions in this debate lie not within the biology of human brains but rather in the cultures those brains have created.*

The genetic theory of intelligence, especially the claim that racial differences are due to genetic variations (e.g. Jensen, 1969), has always been condemned by those of a left-wing persuasion; they see it as reinforcing, and even fuelling, the racism and racial inequalities that are responsible for the intellectual differences in the first place. However, in the case of homosexuality, things are much less clear-cut. If scientific evidence shows that homosexuality is genetically determined, this means that gays (and, presumably, lesbians too) *do not choose* their sexual orientation: they 'cannot help it'. This could, however, be used *against* gays and lesbians: if they cannot choose to be different (i.e. heterosexual), then they are *more* – not less – of a threat. The genetic view is usually a chance to blame the victim, a way of excusing injustice (Byrne, 1994).

Many gays and lesbians fight for the right to choose their sexual preference, so it may be very surprising to find LeVay, a homosexual and eminent biologist, advocating the search for 'gay genes'. He believes that, if successful, the scientific evidence will make society as a whole more, not less, tolerant, precisely because it will show that homosexuals do not choose to 'be that way'. However, LeVay and Hamer (1994) recognize that:

> . . . *increasing knowledge of biology may eventually bring with it the power to infringe on the natural rights of individuals and to impoverish the world of its human diversity. It is important that our society expand discussions of how new scientific information should be used to benefit the human race in its entirety.*

SUMMARY

○ The debate about heredity and environment (or the nature–nurture debate) is concerned with some of the most fundamental questions that human beings ask about themselves.

○ In its broadest sense, the debate is concerned with both the human species as a whole (compared with other species) and with individual differences between people. It is in the latter sense that the nature–nurture debate takes place.

○ Nativists believe that heredity determines certain abilities/capacities, while empiricists believe that the mind, at birth, is a *tabula rasa,* which is gradually 'filled in' by learning and experience.

○ Examples of nativism in psychology include the Gestalt psychologists, Gesell's concept of maturation, and Chomsky's language acquisition device (LAD). Behaviourism represents a very influential and extreme form of empiricist theory within psychology.

○ 'Is it nature or nurture?' is an oversimplified question, while 'How much?' is a more complex question, concerned with the relative importance of heredity and environment. It presupposes that both are involved, consistent with an interactionist position, and is linked to the 'individual differences' form of the debate.

○ Attempts to quantify the relative contributions of genes and environment are the main focus of behavioural genetics, which uses methods such as twin studies, adoption studies and other studies of family resemblance.

○ While genetic variability is the raw material of evolution, evolution doesn't imply genetic variation within a species, and vice versa.

○ The basic units of hereditary transmission are genes, large molecules of deoxyribonucleic acid (DNA). They occur in pairs and are situated on the chromosomes.

○ Genes have two major functions: self-duplication and protein synthesis. The body's non-reproductive cells duplicate through mitosis, while the reproductive/germ cells duplicate through meiosis.

O Structural genes code for proteins and enzymes, and form the basis of classical genetics. Regulator genes (the majority) communicate closely with the environment and change in response to it.

O In a psychological context, 'environment' usually implies external, post-natal influences impinging on a passive individual.

O Instead of seeing the environment as independent of/separate from the individual, people may be seen as making their own environments. This is demonstrated by gene–environment correlations, non-shared psychosocial experiences, attaching their own meaning to events/experiences, and gene–environment interaction. Related to these are niche-picking and niche-building.

O Behaviour genetic research not only shows beyond doubt that genetic factors are involved in complex human behaviour and psychological characteristics, it also provides the strongest evidence for the importance of environmental factors. While the nature–nurture debate may be 'over', eugenics may be back in fashion.

O Molecular genetics (MG) involves the attempt to identify specific genes responsible for individual differences. The research on which such claims are based seems to ignore polymorphisms, and pleiotropic and contingent expression. It also assumes the additive nature of genetic influence.

O Another problem with MG is defining and measuring the phenotype for which the genes are being sought. Heritability estimates for schizophrenia are influenced by what criteria for diagnosing it are used, a problem that rarely occurs with physical diseases. One solution to this problem is to look for the genetics of endophenotypes.

O Genetic research into homosexuality raises several (more general) important social and political issues, including why the research is seen as so important in the first place, and whether society becomes more or less tolerant of homosexuality if it is found that gays 'can't help it'.

USEFUL WEBSITES

http://www.sanger.ac.uk
http://genetics.nature.com
www.guardian.co.uk/genes
http://en.wikipedia.org/wiki/Nature_versus_nurture
www.feralchildren.com/en/nature.php

RECOMMENDED READING

Ceci, S.J. and Williams, W.M. (eds) (1999) *The Nature–Nurture Debate: The Essential Readings.* Oxford: Blackwell.

Gerhardt, S. (2004) *Why Love Matters: How affection shapes a baby's brain.* Hove: Routledge.

Gross, R. (2008) *Key Studies in Psychology* (5th edn). London: Hodder Education. (Chapters 26, 28, 34, 35.)

Pinker, S. (2003) *The Blank Slate: The Modern Denial of Human Nature.* Harmondsworth: Penguin Books Ltd.

Plomin, R. (1994) *Genetics and Experience: The Interplay between Nature and Nurture.* Thousand Oaks, CA: Sage.

Rolls, G. (2005) *Classic Case Studies in Psychology.* London: Hodder Arnold. (Chapter 12.)

CHAPTER 6

PSYCHOLOGY, WOMEN AND FEMINISM

At first sight, it may not seem obvious what a chapter with the title 'Psychology, women and feminism' would be about, or why such a chapter should be necessary. But in a very real sense, what it is about is what makes it necessary, namely the very strong and pervasive *masculinist bias* within psychology, which, in turn, reflects – and to some degree may contribute to – the superior power and status of males in western society.

While feminism is a social and political movement that arose outside psychology (often used synonymously with the women's movement of the 1970s in particular), many who would describe themselves as feminists were, and are, academics who criticized their particular discipline for being 'gender blind' (Kelly, 1988). If what feminists have in common is a condemnation of the oppression of women (in any and all its forms), then we would expect that those engaged in occupations and professions (including psychology) would be critical of such treatment of women as it goes on within their occupation or profession.

However, feminist thinkers and writers are not just against oppression of and discrimination against women, they are also for the recognition of the achievements, contributions and experience of women as being valid and important in their own right, and not just as matters to be understood and evaluated in comparison with men. Feminist psychologists, therefore, are female psychologists who criticize psychology as a discipline – its methods, theories and applications – from a feminist perspective.

WHAT IS FEMINIST PSYCHOLOGY?

According to Wilkinson (1989), definitions of feminist psychology vary widely, in both substance and inclusiveness. For example, in the USA, the terms 'feminist psychology' and the 'psychology of women' are often used synonymously: psychological research on women, and its practitioners, are automatically described as 'feminist'. However, in the UK, these areas are generally more clearly distinguished.

This chapter as a whole explores some of the major criticisms of psychology made from a feminist perspective. Briefly, these include:

- a great deal of psychological research is conducted on all-male samples, but then it either fails to make this clear or reports the findings as if they applied to women and men equally
- some of the most influential theories within psychology as a whole are based on studies of males only, but are meant to apply equally to women and men
- if women's behaviour differs from men's, the former is often judged to be pathological or abnormal or deficient in some way, since the behaviour of men is, implicitly or explicitly, taken as the 'standard', the norm against which women's behaviour is compared
- psychological explanations of behaviour tend to emphasize biological (and other internal) causes, as opposed to social (and other external) causes, thereby giving (and reinforcing) the impression that *psychological sex differences* are inevitable and unchangeable, at the same time reinforcing widely held

stereotypes about men and women. As well as being objectionable in themselves, such stereotypes contribute to the oppression of women

● heterosexuality – both in women and men – is taken (either implicitly or explicitly) to be the norm, so that homosexuality is seen as abnormal.

In short, feminist psychologists see psychology as being *sexist* (women are regarded as inferior to men and are discriminated against because they are women) and *heterosexist* (gay men and lesbian women are considered to be abnormal and are discriminated against *because* they are gays or lesbians). Feminist psychologists also consider that while psychology, as a science, claims to be 'neutral', 'objective' and 'value-free', it is actually *value-laden*, taking men as the 'universal' standard, the centre around which everything else revolves. So, apart from being sexist and heterosexist, psychology is also *androcentric* (male-centred).

According to Moghaddam (2005):

> *Feminist psychology attempts to harness the power of psychology to improve the status of women. But in order to be able to use psychology to bring about change in the wider world, feminist psychologists believe they must also bring about change in psychology. This is because . . . traditional psychology still reflects many of the gender biases of the larger society, albeit in subtle and implicit ways . . . Feminist psychology is explicitly political and nourished by the feminist movement.*

SEXISM WITHIN PSYCHOLOGY

In 1974, Bernstein and Russo published an article in *American Psychologist* called 'The history of psychology revisited: Or, up with our foremothers'. It consisted largely of a quiz, which their psychology colleagues failed miserably! The questions were as follows:

(a) Who were the first persons to use the term 'projective technique' in print?
(**Answer:** Lois Murphy and Ruth Horowitz)
(b) Who was the first person to develop child analysis through play?
(**Answer:** Hermine von Hug-Hellmuth)
(c) Who developed the Cattell Infant Intelligence Test Scale?
(**Answer:** Psyche Cattell)
(d) What do the following have in common?
The Bender–Gestalt Test, the Taylor Manifest Anxiety Scale, the Kent–Rosanoff Word Association Test, the Thematic Apperception Test (TAT), and the Sentence Completion Method.
(**Answer:** A woman was either the senior author or the sole author of each test/method)
(e) The following are the last names of individuals who have contributed to the scientific study of human behaviour. What else do these names have in common?
Ausubel, Bellak, Brunswick, Buhler, Dennis, Gardner, Gibson, Glueck, Harlow, Hartley, Hoffman, Horowitz, Jones, Kendler, Koch, Lacey, Luchins, Lynd, Murphy, Premack, Rossi, Sears, Sherif, Spence, Staats, Stendler, Whiting, Yarrow.
(**Answer:** They are the surnames of female social scientists)

While you may have recognized some of the names in the last question, this may only be because they had more famous and familiar husbands with whom they jointly published research (e.g. Gardner and Gardner, Harlow and Harlow, Kendler and Kendler, Luchins and Luchins, and Sherif and Sherif): we automatically infer that the 'Harlow' in the list is Harry Harlow (of rhesus monkey fame) and that the 'Sherif' is Muztafer Sherif (of the autokinetic effect in conformity fame). We're *all* guilty!

Similarly, there is a strong tendency to assume that a psychologist whose name is unfamiliar to you is male. Even though statistically it is very likely that you will be correct, this is not the basis for making such assumptions. Instead, it reflects a masculinist bias, the belief that the contributions made by men to psychology are more important than those made by women. As Scarborough and Furumoto (1987, in Paludi, 1992) state, the history of psychology is the history of male psychology.

If the names in the answers to questions a–c are not what you would call 'household names', this is precisely because the psychological literature's treatment of women psychologists has kept them invisible (Paludi, 1992):

> *The histories written by psychology's academicians are neither accurate nor complete, neglecting as they do the most important contributions made by women . . . they do not include Mary Calkin's theory of self nor her invention of the method of paired associates, they do not mention Christine Ladd-Franklin's developmental theory of colour vision . . . Additionally, they fail to mention the monumentally important books of Margaret Washburn on animal behaviour . . . and they totally ignore Magda Arnold's comprehensive theory of emotions and Margaret Harlow's contribution to an understanding of the importance of tactile stimulation in mothering.*
>
> (Stevens and Gardner, 1982, in Paludi, 1992)

Figure 6.1 Mary Calkins and Margaret Washburn; if these women are not household names, it is because psychological literature's treatment of women psychologists has kept them invisible

Mary Calkins was also the first person to explicitly recognize, and vividly describe, primacy-recency effects in memory (although she never actually used these terms) (Jackson, 1992).

Jackson (1992) points out that during the earliest days of the discipline of psychology (the mid-1800s), discrimination against women was overt: they were simply banned from participating. Calkins was excluded, in 1890, from a graduate psychology programme on the grounds that she was a woman. Similarly, both Calkins and Ladd-Franklin were refused their PhDs, even though they had completed their theses.

Washburn was the first white American woman to receive a PhD in psychology, in 1908 (1904, according to Paludi); Inez Prosser was the first black American woman, receiving her PhD in 1933 (Jackson, 1992)! Washburn was also the second woman President of the American Psychological Association (APA), in 1921, but despite this, she was denied an academic post at a research university (Paludi, 1992). This reflects the prevalent view at the time that too much intense brain activity as required by higher education would weaken women's reproductive capacities, making them unsuitable candidates for professional degrees (Morawski, 1994, in Davis and Gergen, 1997).

The rediscovery of women psychologists

Their colleagues' poor performance on their quiz led Bernstein and Russo (1974) to conclude that women psychologists needed to be *rediscovered*. According to Paludi (1992), in response to the neglect of women's contributions to psychology and to the recognition that women's history has the potential to transform women's self-understanding, a sub-field of women's history in psychology has evolved in recent years. This draws on Lerner's (1979) model, namely (i) finding lost or overlooked women and putting them back into the history (*compensatory history*), (ii) noting women's contributions (*contribution history*), and (iii) noting how history is constructed through a male (androcentric) perspective and reconstructing it from the perspective of women (*reconstruction history*) (see Chapter 11).

In the USA, the Association for Women in Psychology (AWP) was formed in 1969, and in 1973 the APA formed the Division of the Psychology of Women (Division 35), which publishes its own journal, *The Psychology of Women Quarterly* (*PWQ*). Parlee (1991) asks how far *PWQ* has helped to develop a psychology for women or a psychology of gender that is different from mainstream (or 'malestream') psychology. Compared with mainstream journals, articles in *PWQ* have (i) more often involved women of different ages, sexual orientations and from different ethnic backgrounds, (ii) less often involved just experimental research designs, and (iii) have paid somewhat more attention to the context of behaviour (as opposed to biological or personality variables). (Both (ii) and (iii) are discussed in more detail below.) However, Parlee feels that these differences represent only a superficial change.

This view is endorsed by Wilkinson (1989), who asks why there has been a lack of change within mainstream psychology in response to the 'feminist critique'. The answer, she says, is essentially to do with legitimacy: feminist research is not seen by the mainstream to be 'legitimate science' and so is largely dismissed. Not only is it not seen as legitimate, but, because of the commitment of feminist research to social and political change for the benefit of women, it provides a convenient 'handle' for the labelling of feminist research as 'purely political'. This false polarization of 'science' and 'politics' removes the need to take feminist arguments seriously, and protects mainstream researchers from having to acknowledge the political dimension of their practice (Wilkinson, 1989) (see Chapters 5, 10 and 14). The Division of the Psychology of Women also has a Section on the Psychology of Black Women, as well as Committees on the Psychology of Latinas and Asian-American Women.

In her presidential address to the APA in 1987, Bonnie Stricklund pointed out that women now constitute about one-third of all employed psychologists and more than half of those gaining PhDs in psychology each year. Compared with the overt discrimination of the early years of psychology, this represents a radical change. She predicted that psychology would become the first science to be 'feminized' – that is, it would have more women than men. This would allow the investigation of a set of research problems that were not consistent with, or could not be solved by, the androcentric paradigm – such as women's friendships with other women, rape, sexual harassment, battered women, eating disorders, and sexism within psychopathology (Paludi, 1992).

One manifestation of sexism within psychology is the devaluation (by men) of the areas of the discipline in which women are traditionally more numerous and which they seem to prefer, compared with the traditionally 'male' areas. The former include person-oriented/service-oriented fields, such as educational, developmental and clinical psychology, and counselling, while the latter are the academic/experimental areas, including learning and cognitive psychology, which are regarded (by men) as more scientifically rigorous and intellectually demanding (Paludi, 1992). This is consistent with the more general observation that professions dominated by women are seen as low status (at least by male practitioners) (Wilkinson, 1989).

Could it be that women are 'channelled' into certain fields of psychology, which are then defined as 'inferior', simply because they're populated mainly by women? People who play a key role in this process are gatekeepers – individuals, such as heads of university psychology departments, with the power and authority to decide who is employed to teach and do research, and in what areas of the discipline. In psychology, the gatekeepers are usually men.

HETEROSEXISM IN PSYCHOLOGY

Many radical feminists, both within and outside psychology, are lesbians. Not surprisingly, lesbian feminist psychologists tend to focus their criticisms on the neglect of the topic of homosexuality, and on discrimination against lesbians and gays, both staff and students.

Figure 6.2 Celia Kitzinger and Sue Wilkinson outside the High Court in London in 2006. Despite having been legally married in Canada in 2003, their attempt to have this recognized in the UK was rejected. The judge ruled that, although being treated differently from heterosexual couples represents discrimination, this is justified in order to protect the traditional definition of marriage as between a man and a woman, primarily to produce children. Their marriage was being 'reduced' to a Civil Partnership (which became UK law in 2005).

According to Celia Kitzinger (1990), homosexuality hardly features in undergraduate psychology courses. She quotes Louise Clarke (1989), a lesbian student at one of the 'new' universities in London, who says that:

There are . . . lesbians/gay men in every college of higher education, whose needs are barely acknowledged, let alone met. Our existence should be acknowledged and reflected not just in the lecture room, but also in the curriculum.

Kitzinger goes on to say that for gay and lesbian students and staff alike, academic psychology departments can be deeply oppressive places. Although teaching unions have anti-discrimination policies and oppose Section 28 of the Local Government Act (outlawing the 'promotion' of homosexuality and the teaching of the 'acceptability of homosexuality as a pretended family relationship'), universities still embody anti-gay attitudes. Psychologists who 'come out' run the risk of verbal abuse and threats of violence. Kitzinger advocates that policies should be implemented comparable to those dealing with gender, race and disability discrimination, to protect lesbians and gays wherever psychologists work.

The APA Gay and Lesbian Studies Division was established in 1984. In the UK, the British Psychological Association (BPS) has a Psychology of Women Section (POWS), set up in 1987, and there also exists the more informal Women in Psychology organization. According to Kitzinger and Coyle (2002), publication of their book, *Lesbian and Gay Psychology: New Perspectives*, marks the 'coming of age' of British lesbian and gay psychology. It celebrates the founding of the BPS's Lesbian and Gay Psychology Section in 1998, after nine years of campaigning and three rejected proposals.

THE FEMINIST CRITIQUE OF SCIENCE

If certain areas of psychology (such as cognitive) are regarded (by men) as scientifically more rigorous and intellectually demanding, we need to ask just what is meant by 'scientifically rigorous'. What view of science is assumed by those who would make such a claim? What is the 'malestream' or androcentric account of the nature of science?

Basically, it sees the scientist as pursuing 'the truth' through the use of highly controlled, experimental methods. The scientist is able to discover 'what the world is really like', in some objective sense (how things are when not being observed and measured by scientists). Because the scientist is only interested in objective truth ('facts'), science, according to this perspective, is said to be value-free: the scientist's values, biases and so on have no influence on the scientific process. This positivist approach applies as much to the study of people as it does to the physical world (see Chapters 10 and 14).

But can scientific inquiry be neutral, totally free of bias, wholly independent of the value system of the human scientists who are doing the science? According to Prince and Hartnett (1993):

Decisions about what is, and what is not, to be measured, how this is done, and most importantly, what constitutes legitimate research are made by individual scientists within a socio-political

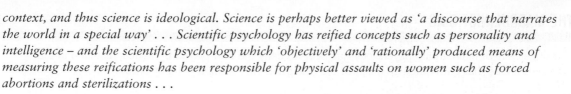

context, and thus science is ideological. Science is perhaps better viewed as 'a discourse that narrates the world in a special way' . . . Scientific psychology has reified concepts such as personality and intelligence – and the scientific psychology which 'objectively' and 'rationally' produced means of measuring these reifications has been responsible for physical assaults on women such as forced abortions and sterilizations . . .

Prince and Hartnett point out that, between 1924 and 1972, over 7500 women in the state of Virginia alone were forcibly sterilized – in particular, 'unwed mothers, prostitutes, the feeble-minded, children with discipline problems'; the criterion in all cases was the woman's mental age as measured by the Stanford–Binet intelligence test (Gould, 1981).

When some human ability or quality, such as intelligence, is treated as if it had a separate, independent, objective existence (reification), such that it can be measured in an objective way, scientific 'findings' relating to that ability/quality can then be used to promote and justify discrimination against groups in society. But intelligence, personality and so many more of the 'things' psychologists study are hypothetical constructs, abstract concepts used to help explain and predict behaviour, but not directly, or literally, observable.

The very decision to study intelligence, and to develop tests designed to measure it, indicates that (some) psychologists believe that not only is this possible but (much more relevant to the view of science as value-free) that it is important to do so! Such decisions are not made in a politico-cultural vacuum and so cannot be seen as objective, neutral and value-free. As Weisstein (1993b) says:

. . . our ideas are filtered through our cultural and social categories, the ongoing social context and our own social rank.

According to Nicolson (1995), *the scientific method is gender-biased* (see Chapters 10 and 14). She argues that:

Psychology relies for its data on the practices of socialized and culture-bound individuals, so that to explore 'natural' or 'culture-free' behaviour (namely that behaviour unfettered by cultural, social structures and power relations) is by definition impossible, which is a state of affairs that normally goes unacknowledged . . .

'Normally' denotes mainstream, positivist psychology.

Far from advocating that psychology should be value-free, objective and 'scientific', many feminist psychologists argue that we should stop denying the role of values, and acknowledge that psychological investigation must always take wider social reality into account. They call for a new value-laden approach to research: unless and until psychology 'comes clean' about its values and biases, it will never be able to adequately reflect the reality of its subject matter, namely human beings.

In the 1993 preface to her classic *In A Different Voice* (first published in 1982), Carol Gilligan says that at the core of her work on moral development in women and girls was the realization that within psychology, and in society at large, 'values were being taken as facts'. She continues:

In the aftermath of the Holocaust . . . it is not tenable for psychologists or social scientists to adopt a position of ethical neutrality or cultural relativism – to say that one cannot say anything about values or that all values are culturally relative. Such a hands-off stance in the face of atrocity amounts to a kind of complicity . . .

While the example she gives is clearly extreme, it helps to illustrate the argument that, not only do psychologists (and other scientists) have a responsibility to make their values explicit about important social and political issues, but their failure to do so may (unwittingly) contribute to prejudice, discrimination and oppression.

THE MASCULINIST BIAS

The major 'sin' of mainstream psychology has been to deny the part played by values, resulting in the masculinist bias that permeates so much of the discipline. This takes a number of forms.

'Women want first and foremost to be mothers'

As we have seen, most psychologists are male, and the predominant research methodology used is the experiment, which is supposed to be objective and value-free. But we have also seen that deciding what is worth investigating is itself a value judgement, and this is particularly clear when male psychologists investigate aspects of female behaviour, such as motherhood.

For example, according to Bettelheim (1965):

> . . . we must start with the realization that, as much as women want to be good scientists or engineers, they want first and foremost to be womanly companions of men, and to be mothers.

Similarly, Bowlby (1953) linked motherhood inextricably to being at home, white, 20–30 years old, middle class and married. But what about the parent and infant studies of non-married, single, gay, lesbian and black parents (Jackson, 1992)?

In the twenty-first century, a lesbian sexual orientation is no longer considered to be a reason to deny a mother custody of her children. In the UK, gay and lesbian couples are eligible to adopt children. Lesbian mothers also have access to assisted reproduction clinics to allow them to conceive a child without the involvement of a male partner. This change in social attitudes has come about largely through the efforts of the women's movement and the gay liberation movement beginning in the 1970s (Golombok, 2002).

Golombok believes that psychology has also had a part to play. There will always be some people who believe that it's morally wrong for lesbian women to rear children – whatever the outcome for the child. Others object on the grounds that the children would suffer. But psychological research (including Golombok's own) to the contrary has brought about a change of mind:

> Mothers no longer have to choose between their partner and their child, and children who would otherwise have remained in care are being adopted or fostered into loving homes. Psychological research has helped tackle the injustices and prejudice that has damaged people's lives. That is why I study lesbian mothers.
>
> (Golombok, 2002)

(See 'Essentialism revisited', page 101.)

The male standard

Men are taken as some sort of standard or norm, against which women are compared and judged. According to Tavris (1993):

> In any domain of life in which men set the standard of normalcy, women will be considered abnormal, and society will debate woman's 'place' and her 'nature'. Many women experience tremendous conflict in trying to decide whether to be 'like' men or 'opposite' from them, and this conflict is itself evidence of the implicit male standard against which they are measuring themselves. This is why it is normal for women to feel abnormal.

She gives three examples.

1 Women and men have the same moods and mood swings, but only women get theirs packaged into a syndrome. Women's hormones have never been reliably related to *behaviour*, competence or anything to do with work, while men's *are* related to a variety of antisocial behaviours. Despite this, women may suffer from PMS (pre-menstrual syndrome) but there's no male equivalent (such as 'hyper-testosterone syndrome').

2 In 1985, the American Psychiatric Association proposed two new categories of mental disorder for inclusion in the revised (third) edition of DSM (*Diagnostic and Statistical Manual of Mental Disorders*), the official classification system used by American psychiatrists. One of these was *masochism*, which in DSM II was one of the psychosexual disorders, in which sexual gratification requires being hurt or humiliated. The proposal was to extend the term so that it became a more pervasive personality disorder, in which a person seeks failure at work, at home and in relationships, rejects opportunities for pleasure, puts others first, thereby sacrificing his/her own needs, playing the martyr, and so on. While not intended to apply to women exclusively, these characteristics are associated predominantly with the female role. Indeed, Caplan, in 1985, appeared before an American Psychiatric

Figure 6.3 The fact that Eve was made from Adam's rib illustrates the point that men are the standard by which women are all too often judged

Association hearing on the proposed disorder, and argued that it represented a way of calling psychopathological the behaviour of women who conform to social norms for a 'feminine woman' (the 'good wife syndrome'; Caplan, 1991). In short, such a diagnostic label was biased against women and perpetuated the myth of women's masochism. After a year-long debate, the label was changed to self-defeating personality disorder and was put in the Appendix of DSM-III-R, under the heading 'Proposed Diagnostic Categories Needing Further Study'. As Zimbardo (1992) argues, this example shows the political and ideological implications of diagnosing certain behaviour patterns as mental disorders (see Chapter 7). At the same time, there was no proposal for a parallel diagnosis for men who conform to social norms for a 'real' man (the John Wayne type, or 'macho personality disorder'). However, in 1991, Pantony and Caplan formally proposed that delusional dominating personality disorder be included in DSM IV, which was at the time being prepared (and was subsequently published in 1994). The Committee soundly rejected the proposal, on the grounds that 'there is no clinical tradition' for such a disorder (Caplan, 1991; Tavris, 1993).

3 When men have problems (such as drug abuse) and behave in socially unacceptable ways (as in rape and other forms of violence), the causes are looked for in their upbringing. Women's problems, on the other hand, are the result of their psyche or their hormones. This corresponds roughly to an internal attribution in the case of women and an external attribution in the case of men. The further implication is that for men, it could have been different (they are the victims of their childhoods, etc.), while for women it couldn't (because 'that's what women are like').

According to Tavris (1993), the view that man is the norm and woman is the opposite, lesser or deficient ('the problem') constitutes one of three currently competing views regarding what she calls the 'Mismeasure of Woman' (meant to parallel Gould's *The Mismeasure of Man* (1981), a brilliant critique of intelligence testing: see Gross, 2008). It is the view that underlies so much psychological research designed to discover why women are not 'as something' (moral, intelligent, rational) as men. According to Tavris (1993):

> *The bias of seeing women's behaviour as something to be explained in relation to the male norm makes sense in a world which takes the male norm for granted.*

Moreover, the male norm frames the very questions investigators ask; the answers to these questions then create the impression that women have 'problems', 'deficiencies', etc. if they differ from the norm (see Box 6.1).

The male standard as the norm also underlies the enormous self-help industry, whereby women consume millions of books advising them how to be slimmer, more beautiful, independent or whatever. Men, being normal, feel no need to 'fix' themselves in corresponding ways (Tavris, 1993).

Consistent with this view is a study by Broverman *et al.* (1979, in Jackson, 1992), which asked several psychiatrists to define a healthy adult, a healthy adult male and a healthy adult female. The first two definitions were very similar, being defined by traits such as assertiveness, aggression, ambition and task-orientation. But healthy women were viewed as being caring, expressive, nurturing and affiliative. Women, therefore, are in a double bind. As healthy women, they fall outside the norm for healthy adults; if they assume male characteristics, they step outside the definition of a healthy woman (Jackson, 1992).

Accentuating the sex differences

In psychology in general, but perhaps in the study of gender in particular, there is a strong bias towards publishing studies that have produced 'positive' results (where there is a significant difference: see Chapter 14). So, in the case of gender, studies that find sex differences will be published, while those that don't, won't. The far more convincing evidence for 'sex similarity' is, therefore, ignored, creating the very powerful impression that differences between men and women are real, widespread and 'the rule'. Indeed, the very term 'sex similarities' sounds rather odd (Jackson, 1992; Tavris, 1993; Unger, 1979).

Sexism in research

Pointing out the sexist bias in psychological research is as much an *ethical* as a scientific/practical criticism: we have already seen how damaging to women sexist research can be (see also Chapter 9).

The APA Board of Social and Ethical Responsibility for Psychology set up a Committee on Nonsexist Research, which reported its findings as Guidelines for Avoiding Sexism in Psychological Research (Denmark *et al.*, 1988). According to Denmark *et al.*, gender bias is found at all stages of the research process: (i) question formulation; (ii) research methods and design; (iii) data analysis and interpretation; (iv) conclusion formulation. The principles set out in the Guidelines are meant to apply to other forms of bias too : race, ethnicity, disability, sexual orientation and socioeconomic status.

Question formulation

Gender stereotypes associated with the topic being studied can bias the questions that are asked (and the research outcomes). For example, leadership is often defined in terms of dominance, aggression and other styles that stress stereotypically male characteristics. To correct this problem, researchers should recognize the existence of a range of leadership styles, including those that stress egalitarian relationships, negotiation, conflict resolution and consideration of others.

BOX 6.1 SOME EXAMPLES OF TYPICAL FINDINGS FROM THE LITERATURE ON PSYCHOLOGICAL SEX DIFFERENCES (TAVRIS, 1993)

- Women have lower self-esteem than men.
- Women do not value their efforts as much as men.
- Women are less self-confident than men.
- Women are more likely to say they are hurt than to admit they are angry.
- Women have more difficulty developing a 'separate sense of self'.

Most people would agree that it is desirable for women to have high self-esteem, to value their efforts more, and so on. So such studies usually conclude with discussion of 'the problem' of why women are so insecure and what can be done about it.

But had these studies used *women* as the basis of comparison, the same findings might have produced different conclusions about what the 'problems' are.

- Men are more conceited than women.
- Men overvalue the work they do.
- Men are not as realistic as women in assessing their abilities.
- Men are more likely to accuse/attack others when unhappy, instead of stating that they feel hurt or looking for sympathy.
- Men have more difficulty in forming and maintaining relationships.

If these 'translations' of the first set of statements sound biased and derogatory, this is precisely the point Tavris is trying to make: describing women's deficiencies is not usually seen as biased and derogatory, because the male norm is the standard against which women are being judged. As soon as a female norm is used to set the standard, the bias becomes apparent; only then do we become aware of the bias that was there all the time!

Why has it been so difficult to notice the same negative tone in the way we talk about women? The answer is that we are used to seeing women as the problem, and to regarding women's differences from men as deficiencies and weaknesses.

(Tavris, 1993)

Tavris argues that, after centuries of trying to 'measure up', many women feel exhilarated by having female qualities and experiences valued and celebrated. *Cultural feminists,* while regarding man as the norm, see woman as opposite but better ('the solution'); this represents the second current version of the 'mismeasure of woman'.

Again, questions derived from, or constrained by, existing theory and research based on male samples, thus not taking women's experiences into account, are likely to result in explanations of female behaviour that are not very meaningful. For example, the hypothesis that aggressive stimuli increase sexual arousal is based on results using male participants only; it is essential either to use female participants as well as male, or to point out the difficulties of generalizing these results to women.

Finally, it is assumed that topics relevant to white males are more important and 'basic', whereas those relevant to white females, or ethnic-minority females or males, are more marginal, specialized or applied. For example, research on the effects of television violence on aggression in boys is considered basic, while research on the psychological correlates of pregnancy or the menopause is not. (This relates to what we noted earlier regarding the value-laden nature of psychology and the need to recognize the biases involved in research, instead of trying to deny them.)

Research methods and design

The selection of research participants is often based on stereotypic assumptions, and does not allow for generalizations to other populations. For example, in studies of contraception, female-only samples are used, on the assumption that males aren't (or needn't be) responsible for contraception. But both sexes should be studied before drawing any conclusions about the factors that influence the use of contraception.

Sometimes male samples are used because of practical convenience. For example, male animals are often preferred as subjects in experiments because the oestrous cycle in females disrupts responses in certain types of behavioural or biological tests. Generalization to females must then be made only with great caution.

In a surprisingly large number of studies, the gender and race of the participants, researchers and any confederates/stooges who may be involved, are not specified. As a consequence, potential interactions between these variables are not accounted for. For example, men tend to display more helping behaviour than women in studies involving a young female confederate who needs help. These findings could be a function of either the gender of the confederate or an interaction between the confederate and the participant, rather than gender differences between the participants (which is the usual conclusion that is drawn).

Data analysis and interpretation

As we noted in the section on 'Accentuating the sex differences', above, when sex differences *aren't* found, the findings tend to remain unreported. Not only should they be, but conversely, when any *non-hypothesized* gender differences are found, they should be reported. In both cases, the findings should be reported so that replications can be carried out.

Gender differences are sometimes claimed to be present when a significant correlation is found between two variables for, say, men, but not for women. Instead of testing to see if there is a significant difference between the two correlations, it is simply assumed (because the findings fit the stereotypes).

Finally, significant gender differences may be reported in a very misleading way, because the wrong sort of comparisons are being made. For example, 'The spatial ability scores of women in our sample are significantly lower than those of men, at the 0.01 level'. We might conclude from this that women cannot/should not become architects or engineers. However, 'Successful architects score above 32 on our spatial ability test . . . engineers score above 31 . . . 12 per cent of women and 16 per cent of men in our sample score above 31; 11 per cent of women and 15 per cent of men score above 32.' What conclusions would you draw now?

Conclusion formulation

Results based on one sex only are then applied to both. This can be seen in some major psychological theories, notably Erikson's psychosocial theory of development and Kohlberg's theory of moral development. Grosz (1987, in Wilkinson, 1989) would describe these as 'phallocentric' theories, involving 'the use of general or universal models to represent the two sexes according to the interests and terms of one, the male'.

Discussing Erikson's theory, which was based on the study of males only, Gilligan (1982) states that:

> . . . *psychological theorists . . . Implicitly adopting the male life as the norm . . . have tried to fashion women out of a masculine cloth . . . In the life cycle . . . the woman has been the deviant . . .*

Erikson (1950) describes a series of eight developmental stages meant to be universal – that is, they apply to both women and men, in different cultures and so on. For example, the conflict between *identity* and *role confusion* (which occurs during adolescence) precedes that between *intimacy* and *isolation* (young adulthood). But he acknowledges (Erikson, 1968) that the sequence is different for the female: she holds her identity in abeyance as she prepares to attract the man by whose name she'll be known, by whose status she'll be defined, the man who'll rescue her from emptiness and loneliness by filling 'the inner space'. For men, achieving a sense of identity *precedes* intimacy with a sexual partner; but for women, these tasks seem to be *fused,* and intimacy goes along with identity: 'the female comes to know herself as she is known, through her relationships with others' (Gilligan, 1982).

Yet despite his observation of sex differences, Erikson's epigenetic chart of the life-cycle stages remains unchanged: 'identity continues to precede intimacy as male experience continues to define his [Erikson's] life-cycle concept' (Gilligan, 1982).

Similarly, Kohlberg's six-stage theory of moral development was based on a 20-year longitudinal study of 84 boys (starting in 1955), but he claims universality for his stage sequence. Girls and women rarely attain a level of moral reasoning above the third stage (good boy–nice girl orientation), which is supposed to be achieved by most adolescents and adults. This leaves females looking decidedly morally deficient. But Gilligan argues, based on her own studies of females (see above), that men and women have qualitatively different conceptions of morality. When presented with hypothetical moral dilemmas, such as the famous case of Heinz (whose wife is dying from cancer and can only be saved by a drug which Heinz can obtain only through stealing it), both boys and girls typically want his wife to live. But the 'female' solution is to 'find some other way' besides stealing the drug, and the emphasis is put on the notions of care, responsibility and relationships. By contrast, males are more likely to condemn the druggist for asking so much money for the drug (which is his invention), stressing rights and rules.

WHAT'S DIFFERENT ABOUT FEMINIST RESEARCH?

According to Davis and Gergen (1997):

. . . Ideally, from the empirical point of view, subjects are taken out of their normal environments and placed in a situation designed by the researcher. In order to maintain scientific rigour, the scientist controls as many aspects of the research situation as possible, and then manipulates significant variables in order to discover the causal relations among variables. Studying 'real' people in their ordinary settings is not ideal for developing scientifically sophisticated results, from the empiricist viewpoint . . .

The very terms used by psychologists – such as 'subject', 'manipulate' and 'control' – imply the masculinist-biased nature of the field: the dominance, status and power of the experimenter and the subordinate role of the participant (Paludi, 1992) (see Chapter 10). Most psychologists have been, and still are, trained within a paradigm that is positivistic and behaviouristic, being taught that:

. . . effects derived from orderly determinist causes, that the subjective aspects of behaviour were irrelevant, and that the best studies required maximal distance between experimenter and subject . . . If I thought of sex professionally at all, I saw it as a variable which could neither be manipulated or controlled and therefore of very little scientific interest. Even the rats were male.

(Unger, 1984, in Unger, 1993)

But from the feminist perspective, these results are not about real people in their life circumstances but are artifacts of scientific manipulations. Also, these kind of laboratory-based studies:

. . . discourage any relationship between the scientist and subject, thus people are objectified (as 'things') for research purposes . . .

(Davis and Gergen, 1997)

From a feminist standpoint, researchers must become actively involved in the research process, taking the perspective of the participants; they are *not* detached investigators but became an integral part of the whole process. According to the Task Force of APA Division 35, feminist research in psychology tends to be '... co-operative, participative ... interdisciplinary [and] non-hierarchical ... [beginning] with personal experience' and recognizing that 'truth is not separate from the person who speaks it' (in Wilkinson, 1989). The *feminist standpoint position* (FSP) (Harding, 1986):

> *... emphasizes the importance of knowledge-gathering as a personal activity, in which the researcher and the researched are recognized as in relation to one another. Both must take into account their own experiences, gained from their own perspectives, not from some universal standpoint, the so-called 'God's-eye view', which the objectivity-seeking empirical psychologists value (Haraway, 1988) ...*

> *(Davis and Gergen, 1997)*

According to Tavris (1993), two new directions taken by feminist researchers in recent years are (i) looking outward at gender *in context*, and (ii) looking inward at gender *as narrative*.

Gender in context

This relates to the debate within the psychology of personality as to the relative influence of individual traits and situational factors on behaviour (see Chapter 4). It can be seen as the application of that debate to the particular issue of gender differences.

A major figure in the debate is Weisstein (1971, in Weisstein, 1993a). While she was not the first person to discuss the role of ideology and social context in the construction of the female psyche (that person probably being Simone de Beauvoir, 1953), her article entitled 'Psychology constructs the female' was the first to provide a challenge to psychology's essentialist views regarding maleness and femaleness (Unger, 1993).

The central argument in Weisstein's critique was that psychology can have 'nothing of substance to offer' to either 'a study of human behaviour' (male or female) or a vision of 'human possibility', because it insists on looking for 'inner traits' when it ought to be looking 'for social context'. In doing so, psychology has functioned as 'a pseudo-scientific buttress for our cultural sex-role notions', which include not only our ideas about the 'nature of women' but also about 'the nature of homosexuality'. Consequently, psychology has helped to justify and reinforce many of the prejudices inherent in a 'patriarchal social organization', such as the USA (and western culture generally).

By placing the emphasis on internal, individual causes of behaviour, psychologists, unwittingly, help to promote a view of society as composed of so many individuals removed from the political, economic and historical context in which human behaviour takes place. It reinforces the popular view that 'people are as they are', including, of course, the 'nature' of women and men, making behavioural change virtually impossible. According to Bem (1993a):

> *Psychology may be so predisposed as a discipline to individualize and decontextualize the phenomena it studies (including gender, sexuality, race and class) that it necessarily depoliticizes those phenomena and thereby functions both as a collaborator in the social reproduction of the status quo and as an obstacle to social change.*

Bem gives the example of 'battered woman's syndrome'. (See Box 6.2, page 100.)

Bem is probably best known for her work (during the 1970s) on *androgyny*, the blending within the same individual man or woman of masculine and feminine characteristics. Her later *gender schema theory* (1984) sees androgyny as a disposition to process information in accordance with relevant non-sex principles (in

Figure 6.4 This Cowan Kemsley Taylor advertisement was censored by every national newspaper. It appeared once, in *Girl about Town* magazine

contrast with traditional, 'masculine' men and 'feminine' women, who spontaneously think of things in sex-typed terms) (see Gross, 2008).

By the mid-1980s, Bem began to feel 'theoretically hemmed in', partly because of her own 'overly narrow focus on how gender stereotypes in the head constrain both sexes' (Bem, 1993b). This left out the social institutions that push women and men into different and unequal roles, and the (rather obvious) fact that, because most societies are male-dominated, women are a lot more constrained by these social institutions than men. She describes her book, *The Lenses of Gender* (1993b), as 'a contextualized and constructivist analysis of how biology, culture, and individual psyche all interact in historical context to systematically reproduce not only the oppression of women, but of sexual minorities too'.

In it, she argues that there are hidden assumptions embedded in cultural discourses, social institutions and individual psyches, which shape not only perceptions of reality, but the material aspects of reality itself (for example, unequal pay, inadequate daycare facilities for children). These assumptions take the form of three kinds of lenses:

BOX 6.2 'BATTERED WOMAN'S SYNDROME'

Creation of the concept of 'battered woman's syndrome' has helped battered women in the USA to conduct a legal defence when accused of murdering their batterers, and has captured some of the helplessness they undoubtedly feel. But it has achieved this by *pathologizing* the women themselves, rather than trying to expose the institutional context in which they live and in which their ultimate act of self-defence occurs.

A less individualized and depoliticized approach would be to argue not that the woman herself is sick (which necessarily deflects attention away from the 'sickness' of her institutional context), but that there is something fundamentally male-centred about the US legal definition of self-defence. A defendant may be found innocent of homicide (murder) only if s/he perceived imminent danger of great bodily harm or death, and responded to that danger with only as much force as was necessary to defend against it. Feminist legal scholars point out that this definition fits the scenario in which two men are involved in an isolated episode of sudden violence much better than the battered woman scenario. She is put at an immediate and fundamental disadvantage by virtue of the fact that her victimization has been taking place over an extended period of time: the perceived danger may be no greater at the time the killing takes place than on many previous occasions. In other words, the act is the culmination of (usually) years of terror.

(Based on Bem, 1993a)

1 *androcentrism*, or male-centredness (see above)
2 *gender polarization*, which superimposes a male/female dichotomy on almost every aspect of human experience (such as modes of dress, social roles, ways of expressing emotion, experiencing sexual desire)
3 *biological essentialism*, which rationalizes and legitimizes the other two lenses by treating them as the inevitable consequences of the intrinsic biological nature of women and men.

Her *enculturated lens theory* tries to explain how we either acquire the culture's lenses and construct a *conventional* gender identity, or we construct a *gender-subversive* identity:

> *We must reframe the debate on sexual inequality so that it focuses not on the differences between women and men but on how male-centred discourses and institutions transform male–female difference into female disadvantage.*

(Bem, 1993)

SO HOW *IS* GENDER CONSTRUCTED?

Weisstein's (1971, 1993a) article foreshadowed the paradigm shift within psychology, from the view that reality constructs the person to the view that the person constructs reality (Buss, 1978, in Unger, 1993). She, together with a few other pioneers, explicitly used the term 'social constructionism' to question the bases of psychological knowledge.

One form that this construction of gender can take is social expectations of behaviour – both other people's expectations of our behaviour and our expectations of our own behaviour. More specifically, expectations can influence behaviour through the self-fulfilling prophecy, and Weisstein cites classic studies by Rosenthal and his co-workers (Rosenthal, 1966; Rosenthal and Jacobson, 1968), which demonstrate how expectations can change experimental outcomes (see Chapter 11):

> *. . . even in carefully controlled experiments, and with no outward or conscious difference in behaviour, the hypotheses we start with will influence enormously the behaviour of another organism.*

(Weisstein, 1971, 1993a)

Weisstein also discusses Milgram's obedience experiments as demonstrating the very powerful influence of the social situation on the behaviour of individuals (see Chapter 4).

In line with this continuing shift towards studying the importance of context, more recent studies of gender have consistently shown that the behaviour we associate with 'gender' depends more on what an individual is doing than on biological sex (e.g. Eagly, 1987). For example, Maccoby (1990, in Tavris, 1993) re-analysed studies that used to show that little girls are 'passive' and little boys are 'active'. She concluded that boys and girls do not differ, as groups, in some consistent, trait-like way: their behaviour depends on the gender of the child they're playing with. Girls (as young as three) are only passive when a boy is present, but they're just as independent as boys when in an all-girl group. According to Tavris (1993), results like these suggest that:

> . . . *gender, like culture, organizes for its members different influence strategies, ways of communicating and ways of perceiving the world. The behaviour of men and women often depends more on the gender they are interacting with than on anything about the gender they are – a process that West and Zimmerman (1987) call 'doing gender'.*

However, a major aspect of the context of people's lives is the *power* they have (or lack) in influencing others, and in determining their own lives. Clearly, the 'two cultures' of women and men *are not* equal in power, status and resources. Tavris (1993) believes that many behaviours and personality traits thought to be typical of women (such as the ability to 'read' non-verbal cues, and the tendency to blame themselves for their shortcomings and to have lower self-esteem than men), turn out to be typical of women – and men – who lack power; they seem to be the *result* of powerlessness, *not* the cause.

Essentialism revisited

According to Kitzinger and Coyle (2002):

> *The social constructionist/essentialist debate has been described as the 'hottest' philosophical controversy to hit psychology in years . . . and it is a controversy in which lesbian and gay psychology has been deeply enmeshed.*

It is sometimes difficult to see certain research as 'essentialist' because it is simply good psychology as traditionally done. An example of such research is a study by Tasker (2002) of lesbian and gay parenting. Its essentialism is indicated by its aim: 'empirically to evaluate the basis on which lesbian mothers were commonly refused custody' – that is, to compare children from lesbian families with those from heterosexual-mother families in terms of family relationships, mental health, peer relationships and psychosexual development. In effect, the questions Tasker addresses are whether or not children of lesbians have worse family relationships, suffer more mental health problems, have to endure more bullying and are more likely to be homosexual themselves (these being factors that are often cited as reasons for denying custody to lesbian mothers). Her findings are reported as offering new 'facts' about family life, such as 'the quality of family relationships is more important than family structure in terms of the child's psychological well-being'.

Kitzinger and Coyle see Tasker's study as contributing to 'positive' representations of lesbian parenting. They contrast this with a study by Clarke (2002), which interrogates such representations. Clarke proceeds not from the 'neutral' position of the scientist but from a politically engaged feminist perspective. She asks about the political effects of making the kind of argument that Tasker makes (scientific evidence concerning the development of children raised by lesbian mothers). Rather than asking about the truth value of claims made in support of lesbian and gay families (are they empirically true or false?), Clarke explores the strategies people use to defend lesbian and gay parenting, and discusses the political costs and benefits of these different strategies.

So, for example, where Tasker claims that the quality of family relationships is more important than parents' sexual orientation, Clarke represents this kind of claim as a 'discourse', which emphasizes the importance of love, security and stability over any particular family structure. Accordingly, families can assume any shape or form, provided they are loving and stable environments. Clarke's assessment of this discourse is not in terms of 'truth' but rather the rhetoric; for example, she argues that it runs the risk of being 'defensive' and judgemental of lesbian and gay families in accordance with 'heterosexual norms and expectations' (see Chapter 7).

In sum, whereas Tasker is aiming to uncover something approximating to 'truths' about lesbian and gay parenting, Clarke treats these truth claims as 'discourses' to be assessed not in terms of their facticity, but in terms of their rhetorical force and political implications (Kitzinger and Coyle, 2002).

Gender as narrative

The other major recent direction that feminist research has taken is to focus on the *life story*, which Sarbin (1986) describes as the key metaphor in understanding human behaviour. Our plans, memories, love affairs and hatreds are guided by narrative plots, with women and men differing greatly in the narrative plots they tell about their lives. (These can be seen as an important move towards *idiographic methods* of studying gender, and away from the *nomothetic methods* used by psychologists wanting to establish gender *differences* from the androcentric perspective: see Chapter 3.)

Where do the narratives come from? What functions do they serve for the story-teller? Why do so many women today feel safe telling stories that place their fate in the stars or PMS rather than in their own hands – or society's? However, life stories can change; how and why they do is at the heart of psychology and politics (Tavris, 1993).

SO ARE WOMEN AND MEN DIFFERENT – AND IF SO, HOW?

According to the third of the current versions of the mismeasure of woman, there is no problem, because man is the norm and woman is just like him. According to Tiefer (1992, in Tavris, 1993), this assumption pervades the diagnosis of sexual disorders in DSM: 'Men and women are the same, and they're all men.'

Tavris believes that the study of gender has entered a 'transformationist' era (citing Crawford and Mararcek, 1989), whereby we should 'stand back from the fray' and accept that we shall never know the essence of male and female. These are endlessly changing and depend both on the eye of the observer and the conditions of our lives. Instead of asking 'Do men and women differ?' (which is literal and limited), this approach asks, 'Why is everyone so interested in differences? Which differences? What function does belief in differences serve? What are the consequences of believing that women are emotionally and professionally affected by their hormones, but men aren't, or that women are the love experts and that men are incapable of love and intimacy? Where do these beliefs come from, and who benefits (and loses) from them?'

While cultural feminism is an important step forward in the study of gender, it runs the risk of replacing one set of stereotypes with another: the 'woman-is-better' school, like the 'woman-is-deficient' school, assumes a fundamental opposition between the sexes. Thinking in opposites leads to what philosophers call 'the law of the excluded middle': most actual women and men fall somewhere in between the stereotypical opposites regarding psychological qualities, abilities, traits, and so on.

The debate about gender and gender differences is not about whether or not women and men differ. Of course they do. As in the debate about racial differences in IQ, what is controversial is how we should interpret such differences (when they are found). Do they reflect permanent, biological, intra-individual traits and characteristics, or should they be understood in relation to life experiences, social contexts, resources and power, which can and do change culturally and historically?

By setting aside predetermined categories, we have learned that there is no one right way to be lesbian, straight or gay, no one right way to be.

(Tavris, 1993)

CONCLUDING COMMENTS: WHAT'S BETTER ABOUT FEMINIST PSYCHOLOGY?

Wilkinson (1989) maintains that there are three major improvements that feminist psychology can make to mainstream psychology:

1 it identifies hitherto unrecognized sources of bias (such as Gilligan's critique of Kohlberg)
2 it increases critical thinking
3 it broadens the scope of research by (i) looking at under-researched areas (such as violence against women), and (ii) generating new ways of looking at old problems.

This, in turn, offers the possibility of an 'extra dimension' to psychological knowledge: by looking at human experience from women's perspective, we can enrich and extend our understanding of the whole of human functioning and its possibilities (Wilkinson, 1989).

Wilkinson's assessment is endorsed by Moghaddam (2005), who contends that:

Feminist psychology is a great idea because it has helped transform the way psychologists conceptually approach the study of females and males. It is no longer acceptable for researchers to adopt the male as the norm according to which the female must be judged, or to work on the general assumption of male superiority, Moreover, there is greater interest in studying females in and for themselves, rather than just in comparison with males . . .

However, he also notes that the impact of feminist psychology remains at the broad conceptual and political level, rather than at the level of specific empirical findings. Nor, he believes, have feminist psychologists had much impact on research methods.

Feminist psychologists share the commitment to reform and social change of the modern feminist movement; not only do they want to understand human behaviour, they want to change it in fundamental ways. This has important implications for their position on relativism.

The most influential feminist psychologists are not relativistic, if by 'relativism' is meant that all values have equal merit. Feminist psychologists believe that some values should have priority, because they are better than other values. For example, different kinds of gender relations do not have equal merit. It is better for women to gain freedom and equality than to remain shackled by traditional gender roles . . .

(Moghaddam, 2005)

This kind of anti-relativist position is fundamentally opposed to *cultural relativism*, whereby the values of different cultures can be assessed only within the context of the cultural group itself, and universal criteria for evaluating behaviour are rejected. Moghaddam gives the example of Iranian men (most of whom are Shi'a Muslims) being permitted several wives, while those in western countries are legally permitted only one (see Chapter 8).

. . . In this, and many other cases, according to cultural relativism, what is 'wrong' behaviour in one culture could be 'correct' behaviour in another. Feminist psychologists . . . reject such relativism . . .

(Moghaddam, 2005)

If feminist psychologists charge psychology with being biased (towards men), they can themselves be charged with the equivalent 'crime'. The crucial difference is that feminist psychologists are openly, avowedly *feminist* (as part of their political agenda), while traditional, mainstream, *masculinist* psychology claims to be *value-free* (in keeping with its apolitical, 'objectivity' agenda).

SUMMARY

- Feminism, as a social and political movement, condemns the oppression of women and strives for the recognition of women's achievements, contributions and experience as valid and important in their own right.

- Feminist psychologists see psychology as sexist and heterosexist, value-laden and androcentric.

- The masculinist bias holds the contributions made by men to psychology to be more important than those made by women; the history of psychology is the history of male psychology.

- Women's history in psychology comprises compensatory, contribution and reconstruction history.

- The 'feminist critique' has had little impact on mainstream psychology, because it is not seen as legitimate science and is dismissed as 'purely political'.

- Despite the growing numbers of female psychologists, they still work in predominantly person-oriented/ service-oriented areas, compared with the traditionally male academic/experimental areas.

- This could reflect sexism among male psychologists, who regard 'female' areas of psychology as scientifically/intellectually inferior; gatekeepers are also predominantly male.

- Many radical feminist psychologists are lesbians, who criticize mainstream psychology for its heterosexism.

- The feminist critique of science challenges the fundamental assumptions of the positivist approach, which sees scientific inquiry as objective and value-free. But psychologists' decisions about what they should study reflect values and are related to a particular politico-cultural context.

- Feminist psychologists advocate a value-laden approach to research, so that values will no longer be mistaken for facts. If psychologists fail to make their values explicit about important social/political issues, they may (unwittingly) contribute to prejudice and discrimination.

- The masculinist bias can take the form of (i) deciding what is worth investigating about women, (ii) taking men as a standard/norm against which to compare and judge women, and (iii) only publishing the results of studies that have found evidence of sex differences.

- Gender bias can be found at all stages of the research process: question formulation, research methods/ design, data analysis/interpretation and conclusion formulation.

- Results regarding sex differences are often reported/interpreted in line with stereotyped expectations, or they may be reported in a very misleading way, because the wrong sort of comparisons are being made. Group (mean) scores often obscure important individual differences within each group.

- Feminist researchers become actively involved in the research process, taking the perspective of the participants; they reject the detached experimenter role and do not see themselves as of higher status, or more powerful, than the 'subject'.

O Feminist critics of mainstream psychology believe that it has overemphasized internal, individual causes of behaviour and neglected social context; this helps to reinforce the status quo and the belief that people cannot change.

O Bem's enculturated lens theory sees gender/gender identity as being constructed in a way that disadvantages women. Three 'lenses' through which this is done are androcentrism, gender polarization and biological essentialism.

O One way in which gender is constructed is through social expectations of behaviour, specifically self-fulfilling prophecies.

O Many behaviours/personality traits thought to be typical of women are, in fact, typical of people who lack power and so are the result, not the cause, of powerlessness.

O Feminist research tends towards idiographic methods, such as the recent focus on the life story.

O According to cultural feminism, women are opposite to but better than men, who are the norm. This threatens to replace one set of stereotypes with another, and assumes a fundamental opposition between the sexes. All feminists are anti-relativism.

O The crucial question is not whether sex differences exist but how they should be interpreted.

USEFUL WEBSITES

http://web.lemoyne.edu/~hevern/narpsychnarpsych.html
http://www.socialpsychology.org/social.htm#sexuality

RECOMMENDED READING

Coyle, A. and Kitzinger, C. (eds) (2002) *Lesbian and Gay Psychology: New Perspectives.* Oxford: BPS/Blackwell.

Gergen, M.M. and Davis, S.N. (eds) (1997) *Toward a New Psychology of Gender: A Reader.* New York: Routledge.

Paludi, M.A. (1992) *The Psychology of Women.* Dubuque, IA: WCB Brown & Benchmark.

Tavris, C. (1993) The mismeasure of women. *Feminism & Psychology, 3*(2), 149–68. (There are several other important articles in the same issue.)

Trew, K. and Kremer, K. (eds) (1998) *Gender and Psychology.* London: Arnold.

Ussher, J.M. (1997) *Fantasies of Femininity: Reframing the Boundaries of Sex.* London: Penguin Books.

CHAPTER 7

NORMALITY AND ABNORMALITY

Most of this chapter is devoted to trying to define the terms 'normal' and 'abnormal' and to establish the relationship between them. While it is always important to be clear about the meaning of the terms we use in discussion of any psychological topic, here it is essential, because the whole field of abnormal psychology rests upon the assumption that a distinction can be made between normality and abnormality.

As with many terms and concepts, examples can help to get a discussion started and may help to raise some of the important issues. So, if you were asked to give some examples of the kinds of behaviour and experience that fall under the heading of abnormal psychology, you would probably include schizophrenia, anxiety, panic attacks, homosexuality, sexual fetishes, depression and hallucinations. While the list of possible examples is very much longer, these make it reasonably clear what the field of abnormal psychology is about (its 'scope'). However, giving examples is the easy bit! What we really want to know is: what do they all have in common that makes us want to call them abnormalities in the first place? Does there have to be anything that links them, or can they all illustrate abnormality for different reasons? Do psychologists and psychiatrists consider the meaning of normality and abnormality, or do they just assume that schizophrenia, say, is abnormal and concentrate on investigating its causes, diagnosing and treating it? Is it possible to define and diagnose abnormality in an objective way, without allowing our values to bias the judgements we make? What are some of the practical and ethical implications of labelling a person's behaviour as abnormal?

The attempt to give answers to these very complex questions forms the basis of this chapter.

ABNORMALITY, DEVIANCE AND DIFFERENCE

According to Littlewood and Lipsedge (1989), every society has its own characteristic pattern of normative behaviour and beliefs – that is, expectations about how people should behave as well as what they should think. These norms define what is acceptable and permissible, as well as what is desirable. It might be useful to think of this as a scale or continuum, as shown in Figure 7.1.

Unacceptable.......Tolerable.......Acceptable/permissible.......Desirable.......Required/obligatory

Figure 7.1 The continuum of normative behaviour

At the left-hand end of the scale, behaviour is either illegal (such as burglary or fraud) or breaches fundamental moral or religious principles (adultery, abortion) or both (child sexual abuse, rape, bigamy). There is usually little room for disagreement as to whether or not something is illegal, but there will usually be more debate about the immorality of (illegal) acts: the vast majority of people will condemn child abuse and rape (including, very often, the perpetrator of the act), but people have very different views regarding the smoking of marijuana. (Ever since the re-classification of cannabis in the UK (2004) from a class B to a class C drug, many have called for it to be re-classified again, back to class B. This is largely in response to evidence regarding its long-term effects – see Gross, 2005 – but whether this reflects a change in moral opinion is another issue. The UK government has indeed decided to make it Class B once again.)

Behaviour deemed tolerable is at the fringes of illegality and/or immorality; examples might include gambling, drinking (large amounts of) alcohol, going to pole-dancing clubs, joining a squat, and living with one's sexual partner (as opposed to getting married).

Getting married is, of course, also acceptable/permissible, and desirable, as far as most people are concerned (despite a recent drop in its frequency and the very high divorce rate). To the extent that most people will get married (at least once in their lives), that we usually assume that adults are married (unless we have good reason to believe otherwise), and that there is an implicit judgement made about people who do not get married ('there must be something wrong with them'), getting married can also be seen as required/obligatory.

This example brings us back full circle to what is unacceptable. This was defined earlier in terms of illegality and immorality, but perhaps there is another criterion by which we make this judgement. Clearly, it is not illegal to remain single (there is no actual, literal, law against it), nor is any religious or moral law being broken (assuming that instead of being married one isn't cohabiting or 'living in sin'). But it is still somehow socially unacceptable, it is 'not quite right', it may make us feel a little uneasy, less sure about how to relate to this person than when we are interacting with individuals whom we know (or believe) are married.

Our first reaction to learning that someone is unmarried might be to wonder whether s/he is gay or lesbian. This may be a perfectly logical explanation, but at the same time it raises even more fundamental questions about acceptability and normality (see below). Similarly, if the person is painfully shy, or badly disfigured or has a disability, or is a nun or a priest, we can easily understand his or her unmarried state.

But what if none of these explanations is available to us? This is when the unacceptability of the 'behaviour' becomes an issue: being married is, for most people, part of their definition of 'reality', the 'natural order' of things.

Perhaps the unacceptability of schizophrenia, homosexuality, and the other examples given above, also lies in the way they threaten and challenge our basic view of the world, what Scheff (1966) called residual rules: the 'unnameable' expectations we have regarding such things as 'decency' and 'reality'. Because these rules are themselves implicit, taken for granted, and not articulated, behaviour that violates them is found strange and sometimes frightening – but it is usually very difficult to say why!

Similarly, Becker (1963) believes that the values on which psychiatric intervention is based are, generally speaking, middle-class values regarding decent, reasonable, proper behaviour and experience. These influence the process of diagnosis of patients, who, in state-funded – National Health Service (NHS) – hospitals, at least, are mainly working class. (We return to the question of the objectivity of psychiatric diagnosis below.)

In addition to the breaking of residual rules, the mere fact of being different may contribute to the unacceptability of schizophrenics and others deemed 'abnormal'. If every society has its own characteristic pattern of normative behaviour and beliefs, then 'outsiders' (those who deviate from these norms), even if they are not seen as physically dangerous, are threatening simply because they are different. As a way of confirming our own identity (which is so much bound up with these norms), we push the outsiders even further away, and 'By reducing their humanity, we emphasize our own' (Littlewood and Lipsedge, 1989).

'Outsiders in our midst' include criminals (those who break the 'law of the land'), those whose behaviour and beliefs conflict with our moral code, and those, like the mentally ill, who break residual rules. All three groups can be regarded as deviants, since their behaviour is considered to deviate from certain standards as held by the person making the judgement. While criminal behaviour is sometimes seen as being caused by psychological disturbance, it is important to distinguish between social deviance (non-conformity) and mental disorder or abnormality (Zimbardo, 1992).

Neither deviant behaviour, e.g. political, religious, or sexual, nor conflicts that are primarily between the individual and society, are mental disorders unless the deviance or condition is a symptom of a dysfunction (i.e. impairment of function) in the person.

The above is a quote from the revision of the third edition of the *Diagnostic and Statistical Manual (of Mental Disorders),* published by the American Psychiatric Association (1987), abbreviated to DSM-III-R. It is the official system for classifying and diagnosing mental disorders used by American psychiatrists and is used widely throughout the world (including the UK). This – and the latest edition, DSM-IV-TR (2000) – is discussed throughout the rest of the chapter (see also Chapter 6).

Although some clinical psychologists and psychiatrists are interested in the causes and treatment of criminality as a form of social deviancy, the main focus of abnormal psychology is the kinds of unacceptable behaviour and experience that are variously called mental illness, emotional disturbance, behaviour disorder, mental disorder, or psychopathology (literally, 'disease of the mind', or psychological abnormality).

CRITERIA FOR DEFINING PSYCHOLOGICAL ABNORMALITY

So far, the discussion has suggested a number of possible criteria for defining psychological abnormality and has considered their usefulness and validity. In this section, we take another look at these criteria (although from a slightly different angle), and discuss some additional ones. Many of these have been proposed by a number of writers (e.g. Cullberg, 2006; Davison and Neale, 2001; Miller and Morley, 1986; Rosenhan and Seligman, 1989), and so particular points will not usually be attributed to specific authors.

The statistical infrequency criterion (or deviation from the average)

According to this criterion, what is *average* determines what is *normal*: behaviour is abnormal to the extent that it falls outside the middle ranges (what the majority of people do). In other words, it is *extreme*. Take the example of people with learning difficulties ('mental retardation'). As measured by intelligence (IQ) test scores, those with a score below 70 or 75, who represent the lowest 2 per cent of the whole population, are considered to be retarded; their scores are, clearly, extremely low and so, according to this criterion, their intelligence is abnormally low (see Figure 7.2).

But what about those individuals whose scores are extremely *high*? According to the statistical criterion, they should be thought of as equally abnormal because their scores (the 2 per cent scoring 130 and above) are as

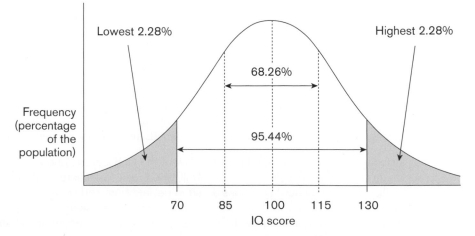

Figure 7.2 Normal distribution curve for IQ, given a mean of 100 and a standard deviation of 15 IQ points

extreme as those scoring 75 and below. Those who score extremely high are usually described as 'gifted', a somewhat more positive label than 'mentally retarded', yet the two groups are statistically equally abnormal. Clearly, there is more to abnormality than mere statistics!

Also, just how far from the population mean does an individual need to be to be considered abnormal? As Miller and Morley (1986) point out, any chosen cut-off point is necessarily arbitrary: what is the significance of 75/70 as the boundary between mental normality and retardation?

A further problem with this criterion is that most kinds of abnormality that psychologists are interested in (see the list above) simply cannot be measured in the way that intelligence can (or, at least, is). In other words, the statistical criterion assumes that psychological characteristics in general can be viewed as dimensional (measured on at least an ordinal scale), such that individual scores can all be placed somewhere on the same scale. This in itself is a complex and controversial issue in relation to the normality/abnormality debate, which we return to below.

Abnormality as personal distress

From the perspective of the individual, abnormality is the subjective experience of intense anxiety, unhappiness, depression or a whole host of other forms of personal distress or suffering. While this may often be the only indication that anything is wrong (and may not necessarily be obvious to others), it may be a sufficient reason for someone to seek professional help. As Miller and Morley (1986) say:

> . . . people do not come to clinics because they feel that they have met some abstract definition of abnormality. For the most part they come because their feelings or behaviour cause them distress.

However, the converse may also sometimes be true. Someone whose behaviour is obviously 'mad' as far as others are concerned, may be unaware of how others see him/her and may experience little or no subjective distress. This 'lack of insight' (self-awareness or understanding) is often taken to be a characteristic of *psychotic mental disorder* (as opposed to *neurotic disorder*), and illustrates 'the fish is the last to discover water' phenomenon.

Abnormality as others' distress

It might at first seem very strange, if not illogical, to define one person's abnormality in terms of another person's distress. But, as we have seen in discussing the personal distress criterion, the person seen by others as behaving abnormally may be the last to recognize that there is a problem, so others' concern acts as a counterbalance to the former's lack of concern.

This criterion also suggests that, as with all behaviour, abnormality is interpersonal and not simply intrapersonal/intrapsychic. Behaviour takes place between people, in social situations, and is not merely a reflection of the personal qualities or characteristics of the individual actor (see Chapters 4 and 14).

From a practical and ethical point of view, this criterion can be seen as double-edged. Others' distress may be both a 'blessing' (literally a life-saver on occasions, for someone lacking insight into his/her own self-destructive behaviour, for example) and a curse (for example, parents' distress regarding a son or daughter's homosexuality, with which the child him/herself may feel perfectly comfortable). While the former may be termed empathic concern, where the 'helper' has an altruistic desire to reduce the other's distress, in the latter, personal distress produces an egoistic desire to reduce one's own distress. The question is, whose distress is really the focus of the attempt to intervene?

BOX 7.1 LAING AND ANTI-PSYCHIATRY

One of the most outspoken critics of conventional medical psychiatry during the heyday of the *anti-psychiatry movement* in the 1960s was the Scottish psychiatrist R.D. Laing. According to his *family interaction model* (1961), schizophrenia can only be understood as something that occurs *between* people, rather than as something taking place *inside* a person (as the medical model maintains: see below). Schizophrenia refers to an *interpersonal ploy* used by some people (parents, doctors, psychiatrists) in their interactions with others ('the schizophrenic').

To understand individuals, we must study not individuals but interactions between individuals, and this is the subject matter of *social phenomenology*. The family interaction model was consistent with research by Bateson *et al*. (1956), which showed that schizophrenia arises within families that use 'pathological' forms of communication, in particular, contradictory messages (*double binds*).

More directly relevant to the 'distress criterion' is a later explanation of schizophrenia, namely Laing's (1967) *conspiratorial model*, according to which schizophrenia is a *label*, a form of violence perpetrated by some people against others. The family, GPs and psychiatrists conspire against the schizophrenic in order to keep him/her in check: by treating them as patients who are sick, 'imprisoning' them in a psychiatric hospital, where they're degraded and invalidated as human beings, these people are able to maintain their definition of reality (the *status quo*). (*Residual rules* again?) The threat posed by the behaviour and experience of the 'patient' is contained within a medical framework: 'If they act and think like that they must be sick, which means that we're all right and everything is still all right with the world as we know it.'

According to Laing's *psychedelic model* (1967), the schizophrenic is, in fact, an exceptionally eloquent critic of society and schizophrenia is 'itself a natural way of healing our own appalling state of alienation called normality'.

Abnormality as unexpected behaviour

According to Davison and Neale (2001), it is abnormal to react to a situation or an event in ways that could not be predicted or reasonably expected (given what we know about human behaviour). For example, anxiety disorders are diagnosed when the anxiety is 'out of proportion to the situation'. While this might seem like a very reasonable and useful criterion, it could be claimed that it raises as many questions as it answers. In particular, who is to say what is 'in proportion'? Is this just another form of the statistical criterion whereby what is a reasonable, acceptable, response is simply how *most people* would be expected to respond? By this criterion, *under*reacting is just as abnormal as *over*reacting, and yet the way Davison and Neale describe it suggests very strongly that only the latter is a problem. So, by what other criteria do we judge a reaction to be normal or abnormal? (See Box 7.2.)

Abnormality as highly consistent/inconsistent behaviour

If we have generalized expectations about how people are typically going to react to particular (kinds of) situation, as when we define abnormality as unexpected behaviour, then a person's behaviour is predictable to the extent that we know about the situation. However, not all situations are equally powerful influences on behaviour, and so cannot be used equally to predict a person's behaviour. In some situations, individual differences play a much larger role in influencing behaviour, and this makes behaviour less predictable. Consequently, it is 'normal' for any individual's behaviour to be partially predictable (high *intra-individual consistency*) and, at the same time, partially unpredictable (low *intra-individual consistency*).

If we accept this argument, then we can reasonably further argue that it is abnormal for a person to display either extremely predictable or extremely unpredictable behaviour. If someone acts so consistently that they seem to be unaffected by a situation, including the other people involved, this would strike most people as very odd; it is almost as if we are dealing with more of a machine than a person! Someone who is paranoid, for example, might see the world almost entirely in terms of others' malevolent intentions, which may, in turn, elicit certain kinds of responses in others; these responses may reinforce the attribution of negative intent, thus producing a vicious cycle.

Equally, it is difficult to interact with someone who, for whatever reason, is very unpredictable, since our dealings with others require us to make assumptions and have expectations about their responses. Schizophrenics are often perceived, by the lay person, as embodying this kind of unpredictability, which is unnerving and unsettling. Again, this perception, together with the related expectation of unpredictability, may to some degree contribute to that unpredictability.

In both cases, the assessment being made is as much a reflection of the perceiver making the judgement as of the person whose behaviour is being judged. Perhaps the term consistency should be applied to the actor's behaviour, and predictability to the perceiver's judgement. But regardless of the term that is used, the basic argument is the same: to understand behaviour we must always take the actor and the situation (including other people) into account (see Chapter 4). We return to this point later on when we look at the process of psychiatric diagnosis.

Abnormality as maladaptiveness or disability

When people's behaviour prevents them from pursuing and achieving their goals, or does not contribute to their personal sense of well-being, or prevents them from functioning as they would wish in their personal, sexual, social, intellectual and occupational lives, it may well be seen as abnormal for that reason.

For example, substance-use disorders are defined mainly by how the substance abuse produces social and occupational disability, such as poor work performance and serious marital arguments. Phobias can be maladaptive or disabling in this way; for example, fear of flying might prevent someone from taking a job promotion (Davison and Neale, 2001).

So, according to this criterion, it is the consequences of the behaviour that lead us to judge the behaviour to be abnormal, rather than the behaviour itself. At the same time, such behaviours may be very distressing for the person concerned; by their nature, phobias are negative experiences because they involve extreme fear, regardless of any practical effects of the fear.

In a similar vein, Barker (2003) argues that the crucial issue is how people respond to the experience of mental distress. See Box 7.2.

An interim summing up: What have we learned so far?

We have now considered six criteria for defining behaviour as abnormal:

1 statistical infrequency involves a comparison with other people's behaviour
2 abnormality as personal distress involves the consequences for self of the behaviour in question
3 abnormality as others' distress involves looking at the consequences for others of the behaviour in question
4 abnormality as unexpected behaviour involves another kind of comparison with others' behaviour
5 abnormality as highly consistent/inconsistent behaviour also involves making comparisons, this time between both the actor and others, and between the actor and him/herself on different occasions
6 abnormality as maladaptiveness or disability is concerned with the consequences for the actor of his/her behaviour.

But what is different about abnormality as personal distress (the second criterion)? While the other criteria could be seen as having an external focus (they look outwards from the behaviour in question towards

BOX 7.2 THE POSITIVE – AND TEMPORARY – SIDE OF MADNESS

Some of the experiences associated with 'serious' forms of madness – such as hearing voices, seeing visions or descending to the depths of despair – have been used by people over the centuries as the basis for creative experiments in art, literature and even the sciences (Barker, 2003). Perhaps the most famous example is the painting of Vincent Van Gogh.

> . . . If they can use this [madness] constructively as part of the development of their life story, it may be distressing, but is still of value. If people cannot make sense of, or otherwise learn from, the experience, then it is deemed to be worthless . . .
>
> (Barker, 2003)

Only if this happens will attempts be made to eliminate the experience, especially if it is not just worthless but causes the person discomfort and emotional pain.

Another way of looking at the positive potential of 'madness' is to consider its duration – and what causes it. Sometimes, our response to a situation may be *extreme*, without necessarily being 'out of proportion' (see text above). If the situation is extreme (such as a soldier serving in Iraq or Afghanistan and regularly witnessing colleagues' horrific injuries and the risk of being killed themselves), then an extreme reaction (such as post-traumatic stress disorder/PTSD), while technically a psychological disorder (see text below), is a perfectly 'reasonable' reaction to such a situation. PTSD tends to be long-lasting, but some extreme reactions can be temporary and are best described as a response to a *crisis*, which, according to Cullberg (2006) 'oscillates between the psychically normal and the psychiatric'. Such reactions are often temporary, plausible and acceptably reasonable given the external circumstances (see Chapter 2, pages 34–6.)

something else), the personal distress criterion has an internal focus (it begins and remains with the person whose behaviour is in question).

While a simple definition of abnormality that captures it in its entirety seems impossible to give (see, for example, Davison and Neale, 2001), and no single criterion is necessary (see Zimbardo, 1992), this distinction between external and internal focus is important. Discussions of abnormality often seem to assume that certain behaviours and experiences are abnormal in and of themselves, without any reference to any external criterion. Examples might include all those in our original list, although some of these – such as homosexuality (see below) – will be considerably more controversial than others when seen from this perspective. None of the criteria discussed so far addresses this issue.

THE CASE OF HOMOSEXUALITY: NORMAL OR ABNORMAL?

Let's apply the criteria we have discussed so far to the case of homosexuality, in order to expose their limitations and to introduce some important additional ones.

As far as statistical infrequency is concerned, it is very likely that most people, especially perhaps those who believe that homosexuality is abnormal, also believe that lesbians and gay men (especially lesbians!) represent a very small minority of the adult population. But even if it turned out that the majority of adults were homosexual (or had had at least one homosexual relationship), most people would continue to believe it to be abnormal – the very use of the term 'queer' conveys a negative attitude towards homosexuals (its other main meaning is 'ill'). In other words, there is more to judging homosexuality to be abnormal than 'deviation from the average'.

In relation to personal distress, while there are undoubtedly some homosexuals who experience conflict and distress about their sexuality, there are probably as many for whom being gay or lesbian feels as 'right' as being heterosexual does for most 'straights'. This, together with the fact that many of those in conflict are so because of society's homophobic attitudes (the irrational fear and extreme intolerance of homosexuality) and heterosexism (inequality and discrimination based on people's sexual preference or orientation), suggests that 'being homosexual' is not distressing in itself. It is not an inherent feature of preferring members of one's own sex as sexual partners to experience distress, unlike the person with a phobia, for example (but see Box 7.3). Indeed, it is as likely to be as pleasurable as a heterosexual's attraction to someone of the opposite sex. (The 'flip side' of the belief that being homosexual isn't inherently distressing is the homophobic assumption that any gay man will 'fancy' any male (gay or straight), so that no one is 'safe'.)

BOX 7.3 IS HOMOSEXUALS' DISTRESS HOMOSEXUAL DISTRESS?

According to Taylor (2002), men (and by the same token women) who identify – or are struggling to identify – as gay (or lesbian) appear to be more vulnerable to certain forms of psychological and emotional distress than men and women who identify as heterosexual. Much of this distress is, undoubtedly, the result of factors that have nothing to do with sexual identity or orientation and everything to do with being human. Indeed:

> *. . . an insistence upon consistently sexualising the emotional difficulties of gay men would constitute naïve reductionism and would be potentially oppressive. While sexuality may be a constituent part of a person's identity – especially when the sexuality is constructed as being in some way 'different' – we are not simply the uncomplicated product of our sexualities . . .*

(Taylor, 2002)

Nevertheless, this unequal distribution of psychological distress suggests that certain processes are operating here. As a clinical psychologist, Taylor observes that many men present with difficulties, dilemmas and conflicts that are intrinsically tied to their sexual identities. Sometimes, these difficulties seem to be a direct response to negative societal representations of and behaviour towards homosexuality (homophobia and heterosexism). Sometimes they appear to be the consequence of participation within a specific subculture and the internalizing of negative stereotypes and other representations of 'gayness' (Taylor, 2002).

Assuming that homosexuals themselves do not, typically, or inevitably, experience distress, why should other people do so 'on their behalf', which is what happens, according to 'abnormality as other people's distress'? It is clearly false (as well as patronizing) to claim that homosexuals 'don't realize what they're doing' (as in, say, the case of drug addicts or others engaging in self-destructive behaviour), such that they need to be 'saved from themselves'. We need to look elsewhere for the source of others' distress.

Such an explanation is most unlikely to be found in 'abnormality as unexpected behaviour': it does not make very much sense to see homosexuality as an overreaction to some event. What could such an event be? If it were discovered, for example, that homosexuals have typically experienced some kind of trauma in early childhood that caused their homosexuality, we would not then want to call this outcome an overreaction: it would be seen as a 'normal' reaction to that kind of trauma. (Although 'normal' here might seem to beg the question, the idea of homosexuals as a group all reacting in the same way at least suggests that homosexuality as a reaction to certain childhood trauma is not a deviation.)

While research may not have found any evidence for traumatic events as a causal influence on the development of homosexuality, Bieber *et al.* (1962) claim to have found a difference between male homosexuals and heterosexuals, namely that the former are brought up by a 'close-binding intimate mother' and a father who displays 'detachment-hostility'. This difference is referred to as a pathogenic ('disease-producing') factor, which is responsible for the pathological condition of homosexuality. But we judge this pattern of child-rearing to be pathological only if we have already judged its outcome to be pathological. In other words, only if we already regard homosexuality to be abnormal will we regard any difference between homosexuals and heterosexuals (and which we think causes homosexuality) as itself abnormal (Davison and Neale, 1994). This is clearly a circular argument which begs the whole question of the normality or abnormality of homosexuality.

Regarding the abnormality as highly consistent/inconsistent behaviour criterion, there is no reason to believe that homosexuals, as a group, compared with heterosexuals, are any more or less consistent or predictable in their overall behaviour. So, this criterion does not move us on any further in our search for the reasons behind the belief that homosexuality is abnormal.

This leaves just abnormality as maladaptiveness or disability. Unlike the case of someone with a phobia, the negative consequences suffered by homosexuals aren't to do with being homosexual, but stem from society's response to the homosexual. Whereas someone with a phobia of flying might be unable to visit faraway lands as a direct result of the phobia (almost as an extension of the phobia), quite independently of any external factors or influences, the homosexual is confronted by homophobia and heterosexism, which aren't part of being homosexual. It is social attitudes towards homosexuals that constitute the maladaptiveness/disability of homosexuality, not the 'handicapping' nature of being gay. (However, homophobia and heterosexism can become internalized to form part of the individual homosexual's self-concept: see Box 7.3 above.)

So, we are left still needing to know by what criteria homosexuality is judged to be abnormal (and where homophobia and heterosexism 'come from'). This brings us on to the deviation from the norm criterion.

Abnormality as deviation from the norm

This implies that, regardless of how other people behave (the statistical criterion), abnormality involves not behaving, feeling or thinking as one *should*. 'Norms' have an 'oughtness' about them: they convey expectations about behaviour, such that what is normal is *right*, *proper*, *natural*, *desirable*, and so on (see Figure 7.1). Clearly, these terms all convey *value judgements*. They are not neutral, value-free, objective descriptions or assessments of behaviour, but reflect beliefs concerning what are essentially *moral/ethical issues*.

Sometimes, it is very obvious how a particular behaviour deviates from a norm, and it is equally obvious what the norm is. For example, murder is a crime, and the law that makes it a crime embodies the moral law − 'Thou shalt not murder.' As with most crime, the behaviour is labelled as 'bad', making clear that legal/moral norms have been breached. However, there is no law against being schizophrenic, or having panic attacks, or being depressed, nor is it obvious what moral law or ethical principle is being broken in these cases. It seems that we might be dealing, once more, with residual rules (see above).

Up until the 1960s in the UK, homosexuality among consenting adults was illegal. That law, presumably, embodied the pre-Christian Jewish and early Christian condemnation of sex outside marriage and for any purpose except reproduction, even as an expression of love between husband and wife (Doyle, 1983). Now it is legal (at least between consenting adults over the age of 18), but homophobia and heterosexism continue to reflect these religious roots. (Interestingly, repeated attempts in the UK to bring down the age of consent between consenting homosexuals to 16, and hence bring it in line with that for heterosexuals, have failed.)

So, behaviour may be judged abnormal quite independently of its legal status (including its legal history), because it seems to breach certain fundamental religious−moral principles (even though it may not be easy to identify these principles or even to articulate them). However, in western culture, unlike many non-western cultures, a sharp distinction is made between legal, religious and medical aspects or definitions of normality. Disease, illness and pathology (bodily and psychological) are dealt with by the medical profession; they're the province of doctors and psychiatrists (as opposed to priests): mental disorder has become medicalized. Religion and illness are in separate 'cultural compartments': illness is an entirely secular matter.

However, many human situations and forms of human distress that are conceptualized in the West as 'illness' are seen in religious and/or philosophical terms in Indian culture, for example, which also stresses harmony between the person and his/her group as indicating health. In African culture, the concept of health is more social than biological:

> In the mind of the African, there is a more unitary concept of psychosomatic interrelationship, that is, an apparent reciprocity between mind and matter. Health is not an isolated phenomenon but part of the entire magico-religious fabric; it is more than the absence of disease. Since disease is viewed as one of the most important social sanctions, peaceful living with neighbours, abstention from adultery, keeping the laws of gods and men, are essentials in order to protect oneself and one's family from disease.
>
> (Lambo, 1964, in Fernando, 1991)

The spiritual and physical worlds are not separate entities, as they are in western culture; mind and body do not exist separately, and no distinction is made between 'bodily illness' and 'mental illness' (see Chapter 12).

However, although ideas about health and illness vary across cultures on a number of parameters, every culture possesses a concept of illness as some kind of departure (or deviation) from health. Yet, according to Fernando (1991):

> The overall world view within a culture, appertaining to health, religion, psychology and spiritual concerns determines the meaning within that culture of 'madness', mental illness and mental health.

So, thinking about, and treating, psychological abnormality from a medical, biological, perspective, is itself a cultural phenomenon. This leads on to an eighth major criterion of abnormality, namely abnormality as mental illness or mental disorder (see below).

Abnormality as an exaggeration of normality

A ninth criterion emerges from the study of personality. According to Claridge and Davis (2003), the development of a psychological disorder can be seen as a particularly dramatic example of how 'apparently quite stable propensities to action, motivations, and other characteristics that constitute the personality can be thrown into disarray'. This is especially true in the case of serious (psychotic) mental illness (such as schizophrenia), but also in other (neurotic) disorders (such as obsessive-compulsive disorder).

As discussed in Chapter 4, psychologists tend to see personality as composed of a collection of traits, relatively stable tendencies, inherent within the individual, which define 'typical' ways of behaving, thinking and feeling. Some – notably Eysenck – prefer to define and measure personality in terms of a small number of dimensions (such as introversion–extroversion), which subsume a larger number of traits (they summarize 'underlying' traits). These dimensions apply to everyone, allowing people to be compared with each other (a nomothetic approach), but people can also be regarded as unique, in that they differ in the profiles they display across these various dimensions (an idiographic approach: see Chapter 3).

What both the trait and dimensional approaches assume is continuity in the features (broad or narrow) they use to describe personality. In other words, individuals are more or less X, Y or Z, being ranged at various points along a continuum ('more or less extrovert', or 'more or less sociable'). Claridge and Davis (2003) believe that this approach is tailor-made for helping us understand psychological disorders:

> The clinically abnormal can easily be visualized as, in some regard, an extension of the normal, defining the extremes of the dimensions that describe personality.

In other words, there is only a *quantitative* difference (one of degree) between 'normal' people and those diagnosed with mental disorders (in rather less 'technical' language, 'we're all a little bit mad' or 'some of us are madder than others'). Eysenck was very critical of the psychiatric construction of psychological abnormality

as discrete (distinct) disease entities that prevailed in the 1960s. Unlike the anti-psychiatrists (such as Laing: see Box 7.1), Eysenck argued strongly for the essentially *biological* roots of mental disorder. But unlike most psychiatrists, he argued that the biology of mental illness was an extension of the biology of the personality dimensions that predispose to illness (Eysenck, 1960). Some empirical support for this dimensional approach, from a rather surprising quarter, is described in Box 7.4.

BOX 7.4 ARE WE ALL A LITTLE BIT SCHIZOPHRENIC?

Ochert (1998) describes research by Steel (at the Institute of Psychiatry in London) into schizophrenia-like personality traits ('schizotypy'). He regards the symptoms of schizophrenia as a 'severe manifestation of personality traits that exist within the normal population'.

Everyone has some degree of schizotypy, as assessed by the Oxford-Liverpool Inventory of Feelings and Experiences (O-LIFE). 'High schizotypes' are normal people who answer questions in much the same way as schizophrenics, and who may be particularly vulnerable to schizophrenia. Their brains may operate in similar ways to schizophrenics' brains, and there is evidence that both groups have difficulty weeding out irrelevant information. They also share a tendency to be less affected by expectations built up from past events. Steel believes that this and other schizotypal traits may make people more creative, but he has no doubt that schizophrenics are actually suffering. He hopes that greater understanding might translate into better therapies, not least by making it 'more normal to be abnormal' (Ochert, 1998).

However, the picture is not quite as simple as Steel (see Box 7.4) paints it.

- Claridge and Davis (2003) point out that people with mental disorders are not *merely* individuals occupying one end of some normal personality dimensions (even if the latter do describe part of their condition). For example, someone with agoraphobia would almost certainly score high on a rating scale or personality inventory of *trait anxiety*. But by the time they have been formally diagnosed as agoraphobic (and probably even before), such individuals will have developed new, pathological behaviours (symptoms), such as refusal to leave home and expressing irrational fears they did not previously have. In other words, 'they are now *more* than just people of very anxious personality; so new facts are needed to explain the transition from extreme *trait* anxiety to *symptomatic* anxiety'.
- The preferred approach amongst psychiatrists is the *categorical* approach, which forms the basis of attempts to classify mental disorders, such as DSM and ICD (see below). But the authors of DSM themselves admit that it falls short of standards for a strictly categorical model of the kind that works well in physical medicine. They defend it largely on *practical* grounds (such as providing a system for communication between clinicians and others involved in the care of psychiatric patients), but its *scientific* value is much more doubtful (see Box 7.5).
- Claridge and Davis also draw attention to a distinction between psychological disorders and *neurological diseases* (such as Alzheimer's and Huntington's). (This relates to the further distinction between functional and organic mental disorders discussed below.) Both categories appear in the major classification systems (DSM and ICD), but there are important differences in how the nervous system is implicated in the two types of disorder. (i) In *neurological* disorders, illness results from some pathological process, either one that's already known or that can be confidently assumed, and, therefore, at some future point, discovered. They are like any other physical disease – they just happen to affect the brain, often producing progressive deterioration in mental functioning. They destroy healthy brain, partly or completely, and are incompatible with full health. (ii) In *psychological* disorders, the biology is much more continuous with the biology of health.
- According to McGhee (2001), discussion of mental disorders often focuses on *absences*, while actual diagnostic categories for specific disorders focus on the *presence* of symptoms. For example, the mentaslly ill are often described as *not* following society's behavioural norms (they are *deviant*), *not* functioning effectively (they are *dysfunctional*), and so on. But diagnosis is made in terms of present,

identifiable symptoms, such as hearing voices, anxiety, anger outbursts, and so on. So, specific disorders may be distinguishable from each other in terms of what the sufferer displays, but:

> *. . . according to psychologists, the mentally ill do not seem to have anything in common with one another, apart from the fact that they are different from some notional standard of normal functioning. If this is the case, then we should treat very sceptically any general claims about the 'mentally ill'.*

> (McGhee, 2001)

BOX 7.5 SOME PROBLEMS WITH THE DIAGNOSIS OF MENTAL DISORDERS

(a) When someone with cystitis suffers hair loss, there is factual evidence that each disease/condition has a distinct aetiology (causation) – and they also *look* very different. But in psychiatry, 'comorbid disorders can often seem suspiciously similar, as though they share some common cause or underlying mechanism' (Claridge and Davis, 2003). So, *comorbidity* refers to having more than one disorder/ disease, and Claridge and Davis give the example of eating disorders and substance-use disorder, which often occur together.

(b) The distinction between illness or dysfunction and health is an issue in relation to physical disease, but in the context of psychological disorders it takes on even greater force. Psychological disorders are uniquely different:

> *In physical diseases the primary fault lies in just one part of the organism and the evidence for its failure or deficiency is usually fairly objective. Psychological disorders, on the other hand, are defined more in terms of the person's whole behavioural and mental functioning . . .*

> (Claridge and Davis, 2003)

This means that what is judged psychologically abnormal can sometimes seem quite arbitrary and may often depend on changing social criteria regarding what is healthy and unhealthy. In other words, 'the idea of "disease process" as the sole cause of psychological disorders is less helpful than in the case of physical illness' (Claridge and Davis, 2003).

(c) Similarly, Boyle (2007) argues that psychiatric diagnosis is based on assumptions which became acceptable during the late nineteenth and twentieth centuries that:

> *. . . troublesome behaviours, emotions and psychological experiences will form the same kinds of pattern, conform to the same theoretical frameworks, as bodily complaints; that these behaviours and emotions are outward symptoms of an underlying internal dysfunction which, together with signs (objective, measurable bodily antecedents), will cluster into syndromes . . .*

However:

> *. . . our body parts . . . don't have language or emotions, form beliefs, make relationships, create symbols, search for meaning, or plan the future. Small wonder that a theoretical framework developed for understanding bodily problems has proved so inappropriate for the task of understanding psychological experience and behaviour . . .*

> (Boyle, 2007)

Boyle also criticizes psychiatric diagnosis in terms of the way it distorts research. For example, it directs research efforts to the 'ill' or 'deficient' individual in whose brain or psyche the fundamental cause of their disorder is assumed to be. (It is this kind of research that is most widely reported in textbooks and the media.)

> . . . Yet there is strong evidence that emotional distress and behavioural problems, even the most bizarre, are understandable responses to or ways of actively trying to manage adverse circumstances and relationships . . . The theoretical and practical implications of this evidence are often minimized by, for example, presenting adverse environments and relationships largely as consequences of 'having a mental disorder' rather than as antecedents of a range of meaningful and purposive – if problematical – responses to adversity . . .
>
> (Boyle, 2007)

In other words, the individual, rather than his/her life circumstances, is 'blamed' for the disorder. As Harper *et al.* (2007) point out, researchers have found strong associations between ethnicity, gender, social class, sexual abuse and many forms of distress, which suggests that:

> . . . the brain–body is an open system that cannot be comprehensively understood outside of its social context. Psychiatric diagnoses ignore such research in favour of the individualization of distress, forcing it into categories of dubious validity, and then implicitly associating it with underlying biomedical pathologies
>
> (Bentall, 2004; Boyle, 2002).

Psychiatric symptoms as psychological processes that go wrong

A different kind of criticism comes from Bentall (2007), who cites research into the psychological processes involved in psychotic complaints ('symptoms') suggesting a very different view of the psychotic disorder itself.

In relation to auditory-verbal hallucinations, some researchers have attempted to directly measure source monitoring (the capacity to distinguish between self-generated thoughts and externally-presented stimuli). One idea is that hallucinating patients have dysfunctional metacognitive beliefs (beliefs about their own mental processes) that lead them to make self-defeating efforts to control their thoughts; this makes the thoughts seem unintended, and therefore alien. A second proposal is that source monitoring errors reflect a general failure to monitor one's own intentional states, as demonstrated by voice-hearing psychotic patients' greater ability to tickle themselves compared with non-psychotic controls (Blakemore *et al.*, 2001, in Bentall). More direct evidence supporting this account comes in a series of electrophysiological studies which show that hallucinating patients do not display the same dampening in the auditory perception areas of the temporal lobe that is seen during talking and inner speech (Ford and Mathalon, 2004, in Bentall).

Patients with delusions appear to perform normally on conventional measures of reasoning (Bentall and Young, 1996; Corcoran *et al.*, 2006; both in Bentall). The psychological abnormality that has been most reliably linked to delusional thinking is a tendency to 'jump to conclusions' when reasoning about probabilities: they request less information before reaching a decision compared with non-delusional controls. Deficits in theory of mind (ToM: see Chapter 1 and Gross, 2005, 2008) skills have been specifically implicated in persecutory delusions.

Bentall (2003) argues that, once hallucinations, delusions and the other manifestations of psychosis ('madness') have been adequately explained, there will be no 'schizophrenia' left behind that also requires explanation. This leads us, logically, to ask if mental disorders exist at all (in the way that bodily diseases do).

THE OBJECTIVE NATURE OF MENTAL DISORDERS: DO THEY EXIST?

At the heart of the 'abnormality as mental illness' criterion is the *medical model*. The use of the term 'psychopathology' to refer to the particular kind of deviancy that psychiatrists and clinical psychologists are concerned with ('mad', not 'bad') reflects the medical model. Also central to the model is the classification and diagnosis of mental disorders, the treatment of psychiatric patients in psychiatric hospitals, and the use of other medical terminology and practices (Maher, 1966).

All systems of classification stem from the work of Emil Kraepelin (1913), who published the first recognized textbook of psychiatry in 1883. He proposed that certain groups of symptoms occur together sufficiently often to merit the designation 'disease' or 'syndrome', and he went on to describe the diagnostic indicators associated with each syndrome. His classification helped to establish the organic (bodily) nature of mental disorders, and this is an integral feature of the medical model. See Box 7.6.

BOX 7.6 ORGANIC *VS* FUNCTIONAL DISORDERS

Kraepelin's system laid the foundation for all subsequent classification systems (in particular DSM in America, and the World Heath Organization's ICD – International Classification of Diseases). Until recently, psychiatrists distinguished between:

- *organic mental disorders,* in which biological factors are clearly involved (usually taken to be causal factors), such as Alzheimer's disease and senile dementia, and
- *functional mental disorders*, in which the role of biological factors is much less obvious.

What 'functional' conveys is that there is no demonstrable physical basis for the abnormal behaviour, and that something has gone wrong with the way the person functions in the network of relationships that make up his/her world (Bailey, 1979).

This distinction is related to another that has traditionally been made (also recently dropped), namely that between *neurosis* and *psychosis*.

The great majority of neuroses and psychoses have traditionally been thought of as functional disorders; the examples given above of organic disorders have usually been referred to as *organic psychoses*. Although neuroses and psychoses have not been *defined* in terms of the role of biological factors (otherwise *all* psychoses would be organic, and *all* neuroses functional), the different methods of *treatment* used strongly suggest how their likely causes are perceived. While neuroses (such as phobias, panic attacks and multiple personality/dissociative identity disorder) are typically treated using *psychological techniques* (psychotherapy, behaviour therapy), psychoses (such as schizophrenia and major depression) are mainly treated using *physical/organic methods* (antipsychotic medication, antidepressants, electroconvulsive therapy/ECT).

Most *biologically oriented* psychiatrists (the large majority of psychiatrists as a whole) have always believed that schizophrenia (as well as the other functional psychoses) is actually organic, and that it is only a matter of time until medical science discovers the biological causes and mechanisms involved. This argument is supported by classic cases such as *general paresis of the insane* (GPI). This was recognized as a clinical syndrome (in summary, dementia) long before the physical cause was discovered (namely, untreated syphilis). This discovery represents an important landmark in the history of psychiatry because it stimulated a search for organic causes of other syndromes (Gelder *et al.,* 1989). Also, many illnesses that were once thought to have a supernatural or psychological origin have now become generally accepted as physical; for example, epilepsy was for centuries thought to be of divine origin (Littlewood and Lipsedge, 1989: see Chapter 13).

Contrary to this view, however, socially oriented psychiatrists argue that mental disorders, such as GPI, always had an 'organic feel' about them – they are only found associated with easily recognized bodily abnormalities.

Conversely, Charcot and Freud helped hysteria (for so long thought to be caused by abnormalities of the womb) to be generally accepted as psychological in origin (Littlewood and Lipsedge, 1989).

If mental disorders 'exist' in some objective sense – that is, independently of cultural norms, values and world views – then the most likely candidates will come from those believed to be organic in origin. Just as modern medicine is based on the assumption that physical disease is the same throughout the world, and that definition, classification, causation and diagnosis are largely unaffected by cultural factors, so biologically oriented psychiatrists contend that psychoses, in particular schizophrenia and depression, are also 'culture-free'.

The cross-cultural study of mental disorder

During the 1970s and 1980s, psychiatrists and clinical psychologists became increasingly interested in 'cultural psychiatry' (otherwise known as 'transcultural psychiatry', or 'comparative psychiatry'). Bhugra and Bhui (2001) define *comparative psychiatry* as:

> . . . *the study of the relations between psychiatric disorder and the psychological traits and characteristics of people, the cultures and societies they come from and the interaction between various factors arising from this.*

It also deals with cultural factors in the genesis and management of psychiatric disorders. Although comparative psychiatry was originally proposed as an academic discipline, it is essential that any academic findings and views are put into practice in the delivery of healthcare to people from ethnic minorities and even to members of ethnic majority groups that differ from those to which the clinicians themselves belong (Bhugra and Bhui, 2001) (see below).

According to Berry *et al.* (1992), the central issue in the cross-cultural study of psychopathology is whether phenomena such as schizophrenia are (i) absolute (found in all cultures in precisely the same form), (ii) universal (present in some form in all cultures, but subject to cultural influence regarding what factors bring them on, how they're expressed and so on), or (iii) culturally relative (unique to particular cultures and understandable only in terms of those cultures).

Absolute phenomena

Of the three possibilities, this is the only one that corresponds to a 'culture-free' view of abnormality. But even in the case of a disorder that may appear to be totally 'biological', such as the physiological response to alcohol, cultural factors seem to play a part. For example, cultural norms regarding what, where and how much to drink result in quite different expressions of alcohol use across cultural groups:

> *We may conclude that it makes little sense to even consider a culture-free abnormal behaviour, since cultural factors appear to affect at least some aspects of mental disorders, even those that are so closely linked to human biology.*
>
> *(Berry* et al., *1992)*

Universality

This is a more likely candidate for capturing the nature of psychopathology and is supported, in particular, by studies of schizophrenia and depression. We will look at the former here.

Schizophrenia is the most commonly diagnosed mental disorder in the world, and of the major disorders, the largest number of culture-general symptoms has been reported for schizophrenia (e.g. World Health

Organization, 1973, 1979; Draguns, 1980, 1990). These two findings constitute one of the major arguments for the biological basis of this disorder.

The core symptoms include: (i) poor insight into the reasons for one's problems and one's current thinking; (ii) thinking aloud; (iii) incoherent speech, one phrase or sentence apparently bearing no relationship to others; (iv) giving unrealistic information that would be contradicted by objective facts if the person were able to consider them; (v) widespread, bizarre and/or nihilistic delusions (feeling that existence is useless and nothing is worth living for); (vi) flattened mood and limited ability to form emotional ties with others (Brislin, 1993). But even with this large core of culture-general symptoms, there are at least three possible ways in which culture-specific factors can influence schizophrenia: (a) the form that symptoms will take; (b) the specific reasons for the onset of the illness; (c) the prognosis.

The form that symptoms will take

When schizophrenics complain that their minds are being invaded by unseen forces, in North America and Europe these forces keep up to date with technological developments. So, in the 1920s, these were often voices from the radio, in the 1950s they often came from the television, in the 1960s it was satellites in space, and in the 1970s and 1980s spirits were transmitted through microwave ovens. In cultures where witchcraft is considered common, the voices or spirits would be directed by unseen forces under the control of demons.

Citing Katz et al. (1988), Brislin points out that the exact form taken by the symptoms of schizophrenia can be understood by looking at predominant cultural values. In Ibadan, Nigeria, the symptoms shown by schizophrenics emphasized a highly suspicious orientation towards others, with many bizarre fears and thoughts. For many Nigerians it is normal to view illness as caused by unseen evil forces, and sometimes those forces are directed at a person by enemies and witches. This paranoid aspect of the schizophrenic's symptoms is an exaggeration of this normal view, a distortion of the 'normal' state. This, of course, is directly relevant to the dimensional vs categorical views of abnormality discussed earlier.

Reasons for the onset of illness

One view of schizophrenia is that we inherit a predisposition towards the disorder (we're 'at risk'), while the actual symptoms are triggered by stress (see Draguns, 1990).

Day et al. (1987, in Brislin, 1993) studied schizophrenia in nine different locations in the USA, Asia, Europe and South America. Acute schizophrenic attacks were associated with stressful events, which could be described as external to the patients (and not initiated by them), and they tended to cluster within a two- to three-week period before the onset of obvious symptoms (such as the unexpected death of a spouse, losing one's job, and parental divorce). Some stressful events were interpretable only if the researchers had considerable information regarding the cultural background of the sample.

The prognosis

Lin and Kleinman (1988, in Brislin, 1993) found that the prognosis for successful treatment of schizophrenia was better in non-industrialized than industrialized societies. Why should this be? Wouldn't we expect the opposite to be true, given the superior resources available in the latter?

To be a functioning member of a 'highly industrialized' nation, certain skills are needed that are very difficult for the schizophrenic to demonstrate, and many of the core symptoms involve relating to others. Individualism is valued in highly industrialized societies (see Chapter 8), and it is up to the individual to develop rapport and emotional ties with others. Yet there is no automatic support group available to help with this. In the past, there might have been the nuclear family, but its members are often so affected by divorce and intra-familial conflict that it can be a source of stress rather than support.

Along with this heavy emphasis on independence, self-reliance, and personal freedom, individualistic value orientations also tend to foster fierce competition, frequent life changes, and alienation, and they do not usually provide the kind of structured, stable, and predictable environments that allow schizophrenic patients to recuperate at their own pace and to be reintegrated into the society.

(Lin and Kleinman, 1988, in Brislin, 1993)

In contrast, the slower lifestyle and more integrated collectives commonly found in less industrialized nations may provide a more supportive environment for schizophrenics; this includes the greater likelihood of finding productive work (for example, in the family farm or business). This is clearly important for developing a sense of self-worth. Also, 'colleagues' will be more tolerant of mistakes than would an employer or colleagues in large, impersonal organizations. Brislin concludes by saying:

As part of their socialization, people learn to express psychological disturbances in ways that are acceptable within their culture, in ways that will be understood, and in ways that will evoke sympathy from others.

What Brislin seems to be implying is that: (i) there is a crucial element of learning involved in abnormality, although this does not, of course, rule out the role of biological factors; (ii) abnormal behaviour and experience are not random or arbitrary or meaningless, but make perfectly good sense in terms of the culture in which they are manifested; and (iii) there is a continuity between normal and abnormal behaviour (including schizophrenia), since both are, at least in part, acquired through the same process of socialization.

Although these observations are consistent with how universal abnormality has been defined by transcultural psychiatrists, Berry *et al.* (1992) point out two major limitations of the studies that provide the bulk of the evidence.

1 Studies such as the International Pilot Study of Schizophrenia (World Health Organization, 1973), which compared the prevalence of schizophrenia in Columbia, (the former) Czechoslovakia, Denmark, India, Nigeria, Taiwan, the UK, the USA and (the former) USSR involved the use of diagnostic instruments, concepts and researchers that all belonged to western psychiatry.
2 The patient populations involved were not representative of world cultural variation (and were themselves, to some extent, acculturated to a western way of life).

Cultural relativity

A large number of studies have found that, in a wide range of non-western cultures, there are apparently unique ways of 'being mad' (Berry *et al.*, 1992): there are forms of abnormality that are not documented and recognized within the classification systems of western psychiatry. These 'exotic' disorders are usually described and interpreted in terms that relate to the particular culture in which they're reported. The local, indigenous, name is used, which then gradually enters the (western) psychiatric literature. They are commonly referred to as *culture-bound syndromes* (CBSs: see Box 7.7).

Again, researchers distinguish between modern, scientific psychiatry and traditional ethnopsychiatry (the study of culture-relative/culture-specific disorders), seeing the former as telling us about authentic illness, while the latter tells us about illness that is contaminated/distorted by culture. Fernando (1991) believes that anthropology and psychiatry have colluded in regarding psychiatric disorders seen in western (white) societies as being on a different plane from those seen in non-western (black, 'primitive') societies:

When culture 'distorts' a syndrome beyond a certain point, a CBS is identified. Practitioners go along with this approach seeing symptom constellations in the West as the standard and those in other cultures as anomalies . . .

BOX 7.7 CULTURE-BOUND SYNDROMES (CBSS)

Culture-bound syndromes are studied mainly by anthropologists, who focus on 'culture-specific' disorders, stressing the differences between cultures. This contrasts with the approach of traditional (biological) psychiatrists, who tend to focus on 'universal' disorders, stressing the similarities. So, when a 'new' condition is observed in some non-western society (people perceived as being alien to western culture), the syndrome itself is perceived as alien to the existing classification system, sufficiently 'outside' the mainstream that it may be *unclassifiable*. The fact that they may be quite common within a particular culture makes no difference – if they are (apparently) limited to other cultures, they are excluded from the mainstream classification of mental disorder.

Since the disorder occurs in groups seen as alien in primarily racial terms, the concept of a CBS is, therefore, one that has been generated by the ideology of western psychiatry:

> *Psychopathology in the West is seen as culturally neutral and psychopathology that is distinctively different (from that seen in the West) as 'culture-bound'.*

> *(Fernando, 1991)*

This represents a form of *ethnocentrism* within western psychiatry, and in keeping with this view, Fernando believes that the concept of a CBS has a distinctly racist connotation.

Similarly, Littlewood and Lipsedge (1989) argue that it is wrong to look at beliefs about madness in other cultures as if they are only more or less accurate approximations to a 'scientific' (accurate, objective) description. A cultural understanding of mental disorder is as important in western as in any other culture, and, indeed, some general features of those 'ritual patterns' usually classed as CBSs are applicable to western neurosis (Littlewood and Lipsedge, 1989). It has been suggested that anorexia nervosa and pre-menstrual syndrome (PMS: see Chapter 6) may be western CBSs (Fernando, 1991).

Ironically, in at least two cases, CBS names have become part of the common vocabulary in English-speaking western societies. Amok involves wild, aggressive behaviour, usually short-lived, and usually confined to males, involving attempts to kill or injure. It was identified in Malaysia, Indonesia and Thailand, the Malay word 'amok' meaning 'to engage furiously in battle'. It has obvious similarities to the Viking behaviour called berserker, practised just before going into battle (Berry *et al.*, 1992). You do not have to come from South-East Asia, or be a Viking, in order to 'run amok' or 'go berserk'!

THE CULTURE-BOUND NATURE OF PSYCHIATRY

If western psychiatry is, inevitably, influenced by western cultural beliefs and values (since it is part of that culture), then it cannot claim to be objective, scientifically 'detached' and value-free. If we accept this argument, it should follow that: (i) psychiatric definitions and the classification of mental disorders will change over time, reflecting changes in cultural beliefs and values; and (ii) the process of psychiatric diagnosis will be influenced by wider cultural beliefs and values.

Changing views of homosexuality

Psychological abnormality has not always been explained and dealt with in western culture by medicine. During the Middle Ages (roughly AD 500–1500), when religion was the dominant force in almost all aspects of European life, what we now call mental disorder was seen as possession by the Devil. It was the time of witch-hunts and burning witches at the stake, the Spanish Inquisition, and brutal exorcisms to drive out the Devil (Holmes, 1994). The 1500s marked the beginning of widespread recognition that disturbed people needed care, not exorcism and condemnation, but it was not until the middle of the 1800s that 'modern' psychiatry began to emerge, seeing psychological abnormality as comparable to bodily, physical, illness with organic origins (*somatogenesis*: see above).

Figure 7.3 During the Middle Ages, what we would now call mental disorder was seen as possession by the Devil or as witchcraft

In DSM-IV (1994), the category 'Organic Mental Disorders', which had appeared in DSM-III-R (1987), was omitted and replaced by 'Delirium, Dementia, Amnesic and Other Cognitive Disorders'. According to Davison and Neale (1994), the thinking behind this change was that the term 'organic' implies that the other major categories do not have a biological basis. Since research had shown the influence of biological factors through a whole range of disorders, it was no longer considered appropriate to use the term 'organic' (it was now thought to be misleading). To this extent, mental disorder became even more medicalized than it had ever been.

What this shows is that mental disorders, and how they are classified, are not 'set in stone'. Assuming that the behaviour and experience of people with disorders do not change radically (at least within the same cultural group over relatively short periods of time), it is not the 'reality' of mental disorders that changes but how psychiatrists define and interpret that reality. We have seen how those definitions and interpretations reflect wider cultural beliefs and values, and there is perhaps no better demonstration of this process than the case of homosexuality.

DSM-II (1968) included homosexuality as a sexual deviation. In 1973, the Nomenclature Committee of the APA, under pressure from many professionals and gay activist groups, recommended to the general membership that the category should be removed and replaced with sexual orientation disturbance. This was to be applied to gay men and lesbians who are 'disturbed by, in conflict with, or wish to change their sexual orientation'. The change was approved, but not without vehement protests from several eminent psychiatrists, who maintained the traditional view that homosexuality is inherently abnormal.

When DSM-III was published in 1980, another new term, ego-dystonic homosexuality (EDH), was used, referring to a person who is homosexually aroused, finds this arousal to be a persistent source of distress, and wishes to become heterosexual. Since homosexuality itself was no longer a mental disorder, there was no discussion in DSM-III of predisposing factors (as there was for all disorders). But predisposing factors for EDH were included, and were, primarily, those negative societal attitudes (homophobia and heterosexism) that have been internalized by the homosexual individual. So, according to DSM-III, a homosexual is abnormal if s/he has been persuaded by society's prejudices that his/her sexual orientation is inherently abnormal, but at the same time denies that homosexuality in itself is abnormal (Davison and Neale, 2001).

For whatever reasons, very little use was made of the EDH category. Less surprisingly, no such category as 'ego-dystonic heterosexuality' has ever been used (Kitzinger, 1990).

When DSM-III was revised (DSM-III-R, 1987), the APA decided that even the watered-down EDH should no longer be included. Instead, 'Sexual Disorder Not Otherwise Specified' includes 'persistent and marked distress about one's sexual orientation'. This has been retained in DSM-IV. This new category does not specify a sexual orientation, so ego-dystonic heterosexuality is a diagnostic possibility; however, Davison and Neale (2001) believe that, in practice, this is as unlikely to be made as EDH.

Psychiatric diagnosis as a social process

According to Fernando (1991), the diagnostic interview consists, primarily, of (i) taking the patient's history, and (ii) assessing the patient's current 'mental state'.

The history is often thought of as comprising objective facts, but, in reality, it is a highly selective account of whatever information has been acquired from the patient and others, and it is the psychiatrist who does the crucial sorting out. The psychiatrist also influences the content of the history, in two interrelated ways.

1 The type and extent of information given by the patient and others are fashioned by the perceptions of the psychiatrist about the people providing the information, and vice versa. For example, if a black Asian patient says little about an arranged marriage (because s/he thinks it will be disapproved of by the white psychiatrist), this will usually be interpreted as a negative quality of the patient (secretiveness or deviousness) rather than a quality of the doctor.
2 The picking and choosing that occurs during the history-taking depends on the beliefs, value judgements, understanding and knowledge of the psychiatrist. White, middle-class psychiatrists are unlikely to have personal experience of predominantly black areas (such as Harlem in New York, Tower Hamlets in London and St Paul's in Bristol), and so will be unaware of the pressures impinging upon black people who live there. This is likely to result in a misinterpretation of their lifestyles and behaviour, which often reinforces their racist attitudes.

The assessment of the patient's 'mental state' is probably the major determinant of the final diagnosis. What the patient reports of his/her experiences is taken to depict an inner state of mind. The validity of such an inference is dubious even when there is excellent rapport and full understanding between patient and psychiatrist, but in a multi-cultural setting this is highly unlikely. Fernando (1991) argues that:

The meanings attached to experiences and perceptions, the concept of illness, and the overall significance of the interview situation . . . are but some of the parameters along which variation must occur when cultural differences are present between the participants of an interaction.

Deductions made from an 'examination' of the mental state cannot be viewed as equivalent to a medical description of the state of a bodily organ:

What a doctor 'finds' in a 'mental state' is as much a reflection of the observers as the so-called patient. It is the result of an interaction rather than a one-sided observation.

(Fernando, 1991)

According to Kareem (1978, in Mohamed, 2000):

The fact of being from another culture involves both conscious and unconscious assumptions, both in the patient and the therapist . . . for the successful outcome of therapy it is essential to address these . . . assumptions from the beginning.

To help patients change, therapists must possess an understanding of the psychology, pathology and social experiences of individuals, including themselves. They need a deep level of self-awareness that enables them to recognize all the assumptions they bring with them. This includes facing the oppression, discrimination, stereotyping and racism within their society and their role in it. However, ignoring someone's blackness (as with their gender or sexual orientation) as if it were irrelevant involves denying major aspects of that person's experiences. In order to avoid having to deal with material that white therapists might perceive as frightening or too challenging, they may tend to try to match culturally different clients with therapists from a similar background, instead of developing their own transcultural skills. However,

. . . the idea that black clients can only be seen by black therapists may serve to protect white therapists from having to confront issues about their own prejudices and racism.

(Mohamed, 2000)

SUMMARY

○ The whole field of abnormal psychology rests upon the assumption that a distinction can be made between normality and abnormality.

○ It is relatively easy to give examples of psychological abnormality, but much more difficult to provide precise definitions.

○ All behaviour can be placed somewhere on a continuum, running from unacceptable, through tolerable, acceptable/permissible, to desirable and required/obligatory.

○ 'Unacceptable' conveys 'not decent and proper' (residual rules). Because these rules are implicit, we cannot easily say why schizophrenia or homosexuality is strange and frightening.

○ It is important to distinguish between social deviance and mental disorder/abnormality; only the latter involves an impairment of function in the person.

○ The statistical infrequency criterion (or deviation from the average) assumes that psychological characteristics in general are dimensional.

○ Those judged to be suffering from psychotic mental disorder may not experience any personal distress at all.

○ Defining abnormality as other people's distress suggests that abnormality, like normality, is interpersonal. According to Laing's conspiratorial model of schizophrenia, schizophrenia is a label applied by other people to protect them against the threat posed by the patient's behaviour/experience.

○ Abnormality as maladaptiveness/disability focuses largely on the consequences of behaviour, namely what it prevents the individual from achieving – personally, sexually, socially, intellectually or occupationally.

○ According to the deviation from the norm criterion, abnormality involves not behaving, feeling or thinking as one should. This involves value judgements and relates to residual rules.

○ The abnormality as exaggeration of normality criterion is based on the dimensional view of mental disorder, as opposed to the categorical view. These are favoured by (western) psychologists and psychiatrists respectively.

○ Although now no longer illegal, homosexuality still breaches certain fundamental religious–moral principles; homophobia and heterosexism continue to reflect these religious roots.

○ In western culture, unlike many non-western cultures, a sharp distinction is made between legal, religious and medical definitions of normality; mental disorder has become medicalized. In African culture, however, no distinction is made between bodily and mental illness.

○ At the heart of the abnormality as mental illness criterion is the medical model. This involves the classification/diagnosis/treatment of psychopathology, stemming from the work of Kraepelin.

○ Two traditional distinctions made within psychiatry are organic vs functional disorders, and neurosis vs psychosis. Psychoses are mainly treated using physical methods, which implies a belief that they are biologically caused.

○ Any attempt to model psychological disorders on organic (bodily) disease seems doomed to fail. While the latter can be defined objectively, the former can be understood only within their socio-cultural context.

O The central issue in comparative psychiatry is whether phenomena such as schizophrenia are absolute ('culture-free'), universal ('culture-general') or culturally relative (unique to particular cultures).

O Although schizophrenia is the most commonly diagnosed mental disorder in the world, culture-specific factors could influence schizophrenia in relation to (i) the form the symptoms will take, (ii) the specific reasons for the onset of the illness, (iii) the prognosis.

O The evidence that supports the view of abnormality as universal is of limited value because of the use of culturally biased diagnostic instruments and samples.

O Many studies have found unique ways of 'being mad' in a wide range of non-western cultures. These culture-bound syndromes (CBSs) are excluded from mainstream, western psychiatric classification, according to which psychopathology is seen as culturally neutral. This represents a form of ethnocentrism, since 'western symptoms' are seen as the 'standard'.

O Western psychiatry is influenced by western cultural beliefs and values and so is not objective and value-free. This is reflected in changing definitions among psychiatrists regarding the 'status' of homosexuality as a mental disorder.

O The cultural nature of psychiatry can also be seen if psychiatric diagnosis is understood as a social process. Assessment of the patient's 'mental state' is not equivalent to a medical description of a bodily organ but is the product of an interaction between individuals who often possess widely divergent beliefs, values and cultural experiences.

USEFUL WEBSITES

www.nsf.org.uk
www.hants.gov.uk/istcclr/cch33222.html
www.understandingpsychosis.com
www.critpsynet.freeuk.com/index.htm
www.hearing-voices.org
http://tinyurl.com/6yuvb

RECOMMENDED READING

Bentall, R.P. (2003) *Madness Explained: Psychosis and human nature.* London: Penguin Books Ltd.

Boyle, M. (2007) The problem with diagnosis. *The Psychologist, 20*(5), 290–2.

Davison, G.C., Neale, J.M. and Kring, A.M. (2004) *Abnormal Psychology* (9th edn). New York: John Wiley & Sons Ltd.

Gross, R. (2008) *Key Studies in Psychology* (5th edn). London: Hodder Education. (Chapters 31, 33 and 36.)

May, R. (2007) Working outside the diagnostic frame. *The Psychologist, 20*(5), 300–1.

Miller, L. and Morley, S. (1986) *Investigating Abnormal Behaviour.* London: Lawrence Erlbaum Associates.

CHAPTER 8

CROSS-CULTURAL PSYCHOLOGY

CULTURE AS PART OF THE NATURE–NURTURE DEBATE

When discussing the *heredity–environment* (nature–nurture) issue in Chapter 5, we distinguished between two levels at which the debate has taken place:

1 the *species level*
2 the *individual* (or, more accurately, the *individual differences*) *level*.

The former relates to questions such as: Are particular abilities, such as language, unique to human beings, and if so, is it part of our biological make-up? Or is it an acquired ability? Or does it involve an interaction between biological factors and environmental ones?

The latter relates to questions such as: How do we account for the fact that people vary in intelligence? Are these differences largely due to differences in genetic make-up between people, or to differences in their environmental experience, or to an interaction between the two?

The concept of culture and cultural differences provides a third level at which the nature–nurture issue may be debated, intermediate between the other two. All human beings are born into a particular cultural environment, and culture (to be defined below) may be regarded as unique to human beings (also see below). This corresponds to level 1. To the extent that different cultures provide their members with different experiences, they represent an important source of individual differences; this, of course, corresponds to level 2.

So, culture is part of the experience of every human being (and is a distinctive feature of human behaviour), but at the same time cultures differ, providing people with different experiences. To ask in what ways differences in culture are related to differences in behaviour is to ask about nature–nurture at level 3.

Accepting that most psychologists believe that both nature and nurture are always involved in any human behaviour, cross-cultural psychologists argue for the centrality of learning. According to Segall *et al.* (1999):

Human behaviour can best be understood as the product of learning, particularly learning that results from experiences with other people or with ideas, institutions, or other products of the behaviour of other people. In short, we are largely what we are because of culturally based learning . . .

Our sociocultural nature reflects a highly developed capacity to benefit from the lessons of experience, our own and our culture mates. No other animal has this capacity to the same extent . . . No other animal learns as much. As a result, we display many forms of behaviour that are uniquely human, many of which are part of what we call culture . . .

Each person is the product of the twin processes of *enculturation* and *socialization*.

- *Enculturation* (Herskovits, 1948) refers to all the learning that occurs in human life because of what is available to be learned – that is, without any direct, deliberate teaching. This is demonstrated in observational learning (e.g. Bandura, 1971), where we (especially children) learn through modelling the behaviour of others (in particular, adults). Conformity (e.g. Asch, 1951) is another example.
- *Socialization* was defined by Child (1954) as:

> *the whole process by which an individual, born with behavioural potentialities of enormously wide range, is led to develop actual behaviour which is confined within a much narrower range – the range of what is customary and acceptable for him according to the standards of his group.*

This definition reminds us that all human beings are capable of a far greater repertoire of behaviours than any single person ever displays. As Segall *et al.* (1999) put it:

> *Each of us, because of the accident of birth, begins life in a particular social context, within which we learn to make certain responses and not others.*

They say that the most dramatic illustration of this is our *language* (see below).

A useful way of thinking about culture and environment is Bronfenbrenner's (1979, 1989) ecological model, intended mainly to help explain child development. According to this model, there are four levels, with interactions possible both within and between:

1 the *microsystem* – the immediate setting in which the individual is directly involved; for instance, face-to-face interactions between a mother and child
2 the *mesosystem* – the total system of microsystems that impinge on a particular child; for example, experiences at school and at home are bound to influence each other
3 the *exosystem* – interactions between settings in which at least one setting does not directly involve the individual; for example, the child's home and the parents' place of work
4 the *macrosystem* – the overall system of micro-, meso- and exosystems that characterizes a particular culture or subculture. 'The ecological environment is conceived as a set of nested structures, each inside the next, like a set of Russian dolls' (Bronfenbrenner, 1979). So, interactions between two individuals, such as mother and child, are influenced by the social context within which they occur (usually the family). In turn, the family exists and functions within a broader social setting (for example, socioeconomic status, racial background), which is itself part of an even broader, cultural, context.

WHAT IS CROSS-CULTURAL PSYCHOLOGY?

The study of microsystems has mainly been carried out by psychologists, while the 'larger' units (mesosystems and exosystems) have traditionally been the focus of sociologists and anthropologists. To the extent that *cross-cultural psychologists* are interested in studying variability in behaviour among societies and cultural groups around the world (Smith and Bond, 1998), they have more in common with sociologists and social anthropologists than with other (more traditional) psychologists. In terms of Bronfenbrenner's model, it is the *interrelationship* between the different levels that makes the cross-cultural approach different from that of other psychological approaches to the study of behaviour.

Absolutism vs relativism

According to Jahoda (1978), the immediate (and modest) goals of cross-cultural psychology (CCP) are (i) to describe varieties of social behaviour encountered in different cultural settings and to try to analyse their

origins, and (ii) to sort out what is similar across different cultures and, thus, likely to be our common human heritage (the *universals* of human behaviour).

Segall *et al.* (1999) see cross-cultural psychologists as trying to determine how sociocultural variables influence human behaviour. To do so, they sometimes focus on behavioural differences across cultures, and sometimes on universal patterns of behaviour. But the ultimate goal is always to discover how culture and individual behaviour relate. To reach this goal, cross-cultural psychologists are confronted by different general orientations, which they refer to as extreme absolutism and relativism.

BOX 8.1 ABSOLUTISM VS RELATIVISM

Absolutism is associated with much traditional, 'mainstream', scientific psychology as it has been conducted in most European and US universities during the twentieth century; *relativism* is the approach central to anthropology during this same time frame.

CCP is located between the two, borrowing some aspects of each. For example, *cultural relativism* (Boas, 1911), extended by Herskovits (1948), was meant primarily to warn against invalid cross-cultural comparisons, flavoured by ethnocentric value judgements (see text below). Berry *et al.* (1992) 'borrowed' the term relativism to denote one pole of a dichotomy, with absolutism at the other pole.

- *Relativists* give more weight to cultural factors than to biological ones, while the reverse is true for *absolutists*.
- *Relativists* attribute group differences mainly to cultural differences, while *absolutists* attribute them mainly to non-cultural factors.
- *Relativists* have little/no interest in intergroup similarities, while *absolutists* believe that species-wide basic processes cause many similarities between groups ('the search for the psychic unity of mankind').
- *Relativists* advocate strictly 'emic' research, arguing that context-free categories and their measurement are impossible. They try to avoid all comparisons, which, if made at all, would be as non-evaluative as possible. *Absolutists* attempt to use context-free measurements, using standardized psychological instruments, which results in 'imposed etics' (see text below).

(Based on Segall et al.*, 1999)*

As with most dichotomies, few scholars are either extreme relativists or absolutists. For years, however, many US and European experimental psychologists stubbornly denied that cultural factors affected psychological processes. They proceeded to accumulate culture-bound findings they believed to be universally valid for all humankind. In parallel, some *cultural psychologists* place themselves quite close to the relativism end, emphasizing that psychological processes and structures vary in such fundamental ways in different cultural contexts that they are beyond comparison (or nearly so). Or they will suggest that culture should not be treated as existing outside individuals, where it can influence their behaviour, but *inside* (Greenfield, 1997; Miller, 1997; see below).

Segall *et al.* conclude by saying that most cross-cultural psychologists are somewhere in between these two extremes, where they try to strike a balance:

> *. . . revealing an orientation that borrows from both of the poles. Cross-cultural psychologists expect both biological and cultural factors to influence human behaviour, but, like relativists, assume that the role of culture in producing human variation both within and across groups (especially across groups) is substantial.*

Like absolutists, cross-cultural psychologists allow for similarities, due to species-wide basic processes, but consider their existence subject to empirical demonstration. When doing our research among different human groups, we adapt standard instruments to local conditions and make controlled nonevaluative comparisons, employing 'derived etics' . . .

(Trans)cultural and cross-cultural psychology: emphasizing differences

If knowledge is culturally created, then we should not assume that our ways of understanding are necessarily any better (closer to 'the truth') than other ways. Yet this is precisely what mainstream (social) psychology has done. According to Much (1995), a new *(trans)cultural psychology* has emerged in North America (e.g. Bruner, 1990; Cole, 1990; Shweder, 1990) as an attempt to overcome the bias of *ethnocentrism* that has too often limited the scope of understanding in the social sciences (see below).

Shweder (1990) makes the crucial distinction between 'cross-cultural psychology', which is a branch of experimental social, cognitive and personality psychology, and 'cultural psychology'. Most of what's been known as 'cross-cultural' psychology has presupposed the categories and models based on (mostly experimental) research with (limited samples of) Euro-American populations. It has mostly either 'tested the hypothesis' or 'validated the instrument' in other cultures, or 'measured' the social and psychological characteristics of members of other cultures with the methods and standards of western populations, usually assumed as a valid universal norm. The new 'cultural psychology' rejects this universalist model (Much, 1995).

Cole (1996) refers to the results of the last 100 years of psychological research, including cross-cultural experimental studies, as the 'first psychology'. We should not discard these results, since:

> *Cross-cultural studies, especially when they are sensitive to the local organization of activity, can serve to refute ethnocentric conclusions that 'those people' suffer from general cognitive deficits as a consequence of cultural inadequacies. From time to time they may even induce adherents of the first psychology to rethink their conclusions and their experimental methods . . .*

However, he advocates a return to the early decades of psychology, particularly Wundt's *Volkerpsychologie* (see Chapter 10). Wundt argued that the methods of natural science could only be applied to the most elementary, universal, and therefore timeless, aspects of human behaviour. Genetic (historical and developmental) methods are needed to study culturally mediated and historically dependent 'higher psychological processes'. He seemed to have anticipated modern objections to cross-cultural research even before the first such study was conducted. But the road Wundt advocated was not taken – that is,

> *. . . the road along which culture is placed on a level with biology and society in shaping individual human natures. The name correctly given to that enterprise is cultural psychology, a major late twentieth-century manifestation of the second psychology.*

> (Cole, 1996)

The biases of mainstream psychology: emphasizing similarities

It has become almost a standing joke that experimental (social) psychology is really the psychology of the American undergraduate/psychology major. Apart from their accessibility, the main argument used to justify the practice of studying mostly student behaviour is based upon a sweeping *universalist assumption*: since we are all human, we are all fundamentally alike in significant psychological functions, and cultural/social contexts of diversity do not affect the important 'deep' or 'hardwired' structures of the mind. The corollary of this assumption is that the categories and standards developed on western European and North American populations are suitable for 'measuring', understanding, and evaluating the characteristics of other populations.

By contrast, a genuinely transcultural psychology ('the interplay between the individual and society and [symbolic] culture' (Kakar, 1982, in Much, 1995)) would base its categories, discriminations and generalizations upon empirical knowledge of the fullest possible range of existing human forms of life, without privileging one form as the norm or standard for evaluation. This is related to the emic–etic distinction (see below).

131

CCP (despite the criticism from (trans)cultural psychologists) is important because it helps to correct the fundamental ethnocentrism within psychology as a whole (including social psychology, which 'ought to know better'). This refers to the strong human tendency to define 'reality' by using our own ethnic/cultural group's norms and values to define what's 'natural' and 'correct' for everyone (Triandis, 1990).

Psychology as a discipline has been largely dominated by psychologists from the USA, the UK and other western cultures, and the large majority of participants in psychological research have been members of those same cultures.

> *Historically, both researchers and subjects in social psychological studies have shared a lifestyle and value system that differs not only from that of most other people in North America, such as ethnic minorities and women, but also the vast majority of people in the rest of the world.*
>
> (Moghaddam et al., 1993)

Yet the findings from this research, and the theories based upon it, have been applied to *people in general*, as if culture makes no difference. An implicit, assumed, equation is made between 'human being' and 'human being from western culture', and this is commonly referred to as the *Anglocentric* or *Eurocentric bias*.

When members of other cultural groups have been studied, it has usually been so that they can be compared with western samples, using the behaviour and experience of the latter as the standard. (This is an exact parallel to the masculinist or androcentric bias in mainstream psychology, whereby men's behaviour and experience have been taken, by male psychologists, as the standard against which women have been judged; see Chapter 6.)

In both cases (the Anglocentric and masculinist biases), the failure to recognize and acknowledge the bias creates the misleading and false impression that what's being said about behaviour can be generalized without qualification. Cross-cultural psychologists do not equate 'human being' with 'member of western culture' because, for them, cultural background is the crucial independent variable.

Smith and Bond (1998) analysed the best-selling US social psychology textbook (Baron and Byrne, 1994) and the best-known European social psychology text (Hewstone *et al.*, 1996), to see in which countries the studies referred to were carried out. In the former, a full 94 per cent are American, and even in the latter 75 per cent are American. The same figures apply to another widely used text, written by social psychologists from Australia and New Zealand (Hogg and Vaughan, 1995). In all three cases, all but 2–3 per cent of the non-American studies were conducted outside western Europe, Australia or New Zealand. This means that only about 10 per cent of the world's population is being sampled (Smith and Bond, 1998).

While this may not be a problem in, say, physics, it very definitely is in the study of behaviour (particularly social behaviour). Instead of an objective, universal account of behaviour, what is presented is a predominantly North American, and to a lesser degree European, picture of human behaviour!

This is not to say that the search for universal principles of human behaviour is, in itself, invalid; it is certainly consistent with the 'classical' view of natural science, according to which the scientist's ultimate goal is to discover laws of nature, to which there are no exceptions (see Chapters 3 and 10). Furthermore, if universal principles of behaviour are to be found, they can be found by anyone, regardless of race, gender or social class. But this could only be achieved if the researchers adopted a non-ethnocentric approach. Unfortunately,

> *. . . ethnocentrism, involving a belief in the superiority of one's own cultural group, has influenced research in social psychology so that even some of the most established findings in social psychology do not stand up to the test when assessed in cultures outside North America . . .*
>
> (Moghaddam et al., 1993)

Some examples of these apparent social psychological 'facts' are considered later in the chapter.

WHAT IS THIS THING CALLED CULTURE?

Based on Herskovits (1948), culture is usually defined as the 'man-made part of the environment' (Segall *et al.*, 1999), or (more politically correctly) the 'human-made part of the environment' (Moghaddam *et al.*, 1993). According to Triandis (1990), it has two major aspects: *objective* (e.g. roads, bridges, cooking pots and military weapons, musical symphonies and poetry – examples given by Moghaddam *et al.*) and *subjective* (e.g. beliefs, attitudes, norms, roles and values). The examples of objective aspects suggest that this category should be subdivided into *physical/material* and *social/non-material*.

So, culture is the part of the environment made by humans. But, in turn, culture helps to 'make' humans:

> *In essence, humans have an interactive relationship with culture: we create and shape culture, and are in turn influenced by our own cultural products.*
>
> *(Moghaddam* et al.*, 1993)*

While our culture is already 'there' when we arrive in the world (we are born into our culture), this does not mean that it is static. Jahoda (1978) cites the famous geneticist, Waddington, who referred to culture as an 'information-transmitting system', which provides humans with an evolutionary system distinct from the biological one governing the animal world:

> *There is no evidence that our Stone Age ancestors were biologically very different from modern man, and most of the vast transformations that have taken place appear to have been the outcome of cultural evolution which is social rather than genetically transmitted . . .*
>
> *(Jahoda, 1978)*

Of course, the rate of cultural evolution is far greater in some societies than others. A common distinction is made between western culture, which is characterized by very rapid change (of both material and social/non-material aspects), and traditional (non-western) culture, where the rate of change is very much slower. In turn, 'traditional' has come to mean something like 'resistant to the influence of western culture', but this seems to be a matter of degree only: nowhere is immune from western influence.

Broadly speaking, 'culture' can refer to groups of nations (e.g. the USA, Canada and all the member states of the European Community, are 'western') or a single one, or it can refer to sub-units (or subcultures) within a nation, such as tribes, social classes and castes. Rohner (1984, in Smith and Bond, 1998) makes the important distinction between culture and social system. The former refers to an organized system of meanings that members attribute to the persons, objects and events comprising that culture, while the latter refers to the behaviours found within a culture. Society is defined as:

> *the largest unit of a territorially bounded, multi-generational population, recruited largely through sexual reproduction, and organized around a common culture and a common social system.*
> *(Rohner, in Smith and Bond, 1998)*

This definition acknowledges the degree to which culture and social system are interwoven.

Much cross-cultural research is in fact based on 'national cultures', which, of course, often comprise a number of separate subcultures. These may be demarcated by religion (as in Northern Ireland), by language (as in Belgium) or by race (as in Malaysia and Singapore). But studies in this area often provide little more detail about the participants than the name of the country (national culture) in which the study was conducted.

According to Smith and Bond (1998), this involves two 'penalties'. First, when we compare national cultures we can lose track of the enormous *diversity* found within many of the major nations of the world, and differences found between any two countries might well also be found between carefully selected subcultures

Figure 8.1 The national culture of Northern Ireland is dominated by the subculture of religion

within those countries. Second, there is the danger of implying that national cultures are unitary systems, free of conflict, confusion and dissent. This, of course, is rarely the case.

So, if we should distinguish between culture and country/national culture, how can we define 'culture'? Or, as Brislin (1993) puts it, what are the fundamental features of culture? Brislin proposes a checklist of 12 features (see Box 8.2), some of which overlap with the definitions we have already considered.

Since Brislin's checklist is to do with the fundamental features of culture, the emphasis is on what different cultures have *in common*. Only point 12 relates to differences between cultures; one way of trying to distinguish between cultures is to see how the concept of time is used and understood in different cultures (see Gross, 2003). However, as important as it is, time represents a fairly specific feature of cultural life. Are there any more general features or dimensions that can help us to understand the differences between cultures?

BOX 8.2 A CHECKLIST OF FUNDAMENTAL FEATURES OF CULTURE

1 Culture consists of ideas, values and assumptions about life that guide specific behaviour.
2 Culture consists of those aspects of the environment that people make. (But people's responses to aspects of the environment that are *natural*, such as the climate, also constitute part of the environment.)
3 Culture is transmitted from generation to generation, with the responsibility being given to parents, teachers, religious leaders and other respected elders in a community.
4 There will be childhood experiences that many people in a community remember happening to them.
5 Aspects of one's culture are not commonly discussed by adults; since culture is widely shared and accepted, there is little reason to.
6 Culture can become clearest in well-meaning clashes – that is, interactions among people from very different backgrounds. Each may behave quite 'normally' as far as their own culture is concerned, but not as judged by the other culture.
7 Culture allows people to 'fill in the blanks' when presented with a basic sketch of familiar behaviours or situations.
8 Cultural values remain despite compromises and slip-ups. Even though we can list exceptions, the cultural value is seen as a constant that continues to guide specific behaviours.
9 People react emotionally when cultural values are violated, or when a culture's expected behaviours are ignored.
10 There can be both acceptance and rejection of a culture's values at different times in a person's life. For example, rebellious adolescents and young adults come to accept a culture's expectations after having children of their own.
11 When changes in cultural values are contemplated, people are likely to react by saying, 'This will be difficult and time-consuming.' In other words, people tend to resist cultural change.
12 When comparing proper and expected behaviour across cultures, it's possible to observe certain sharply contrasting beliefs or orientations; for example, the treatment of time, and the clarity of rules or norms for certain complex behaviours.

(Based on Brislin, 1993)

Dimensions of cultural difference

Two very useful attempts to identify the key dimensions in terms of which cultures differ, allowing them to be compared, are those of Hofstede (1980) and Triandis (1990). For Hofstede (1980), culture is 'the collective programming of the mind which distinguishes the members of one group from another'. He conducted a large-scale study of several thousand IBM employees in 40 different countries, and identified four dimensions:

1 *power distance*: the amount of respect and deference shown by those in both superior and subordinate positions
2 *uncertainty avoidance*: the focus on planning and stability as ways of dealing with life's uncertainties
3 *individualism–collectivism*: whether one's identity is defined by personal choices and achievements (*individualism*) or by characteristics of the collective groups to which one is more or less permanently attached (*collectivism*)
4 *masculinity–femininity*: the relative emphasis on achievement (*masculinity*) or interpersonal harmony (*femininity*).

When a culture is described as, say, collectivist, we do not mean that any two members of the culture must be equally collectivist, or that either one of them must necessarily be more collectivist than someone from an individualist culture. We are looking at the mean score of a large number of individual scores, such that a collectivist culture displays collectivism to a greater degree than individualism, and more than an individualist culture does. These are *dimensions* rather than categories or types; it is the manifestation of these characteristics and behaviours *relative* to each other and relative to other cultures that matters (see Figure 8.2).

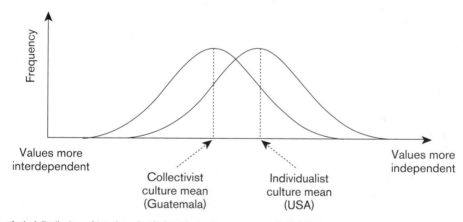

Figure 8.2 Hypothetical distributions of interdependent/independent value scores in a collectivist and an individualist national culture

In 1983, Hofstede expanded his sample to include 50 national cultures, although he omitted the former Soviet Bloc countries, as well as most of Africa. However, in terms of global coverage, his study is unrivalled, and the individualism–collectivism dimension has attracted many cross-cultural researchers in recent years (Smith and Bond, 1998).

Cultural syndromes

One of these cross-cultural researchers is Triandis, who replicated some of Hofstede's results with 15 samples from different parts of the world (Triandis *et al.*, 1986, in Triandis, 1990). Triandis sees 'culture' as comprising *cultural syndromes*, which he defines as 'a pattern of values, attitudes, beliefs, norms and behaviours that can be used to contrast a group of cultures to another group of cultures'. Three major cultural syndromes are *cultural complexity*, *individualism–collectivism* and *tight vs loose cultures*.

Cultural complexity

The more complex the culture, the more people must pay attention to time, which is one of the examples given by Brislin (1993; see above). This is related to the number and diversity of roles that members of the culture typically play: the more numerous and diverse the roles, the more important it is that time be allocated in an appropriate way.

Cultures that are more industrialized and technological, such as Japan, Sweden and the USA, tend to be more focused on time. To this extent, therefore, more industrialized and technological cultures are more complex cultures. The concept of time also differs between cultures. Typically, in the West, time is seen as linear (it 'travels' in a straight line, from past, through present, to future), while in many non-western cultures it is seen as circular (it occurs in recurring cycles).

Another feature of complexity is specificity vs diffusion: the more complex, the more specific roles become. For example, because of the role of religion in certain cultures (e.g. the Arab world in general, and Iran), a person's religion is a major determinant of his/her social behaviour. But in western cultures, there is a fairly clear demarcation between the religious and the non-religious (i.e. the secular).

Individualism vs collectivism

Triandis believes that this is the most promising of the many dimensions of cultural variation that have been proposed, in the sense of being the most likely to account for a great deal of social behaviour. As we saw earlier, people in every culture have both types of tendency, but the relative emphasis in the West is towards individualism, and in the East towards collectivism.

When Triandis *et al.* (1986, see Triandis, 1990) replicated some of Hofstede's findings, they found four additional factors related to the main construct. Family integrity (e.g. 'children should live at home with their parents until they get married') and interdependence (e.g. 'I like to live close to my good friends') are both related to collectivism, while self-reliance with hedonism (e.g. 'if the group is slowing me down, it's better to leave it and work alone; the most important thing in my life is to make myself happy') and separation from in-groups (indicated by agreement with items showing that what happens to extended family members is of little concern) are both related to individualism. Other 'defining attributes' (Triandis, 1990) include the following:

- *Collectivists* pay much more attention to an identifiable in-group and behave differently towards members of that group compared with out-group members. The in-group can best be defined by the common fate of members; often, it is the unit of survival, or the food community, so that if there is no food, all in-group members starve together. In most cultures, the family is the main in-group, but in some the tribe or country can be just as important, and in still others, the work group (e.g. Japan), reflecting the incredible economic success enjoyed by that culture.
- For *collectivists*, in-group goals have primacy over individual goals. For *individualist* cultures, it is the other way round, and the former often perceive the latter as 'selfish'.
- *Collectivists'* behaviour is regulated largely by in-group norms, while that of *individualists* is regulated largely by personal likes and dislikes and cost–benefit analyses. Thus for 'traditional' behaviours, such as having children, *norms* (which have an *outward-looking*, group reference) should be more important in collectivist cultures, while *attitudes* (which have an *inward-looking*, personal reference) should be more important in individualist cultures. Lower-class groups, in most societies, are more collectivist than upper-class groups.
- *Collectivists* emphasize social hierarchy much more than *individualists*; usually the father is 'head of the household' and women are generally subordinate.
- *Collectivists* emphasize harmony and 'saving face'. They favour homogeneous in-groups, in which there are no internal disagreements, so that a 'united front' is shown to out-groups. But in *individualist* cultures, disagreements within the in-group are acceptable and often help to 'clear the air'.

- *Collectivist* cultures stress in-group fate and achievement, and interdependence within it. Self-reliance implies 'I'm not a burden on the in-group', while in *individualist* cultures it conveys 'I can do my own thing'. There is generally much more emotional detachment from the larger in-group in individualist cultures.

- For *collectivists*, the self is an appendage, or extension, of the in-group, while for *individualists* it is a separate and distinct entity (see Chapter 3). When asked to complete statements that begin 'I am', collectivists typically give more in-group-related answers (e.g. 'I am a son', 'I am a Roman Catholic'), while individualists typically give more personal-attribute answers (e.g. 'I am kind', 'I am hard-working'). In *collectivist* cultures, people usually belong to a small number of in-groups that influence them significantly; but in *individualist* cultures, behaviour is rarely greatly influenced by any one in-group in particular, because there are usually so many, and they often make conflicting demands on the individual.

- In *collectivist* cultures, *vertical relationships* (e.g. parent–child) take priority over *horizontal relationships* (e.g. spouse–spouse) when there's conflict between them. The reverse is true in *individualist* cultures. *Collectivists* stress family integrity, security, obedience and conformity, whereas *individualists* stress achievement, pleasure and competition. Consistent with these differences, *individualist* cultures use child-rearing methods that encourage autonomy and self-reliance, while *collectivist* cultures encourage children to be obedient and dutiful, and to make sacrifices for the in-group.

Roughly speaking, *capitalist* politico-economic systems are associated with *individualism*, and *socialist* societies are associated with *collectivism*. There is also evidence which shows that urban environments, compared with rural ones, within the same societies, seem to encourage competitiveness, one of the major features of individualism (Smith and Bond, 1998).

Tight vs loose cultures

In *tight* cultures, people are expected to behave according to clearly defined norms, and there is little tolerance of deviation from those norms; in *loose* cultures, there is a good deal of freedom to deviate. (This is relevant to the whole question of normality/abnormality, including mental disorder: see Chapter 7.)

The concept of tightness has much in common with Hofstede's (high) uncertainty avoidance (see above). Japan is the prototype of a tight culture (although tightness is not a feature of every aspect of social life), and Thailand is the prototype of a loose culture. Tightness is also associated with cultural homogeneity – that is, there is very little mixing of ethnic groups from a variety of cultural backgrounds, and the culture is relatively 'pure'. By contrast, looseness is associated with cultural heterogeneity. Hofstede found evidence of looseness (low uncertainty avoidance) in Hong Kong and Singapore, two cultures in which East (China) meets West (Britain).

In addition to these three major dimensions of cultural diversity, Triandis (1990) discusses three more specific dimensions.

1 *Masculinity vs femininity* is also one of Hofstede's four main dimensions, which he described in terms of work-related goals (Japan is masculine and Sweden feminine). There is an interesting similarity between masculinity and *individualism*, on the one hand, and femininity and *collectivism* on the other. *Masculine* cultures stress getting the job done, achievement, progress, advancement, and being strong and effective, while *feminine* cultures stress quality of life, good interpersonal relationships, nurturing, concern for others, and being kind and caring (see Chapter 6).

2 Regarding *emotional control vs emotional expressiveness,* in cultures such as Japan, where people are expected to express mostly pleasant emotions (even in unpleasant situations), people do very well in controlling their emotions, By contrast, in cultures such as southern Europe, where people are not expected to control their emotions, they often feel good about expressing themselves openly.

There is some evidence that people in Africa, and places near Africa, express their emotions freely, and that the further people live from where human beings first developed, the more emotional control they have. If human beings originated in Africa (a widely held belief among anthropologists), then as they migrated to remote corners of the world, they had to learn to control the unfriendly environments they encountered – and themselves. Self-control became a value, and emotional control was a manifestation of that value.

3 *Contact vs no-contact cultures* refers to cultural differences in terms of what Hall (1959, 1966) called *proxemic rules*. These prescribe the amount of physical distance between people in everyday interactions, according to the situation and the relationship between the people involved. How close we are 'allowed' to sit or stand next to others (particularly strangers) constitutes an important feature of non-verbal communication. Misunderstandings between members of different cultural groups (and unfavourable first impressions) can arise from a failure to appreciate the appropriate proxemic rules that apply on a particular occasion.

Table 8.1 Major dimensions of cultural difference

Power distance	Hofstede (1980)
Uncertainty avoidance	Hofstede (1980)
Tight vs loose cultures	Triandis (1990)
	Triandis et al. (1986)
Individualism–Collectivism	Hofstede (1980)
	Triandis (1990)
	Triandis et al. (1986)
Masculinity–Femininity	Hofstede (1980)
	Triandis (1990)
	Triandis et al. (1986)
Cultural complexity	Triandis (1990)
	Triandis et al. (1986)
Emotional control vs emotional expressiveness	Triandis (1990)
	Triandis et al. (1986)
Contact vs no-contact cultures	Triandis (1990)
	Triandis et al. (1986)

DOING CROSS-CULTURAL RESEARCH: CONCEPTUAL AND METHODOLOGICAL ISSUES

The emic–etic distinction

As we have seen, CCP (like psychology as a whole) involves the study by (mostly) members of one cultural group (western psychologists) of members of non-western cultural populations. This perhaps makes it inevitable (even if it doesn't make it justifiable) that, when a western psychologist studies members of some other culture, s/he will use theories and measuring instruments developed in the 'home' culture. These can be used for studying both cross-cultural differences *and* universal aspects of human behaviour. For example, aggression is a cultural universal – but *how it is expressed* may be culturally specific.

Similarly, there are good reasons for believing that a mental disorder such as schizophrenia is universal, with core symptoms found in a wide range of cultural groups, but also with culture-specific factors influencing the form the symptoms take, the specific reasons for the onset of the illness, and the likely outcome of the illness (the prognosis) (Brislin, 1993: see Chapter 7).

The distinction between culture-specific and universal behaviour is one version of what has come to be known in cross-cultural psychology as the emic–etic distinction. This also refers to problems inherent in the cross-cultural use of instruments developed in a single culture (Segall *et al.*, 1999).

BOX 8.3 THE EMIC–ETIC DISTINCTION

The terms 'emic' and 'etic' are based on the distinction made in linguistics between *phonemics* (the study of sounds as they contribute to the meaning of a language) and *phonetics* (the study of universal sounds used in human language, independently of their relationship to meaning) (Pike, 1954).

As applied to the study of cultures, *etics* refers to *culturally general concepts*, which are easier to understand (because, by definition, they are common to all cultures), while *emics* refers to *culturally specific concepts*, which include all the ways that specific cultures deal with etics. It is the emics of another culture that are often so difficult to understand (Brislin, 1993).

According to Pike (1954), the terms should be thought of as referring to two different viewpoints regarding the study of behaviour: the etic approach studies behaviour from *outside* a particular cultural system, and the emic approach studies behaviour from the *inside* (Segall *et al.*, 1999).

While both viewpoints represent part of CCP, does the distinction help us to understand how research is actually carried out? According to Berry (1969), research has to begin somewhere and, inevitably, this usually involves an instrument or observational technique rooted in the researcher's own culture (an emic for that culture). When such an emic is brought in from an outside culture, is assumed to be valid in the alien culture and so is seen as a valid way of comparing the two cultures, an imposed etic is being used (Berry, 1969).

Many attempts to replicate American studies in other parts of the world involve an imposed etic; they all assume that the situation being studied has the same meaning for members of the alien culture as it does for members of the researcher's own culture (Smith and Bond, 1998). The number of failures to replicate the findings obtained using American samples illustrates very clearly that this assumption is often false! (Some examples of such failures are discussed at the end of the chapter.)

An (imposed) etic approach is more likely to be used, since the researcher brings with him/her ready-made theories and measuring instruments in an attempt to identify universal behavioural patterns. But this is also the approach that involves the danger of the researchers imposing their own cultural biases and theoretical framework on the behaviour of people from a different cultural group. The danger is that the biases and framework may simply not 'fit' the phenomena being studied, resulting in their distortion.

Brislin (1993) gives the example of 'raising responsible children' as an etic, and 'encouraging independent thinking' as an emic designed to achieve it. While the etic may be reasonable (relevant to all cultures), it is simply wrong to believe that the emic will also be: different cultures may use very different means to achieve the same goal. We cannot simply assume that 'one's own emics are part of the culturally common etic'. This is, of course, an imposed etic.

Another example is the concept of intelligence. Brislin suggests that the etic is 'solving problems, the exact form of which hasn't been seen before', a definition likely to be generally acceptable across cultures (partly because it is at least consistent with the fact that what constitutes a 'problem' differs from culture to culture). However, is the emic of 'mental quickness' (for example, as measured by timed IQ tests) universally valid? Among the Baganda people of Uganda, intelligence is associated with slow, careful, deliberate thought (Wober, 1974, in Brislin, 1993), nor is it necessarily valid for all schoolchildren within a culturally diverse country like the USA (Brislin, 1993).

Some possible solutions to the 'imposed etic' problem

Instead of using imposed etic measures, Berry (1969) outlines a strategy for reaching a more valid set of *derived etic* generalizations; this strategy basically consists of a number of parallel emic studies within a series of national cultures. This focuses on culture-specific phenomena, such as the behaviours, values, customs and traditions of the particular national cultures included. This is the approach typically used in ethnographic anthropological research (*ethnography* being 'fieldwork'), which provides a rich source of information about the culture, which can then be used as a basis for CCP (Berry *et al.*, 1992). Typically, participant observation is used, together with local people serving as informed observers, as well as local test construction, in an attempt to tap the culture's own indigenous system of classification or 'subjective culture' (Triandis, 1972).

If the 'subjective cultures' of different national cultures show similarities (there is a convergence between the results obtained within each culture), we can be more confident that we have identified processes that are equivalent, and we are in a position to make a derived etic generalization, at least with regard to the particular cultures that have been sampled (Smith and Bond, 1998).

The problem of equivalence

The emic–etic distinction implies that social psychology cannot discover cultural universals unless it adopts a cross-cultural approach. The methods used by psychologists need to be adapted, so that researchers can study the same processes in different cultures (Moghaddam *et al.*, 1993).

But how do we know that we are studying the same processes? What does 'same' mean in this context? For Brislin (1993), the question is: 'Do the concepts being investigated, and especially the way the concepts are being measured, have the same meaning in the different cultures?' He describes three approaches that have been used to deal with this fundamental issue of equivalence: translation, conceptual and metric.

Translation equivalence

Discovering whether concepts can be easily expressed in the languages of the different cultures being studied represents a first step in dealing with the issue of equivalence. If material does not translate well, this might be because emic aspects are involved with which the translators are unfamiliar. Alternatively, there may not be readily available terms in the language to capture certain aspects of the concept being translated.

A common method used in trying to overcome this problem is *back-translation*. The material in the original language (usually English) is carefully prepared (e.g. a questionnaire on child-rearing practices), then a bilingual person translates it into the target language. A second bilingual person (unfamiliar with the efforts of the first) then translates it from the target language (back) into English. The two English versions are then examined in order to see what 'comes through' clearly. If the two English versions are equivalent, it is assumed that the target-language version is adequate. By studying the back-translated original-language (English) version, researchers can gain insights into what can and cannot easily be expressed in the target language (see Figure 8.3).

Conceptual equivalence

The material that proceeds smoothly through the multiple steps of back-translation is said to be *translation equivalent*. *Conceptual equivalence* begins with the assumption that there will probably be different aspects of a concept that serve the same purpose in different cultures. This often begins by identifying the etic aspects, followed by a further identification of the emic aspects related to the etic in the various cultures being studied.

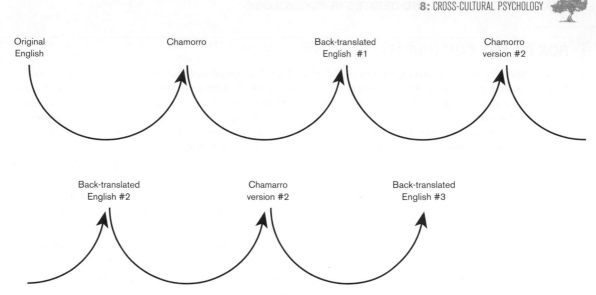

Figure 8.3 An example of back-translation between English and Chamorro (the native language of Guam, an island in the northern Pacific) (From Brislin, *Understanding Culture's Influence on Behavior*, 1E. © 1993 Wadsworth, a part of Cengage Learning, Inc. Reproduced by permission. www.cengage.com/permissions)

To take an earlier example, the etic for 'intelligence' might be 'solving problems the exact form of which haven't been seen before', while the emic might include 'mental quickness' (USA and western Europe), 'slow, careful, deliberate thought' (the Baganda people of Uganda: Wober, 1974), and 'responsibility to the community (getting along well with others)' (the Chi-Chewa people of Zambia: Serpell, 1982).

All these emics are conceptually equivalent – that is, they all form part of the definition of intelligence as used by respected adults in the various cultures, and might be elicited by asking such adults, 'Which young people in your community are considered intelligent?'

Metric equivalence

While conceptual equivalence centres on the analysis of different behaviours that can all demonstrate the same general concept, *metric equivalence* centres on the analysis of the same concepts across cultures, based on the assumption that the same scale (after proper translation procedures have been carried out) can be used to measure the concept.

For example, after careful translation, an IQ test produces a score of, say, 120 for an American woman and for a woman in Chile. The assumption is that the intelligence scale (metric) is measuring exactly the same concept (intelligence) in the two countries, and that a score in one country can be directly compared with that in another. But even if translation has been carried out satisfactorily, this is no guarantee of conceptual equivalence and, surely, this is the most important criterion by which to assess the cross-cultural equivalence of an IQ test (as well as being a requirement for metric equivalence). While translation equivalence has actually been used in cross-cultural research (and isn't particularly controversial), conceptual and metric equivalence are largely theoretical and are much more controversial (they beg more questions than they answer).

Even if conceptual equivalence can be established, there remains the question of who constructs the test – a western psychologist (in which case the test must be translated, still begging the question of metric equivalence) or a local test constructor (which removes the need for translation). In either case, we seem to be left with the question of whether the test is culture-fair.

BOX 8.4 ARE CULTURE-FAIR TESTS POSSIBLE?

According to Frijda and Jahoda (1966, in Segall *et al.*, 1999), a culture-fair test could: (i) be a set of items that are equally unfamiliar to all possible persons in all possible cultures, so that everyone would have an equal chance of passing (or failing) the items; or (ii) comprise multiple sets of items, modified for use in each culture to ensure that each version of the test would contain the same degree of familiarity. This would give members of each culture about the same chance of being successful with their respective version. While (i) is a virtual impossibility, (ii) is possible in theory, but in practice very difficult to construct.

Clearly, culturally mediated experience always interacts with a test's content to influence test performance.

The root of all measurement problems in cross-cultural research is the possibility that the same behaviours may have different meanings across cultures or that the same processes may have different overt manifestations. As a result, the 'same' test, be it a psychometric one or another type of instrument, might be 'different' when applied in different cultures. Therefore the effort to devise culturally fair testing procedures will probably never be completely successful. The degree to which we are measuring the same thing in more than one culture, whether we are using the same or different test items, must always worry us.

(Segall et al., 1999)

The view that 'tests of ability are inevitably cultural devices' (Cole, 1985) is related to Segall *et al.*'s claim that the 'same' test might actually be 'different' when applied across cultures. What none of the three types of equivalence takes into account is the *meaning of the experience of taking an intelligence test* (what we could perhaps call 'experiential equivalence'). Taking tests of various kinds is a familiar experience for members of western culture, both within and outside the educational context, but what about cultures in which there is no generally available schooling? How can we measure intelligence independently of people's responses to taking the test itself? The very nature or form of the tasks involved in an intelligence test (as distinct from the content) has a cultural meaning, as illustrated by Glick's report of research with the Kpelle people (1975, in Rogoff and Morelli, 1989).

Participants were asked to sort 20 objects into groups. They did this by using functional groups (e.g. knife with orange, potato with hoe), instead of category groups, which the experimenter thought more appropriate. When their way of classifying the objects was challenged, they often explained that this was how a wise man would do it. 'When an exasperated experimenter asked finally, "How would a fool do it?", he was given back sorts of the type that were initially expected – four neat piles with food in one, tools in another, and so on' (Glick, 1975, in Rogoff and Morelli, 1989).

This is a kind of 'putting two fingers up' at the researcher for being ethnocentric, imposing an etic, and making culturally inappropriate assumptions. Being asked to perform a task outside its usual context (from practical to abstract) could so easily produce the conclusion that the people being studied lack the basic ability to classify, when it is the inappropriateness of the task that is at fault.

Advantages of cross-cultural research

It has become almost a truism among cross-cultural researchers that the development of concepts and theories of human behaviour demands that behaviour be studied all over the world. This might seem like common sense, but we have seen already in this chapter that psychologists often appear to believe it is perfectly legitimate to investigate behaviour in one culture (or using one gender: see Chapter 6) and then generalize to other cultures (or to the other gender).

Highlighting implicit assumptions

An important function of cross-cultural research is to allow investigators to look closely at the impact of their own belief systems ('folk psychology') on scientific theories and research paradigms. When participants and researchers are from the same population, interpretations of the behaviour under investigation may be constrained by implicit cultural assumptions.

Working with people from a quite different background can make us aware of aspects of human activity that we normally would not notice, either because they are missing in the 'new' culture, or because they are arranged differently. In this way, we become aware of our assumptions, helping us recognize that human functioning cannot be separated from its contexts, both cultural and more immediate (Rogoff and Morelli, 1989). The case of the Kpelle being asked to sort objects is an insightful (and very amusing) example of this.

Separating behaviour from context

One consequence of researchers being unable to stand back from their own cultural experience is that, when studying behaviour within their own culture, they tend to focus on the behaviour rather than on the situation or context. This results in the *fundamental attribution error* (FAE: Ross, 1977) – that is, seeing the behaviour as reflecting the personal dispositions of the actor (see Chapter 4). The researchers are so familiar with these situations and contexts that it's difficult for them to appreciate the impact they have on behaviour. For example, researchers comparing minority-group children in the USA with mainstream children often assume that mainstream (white, middle-class) skills and upbringing are normal and superior. This results in a 'deficit model' view of minority groups, who are seen as needing intervention to compensate for their deficiencies (Rogoff and Morelli, 1989).

However, when studying other cultures, it may be far easier to make this separation of behaviour from situational context, since many situations will be new, unfamiliar and fresh in their eyes (Brislin, 1993). This increased sensitivity to context may help to counteract the ethnocentrism found when studying minority groups within the researcher's own national culture.

Extending the range of variables

Studying members of only one culture, or a small number and range of cultures, limits the range of variables and concepts that can be explored. For example, trying to find out what effect having a television set in the home has on school achievement is very difficult to do just by studying American or British samples, since the vast majority of families have (at least) one!

Again, research suggests that members of *individualist* cultures (which includes the vast majority of psychologists) are much more likely to explain behaviour in terms of personality traits (and so see behaviour as consistent across situations), while those from *collectivist* cultures use a more complex analysis, whereby the same person may act differently in different situations (e.g. Schweder, 1991, in Brislin, 1993). The point here is that, if only individualist cultures were studied, we would regard the explanation of behaviour as reflecting personality traits as a universal tendency (Brislin, 1993; see Chapter 4).

Figure 8.4 A researcher would have to go a long way to find a corner of the Earth which did not have access to television

Separating variables

Cross-cultural research can also help to separate out the effects of variables that may usually be confounded within a particular culture. According to Rogoff and Morelli (1989):

> *Cross-cultural research . . . allows psychologists to use cultural variation as a natural laboratory to attempt to disentangle variables that are difficult to tease apart in the US and to study conditions that are rare in the US.*

For example, how do gender differences manifest themselves under different cultural conditions? To what extent is cognitive development a function of schooling as distinct from age (two variables that cannot be separated where schooling is freely available and compulsory)?

A very famous example is Freud's theory of the Oedipus complex, as it applies to little boys: the son experiences extreme jealousy of his father (over the father's 'possession' of the mother) and at the same time extreme fear of the father (who is more powerful and, in the child's view, will punish him by castration if he continues to compete with the father for the mother's affections). Among the Trobriand islanders of the South Pacific, Malinowski (1929) found that the mother's brother, not the child's father, is the major figure of authority, although the father continues to have a normal sexual relationship with the mother. Under these circumstances, sons tend to have a very good relationship with their father, free of the love–hate ambivalence Freud saw as an inevitable feature of the Oedipus complex. But the relationship with the uncle is not usually so good.

What this suggests is that not only is the Oedipus complex not universal, as Freud claimed it was, but that sexual jealousy and rivalry, as a major component in the whole 'family drama', may play a much less important role than he believed.

Testing theories

Finally, a major function of cross-cultural research is to test out theories developed in the West, in order to see whether they apply to other cultural groups. Most of the major theories within psychology, such as those of Freud and Piaget, are meant to be universal, but we've just considered one example of a cross-cultural study that casts doubt on one of the fundamental elements of Freud's psychosexual theory of personality.

While the USA is still the world centre of psychology, and of social psychology in particular, some of the models of social behaviour that have come out of the USA may have little relevance or appeal in a different cultural context. For example, Thibaut and Kelley's (1959) analysis of social relationships in terms of the exchange of rewards is a:

> *. . . kind of rational, market-based model . . . [which] is shaped by the values of middle-class, US culture, and often it is only when people from other backgrounds become familiar with middle-class, US culture that such models make sense to them.*
>
> (Moghaddam et al., 1993)

Since the late 1960s, European social psychology has developed its own character, with Tajfel (regarded generally as the 'father' of European social psychology) and Harré in England, Moscovici in France and Doise in Switzerland among the leading figures. It 's become more social than its American counterpart: there 's a greater focus on larger societal issues, such as intergroup relations, unemployment and ideology (Moghaddam et al., 1993).

Festinger's (1957) cognitive dissonance theory has generated an enormous amount of research and theorizing in America (see Gross, 2005), but it does not explain behaviour very well in some non-western cultures, including Japan. For example, how well a person handles a supposed 'inconsistency' is considered a sign of maturity and broad-mindedness. Japanese children are brought up to accept inconsistency, whereas the focus of the theory is on how people attempt to reduce the dissonance that results from perceived inconsistencies.

According to one estimate, only about 13 per cent of all the research reported in the leading American journals of social psychology are field studies. Because these are conducted in contexts that are culturally richer than laboratory studies, we need to be even more attentive to the role of cultural factors when interpreting the results (Moghaddam *et al.*, 1993). A good example of this is the famous 'Robber's Cave' experiment of intergroup conflict involving boys at a summer camp in America (Sherif *et al.*, 1961). The very fact that it was conducted in this setting is significant, since boys' summer camps play a certain role in North American culture not found elsewhere.

The study also illustrates the importance of taking into account what the participants see as the appropriateness of different types of behaviour in certain settings. The boys interpreted the situation as one where both competition and cooperation for scarce resources were appropriate; which strategy was used depended on which best served their material interests (e.g. they competed for the knives awarded to the winners of the tournament, but cooperated by, literally, pulling together to get their bus out of the mud). Such interpretations have a cultural bias (Moghaddam *et al.*, 1993. See Box 8.5).

BOX 8.5 NON-AMERICAN REPLICATIONS OF THE ROBBER'S CAVE FIELD EXPERIMENT

Diab (1970, in Smith and Bond, 1998) replicated this study in Lebanon and tried to follow the procedure used by Sherif *et al.* as closely as possible (using a summer-camp setting, with 11-year-old boys, and the same planned stages of group formation, intergroup competition and, finally, group cooperation).

Two randomly created groups of nine (Muslims and Christians in each group) developed very different 'cultures': 'The Friends' were warm and cooperative, while 'Red Genie' were highly competitive and stole things from one another, not just from The Friends. It proved impossible to get the two groups to cooperate in stage three (as Sherif *et al.* had managed to do); when Red Genie lost the tournament, they stole the knives, threatened The Friends with them, and tried forcibly to leave the camp. The study had to be abandoned.

Tyerman and Spencer (1983) failed to find any spirit of competition in their replication involving English boy scouts. They point out that the culture of each specific group will depend not just on externally imposed incentives of competition and cooperation but also on established traditions and local cultures that form a background to specific events within each group.

The summer camp is a North American phenomenon, although we could find 'stimulus equivalents' in other cultures. However, the formation of friendships rigidly within one's own age group is more characteristic of industrialized societies, compared with traditional cultures, where friendships tend to be extensions of family networks. Such cultural differences help to explain why it has proved so difficult to replicate Sherif *et al.*'s study outside North America (Moghaddam *et al.*, 1993).

SOME CONCLUDING COMMENTS

As we noted when discussing culture-fair intelligence tests, the participant's familiarity with taking tests of any description, together with his/her concept of a test and understanding of the test situation, are all crucial factors when evaluating test performance. Similarly, the tradition of political polls, consumer surveys and so on cannot be taken for granted when conducting research outside western countries; social science may not be practised at all, or it may be highly politicized.

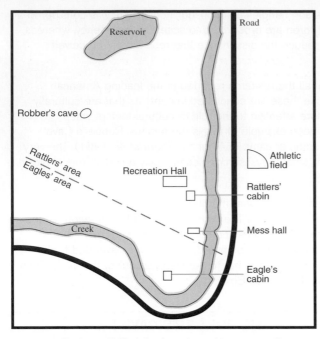

Figure 8.5 The famous 'Robber's Cave' experiment of intergroup conflict involved boys at summer camp in America, a culturally significant factor

These factors make it essential that novel methodologies are developed (instead of questionnaires, laboratory experiments, etc.), relationships with cultural informants are carefully nurtured, and participants carefully trained before data collection begins. The cultural context of 'doing social science' must be thoughtfully assessed by the social scientist to ensure that the outcome of the resulting research has a claim to validity (Smith and Bond, 1998).

But it is not just methods of investigation that may be inappropriate or invalid when used outside the western cultural context from where they've arisen. According to Danziger (1997):

> There is a substantial body of cross-cultural evidence which throws doubt on the universal validity of many of the categories with which the discipline of Psychology has been operating . . . these categories do not occupy some rarefied place above culture but are embedded in a particular professional sub-culture. There is a certain arrogance in taking it for granted that, alone among a myriad alternative ways of speaking about individual action and experience, the language of twentieth century American Psychology accurately reflects the natural and universal structure of the phenomenon we call 'psychological' . . .

SUMMARY

O The concept of culture/cultural differences represents a third level at which the nature–nurture debate takes place, intermediate between (i) the species level and (ii) the individual differences level.

O According to Bronfenbrenner's ecological model, there are four interacting levels: microsystem, mesosystem, exosystem and macrosystem.

O Cross-cultural psychologists study variability in behaviour among societies/cultural groups around the world, as well as the universals of human behaviour. They fall somewhere between the extremes of absolutism (associated with experimental psychology) and anthropology's relativism.

O Learning, in the form of enculturation and socialization, is fundamental to human behaviour.

O Cross-cultural psychology helps to correct ethnocentrism within psychology, whereby an implicit equation is made between 'human being' and 'human being from western culture' (the Anglocentric/Eurocentric bias).

O Culture is usually defined as the man/person-made part of the environment, both the material and non-material/social aspects. Human beings both create culture and are influenced by it.

○ Culture is not static but provides humans with an evolutionary system distinct from the biological system of animals. Cultural evolution is socially rather than genetically transmitted.

○ Much cross-cultural research is based on national cultures (denoted by the name of a country). This obscures the enormous diversity within a national culture and implies that national cultures are unitary, harmonious systems.

○ Hofstede identified four central dimensions of culture: power distance, uncertainty avoidance, individualism–collectivism and masculinity–femininity.

○ Overlapping with these are Triandis's cultural syndromes, namely cultural complexity, individualism–collectivism and tight vs loose cultures. He also discusses three more specific cultural dimensions: masculinity vs femininity, emotional control vs emotional expressiveness, and contact vs no-contact cultures.

○ The distinction between culture-specific/universal behaviour is one version of the emic–etic distinction. Etics refers to culturally general concepts, while emics refers to culturally specific concepts.

○ The etic approach studies behaviour from outside a particular cultural system, while the emic approach studies behaviour from the inside.

○ When western psychologists use an instrument/observational technique from their own culture (an emic for that culture) to study another culture, an imposed etic is being used.

○ An imposed etic approach is involved when attempts to replicate American studies are made in other countries. It assumes that the situation being studied has the same meaning in all the cultures being tested.

○ One solution to the 'imposed etic problem' is to reach a more valid set of derived etic generalizations, by conducting a number of parallel emic studies in a variety of national cultures, focusing on culture-specific phenomena.

○ Psychologists need to adapt their methods so that they study the same processes in different cultures. This raises the fundamental issue of the equivalence of meaning.

○ Three approaches used to deal with this issue are translation equivalence (often using back-translation), conceptual equivalence and metric equivalence. The first is actually used and not particularly controversial, while the other two are largely theoretical proposals and are much more controversial.

○ Cross-cultural research allows investigators to examine the influence of their own beliefs/assumptions, revealing how behaviour cannot be separated from its cultural context and the impact of situational factors.

○ Cross-cultural research expands the range of variables/concepts that can be explored, and allows the separation of the effects of variables that may be confounded within a particular culture.

○ Only by conducting cross-cultural research can western psychologists be sure that their theories and research findings apply outside their own cultural context. Sherif *et al.*'s 'Robber's Cave' experiment has failed the 'replication test' outside North American settings.

○ Research methods need to be made relevant to the particular cultural setting in which they are used, and western psychologists must not assume that their concepts and categories capture the nature of human behaviour and experience in non-western cultures.

USEFUL WEBSITES

http://www.socialpsychology.org/social.htm#cultural
http://www.iupui.edu/#authkb/ewthnocen.htm

RECOMMENDED READING

Brislin, R. (1993) *Understanding Culture's Influence on Behavior.* Orlando. FL: Harcourt Brace Jovanovich.

Cole, M. (1996) *Cultural Psychology: A Once and Future Discipline.* Cambridge, MS: Harvard.

Moghaddam, F.M. (1998) *Social Psychology: Exploring Universals Across Cultures.* New York: W.H. Freeman & Co.

Segall, M.H., Dasen, P.R., Berry, J.W. and Poortinga, Y.H. (1999) *Human Behaviour in Global Perspective: An Introduction to Cross-Cultural Psychology* (2nd edn). Needham Heights, MA: Allyn & Bacon.

Smith, P.B. and Bond, M.H. (1998) *Social Psychology across Cultures* (2nd edn). Hemel Hempstead: Prentice Hall Europe.

CHAPTER 9

PSYCHOLOGY AND ETHICS

ETHICAL QUESTIONS: WHY DO PSYCHOLOGISTS NEED TO ASK THEM?

Perhaps the most general question we can ask about ethics is: 'Why do ethical issues arise at all?' Answers to this question might include the following:

1 Human beings and non-human animals have feelings and sensations. They are capable of experiencing pain, fear and so on (they are *sentient*, living, things), and so are capable of reacting with pain and fear to certain kinds of aversive (painful) stimulation.

2 Humans are not just sentient, they are also thinking beings. This means that situations that are not literally, or physically, painful or dangerous, may still be experienced as threatening, stressful, offensive, belittling or embarrassing, or may evoke feelings of guilt, self-doubt, inadequacy or incompetence.

3 Any attempt on the part of one person to induce any of the above feelings or sensations in another person (or animal), or the inducement of any of these feelings or sensations in one person (or non-human animal) as a result of the neglect or negligence of another, is usually condemned as immoral or morally unacceptable.

These points may seem perfectly reasonable, and perhaps fairly 'obvious' (at least once they are pointed out), and it may seem fairly clear in what ways they are relevant to psychology. But we should still ask: 'Why do ethical issues arise for psychologists?' Answers to this question might include the following:

1 Psychologists study human beings and non-human animals.

2 Psychologists often subject – deliberately or otherwise – the human beings and non-human animals they study to situations and stimulation that induce pain, embarrassment and so on.

3 Just as every psychology experiment is primarily a *social* situation (Orne, 1962: see Chapter 11), so every psychological investigation may be thought of as an *ethical* situation. In other words, whenever one person (the researcher) deliberately creates a situation intended for the investigation of the behaviour and/or experience of another person (the 'subject' or participant), there is always the possibility that the person being studied will experience one or more of the feelings and sensations identified above. This may be what the researcher is expecting to happen (it may be a crucial feature of the study), or it may genuinely not be anticipated by the researcher, who is as surprised as everyone else by how the participants respond.

But while we normally associate 'deliberately created situations' with *laboratory studies* (whether experimental or not), ethical issues are not confined to such settings. Indeed, *naturalistic studies* face ethical problems of their own, despite the fact that the researcher is not creating a situation into which other people are brought so that s/he may study their behaviour (see below).

Perhaps the common feature linking the laboratory and naturalistic settings, which makes them both 'ethical' situations, is the difference in the power associated with the roles of researcher and researched. Indeed, according to the latest Code of Ethics and Conduct (2006), published by the British Psychological Society/'BPS':

> ... ethics is related to the control of power. Clearly, not all clients are powerless but many are disadvantaged by lack of knowledge and certainty compared to the psychologist whose judgement they require ...

If this is true in the case of humans studying/working with other humans, it's even more true in the case of humans studying non-human animals! (Again, we return to this issue later in the chapter.)

PSYCHOLOGISTS AS INVESTIGATORS AND PRACTITIONERS

So far, we have discussed ethics in relation to the psychologist's role as scientist or investigator – that is, someone who wishes to find out more about human behaviour and experience. Sometimes this is done for its own sake (because of its intrinsic interest: *pure research*), sometimes as part of an attempt to solve a practical problem (*applied research*). While there is no hard-and-fast distinction between these two kinds of research, the distinction between psychologists as scientists/investigators and as practitioners is important in relation to understanding ethical issues. While many psychologists are both researchers and practitioners, the difference in these two roles needs to be understood when ethics is being discussed.

● The practitioner role refers to the work of clinical, counselling, educational, forensic and industrial/ occupational psychologists, who work in applied, naturalistic settings, such as psychiatric hospitals, schools, the prison service and commercial organizations.
● While all psychologists have responsibilities and obligations towards those they 'work' with, which are common to both the scientist and practitioner roles, there are also important differences in these responsibilities and obligations related to the different roles. This is reflected in the various *codes of conduct* and *ethical guidelines* published by the major professional bodies for psychologists: the BPS and the American Psychological Association (APA).

As shown in Figure 9.1, the *Code of Conduct for Psychologists* (BPS, 1985a), the *Ethical Principles of Psychologists and Code of Conduct* (APA, 2002), the *Code of Conduct, Ethical Principles and Guidelines* (BPS, 2000), and the *Code of Ethics and Conduct* (BPS, 2006) apply to both of the main areas of research and practice, while there are additional documents designed for the two areas separately.

The *Ethical Principles for Conducting Research with Human Participants* (BPS, 1992, which replaced the 1978 version and were incorporated into the *Code of Conduct*, 2000), the *Guidelines for the Use of Animals in Research* (BPS, 1985b), the *Guidelines for Ethical Conduct in the Care and Use of Animals* (APA, 1985), and the *Guidelines for Psychologists Working with Animals* (BPS, 2007a) clearly cover the scientists/investigators role. The *Code of Conduct* (2000) includes a section on 'Guidelines for psychologists working with animals'. The BPS has also published *Guidelines for Ethical Practice in Psychological Research Online* (2007b).

In addition to the *Report of Working Party on Behaviour Modification* (BPS, 1978b) and *Principles Governing the Employment of Psychological Tests* (BPS, 1981), there exists the *Division of Clinical Psychology Professional Practice Guidelines* (BPS, 1995); these all apply to the practitioner role.

Clinical psychologists are by far the most numerous single group of psychologists: more than one-third of all psychologists classify themselves as clinical, and a further 10 per cent call themselves 'counselling psychologists'. The latter tend to work with younger clients in colleges and universities, rather than in psychiatric hospitals (and other mental health facilities), which, typically, accommodate a much greater age range of adults (including many who are psychogeriatric). What clinical and counselling psychologists have in common is responsibility for people with psychological problems.

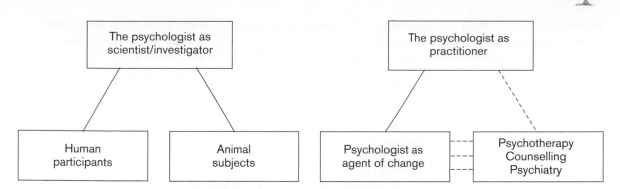

Figure 9.1 Major codes of conduct/ethical guidelines published by the British Psychological Society (BPS) and American Psychological Association (APA)

Because their clients are seeking professional help for a whole range of mental disorders, clinical and counselling psychologists have much in common with psychotherapists, in terms of both therapeutic methods/ techniques used, and ethical issues raised by their work. While psychologists are trained largely to use behaviour therapy/modification (based on the principles of learning theory), counselling psychologists (and other trained counsellors) mainly use methods based on Rogers's client/person-centred therapy. Psychotherapists may have trained initially as psychiatrists, social workers or even psychologists, but all undergo special psychotherapy training (which includes their own psychotherapy). They use psychodynamic techniques derived from Freud's psychoanalytic theory and therapy (see Chapter 14).

The important point here is that, regardless of the particular training the practitioner has received and the particular therapeutic techniques s/he uses, the nature of the relationship between 'helper' and 'helped' is very different from that between researcher and researched. In particular, the helper is attempting to change something, presumably for the benefit of the helped, while the researcher is 'merely' trying to find out (more) about what the researched is already like. This makes the respective situations very different from an ethical point of view.

In the remainder of this chapter, we explore some of the major ethical issues and debates that take place in relation to psychologists as both researchers and as practitioners.

RESEARCH WITH HUMAN PARTICIPANTS

In the Introduction to the *Ethical Principles for Conducting Research with Human Participants* (BPS, 1992: hereafter referred to as 'the *Principles*'), it is stated that psychologists owe a debt to those who agree to take part in their studies; even when people are paid for their time, they should be able to expect to be treated with the highest standards of consideration and respect. This is reflected in the change from the term 'subjects' to 'participants': the former term is impersonal at best. At worst, it is really a less accurate – but more neutral/ acceptable – alternative to 'object': traditional, mainstream, positivist psychology (with the laboratory experiment as the 'method of choice') treats people *as if* they were objects, responding to experimenter-manipulated variables (Heather, 1976; Unger, 1984: see Chapters 10, 11, and 14).

Guidelines, such as the *Principles*, are intended, primarily, to protect the 'rights and dignity' of those who participate in psychological research. The ability to test human participants in research is described as a 'privilege', which will be retained only if 'all members of the psychological profession abide by the *Principles*' (BPS, 2000).

Violation of the *Principles* could also form a basis of disciplinary action, and the Introduction to the *Principles* points out that:

> *In recent years, there has been an increase in legal actions by members of the general public against professionals for alleged misconduct. Researchers must recognise the possibility of such legal action if they infringe the rights and dignity of participants in their research.*
>
> *(BPS, 2000, Paragraph 1.4)*

As a secondary aim, therefore, the *Principles* are designed to protect psychologists themselves; but this protection becomes necessary only if the primary aim is not fulfilled.

The document lists nine major principles that are meant to be followed by anyone engaged in psychological research: all professional psychologists, whether members of the BPS or not, research assistants, and all students, from GCSE, through A-Level and undergraduate, up to postgraduate. These principles concern the following:

- consent
- deception
- debriefing
- withdrawal from the investigation
- confidentiality
- protection of participants
- observational research
- giving advice
- colleagues.

While these are listed separately, many are overlapping. Also, while the sixth principle is called 'Protection of participants', all the principles are aimed, in different ways, at protecting participants.

What are participants being protected from?

As we noted at the beginning of the chapter, people are sentient and thinking creatures, which means they are capable of experiencing a wide range of negative emotions in response to situations that psychologists may create as part of their research. This danger is increased when we consider the difference in the *power* inherent in the roles of researcher and researched (also noted above).

From a feminist perspective (see Chapter 6), researchers should try to reverse the traditional, orthodox, masculine-dominated approach, whereby the experimenter, who is dominant and has superior status and power, manipulates and controls the experimental situation to which the subordinate 'subject' reacts (e.g. Paludi, 1992). This difference in status and power creates a social and emotional distance between them. According to Harré (1993):

> To speak of people as 'males' and 'females', to write of 'running subjects in an experiment' and so on is morally troublesome. It denigrates the men and women who give up their time to assist one in one's studies. It displays a contempt for them as people that I find quite unacceptable. I find it deeply disturbing that students are encouraged to adopt this scientific rhetoric . . .

The BPS changed its *Ethical Principles for Research with Human Subjects* (1978) to *Ethical Principles for Conducting Research with Human Participants* (originally in 1990):

> In the forefront of its considerations was the recognition that psychologists owe a debt to those who agree to take part in their studies and that people who are willing to give up their time, even for remuneration, should be able to expect to be treated with the highest standards of consideration and respect. This is reflected in the change from 'subjects' to 'participants'.
> *(British Psychological Society, 2000)*

While recognizing that to psychologists brought up on the jargon of their profession, the term 'subject' isn't derogatory, 'to someone who has not had that experience of psychological research it is a term which can seem impersonal'.

Feminist research requires the researcher to become actively involved in the research process, taking the perspective of the participants: they are not detached investigators but become an integral part of the whole process (see Chapter 10). Similarly, Eysenck (1994) argues that the human participant is in a rather vulnerable and exploitable position. He quotes Kelman (1972), who believes that 'most ethical problems arising in social research can be traced to the subject's power deficiency'. As well as possessing knowledge and expertise relating to the experimental situation that is not shared with the participant, the experimenter is on 'home ground' (i.e. the laboratory) and the situation is under his/her control.

According to the *Code of Ethics and Conduct* (BPS, 2006):

> . . . ethics is related to the control of power. Clearly, not all clients are powerless but many are disadvantaged by lack of knowledge and certainty compared to the psychologist whose judgement they require . . .

The *Code* defines 'client' as 'any person or persons with whom a psychologist interacts on a professional basis', such as an individual patient, student, or research participant, a couple, family group, educational institution, or a private or public organization (including the Court)'.

Deception, consent and informed consent

The experimenter's 'being in charge' is potentially most detrimental to participants when what they *believe* is going on in the experimental situation (for example, a study of perceptual judgement, as in Asch's 1951 conformity experiments, or a study of the effects of punishment on learning, as in Milgram's 1963 obedience experiments) is not what is *actually* going on, as defined by the experimenter. Because it is the experimenter who manipulates the situation, the participant cannot know that s/he is being deceived; this is a feature of the experimenter's greater power.

The key ethical questions here are: 'Can failure to inform the participant of the true purpose of the experiment ever be justified?', 'Can the end (what the experimenter is hoping to find out) justify the means (the use of deception)?'

If informed consent involves the participant knowing everything that the experimenter knows about the experiment, and if giving informed consent (together with the right to withdraw from the experiment once it has begun) represents some kind of protection against powerlessness and vulnerability, should we simply condemn all deception and argue that it is always, and by its very nature, unacceptable?

According to the *Principles*:

> . . . *To many outside the psychology profession, and to some within it, the idea of deceiving the participants in one's research is seen as quite inappropriate. At best, the experience of deception . . . can make the recipients cynical about the activities and attitudes of psychologists. However, since there are very many psychological processes that are modifiable by individuals if they are aware that they are being studied, the statement of the research hypothesis in advance of the collection of data would make much psychological research impossible . . .*
>
> *(BPS, 2000)*

According to Milgram (1977, 1992), many regard deception as the cornerstone of ethical practice in human experimentation. According to some estimates, more than half the research published in social psychology journals involves some sort of misinformation or lack of disclosure, and although the 'topic' has received less attention in recent years (compared with the 1960s), the debate still goes on (Krupat and Garonzik, 1994).

Milgram cites Kelman (1974), who identifies two quite different reasons for not fully informing the participant.

1 The experimenter believes that if the participant knew what the experiment was like, s/he might refuse to participate (the *motivational reason*). Milgram believes that:

> *Misinforming people to gain their participation appears a serious violation of the individual's rights, and cannot routinely constitute an ethical basis for subject recruitment.*

This corresponds to what the *Principles* calls 'deliberately falsely informing the participant of the purpose of the research. Especially if the information given implies a more benign topic of study than is in fact the case, this is very different from 'withholding some of the details of the hypothesis under test'.

2 More typically, many social psychology experiments cannot be carried out unless the participant is ignorant of the true purpose of the experiment. Milgram calls this the *epistemological reason*; it is the psychologist's equivalent to what the author of a murder mystery does by not revealing the culprit until the very end of a novel – to do so would undermine the psychological effect of the reading experience! (See the quote from the *Principles* above.)

But is this sufficient justification? While readers of murder mysteries *expect* not to find out 'whodunnit' until the very end (indeed, this is a major part of the appeal of such literature), people who participate in psychology experiments *do not* expect to be deceived, and if they did, they presumably would not agree to participate! But are things as cut and dried as this?

What if we found that, despite expecting to be deceived, people still volunteered, or that, not expecting to be deceived, they said that the deception didn't particularly bother them? Would this change the ethical 'status' of deception?

A number of points need to be made in response to this question.

- Mannucci (1977, in Milgram, 1977, 1992) asked 192 lay people about ethical aspects of psychology experiments. They regarded deception as a relatively minor issue, and were far more concerned about the quality of the experience they would undergo as participants.
- Most of the actual participants who were deceived in Asch's conformity experiments were very enthusiastic, and expressed their admiration for the elegance and significance of the experimental procedure (Milgram, 1977, 1992).
- In defence of his own obedience experiments, Milgram (1974) reports that all participants received a comprehensive report when the experiments were over, detailing the procedure and the results, as well as a follow-up questionnaire concerning their participation. (This was part of a very thorough debriefing or 'dehoax'.) Of the 92 per cent who returned the questionnaires (an unusually high response rate), almost 84 per cent said they were glad or very glad to have participated, while less than 2 per cent said they were sorry or very sorry; 80 per cent said they felt that more experiments of this kind should be carried out, and 74 per cent said they had learned something of personal importance.

More specifically, the 'technical illusions' (Milgram's preferred term for 'deception') are justified for one reason only – they are in the end accepted and endorsed by those who are exposed to them:

> *The central moral justification for allowing a procedure of the sort used in my experiment is that it is judged acceptable by those who have taken part in it. Moreover, it was the salience of this fact throughout that constituted the chief moral warrant for the continuation of the experiments.*
>
> *(Milgram, 1974)*

Similarly, the *Principles* maintains that:

> *. . . the central principle was the reaction of participants when deception was revealed. If this led to discomfort, anger or objections from the participants . . . then the deception was inappropriate . . .*

Milgram goes on to say that any criticism of the experiment (or any other research method, for that matter) that does not take account of the tolerant reactions of the participants is hollow:

> *Again, the participant, rather than the external critic, must be the ultimate source of judgement.*
>
> *(Milgram, 1974)*

But this is an *after-the-event* justification or condemnation: shouldn't there be criteria for deciding *in advance* what counts as acceptable/unacceptable deception? To be 'on the safe side' *no* deception should be permitted – but then we would be left with a very restricted methodology to study a very limited range of behaviour and experience (see below).

- In a review of several studies focusing on the ethical acceptability of deception experiments, Christensen (1988, cited in Krupat and Garonzik, 1994) reports that, as long as deception is not extreme, participants do not seem to mind. He suggests that the widespread use of mild forms of deception is justified – first, because apparently no one is harmed and, second, because there seem to be few, if any, acceptable alternatives.
- Krupat and Garonzik (1994) found that, among 255 university psychology students, those who had had at least one experience of being deceived while participating in some psychological research, compared with those who had not, were significantly more likely to expect to be deceived again. But the experience of being deceived *does not* have a significant impact on the students' evaluation of other aspects of participation, such as enjoyment and interest. Consistent with Christensen's and Mannucci's findings, previously deceived participants were not terribly upset at the prospect of being deceived again. Indeed, those who had been deceived at least once said they would be *less* upset at being lied to or misled again. According to Krupat and Garonzik (1994):

It almost seems that these people are accepting deception as par for the course and, therefore, not worthy of becoming upset. To the extent that the ethical issue revolves around subjects' negative reactions to deception, our findings are consistent with that of prior research . . .

● Milgram (1977, 1992) acknowledges that the use of 'technical illusions' (a morally neutral term that he prefers to the morally biased, or 'loaded', 'deception') poses ethical dilemmas for the researcher. By definition, the use of such illusions means that participants cannot give their informed consent, and he asks whether this can *ever* be justified. Clearly, he says, they should never be used unless they are 'indispensable to the conduct of an inquiry', and honesty and openness are the only desirable bases of transactions with people in whatever context.

According to the *Principles*:

Intentional deception of the participants over the purpose and general nature of the investigation should be avoided whenever possible. Participants should never be deliberately misled without extremely strong scientific or medical justification. Even then there should be strict controls and the disinterested approval of independent advisors.

(Paragraph, 4.2)

Again,

It may be impossible to study some psychological processes without withholding information about the true object of the study or deliberately misleading the participants . . .

(Paragraph 4.3)

But does the judgement that deception is indispensable justify its use? In other words, while believing it is crucial may be a *necessary* reason for using it, is it a *sufficient* reason? Milgram gives examples of professions in which there exist exemptions from general moral principles, without which the profession could not function. For example, male gynaecologists and obstetricians are allowed to examine the genitals of female strangers, because they are their patients. Similarly, a lawyer may know that a client has committed a murder but is obligated *not* to tell the authorities, based on the principle of 'privileged communication'. We return to this very important issue when we discuss psychologists as practitioners later in the chapter.

In the case of gynaecology and the law, the underlying justification for 'suspending' more generally accepted moral principles ('It is wrong to examine the genitals of female strangers' and 'If you know that someone has committed a serious crime, you should tell the police') is that, in the long run, society as a whole will benefit (women need gynaecologists and people need lawyers whom they can trust implicitly). In the case of gynaecology and the law, both 'society in general' and the individual patient or client benefit. However, in the case of the psychology experiment, the individual participant clearly is not the beneficiary. So how do we resolve this moral dilemma?

The ethical status of psychological research

Any research that psychologists do is carried out within a whole range of constraints – methodological, ethical, financial, social, cultural and political. As the discussion of feminist and cross-cultural psychology shows (see Chapters 6 and 8), the very questions that psychologists ask about human behaviour and experience reflect a whole range of beliefs, values, presuppositions and prejudices, which, in turn, reflect the particular cultural, gender and other groups to which they belong. While this raises important questions about the objective nature of psychological inquiry (see Chapter 10), it also raises very important ethical issues.

If sexism, heterosexism, the androcentric/masculinist bias, ethnocentrism and racism are all inherent features of what psychologists do when they study human beings, then it could be argued that traditional, mainstream, western, academic, psychology (as well as the applied areas, such as clinical and educational psychology) is inherently unethical. In other words, most psychologists, most of the time, are trying to answer questions which stem from all kinds of prejudices. Most of the time, the psychologists themselves are unaware of these prejudices, but this does not by itself absolve them of the 'crime' ('ignorance of the law is no defence').

Protecting the individual vs benefiting society

The debate about the ethics of psychological research usually focuses on the vulnerability of individual participants and the responsibility of the psychologist towards his/her participants to ensure that they don't suffer in any way from their experience of participating. As we have seen, codes of conduct and ethical guidelines are designed to do just that. According to the *Principles*:

> *Participants in psychological research should have confidence in the investigators. Good psychological research is possible only if there is mutual respect and confidence between investigators and participants. Psychological investigators are potentially interested in all aspects of human behaviour and conscious experience. However, for ethical reasons, some areas of human experience and behaviour may be beyond the reach of experiment, observation or other forms of psychological investigation. Ethical guidelines are necessary to clarify the conditions under which psychological research is possible.*

> *(Paragraph 1.2)*

But how useful and effective are they in achieving these aims? See Box 9.1 (p. 158).

Wider issues about the 'morality' of the questions the researcher is trying to answer through the research are much less commonly asked. These would include the fundamental issue of the values that are, often unconsciously, helping to shape the research questions. If the questions themselves are limited and shaped by the values of the individual researcher, they're also limited and shaped by considerations of methodology – that is, what it is possible to do, practically, when investigating human behaviour and experience. According to Brehm (1992):

> *Given the clarity with which experiments allow us to test our causal ideas, it may seem strange that anyone would ever use anything other than an experimental design. Unfortunately, the same factor that defines an experiment also limits its use: the manipulation of the independent variable. Researchers can control the information that subjects receive in the laboratory about people they have never met, but they cannot manipulate many of the truly important factors in intimate relationships. We cannot create love in the laboratory. We don't know how to do it . . . For the most part, laboratory experiments are limited to explaining relatively emotionless interactions between strangers. Yet, in the study of relationships, we often want to understand intense encounters between intimates.*

Brehm is saying that, in the context of interpersonal attraction, the laboratory experiment *by its nature* is extremely limited in the kinds of questions it will allow psychologists to investigate. Conversely, and just as importantly, there are certain aspects of behaviour and experience that *could* be studied experimentally, but it would be unethical to do so. Brehm gives 'jealousy between partners participating in laboratory research' as an example. Indeed,

> *. . . all types of research in this area [intimate relationships] involve important ethical dilemmas. Even if all we do is to ask subjects to fill out questionnaires describing their relationships, we need to think carefully about how this research experience might affect them and their partner . . .*

BOX 9.1 HOW USEFUL ARE CODES OF CONDUCT AND ETHICAL GUIDELINES?

According to Gale (1995), the fact that both the BPS and the APA codes are regularly reviewed and revised indicates that at least some aspects do not depend on absolute or universal ethical truths. Guidelines need to be updated in light of the changing social and political contexts in which psychological research takes place and the new ethical issues/dilemmas they create. A good example is people's increasing familiarity with the Internet, and psychologists' increasing use of online research (see discussion in text below of the *Guidelines for Ethical Practice in Psychological Research online* (BPS, 2007: see Box 9.4).

Another example is sexual behaviour in the context of AIDS. Information revealed by participants can create conflict between the need to protect individuals and the protection of society at large. For instance, despite the confidentiality requirement, should a researcher inform the sexual partner of an HIV-positive participant? As Gale points out:

> *One consequence of such breaches of confidentiality could be the withdrawal of consent by particular groups and the undermining of future research, demonstrating . . . how one ethical principle fights against another.*

Taking the example of informed consent, Gale argues that however much information is given in advance of the procedure, this can never guarantee that informed consent is given. There is a sense in which you do not truly know what something is like until you have actually experienced it – and that goes for the researchers as much as the participants. Also, how much information can children, the elderly or disabled, or emotionally distressed people be expected to absorb? Even if this wasn't a problem, the status of the experimenter, the desire to please and 'be a good subject' (see Chapter 11) all detract from truly choosing freely in the way that's assumed by the *Principles* (Gale, 1995).

The BPS *Code of Conduct* (which incorporates the *Principles*) is an important guide in monitoring ethical standards and professional practice. But because it applies to all psychologists, regardless of the nature of their work, it is of necessity more general than is always helpful (Joscelyne, 2002). It is specific about some issues, but vague about others, and this can be confusing. For specific issues, such as disclosing an adult client's prior child sexual abuse if there are indications that s/he might be currently abusing a child, the *Division of Clinical Psychology Professional Practice Guidelines* (1995) are far more useful. Another issue that arises within clinical psychology is having a (sexual) relationship with a former client. Again, the *Code of Conduct* is very vague, and so unhelpful, on this (Joscelyne, 2002).

However, Joscelyne was commenting on an earlier form of the *Code*. The most recent *Code of Ethics and Conduct* (2006), while still applying to all psychologists, emphasizes and supports the process of *ethical decision making*. The *Code* is based on four Ethical Principles (*respect, competence, responsibility* and *integrity*), which constitute the main domains of responsibility within which ethical issues are considered. Each Principle is described in (i) a *Statement of Values* (reflecting the fundamental beliefs that guide ethical reasoning, decision making and behaviour); and (ii) a set of *Standards* (which spell out, sometimes in quite a detailed way, the ethical conduct the BPS expects of its members) (see Table 9.1 p. 161).

It is worth pointing out that the *Code of Conduct* (2000) consists of several sections (apart from the Ethical Principles). These include 'Guidelines for psychologists working with animals', 'Guidelines on advertising the services offered by psychologists', and 'Guidelines for penile plethysmography (PPG) usage'. The last refers to the measurement of sexual arousal and involves apparatus being attached to the penis and sexual stimuli being presented. This might be used in the context of assessing paedophilia and sexual dysfunction, so its use is highly sensitive. But it's amusing to note that point nine of the Guidelines states that: 'Stimuli material for PPG assessment should be kept secure and access limited to those using it for professional purposes.'

Figure 9.2 Ethical and methodological constraints on the questions that psychologists can try to answer through the research process

So, the research that psychologists do is partly constrained by practical (methodological) considerations, and also partly by ethical ones: what it may be possible to do may be unacceptable but, equally, what may be acceptable may not be possible. As shown in Figure 9.2, the 'what' of research is constrained by both the' how' and the 'should'.

As we have seen, ethical debates (the 'should') are usually confined to protecting the integrity and welfare of the individual participant. This is what the various codes of conduct and ethical guidelines are designed to try and ensure. But are there wider ethical issues involved? For example, is it possible that by focusing on the protection of (individual) participants, the social groups to which they belong may be harmed in some way? This possibility, and the reasons underlying it, are discussed in Box 9.2 (p. 160).

As important as it surely is to protect individuals, does the 'should' relate to something beyond the particular experimental situation in which particular participants are involved?

The other side of the ethical coin: research that must be done

In our necessary concern with treating subjects well and protecting them from any harmful effects, we must not overlook the other side of the ethical issue: the ethical imperative to gain more understanding of important areas of human behaviour. Intimate relationships can be a source of the grandest, most glorious pleasure we human beings experience; they can also be a source of terrible suffering and appalling destructiveness. It is, I believe, an inherently ethical response to try to learn how the joy might be increased and the misery reduced.

(Brehm, 1992)

Although specifically discussing the study of intimate relationships, Brehm's argument applies to psychology in general but perhaps to social psychology in particular. Her argument is that not only are psychologists obliged to protect the welfare of individual participants, they are also under obligation to carry out socially meaningful research: research that, potentially, may improve the quality of people's lives. Social psychologists in particular have a two-fold ethical obligation: to individual participants and to society at large (Myers, 1994). Similarly, Aronson (1992) argues that, in a real sense, social psychologists are under an obligation to use their research skills to advance our knowledge and understanding of human behaviour for the ultimate aim of 'human betterment'. But they face a dilemma when this general ethical responsibility to society comes into conflict with their more specific ethical responsibility to each individual experimental participant.

BOX 9.2 THE ETHICS OF ETHICAL CODES: UNDERLYING ASSUMPTIONS

According to Brown (1997), a core assumption underlying ethical codes is that what psychologists do as researchers, clinicians, teachers and so on is basically harmless and inherently valuable, because it is based on (positivist) science. Consequently, it is possible for a psychologist to conduct technically ethical research but still do great harm. For example, a researcher can adhere strictly to 'scientific' research methodologies, obtain technically informed consent from participants (and not breach any of the other major ethical principles), but still conduct research that claims to show the inferiority of a particular group. Because it is conducted according to 'the rules' (both methodological and ethical), the question of whether it is ethical in the *broader* sense to pursue such matters is ignored.

For example, neither Jensen (1969) nor Herrnstein (1971) was ever considered by mainstream psychology to have violated psychology's ethics by the questions they asked regarding the intellectual inferiority of African-Americans. Individual black participants were not harmed by being given IQ tests, and might even have found them interesting and challenging; however, Brown (1997) argues that how the findings were interpreted and used:

> *. . . weakened the available social supports for people of colour by stigmatizing them as genetically inferior, thus strengthening the larger culture's racist attitudes. Research ethics as currently construed by mainstream ethics codes do not require researchers to put the potential for this sort of risk into their informed consent documents.*

Jensen's and Herrnstein's research (highlighted by Herrnstein and Murray in *The Bell Curve*, 1994) has profoundly harmed black Americans. Ironically, the book has received a great deal of methodological criticism, but only black psychologists – such as Hilliard (1995) and Sue (1995) – have raised the more fundamental question of whether the mere fact of conducting such studies might be ethically dubious.

Herrnstein and Murray, Rushton (1995), Brand (in Richards, 1996) and others, like the Nazi scientists of the 1930s, claim that the study of race differences is a purely 'objective' and 'scientific' enterprise (Howe, 1997).

Talking about the aim of 'human betterment' raises many important questions to do with basic values. This opens up the ethical debate in such a way that values must be addressed and recognized as part of the research process (something that feminist psychologists advocate very strongly: see Chapter 6). As noted in Box 9.1, the latest version of the *Code of Ethics and Conduct* (BPS, 2006) comprises four major ethical principles, each of which is described in a Statement of Values and a set of Standards. These are summarized in Table 9.1.

Discussion of values may also have provided a solution to the dilemma noted earlier, whereby the individual participant isn't the beneficiary (unlike the gynaecology patient or the lawyer's client). The short-term deception of individual participants (and the distress this might cause) may be necessary if psychologists are to learn things about human behaviour and experience which can then be used to benefit people in general. What form might such benefits take?

In some of the early, and very famous, studies of bystander intervention, people were deceived as to the 'emergency' supposedly taking place. In the Latané and Darley (1968) experiment, steam, meant to resemble smoke, poured into the room where the participants were filling out questionnaires, and in a second study (Darley and Latané, 1968), participants believed that another participant (supposedly in another part of the building and heard via an intercom system) was having an epileptic fit.

Many participants were very distressed by their experience, especially those in the latter experiment. Yet when asked to complete a post-experiment questionnaire (which followed a very careful debriefing), all said they

Table 9.1 Ethical principles and the related Statement of Values (BPS *Code of Ethics and Conduct*, 2006)

Ethical principle:	**Respect**
Statement of values:	*Psychologists value the dignity and worth of all persons, with sensitivity to the dynamics of perceived authority or influence over clients, and with particular regard to people's rights including those of privacy and self-determination.*
Standards:	General respect; Privacy and confidentiality; Informed consent; Self-determination.
Ethical principle:	**Competence**
Statement of values:	*Psychologists value the continuing development and maintenance of high standards of competence in their professional work, and the importance of preserving their ability to function optimally within the recognized limits of their knowledge, skill, training, education, and experience.*
Standards:	Awareness of professional ethics; Ethical decision making; Recognizing limits of competence; Recognizing impairment.
Ethical principle:	**Responsibility**
Statement of values:	*Psychologists value their responsibilities to clients, to the general public, and to the profession and science of Psychology, including the avoidance of harm and the prevention of misuse or abuse of their contributions to society.*
Standards:	General responsibility; Termination and continuity of care; Protection of research participants; Debriefing of research participants.
Ethical principle:	**Integrity**
Statement of values:	*Psychologists value honesty, accuracy, clarity, and fairness in their interactions with all persons, and seek to promote integrity in all facets of their scientific and professional endeavours.*
Standards:	Honesty and accuracy; Avoiding exploitation and conflicts of interest; Maintaining personal boundaries; Addressing ethical misconduct.

believed the deception was justified and that they would be willing to participate in similar experiments again. None reported any feelings of anger towards the experimenter.

A later study (Beaman *et al.*, 1978, in Myers, 1994) built on these earlier experiments. They used a lecture to inform some students about how bystanders' refusal to help can influence both one's interpretation of an emergency and one's feelings of responsibility. Two other groups of students heard either a different lecture or no lecture at all. Two weeks later, as part of a 'different experiment' in a different location, the participants found themselves (accompanied by an unresponsive confederate) walking past someone slumped over or sprawled under a bike. Of those who had heard the lecture about helping behaviour, 50 per cent stopped to offer help, compared with 25 per cent of those who hadn't.

What this suggests, of course, is that the results of psychological research can be used to make us more aware of the influences that affect our behaviour, making it more likely that we will act differently when armed with that knowledge, compared with how we might otherwise have done. In the case of bystander intervention, this 'consciousness-raising' is beneficial in a very tangible way to the person being helped. As for the helper, being more sensitive to the needs of others, and the feeling of satisfaction from actually having helped another person may be seen as benefits too.

We should note that in the Beaman *et al.* experiment, the participants were being deceived, both as to the identity of the unresponsive confederate and the apparent 'victim'. But this can be justified in the same way as any experiment using deception.

How do we decide when to deceive?

The preceding argument implies rejection of the view that deception can never, under any circumstances, be justified. But that does not inevitably lead us to the opposite view, namely that almost any price is worth paying for results that may have profound benefits for humankind (Aronson, 1992). So is there a middle ground?

> *I believe the science of social psychology is important, and I also believe experimental subjects should be protected at all times. When deciding whether a particular experimental procedure is ethical or not, I believe a cost–benefit analysis is appropriate. That is, how much 'good' will derive from doing the experiment and how much 'bad' will happen to the experimental subjects should be considered. Put another way, the benefits to society are compared with the costs to the subjects, and this ratio is entered into the decision calculus . . .*

> *(Aronson, 1992)*

Unfortunately, this comparison is often very difficult to make, because neither the benefits nor the harm are known or calculable. McGhee (2001) identifies several problems faced by any cost–benefit analysis (see Box 9.3).

BOX 9.3 SOME PROBLEMS WITH COST–BENEFIT ANALYSIS (McGHEE, 2001)

- Both costs and benefits are multiple and subjective, some are immediate, others are longer term, and there are difficulties in 'adding them up'.
- Regarding *multiplicity*, every psychology experiment (like every complex social activity) has many outcomes. It is difficult, if not impossible, to *identify* them, let alone assess them. Even if they can be assessed individually, they need to be *aggregated* in some way, because we are trying to assess the experiment as an overall package. For example, how much is deception 'worth' relative to 'new data'?
- Ultimately, costs and benefits can only be *subjectively* assessed. Each individual values different kinds of experiences (gains and losses) differently. Indeed, one person's cost might be another's benefit.
- In *theory-driven* research such as Milgram's (as distinct from applied research), costs tend to be real, while benefits tend to be *potential:*

  > *The distress to the participants in Milgram's studies is real but the prospect of reducing the possibility of another Auschwitz is remote – even if extraordinarily desirable.*

- Similarly, although the benefits may outweigh the costs, for individual participants it is mostly all costs: time, effort, stress, and occasional humiliation and deception; any tangible or practical benefits are unlikely to be for them. The costs, therefore, are linked to specific people, while the identity of those who will benefit is much less obvious.

We need to decide *before* a study takes place whether or not it should go ahead. But very often the full range and extent of costs and benefits will only become apparent retrospectively. (See text above.)

Finally, who should have the right to decide whether the benefits outweigh the costs?

Our judgement about the acceptability of any experimental procedure (including any deception involved) may be (unconsciously) influenced by the outcome. If the results tell us something pleasant or flattering about human nature, the procedure is less likely to be criticized as unethical, while the reverse is true if the results tell us 'something we'd rather not know' (Aronson, 1992). This is to confuse the procedure with the outcome, when they should be assessed independently before being weighed against each other.

There is little doubt that Milgram's experiments told us something about ourselves that 'we'd rather not know'. Aronson agrees with Milgram himself, who is convinced that:

> . . . *much of the criticism [of his obedience experiments], whether people know it or not, stems from the results of the experiment. If everyone had broken off at slight shock or mild shock, this would be a very reassuring finding and who would protest?*

> *(Milgram, 1977, 1992)*

Ironically, our current codes of ethics are a direct consequence of the public and academic debates that followed Milgram's research (McGhee, 2001).

Consistent with this argument is Aronson's observation that the dilemma faced by social psychologists (regarding their obligations to society and to their individual participants) is greatest when investigating such important areas as conformity, obedience and bystander intervention. In general, the more important the issue, (i) the greater the potential benefit for society and (ii) the more likely an individual participant will experience distress and discomfort. The 'missing middle' from this observation is that the more important the issue, the more essential it becomes that deception ('technical illusion') is used. Why? Because the psychologist wants to know how people are likely to behave were they to find themselves in that situation outside the laboratory.

This raises a number of crucial methodological questions (to do with experimental realism, external validity or mundane realism: see Chapter 10). But the key ethical issue hinges on the fact that the use of deception both contributes enormously (and perhaps irreplaceably) to our understanding of human behaviour (helping to satisfy the obligation to society) and at the same time may significantly increase the distress of individual participants (detracting from the responsibility to protect individuals).

So what is the psychologist to do?

Some suggested solutions to the 'double obligation' dilemma

Using deception only when essential

Having accepted that, under certain circumstances, deception is permissible, most psychologists still advocate the principle that it should not be used unless it is considered to be essential to do so (Aronson, 1992; Milgram, 1977, 1992). This is consistent with the BPS's *Principles* (see above).

Accurately reflecting human experience

Milgram (1977, 1992) also believes that if we excluded, on principle, the experimental creation of stress or conflict, and only allowed studies that produced positive emotions,

> . . . *such a stricture would lead to a very lopsided psychology, one that caricatured rather than accurately reflected human experience.*

Historically, the most deeply informative experiments in social psychology include those that examine how participants resolve conflicts of one kind or another, such as the Asch studies of conformity (truth vs conformity), the Latané and Darley bystander intervention studies (getting involved in another's troubles vs not getting involved), and Milgram's own obedience experiments (internal conscience vs external authority). If we excluded the study of such core human issues, we would be causing an 'irreparable loss' to any science of human behaviour.

But what of the accusation that Milgram's experiment may produce diminished self-esteem, or sense of self-worth, in those participants who obey the experimenter all the way up to 450 volts? Milgram's reply is to agree that it is the experimenter's responsibility to make the laboratory session as constructive an experience

163

as possible and to explain the experiment in a way that allows participants to integrate their performance into their self-concept in an insightful way. However, if the experimenter were to hide the truth from the participant, even if this was negative, this would set the experiment completely apart from other life experiences (and, we could add, would simply be dishonest).

BOX 9.4 *GUIDELINES FOR ETHICAL PRACTICE IN PSYCHOLOGICAL RESEARCH ONLINE* (BPS, 2007B)

Advances in technology, such as the Internet, have extended opportunities for research in psychology. The term *Internet Mediated Research* (IMR) covers a wide range of research activities, ranging from purely observational studies (e.g. analysis of people's behaviour in chat rooms), to surveys and *in vivo* quantitative studies (e.g. a comparison of the personality profiles of job applicants and employees), to highly structured and well-controlled experiments (such as those in memory and perception).

IMR requires the application of the same controls, checks and balances that apply to good research in traditional settings; it should also involve the same ethical considerations being given to people who are taking part in the research, whether they are simply being observed or are invited to actively engage in experimental tasks. However, IMR raises *additional* ethical issues; the *Guidelines* supplement, rather than replace, the BPS *Code of Ethics and Conduct* (2006).

In IMR, compared with traditional methodologies, the most salient and critical feature is the absence of physical contact between researcher and participant:

. . . This restricts the researcher's capacity to monitor, support, or even terminate the study if adverse reactions become apparent. For example, experimental research online requires careful consideration of the design of stimulus materials to anticipate possible distress that might go undetected and qualitative analysis of discussion boards requires an awareness that the author of quotations can be identified by using a search engine.

(BPS, 2007b)

Key ethical issues
Depending on the research design, participants in IMR can be (a) identifiable or anonymous; (b) they can explicitly consent to participate, or they can be invisibly observed without their knowledge. These two dimensions (level of identifiability and level of observation) form the basis of the additional ethical issues raised by IMR. The *Guidelines* deals with ten broad areas of ethical concern as follows:

1 Verifying identity
2 Public/private space
3 Informed consent
4 Levels of control
5 Withdrawal
6 Debriefing
7 Deception
8 Monitoring
9 Protection of participants and researchers
10 Data protection.

Several of these areas of concern correspond to the specific *Principles* discussed above, but the *Guidelines* indicate how they pose specific and more complex ethical issues in the context of IMR.

Alternatives to informed consent

Two compromise solutions to the problem of not being able to obtain informed consent are (i) *presumptive consent* (of 'reasonable people') and (ii) *prior general consent*.

● In *presumptive consent*, the views of a large number of people are obtained about the acceptability of an experimental procedure. These people would not participate in the actual experiment (if it went ahead), but their views could be taken as evidence of how people in general would react to participation.
● *Prior general consent* could be obtained from people who might, subsequently, serve as experimental participants. Before volunteering to join a pool of volunteers to serve in psychological research, people would be explicitly told that sometimes participants are misinformed about the true purpose of the study and sometimes experience emotional stress. Only those agreeing, in the light of this knowledge, would be chosen for a particular study (Milgram, 1977, 1992).

This is a compromise solution, because people would be giving their 'informed consent' (i) well in advance of the actual experiment, (ii) only in a very general way, and (iii) without knowing what specific manipulations/deceptions would be used in the particular experiment in which they participate. It seems to fall somewhere between 'mere' consent and full 'informed consent', and could perhaps be called *semi-* or *partially informed consent*.

THE USE OF (NON-HUMAN) ANIMALS IN PSYCHOLOGICAL RESEARCH

Why do psychologists study animals?

Because of the very close relationship between the ethical and the practical aspects of animal experimentation, they are discussed together here.

Figure 9.3 Darwin was ridiculed by the media of the day for his 'outrageous' ideas of evolution

1 Experiments that would not be allowed (or would be very impractical if they were) if they involved human participants, are permitted (or have been in the past) using animal subjects. This, of course, begs the question as to the *ethics* of such animal experiments.
2 Even if animals are not subjected to ethically unacceptable procedures, such as severe sensory deprivation (e.g. Riesen, 1947; Blakemore and Cooper, 1970), total social isolation (e.g. Harlow and Zimmerman, 1959), extreme stress (e.g. Brady, 1958; Seligman, 1974), or surgical procedures and eventually 'sacrifice' (e.g. Olds and Milner, 1954), greater control can still be exerted over the variables under investigation compared with the equivalent human experiment. For example, the Skinner box is an environment totally controlled by the experimenter (see Chapter 14).
3 There is an underlying *evolutionary continuity* between humans and other species, which gives rise to the assumption that differences between humans and other species are merely *quantitative* (as opposed to *qualitative*): other species may display more simple behaviour and have more primitive nervous systems than humans, but they are not of a different order from humans (see Chapter 14). In fact, the mammalian brain (which includes rats, cats, dogs, monkeys and humans) is built on similar lines in all these species, and neurons (nerve cells) are the same in all species, and work in the same way. These similarities of biology are, in turn, linked to behavioural similarities. So, studying the more simple cases is a valid and valuable way of finding out about the more complex ones. Skinner's *analysis of behaviour* is a good example of this approach (again see Chapter 14).

4 Animals are (mostly) smaller and, therefore, easier to study in the laboratory. They also have much shorter lifespans and gestation periods, making it much easier to study their development: many generations can be studied in a relatively short time.

5 Animal studies can provide useful hypotheses for subsequent testing with human participants. For example, Bowlby's theory of attachment (see Gross, 2005) was partly influenced by Lorenz's study of imprinting in geese. Equally important, animals can be used to test cause-and-effect relationships where the existing human evidence is only correlational, as in smoking and lung cancer. This, of course, raises fundamental *ethical* questions.

The *Guidelines for Psychologists Working with Animals* (BPS, 2007a) point out that research is not the only reason psychologists work with animals, even though, not surprisingly, it is what has caused the most controversy and media attention. Animals are sometimes used in practical teaching within psychology degree courses, and increasingly animals are being used in various forms of psychological therapy (including companion animal visiting schemes in hospitals or hospices, pet-keeping within prison rehabilitation schemes, and in behaviour therapy for the treatment of specific animal phobias). Psychologists may also be asked to advise on therapy for animals whose behaviour appears to de disordered in some way, as well as training animals for commercial purposes.

The case for animal experimentation

The main justifications for using animals in experiments are (i) the pursuit of scientific knowledge, and (ii) the advancement of medicine. To justify the use of animals, especially when the procedures used are likely to be very stressful, the research must be rigorously designed and the potential results must represent a significant contribution to our knowledge of medicine, pharmacology, biopsychology or psychology. This is a safeguard against distressing research being carried out for its own sake, or at the whim of the researcher.

Much of the controversy surrounding animal research is focused on its use in medical research. Despite the safeguards that are in place, including the BPS *Guidelines* and the Animals (Scientific Procedures) Act 1986, opponents object to animal experimentation in principle. Supporters – who, not surprisingly, are mainly medical researchers and physiologists – stress the many human diseases and psychological disorders that are now successfully treated or controlled using drugs whose development would have been impossible without animal research (see Gross, 2005).

Some would take the 'medical justification' argument even further. For example, Gray (1991) argues that most people (both experimenters and animal rights activists) would accept the ethical principle that inflicting pain is wrong. However, we are sometimes faced with having to choose between different ethical principles – that is, we have to make moral choices, which may mean having to choose between human and animal suffering. Gray believes that *speciesism* (discriminating against and exploiting animals because they belong to a particular (non-human) species (Ryder, 1990)) is not only justified, but it is our duty to carry out animal research if this may lead to the (long-term) alleviation of human suffering.

Bateson (1986, 1992) proposes a 'decision cube' (similar to Aronson's cost–benefit analysis in human research: see above), involving (i) the quality of the research, (ii) the certainty of medical benefit, and (iii) the degree of animal suffering. The last should only be tolerated if (i) and (ii) are high.

Chimpanzees and animal rights

In recent years, the ethics debate in relation to non-humans has become focused on chimpanzees and other primates, and in the process its scope has widened to include the notion of equality under the law. One strand to this debate involves psychologists' attempts to teach language to chimpanzees (and other great apes). A famous example is described in Box 9.6.

BOX 9.5 *GUIDELINES FOR PSYCHOLOGISTS WORKING WITH ANIMALS* (BPS, 2007A)

Ten major areas that are covered as follows:

1 *Legislation:* The Animals (Scientific Procedures) Act (1986) governs any scientific procedure that may cause pain, suffering, distress or lasting harm to a 'protected' animal. Protected animals comprise all non-human vertebrates and a single invertebrate species (*Octopus vulgaris*). Psychologists working with animals in ways not covered by the Act should aim to maintain standards at least as high as those proposed in the *Guidelines* for research use. In addition, psychologists should be aware that they have a more general duty of care towards any protected animal under the Animal Welfare Act (2006).

2 *Replacing the use of animals:* Alternatives to intact behaving organisms, such as video records from previous work or computer simulations, may be useful – especially in a teaching context. Two specific examples are the 'Ratlife' project (video) and 'Sniffy the virtual rat' (computer simulation).

3 *Choice of species and strain:* Psychologists should choose a species that is scientifically and ethically suitable for the intended use: the species should be chosen for the least amount of suffering while still attaining the scientific objective. The choice must be justified as part of the application for a Project Licence (under the 1986 Act). In addition, different strains of commonly used laboratory rodents have very different physiological and behavioural characteristics that may make them more or less suitable for psychological research.

4 *Number of animals:* The 1986 Act requires use of the smallest number of animals sufficient to achieve the research goals.

5 *Procedures:* (See 'Legislation' above.) Investigators should consider experimental designs that avoid the use of regulated procedures by, for example, enriching rather than impoverishing the environment as the experimental treatment, or by observing naturally occurring harmful conditions. Permission to perform regulated procedures requires a *Project Licence,* which is granted only after weighing the benefits and costs (in welfare terms) to the animal subjects. In addition, the actual performance of a regulated procedure requires a *Personal Licence*, given only after successful completion of appropriate training. When applying for a licence, investigators must also discuss their proposal with a *Local Ethical Review Committee* (which must include a veterinary surgeon). More specifically, the *Guidelines* considers (a) housing conditions, (b) reward, deprivation and aversive stimulation, (c) aggression and predation, (d) fieldwork and (e) anaesthesia, analgesia and euthanasia.

6 *Procurement of animals:* Common laboratory animals must come from Home Office Designated Breeding and Supply Establishments.

7 *Animal care:* The 1986 European Convention (Article 5) provides that:

> *Any animal used or intended for use in a procedure shall be provided with accommodation, and environment, at least a minimum of freedom of movement, food, water and care, appropriate to its health and well being. Any restriction on the extent to which an animal can satisfy its physiological and ecological needs shall be limited as far as practicable.*

8 *Disposing of animals:* Animal subjects may sometimes be passed to colleagues for further study, breeding or as companion animals. If they must be killed during or subsequent to the study, this must be done as humanely and painlessly as possible (as defined by the Act). A veterinary surgeon should be consulted regarding current methods of euthanasia.

9 *Animals in psychology teaching:* Whoever the students are, ethical issues should be discussed with them, and individual students should not be required to perform any experimental manipulation they consider inappropriate. Only advanced undergraduates and postgraduate students would be eligible to apply for a Personal Licence, and any procedures would be carried out only under an existing Project Licence.

BOX 9.5 (CONTINUED)

10 *The use of animals for therapeutic purposes:* (See text above.) In all cases, the same considerations concerning the general care and welfare as detailed for experimental animals apply. But there are also specific considerations, such as the individual animal's temperament and training being suitable for the planned task (e.g. a hospital visiting dog should be calm, placid and sociable with people). Contact with the client/patient needs to be carefully monitored.

BOX 9.6 WASHOE AND THE GARDNERS

In 'Teaching sign language to a chimpanzee' (1969), Gardner and Gardner report their famous research with Washoe, estimated to be between 8 and 14 months when she arrived at their laboratory.

When she was five years old, Washoe was sent away with Roger and Deborah Fouts. The Gardners next saw her 11 years later; when they unexpectedly entered the room Washoe was in, she signed their name, then 'Come, Mrs G', led her to an adjoining room and began to play a game with her which she had not been observed to play since she left the Gardners' home (Singer, 1993).

Observations like this, as well as supporting the argument that non-humans really are capable of language (see Gross, 2005, 2008), raise important ethical questions – in particular:

● How justifiable is the whole attempt to study language in non-humans, since this involves removing the animals from their natural habitat in which they do not spontaneously use language?
● What happens to the chimpanzees after they have served their purpose as experimental subjects?

While these kinds of study are not usually the target for attacks against cruel treatment of animals in psychological research, they nonetheless involve animals that have not chosen to become involved. But perhaps it is the fact that they're great apes, and not just 'other animals', which makes these ethical questions so fascinating and important. This also applies to the other 'strand', which involves the several hundred chimpanzee 'veterans' of American research during the 1970s aimed at developing vaccines for hepatitis B and C. While euthanasia was being considered, the AIDS epidemic in the mid-1980s came to their 'rescue'. Once again, because of their genetic similarity to ourselves, they became 'surrogate human beings' again (Mahoney, 1998).

By the mid-1990s, scientists began turning to human volunteers for the initial testing of HIV vaccines, leaving large numbers of 'redundant' chimpanzees (which have a lifespan of up to 40 years). A report of the US National Research Council (1997) concluded that chimpanzees should be afforded special consideration, on ethical grounds, over other non-humans, and that euthanasia is not an acceptable means of population control (Mahoney, 1998).

The *Great Ape Project* (GAP) is (i) the title of a book (subtitle: *Equality Beyond Humanity*, edited by Singer and Cavalieri, 1993), (ii) a simple but radical idea, to extend the 'community of equals' beyond human beings to all great apes (chimps, gorillas and orang-utans), and (iii) an organization, comprising 34 academics and others, set up to work internationally for the immediate inclusion of the great apes within the community of equals. This refers to the moral community within which we accept certain basic moral rights/principles as governing our relationships with each other and which are enforceable at law.

The central tenet of the GAP is that it is ethically indefensible to deny the great apes the basic rights of (i) the right to life, (ii) protection of individual liberty, and (iii) prohibition of torture (collectively, the *Declaration of Great Apes*). Wise (2000), in a book entitled *Rattling the Cage: Towards Legal Rights for Animals*, argues that

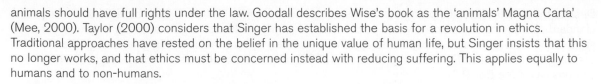

animals should have full rights under the law. Goodall describes Wise's book as the 'animals' Magna Carta' (Mee, 2000). Taylor (2000) considers that Singer has established the basis for a revolution in ethics. Traditional approaches have rested on the belief in the unique value of human life, but Singer insists that this no longer works, and that ethics must be concerned instead with reducing suffering. This applies equally to humans and to non-humans.

PSYCHOLOGISTS AS AGENTS OF CHANGE

We noted at the beginning of the chapter that there are both important similarities and differences as regards the ethical problems faced by psychologists as scientists and as practitioners. These are reflected, respectively, in BPS documents aimed at *all* psychologists (such as the *Code of Ethics and Conduct*, 2006) and those aimed at specific groups (notably, the *Division of Clinical Psychology Professional Practice Guidelines* (1995)).

We also noted that there is considerable overlap between clinical and counselling psychologists, and psychotherapists and psychiatrists, in terms of the ethical dimensions of their work. In the remainder of this chapter, we will discuss some of the major ethical issues common to all these professional groups, namely:

● informed consent
● the influence of the therapist
● behavioural control
● the abuse of patients by therapists.

Informed consent

Where someone is voluntarily seeking help from a psychologist or psychotherapist (as opposed to the position of an involuntary, sectioned, patient in a psychiatric hospital), it might seem that there would not be an issue regarding informed consent. But even here, differences in power between staff and patients and the ability to control one's situation are very real. If we think about what this means in relation to participants in research (namely, being fully aware of the purpose of the study), things begin to look a little less straightforward.

According to Holmes (1992), this is a problem throughout the caring professions. The law in Britain and the USA differs regarding the extent to which doctors are expected to explain in advance every detail of the possible adverse consequences of a procedure or treatment. In the case of psychotherapy, this is especially problematic, for four main reasons:

1 The patient may well be in a vulnerable and emotionally aroused state and, thus, unlikely to be able to make a balanced judgement as to the suitability of the particular form of therapy on offer and/or his or her compatibility with the therapist.
2 Unlike medical procedures, the range of different forms of psychotherapy available tends to be poorly understood by the general public and the media.
3 The lack of any generally agreed standards of training, practice or regulatory procedures within psychotherapy as a whole means that there are no external criteria against which a particular therapy can be assessed.
4 There are special problems of informed consent associated with particular therapies. For example, in psychoanalysis, some degree of 'opacity' is necessary if certain techniques, such as transference, are to be effective. In other words, the therapist must remain partially 'obscure' or 'non-transparent' if the patient is to be able to transfer onto the therapist unconscious feelings for parents (or other key relatives), which are then discussed and interpreted. When assessing patients for treatment, analysts must strike a balance between providing legitimate information on the one hand, and maintaining their 'professional distance' on the other. (See Chapter 14.)

Despite these difficulties, the problems of consent can be overcome. Holmes (1992) believes that recognized standards of training and practice would help. Indeed, most psychotherapy organizations in Britain favour a state-recognized profession of psychotherapy and are actively trying to achieve this goal through the UK Standing Conference on Psychotherapy. Masson (1992) proposes that there should be a 'psychotherapy ombudsman'. (See Box 9.7.)

BOX 9.7 THE BRITISH ASSOCIATION FOR COUNSELLING AND PSYCHOTHERAPY (BACP)

History
The British Association for Counselling (BAC) was founded in 1977. It grew from the Standing Conference for the Advancement of Counselling, a grouping of organizations inaugurated in 1970 at the instigation of the National Council for Voluntary Organizations. In 2000, the BAC recognized that it no longer represented just counselling, but also psychotherapy. It changed its name to the *British Association for Counselling and Psychotherapy* (BACP). The change of name also acknowledged that counsellors and psychotherapists wished to belong to a unified profession that could meet their common interests.

BACP is the largest and broadest body within the sector. Its remit is to protect the public while also developing and informing its members. Its work ranges from advising schools on how to set up a counselling service, assisting the NHS on service provision, working with voluntary agencies, to supporting independent practitioners.

Objectives
The BACP's objectives are to:

a promote and provide education and training for counsellors and/or psychotherapists working in either professional or voluntary settings, with a view to raising the standards of counselling and/or psychotherapy for the benefit of the community, in particular the recipients of these services; and

b advance the education of the public in the part that counselling and/or psychotherapy can play generally and in particular to meet the needs of those members of society where development and participation in society is impaired by mental, physical or social handicap or disability.

Ethical Framework for Good Practice in Counselling and Psychotherapy
The BACP sets, promotes and maintains standards for the profession. The *Ethical Framework* (2002), together with the *Professional Conduct Procedure*, ensures that members abide by an accepted and approved code of conduct and accountability. The basic principles are as follows:

- Fidelity: honouring the trust placed in the practitioner.
- Autonomy: respect for the client's right to be self-governing.
- Beneficence: a commitment to promoting the client's well-being.
- Non-maleficence: a commitment to avoiding harm to the client.
- Justice: the fair and impartial treatment of all clients and the provision of adequate services.
- Self-respect: fostering the practitioner's self-knowledge and care for self.

Statutory regulation
In 2005, the Department of Health funded BACP and the United Kingdom Council for Psychotherapy (UKCP) to conduct research into the provision of counselling and psychotherapy training in the UK and the standards of that training and the codes of ethics, practice and conduct processes of all affiliated organizations. Part of this regulation is a *core curriculum:* this comprises elements that the BACP believes should be present in all training courses for counsellors and psychotherapists. It is hoped that by adopting the core curriculum, it will be possible to achieve some *standardization* in training while allowing courses to retain their own identity and individuality.

Most patients probably gravitate towards the therapies and therapists they feel comfortable with, and word-of-mouth recommendations are very important in private practice. At least you only pay for one session at a time – it is not like buying a used car (Holmes, 1992)!

The influence of the therapist

Psychologists are aware of the subtle coercion that can operate on hospitalized psychiatric patients – even voluntary ones. The in-patient is subjected to strong persuasion to accept the treatment recommendations of professional staff. As Davison and Neale (2001) observe,

> . . . *even a 'voluntary' and informed decision to take psychotropic medication or to participate in any other therapy regimen is often (perhaps usually) less than free.*

The issue of the influence of the therapist on the patient/client has been central to a long-standing debate between traditional (psychodynamic) psychotherapists and behaviour therapists (who, as we saw earlier, are usually clinical psychologists by training).

Many psychotherapists believe that behaviour therapy is unacceptable (even if it works), because it is manipulative and demeaning of human dignity. By contrast, their own methods are seen as fostering the autonomous development of the patient's inherent potential, helping the patient to express his/her true self, and so on. Instead of an influencer, they see themselves as a kind of psychological midwife, present during the birth, possessing useful skills, but there primarily to make sure that a natural process goes smoothly (Wachtel, 1977).

According to Wachtel, however, this is an exaggeration and misrepresentation of both approaches. For many patients, the 'birth' probably would not happen at all without the therapist's intervention, and s/he undoubtedly does influence the patient's behaviour. Conversely, behaviour therapists are at least partly successful because they establish an active, cooperative relationship with the patient, who plays a much more active role in the therapy than psychotherapists believe.

Wachtel argues that all therapists, of whatever persuasion, if they are at all effective, influence their patients. Both approaches comprise:

> . . . *a situation in which one human being (the therapist) tries to act in such a way as to enable another human being to act and feel differently than he has, and this is as true of psychoanalysis as it is of behaviour therapy.*

For Wachtel, the crucial issue is the *nature* of this influence (not whether it occurs), and there are four crucial questions that need to be asked:

1 Is the influence exerted in a direction that is in the patient's interest, or in the service of the therapist's needs?
2 Are some good ends (such as reduction in anxiety) being achieved at the expense of others (such as the patient's enhanced vision of the possibilities that life can offer or an increased sense of self-directedness)?
3 Is the patient fully informed about the kind of influence that the therapist wishes to exert and the kind of ends being sought? (This, of course, relates to informed consent.)
4 Is the patient's choice being excessively influenced by a fear of displeasing the therapist, rather than by what s/he would really prefer?

The *neutrality* of therapists is a myth; they influence their clients in subtle yet powerful ways:

> *Unlike a technician, a psychiatrist cannot avoid communicating and at times imposing his own values upon his patients. The patient usually has considerable difficulty in finding the way in which he would wish to change his behaviour, but as he talks to the psychiatrist his wants and needs become clearer. In the very process of defining his needs in the presence of a figure who is viewed as wise and authoritarian, the patient is profoundly influenced. He ends up wanting some of the things the psychiatrist thinks he should want.*
>
> (Davison and Neale, 1994)

In the above extract, we can add the terms 'psychologist' and 'psychotherapist' to 'psychiatrist'.

According to Davison *et al.* (2004), sometimes therapists' values are subtle and difficult to identify. Wachtel (1997) criticizes both psychoanalysis and the humanistic-existential approaches for their overemphasis on people's need to change 'from within', rather than being assisted, even directed, in their efforts to change as happens in cognitive behaviour therapy (see Chapter 14). By concentrating on people gaining their own insights and making behavioural changes more or less on their own, and by discouraging therapists from influencing their clients by directly teaching them new skills, insight-oriented therapists unwittingly teach an ethic of aloneness devoid of social support. Wachtel asks whether this is an appropriate message to convey to patients and to society at large.

> *. . . many [insight] therapists who criticize behaviour therapy as an agent of cultural norms are themselves upholding one of the basic tenets of our capitalistic society, when they stress change based solely on autonomous action and deride the need for direct assistance from others . . . It is, after all, just as human to be able to turn to others as it is to stand alone.*
>
> (Wachtel, 1997)

Behavioural control

While a behavioural technique such as *systematic desensitization* (SD, based on classical conditioning) is largely limited to the reduction of anxiety, at least this can be seen as enhancing the patient's freedom, since anxiety is one of the greatest restrictions on freedom. By contrast, methods based on *operant conditioning* can be applied to almost any aspect of a person's life (largely because they are applied to *voluntary* as opposed to *reflex* or *respondent* behaviour: see Chapter 14).

Those who use operant methods, such as the token economy (TE), often describe their work rather exclusively in terms of behavioural control, and they subscribe to Skinner's (1971) view that freedom is only an illusion (see Chapter 11). Wachtel (1977) believes that when used in institutional settings (as with long-term schizophrenic patients in psychiatric hospitals), the TE is so subject to abuse that its use is highly questionable. It may be justifiable (i) if it works, and (ii) if there's clearly no alternative way of rescuing the patient from an empty and destructive existence. But as a routine part of how society deals with deviant behaviour, this approach raises very serious ethical questions.

One of these relates to the question of power. As we noted earlier, even voluntary patients are powerless relative to the institutional staff; patients who become involved in TE programmes are likely to be involuntary, very long-term, highly institutionalized. According to Wachtel:

> *. . . reinforcement is viewed by many – proponents and opponents alike – as somehow having an inexorable controlling effect upon the person's behaviour and rendering him incapable of choice, reducing him to an automaton or duly wound mechanism . . .*

The alarming feature of the TE is the reinforcing agent's power to physically deprive uncooperative patients of 'privileges'.

Applied behaviour analysis (ABA) and punishment

Another application of operant conditioning is *applied behaviour analysis* (ABA), often referred to simply as 'behaviour modification'. This is commonly used with autistic and brain-damaged children and adults, and punishment techniques may be involved, especially when the client displays self-injurious behaviour. O'Donohue and Ferguson (2001) believe that a common misconception about ABA is that it uses a great deal of punishment such as electric shock:

> *The caricature of these approaches is a cattle-prod-wielding Nurse Ratchett who shocks and threatens to punish in order to coerce behaviour change . . .*

Although punishment is sometimes used, psychologists who use ABA follow Skinner's recommendations and rarely use it as a first choice (see Chapter 14). It often induces escape and avoidance behaviour, anger and fear. Also, it is not a constructive learning mechanism: while it decreases the frequency of some behaviours, it does not increase the frequency of more desirable behaviours. So, applied behaviour analysts prefer to use a *reinforcement-based* intervention. Reinforcement does not always work, though, and sometimes the undesirable behaviour is so serious that punishment *must* be used (O'Donohue and Ferguson, 2001).

Leslie (2002) observes that, although punishment is a 'normal' part of everyday attempts to modify others' behaviour, it becomes controversial in applied settings. While it can be effective,

> *. . . it should be a technique of last resort, both because the situation in which it occurs may become aversive and lead to escape or aggression, and because of the public debate that surrounds its use.*

Some critics have condemned punishment in particular, and ABA in general, as evil and controlling. But these attacks are based partly on misinformation, partly on a small number of cases of abuse, and partly on ideological objections to all scientific accounts of human behaviour (see Chapter 14). But this only strengthens the need for applied behaviour analysts to explain how and why their practices *are* ethical (Leslie, 2002).

Leslie refers to ethical guidelines that have been developed for the use of behavioural treatments (citing Van Houten *et al.*, 1988). These are primarily intended to protect the human rights of the clients involved, and comprise six fundamental rights of individuals for whom behavioural intervention is provided. These are the rights to:

- a therapeutic environment
- services whose overriding goal is personal welfare
- treatment by a competent behaviour analyst
- programmes that teach fundamental skills
- behavioural assessment and ongoing evaluation, and
- the most effective treatment procedures available.

As the guidelines indicate:

> *. . . professionals who practise applied behaviour analysis are fundamentally interested in improving the lives of the people they work with and of society in general. Regrettably, there will, from time to time, be individuals in any discipline who will violate professional guidelines, and such individuals should not be allowed to practise behaviour analysis.*
>
> *(Leslie, 2002)*

173

The abuse of patients by therapists

In recent years, there has been a wave of criticism of psychotherapy (especially of the Freudian variety) from a number of directions, and these have included criticism of its ethical shortcomings. One particularly controversial and much publicized aspect of psychodynamic therapy is the *false-memory debate* and the related *false-memory syndrome*. The False Memory Syndrome Foundation (in the USA) and the British False Memory Society were founded in the early 1990s, largely by parents accused by their grown-up children of having sexually abused them when they were children. The accusing children discovered repressed memories of child sexual abuse during the course of psychotherapy; hence, from their and their therapists' perspectives, these are *recovered memories* (RMs).

However, from the perspective of the accused parents, these are false memories (FMs), implanted by therapists into the minds of their emotionally vulnerable patients/clients. These unethical, unscrupulous therapists are, in turn, accused by parents of practising recovered-memory therapy, which induces false-memory syndrome (FMS). (See Gross, 2005.)

One of psychoanalysis's most outspoken critics is an American, ex-Freudian psychoanalyst, Jeffrey Masson. Masson (1992) believes there is an *imbalance of power* involved in the therapeutic relationship. Individuals who seek therapy need protection from the constant temptation to abuse, misuse, profit from and bully on the part of the therapist. The therapist has almost absolute emotional power over the patient, and in his *Against Therapy: Emotional Tyranny and the Myth of Psychological Healing* (1988), he catalogues example after example of patients' abuse – emotional, sexual, financial – at the hands of their therapists.

Naturally enough, Masson's attack has stirred up an enormous controversy. Holmes (1992) agrees with the core of Masson's argument, namely that:

> *. . . no therapist, however experienced or distinguished, is above the laws of the unconscious, and all should have access to supervision and work within a framework of proper professional practice.*
>
> *(Masson, 1992)*

In defence of psychotherapy, Holmes (1992) points out that exploitation and abuse are by no means confined to psychotherapy: lawyers, university teachers, priests and doctors are also sometimes guilty. All these professional groups have ethical standards and codes of practice (often far more stringent than the laws of the land), with disciplinary bodies that impose severe punishments – usually expulsion from the profession. As Leslie (2002) argues in the case of ABA, we should not condemn an entire profession because of the transgressions of a small minority. Also, as we noted in Box 9.7, there is an increasing move towards regulation of (and by) the BACP and other bodies responsible for the practice of counselling and psychotherapy; this includes those individuals working in private practice.

SUMMARY

- ○ Ethical issues arise because (i) human beings and animals are sentient, living things, and (ii) human beings are thinking creatures, capable of experiencing embarrassment, guilt and so on.

- ○ Ethical issues arise for psychologists because (i) they study human beings and animals, (ii) they often subject the people/animals they study to painful/embarrassing situations/stimulation, (iii) every psychological investigation can be thought of as an ethical situation.

- ○ The BPS and APA both publish various codes of conduct and ethical guidelines, some of which apply to the roles of both scientist/investigator and practitioner jointly, while others apply to one or the other.

O Guidelines such as the BPS's *Ethical Principles* are intended, primarily, to protect the 'rights and dignity' of participants. These include deception, consent/informed consent, withdrawal from the investigation, and debriefing.

O Feminists argue that the power difference between researcher and researched should be reversed by the researcher becoming actively involved in the research process, as opposed to a detached manipulator/controller of the experimental situation.

O According to Milgram, the motivational reason for deceiving participants is quite unacceptable, but the epistemological reason is justified.

O Milgram believes that 'technical illusions' are justified only if they are in the end accepted/endorsed by those exposed to them. But since their use prevents participants from giving their informed consent, they should only be used if absolutely essential.

O The questions that psychologists try to answer through their research are shaped partly by their values, and partly by methodological considerations. The research itself is constrained by what is possible and what is ethically acceptable.

O Ethical debates usually concentrate on the need to protect the integrity/welfare of the individual participant. But psychologists are also obliged to carry out socially meaningful research (the 'ethical imperative'). This twofold obligation can present psychologists with a dilemma over whether or not they should use deception.

O Generally, the more socially significant the issue, the greater the need for deception, and the more likely that an individual participant will experience distress.

O Some possible solutions to this dilemma include: (i) only use deception if the scientific/medical justification is extremely strong; (ii) the use of presumptive consent and prior general consent.

O While ethical codes serve to protect individual participants, underlying assumptions may harm the social groups they represent. Formal codes neglect wider issues regarding the ethical acceptability of socially sensitive research.

O In the case of animal experimentation, ethical and practical issues are very closely tied.

O Some of the reasons for using animals in research include: (i) the greater control over variables; (ii) the evolutionary continuity between humans and other species; (iii) the convenience and speed of studying animals' development; and (iv) the testing of cause-and-effect hypotheses from human correlational research.

O The main justifications for using animals are: (i) the pursuit of scientific knowledge; (ii) the advancement of medicine.

O Many drugs used in the treatment of human diseases could not have been developed without animal research, and this may be seen as a sufficient justification for the use of animals.

O According to Gray, not only is speciesism justified, it is our duty to carry out animal research if this may result in the alleviation of human suffering.

O Safeguards for animals used in research include the BPS's *Guidelines* and the Animals (Scientific Procedures) Act. Animals are used for a variety of purposes apart from research; the *Guidelines* aim to protect them all.

○ The Great Ape Project argues that the great apes should be given the basic rights of life, freedom and protection from torture.

○ As agents of change, clinical psychologists (along with counselling psychologists and psychotherapists) face the ethical issues of informed consent, the influence of the therapist, behavioural control, the abuse of patients, confidentiality and 'privileged communication'.

○ Subtle forms of coercion can operate on hospitalized psychiatric patients (including voluntary ones) to accept particular forms of treatment.

○ Many psychotherapists see behaviour therapy as manipulative and demeaning of human dignity, but view their own methods as helping patients to become autonomous. All therapists influence their patients, however, and it is the kind of influence involved that matters. Insight-oriented therapists may be guilty of reinforcing capitalistic values.

○ The token economy (TE), as a form of behavioural control, is ethically highly dubious. One objection is the powerlessness of patients relative to the staff operating the programme; another is the patient's reduction to an automaton who lacks choice.

○ Applied behaviour analysis (ABA) has been condemned for its use of punishment techniques. However, these are used only as a last resort to stop seriously harmful behaviour.

○ Masson condemns psychotherapists for abusing the power they have over their patients. Particularly controversial is the debate over false memories. However, exploitation/abuse can be found in a small minority within all professions.

USEFUL WEBSITES

http://www.apa.org/ethics/code.html
www.bps.org.uk
http://www.bacp.co.uk/ethical_framework/ethics.php
http://altweb.jhsph.edu
http://www.aalas.org
http://www.apa.org/science/anguide.html

RECOMMENDED READING

British Psychological Society (1995) *Division of Clinical Psychology Professional Practice Guidelines.* Leicester: BPS.

British Psychological Society (2006) *Code of Ethics and Conduct.* Leicester: BPS.

British Psychological Society (2007a) *Guidelines for Psychologists Working with Animals.* Leicester: BPS.

British Psychological Society (2007b) *Guidelines for Ethical Practice in Psychological Research Online.* Leicester: BPS.

Milgram, S. (1974) *Obedience to Authority.* New York: Harper & Row. (Especially Appendix 1: 'Problems of ethics in research'.)

Milgram, S. (1992) *The Individual in a Social World: Essays and Experiments* (2nd edn). New York: McGraw-Hill. (Especially Chapters 10, 12 and 15.)

Wise, R. (2000) *Rattling the Cage: Towards Legal Rights for Animals.* London: Profile Books.

CHAPTER 10

PSYCHOLOGY AS SCIENCE

SCIENCE AS A RECURRENT THEME

Explicitly or implicitly, the nature of science and psychology's status as a science are discussed throughout this book. Chapter 1 looks at the ways in which everyone may be thought of as a psychologist, by examining common-sense psychology and how this is both similar to, and different from, scientific psychology. According to Heider, the lay person assigns causes to behaviour and, to that extent, acts like a naïve scientist.

Identifying the causes of a phenomenon as a way of trying to explain it (as well as a means of predicting and controlling it) is a fundamental part of 'classical' science (see below). This is related to *determinism*, which is discussed in relation to free will in Chapter 11.

The three aims of explanation/understanding, prediction and control are discussed in Chapter 3 in terms of their appropriateness for a science of psychology. The idiographic and nomothetic approaches refer to two very different views as to what it is about people that psychologists should be studying, and the methods that should be adopted to study them. These two approaches correspond to the *social sciences/humanities* and natural/physical sciences respectively. This distinction is much less clear-cut than it was once thought to be; indeed, the view of natural science current at the time that Windelband originally made the distinction between the Geisteswissenschaften ('moral sciences') and the *Naturwissenschaften* ('natural sciences') is now considered by many scientists and philosophers to be outmoded. Ironically, psychologists may still be trying to model their discipline on a view of physics (in particular, and natural science in general) which physicists themselves no longer hold. More of this below.

Chapter 6 considers how feminist psychologists have exposed a major source of bias within both the research and theorizing of 'mainstream' academic psychology, as well as within the psychology profession itself. That bias is *androcentrism*, or male-centredness. From the perspective of classical, orthodox, mainstream scientific psychology, there are very powerful reasons for 'keeping quiet' about it, namely that science is meant to be *unbiased, objective and value-free*. This view of science is called *positivism*, something that feminist psychologists explicitly reject when they advocate a study of human beings, in which the researchers 'come clean' about their values.

Positivism is also involved in the attempts of clinical psychologists and psychiatrists to define, classify, diagnose and treat psychological disorders in an objective, value-free or value-neutral way (comparable to what goes on in general medicine: see Chapter 7). In other words, definitions of abnormality are influenced by a wide range of cultural beliefs, values, assumptions and experiences, but as long as practitioners remain unaware of their influence, they will perceive what they do as being objective. The belief that it is possible to be objective about psychological disorders reflects the positivist scientific training of clinical psychologists and psychiatrists.

The fact that the cultural (as well as the class, ethnic and gender) background of practitioners is usually different from that of the majority of their patients/clients, introduces a strong *ethnocentric bias* to the area of abnormal behaviour. This is often even more apparent when western psychologists travel to other cultures in order to study the behaviour and experience of members of those other cultures (see Chapter 8). While cross-cultural psychology can serve as an important counterbalance to the equation of 'human' with 'member of western culture', it is even more difficult (both theoretically and in practice) for a member of one culture to objectively study a person from another culture than when the researcher and the person being investigated share a common culture (although even here the differences may be greater than the similarities).

In Chapter 9 on ethics, reference is made to Orne's (1962) claim that every psychology experiment is a social situation. Whatever topic is being investigated or hypothesis tested, there is an interaction between two (or more) people who bring with them to the experimental situation a whole set of expectations, questions and other cognitive processes (both conscious and unconscious) and behaviours, just as they do to other social situations. In other words, what is going on in the minds, and between the minds, of the people involved inevitably affects the outcome, making the experiment something less than a wholly objective situation. This is often contrasted with experiments in the natural sciences, which are interpreted according to the classical, positivist view of science in which objectivity plays such a crucial role. But this, in turn, is considered by many to be an oversimplification – indeed a misrepresentation – of what goes on even in the natural sciences (see below).

Chapter 13 considers some of the issues surrounding the study of paranormal ('unusual' or anomalistic) phenomena and experiences. These issues include some basic questions about the nature of science and the validity of using scientific methods to study human experience.

Finally, Chapter 14 considers major theoretical approaches within psychology. One of the major criteria used to assess these is how 'scientific' their methods (and the resulting theories) are. But this criterion is applied only by those who adopt a positivist approach, and both psychodynamic and social constructionist approaches show that there are different 'takes' on what science means. Importantly for parts of this chapter, social constructionists argue that not only is knowledge (including scientific knowledge) socially constructed, but science itself is a socially constructed, socially mediated activity. Theories about 'the world' are as much a reflection of the social nature of science as they are a reflection of the world itself.

A BRIEF SKETCH OF THE HISTORY OF SCIENCE

Many of the basic principles and assumptions of modern science, as well as some fundamental 'common-sense' assumptions we make about the world, can be attributed to the French philosopher Descartes (1596–1650). He divided the universe into two fundamentally different realms or 'realities': (a) physical matter (*res extensa*), which is extended in time and space, and (b) non-material, non-extended mind (*res cogitans*). This view is known as *philosophical dualism*, and the opposed view, that only matter exists, is called *materialism* – both views (and others relating to the mind–body/brain issue) are discussed in detail in Chapter 12.

This distinction between matter and mind allowed scientists to treat matter as inert and completely distinct from themselves, which meant that the world could be described objectively, without reference to the human observer. Objectivity became the ideal of science; Comte's extension of it (in the mid-1800s) to the study of human behaviour and social institutions became known as *positivism* (see below).

Descartes believed that the material world comprised objects assembled like a huge machine and operated by mechanical laws that could be explained in terms of the arrangements and movements of its parts. This view of the world is called *mechanism* ('machine-ism'). Descartes extended this mechanistic view of matter to living organisms. He compared animals to clocks composed of wheels and springs, and later extended this view to the human body, which he saw as a machine, part of a perfect cosmic machine, controlled, at least in principle,

Figure 10.1 Describing the world objectively became easier with the invention of such instruments as the ruler of Ptolemy for measuring the distance from the ground to the zenith

by mathematical laws. Descartes also believed that complex wholes may be understood in terms of their constituent parts, and so was one of the first advocates of reductionism (see below and Figure 10.2 overleaf).

Because the mind is non-material, it cannot be studied in the way that the physical world is studied. Descartes believed that the mind could only be approached by *introspection* – that is, looking inwards at one's own thoughts and ideas.

Newton later formulated the mathematical laws and mechanics that were thought to account for all the changes observable in the physical world. The mechanical model of the universe subsequently guided all scientific activity for the next 200 years. By the end of the nineteenth century, Nietzsche (1844–1900) captured the spirit of the age by declaring that 'God is dead', meaning that traditional religious values had been largely negated, replaced by science as the ultimate authority within western culture.

Science and empiricism

In addition to positivism, determinism, mechanism, materialism and reductionism, *empiricism* represented another fundamental feature of science (and a major influence on its development). This refers to the ideas of the seventeenth-century British *empiricist* philosophers – in particular, Locke, Hume and Berkeley. They believed that the only source of true knowledge about the world is *sensory experience* – what comes to us through our senses or what can be inferred about the relationships between such sensory facts. This belief proved to be one of the central influences on the development of physics and chemistry.

The word 'empirical' is often used synonymously with 'scientific', implying that what scientists do is carry out experiments and observations as means of collecting data or 'facts' about the world. This, in turn, implies other very important assumptions about the nature of scientific activity and its relationship to the phenomena under investigation:

● an empirical approach is different from a *theoretical* one, since the latter does not involve the use of experiment, measurement and other forms of data collection
● philosophers, rather than scientists, use theory and rational argument (as opposed to data collection) to try to establish the truth about the world
● the truth about the world (the objective nature of the world – what it's 'really like') can be established through properly controlled experiments and other empirical methods. In other words, science can tell us about reality as it is *independently* of the scientist and of the activity of trying to observe it.

Logical positivism

Logical positivism (LP) was the dominant philosophy of science from the 1920s to the 1960s, associated with a group of scientists, mathematicians and philosophers known as the 'Vienna Circle; a central figure in the movement was the English philosopher A.J. Ayer.

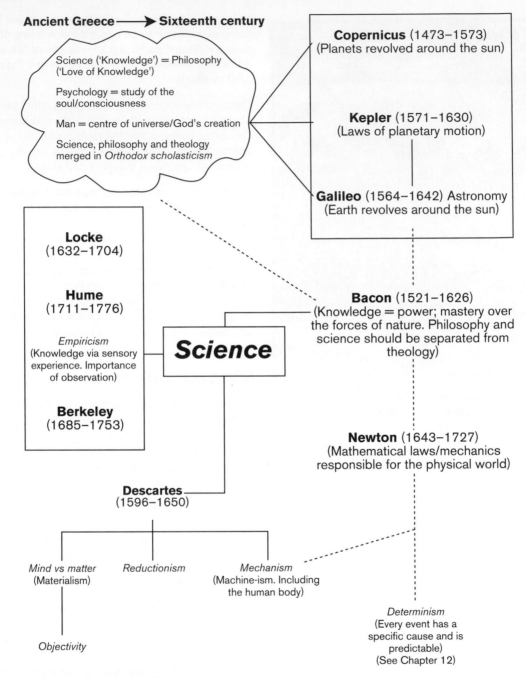

Figure 10.2 Influences on the development of science

An extreme form of 'operationalism', LP maintains that the meaning of a statement can be defined in terms of the operations needed to verify it. In other words, for sentences to have meaning, it must be possible, at least in principle, to demonstrate their truth or falsity (e.g. 'The liquid in the test tube is coloured red'; 'Intelligence is what an intelligence test measures': Bem and Looren de Jong, 1997). If a statement does not specify how it could be proven true or false, then it is just meaningless nonsense. If meaning can be described in terms of specifiable operations on the physical world, without reference to observers, then 'objective knowledge' is possible. According to Ayer (1936), sensory experience is all-important, which places LP firmly in the traditions of classical empiricism and realist theories of perception (according to which objects are as we perceive them to be). In fact, Gregory (1981) believes that LP makes sensory experience even more crucial than did Locke and the other British empiricist philosophers (see Chapter 5) – they at least allowed meaning to non-sensory statements. What LP allows is that observation/experimentation can help discover knowledge without the need for underlying beliefs for interpreting observations. This corresponds to the second and third points above.

The role of theory

While the first point is true and non-controversial, the second and third points are much more the subject of debate among scientists and philosophers of science. Although the use of empirical methods is a defining feature of science and does distinguish it from philosophy, the use of theory is *equally* crucial. This explains why many would reject the view of science as involving the discovery of 'facts' about the world, which are uninfluenced by the scientist's *theories*. These may deal with what causes the phenomenon under investigation (corresponding, perhaps, to most people's understanding of what a 'scientific theory' is), but in a broader sense theories also 'include' and reflect the biases, prejudices, values and assumptions of the individual scientist, as well as those of the scientific community to which s/he belongs. To the extent that such characteristics of the scientist influence the scientific process, it cannot be regarded as objective.

If this is true in the cases of physics and chemistry, it is even more likely to be true of Psychology (with a capital 'P'), where human beings are studying other human beings. Unconscious biases (such as androcentrism, sexism and ethnocentrism) come into play here, which is less likely to be true of the physicist or chemist investigating aspects of the physical world. But in Psychology's attempt to model itself on the natural sciences, people have been regarded and treated as if they were part of the natural world. The difficulties of using this approach are discussed later in the chapter.

Ayer has since abandoned his radical brand of LP. According to Gregory (1981):

> . . . He [Ayer] no longer believes that operational criteria can be found that will separate the wheat of facts from the weeds of subjective ethics and aesthetics. This implies that clear distinctions between sense and nonsense (or between objective and subjective) cannot be made by simple rule-following. These distinctions depend on assumptions, which themselves change according to the 'philosophic atmosphere' . . .

Kuhn (1962, 1970) and other philosophers of science (e.g. Feyerabend, 1965) claim that empirical observations are 'theory-laden': our theory *literally* determines how we see the world. This means that no observation can be objective (i.e. *unbiased*) and 'facts' do not exist independently of a 'theoretical lens' without which *data* have no meaning (Deese, 1972). What scientists gather are data – *not* 'facts' which somehow already exist in the way that fossils are (literally) unearthed. 'Facts' are *interpretations* of data, and theories are what provide the interpretations.

But while 'facts' (as commonly misunderstood) cannot change (and have always 'existed' in their current form), theories can – and do. This means that scientific knowledge is only ever temporary: as theories change, so do the 'facts'.

Paradigms and scientific revolutions

This view of the *provisional* nature of our knowledge lies at the heart of Kuhn's theory of *scientific revolutions*. 'Philosophic atmosphere' (James, 1907) in the quote above from Gregory (1981) comes very close to what Kuhn (1962, 1970) means by a *paradigm*. A paradigm is a framework that determines which data are legitimate, what methods may be used, what terminology may be used when stating results, and what kinds of interpretation are allowed. It also embraces the *social organization* of research, the overall 'culture' of the particular discipline dominated by that paradigm. As Bem and Looren de Jong (1997) put it:

> . . . *Students and junior researchers are trained to adopt the frame of reference, the vocabulary and the methods and techniques of the existing community. . . . research communities can be as authoritarian and dogmatic as the Catholic Church or the Mafia . . .*

For Kuhn, theory is part of a greater structure of methods, frameworks, concepts, professional habits and obligations, and laboratory practices. Without such a structure, there would be no research problems – and no research. Facts exist only in the context of a paradigm (see above), making it impossible to choose between competing theories based on their empirical adequacy.

Kuhn rejects the claim by logical positivists that scientific progress occurs through the steady accumulation of scientific knowledge. Taking a historical perspective, Kuhn argues that a discipline can be described as a true science only once it has an established paradigm. Before this stage is reached, it is pre-paradigmatic; after the paradigm is established, a stage (or state) of normal science exists. When results begin to be found that do not fit the paradigm, a crisis eventually triggers a revolution, which involves a paradigm shift and then a return to normal science.

But are paradigm shifts really comparable to revolutions? While this is probably Kuhn's most shocking and controversial claim, it is difficult to criticize his concept of normal science:

> . . . *Doing research is essentially puzzle solving, filling in the gaps in a generally accepted framework by applying the generally accepted methods and interpretations . . . research is working out the paradigm under the assumption that there is a well-defined solution to the remaining uncertainties which can be found by the usual methods . . .*
>
> (Bem and Looren de Jong, 1997)

Kuhn compares a paradigm to a world view: a change of concepts and procedures can transform objects into something else – the data themselves change. Here, the notion of *theory-ladenness* is taken to its limits.

As applied to Psychology, Kuhn, like many others, has described it as pre-paradigmatic. There is little agreement among psychologists regarding the fundamentals of their science. Instead, there are several distinct and competing theoretical approaches, including the *psychoanalytic, behaviourist, Gestalt, psychodiagnostic/psychometric*, and the *cognitive* (Kitchener, 1996: see Chapter 14).

The problem of relativism

While not everyone would necessarily agree with Kitchener's list, many – but not everyone – would agree in principle. However, if, as we noted above, there is no rational, objective way of comparing and choosing between competing theories in terms of how well they 'fit the facts', and if all knowledge is *constructed* (defined in terms of particular theories), then we are faced with the problem of *relativism*. Part of this problem is that we cannot distinguish between a good and a poor paradigm (Agassi, 1996). If a paradigm is simply a way of doing research that all (or most) of those working within a particular field operate within, then its inherent worth becomes irrelevant:

. . . the goodness of a paradigm is not a matter of a fixed criterion: any idea is good as long as it is upheld by the scientific leadership . . . what matters is the command of the scientific leadership, not any specific idea. The reason for that . . . is that there must be coordination between researchers, that this coordination requires control, and that the best arrangement is when the scientific leadership controls the research of the rank and file . . .

(Agassi, 1996)

However much Kuhn has exaggerated the importance of researchers 'towing the paradigm line', the concept is still useful in highlighting the *social* nature of scientific activity (see below, pages 193–8).

Lakatos (1970) has attempted to combine Kuhn's analysis of paradigms with the possibility of avoiding the problem of relativism. He does this by allowing for progress and rationality in terms of competition between *research programmes*, defined as a complex of theories which succeed each other over time. A set of hard-core hypotheses, which are essential and not open to criticism, is protected by a belt of auxiliary hypotheses that can be modified to explain deviant results. The test for superiority of one programme over another is whether the empirical content increases. When new hypotheses work, open new areas and trigger new research, a programme is considered to be progressive (Bem and Looren de Jong, 1997).

In the opposite extreme, Feyerabend's (1978) *methodological anarchism* is a radicalization of relativism: 'anything goes' in methodology and framing hypotheses which go against established theories is the way science proceeds. No hypothesis should be rejected as falsified or unconfirmed; on the contrary, notoriously unscientific ideas, such as voodoo, magic or alternative healing, should be given a try. The acceptance of new scientific ideas is as much due to social and accidental factors as to rational methods, and methodological rules hold back progress (see Chapter 13). Feyerabend's maxim was 'Always contradict!' Perhaps not surprisingly, he became a kind of cult figure in Californian counterculture in the late 1970s.

Feyerabend wished to blow up the established ideology from the inside:

. . . Big science is successful because it controls the resources to churn out ever more results that confirm it. The competition lacks the laboratories and the manpower to produce its own evidence, and hence has no data to show. So it is only natural that new hypotheses should clash with accepted wisdom, and seem ill-supported by the evidence. However, lack of confirmation is . . . no disadvantage. Rather, being counterintuitive is highly desirable, since that is the way to unsettle the established ideologies, and realize real progress . . .

(Bem and Looren de Jong, 1997)

But we are still left asking why it is that established science has delivered such impressive results, while alchemy, voodoo and witchcraft have not. What distinguishes the former from the latter (Bem and Looren de Jong, 1997)?

An unbroken lineage: origin myth 1

Just as psychological concepts and categories are culturally relative (see Chapter 8), so they are *historically* relative. The notion of an 'unbroken lineage' reinforces the idea that Psychology has a history as long as any other science, with the Ancient Greek philosophers being seen as concerned with the same problems and issues as present-day psychologists (Jones and Elcock, 2001). People are praised or criticized according to how their ideas fit with modern conceptions of Psychology. But Jones and Elcock describe this as an 'origin myth'.

According to Danziger (1997), modern Psychology is deeply ahistorical – it fails to see psychological categories and concepts from a historical perspective. Why? One reason is Psychology's wishful identification with natural science. As Danziger says:

Psychological research is supposed to be concerned with natural, not historical, objects, and its methods are considered to be those of natural science, not those of history. Psychology is committed to investigating processes like cognition, perception and motivation, as historically invariant phenomena of nature, not as historically determined social phenomena. Accordingly, it has strongly favoured the experimental approach of natural science and rejected the textual and archival methods of history . . .

Related to this is the implicit belief in scientific progress. (See Kuhn's theory of scientific revolutions above.) As a scientific discipline develops, so knowledge accumulates and we move closer to 'the truth':

. . . the past simply consists of that which has been superseded. The main reason for bothering with it all [the historical course of science] is to celebrate progress, to congratulate ourselves for having arrived at the truth which the cleverest of our ancestors could only guess at.

(Danziger, 1997)

Implicit in this view is the assumption that psychological domains, such as 'intelligence', 'personality' and 'motivation', truly reflect the actual structure of a timeless human nature. So, even though pre-twentieth-century writers may not have organized their reflections around such topics, they are still presented as having had theories about them. If changes in such categories are recognized at all, their *present-day form* is what is taken to define their true nature: older work is interesting only in so far as it 'anticipates' what we now know to be true. But as Danziger says:

The essence of psychological categories (insofar as they have one) lies in their status as historically constructed objects. There are no 'perennial problems' driving through the history of Psychology through the ages . . . At different times and in different places psychologically significant categories have been constructed and reconstructed in attempts to deal with different problems and to answer a variety of questions, many of them not essentially psychological at all . . .

Even the categories of physics are historical constructions, and so are subject to change.

Danziger (1997) examines how Aristotle, one of the Ancient Greek philosophers, used concepts such as 'psyche', which have become equated with 'mind' through translation from Greek into Latin, then into various modern languages. He concludes that:

Many of the fundamental categories of twentieth-century Psychology are, to all intents and purposes, twentieth-century inventions. Such concepts as 'intelligence', 'behaviour' and 'learning' were given such radically changed meanings by modern Psychology that there simply are no earlier equivalents.

In other cases, such as 'motivation' and 'social attitudes', use of the terms themselves is new, describing previously unsuspected phenomenological domains:

The coming of modern Psychology was associated with a revolutionary restructuring of the network of categories employed in the conceptualization of human experience and conduct.

But some, unquestionably psychological, categories were retained with little or no change in meaning from an earlier period, such as 'emotion', 'motive', 'consciousness' and 'self-esteem'. These examples point to an older layer of psychological concepts that predated the emergence of Psychology as a discipline. However:

The very notion of 'Psychology' does not exist before the eighteenth century. Of course, there was no lack of reflection about human experience and conduct, but to imagine that all such reflection was 'psychological' in our sense is to project the present on to the past. Before the eighteenth century there was no sense of a distinct and identifiable domain of natural phenomena that could be systematically known and characterized as 'psychological'. There were theological, philosophical, rhetorical, medical, aesthetic, political categories, but no psychological categories.

Danziger's analysis implies that psychological concepts and categories *do not* refer to 'natural kinds' – that is, 'groups of naturally occurring phenomena that inherently resemble each other and differ crucially from other phenomena'. In other words, they are *constructions*, used to make sense of observable behaviour. But while they may not refer to 'real', objectively existing phenomena, they nevertheless have the power to influence people's behaviour and experience (that is, their psychology). This unique feature of Psychology is discussed below.

SOME (OTHER) INFLUENCES ON THE DEVELOPMENT OF PSYCHOLOGY

Philosophy

Richards (2002) identifies a number of major philosophical theories, prior to 1850, which made significant contributions to the body of psychological concepts that psychologists had to work with. These include *associationism*, which is logically distinct from, but commonly linked with, empiricism (see above), and Scottish 'common-sense' *realism*.

According to Locke (1690) and other British empiricists (see Figure 10.2), all psychological phenomena originate in, and consist of, atom-like, 'corpuscular' sensations, which are built up into complex ideas through a few simple 'laws of associationism'. Although meant to explain how the mind operates, associationism was, ironically, first seized upon by Watson, the founder of behaviourism. The conditioned response represented the 'atom', or basic unit, from which all (learned) behaviour is ultimately derived, but mental processes should be removed from a scientific psychology altogether (see below). Scottish 'common-sense' realism identified several innate 'powers' of the mind, but perhaps its more important contribution to psychology was its *practical* orientation, including an interest in child development and social psychological phenomena (Richards, 2002).

Physiology

These philosophical theories were not trying to account for psychological phenomena as we understand them today – that is, they were not an early form of 'scientific' (or 'natural philosophical') psychology. For the beginnings of 'research', as we now use the term, we need to look to physiology (Richards, 2002). By the late 1700s, physiology was making serious progress in conceptualizing biological processes, and as it did so, various psychological issues took shape. These included a growing debate about brain functioning, with Gall's 'craniology' or 'phrenology' assuming great popularity as a 'scientific' approach to 'character' from about 1800 to the early 1850s (especially in Scotland, where it mapped onto 'common-sense' realism's belief in innate mental powers).

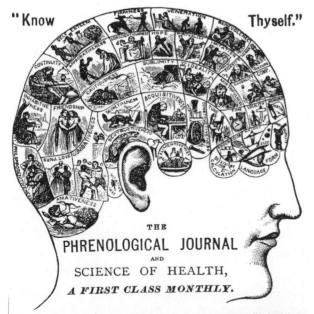

Specially Devoted to the "SCIENCE OF MAN." Contains PHRENOLOGY and PHYSIOGNOMY, with all the SIGNS of CHARACTER, and how to read them;" ETHNOLOGY, or the Natural History of Man in all his relations

Figure 10.3 A phrenology map of the brain

185

Richards believes that, in many ways, phrenology was a 'dry run' for psychology. Although traditionally dismissed as naïve pseudo-science, phrenology is now understood to have played a vital contextual role in popularizing the idea of a secular 'science of the mind', as well as pioneering the 'functionalist' approach (as reflected in the localization of brain function).

Other physiological discoveries that had important implications for psychology included:

- the distinction between afferent and efferent nerves (1820s)
- reflex action (1830s–1840s), which put the possibility of 'unconscious' (automatic) action clearly on the map, as well as the possibility of theorizing about the biological basis of learning
- experimental study of the senses.

In the case of the last, Weber, in the early 1800s, brought the experimental approach across from physiology to psychological issues, such as reaction times and sensory thresholds. This laid the foundation for the work of Fechner and Wundt in the 1850s, which is generally held to represent the birth of experimental psychology (see below). Richards believes that Fechner's (1860/1966) *Elements of Psychophysics* marked the advent of experimental psychology. Psychophysics is the study of the relationship between sensory stimuli and people's experience of them.

From around 1800, such developments in physiology began to make increasing inroads into philosophy's academic monopoly on psychological issues. But both philosophy and physiology 'may be seen as Psychology's major roots' (Richards, 2002).

Evolutionary theory

According to Richards, something was needed to integrate these various developments, and this came in the form of evolutionary thought, triggered by Spencer and Darwin in the 1850s (see Chapter 14). Richards argues that:

> *The role of evolutionary thought is absolutely crucial to the birth of modern Psychology and modern 'psychology' too in fact.*

Throughout Richards's account, he distinguishes between the academic discipline of 'Psychology' and what this discipline attempts to explain, namely people's behaviour and experience (their 'psychology'). This 'Big P'/'Little P' distinction (as made, in particular, in this chapter) is actually quite crucial in discussing the uniqueness of Psychology as a scientific discipline (see below).

Some key evolutionary ideas are summarized in Box 10.1.

THE DEVELOPMENT OF PSYCHOLOGY AS A SCIENCE: THE EARLY DAYS

The secularization of science and philosophy had profound implications for the western perspective on human beings. According to Graham (1986):

> *By the nineteenth century, thinking was essentially analytic, reductionist, objective and positivistic in the sense that it was held that the only valid knowledge is scientific knowledge or positive fact which is objectively verifiable . . .*

The emergence of Psychology as a separate discipline, distinct from philosophy, clearly reflected this scientific 'mentality' or *Zeitgeist* ('spirit of the time'), but at first the subject matter was what it had traditionally been, namely 'non-material consciousness' (Graham, 1986).

BOX 10.1 SOME KEY IDEAS FROM EVOLUTIONARY THEORY

- Humans are descended from primates and so can be considered *zoologically*. We are not semi-divine or beyond the scope of scientific enquiry.
- The raw material for natural selection is the occurrence in each generation of *random variations* ('spontaneous variation'). The 'gene' concept later clarified this, but the lack of genetic understanding handicapped evolutionary theory until the 1920s (see Chapter 5).
- Each individual's development, from conception to maturity, repeats ('*recapitulates*') the evolutionary stages of the species ('*ontogeny* reflects *phylogeny*'). This is referred to as the '*biogenetic law*'.

These ideas galvanized interest in 'human nature', which took various forms, including the following:

1 Investigating the evolution of 'mind': how far are human characteristics present in rudimentary form in 'lower' animals, and, conversely, how far have humans retained 'lower' traits? This led to the development of Comparative Psychology, one aspect of which was a fascination with instincts (see Chapter 14).

2 Focusing attention on the diversity of human 'stock' as raw material from which future generations would be 'naturally selected'. This underlay Galton's pioneer studies of *individual differences* and the development of statistical procedures for analysing them. Galton was also the founder of *eugenics* (see Chapter 5).

3 Studying children as a means of looking back in time and tracking the evolution of humankind. A good example is G. Stanley Hall's (1904) recapitulation theory of adolescence.

4 Understanding the structure of the brain in terms of older and newer components; the human brain has evolved by successive additions/modifications to those of lower organisms.

(Based on Richards, 2002)

University courses in scientific psychology were first taught in the 1870s, before which time there were no laboratories explicitly devoted to psychological research. According to Fancher (1979), the two professors who set up the first two laboratories deserve much of the credit for the development of academic psychology, namely Wilhelm Wundt (1832–1920) in Germany and William James (1842–1910) in the USA.

Wundt's contribution: founding father or origin myth 2?

In the light of physiology's influence on the development of Psychology, it is not too surprising to learn that Wundt was a physiologist. He (sometimes along with James, sometimes alone) is generally regarded as the 'founder' of the new science of Experimental Psychology. As he wrote in the preface to his *Principles of Physiological Psychology* (1874, 1974), 'The work I here present to the public is an attempt to mark out a new domain of science' (in Fancher, 1979). In 1879, he converted his 'laboratory' at Leipzig University (in fact, a small, single room used as a demonstration laboratory, in a rather run-down old building) into a 'private institute' of Experimental Psychology. For the first time, a place had been set aside for the explicit purpose of studying psychology and conducting psychological research. Hence, 1879 is the year that is commonly cited as the 'birth date' of Psychology as a discipline in its own right. The institute soon began to attract people from all over the world, who returned to their own countries to establish laboratories modelled on Wundt's.

In his preface to *Contributions to the Theory of Sensory Perception* (1862), Wundt outlined the possibility of an experimental Psychology, whose aim would be to vary systematically the stimuli and conditions that produce differing mental states. It should be possible to manipulate and observe the facts of consciousness, just like those of physics, chemistry or physiology. In his *Principles of Physiological Psychology*, he argued that conscious mental states could be analysed by carefully controlled techniques of *introspection*. Introspection was a rigorous and highly disciplined technique designed to analyse conscious experience into elementary sensations and feelings. Participants were always carefully trained, advanced Psychology students. Wundt founded the journal *Philosophische Studien* ('Philosophical Studies'), which, despite its name, was the world's

187

first to be primarily devoted to Experimental Psychology. This demonstrated the popularity and success of the 'new psychology'.

The limits of introspection

However, Wundt believed that introspection was only applicable to *psychophysiological* phenomena (sensations, reaction times, attention and other 'lower mental processes' – that is, immediate objects of conscious awareness). Memory, thinking, language, personality and social behaviour belong to the *Geisteswissenschaften* (social sciences), rather than the *Naturwissenschaften* (natural sciences: see Chapter 3). Specifically, he argued that human minds exist within human communities, so in order to study memory, thinking and other 'higher' mental processes, as well as cultural practices, one needs to study communities of people (*Volkerpsychologie*); introspection under controlled laboratory conditions is not an option and can only be used to study the 'lower' mental processes.

By making these distinctions, Wundt was limiting the scope of scientific/Experimental Psychology. But, according to Jones and Elcock (2001), the experiment and the laboratory are portrayed as being of paramount importance in Psychology's construction of itself as a natural science like physics and chemistry. Consequently, Wundt's advocacy of this approach for the study of certain psychophysiological processes has been inflated, creating an 'origin myth', a distorted account of how Psychology 'began'. As we have seen, there was a lot more to Wundt's picture of Psychology as a whole than just those aspects emphasized by the origin myth.

Even those American students who came to Leipzig to study under Wundt failed to establish his introspective methodology permanently back in their own country. Wundt has dominated English-speaking psychologists' picture of late nineteenth-century psychological thought without good foundation (Richards, 2002). He left no lasting legacy, in terms of either theory or empirical discoveries, and although he helped to put experimental Psychology 'on the map', beyond that:

> . . . *his status appears to derive more from the symbolic significance he acquired for others than the success of his Psychology. The discipline wanted a founding father with good experimental scientific credentials, and his American ex-students naturally revered him as their most influential teacher even while subsequently abandoning most of what he taught them . . .*

> *(Richards, 2002)*

The best-known criticism of Wundt's approach to scientific Psychology came from Watson, the American founder of behaviourism (more of which below). But there were underlying cultural differences between Germany and America, which made it difficult for American psychologists to accept Wundt's work wholeheartedly. Wundt, as a representative of the German intellectual tradition that was interested in the mind *in general*, wanted to discover the universal characteristics of the mind that can account for the universal aspects of human experience. But Fancher (1979) argues that, by contrast:

> *Americans, with their pioneer tradition and historical emphasis on individuality, were more concerned with questions of individual differences . . . and the usefulness of those differences in the struggle for survival and success in a socially fluid atmosphere. These attitudes made Americans especially receptive to Darwin's ideas about individual variation, evolution by natural selection, and the 'survival of the fittest' when they appeared in the nineteenth century . . .*

The contribution of James

James was 'perhaps the greatest writer and teacher psychology has ever had' (Fancher, 1979). He trained to be a doctor, never founded an institute for psychological research, and in fact did relatively little research himself. But he used his laboratory to enrich his classroom presentations, and his classic textbook, *The*

Principles of Psychology (1890), was a tremendous popular success, making Psychology interesting and personally relevant. *The Principles of Psychology* includes chapters on brain function, habit, the stream of consciousness (see Chapter 12), the self (see Chapter 4), attention, association, the perception of time, memory, perception, instinct, free will (see Chapter 11) and emotion. The book has given us the immortal definition 'Psychology is the science of mental life.'

After its publication, James became increasingly interested in philosophy and thought of himself less and less as a psychologist. However, he was (in 1894) the first American to call favourable attention to the recent work of the then still rather obscure neurologist from Vienna, Sigmund Freud (Fancher, 1979). According to Fancher, James did not propose a theory so much as a *point of view* (as much philosophical as psychological), which directly inspired functionalism. This was particularly popular with American psychologists. According to functionalism, ideas had to be meaningful to people's lives, and James emphasized the functions of consciousness over its contents. He believed in free will, but this conflicted with his belief in Psychology as a natural science (see Chapter 11). Functionalism, in turn, helped to stimulate interest in *individual differences*, since they determine how well or poorly individuals will adapt to their environments.

James's theory of emotion (see Gross, 2005) proposed that behaviour (such as running away) produces changes in our conscious experience (such as the emotion of fear). This implied that consciousness might be less important to psychology than had previously been thought. While this conflicted with James's belief in free will, it helped lead American Psychology away from a focus on mentalism and towards behaviour (Leahey, 2000).

Behaviourism: revolution or origin myth 3?

When John B. Watson first took over the psychology department at Johns Hopkins University in 1909, he continued to teach courses based on the work of Wundt and James, while conducting his own research on animals. But he became increasingly critical of the use of introspection. In particular, he argued that introspective reports were unreliable and difficult to verify: it is impossible to check the accuracy of such reports, because they are based on purely *private* experience, to which the investigator has no possible means of access. Surely this was no way for a *scientific* Psychology to proceed!

The only solution, as Watson saw it, was for Psychology to redefine itself (see Box 10.2, page 190).

In 1915, Watson was elected president of the American Psychological Association (APA), and his presidential address dealt with his recent 'discovery' of Pavlov's work on conditioned reflexes in dogs. He proposed that the conditioned reflex could become the foundation of a full-scale human Psychology:

> . . . *encompassing everything from habit-formation to emotional disorders. Whereas his behaviourism had been at first little more than a point of view, it promised to become a full-fledged program of research with apparently limitless horizons.*
>
> *(Fancher, 1979)*

Although Wundt had been influenced by empiricism through its impact on science as a whole (including physiology), it was behaviourism that was to embody empiricist philosophy within Psychology. The extreme environmentalism of Locke's empiricism (the mind at birth is a *tabula rasa*, or 'blank slate', on which experience makes its imprint) lent itself very well to the behaviourist emphasis on learning (through the process of conditioning). Despite rejecting the mind as valid subject matter for a scientific Psychology, what the environment shapes simply moves from 'the mind' to observable behaviour (see Chapters 5 and 14).

Behaviourism also embodied the positivism of the Cartesian–Newtonian tradition (Cartesian = from Descartes), in particular the emphasis on the need for scientific rigour and objectivity. Human beings were now being conceptualized and studied as 'natural phenomena', with their subjective experience, consciousness

BOX 10.2 WATSON'S 'BEHAVIOURIST MANIFESTO'

In his 1913 article, 'Psychology as the behaviourist views it' (often referred to as the 'Behaviourist Manifesto'), Watson declared that:

> *Psychology as the behaviourist views it is a purely objective natural science. Its theoretical goal is the prediction and control of behaviour. Introspection forms no essential part of its methods, nor is the scientific value of its data dependent upon the readiness with which they lend themselves to interpretation in terms of consciousness. The behaviourist, in his efforts to get a unitary scheme of animal response, recognizes no dividing line between man and brute. The behaviour of a man, with all its refinement and complexity, forms only a part of the behaviourist's total scheme of investigation.*

Three features of this 'Behaviourist Manifesto' deserve special mention.

1 Psychology must be purely objective, excluding all subjective data or interpretations in terms of conscious experience. Whereas traditional Psychology used objective observations of behaviour to *supplement* introspective data, Watson argued that these should be the *sole* and *exclusive* subject matter. He was redefining Psychology as the 'science of behaviour', instead of the traditional 'science of mental life'.

2 Whereas traditional Psychology aimed to *describe* and *explain* conscious mental states, Watson's goals were to *predict* and *control* overt behaviour, as they were for the other major behaviourist psychologist, B.F. Skinner (see Chapters 3, 9 and 11).

3 Watson wanted to remove the traditional distinction between human beings and non-human animals. If, as Darwin had shown, humans evolved from more simple species, then it follows that human behaviour is simply a more complex form of the behaviour of other species. In other words, the difference is merely *quantitative* (one of degree), rather than *qualitative* (one of kind; see Chapter 9). Consequently, rats, cats, dogs and pigeons became the major source of psychological data. Since 'psychological' now meant 'behaviour' rather than 'consciousness', animals that were convenient to study, and whose environments could easily be controlled, could replace people as experimental subjects.

and other characteristics that had for so long been taken as distinctive human qualities being removed from the 'universe'. There was no place for these things in the behaviourist world.

But was Watson really, single-handedly, responsible for redefining/reinventing Psychology as the science of behaviour? According to Jones and Elcock (2001):

> *When behaviourism arose as an identified school of Psychology, the discipline had already adopted a behaviourist orientation. This shift was driven in part by a desire for application and by the wider social context . . .*

There had been increasing acceptance of reflex theories derived from physiology, which was reinforced by Dewey's (1896) 'The reflex arc concept in Psychology'. He saw stimulus, sensation and response as coordinated behaviours that allowed the organism to adapt to the environment. Sensation was a form of behaviour that interacted with other concurrent behaviours. There was evidence of associations between incoming afferent (sensory) and outgoing efferent (motor) nerves without the intervention of consciousness. This suggested that consciousness was a mere *epiphenomenon* (see Chapter 12) with no causal powers. By 1905, functionalism had replaced introspectionism (Wundt's *structuralism*) as the dominant approach within American Psychology, which was now seen as allied to biology rather than philosophy. By 1911, Angell proposed that Psychology should be 'a general science of behaviour' (Jones and Elcock, 2001).

So, rather than a revolutionary break with the past, behaviourism is best regarded as the logical culmination of changes that had been taking place during the preceding 15–20 years. Historians of Psychology have exaggerated the shift to behaviour as a way of strengthening behaviourism's claims to validity. Its claimed dominance was both less complete and more gradual than usually presented. The claims based on the famous case of 'Little Albert' (Watson and Rayner, 1920) became exaggerated over time and added to behaviourism's origin myth (Jones and Elcock, 2001).

Despite challenges from both the psychometric (mental testing) approach and Gestalt Psychology during the 1920s, behaviourism did come to dominate Experimental Psychology from the 1930s onwards. According to Jones and Elcock, this was due partly to Watson's attempts to persuade the public through magazines, popular books and radio broadcasts, and the introduction of Pavlov's work to the US audience (it wasn't translated into English until the mid-1920s). According to Danziger (1997), there were also more deep-rooted, 'political' and conceptual reasons for behaviourism's appeal.

The two categories of 'learning' and 'behaviour' came to establish the claim that there were phenomena of importance common to all fields of Psychology. Then these common phenomena could be studied in order to discover the principles that unified the discipline. Of the two, 'behaviour' was the more foundational: it became the category the discipline used to define its subject matter. As Danziger (1997) puts it:

> *Whether one was trying to explain a child's answers on a problem-solving task, an adult's neurotic symptomatology, or a white rat's reaction to finding itself in a laboratory maze, one was ultimately trying to explain the same thing, namely, the behaviour of an organism. Classifying such diverse phenomena together as instances of 'behaviour' was the first necessary step in establishing the claim that Psychology was one science with one set of explanatory principles . . .*

'Learning' and 'behaviour' became almost inseparable for several decades, and the 'laws of learning' 'provided the core example of those behavioural principles that were supposed to unify the discipline'. But Danziger is at pains to distinguish between 'behaviour' and 'behaviourism'. The history of the *category* must not be confused with the history of the *movement*. Historically, behaviourists had no monopoly on the category of behaviour: it existed as a scientific category before they picked it up and 'nailed it to their masthead'. But:

> *One did not have to be a card-carrying member of one of the behaviourist schools to agree to the definition of Psychology as the science of behaviour.*

Though influenced by behaviourism, most psychologists *did not* identify themselves as behaviourists, and indeed rejected many of its specific claims (Danziger, 1997).

WHAT SHOULD THE SUBJECT MATTER OF PSYCHOLOGY BE?

The need to study the whole person

According to Ornstein (1975), in the process of refining its methods Psychology discarded its essence, namely consciousness. Fromm (1951, in Graham, 1986) argues that Psychology, in:

> *. . . trying to imitate the natural sciences and laboratory methods of weighing and counting, dealt with everything except the soul. It tried to understand those aspects of man which can be examined in the laboratory, and claimed that conscience, value judgements, and knowledge of good and evil are metaphysical concepts, outside the problems of psychology; it was often more concerned with insignificant problems which fitted the alleged scientific method than with devising new methods to study the significant problems of man. Psychology thus became a science lacking its main subject matter, the soul.*

According to Graham (1986), eastern Psychology is rooted in the tradition of mysticism, with an emphasis on the spiritual, the subjective and the individual, and its dominant ethos is necessarily *humanistic*. By contrast, as we have seen, western Psychology is rooted in the tradition of science, stressing the material, the objective and the general, and its predominant ethos (especially since the rise of behaviourism) is *mechanistic* and *impersonal*.

Graham regards the fundamental difference between them as one of perspective: mystical insight (observing from within) and scientific outlook (observing from without). While traditional eastern psychologies fully recognize the double aspect of human existence – the inner world of subjective experience, and the outer, public world of overt behaviour (an essential dualism) – western Psychologists have failed to acknowledge these two fundamentally different realities. In order to gain acceptance as a science, it was seen as necessary to:

> . . . *suppress the human face of psychology, thereby extinguishing its essence, and as Heather (1976) suggests, effectively murdering the man it claims to study.*
>
> (Graham, 1986)

Since scientific method is implicitly *reductionist* (from the Latin *reductio*, meaning to 'take away'), Psychology, in:

> . . . *reducing the study of man to those of his aspects which are 'objective facts' – his physical behaviours – and precluding any examination of his experience, takes away from man what is essentially and fundamentally his humanness. Man is thereby reduced to a mere thing or object, from which, Heather (1976) suggests, it is but a small step to accepting the idea that man is a machine, and nothing but a machine.*
>
> (Graham, 1986)

The importance of free will

The popular definition of psychology as the study of 'what makes people tick' reflects this mechanistic view of the person, which derives from the nineteenth-century mechanistic view of the universe central to the physical sciences.

To the extent that both Freud's psychoanalytic theory and behaviourism see people as being controlled by forces over which they have little or no control, they both depict people as machine-like. The person is pulled, in a puppet-like way, either by internal (unconscious) or external (environmental contingencies of reinforcement) 'strings'. In this way, both theories are deterministic (see Chapter 11). The debate regarding whether people have free will is crucial in trying to establish the appropriate subject matter of psychology. If we believe people have personal agency and are responsible for their actions, that they are not mere passive responders to forces beyond their control (internal or external) but actively influence what they do and what happens to them, then a deterministic account (such as Freud's or Watson's) simply will not do. A mechanistic view of people, whether this is meant to be taken literally ('people are machines') or just metaphorically ('people are *like* machines'), reduces them to something less than human, and this is implied by the use of the term 'subject' (see Chapter 9).

Humanistic psychology

It was as a reaction against such a mechanistic, dehumanizing view of the person that humanistic psychology emerged, mainly in America, during the 1950s. In fact, the term was first coined by John Cohen, a British psychologist, who wrote a book called *Humanistic Psychology* in 1958, aimed at condemning 'ratomorphic robotic psychology' (Graham, 1986).

Abraham Maslow, in particular, gave wide currency to the term in America, calling it a 'third force' (the other two being behaviourism and psychoanalytic theory). However, he did not reject these approaches but hoped that his approach would act as a unifying force, integrating subjective and objective, the private and public aspects of the person, and providing a complete, holistic psychology. He insisted that a truly scientific Psychology must embrace a humanistic perspective, treating its subject matter as fully human. This meant:

- acknowledging individuals as perceivers and interpreters of themselves and of their world, trying to understand the world from the perspective of the perceiver (a *phenomenological* approach), rather than trying to study people from the position of a detached observer; other psychologists whose ideas were influenced by phenomenology include Kelly (see Chapter 1) and Allport (see Chapter 3)
- recognizing that people help determine their own behaviour, and are not simply slaves to environmental contingencies or to their past
- regarding the self, soul or psyche, personal responsibility and agency, choice and free will, as legitimate issues for psychology.

Maslow's theory is commonly referred to as a 'psychology of being', while Carl Rogers's (the other key humanistic psychologist) theory is a 'psychology of becoming'. Although both saw human beings as possessing the need for *self-actualization* (a unique human characteristic), for Maslow this represented an end in itself, while for Rogers it was the process of becoming a 'fully functioning person' that was of major interest and importance. Rogers (1961) described self-actualization as:

. . . the mainspring of life . . . It is the urge which is evident in all organic and human life – to expand, extend, become autonomous, develop, mature.

Just as Maslow hoped to be able to bring behaviourism and Freudian theory together through his humanistic approach, so Rogers never rejected the rigour of empirical methods. Indeed, he used and advocated the use of empirical methods in the assessment of psychotherapy, in particular the *Q-sort* (see Chapters 3 and 14). But he did maintain that *experience* must be included in any attempt to understand man and the universe: there can be no scientific knowledge without experiential knowledge.

Similarly, Rollo May (1967) argued that humanistic psychology is not hostile to science, although he urged that Psychologists need to recognize the limits of traditional scientific methods, and that they should try to find new methods that will more adequately reveal the nature of man. Although not derived from a humanistic perspective as defined above, new methods for studying people are increasingly being used and developed that represent a significant move away from the traditional, mechanistic, laboratory-based methods that are seen as distorting our understanding of human beings. Some of this new paradigm research will be discussed later in the chapter.

THE SOCIAL NATURE OF SCIENCE

Experimenters and participants are people first

A major criticism of traditional empirical methods, especially the laboratory experiment, has focused on the *artificiality* of the laboratory situation and the tasks that people are often asked to perform there in the name of science. The experimental set-up is so far removed from what people are likely to encounter in everyday situations that their behaviour inside the laboratory is a very poor indicator of how they are likely to behave outside, in the real world. Since it is the real world we are interested in, experiments can tell us very little of any value. This relates to the *external validity* of experiments.

However, this criticism assumes that what happens in the experiment is valid within the parameters of the laboratory situation. In other words, the observed behaviour (the dependent variable) is affected by the experimental manipulation (the independent variable) and nothing else (a well-controlled, properly run experiment has *internal validity*). This assumption is necessary as part of the objectivity claimed for empirical research. The experimenter does not influence the participants' behaviour (the outcome of the experiment) except to the extent that s/he decides what hypothesis/hypotheses to test, which variables to operationalize (and how to do this), which design to use, who the participants are to be (and how many), how to run the procedure, collate and interpret the results, and so on. But isn't this a very significant 'except'?

Observing the world as it is?

The whole situation is the creation of the experimenter and, to this extent, s/he cannot be considered to be objective within that situation. All kinds of biases, preferences, attitudes, beliefs, expectations and so on are reflected in the choices and decisions that go to create the experiment. If 'objectivity' requires that the researcher observe the world *as it is*, playing no part in what is studied and how it is studied, then clearly objectivity is a non-starter, whether in physics, chemistry or Psychology.

Is it *possible* for science to be a 'cool, passionless, absolutely objective exploration of an external reality' (Gould, 1987)? Since all scientists are people, and since science is a human activity, part of human behaviour (at least in western culture), the answer would seem to be 'No!' Gould argues that:

> *We scientists are no different from anyone else. We are passionate human beings, enmeshed in a web of personal and social circumstances . . . unless scientists understand their hopes and engage in vigorous self-scrutiny, they will not be able to sort unacknowledged preference from nature's weak and imperfect message . . .*

In other words, the world *does not* reveal itself to us as it is; scientists have to discover ways of explaining the world that best enable them to predict and control it (at least in the case of the natural sciences). To do this most efficiently, they must be able to separate their biases and prejudices from the 'accuracy' of those explanations. Related to this is what Kitzinger (1987) calls the 'mythologizing of expertise'. Scientific expertise brings with it the power to define reality. Of all the accounting strategies open to scientists, it is the myth of the unbiased, neutral scientific expert that credits scientists with access to knowledge denied to ordinary mortals. She gives examples from research into homosexuality of how 'scientific' and 'lay' concepts have been related in a way that serves to reinforce the status of the scientist. 'Stereotypes often depict . . . but current research shows . . .' and 'It is a popular myth that . . . but the data indicate . . .' The scientist clearly has access to 'the truth' through his/her expertise, which is denied to the lay person. This myth ignores the essentially *social* and *sociological* nature of scientific activity and knowledge (see below).

The experimental drama

What makes the laboratory experiment such an unnatural and artificial situation is the fact that it is almost totally structured by one 'participant' (the experimenter). (See Chapter 9 for a discussion of the ethical implications of the *power differences* between the people involved in psychological research.)

As important as the assumption regarding the objectivity of the experimenter is the assumed 'objectness' of the human 'subject', who is implicitly denied subjectivity, agency and intentionality (Graham, 1986). For the experimental situation to be considered an objective study of human behaviour, the person being studied must be thought of, and treated as, a passive responder to whatever stimuli are presented. The only factors that matter (that influence his/her responses) are the variables manipulated by the experimenter, and that are objectively defined (operationalized). This view of the person really does suggest that 'object' would be a more fitting term than 'subject'; it would be no more offensive and dehumanizing than 'subject' and a lot more descriptively accurate!

Experimenter bias and the self-fulfilling prophecy

But is this a valid representation of the actors involved in the experimental drama? Might the experimenter be contributing something more to the situation than what has already gone into the planning and design of the experiment, things to do with the fact that s/he is a human being, a social animal? And might the 'subject' be rather more actively involved, ultimately influencing the outcome of the experiment, contrary to his/her 'object-ness'?

According to Rosenthal (1966):

> *It appears indisputable that the humanness of both the experimenter and the subject interact in numerous ways which are likely to have a profound effect on experimental outcomes. The experimenter's appearance, sex, age, mood, manner, race, social class, dialect and dress are all likely to influence the subject so that instead of the experimenter being an external 'objective' observer, he is, in effect, a participant who actively contributes to the behaviour that he wishes passively and objectively to observe and record . . .*

Rosenthal uses the word 'actively' to describe the way that various characteristics of the experimenter may affect the subject's behaviour, but those characteristics are essentially static, unchanging characteristics, over which s/he has little control (what the experimenter *is like*). However, such characteristics are correlated with the experimenter's behaviour, and will also influence the subject's perception of, and response to, the experimenter. (This is what 'actively' implies.) For example, Rosenthal (1967, in Valentine, 1992) described the pattern of behaviour that female experimenters show towards male subjects as 'interested modesty', while that shown by male experimenters towards female subjects was described as just plain 'interested'. They took significantly longer to prepare stimulus materials for presentation to female subjects than to males. Sex differences reveal themselves in a wide range of non-verbal behaviours.

Perhaps of even greater significance is the way that the experimenter's expectations can influence the outcome of the experiment, serving as a *self-fulfilling prophecy*. This is referred to as experimenter bias. Such effects have been demonstrated in a wide range of experiments, including reaction time, psychophysics, verbal conditioning, personality assessment, person perception, learning and ability, involving both humans and rats (Rosenthal and Rubin, in Valentine, 1992). What they consistently show is that, if one group of experimenters is testing one hypothesis and another group tests the opposite hypothesis, both groups will obtain results in line with their respective hypotheses. These results are not due to the mishandling of data by biased experimenters but, somehow, the bias of the experimenter creates a changed environment in which subjects actually behave differently. Perhaps the most famous demonstration of such bias involving humans is the 'Pygmalion' experiment by Rosenthal and Jacobson, 1966 (written up in book form as *Pygmalion in the Classroom*, 1968: see Box 10.3).

BOX 10.3 ROSENTHAL AND JACOBSON'S (1968) 'PYGMALION' EXPERIMENT

In a natural classroom situation, children whose teachers were told they would show academic 'promise' during the next academic year showed significantly greater gains in IQ than children for whom such predictions were not made (although this group also showed substantial improvements). The children were, in fact, *randomly* allocated to the 'academic promise' and the control (no such prediction) conditions. The teachers' expectations of gains in the first group actually produced the predicted improvements, demonstrating a *self-fulfilling prophecy*.

As to the mechanism, it is likely that the children who were expected to excel received more attention, encouragement, praise and so on than those who weren't. This, in turn, affected their self-concept and motivation in a positive way, reflected in the actual gains in IQ.

Demand characteristics

A way of trying to understand what the participant contributes to the experiment is through the concept of *demand characteristics* (Orne, 1962). Whereas the mechanistic model stresses what is *done to* the (passive) subject, Orne is interested in what the human subject/participant *does*, which implies a far more *active* role. Participants' performance in an experiment could almost be thought of as a form of *problem-solving behaviour* since, at some level, they try to work out the true purpose of the experiment and to respond in a way that will support the hypothesis being tested. In this context, the totality of cues that convey an experimental hypothesis to the participant become significant influences on his/her behaviour. Orne calls the sum total of these cues the *demand characteristics* of the experimental situation.

These cues include:

> . . . the rumours or campus scuttlebut [gossip] about the research, the information conveyed during the original situation, the person of the experimenter, and the setting of the laboratory, as well as all explicit and implicit communications during the experiment proper.
>
> *(Orne, 1962)*

Orne goes on to point out that the experimental procedure itself may provide cues. For example, if a task is presented twice, with some intervening task (in other words, a repeated measures design), then even the dullest college student will realize that some change in performance is expected on the second task compared with the first.

It is very difficult in practice to find truly naïve participants who do not believe they have at least some familiarity with Psychology, or who cannot work out the purpose of the experiment from the procedure. The crucial point is not whether participants are correct in their attempts to 'suss out' what is going on but the mere fact that such an attempt is being made at all. It means that participants are not the passive responders implied by the mechanistic model.

This tendency to identify the demand characteristics is related to the tendency to play the role of 'a good experimental subject', wanting to please and cooperate with the experimenter, and not to 'upset the experiment'. It is mainly in this sense that Orne sees the experiment as a social situation, in which the participants (experimenter and 'subject') play different, but complementary, roles; for the interaction to proceed relatively smoothly, each participant must have some idea of what the other(s) expects of him/her.

The cultural nature of experiments

The experiment is a rather special type of social situation, with its own rules and norms (some explicit, some implicit). As Moghaddam *et al.* (1993) point out, when we agree to participate in a laboratory experiment, we are not entering a cultural vacuum. We have a host of ideas and expectations about what an experiment is, the role and nature of Psychologists, science, and so on. What makes an experiment 'possible' is a set of shared understandings as to the nature of science, and the respective roles of investigator and 'subject' (what Moghaddam, 2005, calls 'implicit research knowledge'). This, in turn, detracts from science's claim to complete objectivity: science itself is a *culture-related phenomenon*.

The sociology of scientific knowledge

The sociology of scientific knowledge (SSK) focuses on the practices that help construct scientific knowledge. While aimed mainly at physics and biology, Danziger (e.g. 1990, 1997), Richards (e.g. 2002) and others have applied it to Psychology. As with feminism (see Chapter 6), SSK has influenced both how science is understood and how some researchers within Psychology work (Jones and Elcock, 2001). Edwards (1997) and Potter (1996) use SSK within their social constructionist approaches (see below and Chapter 14).

According to Danziger (1997):

A scientific fact is always a fact under some description. The discursive framework within which factual description takes place is as much a part of science as its hardware and its techniques of measurement. To be effective, such a framework must be shared . . . Any reference to the 'facts of the world' has to rely on some discursive framework in use among a particular group of people at a particular time. Facts are there to be displayed, but they can only be displayed within a certain discursive structure . . .

Strictly speaking, there are no 'raw data' in science: by the time measurements and observations are made and recorded, an enormous amount of selection, classification, prediction and so on have already taken place. Consistent with what we have said earlier about experimenter bias and demand characteristics, Danziger (1990) claims that:

. . . neither experimenters nor their subjects enter the investigative situation as social blanks to be programmed in an arbitrary manner. Both are the products of a distinctive historical development that has left a heavy sediment of blind faith and unquestioned tradition . . .

Experimenters' expectations and participants' search for demand characteristics operate within a particular social framework that has to be taken for granted in such studies. The framework is provided by the traditions and conventions of psychological experimentation, which, over time, are now well understood by all experimenters and most participants:

In those societies in which it is practiced on any scale, the psychological experiment has become a social institution recognized by most people with a certain level of education. As in all social

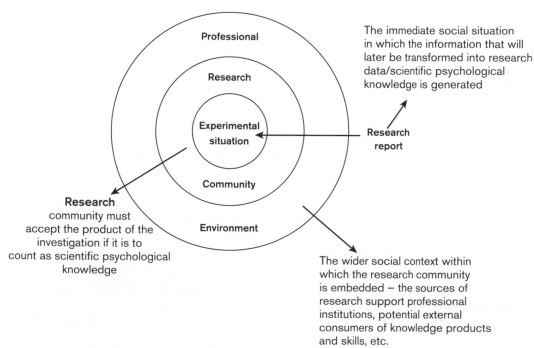

Broader cultural, political, economic contexts

The immediate social situation in which the information that will later be transformed into research data/scientific psychological knowledge is generated

Research report

Research community must accept the product of the investigation if it is to count as scientific psychological knowledge

The wider social context within which the research community is embedded – the sources of research support professional institutions, potential external consumers of knowledge products and skills, etc.

Figure 10.4 The social contexts of investigative practice (based on Danziger, 1990)

institutions the interaction of the participants is constrained by institutional patterns that prescribe what is expected and permitted for each participant . . .

(Danziger, 1990)

This echoes Moghaddam's discussion of the cultural context of the laboratory experiment (see Box 10.4). If the experiment is to be 'successful', everyone must follow the same 'rules'. Hardly more than a hundred years ago, the institution of the psychological experiment was as unknown everywhere as it might be now in parts of the 'Third World' . Ultimately, the experiment is part of the history of those societies that produced it (Danziger, 1990).

BOX 10.4 THE CULTURAL CONTEXT OF THE PSYCHOLOGY LABORATORY

Moghaddam (2005) identifies two main ways in which the Psychology laboratory reflects western, and particularly US, culture:

1 Imagine going to a village in a non-western country, and asking villagers, who may be illiterate, economically poor and technologically unsophisticated, to participate in a laboratory experiment. Typical responses from villagers are likely to be: 'Who are you, a government agent?' 'What is a laboratory? From what you say it sounds like a kind of prison', 'What law have I broken that you want to put me in a room by myself?' Even if you offer to pay, such villagers will be very suspicious about your intentions and will be bewildered as to what you want from them. Western populations are generally far more knowledgeable, and better prepared for participation in laboratory experiments.

> *. . . This higher level of implicit research knowledge is part of Western industrial culture and goes hand in hand with the extensive use of laboratory methods in psychology. The implication is that the laboratory method is not suitable for research in all societies and all groups, so there are possible limitations to basing a science of human thought and action on this method.*
>
> (Moghaddam, 2005)

2 The USA is the most *individualistic* major society in the world, dominated as it is by an ethos of 'self-help' and 'individual responsibility (see Chapter 8). The 'American Dream' espouses an ideal of individual mobility: anyone can make it, provided s/he has personal ability, is hard-working and so on. Given this cultural background, it is perhaps inevitable that the use of the Psychology laboratory has been influenced by individualism and reductionism:

> *. . . The assumption has been that one can come to a valid understanding of human behaviour by studying individuals in isolation, and that the causes of behaviour lie within, and can be reduced to, factors inside individuals.*
>
> *Social relationships are seen as secondary and unimportant in explaining behaviour. For example, in studying memory . . . it is 'isolated minds' remembering and not collective remembering that is important. Also, the context of behaviour is ignored . . . The implication is that the laboratory experiment can inform us about certain underlying psychological processes but not necessarily about what will happen in the world outside the laboratory. Thus we need to constantly move back and forth from laboratory research to explorations in the outside world.*
>
> (Moghaddam, 2005)

THE UNIQUENESS OF PSYCHOLOGY

According to Jones and Elcock (2001), studying Psychology as a social activity has one 'reflexive twist' that is not involved in the case of other sciences. This is to do with how 'Psychology' affects 'psychology'.

According to Richards (2002), the boundaries between the history of science, the philosophy of science and the sociology of knowledge have become blurred, partly because they've acquired an increasingly 'psychological' character. Understanding 'scientific behaviour' raises issues of perception (e.g. how one makes sense of what one is seeing when it has not been seen before), cognition (e.g. how scientists really create their theories and decide what their results mean), personality (e.g. what motivates scientists to devote their lives to a particular topic), communication (e.g. how scientists succeed or fail in getting their work accepted as valid, and how controversies are resolved), and group dynamics (e.g. how scientific disciplines are organized and managed). Richards believes this puts Psychology itself in a rather odd position relative to other sciences, because 'as the science of human behaviour, its subject matter logically includes scientific behaviour'.

Compared with the natural sciences, Psychology is in a quite ambiguous position, since 'while trying to operate as a normal science, it is also on the outside looking in'. Looking at science as a product or expression of specific social contexts has been developed into a way of looking at human behaviour and ideas in general, and this has merged into social constructionism (see Chapter 14). According to Richards:

> . . . *psychology itself must be one of the routes by which this process of 'social construction' operates. The history of Psychology thereby becomes one aspect of the history of its own subject-matter, 'psychology'. The historian of Psychology is not only looking at the history of a particular discipline, but also at the history of what that discipline purports to be studying. Whereas in orthodox sciences there is always some external object of enquiry – rocks, electrons, DNA, stars – existing essentially unchanging in the non-human world (even if never finally knowable 'as it really is' beyond human conceptions), this is not so for Psychology. 'Doing Psychology' is the human activity of studying human activity, it is human psychology examining itself – and what it produces by way of new theories, ideas and beliefs about itself is also part of our psychology . . .*

Richards is describing the 'reflexivity' or self-referring relationship that is unique to Psychology as a (scientific) discipline. The discipline of Psychology actually contributes to the dynamic psychological processes by which human nature constantly 'recreates, re-forms, and regenerates itself, primarily in western cultures'. Again, 'Psychology is produced by, produces, and is an instance of its own subject-matter'.

Language and the nature of psychological kinds

Changes in psychological terminology signify psychological changes in their own right. In one sense, what we are studying is quite literally language: previous accounts of psychological phenomena are only available in that form. In discussing science in general, Danziger (1997) makes a similar point when he says that the most basic instrument of scientific investigation is language. The entire investigative process is so immersed in language that it is simply taken for granted, and its role becomes invisible. But if this is true of science in general, in the case of Psychology it becomes absolutely critical.

According to Danziger, the notion of 'natural kinds' may be peculiarly inappropriate for Psychology:

> *If we change our identification of a chemical compound as a result of advances in techniques of analysis, this changes our knowledge of the compound but the compound itself remains the same compound it always was. But the objects represented in psychological language are generally not like that. A person who learns not to think of his or her actions as greedy or avaricious but as motivated by a need for achievement or self-realization has changed as a person . . . The sorts of*

things that Psychology takes as its objects, people's actions, experiences and dispositions, are not independent of their categorization.

Identifying actions, dispositions and so on is not like sticking labels on fully formed specimens in a museum. So many psychological categories have a taken-for-granted quality about them because the labels we use appear to describe something 'essential' – that is, 'emotions', 'motives', 'cognitions' look as though they are really distinct in some objective, fundamental way. But they only seem 'natural' to members of that particular linguistic community. This sense of natural must not be confused with the concept of 'natural kinds'. For Danziger (1997):

> *Natural kinds have nothing to do with culture, whereas the natural-appearing kinds of Psychology have everything to do with it.*

Similarly, Richards (2002) argues that:

> *To classify and explain the psychological in a new way is to be involved in changing the psychological itself. To think about oneself differently is to change oneself.*

Richards does not believe in some independent psychological 'reality' beyond the language used to describe it more or less 'accurately'. This does not mean that language is all there is, but:

> *Psychological language is itself a psychological phenomenon – a psychological technique for both talking about other psychological phenomena and for giving them form and meaning.*

One implication of this view is that nobody prior to Freud had an Oedipus complex, and nobody before Pavlov or Watson was ever classically conditioned. If we disagree with this conclusion it is because (in Danziger's terms) we are confusing natural kinds with natural-appearing kinds. However similar to such phenomena previous ones appear to be in retrospect,

> *. . . they were not terms in which the psychology of people prior to their introduction was actually structured. They had no psychological reality.*
>
> *(Richards, 2002)*

The very act of introducing such concepts provided people with new terms in which to experience themselves; only then can they properly be said to refer to really occurring psychological phenomena. The same holds true for much of everyday psychological language ('folk psychology'): nobody 'went off the rails' before the advent of railways, and people who agreed with each other were not 'on the same wavelength' before radios were invented (Richards, 2002).

A SHIFT TOWARDS STUDYING PEOPLE AS PEOPLE

The various criticisms of the positivist, mechanistic, behaviourist-dominated scientific Psychology began to be drawn together during the late 1960s, culminating in Harré and Secord's (1972) *The Explanation of Social Behaviour*. This book is widely seen as marking the beginning of a 'new paradigm' in Psychology (Harré, 1993). Harré and Secord called their new approach *ethogenics*, partly to indicate the break from experimentation they were advocating, but also to acknowledge the importance of context and convention in everyday life. They had been particularly influenced by Garfinkel's (1967) *Ethnomethodology* and Goffman's dramaturgical analysis of social interaction (in books such as *Stigma*, 1963, and *The Presentation of Self in Everyday Life*, 1971). Both Garfinkel and Goffman had developed methodologies that were appropriate to the nature of the phenomenon they were studying, namely human beings.

New paradigm research

New paradigm research (NPR: Reason and Rowan, 1981) refers to the attempt to integrate naïve enquiry (the kind of ordinary day-to-day thinking that everyone engages in: see Chapter 1) and orthodox research, making it 'objectively subjective'. It openly opposes the positivist, deterministic, reductionist, mechanistic approach (which they call '*quantophrenia*'), which typically produces statistically significant but humanly insignificant results. They insist that in the field of human enquiry, it is preferable to be deeply interesting than accurately boring. They oppose deception and debriefing, manipulation and mystification. But at the same time they advocate that certain aspects of conventional methods and procedures, in particular certain aspects of report writing, be expanded and developed. For example, the 'Introduction' and 'Discussion' sections should be written with as much care and attention as is usually given to the main part of the investigation ('Procedure' and 'Results'), involving literature searches within sociology, the natural sciences, literature, philosophy, theology and history. They should become part of the research process itself, so that research reports become:

> . . . *a statement of where the researchers stand, not only theoretically, but politically, ideologically, spiritually and emotionally in as much that they discuss the many influences which have shaped the thinking and feeling which has led to the current investigation.*
>
> *(Graham, 1986)*

Another new direction taken by NPR is *collaborative/participative research*, or *cooperative inquiry*, in which both the researcher and the participant actively contribute to the planning, execution and interpretation of the research. According to Heron (1982, in Graham, 1986):

BOX 10.5 DISCOURSE ANALYSIS (DA)

DA brings together a wide variety of perspectives and influences, from philosophy, linguistics, artificial intelligence, anthropology and sociology (as well as various aspects of Psychology). Some of its main features include the following:

1 'Talk' (both conversation between people and written language) is worthy of study in its own right, and as a way in which people (attempt to) achieve their goals. This contrasts sharply with the traditional view of language as an index of external reality or of a person's inner states.

2 The prime source of data in DA is conversation, either in natural settings or in interviews, but the emphasis is very different from that of traditional social psychological methods; for example, instead of treating what people say in interviews as acceptable substitutes for actual observation of behaviour, it is the interview data *themselves* that are of interest (the 'subject matter').

3 DA also avoids hypothesis testing and the use of pre-defined coding schedules (as is usual in observational studies). In this sense, it is mainly *inductive* (as opposed to *hypothetico-deductive*) and *data-driven* (as opposed to *theory-driven*).

4 One use of DA is in the scrutiny of psychological theories (such as Freud's, Skinner's and Piaget's) in order to show how they use language to create a convincing theoretical account of human behaviour. One 'strategy' is to use *metaphors* in such a way that they are taken literally, apparently referring to the 'external reality' of behaviour that the theory is trying to account for. (See Soyland's (1994) *Psychology As Metaphor*.)

5 In everyday life, as well as in putting forward psychological theories and politics, we are often trying to get our account/version of the truth accepted by others as 'fact' or '*the* truth'. This is one sense in which language is seen primarily as a form of *social action* (rather than primarily a *representation* of reality, including what people *really* think about the issue being discussed).

(Based on Lalljee and Widdicombe, 1989)

> *The way of co-operative enquiry is for the researcher to interact with the subjects so that they do contribute directly both to hypothesis making, to formulating the final conclusions, and to what goes on in between. This contribution may be strong, in the sense that the subject is co-researcher and contributes to creative thinking at all stages. Or it may be weak, in the sense that the subject is thoroughly informed of the research proposals at all stages and is invited to assent or dissent, and if there is dissent, then the researcher and subject negotiate until agreement is reached. In the complete form of this approach, not only will the subject be fully fledged co-researcher, but the researcher will also be co-subject, participating fully in the action and experience to be researched.*

(The continued use of 'subject' seems totally incompatible with the approach being advocated, with 'participant' being the obvious alternative.)

Another major innovation within NPR is discourse analysis (DA: see Box 10.5, page 201).

According to Edwards and Potter (1992), DA extends beyond a specific method into a fairly radical rethink about traditional psychological topics, which they call discursive psychology (DP: see Chapter 14). So, memory and attribution theory are treated as processes of discourse between people: memories are not close or not-so-close attempts at recalling 'the facts', but are motivated constructions by people with a 'stake' in producing an 'account' that may, for example, suit their defence against blame and accountability (Coolican, 1994). We cannot simply take what people say as revealing what they think, as if their talk provided a window through which we could peer at their cognitive processes: we must first understand what their talk is trying to do, what it is trying to achieve in a particular social context, at a particular time.

THE CHANGING FACE OF SCIENCE

In his 1983 presidential address to the British Psychological Society, Hetherington (cited by Graham, 1986) stressed the need for a *paradigm shift* in Psychology and the development of its own methods. The methods of natural science can at best provide only a partial knowledge of why people behave as they do, and since Psychology is part natural science and part interpretative science, it needs to develop methods that are adequate for the study of human beings as organisms, as members of social organizations, and as people with whom we engage in dialogue.

Hetherington cited James's (1890) observation that 'the natural science assumptions are provisional and revisable things'. In other words, scientific 'facts' are not 'set in stone' but are constantly being changed, not because the world changes but because our theories and explanations change.

As we have seen, new methods of studying people are being developed, and no doubt Hetherington would approve of these developments. However, the great irony about this new paradigm is that what it is replacing (or partially replacing, since most Psychologists still subscribe to the positivist methodology) may itself have been out of date for some time. The natural science on which Watson so explicitly and vigorously based Psychology (originally in 1913) is in many ways not the natural science of the present day (or even of the recent past).

A number of physicists and other scientists, philosophers of science and other academics (beginning probably with Einstein's 1905 theory of relativity) are moving away from the Cartesian–Newtonian view of a clockwork universe, which is completely predictable and determinate, towards a view of the universe as much more uncertain and unpredictable. A major 'ingredient' in this 'new physics' is Heisenberg's Uncertainty Principle. According to this, there are limits beyond which there can be no certainty, not because of the lack of precision in our measuring instruments or the extremely small size of the entities being measured – but by virtue of the study itself. More specifically, all attempts to observe sub-atomic particles, such as electrons, alter them: at the sub-atomic level, we cannot observe something without changing it, because the universe does not exist independently of the observer trying to measure it.

If most psychologists are still trying to model themselves on a physics based on Descartes and Newton, then they are out of date and out of touch, and if they want their science to reveal what people are 'really like', in some absolute, objective, way, they are also out of luck.

SUMMARY

○ Mainstream, academic Psychology has been very strongly influenced by the classical, positivist, view of science, according to which science is meant to be unbiased, objective and value-free. This can also be seen in the practice of psychiatry and clinical psychology.

○ Descartes divided the universe into *res extensa* (physical matter) and *res cogitans* (non-physical mind). This is philosophical dualism, which allowed scientists to describe the physical world objectively, without reference to the human observer.

○ Descartes also introduced mechanism into science and extended this view of matter to living organisms, including the human body. He was also one of the first people to advocate reductionism.

○ As applied to the study of human behaviour/social institutions, objectivity came to be called positivism (Comte). Another fundamental feature of science is empiricism, which claims to be able to tell us about reality independently of scientific activity.

○ Logical positivism (LP) defines the meaning of statements in terms of the operations needed to verify them. Its emphasis on the role of sensory experience implies that science can reveal 'reality' as it is, independent of the scientist and the activity of observing it.

○ Opposed to LP is the view that 'facts' do not exist objectively or independently of theory, which is needed to interpret data.

○ Theory is central to Kuhn's concept of a paradigm, but there is much more involved than just theory. Only when most workers within a particular field/discipline subscribe to a particular paradigm can it be described as a science. Scientific revolutions occur through paradigm shifts, after which there is a return to normal science.

○ Responses to Kuhn's theory include Lakatos's account of research programmes and Feyerabend's methodological anarchism.

○ Psychological concepts are both culturally and historically relative. Many current psychological concepts/ processes are historically constructed social phenomena, rather than part of a timeless human nature.

○ Philosophy, physiology and evolutionary theory were the major influences on Psychology's emergence as a separate discipline.

○ Wundt, traditionally regarded as Psychology's founding father, advocated the use of introspection only for the investigation of psychophysiological phenomena ('lower mental processes'). 'Higher mental processes', including social and cultural behaviour, required different methods.

○ While Wundt was interested in universal aspects of the mind, American psychologists were influenced by Darwin's theory of evolution and James's theory of functionalism, which helped to stimulate interest in individual differences.

○ Watson rejected introspectionism on the grounds that it's based on purely private experience. To be an objective, natural science, Psychology must replace consciousness with behaviour as its subject matter. Behaviourism combined the extreme environmentalism of Locke's empiricism and the positivist emphasis on objectivity.

○ The idea that Watson was responsible for the 'behaviourist revolution' represents an origin myth. The concept of 'behaviour' had been used by Psychologists long before Watson's 'Behaviourist Manifesto', although most did not identify themselves as behaviourists.

○ Traditional psychologies of the East recognize the double aspect of human existence: the inner world of subjective experience/the outer world of overt behaviour. But western psychologists, by excluding the former, reduce 'man' to a mere thing/object/machine.

○ Humanistic psychology emerged as a reaction against the mechanistic, dehumanizing image of the person that was contained in both behaviourism and Freud's psychoanalytic theory. Both Maslow and Rogers advocated a phenomenological approach and believed in the fundamental human need for self-actualization.

○ Humanistic psychologists do not reject science but urge that there can be no scientific knowledge without experiential knowledge, and that appropriate methods must be found to study people as they are.

○ Even if laboratory experiments lack external validity, they are still seen as having internal validity; this assumption is necessary if empirical research is to be considered objective. But the world does not reveal itself to us as it is.

○ Both the experimenter and the 'subject'/'object' contribute much more to the outcome of the experiment than is compatible with the positivist account of scientific research. Examples of the social dimension of psychological experiments include experimenter bias, which can produce a self-fulfilling prophecy, and demand characteristics.

○ There also needs to be a shared understanding of what 'science' is in order for an experiment to be possible, making science itself a culture-related phenomenon. The psychological experiment has become a social institution in many western countries, and so is also history-related.

○ Psychology is unique among the sciences, because the study of scientific activity is part of its subject matter, and because changes in Psychology the discipline affect psychology the subject matter. This refers to Psychology's reflexivity.

○ Psychological concepts and categories are not 'natural kinds', as is the case in the natural sciences. But they often appear to be describing something that has an objective, independent existence.

○ Criticisms of the positivist approach culminated in Harré and Secord's ethogenics, which marked a new paradigm. New paradigm research (NPR) attempts to integrate 'everyday psychology' and orthodox research.

○ Collaborative/participative research/co-operative enquiry involves both the researcher and the participant actively contributing to the planning/execution/interpretation of the research.

○ Discourse analysis (DA) sees the study of conversation/written language as important in its own right. Edwards and Potter have extended DA from a method to a new way of thinking about traditional topics – discursive psychology (DP) – which sees language as a form of social action.

○ Ironically, while Psychology has always modelled itself on 'classical physics', physics itself no longer adopts a 'classical' view of science. Physicists now believe that the world cannot be studied objectively, independently of attempts to measure it.

USEFUL WEBSITES

http://psychology.dur.ac.uk/eshhs/
www.chss.montclair.edu/psychology/museum/museum.html
http://www.nova.edu/ssss/QR/web.html
http://www.qualitativeresearch/uga.edu/QualPage/

RECOMMENDED READING

Danziger, K. (1990) *Constructing the Subject: Historical Origins of Psychological Research.* New York: Cambridge University Press.

Danziger, K. (1997) *Naming the Mind: How Psychology Found its Language.* London: Sage. (Especially Chapters 1–4, 6, and 9–10.)

Deese, J. (1972) *Psychology as Science and Art.* New York: Harcourt Brace Jovanovich.

Fancher, R.E. (1996) *Pioneers of Psychology* (3rd edn). New York: Norton.

Gough, B. and McFadden, M. (2001) *Critical Social Psychology: An Introduction.* Basingstoke: Palgrave.

Jones, D. and Elcock, J. (2001) *History and Theories of Psychology: A Critical Perspective.* London: Arnold.

Richards, G. (2002) *Putting Psychology in its Place: A Critical Historical Overview* (2nd edn). Hove: Routledge. (Especially Chapters 1–5 and 7.)

Rosnow, R.L. and Rosenthal, R. (1997) *People Studying People: Artifacts and Ethics in Behavioral Research.* New York: W.H. Freeman & Co.

CHAPTER 11

FREE WILL AND DETERMINISM

WHY ARE PSYCHOLOGISTS INTERESTED?

Historical reasons

The debate about free will and determinism has been a central feature of western philosophy, at least since Descartes (1596–1650: see Chapter 10). Given psychology's intellectual and historical roots in philosophy, it would be very surprising if psychologists were not interested in the issue for this reason alone.

To understand the causes of behaviour

Identifying the causes of phenomena, as part of the attempt to explain them, is a fundamental part of 'classical' science (see Chapter 10). According to the philosophical doctrine of *determinism*:

> . . . in the case of everything that exists, there are antecedent conditions, known or unknown, given which that thing could not be other than it is . . . More loosely, it says that everything, including every cause, is the effect of some cause or causes; or that everything is not only determinate but causally determined . . . if true, it holds not only for all things that have existed but for all things that do or ever will exist.
>
> *(Taylor, 1963)*

'Everything that exists' includes people and their thoughts and behaviour, so a 'strict' determinist believes that thought and behaviour are caused no differently from (other) 'things' or events in the world. But this, of course, begs the question: 'Are thoughts and behaviour the *same kind of thing or event* as chemical reactions in a test tube, a volcanic eruption, or the firing of neurons in the brain?' We do not usually ask ourselves if the chemicals 'agreed' to combine in a certain way, or if the volcano just 'felt like' erupting, or if the neurons 'decided' to fire. To do so (assuming we weren't being witty or in some other way not wanting to be taken literally) would involve us in the 'sin' of *anthropomorphizing* – that is, attributing human abilities and characteristics to non-human things (including animals). No one seriously believes that chemicals can agree, or that volcanoes have feelings, or that neurons can make decisions. But we do attribute these abilities to people, they are part of our concept of a person, and this concept forms an essential part of 'everyday' or common-sense psychology (see Chapter 1).

For these reasons, psychologists must take seriously the common-sense view that people make decisions, agree (or not) with each other, and, in a whole host of ways, exercise their free will. And having free will depends upon having 'a mind': deciding, agreeing and so on are precisely the kinds of things we do with our minds; they are mental processes or events. However, while it may be necessary to 'have a mind' in order to be able to decide, agree and so on (free will implies having a mind), having a mind doesn't imply free will: our

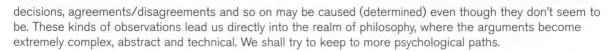

decisions, agreements/disagreements and so on may be caused (determined) even though they don't seem to be. These kinds of observations lead us directly into the realm of philosophy, where the arguments become extremely complex, abstract and technical. We shall try to keep to more psychological paths.

To investigate the influence of mental events on behaviour

Even if we accept that human thinking and behaviour are different from natural, physical phenomena, and that they are not determined (caused) in the same way (or that a different kind of explanation is required), for most of its history as a separate discipline, psychology has operated *as if there were no difference.* Since 1913, anyway, when Watson launched the behaviourist 'movement', psychologists have been trying to emulate the natural sciences, and the most obvious form this has taken has been the use of empirical methods, in particular the laboratory experiment. The use of such methods to study people implicitly adopts a view of human behaviour as determined, and is closely related to the positivist and mechanistic nature of experimental research (see Chapter 10). But does this mean that all, or most, psychologists are behaviourists?

In one important sense, the answer is 'yes'. *Methodological behaviourism* refers to the belief in the importance of empirical methods, especially the experiment, as a way of collecting data about human thought and behaviour which can be quantified and statistically analysed. Most psychologists today would probably describe themselves as behaviourists in this sense.

However, most psychologists since the late 1950s would deny that they are behaviourists in the other important sense, namely *philosophical behaviourism*. In its most extreme form, as represented by Watson, the very existence of mind is denied; thinking, for example, is nothing but a series of vocal or sub-vocal and verbal responses (i.e. 'mind' is *reduced to behaviour*). As we saw above, if you reject the mind, you consequently reject free will too: without a mind, there can be no deciding, choosing and so on (see Chapters 10 and 14).

A less extreme view is adopted by Skinner. Despite his extreme environmentalism, and calling his approach radical behaviourism, Skinner does not deny the existence of mental processes. What he denies is the common-sense explanation of the role of mental events in relation to behaviour (see Chapter 14). For Skinner, they are irrelevant in trying to predict and control behaviour; they are mere epiphenomena, 'by-products' of behaviour, totally lacking any influence over behaviour. This is one attempt to solve the 'mind–body' (or 'mind–brain') problem (see Chapter 12). The important point here is that, along with his denial of the influence of mental events over behaviour, Skinner rejected the notion of free will. While not denying that people believe they make choices, he argued that this belief is an illusion (see below).

While philosophical and radical behaviourism involve an *explicit* rejection or denial of free will, this is implicit in the case of methodological behaviourism. Some, perhaps a majority, of methodological behaviourists might actually express a belief in free will and at the same time believe in the validity of the experimental methods they use to study human behaviour, and this might seem contradictory. They may reject their critics' claim that the use of those methods implies a deterministic, mechanistic model of people, in which case there is no contradiction. Alternatively, they may draw a distinction between (i) 'people as they live their lives on a day-to-day basis', where free will is certainly assumed, and (ii) 'people as subjects in psychological experiments', where the question of free will does not arise or is not relevant. William James drew a similar distinction himself (see below).

These 'solutions' raise more problems and questions in their turn, but the best we can hope for is 'solutions', rather than 'the solution' (which is true of all major philosophical issues and debates).

To diagnose mental disorders

When psychologists and psychiatrists discuss abnormality, and diagnose and treat mental disorders, they often make judgements about free will and determinism, either implicitly or explicitly (see Chapter 7).

In a general sense, mental disorders can be seen as the partial or complete breakdown of the control a person normally has over his/her behaviour, emotions and thinking. For example, *compulsive* behaviour, by definition, is behaviour the person cannot help but is 'compelled' to do. People are '*attacked*' by panic, *obsessed* by thoughts of germs, become the *victims* of thoughts that are inserted into their minds from outside and are under external influence (one kind of passivity experience and thought disturbance in schizophrenia). In all these examples, things are *happening to* or *being done to* the individual (instead of the individual *doing them*), both from the point of view of the individual concerned and that of the psychologist or psychiatrist.

Being judged to have lost the control that we think of as a major feature of normality ('being of sound mind'), either temporarily or permanently, is a legally acceptable defence in cases of criminal offences.

Forensic psychiatry deals with the assessment and treatment of mentally abnormal offenders. There are several clauses within the Mental Health Act (1983) that provide for compulsory detention of prisoners (either while awaiting trial or as part of their sentence) in hospital. Psychiatrists, as expert witnesses, can play an important role in advising the court about: (i) fitness to plead; (ii) mental state at the time of the offence; (iii) diminished criminal responsibility (Gelder *et al.*, 1989; see Box 11.1).

In the case of Peter Sutcliffe, the 'Yorkshire Ripper', the jury found him guilty of the murder of 13 women and the attempted murder of seven others, despite the defence that he heard the voice of God telling him to get rid of prostitutes. He was sentenced to 20 concurrent terms of life imprisonment, which he served initially in an ordinary prison before being sent to Broadmoor Special Hospital.

BOX 11.1 THE McNAUGHTON RULES AND DIMINISHED RESPONSIBILITY

The defence of diminished responsibility (for murder) was introduced in England and Wales in 1957 and has largely replaced 'Not guilty by reason of insanity' (NGRI), which was based on the so-called McNaughton Rules. In 1843, Daniel McNaughton shot and killed Edward Drummond, private secretary to the then prime minister, Sir Robert Peel. He shot Drummond by mistake, intending to shoot Peel. In the Old Bailey trial, the defence of NGRI was made on the grounds that McNaughton had suffered delusions for many years; his paranoia focused on the Tory Party and he decided to kill Peel. In accordance with the judge's summing-up, he was found NGRI. However, he was admitted to Bethlehem Hospital and later transferred to the Criminal Lunatic Asylum, Broadmoor, soon after it was opened.

There was a public outcry at the decision, which was debated in the House of Lords. This resulted in the McNaughton Rules, which although having no statutory basis were given the same status by the courts as an actual law. However, they were considered to present far too narrow a concept of insanity (working to the disadvantage of the mentally ill), and the Homicide Act 1957 introduced the plea of diminished responsibility for murder charges. If accepted, there is no trial and a sentence of manslaughter is passed; if not, a trial is held and the jury must decide whether at the material time (the time when the actual crime(s) was/were committed) the accused was suffering from an abnormality of mind and, if so, whether it was such as to *substantially impair his/her responsibility*.

To discuss moral accountability

Underlying the whole question of legal – and, by the same token, moral – responsibility, is the presupposition that people are, at least some of the time, able to control their behaviour and to choose between different courses of action. Otherwise, how could we ever be held responsible/accountable for any of our actions? We only need expert witnesses (like psychiatrists) to help juries decide whether or not the accused was suffering from a mental abnormality that, at the time the crime was committed, substantially impaired his/her responsibility, because it is not clear *in this particular case*. But usually it is. In most everyday situations and

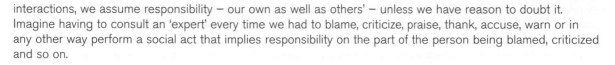

interactions, we assume responsibility − our own as well as others' − unless we have reason to doubt it. Imagine having to consult an 'expert' every time we had to blame, criticize, praise, thank, accuse, warn or in any other way perform a social act that implies responsibility on the part of the person being blamed, criticized and so on.

Descartes made the fundamental distinction between mind and body − the former being non-physical, the latter being physical and essentially a machine (*philosophical dualism*: see Chapters 10 and 12). According to Descartes, the person is an agent whose behaviour is governed by no other law than that which the agent himself creates:

> *But the will is so free in its nature, that it can never be constrained . . . And the whole action of the soul consists in this, that solely because it desires something, it causes a little gland to which it is closely united to move in a way requisite to produce the effect which relates to this desire.*
>
> *(Descartes, 1649, in Flanagan, 1984)*

The 'little gland' that Descartes refers to is in fact the pineal gland/body, situated near the corpus callosum (which joins the two hemispheres of the brain). This is now generally accepted as playing an important role in sleep, but *not* as the 'seat of the mind', the meeting point between the mind and the body, as Descartes believed.

The mind, via the pineal body, uses its immaterial (non-physical) powers to move the material body; this is what happens every time we behave in a voluntary way. The mind itself, however, is self-moved. Flanagan (1984) believes that one of the main consequences of dualism, and what most people would regard as its main advantage, is that it makes sense of the intuitive (common-sense) distinction between (i) conscious, purposeful, voluntary actions, and (ii) mechanical, unintentional, involuntary actions.

This distinction in turn makes sense of moral discourse:

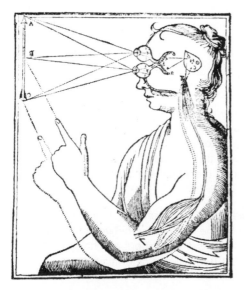

Figure 11.1 The influence of the soul on the machinery of the brain, according to René Descartes, from the 1664 French edition of the *Treatise of Man*. Descartes thought of the pineal gland (the pear-shaped object in the middle of the head) as the point of connection between the soul and the brain. It receives messages from the senses (the eyes in this diagram) by means of waves of vibration through the fluid in the chambers of the brain. In turn, by subtle movements and deflection, conveying the will of the mind, it influences the transmission of signals from the brain to the muscles.

> *When we speak morally . . . we employ an idiom which assumes certain things about human behaviour. At the most general level, the moral idiom assumes that people are capable of controlling their actions − it assumes that we are not mere reflex machines . . . it seems silly to have any expectations about how people ought to act, if everything we do is the result of some inexorable causal chain which began millennia ago. 'Ought', after all, seems to imply 'can', therefore, by employing a moral vocabulary filled with words like 'ought' and 'should', we assume that humans are capable of rising above the causal pressures presented by the material world, and in assuming this we appear to be operating with some conception of freedom, some notion of free will.*
>
> *(Flanagan, 1984)*

This may seem to describe the common-sense understanding of how moral responsibility and free will are related (namely, that it is only because we believe that people have free will that we attribute them with moral responsibility for their actions). But is it necessarily the only view that one could take?

Skinner (1971) claims (consistent with his argument that free will is an illusion) that all the practical sense of doling out rewards and punishments and speaking in moral terms would be maintained even if we gave up our shared belief that human nature is free: we would simply be using them to shape, control and maintain behaviours that we (as a society as well as individually) find pleasing. In other words, the fact that we do usually attribute responsibility to people (based on the assumption that they have free will) does not mean that we have to. (A common argument in support of free will, which could be used against Skinner, is what is called the 'appeal to experience', which we shall consider below.)

Perhaps we need to distinguish between a purely philosophical position (one based on logical analysis, the meaning of concepts and so on) and a more practical position (based on everyday, intuitive, subjective experience). As Koestler (1967) says, whatever one's philosophical convictions, 'in everyday life it is impossible to carry on without the implicit belief in personal responsibility; and responsibility implies freedom of choice'.

To understand the theories of major figures in psychology

Most of the major theorists in psychology have addressed the issue of free will and determinism, including James, Freud, Skinner (as we have already seen), Fromm, Kelly and Rogers. The issue had also been discussed by those working in the field of artificial intelligence, such as Johnson-Laird, and sociobiologists, principally Wilson and Dawkins. This represents perhaps the single major reason for including a chapter on free will and determinism in a book on psychology: to fully appreciate the theories of these major figures we must understand their position regarding this fundamentally important feature of human beings.

According to Morea (1990), the 'story' of Adam and Eve losing their innocence in the Garden of Eden when they chose to eat the fruit from the forbidden tree is a myth suggesting that humans are free. It also suggests how like a god they become in knowing right from wrong and in having a mind. Morea believes that any adequate explanation of human personality must confront these age-old puzzles of free will, morality and mind.

Figure 11.2 Adam and Eve were expelled from the Garden of Eden when they chose to eat the forbidden fruit, a choice which, Morea suggests, indicates that humans are free

Mind, or consciousness, is discussed in Chapter 12. Much of the rest of this chapter concentrates on (a) the relationship between free will and consciousness, and (b) what a number of eminent psychologists and other scientists have said about free will and determinism.

WHAT DO WE MEAN BY FREE WILL?

Valentine (1992) identifies a number of different definitions or senses in which the term is used. These are described below.

Having a choice

The common-sense, lay person's understanding of the term is that the actor could have behaved differently given the same circumstances; this is what 'having a real choice' means. This is something that we normally 'take on trust', an 'article of faith', because it can never be shown to be true.

Not being coerced or constrained

Behaviour is 'free' if it is *uncaused*, implying that if behaviour is caused (i.e. determined), then it cannot be free. However, 'free' and 'determined' are not opposites: the opposite of 'determined' is 'random' (occurring by pure chance). Clearly, when we speak of human actions being 'free', we certainly do not mean that they are 'random'. So, what is the true opposite of 'free'? The answer is 'coerced' or 'constrained': if someone puts a loaded gun to your head and tells you to undress (otherwise you'll be shot), no one – magistrate, priest or onlooker – could condemn your behaviour, since it is obviously done *against your will*; your behaviour was not freely chosen. (This relates to *compatibilism*: see below.)

The view that all acts are caused, but only those that are not coerced or constrained are free, is called soft *determinism* (first proposed formally by James, 1890: see below).

Voluntary

We noted earlier that the word 'voluntary' is usually meant to convey behaviour over which we have control, while 'involuntary' implies the opposite. In one sense, the opposite of voluntary is 'reflex', as in the knee-jerk response to a tap on the patella, or the eye-blink response to a puff of air directed at the eye. It is very

BOX 11.2 THE PHENOMENOLOGY OF FREE WILL

Penfield (1958) performed what are now classic experiments involving patients undergoing brain surgery. Their motor cortex was stimulated while they were fully awake, so they could report their experience. Even though the brain region being stimulated was the same as that which is involved when we move our arms and legs under normal circumstances, these patients reported feeling that their limbs were being moved passively, quite a different experience from initiating the movement themselves. This demonstrates that the *subjective experience* (or *phenomenology*) of the voluntary movement of one's limbs cannot be reduced to the stimulation of the appropriate region of the brain (otherwise Penfield's patients would not have reported a difference) – doing things voluntarily simply *feels* different from the 'same' things just 'happening'.

If this is true for bodily movements, then this adds weight to the claim that having free will is an undeniable part of our subjective experience of ourselves as a person. As Koestler (1967) claims, our sense of self is most acute (and important and real for us) where moral decisions and feelings of responsibility for one's past actions (the problem of free will) are involved.

Libet *et al.* (1979) also applied electric shocks to the exposed somatosensory cortex of patients with their skulls open under local anaesthetic. When the cortex is stimulated in this way, the person reports a feeling of touch – numbness, buzzing, or a tingling sensation on the skin of a contralateral part of the body (for example, the left hand when the right side of the somatosensory cortex is stimulated). In one experiment, as a control condition, Libet *et al.* also directly stimulated the skin of the person's other hand (the one on the same side as the brain activation) at the same time as the brain was being stimulated. Participants were asked: 'Given that you are aware of a buzzing feeling in one hand and a real touch on the other, did those occur simultaneously?' The answer was 'no'! The real stimulus to the hand appeared to come first – despite the fact that it took time for the information to run up the nerve from the hand to the brain and was then registered in the brain. Libet *et al.* found that a 300–500 millisecond latency difference (delay) was necessary for participants to experience the two sensations as simultaneous.

From these and other experiments (see text below), Libet concluded that 300–500 milliseconds is how long it takes for consciousness to arise from cortical activity. But this finding is also consistent with Penfield's: stimulating someone's brain produces a different subjective experience compared with the same part of the body being touched – or moving – naturally. Paradoxically, when the brain is directly stimulated it takes longer for this to register consciously than when signals must travel to the brain from the hand – the opposite of what we would expect!

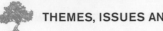

difficult, if not impossible, to prevent these from happening, however hard you try. Clearly, when you undress at gunpoint, your behaviour is not involuntary in this sense, but it is involuntary in the sense that you have been forced into it (it is against your will). So, if behaviour is neither a reflex response to a specific stimulus (knee-jerk), nor coerced (undressing at gun point), then it is free (at least in the soft-determinism sense).

Valentine (1992) observes that there is both phenomenological and behavioural evidence for the distinction between voluntary and involuntary (see Box 11.2).

One demonstration of people's *belief* in their free will is *psychological reactance* (Brehm, 1966; Brehm and Brehm, 1981). This refers to a common response to the feeling that our freedom is being threatened, namely the attempt to regain or reassert our freedom. It is related to the need to be free from the controls and restrictions of others, to determine our own actions and not be dictated to. A good deal of contrary (resistant) behaviour seems to reflect this process ('Don't tell me what to do') (Carver and Scheier, 1992), otherwise known as 'bloody-mindedness'.

Similar to this need to feel free from the controls of others is what has been called *intrinsic motivation* or self-determination (Deci,1980; Deci and Ryan,1987, all in Carver and Scheier, 1992). The central idea is that people have an intrinsic interest in many things, so that they do not need to be offered extrinsic incentives for doing them. Engaging in such activities is motivated by the desire for competence and self-determination.

As far as behavioural evidence for the distinction between voluntary and involuntary behaviour is concerned, Valentine cites a study by Kimble (1964), showing that voluntary eye-blinks can be distinguished from involuntary ones in terms of both form and latency. It is generally agreed that voluntary behaviour is learned, flexible (sensitive to consequences), relatively slow and may involve verbal processes, while involuntary behaviour is automatic, inflexible and may be interfered with by verbalization (see, for example, Shiffrin and Schneider, 1977).

Intentional behaviour based on models

Johnson-Laird (1983) identifies three main levels in the evolution (phylogeny) of automata ('self-operating machines'): the Cartesian (from Descartes), the Craikian (from Craik), and the self-reflective. (The word 'automaton' is often used in a 'derogatory' sense to describe people who seem to show no emotion or who are efficient or self-controlled to such a degree that they appear less than human, as if 'programmed' to behave in pre-determined, highly predictable ways. This contrasts with the common-sense view of the person as being an emotional being who is less than totally predictable, which seems to imply freedom of choice (see Chapters 4 and 7). This non-technical sense of 'automaton' perhaps relates most closely to the Cartesian level as described by Johnson-Laird.)

- The *Cartesian automaton* is an open-loop system, such as bacteria and protozoa, whose behaviour is physically mediated by a direct causal link between stimulus and response. It lacks any kind of awareness or symbolism.
- The *Craikian automaton* is guided by a representation of the external world, constructing a symbolic model of the world in real time – for example, the flight of insects whose flight is controlled by a perceptual model of certain features of the physical environment. This represents a simple kind of awareness or symbolism.
- *Self-reflective automata* are capable of intentional behaviour, which depends on the 'recursive embedding' (repeating process) of models within models (that is, they have a model of a model of a model, and so on). They are self-aware – that is, they have at least a partial model of how their operating system works. For example, humans know they're capable of generating models of future states of affairs and of deciding to bring them about.

Johnson-Laird (1988) believes that freedom consists of the ability to use models of ourselves to select a method of making choices. When you follow a plan, you do not carry out a rigid sequence of actions. Rather, you observe the outcomes of your actions and may, as a result, modify your plan; you may even abandon it. You have the freedom to choose between several options at various points in the execution of your plan (especially if you are using your imagination). Sometimes you adopt a course of action ('our next move') without conscious thought:

> *Level 0: 'You just do it.'* For example: Carry on reading
> Go for a walk

Sometimes, when you are stuck between two equally appealing (or unappealing?) alternatives, you might say to yourself, 'This is ridiculous; I'll have to choose one of them,' and you may then, as a result of this higher-order reflection, make an arbitrary decision (Level 1, meta-level). You might even make sure that it is arbitrary by resorting to some external method, such as tossing a coin or throwing a die (as did the hero of Luke Rhinehart's *The Dice Man*). At the meta-level, you think about what to do and make a decision based, say, on a simple preference:

> *Level 1 (meta-level): By assessing preferences, you choose from*:
> *Level 0*: Carry on reading
> Go for a walk

How did you arrive at this Level 1 method of choice? You did not think consciously about all the different ways you could make a choice and then choose the 'best' method; it simply came to mind as the right way to proceed. Perhaps most methods of choosing are selected this way. But they needn't be; you can confront the issue consciously (Level 2, meta-meta-level) and reflect on which of the methods of choice you will use. You might try to make a rational choice from among them:

> *Level 2 (meta-meta-level): Making a rational assessment, you choose from*:
> *Level 1 (meta-level):* Assessing preferences
> Taking your partner's advice ⎫ to choose from
> Tossing a coin ⎭
>
> *Level 0*: Carry on reading
> Go for a walk

Why did you decide to choose rationally from among the various methods of choice? Once again, it just came to mind as the right way to proceed. The method of decision at the highest level is always chosen *implicitly* (not consciously): if it were chosen consciously, there would have to be a still higher level at which *that* decision was made. In theory, there would be no end to the hierarchy of decisions about decisions about decisions, etc. (an infinite regress), but the business of everyday life demands that you do something, rather than get lost in speculation about how to decide what to do. The buck must stop somewhere! According to Johnson-Laird (1988):

> *We are free, not because we are ignorant of the roots of many of our decisions, which we certainly are, but because our models of ourselves enable us to choose how to choose. Amongst the range of options are even those arbitrary methods that free us from the constraints of an ecological niche or a rational calculation of self-interest . . . one demonstrates freedom (if not imagination) in acting arbitrarily . . .*

This example of a hierarchy of decisions about decisions about decisions, and so on, illustrates the *recursive embedding* of models which is necessary for self-reflection or self-awareness. Johnson-Laird believes that it is an open question whether there is more to self-awareness than this embedding of models, as it is whether cognitive scientists will ever be able to construct computer programs that are self-reflective. Self-awareness is, of course, very closely tied to the concept of *consciousness*, and Johnson-Laird sees the embedding of models as directly relevant to that issue also (see Chapter 12).

Garnham (1991), also a cognitive scientist, agrees with Johnson-Laird that we are unaware of all the factors that influence our decisions. But he reaches the opposite conclusion, namely, that 'it is difficult to see a place for genuinely free will in cognitive science'. But in terms of Johnson-Laird's analysis, it is not obvious in what sense we are not making a free choice: we can still 'choose how to choose' without knowing consciously every 'level' involved in the decision-making process.

Deliberate control

Consistent with Johnson-Laird's analysis is the model of processing capacity proposed by Norman and Shallice (1986). In the context of divided attention (an upper limit to the amount of processing that can be performed on incoming information at any one time), they propose three levels of functioning, ranging from:

- *fully automatic processing*, controlled by organized plans (schemata) that occur with very little conscious awareness of the processes involved, through
- *partially automatic processing*, which involves *contention scheduling* (a way of resolving conflicts between competing schemata) and generally involves more conscious awareness, but occurs without deliberate direction or conscious control, to
- *deliberate control* by a supervisory attentional system, which is involved in decision making and trouble shooting, and allows flexible responding in novel situations. This corresponds to free will.

Driving a car is a sensori-motor skill performed more or less automatically (at least if you are an experienced driver) and which does not require deliberate, conscious control – unless some unexpected event throws the performance 'out of gear', such as putting your foot on the brake pedal when there's an obstacle ahead. According to Koestler (1967), this is a 'rule of the game'. However, on an icy road, this can be risky; the steering wheel has a different feel, the whole strategy of driving must be changed, 'transposed into a different key'. After doing it a number of times, this too may become a semi-automatic routine:

> But let a little dog amble across the icy road in front of the driver, and he will have to make a 'top-level decision' whether to slam down the brake, risking the safety of his passengers, or run over the dog. And if, instead of a dog, the jaywalker is a child, he will probably resort to the brake, whatever the outcome. It is at this level, when the pros and cons are equally balanced, that the subjective experience of freedom and moral responsibility arises.
>
> (Koestler, 1967)

As we move downwards from conscious control, the subjective experience of freedom diminishes: 'Habit is the enemy of freedom ... Machines cannot become like men, but men can become like machines' (Koestler, 1967).

Koestler goes on to say that the second enemy of freedom is very powerful emotions (especially negative ones):

> When they are aroused, the control of decisions is taken over by those primitive levels of the hierarchy which the Victorians called 'the Beast in us' and which are in fact correlated to phylogenetically older structures in the nervous system ... It's the arousal of these structures that results in 'diminished responsibility' and 'I couldn't help it'.

To complete Koestler's account of free will, let's return to what we earlier called the 'appeal to experience', one of the commonest (if not one of the philosophically most convincing) arguments in support of the existence of free will. He argues that:

> The subjective experience of freedom is as much a given datum as the sensation of colour, or the feeling of pain. It is the feeling of making a not enforced, not inevitable, choice. It seems to be

Figure 11.3 The story of Jekyll and Hyde illustrates how the arousal of powerful, primitive emotions can lead to the claim of 'diminished responsibility' and 'I couldn't help it'

working from inside outward, originating in the core of the personality. Even psychiatrists of the deterministic school agree that the abolition of the experience of having a will of his own leads to collapse of the patient's whole mental structure . . .

FREE WILL AND CONSCIOUSNESS

Libet's experiments on consciousness and free will

What happens when we do something voluntarily? How does this something happen?

According to Blackmore (2005), if you are asked to hold out your hand in front of you and to then flex your wrist whenever you feel like it – and of your own free will –, then whether you did it or not, you made a decision: either you flipped your hand at a certain point or you didn't. The question then arises: who or what made the decision or initiated the action? Was it your inner self? Was it the power of consciousness?

It certainly feels as though it is our self ('I') that is making the decision and that the decision to flex the wrist is what makes the wrist flex. However, even if an inner self exists (and many objections have been raised to this claim), we have no idea how it could make the action happen. So, Blackmore suggests, perhaps there were just a lot of brain processes, following one after another, that determined whether and when you flexed your wrist.

This certainly fits with the anatomical evidence. When any voluntary act (i.e. non-reflex) is carried out, such as flexing the wrist, many areas of the brain are involved. Activity begins in the prefrontal cortex (PFC), which sends signals to the premotor cortex, which programmes the actions and sends signals to the primary motor cortex. The motor cortex then sends out the instructions that cause the muscles to move. Other areas are involved in specific actions, such as Broca's area (in the left hemisphere for most right-handed people) in speech. Evidence from brain scans in humans reveals that the dorsolateral PFC is uniquely associated with the subjective experience of deciding when and how to act.

So what's the problem?

The problem from a philosophical point of view is that the existence of free will implies that it is 'I' who decides to perform the action – *not* my brain – and the sequence of brain areas that are activated is a direct result of my decision. But what if it could be shown that the brain begins to become activated *before* I have made the (conscious) decision? Wouldn't this seriously detract from belief in free will?

Libet (1985; Libet *et al.*, 1983) asked the question: when someone spontaneously and deliberately flexes his/her finger or wrist, what starts the action off? Is it the conscious decision to act, or is it some unconscious brain process? To find out, Libet asked participants to flex their finger/wrist at least 40 times, at times of their own choosing, and measured:

(i) the time at which the action occurred (M). This can be easily detected by using electrodes on the wrist (electromyogram/EMG)

(ii) the beginning of brain activity in the motor cortex. This can also be detected through placing electrodes on the scalp (electroencephalogram/EEG), which detect a gradually increasing signal (the 'readiness potential'/RP)

(iii) the time at which the participant consciously decided to act (the moment of willing) (W).

The key question is: which comes first?

(iii) is the most difficult to determine. If you ask participants to shout or press a button or do anything else, there will be another lag before this. Also, the decision to shout or press the button may interfere with the main decision being measured. Libet devised a special method for measuring W. He asked participants to note the position of a spot of light (moving around the circumference of a circular screen placed in front of them) at the moment they decided to act. They could then say, after the action was over, where the spot had been at that critical moment.

Libet found that W came about 200 milliseconds (ms) (one-fifth of a second) before the action (consistent with the concept of free will). But the RP began about 300-500 ms before that (that is, 500-700 ms before the action – contrary to what belief in free will would predict). In other words, there was activity in the brain for anything up to half a second before participants were subjectively aware of having made the decision: consciousness lagged behind brain activity.

While these findings seem to contradict the idea of free will, are they really so surprising? According to Blackmore (2005), for a conscious decision to precede any brain activity would be nothing short of magic. It would mean that consciousness could 'come out of nowhere' and influence physical events in the brain (as proposed by dualists such as Descartes, and Popper and Eccles).

Nevertheless, Libet's results caused a storm of debate among philosophers, neuroscientists, psychologists and physiologists, which has been raging ever since – and shows every sign of heating up still further (Banks and Pockett, 2007). As Banks and Pockett put it:

> The issue is this. Libet's clear-cut finding was that his subjects consciously and freely 'decided' to initiate an action only after the neurological preparation to act was well under way. This implies that the conscious decision was not the cause of the action. . .If conscious decisions are not the cause of actions, it follows that we do not have conscious free will. Even worse, because the ability consciously to initiate actions is an essential property of self, the denial of conscious, personal origination of action is a challenge to our sense of selfhood. The implication is that we, our conscious selves, are not free actors with control over our choices in life. We are only conduits for unconsciously made decisions. Libet's one simple experiment has slipped our entire self-concept from its moorings.

However compelling these conclusions may be, they are also counter-intuitive; so much so that Libet himself refused to draw them. Instead, he concluded that, although consciousness clearly couldn't have *initiated* the participants' movements, it was still capable of stepping in and *vetoing* it before it was performed (Libet, 1985, 1999). This rescues free will, but at the cost of seriously restricting its role. (This is discussed further below.)

Criticisms of Libet's experiments

The idea that perceived freedom of action is an illusion has a long philosophical and psychological history (Freud; 1901; Festinger, 1957; Skinner, 1971; Ross and Nisbett, 1991; Gazzaniga, 1997, 1998; Velmans, 2000; Ferguson and Bargh, 2004), but Libet's findings were the first direct neurophysiological evidence to support it.

Much of the research that was stimulated by Libet's experiments was aimed at examining the possibility that his results were flawed in some way. According to Banks and Pockett (2007), questions about Libet's findings fall into three categories:

(i) does the basic finding hold up from a technical point of view: are there any methodological problems?

(ii) can the movement he studied legitimately be considered as an example of free will?

(iii) what exactly are the participants reporting on when they say they decided at a particular moment to make the movement?

As far as (i) is concerned, the work has been repeated in three independent laboratories. Keller and Heckhausen (1990), Haggard and Eimer (1999), and Trevena and Miller (2002) have all repeated the basic experiment and obtained roughly the same result.

Arguably, (ii) is the most relevant as far as this chapter is concerned. The act being studied in Libet's research is a simple finger/wrist movement. It has no consequences and carries no credit or blame or risk, unlike many of the decisions we make in our everyday lives. It seems to be about as free an action as one could think of. However, it is also about the most trivial action one could perform. Does it count as representative of willed action?

While Libet's method could be viewed as a means of abstracting a feature from nature for scientific study, flexing a finger/wrist is so trivial that it is unlike the vast majority of the enormous category of willed decisions. Only at this extreme of willed actions does the RP precede the conscious decision. Indeed, Banks and Pockett cite research evidence showing that there are apparently some differences in brain activity between consequential and inconsequential decisions. Haggard and Eimer (1999) found that neither W nor M was affected when participants were required to choose between moving their right or left hand. But the question of what relation a more complex or personally involving decision has to the RP does not seem to have been addressed, as Libet (2003) acknowledges.

Regarding (iii), Libet's participants could choose only when to act, not which action to perform. Deciding to flex your finger or wrist does not matter, whereas getting out of bed or reading a book, deciding to accept a job offer or how to raise your children do (some more than others) (Blackmore, 2005). All decisions about what movements to make and how to make them were determined before any measurements were made; timing of volition is thus the only aspect open to study in Libet's experiments. In contrast, Haggard and Eimer (1999) and Trevena and Miller (2002) had their participants choose which hand to use as well as when to respond, but with little change in the basic effect.

Because the decision is an unobservable event whose meaning is defined by the participant, the instructions given by the experimenter are important (Banks and Pockett, 2007), Libet's (1983) participants were asked to wait until the timing spot had revolved once and then to 'let the urge to act appear on its own at any time without any preplanning or concentration on when to act' and report the earliest appearance of a conscious 'wanting' or 'urge' to make particular movements. According to Banks and Pockett:

> . . . *This suggests that W is more a passive registration of the onset of a feeling than an act of will . . . If so, one could argue that this experiment is a measure of the participant's self-defined criterion about where in the RP to report an 'urge', not a measure of the timing of volition . . .*

Another possibility is that the assumption that brain events have a time course that exactly mirrors our experience is mistaken, especially since most of our brain's activity is unconscious. The metaphor of a mental event as a 'thing' with a definite beginning and end is directly imported from folk psychology and must be considered at best as pre-scientific. In the absence of a scientific account of the relationship between brain and action, it is difficult to see what participants' W reports actually mean.

The veto response

While Libet rejected the various criticisms of his experiments, as we noted earlier, he also rejected the conclusion that free will is merely an illusion. Based on the observation that his participants sometimes said they'd aborted their movement just before it happened, Libet conducted another experiment which showed

that in such cases the RP started normally, but then flattened out and disappeared about 200 ms before the action was due to happen. From this he argued for the existence of a 'conscious veto; that is, while consciousness couldn't initiate the finger/wrist movement, it could act to *prevent* it. In other words, although we do not have free will, we do have 'free won't' (Gregory, cited in Blackmore, 2003).

More generally, our choices of action (such as ducking to avoid an approaching missile) need to be made faster than could be achieved consciously; that is, such decisions are made preconsciously. However:

> *. . . the mechanisms of consciousness do still have a say: they are able to veto plans that would lead to disadvantage in the long run, and to permit only the beneficial ones to proceed. 'Free will' is thus expressed in the form of selective permission of automatically generated actions, rather than as the (Cartesian) initiation of action by an independent mind (Libet, 1985) . . . Libet's (1994) philosophical conclusion is that consciousness exists as a dualistic mental field.*
>
> *(Rose, 2006)*

Libet (2004) gives obsessive-compulsive disorder and Tourette's syndrome as examples of disorders in which the individual is unable to make the veto response.

Implications of Libet's 'dualism'

Libet argues that this has important implications for freedom and responsibility. Although we cannot consciously control our dispositions or impulses, we can consciously stop ourselves acting them out. So, for example, we cannot control our impulses to commit crime (that is, thinking about committing murder or robbery), but our conscious veto should prevent us from actually doing it. In this way, Libet was able to accept his own experimental findings and at the same time accept the power of consciousness. Indeed, he went further, proposing the 'conscious mental field theory', according to which subjective experience is a unique and fundamental property in nature: something that emerges from brain activity and can in turn act upon and influence that brain activity. This unified and powerful field accounts for the two most difficult features of consciousness – both the unity of our mental life and our sense of free will (Blackmore, 2005).

An evaluation of Libet's account of free will: compatibilism

According to *compatibilists*, free will is not an absolute freedom but the unrestrained ability to act. It doesn't matter if the intention to act is determined by brain processes that operate outside consciousness. The point is that we are free when there are no external constraints (such as a gun to the head) that compel action (Banks and Pockett, 2007: see above).

For these reasons, compatibilism is perhaps the account of free will that sits most comfortably with Libet's research. The fact that the RP precedes is not a problem for compatibilists: the preconscious processes that lead up to a decision, whether conceived as brain processes or unconscious ideas, do not rule out freedom. On the contrary, Libet's findings might be considered to be the first neurophysiological evidence for a compatibilist account of action.

Libet *et al*. (1983) found that Type I (pre-planned) RPs began 500 ms before Type II (spontaneous) RPs. In both cases, the time between W and the response was about the same. The interval between the onset of the RP and W was consequently greater when the response was pre-planned. If the difference between the beginning of the RP and W measures the length of the unconscious preparation, then it would seem that the more we plan an action, the longer we are unconscious of the final preparation to act. By extension, really important decisions might have the longest period of unconscious incubation (they certainly require more pre-planning than trivial ones). Problem solving and artistic creation have long been associated with unconscious thinking (Krippner, 1981, in Banks and Pockett). Banks and Pockett claim that mental activity that is not conscious may have far greater importance in everyday life than in Libet's paradigm, and the

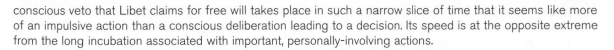

conscious veto that Libet claims for free will takes place in such a narrow slice of time that it seems like more of an impulsive action than a conscious deliberation leading to a decision. Its speed is at the opposite extreme from the long incubation associated with important, personally-involving actions.

According to Velmans's (2000, 2002, 2003) compatibilist account, the unconscious antecedents of conscious motivations are included as part of the self: a person's identity and individuality are reflected in his/her consequent actions and conscious experience. We do not need to be conscious of the decision at the time it is made for it to be free. But for Libet (1999), and many others, free will means conscious free choice.

Conclusions: is free will illusory?

The conclusion that seems most consistent with Libet's experimental findings is that the decision to act is prepared preconsciously, about 350 ms or more before the conscious report of a decision. As Banks and Pockett (2007) say:

> . . . The unwelcome consequence is that the conscious will is not the original determinant of action. Our sense of conscious agency would be illusory in this case, and our sense of ownership of this action is misplaced. The resolution by Velmans, that the preconscious activity is indeed part of the self, posits that the signature of our internal unconscious processes accounts for our gut feelings that these acts are ours and done by us, even though we are not conscious of the origins.

Even if this compatibilist position 'rescues' free will, it still leaves open the question of the *causal efficacy* of consciousness; in other words, how can something 'mental' (non-physical), such as the decision to lift my arm, cause physical events/actions (such as the actual lifting of my arm)? This is discussed further in Chapter 13.

THE VIEWS OF WILLIAM JAMES: SOFT DETERMINISM

James was one of the pioneers of psychology as a separate, scientific discipline (see Chapter 10), but he is remembered as much as a philosopher as a psychologist, which perhaps made him especially qualified to express an opinion on the free will and determinism issue.

In his classic *The Principles of Psychology* (1890), a whole chapter is devoted to the 'will', which he related to attention. He described effort, or the sensation of effort, as the primary subjective indication that an act of will has occurred:

> The most essential achievement of the will . . . when it is most 'voluntary' is to attend to a different object and hold it fast before the mind . . . Effort of attention is thus the essential phenomenon of will.

But should psychology recognize the existence of free will? Is the feeling of effortful attention strictly a mechanistically determined function of the object of thought, or does subjective consciousness supply certain indeterminate, unpredictable influences of its own, independent of the object? Can a scientific conception of the mind be compatible with our ordinary conception of human nature?

James could not find a simple answer to these questions. Belief in determinism seems to fit best with the scientific view of the world, while belief in free will seems to be required by our social, moral, political and legal practices, as well as our personal, subjective experience. In the face of this conflict, James simply distinguished between the scientific and the subjective/everyday realms, claiming that belief in determinism seemed to 'work' best in the former, while belief in free will seemed to work best in the latter. Psychology, as a science, could only progress by assuming determinism, but this does not mean that belief in free will must be abandoned in other contexts:

Science ... must constantly be reminded that her purposes are not the only purposes, and the order of uniform causation which she has use for, and is, therefore, postulating, may be enveloped in a wider order, on which she has no claims at all.

In other words, there is 'more to life than science'. Scientific explanation isn't the only useful kind of explanation. Psychology did not, and could not, provide all the answers. According to Fancher (1996):

He found he could entertain mechanistic ideas and take them seriously scientifically, without fully accepting them personally. In personal life it was useful to think and behave as if he had free will, while as a scientist it was useful to accept mechanistic determinism. Both views were essentially articles of faith incapable of absolute proof or disproof. In the absence of any absolute criterion for judging their 'truth', James decided to evaluate ideas according to their utility within specified and limited contexts ...

Evaluation of ideas in terms of their practical utility or usefulness is the central idea in the philosophical theory of *pragmatism*, which James helped to establish.

A second 'solution' to the conflict is what James called *soft determinism* (what Locke, Hume and others called compatibilism (Flanagan, 1984: see above). According to soft determinism, the question of free will depends on the type(s) of cause(s) our behaviour has, not whether it is caused or not caused. According to James, if our actions have, as their proximate, immediate cause, processing by a system such as conscious mental life (CLM – consciousness itself, purposefulness, personality and personal continuity), then they count as free, rational, voluntary, purposive actions (see Chapter 12).

As far as hard determinism is concerned, CLM is itself caused, so that the immediate causes are only part of the total causal chain that results in the behaviour we're trying to explain. According to this view, if our behaviour is caused at all, there is no sense in which we can be said to act freely.

James's soft determinism is similar to the views of Johnson-Laird, for whom it is neither necessary nor possible to know consciously all the levels involved in the hierarchy of decision making, in order to say that the decision was made freely; it is sufficient to say that the decision was made at a level higher than Level 0 (see above).

THE VIEWS OF SIGMUND FREUD: PSYCHIC DETERMINISM

Although Freud's and Skinner's views on human behaviour are diametrically opposed in most respects, they shared the fundamental view that belief in free will is an illusion. However, in keeping with their theories as a whole, the reasons for holding this belief are very different.

According to James Strachey, one of Freud's translators and the editor of the 'Standard Edition' of Freud's collected works:

Freud's discoveries may be grouped under three headings – an instrument of research, the findings produced by the instrument, and the theoretical hypotheses inferred from the findings – though the three groups were of course mutually interrelated. Behind all of Freud's work, however, we should posit his belief in the universal validity of the law of determinism ... Freud extended the belief [derived from physical phenomena] uncompromisingly to the field of mental phenomena ...

(Strachey, 1962–77)

According to Sulloway (1979), Freud's entire life's work in science (and he very much saw himself as a scientist) was characterized by an abiding faith in the notion that all vital phenomena, including psychical ones, are rigidly and lawfully determined by the principle of cause and effect. Together with his belief that dreams have meaning and can, therefore, be interpreted, the extreme prominence he gave to the technique of free association in his clinical work was perhaps the most explicit manifestation of this philosophical theory.

Sulloway points out that 'free association' is a misleading translation of the German *'freier Einfall'*, which conveys much more accurately the intended impression of an uncontrollable 'intrusion' (*'Einfall'*) by *pre-conscious* ideas into conscious thinking. In turn, this pre-conscious material reflected unconscious ideas, wishes and memories, which was what Freud was really interested in, since here lay the principal cause(s) of his patients' neurotic problems.

It is a great irony that *free* association should refer to a technique used in psychoanalysis meant to reveal the *unconscious causes* of behaviour. The fact that the causes of our thoughts, actions and supposed choices are unconscious (mostly *actively repressed*, made unconscious because of their threatening, disturbing nature) is what accounts for the illusion that we are free. In other words, we believe we have free will, because we are (by definition) unaware of the true, unconscious, causes of our actions. The application of his general philosophical belief in causation to mental phenomena is called *psychic determinism*.

Freud's aim was to establish a 'scientific psychology', and he hoped to be able to achieve this by applying to the human mind the same principles of causality as were in his time considered valid in physics, chemistry and, more recently, physiology. If all mental activity is the result of unconscious mental forces that are instinctual, biological or physical in origin, then human psychology could be formulated in terms of the interaction of forces that were, in principle, quantifiable, and psychology would become a natural science like physics (Rycroft, 1966). (Brown (1961) points out that, strictly speaking, the principle of causality is not a scientific law but rather a necessary assumption without which no science would be possible.)

James, Watson, McDougall (1908) and others among Freud's predecessors or contemporaries all assumed the principle of causation (in McDougall's case, instincts were the major cause). But they distinguished between (i) behaviour for which one or more clear-cut cause(s) were known (or could be readily claimed), and (ii) chance or random events that are the result of many separate and apparently trivial causes, which it would be fruitless or impossible to analyse. It was accepted that most psychological events were of the latter kind and, therefore, could only be discussed in broad descriptive terms, as opposed to being analyzed in detail in any particular case (Brown, 1961).

Freud took exception to this view. In his early studies of hysterical patients, he showed that the apparently irrational symptoms were in fact meaningful when seen in terms of painful, unconscious, memories. They were *not* fortuitous or chance events, and their causes could be uncovered by (psycho)analysis. This same reasoning was then applied to other seemingly random, irrational events, to 'parapraxes' (the 'psychopathology of everyday life, such as slips of the tongue and other 'Freudian slips') and to dreams.

A crucial feature of Freud's theory is that there are no accidents in the universe of the mind:

> *In his view of the mind, every event, no matter how accidental its appearance, is as it were a knot in intertwined causal threads that are too remote in origin, large in number, and complex in their interaction to be readily sorted out. True: to secure freedom from the grip of causality is among mankind's most cherished, and hence most tenacious, illusory wishes. But Freud sternly warned that psychoanalysis should offer such fantasies no comfort. Freud's theory of the mind is, therefore, strictly and frankly deterministic.*
>
> *(Gay, 1988)*

However, Gay's conclusion needs to be qualified.

Some freedom to change

Freud did not deny that human choices are real and, indeed, one of the aims of therapy is to 'give the patient's ego freedom to decide one way or another' (Freud, in Gay, 1988). If we become aware of our previously unconscious memories, feelings and so on, we are freed from their stranglehold (although there is more to therapeutic success than simply 'remembering'). The whole of psychoanalysis is based on the belief that people *can* change.

However, Freud believed that only very limited change is possible, and among the modest aims of therapy is to convert 'neurotic misery into everyday unhappiness'. Yet even such a limited degree of freedom is incompatible with hard determinism:

> *Since he believes that humans are largely not free he cannot hold that there is any moral dimension, since one can be moral only if one is free. In Freud's account the difference between a Stalin and a Gandhi comes down to a difference in biology (which is ridiculous) or a difference in childhoods (which may be relevant but is not the whole explanation) . . . If we believed Freud, we would empty all our prisons and turn them into mental hospitals. We do not do this because we suspect that there is a moral element in human beings, and that sometimes they are free and responsible for what they do . . .*

> *(Morea, 1990)*

Accidents

Freud *did not* deny that 'accidents' can and do occur, in the sense of events brought about by intrusions from 'systems' that have nothing to do with the personality of the 'victim'. For example, being struck by lightning or being aboard a ship that sinks are difficult to attribute to the person him/herself; these are clearly to do with forces beyond the victim's control and are true accidents. But repeated 'accidents', particularly of a similar kind, such as the woman who has a string of 'tragic' marriages, with husband after husband dying within a short time of their wedding, or the person who is seen as 'accident-prone', point to the 'victim' as somehow, unconsciously, helping to bring the event(s) about. These *are not* true accidents.

Multiple causes of behaviour

The Freudian concept of psychic determinism does not propose a simple one-to-one correspondence between cause and effect. *Overdetermination* refers to the observation that much of our behaviour (as well as our thoughts and feelings) has multiple causes, some conscious, some unconscious. By definition, we only know about the conscious causes, and these are what we normally take to be *the* reasons. However, if the causes also include unconscious factors, then the reasons we give for our actions can never tell the whole story and, indeed, the unconscious causes may be more important. According to this view, overdetermination constitutes one aspect of psychic determinism.

The semantic argument

According to Rycroft (1966), the principle of psychic determinism remains an assumption, which Freud made out of scientific faith rather than on actual evidence. Nowhere in Freud's writing does he claim to have predicted in advance the outcome of any choice or decision made by a patient. He denied more than once the idea that it is possible to predict whether a person will develop a neurosis, or what kind it will be. Instead, he claimed that all we can do is determine the cause *retrospectively* (not a very scientific way of going about things, as his critics are fond of pointing out, since predictability is seen as a requirement of a scientific theory). As Rycroft says, this is more reminiscent of a historian than a scientist.

However, Freud successfully claimed that he could show that choices made by patients aren't arbitrary and can be understood as revealing characteristic manifestations of their personality. What he often did, in fact, was to explain patients' choices, neurotic symptoms and so on, not in terms of causes, but by understanding and giving them meaning. The procedure he engaged in was not the scientific one of identifying causes but the *semantic* one of trying to make sense of it:

> It can indeed be argued that much of Freud's work was really semantic and that he made a revolutionary discovery in semantics, viz. that neurotic symptoms are meaningful disguised communications, but that, owing to his scientific training and allegiance, he formulated his findings in the conceptual framework of the physical sciences . . .
>
> *(Rycroft, 1966)*

The 'semantic argument' is supported by the title of what many people consider to be his greatest book, *The Interpretation of Dreams* (as opposed to *The Cause of Dreams*). He was also well aware that his ideas had been anticipated by writers and poets, not scientists.

THE VIEWS OF B.F. SKINNER: FREE WILL AS AN ILLUSION

Skinner's *radical behaviourism* probably represents the most outspoken and extreme expression among psychologists of the view that people are not free, and the most explicit and accessible account of this view is his *Beyond Freedom and Dignity* (1971). In it, he argues that *behavioural freedom is an illusion*.

Radical behaviourists regard their view of behaviour as the most scientific, because it provides an account in terms of material causes, all of which can be objectively defined and measured. Mentalistic concepts, such as free will, are 'explanatory fictions' – that is, they do not account for behaviour (they are not causes, but effects). Also, because they are private, they cannot be defined and measured objectively.

If there is some reason, however tentative, for arguing that Freud was something less than a hard determinist, in Skinner's case there is no doubt whatsoever – he was as hard as they come! Just as Freud believed that freedom is an illusion to the extent that we are unaware of the unconscious causes of our feelings and behaviour, so Skinner claims that it is because the causes of human behaviour are often hidden from us in the environment that the myth or illusion of free will survives. So what is the nature of those causes?

When what we do is dictated by force or punishment, or by the threat of force or punishment (negative reinforcement), it is obvious to everyone that we are not acting freely. For example, when the possibility of prison stops us from committing a crime, there is clearly no choice involved, because we know what the environmental causes of our behaviour are. Similarly, it may sometimes be very obvious which positive reinforcers are shaping our behaviour, such as a bonus for working extra hours.

However, most of the time we are unaware of the environmental causes of our behaviour, so it looks (and feels) as if we are behaving freely. When we believe we are acting freely, all this sometimes means is that we are free of punishments or negative reinforcements; our behaviour is still determined by the pursuit of things that have been positively reinforced in the past. We believe we are free because, most of the time at least, we do what we 'want'; but doing what we want is simply doing what we have previously been rewarded for doing. When we perceive others as behaving freely, we are simply unaware of their reinforcement histories.

But when, for example, people act in a law-abiding way, aren't they choosing to do so, and, by the same token, aren't those who take the criminal route also choosing the rewards of their crime over the possibility of punishment? In other words, isn't Skinner simply assuming that it's the threat of imprisonment and other punishments that determines behaviour, directly, automatically and without the 'mind' of the actor playing any role whatsoever? Skinner does not – and cannot – offer any additional evidence to show that his argument ('when someone appears to be making a choice, we have simply failed to identify the real pay-offs') is more valid than the opposing argument ('when someone appears to be making a choice, it is because they are making a choice!'). As Morea (1990) says, Skinner's argument seems to be of the 'Heads I win, tails you lose' variety:

> Once this is said, and it is the only behaviourist answer to apparently free choices, what seemed like a scientific account begins to look more like faith ... At least the opposite assertion, of a modest degree of free choice, has the advantage of having common sense and human experience on its side.

Skinner in fact suggests that, instead of our behaviour being determined by rewards and the threat of punishment, it is merely shaped and modified by them, allowing for some active part to be played by the actor. This relates to his analysis of behaviour, which is based on operant conditioning. Operant conditioning encompasses what most people think of as voluntary behaviour (see above). Indeed, Skinner (1986) stated that 'operant behaviour is the field of intention, purpose and expectation'. Operant behaviour is also purposive: its function is to change the environment and produce particular consequences. However, according to O'Donohue and Ferguson (2001), purposive behaviour does not imply that the individual has free will, or that behaviour is not caused, because all behaviour is determined. (This argument implies that the opposite of 'determined' is 'free', but recall that the real opposite of determined is 'random'.)

Bettering society and Skinner's attack on 'autonomous man'

As we noted earlier, without free will there cannot be any moral – or legal – responsibility. But Skinner (1971) believes that 'Behaviour is called good or bad ... according to the way in which it is usually reinforced by others.' He more or less equates 'good' and 'bad' with 'beneficial to others' (what is rewarded) and 'harmful to others' (what is punished) respectively. This removes morality from human behaviour, either 'inside' the individual or 'outside', in society. There is only mutual reinforcement, and if we could arrange the reinforcement appropriately, we could create utopia. But in Skinner's utopia (described in his 1948 novel *Walden Two*), how can the planners plan, since you must be free in the first place to be able to plan? For Skinner, 'oughts' *are not* 'moral imperatives' – that is, they do not reflect moral but *practical* guidelines and rules (Morea, 1990).

Skinner's views on bettering society caused an enormous backlash from critical audiences and the general public. This is reflected in his appearance on the cover of *Time* magazine in September 1971. Carl Rogers claimed that Skinner's utopian vision in *Walden Two* was indistinguishable from George Orwell's *Nineteen Eighty-Four*, a nightmarish dystopia, which warns against a punitive society where people are treated as automatons by those in power (O'Donohue and Ferguson, 2001).

Critics saw him as a totalitarian, fascist, 'evil scientist', and at the centre of these attacks was his denial of free will ('autonomous man'). But if we are to improve society, we need to redesign the environment. Only a technology of behaviour can rescue mankind – because social ills are caused by behaviour, it follows that the cure involves changing the variables that control behaviour. For Skinner's critics, any attempt to try controlling behaviour is an infringement of personal liberty. But Skinner regarded the dichotomy between freedom and control (or behavioural engineering) as false: all behaviour is controlled all of the time. For Skinner (1974),

> A scientific analysis of behaviour must, I believe, assume that a person's behaviour is controlled by his genetic and environmental histories rather than by the person himself as an initiating, creative agent ... We cannot prove, of course, that human behaviour as a whole is fully determined, but the proposition becomes more plausible as facts accumulate ... We cannot choose a way of life in which there is no control. We can only change the controlling conditions.

THE VIEWS OF CARL ROGERS: FREEDOM AND THE FULLY FUNCTIONING PERSON

As a humanistic, phenomenological psychologist, Rogers stressed the process of self-actualization and the necessity of adopting the perspective of the other person if we are to understand that person: experience (as distinct from overt behaviour) is all-important (see Chapter 11). In particular, it is crucial to understand the person's *self-concept*, an 'organized, consistent set of perceptions and beliefs about oneself', including our awareness of 'what we are' and 'what we can do'. These influence both our perception of the world and our behaviour. Every experience is evaluated in terms of our self-concept, and most human behaviour can be regarded as an attempt to maintain consistency between our self-image and our actions.

Understanding the self-concept is also central to Rogers's *client-centred therapy*. His experience over many years as a therapist convinced him that real change does occur in therapy; people choose to see themselves and their life situation differently. Therapy and life are about free human beings struggling to become more free. While personal experience is important, it does not imprison us; how we react to our experience is something we ourselves choose and decide (Morea, 1990).

However, we sometimes fail to acknowledge certain experiences, feelings, and behaviours if they conflict with our (conscious) self-image; they are *incongruent* precisely because they are not consistent with our view of ourselves, and they become threatening. So they are denied access to awareness (they remain *unsymbolized*) through actual denial, distortion or blocking. These defence mechanisms prevent the self from growing and changing, and widen the gulf between our self-image and reality (our true feelings, our actual behaviour). As the self-image becomes more and more unrealistic, so the incongruent person becomes more and more confused, vulnerable, dissatisfied and, eventually, seriously maladjusted. Defensiveness, lack of congruence, and an unrealistic self-concept may all be seen as a lack of freedom, which therapy is designed to restore.

Humans are growth-oriented, and will naturally progress towards the fulfilment of their innate potential (*self-actualize*) if psychological conditions are favourable. This contrasts sharply with Freud's view of people as essentially 'savage beasts' (in *Civilization and its Discontents*, 1930), whose aggressive tendencies and unpredictable sexuality can only be controlled by the processes and structures of civilization. Freud was pessimistic about human nature, and saw the instinctual drives of the id (especially sexuality and aggression) as pushing individuals towards the selfish satisfaction of primitive needs or the relief of powerful tensions (the *pleasure principle*). As we saw above, this is a very deterministic view.

However, Rogers's deep and lasting trust in human nature did not blind him to the reality of evil behaviour:

> *In my experience, every person has the capacity for evil behaviour. I, and others, have had murderous and cruel impulses, desires to hurt, feelings of anger and rage, desires to impose our wills on others . . . Whether I, or anyone, will translate these impulses into behaviour depends, it seems to me, on two elements: social conditioning and voluntary choice . . . I believe that, theoretically at least, every evil behaviour is brought about by varying degrees of these elements.*
>
> *(Rogers, 1982, in Thorne, 1992)*

By making the distinction between 'human nature' and 'behaviour', Rogers is able to retain his optimistic view of human beings, but this didn't exclude altogether a deterministic element in his later writings. In *Freedom to Learn for the '80s* (1983), he wrote, 'Yet as we enter this field of psychotherapy with objective research methods, we are, like any other scientist, committed to a complete determinism' (in Morea, 1990). He states that it is becoming clear from science that human beings are complex machines and *not free*. So, how can this be reconciled with self-actualization, psychological growth and the freedom to choose?

225

One proposed solution is a version of soft determinism. Unlike neurotic and incongruent people, whose defensiveness forces them to act in ways they would prefer not to, the healthy, fully functioning person 'not only experiences, but utilizes, the most absolute freedom when he spontaneously, freely and voluntarily chooses and wills that which is absolutely determined' (Rogers, 1983, in Morea, 1990). The fully functioning person chooses to act and be the way s/he has to: it is the most fulfilling.

THE VIEWS OF ERICH FROMM: THE FEAR OF FREEDOM

Fromm was, like Freud, a psychoanalytic theorist and therapist, but, like many other neo-Freudians, he disagreed with Freud on a number of important issues. One of these was the influence of social, cultural and historical forces on human behaviour, as well as the crucial nature of the child's relationships, rather than biological forces within the personality, which were so much stressed by Freud.

In *The Fear of Freedom* (1942; published in 1941 in the USA as *Escape from Freedom*), Fromm argues that we are both part of nature and apart, separate, from it. Human beings created primitive creeds and religious beliefs to enable them to feel less separated from the world, and in Europe, until very recently, the Catholic Church fulfilled this role of providing a sense of security; it mediated between God and humanity, guaranteeing salvation but, in the process, limiting human freedom.

The Reformation and the rise of Protestantism broke the power of the Catholic Church, giving people their freedom, but at what price? According to Morea (1990):

> *Separation – both physical and psychological separation from nature, and psychological separation from dogma and authority – makes people free. But separation makes people alone, and potentially insignificant and lonely.*

At least while Protestantism flourished, people still had a meaningful place in the universe, but with the rise in the nineteenth century of industrialization, capitalism and science, the universe was turned into a machine, with no room for God. This left people alone and insecure, their lives meaningless.

What do we do? One solution is to escape from freedom by creating and becoming part of authoritarian organizations and totalitarian regimes, such as those in Hitler's Germany and Stalin's Russia.

People like Hitler and Stalin gave up their freedom by continuously making 'bad' choices; eventually they could only choose what was wrong. But a fortunate few, because of living lives in which they have made 'good', right choices, opt only for what is right and good: they are no longer free to choose evil or wrongdoing. At both extremes, human behaviour is caused/determined.

Figure 11.4 Millions of people lost their identity and 'escaped from freedom' when they submitted to the Nazi regime in Hitler's Germany

For example, after many years of heavy drinking the alcoholic is no longer free to stop, but most of us aren't yet alcoholics or compulsive gamblers. Only at the end of a long chain of acts does such determinism operate. Earlier along the line we are free, and this is where most of us are, so finely balanced between several contradictory inclinations that we are usually still in a position to choose. But freedom is never absolute; it always depends on the available alternatives.

We all face a fundamental decision: either we accept, even welcome, our freedom, or we can choose to escape from it (our 'ultimate' act of freedom?) by surrendering ourselves and our freedom to a person, ideology or organization. In *The Heart of Man* (1964), Fromm talks about 'soft determinism'. His position is closer to this than to the 'hard' variety, but it often seems that he is not any kind of determinist at all: 'Fromm has to come down on the side of free choice because, if humans are moral beings, we must be free – to choose good or bad, right or wrong. And Fromm continually stresses our moral nature . . .' (Morea, 1990).

THE VIEWS OF GEORGE KELLY: FREEDOM AND PERSONAL CONSTRUCTS

According to Kelly, people are free to the extent that they have *personal constructs* by which to interpret, predict and control the world. But these constructs also restrict freedom, because we can only choose from the constructs we have and, to a very large extent, they *determine* our behaviour:

> *Constructs are the channels in which one's mental processes run. They are two-way streets along which one may travel to reach conclusions. They make it possible to anticipate the changing tide of events . . . constructs are the controls that one places on life – the life within him as well as the life which is external to him. Forming constructs may be considered as binding sets of events into convenient bundles which are handy for the person who has to lug them. Events, when so bound, tend to become predictable, manageable, and controlled.*
>
> *(Kelly, 1955)*

So, constructs are needed if the world isn't to seem totally chaotic and unpredictable. But control is a special case of determinism:

> *A person is to cut a pie. There is an infinite number of ways of going about it, all of which may be relevant to the task. If the pie is frozen, some of the usual ways of cutting the pie may not work – but there is still an infinite number of ways of going about it. But suppose the pie is on the table and there is company present. Certain limiting expectations have been set up about how a meal is to be served. The pie is construed as part of the meal. There are also certain conventions about serving wedge-shaped slices with the point always turned towards the diner. If one accepts all the usual superordinating constructions of the situation, he may, indeed, find his course of behaviour determined and very little latitude left to him. He is not the victim of the pie, but of his notions of etiquette under which the pie-cutting has been subsumed.*
>
> *(Kelly, 1955)*

In Kelly's terms, once we define what we are doing (construe the situation) as 'serving a meal for guests' (a *superordinate construct*), then everything we do as part of that situation, such as cutting a pie, becomes a *subordinate construct* relative to the superordinate one. The way we construe the pie-cutting is *determined by* having subordinated the pie-cutting to the superordinate 'serving a meal for guests'. We are free to define natural events as we wish, but if we want to predict them accurately, we need some kind of construction that will serve the purpose; it is the structure we erect that rules us.

So, we are free in some respects, but not others. Freedom and determinism are two sides of the same coin; neither is an absolute, but relative to something else. Once I see the world in a certain way, what I do inevitably follows (it is determined), but I'm free to change my constructs, just as scientists are free to change their theories (see Chapter 1).

SOCIOBIOLOGY: EXTREME BIOLOGICAL DETERMINISM

This section draws on the critique of sociobiology by Rose *et al.* in *Not in Our Genes* (1984), which is a critique of *biological determinism* in general. Here we concentrate on those aspects that are most relevant to the issue of freedom and determinism.

The central claim of sociobiology is that all aspects of human culture and behaviour, like those of all animals, are coded in the genes and have been moulded by natural selection. Sociobiology is a reductionist, biological determinist explanation of human existence. Its adherents claim, first, that the details of present and past social arrangements are the inevitable manifestations of the specific action of genes. Second, the particular genes that lie at the basis of human society have been selected in evolution; therefore, the traits they determine result in higher reproductive fitness of the individuals that carry them (that is, they are more likely to survive to have offspring that will have genes for those traits: see Chapter 14): 'The academic and popular appeal of sociobiology flows directly from its simple reductionist programme and its claim that human society as we know it is both inevitable and the result of an adaptive process.' What isn't always realized is that, if one accepts biological determinism, nothing needs to be changed:

> . . . *for what falls in the realm of necessity falls outside the realm of justice. The issue of justice arises only when there is choice . . . To the extent that we are free to make ethical decisions that can be translated into practice, biology is irrelevant; to the extent that we are bound by our biology, ethical judgements are irrelevant . . .*

It is precisely because biological determinism removes guilt and responsibility that it has such wide appeal: it is 'our biology' that is to blame, not people, either individually or collectively. This is another instance of one of the recurrent themes of this chapter, namely moral responsibility and responsibility for criminal acts. Aren't sociobiologists obliged to deny them?

To avoid this dilemma, Wilson and Dawkins propose a free will that enables us to go against the dictates of our genes if we so wish. For example, Wilson (1978, in *On Human Nature*) allows that, despite the genetic instructions that demand male domination, we can create a less sexist society (at the cost of some loss of efficiency). He then goes on to speculate on the evolution of culture in *Genes, Mind and Culture* (Lumsden and Wilson, 1981). Similarly, Dawkins (1976, in *The Selfish Gene*) proposes independent evolving cultural units or *memes* (see Box 2.5, page 34).

Rose *et al.* object to these attempts to resolve the 'moral responsibility dilemma', on the grounds that they involve a false dichotomy between biological and cultural/social, just as 'nature–nurture' (see Chapter 5) and 'mind–brain' (see Chapter 12) are false dichotomies. ('Free will–determinism' is another.) What characterizes human development and actions is that they're the product of an immense array of interacting, intersecting causes. Our actions are not random or independent with respect to the totality of those causes as an interacting system, for we are material beings in a causal world:

> *But to the extent that they are free, our actions are independent of any one or even a small subset of those multiple paths of causation: that is the precise meaning of freedom in a causal world. When . . . our actions are predominantly constrained by a single cause, like . . . the prisoner in his cell . . . we are no longer free. For biological determinists we are unfree because our lives are strongly constrained by a relatively small number of internal causes, the genes for specific behaviours or for pre-disposition to those behaviours. But this misses the essence of the difference between human biology and that of other organisms . . . Our biology has made us into creatures who are constantly re-creating our own psychic and material environments, and whose individual lives are the outcomes of an extraordinary multiplicity of intersecting causal pathways. Thus, it is our biology that makes us free.*
>
> (Rose et al., 1984)

DRAWING SOME CONCLUSIONS: FREEDOM AS AN EVOLUTIONARY REALITY

The same starting point can lead to more than one conclusion. Belief in evolutionary forces and genetic influences may lead sociobiologists to largely deny free will, but it can also lead to the opposite conclusion. According to Dennett (2003):

> *Free will is an evolved creation of human activity and beliefs, and it is just as real as such other creations as music and money . . . Recognising our uniqueness as reflective, communicating animals does not require any 'human exceptionalism' that must shake a defiant fist at Darwin . . . We may thus concede that material forces ultimately govern behaviour, and yet at the same time reject the notion that people are always and everywhere motivated by material self-interest.*

Dennett believes that educated people are trapped in a strange kind of double think. On the one hand, they believe that natural science implies determinism, which proves they have no control over their lives. But on the other hand, in their actual daily lives, they mostly assume they *do* have this control. The conflict can create deep, underlying anxiety, confusion, guilt and a sense of futility. This is basically the same dilemma faced by William James, who resolved it (i) by adopting a pragmatic approach, and (ii) by arguing for soft determinism (see above).

Consistent with James's position, Dennett argues that determinism is not fatalism, which teaches that human effort makes no difference to what happens. *Fatalism* is another term for hard determinism, which reflects the view of the mind as a mere epiphenomenon. This is the view that Skinner adopts: mental processes exist, but they have no causal powers (see Chapter 14). Fatalism, however, is clearly false, based on an oversimplified, largely outdated, scientific view of the world. All the sciences, including physics, now find complexity and variety of patterns everywhere. This is related to *scientific pluralism*: the careful, systematic use of different thinking in different contexts to answer different questions. In particular, we are now finding steadily increasing complexity throughout the developing spectrum of organic life. The more complex creatures become, the wider the range of activities open to them. With this increase comes a steadily increasing degree of freedom. According to Dennett:

> *The freedom of the bird to fly wherever it wants is definitely a kind of freedom, a distinct improvement on the freedom of the jellyfish to float wherever it floats, but a poor cousin of our human freedom . . . Human freedom, in part a product of the revolution begat of language and culture, is about as different from bird freedom as language is different from birdsong. But to understand the richer phenomenon, one must first understand its more modest components and predecessors.*

This evolutionary view of human freedom is similar to the one proposed by Rose (1997, in *Lifelines*). Both make the central point that our conscious inner life is not some sort of irrelevant supernatural intrusion on the working of our physical bodies (a 'ghost in the machine'; see Chapter 13) but a crucial feature of their design. We have evolved as beings that can feel and think in a way that makes us able to direct our actions. We operate as whole people, our minds and bodies are aspects of us, not separate items. They do not need to compete for the driving seat (Midgley, 2003).

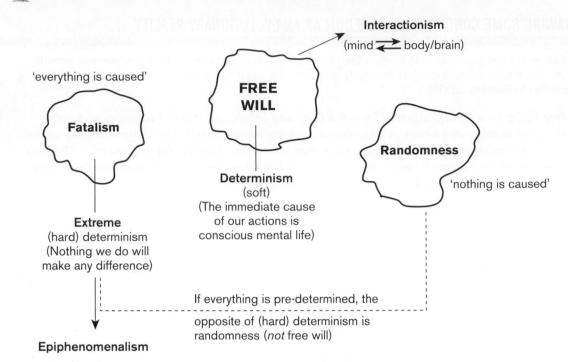

Figure 11.5 The relationship between free will and determinism, showing the link with theories of the mind–brain relationship

SUMMARY

○ Determinism is a central feature of classical science; according to strict determinism, human thought and behaviour are causally determined along with everything else in the world. The opposite of 'determined' is not 'free' but 'random', while the opposite of 'free' is 'coerced/constrained'.

○ It is part of common-sense psychology that people have free will, and to believe that people have free will, we must also believe that they have minds. But our thoughts could be caused.

○ Diagnosis/definition/treatment of psychological abnormality often involve judgements about free will; several kinds of mental disorder seem to involve a loss of control of the patient's behaviour/thinking/emotion.

○ The Homicide Act (1957) introduced the plea of diminished responsibility for murder charges. This implies that most people, most of the time, are responsible for their actions, which, in turn, implies free will.

○ Dualism helps to make sense of the common-sense distinction between conscious/purposeful/voluntary actions and mechanical/unintentional/involuntary actions. This distinction, in turn, is consistent with our everyday assumption that moral responsibility and free will are related.

○ Penfield's experiment in which the motor cortex of fully conscious patients undergoing brain surgery is stimulated, provides phenomenological evidence for the distinction between voluntary/involuntary behaviour.

○ Psychological reactance demonstrates peoples' belief in their free will, as does intrinsic motivation/self-determination.

○ According to Johnson-Laird, despite being unaware of the roots of many of our decisions, we are free because our models of ourselves enable us to choose how to choose (self-reflective automata).

○ In Norman and Shallice's model of processing capacity, deliberate control corresponds to free will. According to Koestler, as we move 'downwards' from conscious control to automatic, habitual behaviour, the subjective experience of freedom diminishes.

○ Despite the conviction that it is our decision to act voluntarily which causes the act to happen, evidence supports the claim that a series of brain processes is the real cause.

○ Libet found that the time at which participants consciously willed to flex their wrist occurred 300–500 milliseconds after the onset of the readiness potential (RP), that is, the beginning of brain activity. This is inconsistent with belief in free will.

○ One criticism of Libet's research is that flexing the wrist is so trivial as to be totally unrepresentative of voluntary action in general.

○ According to Libet's veto response, while consciousness cannot initiate voluntary actions, it can prevent it. People suffering from obsessive-compulsive disorder or Tourette's syndrome are unable to make the veto response.

○ Libet's findings are consistent with compatibilism, which regards the pre-/unconscious antecedents (brain processes or ideas) of conscious motivations as part of the self. We do not need to be conscious of the decision at the time it is made for it to be free.

○ James resolved the conflict between scientific belief in determinism and the common-sense belief in free will by adopting a pragmatic approach in distinguishing between the two realms. He also proposed soft determinism.

○ Freud, like Skinner, saw belief in free will as an illusion. He believed very strongly in psychic determinism. While there is no such thing as an accident in the universe of the mind, he accepted that human choices are real, and psychoanalysis is based on the belief that people can change (although to only a very limited degree).

○ Much of Freud's work was concerned with trying to understand/give meaning to neurotic symptoms and dreams (it was semantic), rather than identifying causes.

○ Skinner's radical behaviourism is probably the most extreme expression among psychologists of the view that people are not free. Most of the time it is not obvious what the environmental causes of our behaviour are, so we believe we are acting freely.

○ According to Rogers, people really do change through client-centred therapy, and choose to see their self and their life-situation differently. Defensiveness, lack of congruence and an unrealistic self-concept all represent a lack of freedom, which therapy is designed to restore.

○ For Fromm, the price we pay for our freedom from dogma and authority is isolation and a feeling of being alone, insecurity and meaninglessness. One way of overcoming these feelings is to create/become part of authoritarian organizations/totalitarian regimes (the 'escape' from freedom).

○ According to Kelly, people are free in that they have personal constructs by which to interpret/predict/control the world. These constructs, however, also restrict freedom, because we can only choose from the constructs we have, and they largely determine our behaviour.

○ By explaining all individual and social behaviour in terms of genes selected through evolution, sociobiologists seem to be denying guilt and responsibility. But Wilson and Dawkins, in order to allow for moral/legal responsibility, propose a free will that allows us to defy our genes if we so wish.

○ Rejecting the false dichotomy between biological and social/cultural, Rose et al. argue that what makes humans unique is that our biology enables us to constantly re-create our own psychic and material environments.

○ Dennett rejects fatalism (hard determinism) in favour of the view that free will is an evolved creation that is as real as other such creations. Scientific pluralism shows that freedom is relative, with more complex creatures having greater degrees of freedom.

USEFUL WEBSITES

http://plato.stanford.edu/entries/freewill
http://en.wikipedia.org/wiki/Benjamin_Libet
http://www.consciousentities.com/libet.htm

RECOMMENDED READING

Banks, W.P. and Pockett, S. (2007) Benjamin Libet's work on the neuroscience of free will. In M. Velmans and S. Schneider (eds) *The Blackwell Companion to Consciousness*. Oxford: Blackwell Publishing.

Blackmore, S. (2005) *Consciousness: A Very Short Introduction*. Oxford: Oxford University Press. (Chapter 6.)

Dennet, D.C. (2003) *Freedom Evolves*. London: Allen Lane.

Flanagan, O.J. (1984) *The Science of the Mind*. Cambridge, MA: MIT Press.

Midgley, M. (2004) Do we ever really act? In D. Rees and S. Rose (eds) *The New Brain Sciences: Perils and Prospects*. Cambridge: Cambridge University Press.

Rose, S. (1997) *Lifelines: Biology, Freedom and Determinism*. Harmondsworth: Penguin.

Rose, S., Lewonton, R.C. and Kamin, L.J. (1984) *Not in our Genes: Biology, Ideology and Human Nature*. Harmondsworth: Penguin.

CHAPTER 12

CONSCIOUSNESS AND THE MIND–BRAIN RELATIONSHIP

CONSCIOUSNESS AND THE SUBJECT MATTER OF PSYCHOLOGY

For the first 30 or so years of its life as a separate discipline, psychology took consciousness (conscious human experience) as its subject matter, and the process of introspection (observation of one's own mind) was the primary method used to investigate it (see Chapter 10).

Probably the first formal definition of the new discipline of psychology (certainly the most commonly quoted) is William James's 'the science of mental life' (1890), which also probably reflects quite accurately the lay person's idea of what psychology is all about. In his 'Behaviourist Manifesto', John Watson (1913) declared that:

> . . . the time has come when psychology must discard all reference to consciousness . . . Its sole task is the prediction and control of behaviour; and introspection can form no part of its method.

On the strength of this doctrine, behaviourists proceeded to purge psychology of all 'intangibles and unapproachables'. The terms 'consciousness', 'mind', 'imagination', and all other mentalistic concepts, were declared unscientific, treated as dirty words and banned from the scientific vocabulary. In Watson's own words, the behaviourist must exclude 'from his scientific vocabulary all subjective terms such as sensation, perception, image, desire, purpose, and even thinking and emotion as they were subjectively defined' (Watson, 1928).

According to Koestler (1967), this represented the first ideological purge of such a radical kind in the domain of science, predating the ideological purges in totalitarian politics, 'but inspired by the same single-mindedness of true fanatics'. This was summed up in a classic dictum by Cyril Burt (1962, in Koestler, 1967):

> Nearly half a century has passed since Watson proclaimed his manifesto. Today, apart from a few minor reservations, the vast majority of psychologists, both in this country and America, still follow his lead. The result, as a cynical onlooker might be tempted to say, is that psychology, having first bargained away its soul and then gone out of its mind, seems now, as it faces an untimely end, to have lost all consciousness.

Has it regained consciousness since the early 1960s when this was written? There is no doubt that 'mind' has once again become respectable, legitimate subject matter for psychologists, since the 'cognitive revolution' (usually dated from 1956), and that introspection has at the same time become an acceptable means of collecting data (at least in conjunction with other, more objective methods).

These developments have coincided with the decline of behaviourism as the dominant force within British and American academic psychology. However, the dominant view of the mind current among cognitive

BOX 12.1 INTROSPECTION, PROTOCOL ANALYSIS AND META-COGNITION

- Even during the time of behaviourism's dominance, *introspection* was not abandoned completely. In particular, it was used in the study of problem-solving. In order to gain access to the conscious processes used to solve a problem, participants were asked to 'think aloud', to provide a sort of 'running commentary' on their attempts to find a solution.

- Ironically, Watson himself was a pioneer in the use of this method, claiming that it was a form of verbal behaviour – not introspection. However, it is not clear what someone 'thinking aloud' is doing, if not introspecting.

- The method was used extensively by Duncker (1945), one of the Gestalt psychologists, and refined as *protocol analysis* by Ericsson and Simon (1984) (see Gross, 2005). Nevertheless, methodologies for utilizing introspection as a source of data have lagged behind those developed for behavioural tasks. Recently, there has been increasing interest in developing such methods.

- Thinking aloud is a form of *meta-cognition*: participants must reflect upon and report their thoughts. Meta-cognition has been used cleverly to provide behavioural measures that reflect consciousness and hence a first-person perspective. For example, when asked to make 'confidence judgements' in *psychophysics* experiments (the study of the relationship between the mental (sensations) and the physical (intensity of a stimulus), pioneered by Fechner in 1860), participants have to think about their perceptions. If the degree of confidence correlates with the accuracy of the judgements, then we can conclude that the participants were conscious of the stimuli rather than just guessing. This is another example of how a behavioural response is being driven by introspection.

(Based on Frith and Rees, 2007)

psychologists and other cognitive scientists, is radically different from the one held by the early psychologists, such as Wundt and James.

Given psychology's philosophical roots, it is not surprising that fundamental philosophical issues continue to be of relevance to modern psychology. Consciousness represents one of these issues, and one form this takes is the problem of mind and brain (or the mind–body problem).

The content of this chapter is drawn from philosophy, neuroscience, artificial intelligence, linguistics and biology, as well as psychology itself; these disciplines all contribute to what has become known (since the early 1990s) as 'consciousness studies' (Schneider and Velmans, 2007).

KNOWING WHERE TO START: DOES CONSCIOUSNESS EXIST?

Much of the attempt to account for the relationship between mind and brain is taken up by trying to describe, define and generally capture the nature of consciousness (and this often takes place separately from the mind–brain issue). But trying to keep them apart is no easy task. For example, Johnson-Laird (1987) states that:

Consciousness lies at the centre of the mind–body problem, because without it there would be no such problem – or, at least if there were, we would be unaware of it.

Similarly:

The mind–body problem is the problem of explaining how states of consciousness arise in human brains. More specifically . . . it is the problem of explaining how subjective feelings arise in the human brain.

(Humphrey, 1992)

Figure 12.1 René Magritte's painting '*A Reproduction Interdite*', 1937, seems to capture the whole idea of psychology being a study of consciousness

It is very difficult in practice, if not also in theory, to begin to describe and define consciousness without trying to relate it to the brain, the 'organ of consciousness'. All psychologists and cognitive scientists, as well as most philosophers, past and present, would accept that without a physical brain, there would be no consciousness (just as without a nervous system of some kind there would be very little in the way of behaviour). In other words, a brain is *necessary* for conscious experience (or a mind), so that 'no brain means no mind'. But we cannot make the logical jump from saying that minds *need* brains, to claiming that minds *are* brains (although the *mind–brain identity theory* makes exactly this claim; see below). Although 'mind' and 'consciousness' are not one and the same, many writers do equate them (e.g. Wise, 2000).

According to McGinn (1999):

> . . . *to any sensible person consciousness is the essence of mind: to have a mind precisely is to endure or enjoy conscious states – inner subjective awareness.*

Many would agree with McGinn. It seems 'obvious' that consciousness exists (after all, how could we even begin to discuss it if we didn't already possess it?). But is this a sufficient 'demonstration'? Can things really be so simple?

Wise (2000) believes that the strongest available argument that you (as well as chimpanzees and baboons) are conscious is 'by analogy':

1 I know I am conscious.
2 We are all biologically very similar.
3 We all act very similarly.
4 We all share an evolutionary history.
5 Therefore, you (and other great apes, and other species too) are conscious.

The basic argument is that 'if it walks like a duck and quacks like a duck . . .'. If something behaves in all respects as if it is conscious, and there is no good reason to believe otherwise, then it (almost certainly) *is* conscious. But doesn't this beg the question? Since we do not have direct access to other people's minds (one of Watson's arguments against the scientific study of consciousness), how can I be sure that this human-looking thing isn't a zombie or an android? (See Chapters 4 and 7, and Box 12.2.)

Dennett (1991) has different reasons for rejecting the possibility of humanoids. He denounces anyone who would distinguish non-conscious, humanlike *zombies* from real humans whose consciousness cannot be observed. This kind of argument, he claims:

> . . . *echoes the sort of utterly unmotivated prejudices that have denied full personhood to people on the basis of the colour of their skin. It is time to recognize the idea of the possibility of zombies for what it is: not a serious philosophical idea but a preposterous and ignoble relic of ancient prejudices. Maybe women aren't really conscious! Maybe Jews!*

235

BOX 12.2 DETECTING ANDROIDS

The depiction of androids or humanoids (a synthetic creature made from biological materials, as opposed to a robot's metal, etc.) is quite common in movies. Famous examples include Arnold Schwarzenegger in *Terminator* (1984) and Ian Holm in *Alien* (1979). Although androids do not currently exist, except in science fiction, scientists at several research laboratories around the world are trying to construct them (for example, the COG Project at MIT's Artificial Intelligence Laboratory).

If anyone succeeded in manufacturing an undetectable android, it would tell us something important about ourselves. It would prove that we are nothing but machines, whose behaviour can be completely explained in scientific terms (Diller, 1999/2000). Assuming that the engineering aspects can be overcome (for example, sufficiently powerful miniature motors can be made to move the android's limbs, electronic sensors can be devised which mimic how human senses work), Diller argues that 'it will always be possible to detect an android that has been designed and built by human beings. There will always be some behaviour that distinguishes a manufactured android from a real human being'.

In order for an android to be built, it first has to be designed, and the designer and design team have to make use of a large number of scientific theories. The android's behaviour is produced by means of these theories, and it will behave in accordance with them. The psychological theories involved not only describe the behaviour, they also *produce* it. But in the case of human beings, psychological theories are only attempts to describe and predict their behaviour: it is impossible for us to know *for sure* how that behaviour is produced. It is this difference between humans and androids which means there will always be behaviours that allow us to differentiate between 'us' and 'them' (Diller, 1999/2000).

Conscious robots: the case for consciousness

Dennett (1991) also believes that *homo sapiens* is a race of conscious robots, machines with information-processing brains that produce higher-order representations of our lower-order processes. These allow us to describe ourselves as having thoughts, feelings, sensations and so on, and this is what being conscious means. Any person, animal or machine with the appropriate machinery would be conscious in the way we are, and for the same reasons. Therefore, consciousness isn't something 'extra', added to the processes that produce behaviour; it just 'comes with the territory'.

If we are robots, it is in a rather special sense. We not only respond knowingly to signals, but we initiate actions in their absence. We can also fail to respond to signals, not because (like mechanical robots) we have broken down, but simply because our attention is elsewhere. As Caldwell (1997) says:

> We are not so much programmed as inventors of our programs as we go. We all of us have our own agendas. We as much create our environments as respond to them. In doing so we also – and continuously – create ourselves.

But we are also to a large degree *unconscious*: much of what we do and most of what goes on inside our heads is inaccessible to consciousness, and our behaviour is often automatic. But we are conscious when we need to be (Caldwell, 1997). (See Box 12.5, page 246.)

Searle (1997) argues that we can never be mistaken (or deluded) about consciousness:

> Where the existence of conscious states is concerned, you can't make the distinction between appearance and reality, because the existence of the appearance is the reality in question. If it consciously seems to me that I am conscious then I am conscious . . .

Wise (2000) extends this argument to consciousness in non-human animals:

> *Most mammals and every primate act in ways that cause most reasonable people to think that they have minds of some kinds . . . It is circular thinking to dismiss this belief as mere anthropomorphism . . . as some do. They begin by assuming that only humans are conscious, then label any contrary claim as anthropomorphic. Why? Because only humans are conscious.*

Although behavioural similarity is no guarantee of mental similarity:

> *. . . when animals who are closely related behave in a way that strongly suggests similarity in mental processes to ours, it seems reasonable and fair to shift the burden of proof to those who would argue that what we are seeing is not what we think we are seeing.*

Wise uses these arguments to support the case for equality under the law for non-humans (see Chapter 9).

A different approach to demonstrating the existence of consciousness is taken by the novelist David Lodge (2002). He quotes Stuart Sutherland, who states (in the *International Dictionary of Psychology*, 1989) that 'Consciousness is a fascinating but elusive phenomenon; it is impossible to specify what it is, what it does, or why it evolved. Nothing worth reading has been written about it'. In making this claim, Sutherland was, inadvertently, dismissing the entire body of the world's literature, because literature is the richest and most comprehensive record of human consciousness we have. Some of those who work in cognitive science agree with Lodge – for example, Chomsky, who claims that 'it is quite possible . . . that we will always learn more about human life and personality from novels than from scientific psychology'.

Lodge contrasts science's pursuit of universal explanatory laws with literature's description:

> *. . . in the guise of fiction the dense specificity of personal experience, which is always unique, because each of us has a slightly or very different personal history, modifying every new experience we have; and the creation of literary texts recapitulates this uniqueness . . .*

> *(Lodge, 2002)*

Here, Lodge is describing the nomothetic/idiographic debate (see Chapter 3).

Why is consciousness a problem?

As soon as we accept that the physical brain is involved in some way in our subjective experience, the philosophical and scientific difficulties start to arise. Why? According to Dennett (1987):

> *Consciousness is both the most obvious and the most mysterious feature of our minds . . . What in the world can consciousness be? How can physical bodies in the physical world contain such a phenomenon?*

One of the fundamental principles of 'classical' science is *objectivity*: the observation and measurement of the world as it is, without reference to the human observer (see Chapter 10). As applied to the study of human behaviour and social institutions, this ideal is referred to as *positivism*. Watson clearly did not believe that the study of consciousness was compatible with such an approach. But most people – scientists and non-scientists alike – would argue that consciousness is an undeniable, indisputable 'fact' about human beings, and if it won't 'go away', it has to be explained. But how?

As Dennett (1987) points out, science has revealed the secrets of many initially mysterious natural phenomena, such as magnetism, photosynthesis, digestion and reproduction, but consciousness seems utterly unlike these. Particular cases of magnetism and other phenomena are, in principle, equally accessible to any observer with the right apparatus, but any particular case of consciousness seems always to involve a

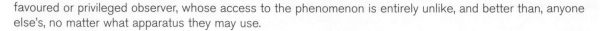

favoured or privileged observer, whose access to the phenomenon is entirely unlike, and better than, anyone else's, no matter what apparatus they may use.

By its very nature, consciousness is *private*, while physical objects (and behaviour) are *public*. While we seem to share a view of the physical world with others (whether as a non-scientist with other non-scientists or as a scientist with fellow scientists), we cannot use that common view for reaching an equivalent view about what goes on inside our heads: the two 'worlds' are simply too different to enable any comparisons to be drawn between them (Gregory, 1981). This relates to what has been called the 'hard problem' of consciousness.

The hard problem of consciousness: experience

According to Chalmers (2007), there isn't just one problem of consciousness. 'Consciousness' is an ambiguous term, referring to many different phenomena, some of which are easier to explain than others. The 'easy' problems of consciousness are those that seem directly accessible to the standard methods of cognitive science, and include:

1 the ability to discriminate, categorize, and react to environmental stimuli
2 the integration of information by a cognitive system
3 the reportability of mental states
4 the ability of a system to access its own internal states
5 the focus of attention
6 the deliberate control of behaviour
7 the difference between wakefulness and sleep.

All of these phenomena are associated with the notion of consciousness, and there is no real argument about whether they can be explained scientifically (in terms of computational or neural mechanisms). This is what makes them 'easy'; this is a relative term which *does not* imply that we have a complete explanation of these phenomena, only that we know how to go about finding one. By contrast:

> *The hard problem of consciousness is the problem of experience. When we think and perceive, there is a whir of information-processing, but there is also a subjective aspect. As Nagel (1974) has put it, there is something it's like to be a conscious organism. This subjective aspect is experience. When we see, for example, we experience visual sensations: the felt quality of redness, the experience of dark and light, the quality of depth in a visual field. Other experiences go along with perception on different modalities: the sound of a clarinet, the smell of mothballs. Then there are bodily sensations, from pains to orgasms; mental images that are conjured up internally; the felt quality of emotion, and the experience of a stream of conscious thought. What unites all these states is that there is something it's like to be in them. . .*
>
> *(Chalmers, 2007)*

Chalmers believes that if any problem qualifies as *the* problem of consciousness, it is this. These experiential states are known as *qualia*.

What do we do about qualia?

According to Edelman (1992), 'The dilemma is that phenomenal experience is a first-person matter, and this seems at first glance, to prevent the formulation of a completely objective or causal account.'

Science is a third-person account. So, how can we produce a scientific account of consciousness that (must) include qualia, the collection of personal, subjective experiences, feelings and sensations that accompany awareness? Qualia are phenomenal states, 'how things seem to us as human beings'. Edelman believes that consciousness manifests itself in the form of qualia.

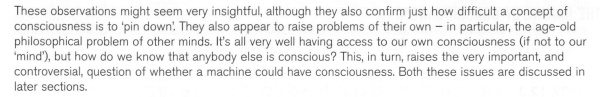

These observations might seem very insightful, although they also confirm just how difficult a concept of consciousness is to 'pin down'. They also appear to raise problems of their own – in particular, the age-old philosophical problem of other minds. It's all very well having access to our own consciousness (if not to our 'mind'), but how do we know that anybody else is conscious? This, in turn, raises the very important, and controversial, question of whether a machine could have consciousness. Both these issues are discussed in later sections.

Edelman's proposed solution to the 'first-person/third-person dilemma' is to accept that other people and oneself do experience qualia, to collect first-person accounts, and to correlate them in order to establish what they all have in common – bearing in mind that these reports are inevitably 'partial, imprecise and relative to . . . personal context'.

A well-known attempt to protect first-person experience (qualia) from reduction to third-person talk (as in neuroscience) is Nagel's (1974) article 'What is it like to be a bat?' (see the quote form Chalmers above). The essence of Nagel's argument is that no amount of descriptive knowledge could possibly add up to the experience of how it feels to be a bat, or what it is like to perceive by sonar. Conscious experience is 'what it's like' to be an organism to the organism. Attempts to reduce that subjective experience must be considered unsuccessful as long as the reducing theory (for example, pain is the firing of neurons in some brain centre) is logically possible without consciousness (the zombie problem). A theory of consciousness should be able to distinguish us from zombies (Bem and Looren de Jong, 1997).

Although we may never know animals' or other people's minds, or have an adequate language to describe subjective experience, this does not mean it isn't real, complex, rich or highly specific in nature. Nagel argues that any solution to the mind–body problem depends on an attempt to gauge or span the subjective–objective gap.

For Humphrey (1992), the problem, specifically, is to explain how and why and to what end the dependence of the non-physical mind on the physical brain has come about (Humphrey, 1992):

> *Somehow, we feel, the water of the physical brain is turned into the wine of consciousness, but we draw a total blank on the nature of this conversion. Neural transmissions just seem like the wrong kind of materials with which to bring consciousness into the world . . . The mind–body problem is the problem of understanding how the miracle is wrought.*
>
> *(McGinn, 1989, in Humphrey, 1992)*

As Chalmers (1996) puts it, how can conscious experience emerge from the grey matter of the brain?

McGinn (1991) concludes that the problem is probably insoluble – either because there actually is no solution, or because human intelligence must always be too limited to grasp it. But Blackmore (2001) argues that, 'there must be something radically wrong with the way we are currently thinking about consciousness or we would not find ourselves with this seemingly intractable problem'. Underlying the views of Humphrey and McGinn, and indeed the whole mind–brain debate, is the fundamental distinction between the physical and the non-physical. It was the French philosopher Descartes who introduced mind–body dualism into western thought in the 1600s, where it has remained ever since. Dualism and other theories of the mind–brain relationship are discussed below.

239

THE NATURE OF CONSCIOUSNESS

Searle (2007) identifies four of the most important features of conscious states.

BOX 12.3 MAJOR CRITERIA FOR DEFINING CONSCIOUS STATES (SEARLE, 2007)

1 Conscious states are *qualitative*, in the sense that there is a qualitative feel to being in any particular conscious state. Some use the term 'qualia' to refer to these qualitative states, but all qualia are conscious states, and all conscious states are qualia.

2 Such states are also *ontologically subjective* in the sense that they only exist as experienced by a human being or non-human animal. While physical objects, as well as natural features such as mountains have an objective (or third-party ontology/existence), conscious states (such as pains and itches) exist only when experienced by a person or animal (they have a subjective or first-person ontology)

3 At any moment in your conscious life, all your conscious states are experienced as part of a *single, unified conscious field*.

4 Most, but not all, conscious states are intentional, in the philosophical sense that they are *about*, or refer to, something (objects or states of affairs). For example, my states of thirst, hunger and visual perception are all directed at something; undirected, generalized feelings of well-being or anxiety *are not* intentional.

5 Conscious states are *real* parts of the real world and cannot be reduced to something else (they are *irreducible*). According to Searle:

> If it consciously seems to me that I am conscious, then I am conscious. We can make lots of mistakes about our own consciousness, but where the very existence of consciousness is in question we cannot make the appearance–reality distinction, because the appearance of the existence of consciousness is the reality of its existence.

6 We cannot reduce consciousness to more fundamental neurobiological processes. Consciousness has a subjective, first-person ontology, while brain processes have an objective, third-person ontology; you cannot show that the former is nothing but the latter. What is not in dispute, however, is that conscious states are caused by brain processes; exactly how this happens is still unknown.

7 Conscious states have *causal efficacy*. (This is discussed further in the text below.)

'Consciousness', and similar terms, are used in a variety of ways. Already in this chapter, 'consciousness', 'conscious human experience', 'subjective experience', 'mental life' and 'mind' have all been used interchangeably. 'Awareness', 'self-awareness' and 'self-consciousness' can be added to that list. But there are some crucial differences between them.

'Mind' and 'consciousness'

Clearly, 'mind' is a much broader concept than 'consciousness', since there is always much more 'going on' than we can detect through introspection at any one time. According to Humphrey (1992), consciousness refers to what is *felt* and what is *present* to the mind, making it quite limited in scope. Rather than embracing the whole range of higher mental functions (perceptions, images, thoughts, beliefs and so on), consciousness is uniquely the 'having of sensations' ('what is happening to me' – *qualia*), all other mental activities remaining outside consciousness.

This view of consciousness can be analysed in terms of three features:

1 consciousness (or conscious awareness) as one level in Freud's psychoanalytic theory of personality
2 consciousness as a form of attention
3 the *cognitive unconscious*.

Consciousness and psychoanalytic theory

Freud believed that thoughts, ideas, memories and other psychic material could operate at one of three levels: *conscious*, *pre-conscious* and *unconscious* (see Chapter 14). These are essentially levels of *accessibility*.

What we are consciously aware of at any one time (what we can report) represents the mere tip of an iceberg. Most of our feelings and memories are either not accessible at that moment (pre-conscious), or are totally inaccessible (unconscious), at least without the use of special techniques, such as free association and dream interpretation. The ego (the 'executive', decision-making, rational part of the psyche, governed by the *reality principle*) represents the *conscious* part of the mind, together with some aspects of the superego (the moral part of the psyche and the source of guilt), namely those moral rules and values we are able to express in words.

The ego also controls the *pre-conscious*, a kind of 'ante-room', an extension of the conscious, whereby things we are not fully aware of right now can become conscious fairly easily if our attention is directed towards them. For example, you suddenly realize that you have had a pain for some time.

The *unconscious* (for Freud the most important type of mental material) comprises (i) impulses arising from the id, the biological, inherited part of the psyche (governed by the *pleasure principle*), (ii) all repressed material, (iii) the unconscious part of the ego (the part involved in dream work, neurotic symptoms and defence mechanisms), and (iv) part of the superego, such as free-floating or vague feelings of guilt or shame that are difficult to explain in a rational way.

Freud depicted the unconscious as a *dynamic* force and not a mere 'dustbin' for all those feelings and memories that are unimportant or too weak to force themselves into awareness. This is best illustrated by the process of repression, whereby what is threatening is actively forced out of consciousness by the ego (Thomas, 1985).

Most psychologists would agree that feelings and memories differ in their degree of accessibility: they can be placed on a continuum of consciousness, with 'fully conscious' at one end and 'completely unconscious' at the other. However, most would not accept Freud's formulation of the unconscious as based on repression. Indeed, other *psychodynamic* theorists, in particular Carl Jung, disagreed fundamentally with Freud's view. Although he accepted the existence of repression, Jung distinguished between the *personal* and the *collective* unconscious, the former being based on the individual's personal experiences, the latter being inherited and common to all members of particular cultural or racial groups (if not all human beings).

Figure 12.2 Dorethea Tanning *'Eine kleine Nacht Musik'*, 1944. The impossible nature of the imagery depicted in the painting is what gives dreams and other unconscious phenomena their distinctive flavour

Consciousness as a form of attention

One way in which experimental psychologists have studied consciousness is through the concept of *attention*. Although consciousness is difficult to describe because it is fundamental to everything we do (Rubin and McNeil, 1983), one way of trying to 'pin it down' is to study what we are paying attention to — that is, what is in the forefront of our consciousness. According to Allport (1980), 'attention is the experimental psychologist's code name for consciousness'.

Focal attention (or focal awareness) is what we are currently paying deliberate attention to, and what is in the centre of our awareness (corresponding to Freud's 'conscious'). All those other aspects of our environment, and our own thoughts and feelings on the fringes of our awareness (which could easily become the object of our focal attention), are within our *peripheral attention* (corresponding to Freud's 'pre-conscious').

This distinction between focal and peripheral attention may be seen as overlapping with the model of processing capacity (Norman and Shallice, 1986), which is intended to explain divided attention, and which is discussed in relation to free will in Chapter 11.

The cognitive unconscious

The concept of focal attention helps us to appreciate how much of our behaviour and mental processes proceed quite automatically, without having to think consciously about what we're doing or deliberately plan each part of our performance.

When we look for examples of 'automatic processing' (Norman and Shallice, 1986), we usually think of the performance of well-practised psycho-motor skills, such as driving, typing and even walking up or down stairs. But just as valid are cases of cognitive processes, such as perception, which usually involves an immediate (and mostly accurate) awareness of something (an object, person or other 'stimulus') in our external environment. In fact, it is difficult to imagine what it would be like if we were aware of exactly how we perceive. Our focal attention or awareness is directed at the identified object (the 'finished product'), not the process of perception itself. Could it be any other way? Trying to discover how we perceive through introspection is unlikely to throw much light on the matter, which suggests that all the underlying processing necessarily takes place outside our conscious awareness. This ensures that we concentrate on what really matters, namely what is going on around us (rather than all the internal processes).

We can take this a step further, and ask whether it is actually necessary to be consciously (focally) aware of an object in order to 'perceive' it? (See Box 12.4.)

A more specific visual deficit, *prosopagnosia*, involves the inability to recognize the human face as such. Although patients with this deficit have no awareness of faces, some, while denying that they can see their spouse's face, will perform on tests in a way that indicates strong discriminative knowledge of that face (Edelman, 1992; Weiskrantz, 2007). In both this and blindsight, a loss of *explicit conscious recognition* is combined with the capacity for *implicit behavioural recognition*.

Johnson-Laird (1988) makes a similar point when discussing decision making (see Chapter 11). At whatever point in the hierarchy (of embedded decisions about decisions, and so on) we make a decision, this will always be made implicitly (and not consciously), since if it were chosen consciously, there would have to be a still higher level at which that decision was made (and so on, *ad infinitum*). In other words, there is always more going on cognitively ('in the mind') than is available to consciousness (or, to adapt a popular phrase, 'there's more involved than meets the inner eye'; see below).

According to Ross and Nisbett (1991), countless experiments point towards the conclusion that the high-level mental activity taken to be involved in attitude change and emotion (see Gross, 2005) in fact goes on outside awareness. Many now believe that most of the processing undertaken by the brain occurs without our awareness (Velmans, 1991). In a much-cited article, Nisbett and Wilson (1977) argued that there is no direct access to cognitive processes at all; instead, there is access only to the ideas and inferences that are the outputs resulting from such processes.

BOX 12.4 BLINDSIGHT: CAN WE SEE WITHOUT REALLY 'SEEING'?

According to Humphrey (1986, 1992), there is increasing evidence that the higher animals, including humans, can in fact show the behaviour of perceiving without being consciously aware of what they are doing. During the 1960s, Humphrey worked with a monkey, called Helen, who had had her visual cortex removed (as part of a study of brain damage in humans; see Chapter 10); however, her lower visual centres were intact. Over a six-month period following the operation, she began to use her eyes again, and over the next seven years, she improved greatly. She was eventually able to move deftly through a room full of obstacles, picking up tiny scraps of chocolate or currants, reaching out to catch a passing fly. Her three-dimensional spatial vision and ability to discriminate between objects (in terms of size and brightness) became almost perfect. However, she did not recover the ability to recognize shapes and colours, and was 'oddly incompetent' in other ways too.

At that time, there were no comparable human cases, but what relevant evidence there was suggested that people would not recover vision. Then, in 1974, Weiskrantz et al. reported the case of D.B., a young man who had recently undergone surgery to remove a tumour at the back of his brain. The entire primary visual cortex on the right side had been removed, resulting in blindness in the left side of the visual field. So, for example, when he looked straight ahead, he could not see (with either eye) anything to the left of his nose. Or could he?

Weiskrantz decided not to accept D.B.'s self-professed blindness at face value. While there was no question that he was genuinely unaware of seeing anything in the blind half of his field, was it possible that his brain was nonetheless still receiving and processing the visual information? What would happen if he could be persuaded to discount his own conscious opinion?

Weiskrantz asked him to forget for a moment that he was blind, and to 'guess' at what he might be seeing if he could see. To D.B.'s own amazement, it turned out that he could do it: he could locate an object accurately in his blind field, and he could even guess certain aspects of its shape. Yet he continued to deny any conscious awareness. Weiskrantz called this phenomenon *blindsight*: 'visual capacity in a field defect in the absence of acknowledged awareness' (Weiskrantz, 1986). Other cases have since been described, and unconscious vision appears to be a clinical reality (Humphrey, 1986).

According to Weiskrantz (2007), the visual parameters that people with blindsight can discriminate include colour, orientation of lines or gratings, simple shapes, motion, onset and offset of visual events. Attention can also be controlled by unseen cues in the blind field controlling the responses to the location of unseen targets. Research has also found that the emotional expression of unseen faces in the blind field can be guessed at better than chance levels. As Weiskrantz says, 'Blindsight has made us aware that there is more to vision than seeing, and more to seeing than vision.'

People have theories about what affects their judgements and behaviour just as they have theories about all kinds of social processes. These theories, rather than any introspective access to mental processes, seem to be the origin of people's reports about the influences on their judgement and behaviour . . .

(Ross and Nisbett, 1991)

Nisbett and Wilson (1977) claim that our common-sense, intuitive belief that we can accurately account for our own behaviour (see Chapter 1) is *illusory*, because what really guides our behaviour is unavailable to consciousness. If true, this conclusion would seem to have serious implications for our belief in *free will*. (Freud's distinction between *our* reasons and *the* reasons has similar implications; see Chapter 11.)

All these various examples of unconscious processing illustrate what Kihlstrom (1987) has called the *cognitive unconscious*. According to Frith and Rees (2007), perhaps the major development in consciousness research during the past 50 years has been the demonstration of unconscious, automatic, psychological processes in perception, memory and action. But the negative side of this development is that:

Just because subjects can detect or discriminate a stimulus, does not mean that they are conscious of it. Their success may be the result of unconscious processes. From their first-person perspective they are just guessing.

(Frith and Rees, 2007)

What can consciousness do?

Blackmore (2001) suggests that consciousness may not have any function, but simply comes with being the kind of organism we are. This, along with Nisbett and Wilson's argument regarding lack of privileged access, appears to threaten our intuitive feeling that our consciousness has some kind of (causal) power – that it *does* things. But does it?

Libet's research (1985; Libet *et al.*, 1983) was discussed in Chapter 11 in relation to free will (see pages 215–19). As we saw, he showed that consciousness lags behind the events of the world; this suggests very strongly that consciousness lacks causal efficacy (that is, it cannot make things happen: causes usually precede their effects). We also discussed criticisms of Libet's research. While Libet's findings may appear to contradict our everyday, common-sense understanding of the role of consciousness, Blackmore asks why we should be surprised: 'If you expected consciousness to have started the process then you are really a believer in magic – in some kind of force that acts on brain stuff.'

However, Midgley (2004) contends that:

> . . . conscious thought has a legitimate and essential place among the causal factors that work in the world. It's not a spooky extra but a natural process. In a species like ours, it is an integral part of normal behaviour . . . Our inner experience is as real as stones or electrons and as ordinary an activity for a social mammal as digestion or the circulation of the blood. The capacity to have this conscious experience, and to use it effectively in making choices, is one that has evolved in us . . . just as normally as our capacities to see, hear and walk.

Disagreeing with Blackmore, Midgley argues that, while needing a brain for conscious thought, the individual *as a whole person* uses his/her brain, just as we use our legs to walk and our eyes and hand in writing. In other words, the 'force that acts on brain stuff' is not some form of magic but is simply the person with a (normal) brain performing actions (i.e. behaving).

We shall say more about the causal efficacy of consciousness on pages 248–50.

'Consciousness' vs 'self-consciousness'

Edelman (1992) distinguishes between *primary* and *higher-order consciousness*, which refer to consciousness and self-consciousness respectively.

- *Primary consciousness* refers to the state of being mentally aware of things in the world, of having mental images in the present. It is not accompanied by any sense of being a person with a past and a future. In other words, to be conscious does not necessarily imply any kind of 'I' who is aware and having mental images. This is why at least some non-human animal species are likely to be conscious, even though they do not possess language. Edelman believes that chimpanzees are almost certainly conscious, and, in all likelihood, so are most mammals and some birds; probably those animals without a cortex (or its equivalent) are not.
- Wise (2000) agrees with Edelman, and with Greenfield (1995), who propose that rather than the 'turning on the light' analogy for consciousness, a better one might be the 'dimmer switch'. This captures the idea that consciousness probably ranges across a vast continuum, and allows for non-humans' possession of primary consciousness. According to Wise, the majority opinion boils down to:

Some consciousness tends to allow one to experience the present, another to realize that one is experiencing the present and to anticipate, to some degree, the future and to think about the past. The International Dictionary of Psychology *(1989) warns against . . . confusing consciousness with self-consciousness – 'to be conscious it is only necessary to be aware of the external world . . .'*

● *Higher-order consciousness* involves recognition, by a thinking subject, of his/her acts or affections. It embodies a model of the personal, and of the past and future, as well as the present. It shows direct awareness of mental episodes without the involvement of the sense organs or receptors. It is what humans have in addition to primary consciousness: we are conscious of being conscious. In order to acquire this capacity, systems of memory must be related to a conceptual representation of a true self (or social self) acting on an environment and vice versa.

This is rather similar to Johnson-Laird's (1988) description of *self-reflective automata*, which are capable of intentional behaviour, which, in turn, depends on the 'recursive embedding' of models within models. To be self-aware is to have at least a partial model of how our operating system works; we represent to ourselves

how we do things (for example, make decisions), rather than 'just doing them'. As well as providing us with self-reflectiveness (or self-consciousness), having 'models of models' gives us the freedom to make choices (see Chapter 11).

Equating consciousness with 'self-consciousness'

Not all descriptions/definitions distinguish between 'consciousness' and 'self-consciousness'. For example, Humphrey (1986) defines 'consciousness' as:

. . . the inner picture we each have of what it is like to be ourselves – self-awareness: the presence in each of us of a spirit (self, soul . . .) which we call 'I'. It's 'I' who have thoughts and feelings, sensations, memories, desires. It's 'I' who am conscious of my own existence and my continuity in time. 'I' who am, in short, the very essence of a human being.

This seems to describe Edelman's *higher-order consciousness.*

Figure 12.3 'Hey, that's *me* in that hat!'
Recognizing oneself in a mirror is an early indication of self-awareness or self-consciousness. It usually appears at about 18 months

Elsewhere, Humphrey (1992) defines consciousness in a way that seems to combine primary and higher-order consciousness: 'To be conscious is essentially to have sensations: that is, to have affect-laden mental representations of something happening here and now to me.'

CAN A MACHINE BE CONSCIOUS? DOES HAVING A BRAIN MATTER?

Many machines 'behave' in ways that, if they were human, would suggest they had mental states. For example, aeroplanes on autopilot can fly themselves; they respond to external 'sensory' information, make 'decisions' about whether to fly, 'communicate' with other aircraft, and even 'know' when they're 'hungry' for fuel, can 'sense' danger, and so on.

But the very fact that the various words in the previous sentence are in speech marks conveys that they are not to be taken literally: only in a *metaphorical* sense do planes make decisions, and that is because they lack consciousness. It is human beings (and possibly some other animal species) who make decisions, communicate and so on, not metal machines. Being sentient (living, breathing, made of flesh and blood)

BOX 12.5 WHERE IS MY MIND'S 'I'?

To be conscious is also to have a point of view on the world. The 'conscious robot' is conscious of his/her own consciousness (Caldwell, 1997). But Dennett (1991) rejects this idea of a *privileged observer* (see text above). There is no mind's 'I' that stands behind all my experience as the condition of its possibility. In the brain's superabundant, often pointless, circuitry, it is impossible to locate a centre, a controller in charge of the whole operation. There is less a 'ghost in the machine' (Ryle, 1949) than a vast, haunted house populated by innumerable ghosts. I don't *have* thoughts – I *am* thoughts. The 'I' is, first and foremost, a *grammatical construction*. In biological terms, our sense of self is no more than a useful fiction (Flanagan, 1992). It would be difficult to live our lives without a sense of self, but it lacks any biological basis, and is merely a superimposition on our biology derived from our social interactions: a solitary human being perhaps would have no self.

Although most psychologists and neuroscientists reject dualism as a philosophical theory (see text below), they still believe in some kind of centre, where everything comes together and 'consciousness happens', some kind of magic finishing line beyond which events 'come into' consciousness, a centre from where 'my' decisions are made and 'my' instructions sent out. But the brain is a massively parallel system with no middle (Blackmore, 2001).

If Dennett, Flanagan and Blackmore are right, who is conscious and what happens to free will and the related legal and moral responsibility? Is free will an illusion after all? But to say that the self does not have a biological basis does not mean that it is not real in other senses (biology isn't the only reality; see Chapters 10 and 14). For Caldwell (1997), to ask questions about responsibility and other ethical questions is:

> . . . *to cease to think of ourselves merely as biological organisms, which is the level at which Dennett primarily moves, but rather as creatures who move in the artificial world which they have constructed for themselves. In this sense . . . the mind is not a natural but an artificial construct, and to look for it in terms of biology or brain science is to look where one is least likely to find it . . .*

seems to be a precondition for primary consciousness, just as primary consciousness is a precondition for higher-order consciousness.

However, isn't there the danger here of confusing (i) the kinds of things in the world that, currently, as far as we know, and according to the criteria we use to judge consciousness, are conscious (human beings and some other species), and (ii) the kinds of things that might, in the future, be considered conscious (due to advances in our ability to construct certain types of machine)? In other words, should we reject the very idea of a conscious machine?

Supporters of what Searle (e.g. 1980) calls *strong artificial intelligence* (AI), believe that 'the future' is already here. Cognitive scientists, such as Turing, Johnson-Laird, Newell, Simon, Minsky and Boden, believe that people and computers turn out to be merely different manifestations of the same underlying phenomenon, namely automatic formal systems. The essence of such systems is the manipulation of symbols according to rules (the *computational theory of mind*/CTM). CTM is the theory underlying strong AI, according to which the computer is not merely a tool for formulating and testing hypotheses concerning the human mind, but, if appropriately programmed, *is* a mind: it literally understands and has other cognitive states – that is, *it is conscious*.

Some of Searle's objections to strong AI and CTM are discussed later, in relation to the mind–brain issue. But one of his arguments is particularly relevant here. Mental states and processes are real biological phenomena in the world, as real as digestion, photosynthesis, lactation and so on; they are caused by processes going on in the brain that are entirely internal to the brain. The intrinsically *mental* features of the universe are just higher-level physical features of the brain. Crucially, in principle only a machine (computer, robot) made of flesh and blood or neuroprotein (a convenient shorthand for the many biochemical substances active in the central nervous system) could be conscious (a view that has been dubbed *carbon/protoplasm chauvinism* by Torrance, 1986).

To Searle, it is obvious that metal or silicon cannot support intelligence or consciousness. But to Boden (1993), and other advocates of strong AI, as well as for most cognitive psychologists, what matters are the *computational functions* performed by 'neuroprotein' (such as message-passing, facilitation and inhibition). If the neurophysiologist can tell us which cells and chemical processes are involved, so much the better, but any other chemistry would do, so long as it enabled these functions to be performed.

From an intuitive point of view, it is far from obvious how the neuroprotein ('that grey mushy stuff inside our skulls') could possibly support intelligence, so just because it is not obvious how metal and silicon could, does not mean that they could not do so. Also, what is intuitively obvious may (and does) change as scientific knowledge advances (Boden, 1993; see Chapters 10 and 14).

A different kind of objection to strong AI, but which is relevant here, involves another distinction between different types of consciousness. '*A (access)-consciousness*' (Block, 1995) refers to the fact that our minds seem to provide a representation of things, such as the world, the past, our plans, in such a way as to allow us to reason, act and communicate. '*P (phenomenal)-consciousness*' describes the distinctive subjective awareness that seems to be a characteristic of those inner representations, but which is not reducible to them. It is what it's like to have the experience of any state (another description of qualia?).

McGhee (2001) believes that, while many systems (including computers) are capable of inner representations that underlie intentional action (A-consciousness), it is more difficult to argue that they have (or ever could have) the subjective awareness that they have these representations (P-consciousness). While it is possible to see how the former could emerge from physical systems (neuroprotein or silicon), this is much more difficult in the case of the latter (McGhee, 2001).

However, a major difference between how the brain processes information (*parallel processing*) and how most computers have been designed to do it (*serial processing*) is also of key relevance to the whole AI debate. Those who oppose the view that computers could be built to have the kind of consciousness that people naturally have stress this crucial difference.

Supporters of AI argue that, at least in principle, computers could be programmed to use parallel processing. In fact, some cognitive scientists would claim that the objection has already been met in practice, in the form of connectionism. This approach models itself on the interconnection of the neurons in the brain ('neural networks') and stresses the role of 'parallel distributed processing' (PDP) (Rumelhart *et al.*, 1986). But Boden (1993) continues to maintain that it is the fact of the processes being carried out by the machine that's crucial for defining intelligence – not what the machine is made of or how the processes are carried out.

However, Eiser (1994) believes that this emphasis on the processes being carried out is mistaken:

> *The error lies in trying to settle the matter by identifying the classes of information-processing operations of which human beings and computers are each capable, whilst ignoring the classes of information with which human and artificial systems actually have to deal . . .*

In other words, it is in the *content* of experience (rather than in an exclusive analysis of process) that an understanding of human consciousness is to be found. This is related to *intentionality*: mental states (beliefs, desires, perceptions, wishes, fears, ideas, as well as intentions) have an *external reference* to something outside themselves, and this is (part of) what we mean by saying that the world is meaningful to us and that we understand it. According to Searle (1980), intentionality is a fundamental feature of consciousness. The

247

symbols that computers manipulate are meaningless for the computer (the meaning has to be provided by a human programmer), which leads to the (inevitable) conclusion that computers (and other machines) do not – and cannot – possess consciousness:

> *If both the machine's processing operations and the information it processed were indistinguishable from those of a human being, so also would be its mind and consciousness. It is the second of these two conditions, rather than the first, which strikes me as the major stumbling block . . .*

In other words, only information that has meaning for the machine carrying out the processing of that information can be considered part of the consciousness of that machine, which is why only human 'machines' can be described as possessing consciousness: 'Computer consciousness – in the sense of self-awareness – is merely science fiction' (Eiser, 1994).

CONSCIOUSNESS AND THE IMPORTANCE OF HAVING A BODY

According to Humphrey (1992), the subject of consciousness, 'I', is an embodied self. In the absence of bodily sensations, 'I' would cease: *Sentio, ergo sum* ('I feel, therefore I am' – this is a variant of Descartes's famous *Cogito, ergo sum*, 'I think, therefore I am'; see below). If there is something distinctive about human consciousness, where should we look for it? According to Eiser (1994):

> *Even if we could build a machine with this full capacity of a human brain [immensely interactive parallelism] we would still be reluctant to attribute to it the kind of consciousness, the sense of self, to which we ourselves lay claim . . . To ask what is special about human consciousness, therefore, is not just a question about process. It is also to ask what is special about our experience of the world, the experience we have by virtue of physical presence in the world . . .*

Any distinction we try to draw between mind and body (mind–body dualism) is, according to Eiser, objectionable precisely because it divorces mental from physical experience. The most continuous feature of our experience is our own body: personal identity (and that of others) depends on physical identity, we feel our body and we feel the world *through* it, and it provides the anchor and perspective from which we experience other things.

This view is very similar to that of the French phenomenologist Merleau-Ponty (1962, 1968). He distinguishes between 'one's own body' (the phenomenal body) and 'the objective body' (the body as object). Experience of our own body is not, essentially, experience of an object. In fact, most of the time, we are not aware of our body as such – it is, as it were, transparent to us. But without our body, we could not be.

Just as sense perception and motor skills function together (as do the different senses), so, for Merleau-Ponty, mind and body, mental and physical, are two aspects of the same thing, namely a person. The mind is embodied in that it can be identified with one aspect of something that has two aspects, neither of which can be reduced to (explained in terms of) the other (Teichman, 1988).

The body provides us with a continuous patterned stream of input, and (simply from the fact that we cannot be in two places at the same time) imposes constraints on the information received by the brain about the outside world (Eiser, 1994). This, in turn, relates to 'aboutness' (or intentionality: see above).

WHAT IS CONSCIOUSNESS *FOR*?

If Searle is correct, and Boden and the other functionalists are mistaken when they claim that our brains *just happen* to be made from neuroprotein (as opposed to silicon or metal), and that whatever they are made of is

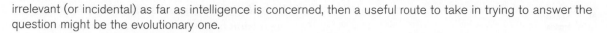

irrelevant (or incidental) as far as intelligence is concerned, then a useful route to take in trying to answer the question might be the evolutionary one.

According to Humphrey (1986), when we ask what consciousness does, what difference it makes to our lives, there are three possibilities that might more or less make sense:

1 It might be making all the difference in the world – it might be a necessary precondition of all intelligent and purposive behaviour, both in humans and animals.
2 It might be making no difference whatsoever – it might be a purely accidental feature that happens (at least) sometimes to be present in (some) animals and has no influence on their behaviour.
3 It might, for those animals that have it, be making the difference between success and failure in some particular aspect of their lives.

Humphrey believes that common sense must back the first of these. Our everyday experience is that consciousness makes all the difference in the world (just as our experience tells us that we have free will): we are either awake, alert and conscious or flat on our backs, inert and unconscious, and when we lose consciousness, we lose touch with the world.

But what about those cases in which consciousness does not seem to be necessary, such as perception, blindsight and automatic processing (see above)? While perception (and other fundamental cognitive and behavioural processes) may not require consciousness, the fact remains that they are very often accompanied by consciousness, and if (as far as we know) most other species lack it, the implication is that it evolved in human beings for some purpose.

Imagine an animal that lacks the faculty of conscious or self-reflexive 'insight'. It has a brain that receives inputs from conventional sense organs and sends outputs to motor systems, and in between runs a highly sophisticated information processor and decision maker. But it has no picture of what this information processing is doing or how it works: the animal is unconscious.

Now imagine that a new form of sense organ evolves, an 'inner eye', whose field of view isn't the outside world but the brain itself. Like other sense organs, it provides a picture of its informational field (the brain) that is partial and selective; but, equally, like other sense organs, it has been designed by natural selection to give a useful ('user-friendly') picture – one that will tell the subject as much as s/he needs to know: this animal is conscious (see Figure 12.3, page 245).

Suppose our ability to look in upon ourselves and examine our own minds at work is as much a part of human biology as our ability to walk upright or to perceive the outside world. Once upon a time there were animals – our own ancestors presumably – who couldn't do it. They gave rise to descendants who could. Why should those conscious descendants have been selected in the course of evolution?

If Darwin's theory is correct, the only answer can be that, like every other natural ability and structure, consciousness must have come into being because it conferred some kind of biological advantage on those creatures that possessed it:

> *In some particular area of their lives, conscious human beings must have been able to do something which their unconscious forbears couldn't; something which, in competition with the other members of their species, distinctly improved their chances of survival – and so of passing on the underlying genetic trait for consciousness to the next generation.*
>
> *(Humphrey, 1986)*

If consciousness is the answer to anything at all, it must be to a biological challenge that human beings have had to meet; could the challenge lie in the human need to understand, respond to and manipulate the behaviour of other human beings?

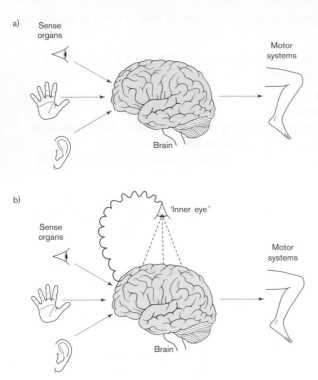

Figure 12.4
a How an animal without insight works (from Humphrey, 1986)
b How the addition of an 'inner eye' affects the animal (from Humphrey, 1986)

In evolutionary terms I suspect that the possession of an 'inner eye' served one purpose before all: to allow our own ancestors to raise social life to a new level. The first use of human consciousness was – and is – to enable each human being to understand what it feels like to be human and so to make sense of himself and other people from the inside . . .

(Humphrey, 1993)

This, of course, is a way of looking at people as natural psychologists (see Chapter 1). It is no accident that humans are both the most highly social creatures to have evolved and are unique in their ability to use self-knowledge to interpret others.

Blakemore (1988) believes that Humphrey's theory raises two important questions.

1   Why does consciousness use such strange symbolism? For example, the biological value of finding a partner obviously has to do with the nitty-gritty of procreation. But we feel we are in love, a sensation that tells us nothing about the crude necessity of reproduction: 'consciousness translates biological necessities into feelings of pain and pleasure, need and emotion'.

2 Why does the inner eye see so little? It gives us only a tiny glimpse, and a distorted one at that, of the internal world (as we saw above, when discussing the cognitive unconscious, much of what our brains do is entirely hidden from the 'spotlight' of consciousness).

For Blakemore, our only answers to these questions is in terms of the structure and organization of the brain: 'to understand the organ that allows us to understand would be little short of a miracle. The human brain makes us what we are. It makes the mind' (Blakemore, 1988).

THE RELATIONSHIP BETWEEN MIND AND BRAIN

What Blakemore, Humphrey, Searle and other physiologists, biologists, psychologists and philosophers seem to be saying is that consciousness is *real*: it is a property of human beings as much as having a particular kind of body, or walking upright on two legs, or having a particular size and type of brain, are properties of human beings. They also seem agreed that, without the human brain, there would be no consciousness – the two seem to have evolved together. But this doesn't mean that the physical brain is in some sense 'primary', with consciousness being 'secondary'.

The logical or philosophical difficulty, as we have seen, is trying to understand how two 'things' are related when one of them (the brain) is physical (has size, weight, shape, location in space and time), while the other (consciousness) seems to lack all these characteristics.

Closely related to this logical/philosophical difficulty is the scientific one of explaining how it is that something non-physical or non-material can influence and produce changes in something physical or material. The classic example given by philosophers of the 'problem' of mind and body is the commonplace, everyday, taken-for-granted act of deciding to lift one's arm. Assuming that it is volitional (an act of free will), how does my 'deciding' or 'intending' to lift my arm bring about the upward physical movement of my arm (which we call 'lifting my arm')?

The problem of causation

The example of lifting my arm is 'classic', partly because it involves the idea of causation: how can a non-physical event (my deciding to lift my arm) cause a physical event (the lifting of my arm)? From a strictly materialist, positivistic, scientific perspective, this should be impossible (see Chapter 10). Science, including psychology and neurophysiology, has traditionally rejected any brand of *philosophical dualism*, which stems from Descartes's belief in the essential difference between the physical and the mental (or non-physical).

However, if consciousness evolved because of its survival value, could it have equipped human beings with such survival value unless it had causal properties (Gregory, 1981) – that is, unless it could actually bring about changes in behaviour? This is one of the more psychologically relevant questions regarding the mind–brain relationship (as opposed to the philosophically relevant – and interesting – questions). There is no doubt (as with free will, and consciousness in general) that our experience tells us our mind affects our behaviour, that consciousness has causal properties.

Lodge (2002) quotes the physicist James Trefil, who states that:

> . . . *no matter how my brain works, no matter how much interplay there is between my brain and my body, one single fact remains . . . I am aware of a self that looks out at the world from somewhere inside my skull . . . this is not simply an observation, but the central datum with which every theory of consciousness has to grapple. In the end the theory has to go from the firing of neurons to this essential perception.*

An example of the 'reality' of non-physical factors (such as expectations, belief, faith) influencing physical processes (including changes in the brain) is the *placebo effect* (see Chapter 13).

An overview of some of the major theories of the mind–brain relationship

Trying to classify the various attempts to 'solve' the mind–body problem is both complex and a matter of some controversy, but it is useful to have some general picture of the types of theory that have been proposed.

According to Armstrong (1987):

> *If we think of mind and body as two opponents in a tug-of-war, then we can distinguish between theories which try to drag body, and matter generally, over into the camp of mind; those which try to drag mind over into the camp of body; and those theories where an equal balance is maintained.*

Dualism

The 'equal balance' theories are dualist. It was Descartes's distinction between the physical body and the non-physical mind that really introduced the mind–body problem into philosophy for the first time. Most alternative theories are an attempt to exorcize the 'ghost in the machine', which is how Ryle (1949), an Oxford philosopher with strong behaviourist leanings, attacked Descartes's belief in the non-physical, non-material mind, with its own separate existence from the body and causal powers to control the body and, hence, behaviour.

Descartes's theory represents a 'pure' form of dualism: the mind can influence the body (through the operation of the pineal gland in the brain), whereas the body cannot influence the mind. By contrast, *interactionists* believe that body and mind influence each other (the influence is two-way).

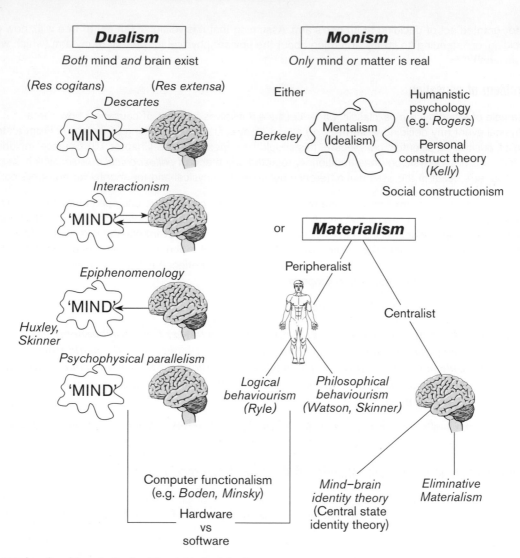

Figure 12.5 An outline of the major theories of the mind–brain relationship

Like Descartes, *epiphenomenologists* believe that the influence is only one-way, but they maintain that it works in the *opposite* direction (the brain influences the mind, but not vice versa). An epiphenomenon is an accompanying event outside the chain of causation (a 'by-product'), and was first proposed by T.H. Huxley, who claimed that consciousness was simply the 'noise of the brain's engine at work, huffing and puffing as it went about the business of processing the information that controls behaviour (Humphrey, 1986).

Skinner was an epiphenomenologist. While accepting the existence of mental phenomena, his *radical behaviourism* involves a denial that they can have any influence on behaviour (they have no explanatory power; see Chapters 10 and 14).

Dualists who believe there's *no* interaction between mind and brain, in either direction, are called (psychophysical) *parallelists*.

Monism

Any theory that is not dualist is monist, implying that there is only *one* kind of reality (not two, as in dualism). Monism can be *mentalist* (trying to drag the body, and matter generally, over into the camp of mind) *or* *materialist* (trying to drag mind over into the camp of body).

According to *mentalism* (or *idealism*), only mental phenomena are real. This idea seems to be contrary to the common-sense belief in the independent existence of an external reality, but it is consistent with psychologists who adopt a *phenomenological approach*. For example, Carl Rogers puts *experience* (and free will) at the centre of his theory of self, and according to Kelly's *personal construct theory*, the world 'is' how it's defined and interpreted by the individual (see Chapters 11 and 14). Also, any *social constructionist* approach has a mentalistic dimension (see Chapters 6 and 14).

The vast majority of monists are materialists, who believe that the only kind of reality is physical. It is best interpreted as the doctrine that the fundamental laws and principles of nature are exhausted by the laws and principles of physics (Armstrong, 1987). Armstrong divides materialism into two major forms, peripheralist and centralist.

Peripheralist materialism

Peripheralist materialism (better known as *logical* or *philosophical behaviourism*) reduces 'the mind' to behaviour. For example, Watson (the founder of behaviourism) claimed that all thought processes are really no more than the sensations produced by tiny movements of the vocal cords, which are too small to produce audible sounds. In fact, he was trying to deny the existence of thought altogether and so reduce it to 'silent speech'.

Ryle's (1949) logical behaviourism, which is consistent with Watson's views, claims that mentalistic terms are simply a grammatical alternative to terms that describe behaviour: sentences about the mind can be translated into sentences about behaviour, without anything being 'left over'. Sometimes, this will involve reference to dispositions to behave – for example, 'John believes it's going to rain' translates into 'John will be disposed to carry an umbrella if he goes out.' According to logical behaviourism, the mind is behaviour plus dispositions to behave (Searle, 1992).

For Ryle, the mind–brain problem is a pseudo-problem, resulting from a purely *grammatical* distinction: matter is normally described using nouns/pronouns, while mind is normally described using verbs/adverbs/adjectives. If, for example, we talk about a person's 'intelligence' instead of his/her 'intelligent behaviour', we create the impression that intelligence exists in some equivalent way to the person's body, because we are using a noun when it is more appropriate to use an adjective. These 'category mistakes' have brought about the non-problem of the mind–brain relationship.

Centralist materialism

Centralist materialism (*mind–brain identity theory* or *central state identity theory*) identifies mental processes with purely physical processes in the central nervous system. According to Place (1956) and Smart (1959), for example, there is no logical absurdity involved in supposing that there might be separate mental, non-physical phenomena, independent of material reality; it just turns out that, as a matter of fact, mental states are identical with states of the nervous system: 'The sciences of biology and psychology ... are an application of physics and chemistry to natural history ... [and] ... organisms are simply very complicated physico-chemical mechanisms' (Smart, 1959, in Teichman, 1988).

A recent example of this rather extreme form of reductionist materialism is *The Astonishing Hypothesis: The Scientific Search for the Soul* (1994), by Francis Crick (one of the co-discoverers of the structure of DNA: see Chapter 5). According to Crick:

You, your joys and your sorrows, your memories and your ambitions, your sense of personality and free will, are in fact no more than the behaviour of a vast assembly of nerve cells and their associated molecules.

Crick's objective is to correlate brain activity and consciousness and, more specifically, to identify which neurons are associated with the mere 'water' of automatism and which with the 'wine' of consciousness. But Smith (1994) asks if Crick's review of all the evidence for the neurophysiological correlates of visual consciousness in primate (including human) brains takes us any further towards a solution to the mind–brain problem: 'How is it that consciousness, that wonder of wonders [Husserl], is correlated with/emerges from/is the "internal" aspect of all this intricate cerebral activity?' The problem of mind and brain, according to Smith, is radically different from other cases of *contingent identity* it's usually compared with, such as:

- a cloud is a mass of water droplets or other particles in suspension
- heat is mean kinetic energy
- a gene is identical with a section of the DNA molecule.

The difference is to do with *reductionism*, and related to this is the issue of deciding exactly what we mean by *identity*.

Even if a perfectly systematic correlation between mind-states and brain-states were found, this would not be sufficient on its own to support the attempt to replace a psychological account of behaviour with an account in terms of neurophysiology (*eliminative materialism*), which represents an extreme reductionist form of materialism. Apart from the objections to reductionism itself, such correlational evidence would be equally consistent with psychophysical parallelism (a form of dualism; see above).

BOX 12.6 TYPE AND TOKEN IDENTITY

It has generally been assumed that mind–brain identity implies what philosophers call *type identity*. This involves the claim that whenever a mind-state of a certain type occurs, a brain-state of a certain type occurs, such that we could study the operation of the human system using one or other framework; the results of our studies could be simply translated from one framework directly into the other. 'Mind talk' would just be an alternative way of describing the same thing as we describe using 'brain talk'.

However, the neurophysiological and neuropsychological evidence points instead towards *token identity*. Although there can never be a mind-state that is not grounded in a brain-state of some kind or other (we cannot have a mind without a brain; see text above), a particular kind of mind-state is sometimes grounded in one kind of brain-state and sometimes in another. We cannot, therefore, substitute a brain-state description for mind-state descriptions, because these ways of looking at the system are not systematically correlated (Harré *et al.*, 1985).

Broadbent (1981, in Harré *et al.*) has shown that we cannot assume that the same neurophysiological mechanisms will be used by two different people when they engage in the 'same' activity of reading: there may be many ways that 'the brain can perform the same task'. Although in a certain sense everyone 'reads with their brain',

. . . a neurophysiological description of brain function cannot displace, or replace, a psychological description: token identity means that there must always be a place for an autonomous psychological account of human action and thought.

(Harré et al., 1985)

Against reductionism: different levels of description

Steven Rose (1992), an eminent biologist interested in the brain, argues in favour of learning how to *translate* between mind language and brain language, and against trying to replace the former with the latter:

> . . . *the mind is never replaced by the brain. Instead, we have two distinct and legitimate languages, each describing the same unitary phenomena of the material world.*

Rose is both a materialist and an *anti-reductionist*. While most reductionists are also materialists, they do not necessarily go together. Like Rose, Freud was a materialist who believed that no single scientific vocabulary (such as anatomy) could adequately describe – let alone explain – all facets of the material world. He upheld the *thesis of the autonomy of psychological explanation*: 'psychoanalysis must keep itself free from any hypothesis that is alien to it, whether of an anatomical, chemical or physiological kind and must operate with purely auxiliary ideas' (Freud, 1919, in Flanagan, 1984).

The fact that there are different 'languages' for describing minds and brains (or different *levels of description*) relates to the question of the relevance of knowing what is going on inside my brain when I think/am conscious:

> *The firing of neurons stands to thought in the same relation as my walking across the room (etc.) stands to my getting some coffee. It is absolutely essential in a causal or physical sense, and absolutely superfluous . . . to the logic of the higher-order description. In short, I can accept that it happens, and then happily ignore it . . .*
>
> *(Eiser, 1994)*

This explains how it is possible to be, simultaneously, a materialist (the brain is necessarily implicated in everything we do and the mind doesn't represent a different kind of reality) and an anti-reductionist (I can describe and explain my thinking without having to 'bring my brain into it' – two separate levels of description are involved). As Chalmers (2007) puts it: '. . .Experience may *arise* from the physical, but it is not *entailed* by the physical.'

CONCLUSIONS: IS FUNCTIONALISM A SOLUTION?

So, from a psychological point of view it is *irrelevant* to establish quite how, in physical terms, the brain goes about being a mind. This view is not too dissimilar from that of the *computer functionalists* (such as Boden, Minsky and others), who, as we noted earlier, stress the importance of the processes carried out by the brain to the exclusion of what the brain is actually made of ('you don't need brains to be brainy'). They attempt to solve the mind–brain problem by distinguishing between *software* and *hardware*: the mind is to software as the brain is to hardware. Since the software/mind is what matters (logical operations involving the manipulation of symbols), the problem of the *relationship* between it and the hardware/brain disappears.

However, as Rose (1992) points out, this separation of mind from its actual material base is in some ways a reversion to Cartesian dualism. But at the same time, by treating the brain as a sort of 'black box', whose internal biological mechanisms and processes are irrelevant, and insisting that all that matters is matching inputs to outputs, it is also behaviouristic. It seems to (re-)create some of the problems it was designed to solve, and to face the same objections as other attempted solutions. Rose concludes by saying:

> *Even if minds and brains have an identical physical reference, our knowledge of brains as brains is neither similar in kind nor comparable in extensiveness to our knowledge of minds as minds. The task of translating the one kind of knowledge into the other is so difficult – both technically and conceptually – that, for most purposes, it is almost certainly not worth the effort.*

Indeed, 'For much of what it conventionally does, psychology might as well be dualist or Cartesian, and might indeed be better for admitting it' (Eiser, 1994).

Rose (2005) rejects the mind–brain dichotomy, which he sees as peculiar to western culture. He claims that:

> *Mental and conscious processes . . . themselves evolved and [are] functionally-adaptive properties essential to human survival, neither descended from heaven, nor functionless add-ons, epiphenomenal consequences of having large brains, but without causal powers . . .*

SUMMARY

○ Psychology began its life as a separate discipline taking consciousness/conscious mental life as its subject matter. This was then rejected by Watson's 'Behaviourist Manifesto'.

○ 'Mind' has once again become legitimate subject matter and introspection is an acceptable means of collecting data, coinciding with the decline of behaviourism.

○ The 'problem of consciousness' arises when we acknowledge that the physical brain is, in some way, involved in our subjective experience.

○ 'Mind' is a much broader concept than 'consciousness'; there is always much more mental activity than we can detect through introspection at any one time.

○ Freud distinguished between the conscious, pre-conscious and unconscious, which, essentially, are levels of accessibility of feelings and memories.

○ Most psychologists accept a continuum of consciousness, but most would not accept Freud's theory of the unconscious as a dynamic force, involving repression of threatening material.

○ One way in which experimental psychologists have studied consciousness is through the concept of attention. An important distinction is made between focal attention (or focal awareness) and peripheral attention.

○ Much of our behaviour/mental processes takes place outside our focal attention/conscious awareness (using automatic processing).

○ The phenomenon of blindsight suggests that it is possible to show the behaviour of perceiving without being consciously aware of what we are doing. In blindsight and prosopagnosia there is a loss of explicit conscious recognition but the capacity for implicit behavioural recognition.

○ Nisbett and Wilson claim that we have access only to the products/outputs of our cognitive processes, most of which fall within the cognitive unconscious. We may not have privileged access to our mental processes, but most psychologists and neuroscientists believe in some kind of centre of consciousness.

○ Edelman distinguishes between primary and higher-order consciousness (or self-consciousness); the latter is similar to Johnson-Laird's self-reflective automata.

○ Consciousness manifests itself as qualia: 'how things seem to us as human beings'.

○ Unlike an android which could be manufactured, and whose behaviour can be completely explained scientifically, humans will always display behaviour that cannot be completely described or explained by psychological theories.

- According to supporters of strong AI, people and computers are merely different manifestations of automatic formal systems/symbol manipulators.

- Searle argues that mental states/processes are real biological phenomena, caused by brain processes; they are higher-level features of the brain, and in principle, only a machine made of neuroprotein could be conscious.

- For supporters of strong AI, the computational functions our brain chemistry allows us to perform is what matters, not the chemistry itself.

- The difference between parallel (brain) and serial processing (most traditional computer programs) is an argument used by those opposed to strong AI. But connectionism is an attempt to meet this objection.

- According to Merleau-Ponty, without our body, we couldn't be. Mental and physical are both aspects of a person, and neither can be reduced to the other.

- The fact that consciousness very often accompanies perception (and other cognitive processes) and is lacking in most other species, suggests that it evolved in human beings for some purpose.

- Humphrey describes consciousness as an 'inner eye', which evolved to provide a 'user-friendly' picture of the brain itself. This provides people with the skills to function as natural psychologists.

- Different theories of the mind–brain relationship try to solve the puzzle of how something non-physical can influence/produce changes in something physical.

- Philosophical dualism, first proposed by Descartes, has traditionally been rejected by positivist, materialist science. Interactionism and epiphenomenology are both forms of dualism; they differ regarding the direction of this influence between mind and brain. Psychophysical parallelists are dualists who deny any mind–brain interaction.

- Any theory that is not dualist is monist. This includes mentalism/idealism, according to which only mental phenomena are real. Phenomenological theories, such as those of Rogers and Kelly, and constructionist theories, can be seen as having a mentalist 'flavour'.

- Most monists are materialists. The peripheralist version is better known as logical/philosophical behaviourism. According to Ryle, the mind–brain problem is a pseudo-problem resulting from a purely grammatical confusion.

- Centralist materialism (mind–brain identity theory/central state identity theory) identifies mental processes with purely physical processes in the central nervous system.

- A difficulty with identity theory is that it implies type identity, while the available evidence points instead towards token identity: 'brain talk' can never displace/replace 'mind talk'.

- Eliminative materialism represents an extreme reductionist form of materialism.

- It is possible to be both a materialist and an anti-reductionist (such as Freud and Rose), because of the independent existence of different levels of description.

USEFUL WEBSITES

http://www.consciousness.arizona.edu/
http://www.fil.ion.ucl.ac.uk/
www.u.arizona.edu/~chalmers/online.html

http://assc.caltech.edu/index.htm
http://www.ai.mit.edu/projects/humanoid-robotics-group
http://www.consciousentities.com/?p=64

RECOMMENDED READING

Blackmore, S. (2003) *Consciousness: An Introduction.* London: Hodder & Stoughton.

Blackmore, S. (2005) *Consciousness: A Very Short Introduction.* Oxford: Oxford University Press.

Blakemore, C. and Greenfield, S. (eds) (1987) *Mindwaves.* Oxford: Basil Blackwell.

Damasio, A. (1999) *The Feeling of What Happens: Body, emotion and the making of consciousness.* London: Vintage.

Eiser, J.R. (1994) *Attitudes, Chaos and the Connectionist Mind.* Oxford: Basil Blackwell.

Gross, R. (2008) *Key Studies in Psychology* (5th edn). London: Hodder Education. (Chapters 17 and 20.)

Humphrey, N. (1992) *A History of the Mind.* London: Vintage.

Ramachandran, V.S. and Blakeslee, S. (1998) *Phantoms in the Brain.* London: Fourth Estate.

Searle, J.R. (1992) *The Rediscovery of the Mind.* Cambridge, MA: MIT Press.

Velmans, M. and Schneider, S. (eds) (2007) *The Blackwell Companion to Consciousness.* Oxford: Blackwell Publishing.

CHAPTER 13

PARAPSYCHOLOGY

PARANORMAL, UNUSUAL AND ANOMALISTIC EXPERIENCES: DEFINING TERMS AND DEFINING THE FIELD

What is parapsychology?

According to Henry (2005a), *parapsychology* (the term introduced in the 1930s to refer to the scientific investigation of paranormal phenomena: Evans, 1987a) is the study of *psychic phenomena*, that is:

> . . . *the exchange of information or some other interaction between an organism and its environment, without the mediation of the senses* . . .

For most psychologists, the sensory systems (vision/sight, audition/hearing, gestation/taste, olfaction/smell, skin or cutaneous senses/touch, and proprioception/kinaesthetic and vestibular senses) are the only means by which we can acquire information about the environment (both physical objects and other people). However, there are some phenomena that seem to involve meaningful exchanges of information, and at the same time appear somehow to *exceed* the capacities of the sensory (and motor) systems as they are currently understood (Rao and Palmer, 1987) (e.g. '*extra*sensory perception').

In addition to extrasensory perception (ESP), the subject matter of parapsychology includes psychokinesis (PK), anomalous ('exceptional') experiences, and apparitional phenomena. ESP and PK are often referred to, collectively, as 'psi' (short for 'psychic ability') and, as we saw above, 'paranormal' is sometimes used to describe the whole range of phenomena studied by parapsychology (as is 'anomalous').

Extrasensory perception (ESP)

The term *extrasensory perception* was introduced in 1934 by J.B. Rhine. This was a general term used to cover three types of communication that supposedly occur without the use of the senses, namely, *telepathy, clairvoyance* and *precognition* ('paranormal cognition' or 'sixth sense'). These, and *retrocognition,* are defined in Box 13.1.

Psychokinesis (PK)

Psychokinesis (movement by the psyche) refers to '. . .the supposed power of the mind to manipulate matter at a distance without any known physical means. . .' (Evans, 1987b), or the apparent ability to '. . . influence events simply by a direct volitional act of some sort, by wanting the event to happen in a certain way . . .' (Morris, 1989). The direction of the influence is from person to environment (the reverse of ESP).

> ## BOX 13.1 THE FOUR TYPES OF EXTRASENSORY PERCEPTION (ESP)
>
> *Telepathy:* '... the transmission of information from one mind to another, without the use of language, body movements, or any of the known senses ...' (Evans, 1987b). It was previously called 'thought transference'.
>
> *Clairvoyance:* '... the acquisition by a mind or brain of information which is not available to it by the known senses, and most important, which is *not known at the time to any other mind or brain ...*' (Evans, 1987b).
>
> *Precognition:* '... the apparent ability to access information about future events before they happen ...' (Morris, 1989).
>
> *Retrocognition:* known information from the past is apparently picked up psychically (Henry, 2005a).
>
> In all cases, the direction of influence is from environment to person.

PK can be split into macro-PK, where solid objects are affected and the result can be seen by the naked eye (such as spoon bending, apports ('gifts' that materialize from non-physical to physical reality) or moving an object purely via intention) and micro-PK, where ultra-sensitive instruments (such as strain gauges and random-number generators/RNGs: see below) are apparently affected by intention, and the significance of the results is assessed statistically.

Macro-PK is still highly controversial; it is an area where experimenters have to take particular care to guard against fraud (Wiseman, 2001: see below).

Naturally occurring PK (recurrent spontaneous PK – RSPK) is associated with phenomena such as poltergeists. Direct mental interaction with a living system (DMILS) refers to PK on a live organism where physiology, such as electrodermal (skin conductance) activity or blood pressure is altered purely by intention. Another example is distant and non-contact healing (Henry, 2005a).

Apparitional phenomena

Apparitions are experienced as *external* to/outside the self, the classic example being a ghost. Sometimes, the apparition appear to be fairly solid, at other times less obviously person-like. In previous centuries, reports of demon visitations were quite common. In the latter half of the twentieth century, reflecting technological developments, similar experiences have often been interpreted as visits by aliens. In non-western cultures, experiences of spirits of some kind are often accepted as part of life; but in the West, such reports are rare (though there are some well-known cases of visions of the Virgin Mary) (Henry, 2005a).

Figure 13.1 A ghostly apparition in the library

Anomalous or exceptional experience

In contrast to apparitions, anomalous experiences (such as out-of-body experiences – OBEs, near-death experiences – NDEs, past-life experiences – PLEs, and coincidence experiences – CEs) are felt as happening to the individual him/herself. There are other anomalous experiences (such as UFOs) and (other) exceptional experiences (such as altered states of consciousness and mystical experiences) that are traditionally studied by researchers other than parapsychologists. This is seen as a reason for categorizing anomalous and exceptional experiences together.

For example, White (1993, in Henry, 2005a) offers a classification of exceptional experiences which brings together phenomena traditionally studied by parapsychologists and others interested in anomalous and exceptional experiences. These are:

- mystical experiences (including peak experiences – see Chapter 14, stigmata, transformational experience)
- psychic experiences (including apports – see above, synchronicity, telepathy, PK, and OBEs – see below)
- encounter-type experiences (including apparitions, angels, UFO encounters, sense of presence)
- death-related experiences (such as NDEs – see below – and PLEs)
- exceptional normal experiences (such as *déjà vu* – and hypnagogia – sometimes spelled 'hypnogogia').

BOX 13.2 A BRIEF HISTORY OF PARAPSYCHOLOGY (PP)

- According to Blackmore (1995), credit for the founding of PP (in the 1930s) was almost entirely due to J.B. and Louisa Rhine (although Louisa is often overlooked; see Chapter 6 for similar examples of neglected women). They were biologists who wanted to find evidence against a purely materialist view of human nature (see Chapter 12).
- They shared the same objectives as *spiritualism*, according to which if souls/spirits survived death of the physical body, they must exist somewhere in the universe, and should, in principle, be contactable (such as through mediums). A substantial number of Victorian scientists associated themselves with this religious movement, but the Rhines wanted to be seen as respectable scientists.
- They renamed the traditional 'psychical research' as 'parapsychology', established a department of PP at Duke University (in the USA), began to develop new experimental methods and defined their terms operationally.

PP AS SCIENCE AND ITS CHANGING CONTENT

According to Roberts and Groome (2001):

> *We live in an age of science. However, there are many types of human experience which continue to defy any scientific explanation, at least in terms of the scientific knowledge that we have at the present time. In some cases we may have a partial explanation, but in other cases the underlying mechanism is completely unknown. These cases which completely defy any normal scientific explanation are referred to as 'paranormal' phenomena. In practice there is considerable overlap between what is regarded as 'paranormal' and what is considered to be merely 'unusual' . . .*

Because scientific knowledge changes so rapidly, and because most parapsychologists consider themselves to be scientists applying the accepted rules of scientific enquiry to difficult-to-explain phenomena, the field of PP is ever-shrinking. For example, hypnosis, hallucinations and lucid dreams (where the dreamer seems to be controlling the dream content) used to be considered part of PP – until psychologists made progress in understanding them. This, in turn, suggests that 'paranormal' implies phenomena that *apparently* lie outside the range of normal scientific explanations and investigations. As Boring (1966) said, a scientific success is a failure for psychical research; in other words, PP is concerned with phenomena that 'mainstream' or 'regular' psychology cannot explain with its currently available models and theories.

Parapsychologists who apply 'normal' scientific methods are following a long tradition of scientists who investigated phenomena which at the time seemed mysterious (Utts and Josephson, 1996), or were given what we would now consider bizarre, 'unscientific' explanations. Gregory (1987) gives the example of thunder and lightning:

> . . . once considered to be the wrath of the Gods, but now understood as the same electricity that we generate and use for wonders of our technology.

So, once 'paranormal' phenomena have been accounted for scientifically, they will no longer be called 'paranormal'. While they are still imperfectly understood in terms of our current/conventional scientific knowledge and theories, it is convenient to call them paranormal: they are understandable *in principle*, but as yet we cannot explain them. This helps distinguish paranormal from 'supernatural' or 'beyond nature', which implies 'incompatible with scientific theorizing and investigation' (Watt, 2001). However:

> . . . the phenomena of psi are so extraordinary and so similar to what are widely regarded as superstitious that some scientists declare psi to be an impossibility and reject the legitimacy of parapsychological inquiry . . .
>
> *(Atkinson* et al., *1990)*

Sometimes, 'extraordinary' can be construed as 'not real', and the history of PP is littered with accusations of fraud on the part of 'believers' by those who, for whatever reason, reject their claims. However, if psi 'really' exists, what does this imply for many of our fundamental scientific beliefs about the world?

While strong opposition to PP is understandable, prejudgements about the impossibility of psi are inappropriate in science. Many psychologists who are not yet convinced that psi has been demonstrated are nevertheless open to the possibility that new evidence may emerge that would be more compelling. Many parapsychologists believe that the case for psi has already been 'proven', or that existing experimental procedures have the potential for proving it (Atkinson *et al.*, 1990).

Who studies paranormal phenomena?

French (2001) describes himself as an *anomalistic psychologist,* not because he is especially unusual (he is a real human being, not a ghost or an alien), but because he studies *anomalistic psychology* (AP). This attempts to explain:

> . . . paranormal and related beliefs and ostensibly paranormal experiences in terms of known (or knowable) psychological and physical factors. It is directed at understanding bizarre experiences that many people have, without assuming that there is anything paranormal involved . . .

One example he gives is that of sleep paralysis. This is a temporary state in which an individual who is either drifting off to sleep or emerging from sleep suddenly realizes that their muscles are totally paralysed. This is frightening enough, but the state is sometimes associated with bizarre and terrifying images of demons, monsters, hags or aliens, and a strong sense of an evil presence. This is a common symptom of narcolepsy, in which the patient suddenly, and uncontrollably, collapses in a state of unconsciousness, any time of the day or night, and in any situation. But many non-narcoleptics suffer from sleep paralysis at least once in their lives.

French argues that while psychology, neurology and other scientific disciplines are rich in explanatory models for many kinds of human experiences, these models are rarely extrapolated to explain unusual experiences. AP tries to do just that. Its aims, he says, would still be valid even if the existence of paranormal forces were to be established beyond doubt, 'because there is little question that most paranormal claims can be plausibly explained in non-paranormal terms'.

Do you have to be a non-believer to study anomalistic psychology?

According to French (2001), the range and variety of topics covered by AP make it an excellent tool for teaching critical-thinking skills. Most people are familiar with these topics via the media, which create a strong pro-paranormal bias. Students can discuss why some sources of evidence should be treated as more reliable than others, as well as alternative explanations for paranormal experiences. A variety of psychological factors, most notably the limitations and biases of human cognition (see Gross, 2005; Gross & Rolls in press), can lead us into drawing faulty conclusions.

Although AP adopts the working hypothesis that paranormal forces do not exist, it allows for the possibility that they do. Most sceptics are not very well informed about parapsychology, and they assume that all apparently positive evidence for psi must be the result of delusion, deception and incompetence (see above). But techniques used by experimental parapsychologists have become much more refined and sophisticated in the light of previous criticisms. Many are easily on a par with the best psychological studies. Some parapsychologists appear to present evidence in support of the existence of paranormal forces even from such apparently well-controlled experiments. Either these findings should be accepted at face value, or critics should try to specify the subtle methodological flaws responsible for the misleading results (French, 2001).

Most psychologists adopt a narrow-minded view that paranormal phenomena do not merit serious study. Notable exceptions include Blackmore, Wiseman and Morris in the UK, and Spanos, Loftus and Lynn in the USA. However, there is a steadily increasing number of journal articles and books on the topic, and both conferences and undergraduate courses are becoming more common (French, 2001).

EXPERIMENTAL INVESTIGATION OF PARANORMAL PHENOMENA

According to Alcock (1981), definitions of ESP and PK are all *negative*, in the sense that they depend on *ruling out* 'normal' communication before the paranormal can be assumed. Progression in PP's experimental methods has necessarily been designed to exclude the 'normal' with even greater confidence. However, this inevitably leaves it open for critics to argue for even more devious ways in which sensory communication or outright fraud might occur (Blackmore, 1995).

Studying ESP through altered states of consciousness (ASC)

Probably the strongest evidence for ESP comes from a line of research that uses altered states of consciousness (ASC) to facilitate ESP performance. The underlying idea behind studying ESP through ASC is described in Box 13.3 (page 264).

Early research: The Rhines' study of telepathy using Zener cards

Throughout the 1930s, the Rhines conducted a lengthy series of *telepathy* experiments, in which the receiver had to guess the identity of a target being looked at by an *agent*. To make the task as easy as possible, a set of simple symbols was developed and made into *Zener cards* (named after their designer) or 'ESP cards'. They come in a pack of 25 cards, comprising 5 circles, 5 squares, 5 crosses, 5 stars and 5 wavy lines.

The rationale for these studies was that they allowed the experimenter to compare the results achieved with what would be expected by chance. So, in a pack of 25 cards comprising 5 of each of 5 distinct symbols, we would expect, on average, 5 to be guessed correctly (i.e. by chance alone). If receivers repeatedly scored above chance over long series of trials, this would suggest they were 'receiving' some information about the cards. This would, in turn, imply that, if the experiments had been sufficiently tightly controlled as to exclude all normal or known sensory cues, then the information must be coming via ESP (Evans, 1987a).

BOX 13.3 ALTERED STATES OF CONSCIOUSNESS (ASC) AND ESP

The basic idea is that normally we live in a very distracting, noisy environment, both internal and external. The ESP information may be like a very weak signal. If it were a strong signal, then we would know all about it already and there would not be a debate as to its existence. In order to help the *receiver* (or recipient) of the ESP to detect the weak ESP signal among the distracting noise, parapsychologists use *noise-reduction techniques*. These include helping the receiver to relax physically and mentally – the 'noise-reduction model' of ESP (Honorton and Harper, 1974; Braud, 1975).

Parapsychologists used noise-reduction techniques because they noticed several converging lines of evidence, which suggested that such states of consciousness facilitated ESP. In the late nineteenth century, many 'spiritual mediums' claimed to be able to obtain information paranormally through trance. More recently, it has been claimed that ESP could be enhanced by using hypnosis (Honorton and Krippner, 1969). Large-scale surveys of *spontaneous* psychic experiences have found that about two-thirds of cases occurred during dream states (Rhine, 1969). When parapsychologists tested for ESP using sleep laboratories, the positive results were very encouraging (Ullman *et al.*, 1973). But studying ESP this way is expensive and time-consuming. An alternative method is the 'Ganzfeld' (see text below and Box 13.6).

(Based on Watt, 2001)

The technique seemed to be successful, and the Rhines reported results that were way beyond what could be expected by chance (Blackmore, 1995); they claimed they had established the existence of ESP. However, these claims produced considerable opposition from the psychological establishment (see Henry, 2005a).

Not only have experimental methods been tightened up since the early days of PP research, making the possibility of fraud much less likely, but new statistical techniques for analysing and interpreting their data have been developed. *Meta-analysis* (MA) has become the leading means of combining the results of studies to provide an overall picture of an area of research, particularly in medicine and the social sciences – including PP (Milton, 2005) (see Box 13.5, page 266).

Free-response ESP

One disadvantage of the early Rhine research was that guessing long series of Zener cards is extremely boring. By contrast, reports of psychic dreams, premonitions and other cases of spontaneous psi were rife. The challenge was to capture these under laboratory conditions (Blackmore, 1995). *Free-response ESP* represents the most important attempt to meet this challenge.

Early experiments used an entirely free choice of image, as in the telepathic drawings of Upton Sinclair and his wife in the 1930s (Henry, 2005a). Upton drew a sketch and his wife attempted to reproduce it: her attempts showed some failures but also many striking similarities. This type of experiment often produces dramatic results with certain receivers drawing an image which seems very close to the original. However, interpreting the results can be problematic. For example, the probability of drawing a house, face or tree is much higher than objects such as a garden swing or a cooker. Also, it can be argued that people who know each other may well be able to use unconscious inference to anticipate what image the other party is likely to draw. Today, parapsychologists get round this problem by randomly selecting the images that people need to guess from a target pool (Henry, 2005a).

Remote viewing

Free-response methods include *remote-viewing (RV) studies* (Targ and Puthoff, 1974, 1977). RV is a form of *clairvoyance*, in which an individual is able to 'see' a specific location some distance away, without receiving any information about it through the usual sensory channels. The experimenter selects a target site at random,

BOX 13.4 THE PROBLEM OF FRAUD

According to Colman (1987), the history of PP is:

. . . disfigured by numerous cases of fraud involving some of the most 'highly respected scientists', their colleagues and participants . . .

For example, Soal (Soal and Bateman, 1954), a mathematician at London University, tried to replicate some of the Rhines' telepathy experiments using Zener cards. Despite his rigid controls and the involvement of other scientists as observers throughout, accusations of fraud resulted in a series of re-analyses of the data. Marwick, a member of the Society for Psychical Research in London, finally proved (in 1978) that Soal *had* cheated (Blackmore, 1995).

Against this, it is misleading to suggest that experimenter fraud is rife in PP, or even that it's more common here than in other disciplines. According to Roe (personal communication), books such as *Betrayers of the Truth* (Broad and Wade, 1982) show that fraud is more likely when the rewards are high and the chances of being caught (publicly exposed) are low. This characterizes mainstream science (especially medicine), and is certainly *not* characteristic of PP.

As far as participant fraud is concerned, some fakirs and stage psychics use tricks, and some mediums are fraudulent. As Henry (2005a) points out:

. . . This is one of the reasons that the modern parapsychological experiment is designed to control procedures so that fraud is effectively ruled out as an explanation. The controls include random automated target selection, automated result recording, predetermining the number of trials, screening and independent judging.

But there remains the question of the number of researchers achieving positive results. Many of the most significant results in PP seem to have been published by a relatively small number of experimenters (including Honorton – see below). As in other disciplines, fraud seems a less plausible explanation if positive results are replicated under well-controlled conditions by many different investigators in different locations. Meta-analysis (MA) offers a tool to assess the overall significance of work undertaken by many different researchers (see Box 13. 5).

Almost all experiments involve ordinary people, based on the assumption that if ESP and PK are genuine abilities or faculties, then, as with most other human abilities/faculties, a small proportion of people will be very bad at the task, most people somewhere near the middle, and a small proportion will be star performers (i.e. psi is *normally distributed*). According to Milton (2005):

People who make special claims of having strong psychic abilities are relatively rarely tested, not only because few of them make credible claims that appear worth testing but also because . . . the possibility that they might be fraudulent . . . requires extensive, time-consuming and potentially expensive experimental controls to rule out the possibility of cheating.

the agent/sender travels to it and attempts to 'send' back images of the chosen site through mental intention. Targ and Puthoff reported a series of field studies involving Pat Price, a former California police commissioner, which sparked a debate between researchers as to whether her successes constituted genuine clairvoyance. While the target sites were usually within 30 minutes of the laboratory (for practical reasons), replications have taken place over thousands of miles (Henry, 2005a).

Despite the controversy, the research was sufficiently convincing for the US military to fund a substantial research programme. The CIA declassified this information and released details of more than 20 years of RV

BOX 13.5 META-ANALYSIS

Meta-analysis (MA) refers to the use of statistical methods to synthesize and describe experiments and their outcomes. Milton (2005) describes five major advantages that MA has over traditional 'research reviews', in which the reviewer describes individual studies and uses his/her (often subjective) judgement to draw an overall conclusion.

Cumulative probability: MA provides a precise estimate of how unlikely it is that the results of the entire group of studies being examined arose by chance alone. In order to make this calculation, the probability associated with each study's outcome is calculated and the probabilities are combined to reflect the overall outcome. In most PP meta-analyses, the results have been highly significant. In large groups of studies, the results go well beyond mere statistical significance and have astronomical odds against having arisen by chance alone (a 'fluke').

File-drawer estimate: a recurring issue within science in general, and PP in particular, is the concern that only successful studies tend to be published (i.e. those that produce significant results), while those that find no effect (or one that is in the opposite direction from the predicted effect) are left in researchers' file drawers (and so *do not* get published: see text below). This is because the editors of academic journals – or even the researchers themselves – believe that negative results are not worth making public. If this is the case, then even a non-existent effect will appear to have been successfully demonstrated: with the usual cut-off point for statistical significance being set at 0.05, on average one in 20 studies will be apparently successful by chance alone. This makes it necessary to know how many studies have been conducted in total (Milton, 2005).

MA allows the calculation of the number of studies with an average zero effect that would have to be in the research 'file drawer' to bring the observed overall result in an MA down to the point at which it became non-significant. In most MAs carried out in PP so far, the file-drawer estimates are so large that selective publication *does not* appear to be a reasonable counter-explanation for the observed results.

Effect size: MA not only focuses on studies just in terms of their significance levels (the traditional approach) but also allows diverse studies to be compared on a single measure, called an *averaged effect size*. When MA is used to assess the effectiveness of treatments for mental disorder, effect size is essentially an indicator of the extent to which people who receive psychotherapy improve relative to those who don't: the greater the difference between these two groups, the greater the effect size (Lilienfeld, 1995). Most PP research wants to know about levels of performance in a certain task *under different conditions* – not just how unlikely the levels of performance were (Rosenthal and Rubin, 1992–93, in Milton, 2005).

Study quality: when an MA is used in PP research, each study is typically assessed on a number of quality criteria, such as whether an adequately tested source of randomness was used in a PK experiment, whether there was an adequate sensory shielding between receiver and target in an ESP study, and so on. Each study does or does not receive a full point for each criterion it passes and the points are added to reflect its overall quality (Milton, 2005).

If psi experiment results were due to poor methodological controls rather than to genuine phenomena, we might expect each study's quality to be negatively related to its effect size; in other words, the better controlled the study, the smaller its outcome. However, in almost all MAs in PP, *no* significant relationships have been demonstrated between overall quality and effect size (Milton, 1995, in Milton, 2005).

Replicability: MA also allows examination of whether only a few experimenters obtain significant results. Where this has been done, a much higher proportion appears to do so than the 5 per cent expected by chance. For example, Honorton and Ferrari (1989) report that 30 per cent of studies and 37 per cent of experimenters obtained statistically significant results.

research (Blackmore, 1996). RV has been put to practical use in 'psychic archaeology' (finding lost sites), criminal investigations, and, most controversially, predicting price fluctuations on the stock-market.

The Ganzfeld

The *Ganzfeld* ('ganz' = 'whole' and 'feld = 'field') is the most successful free-response method used to date, and was first used for psi research by Honorton in 1974. Consistent with the rationale outlined in Box 13.3, Honorton argued that the reason ESP occurs in dreams, meditation and reverie is that they are all states of reduced sensory input and increased internal attention. He tried to find a way of producing such a 'psi-conducive' state without the expense of a dream laboratory. The basic arrangement is described in Box 13.6.

BOX 13.6 THE GANZFELD

Halved ping-pong balls are taped over the receiver's eyes and red light is shone into them, so all that can be seen is a pinkish glow. Soothing sea-sounds or hissing 'white noise' (like a radio that's not properly tuned in) are played through headphones while the participant lies on a comfortable couch or reclining chair. While this does not constitute total sensory deprivation, the Ganzfeld deprives receivers of patterned input, which encourages internal imagery. They typically report a pleasant sensation of being immersed in a 'sea of light'.

A *sender* (an experimenter acting as an agent) is situated in a separate, acoustically isolated, room. A visual stimulus (a picture, slide or brief video sequence) is randomly selected from a large pool of similar stimuli to serve as the *target*. While the sender concentrates on the target (for about 15 minutes), the *receiver* tries to describe it by providing a continuous verbal report of his/her ongoing imagery and free associations. The sender stays in the room

Figure 13.2 Illustration of a Ganzfeld experiment

for another ten minutes. From a separate room, the experimenter can both hear (via a microphone) and see (via a one-way mirror) the receiver, and is blind to the target (does not know what the target is).

At the end of the experimental session, the receiver is presented with four stimuli (one of which is the target) and asked to rate the degree to which each one matches the imagery and associations experienced during the session. A 'direct hit' is recorded if the receiver assigns the highest rating to the target. The sender is then called in and reveals the target. A typical experiment involves about 30 sessions.

In practice, in this and other free-response experiments, the image the receiver draws or describes is rarely identical to the target – but it often has many striking similarities; for example, the shape or colour may be right but the scale or function may be wrong (a cone rather than pyramid, or the sun rather than an orange beach ball) (Henry, 2005a).

Typically, the receiver is asked to rank four images (selected randomly by computer) as to which s/he thinks most resembles the target. Independently, a third party unconnected with the experiment is presented with a transcript of the receiver's continuous verbal report of his/her mentation about the target, plus a copy of the same four images; the person is asked to rank the four images in terms of how closely each matches the transcript. Each of Honorton's 1,000+ targets differs from all the others in terms of the presence or absence of at least one of 10 characteristics (such as colour, humans, animals, architecture, activity versus static). The receiver can be asked 10 questions about his/her image relating to each of these 10 characteristics.

The 'Ganzfeld debate'

Honorton (1985) analysed 28 studies using the Ganzfeld procedure (totalling 835 sessions, conducted in ten different laboratories). He reported a 38 per cent correct selection of the target, which compares with a 25 per cent success rate by chance alone (i.e. by guessing). Statistically, this is highly significant: the chance of obtaining a 38 per cent success rate by chance alone is less than one in a billion (Honorton, 1985).

However, a critical review by Hyman (in the *Journal of Parapsychology*, 1985) pointed out discrepancies in the scoring systems used, and procedural flaws (such as the failure to use proper randomization for selecting the targets). Hyman also claimed to have found correlations between the quality rating of a study and its outcome: the sloppier studies gave 'better' results (see Box 13.5). But in the same journal, Honorton claimed to have found no evidence of such a correlation. Rosenthal provided a commentary on the debate, generally regarded as favouring Honorton's interpretation (Blackmore, 1995).

Hyman and Honorton issued a joint 'communiqué' in 1986, in which they agreed that the studies as a whole fell short of ideal, but that something beyond selective reporting, or inflated significance levels, seemed to be producing the above-chance outcomes. They also agreed that the significant outcomes had been produced by several different researchers. Further replications would decide which of their interpretations was correct.

This 'debate' – 'an outstanding example of productive interaction between critic and researcher' (Morris, 1989) – brought parapsychologists and sceptics together to try to agree what would constitute an acceptable experiment. As a consequence, Honorton designed a *fully automated* Ganzfeld experiment, leaving little scope for human error or deliberate fraud. Several experiments using this procedure produced significant results. These were published, in the form of an MA, in the *Psychological Bulletin* (Bem and Honorton, 1994), one of the (western) world's most prestigious psychology journals. It meant that 'the Ganzfeld had achieved respectability' (Blackmore, 1997b). However, despite many parapsychologists believing that the Ganzfeld is a genuinely repeatable experiment, and that it provides evidence for ESP (e.g. Utts, 1991; Bem and Honorton, 1994), most other scientists still tend to reject the findings.

The Koestler Parapsychology Unit at Edinburgh University is the UK's premier centre for Ganzfeld research. Of the six studies conducted since the unit opened, four have produced statistically significant results. A further MA on Ganzfeld studies conducted up to 1997, comprising over 2,500 Ganzfeld sessions conducted around the world, produced an average effect size of 33 per cent. This appeared to provide impressive evidence for a psi effect. However, an MA of 30 subsequent studies (Milton and Wiseman, 1999) found an effect close to chance. A re-analysis (Bem *et al.*, 2001, in Henry, 2005a) of 40 subsequent studies, including Milton and Wiseman's 30, suggested that those studies that followed the classic Ganzfeld procedure (such as using similar visual targets) did come very close to replicating the original effect size; those trying something different (such as using musical targets) did not.

The reasons for Milton and Wiseman's results are unclear, either in normal or paranormal terms. This suggests that the next step in the search for strong evidence of psi will involve more systematic research to identify what, if any, variables affect performance in Ganzfeld ESP studies – if ESP is, indeed, a genuine phenomenon (Milton, 2005).

SOME RECURRING PHILOSOPHICAL AND METHODOLOGICAL ISSUES

Science and truth

The 'Ganzfeld debate' is a good example of how bias, prejudice, belief and other attributes of the scientist can influence what research s/he does, and how s/he interprets the research findings of other scientists. This detracts from the *positivist* nature of science, according to which scientists discover the true, *objective* nature of the world. According to Roberts (2001), scientists claim that the relationships between events that science describes in some way mirror or approximate to events that are assumed to occur in a world that is real and exists independently of any human sensory contact with it. This is the doctrine of *scientific realism* (see Chapter 10).

In the physical sciences, there is a sense in which scientific realism must be valid, otherwise the technological applications of scientific theories and research couldn't work. Roberts gives the example of knowledge of the mathematical relationships describing motion, which enable a spacecraft to be put into orbit:

> *These mathematical descriptions are not arbitrary . . . they do not depend upon a social or public consensus that they are correct. They must fit with reality in some deep sense – otherwise the spacecraft could not remain in orbit, and the practical possibilities of satellite communications and human space travel could not be brought into being.*

However, there have been many criticisms of scientific realism and the positivist approach (see Chapter 10 for a detailed discussion). According to Roberts, a recurring issue is whether we should think of science in terms of what scientists *actually* do, or in the ideal, abstract terms of what scientists *ought* to do. As indicated above, scientific activity is influenced by many factors, personal, social and political, apart from/in addition to, the actual phenomenon under investigation: it is essentially *creative*. So, how is it possible that science 'works', as in Roberts's spacecraft example? He argues that there is an article of faith involved in science, according to which the 'laws of nature' are in principle comprehensible and consistent throughout the universe. It is difficult to contemplate how science could be 'done' at all without it. There is also a *self-correcting* tendency that helps to distinguish science from other disciplines/activities that might also lay claim to the truth: 'what is being corrected is the mismatch (or potential mismatch) between what is predicted from theory and which may be suggested by observation' (Roberts, 2001).

Is scientific study of psi possible?

The preceding discussion has in effect been about natural/physical science. So, how do scientific realism and the notion of scientific objectivity apply to psychology? These issues are discussed in detail in Chapter 10, but suffice it to say here that there are many good reasons for believing that trying to study human behaviour in the way that natural scientists investigate the physical world is a highly complex, problematical and controversial matter (see also Chapter 14). (This perhaps isn't surprising, given that science was originally invented, constructed and elaborated for the study of natural objects.) This is especially true when the 'behaviour' refers to people's self-reported experiences, such as dreams, NDEs, ESP and alien abductions. (These are, of course, the stuff of para-/anomalistic psychology.) As Roberts (2001) says, 'the private unobservable nature of human experience seems to render it unsuitable for scientific scrutiny'.

Roberts identifies two major ways of systematically investigating (reports of) paranormal experiences.

1 One strategy is to look for correlations between self-reports and other, more easily observable, phenomena, then to try to establish the conditions under which such reports are made. For example, the existence of both sleep and dreaming relies on self-reports of human participants. With sleep, the reports are validated by the appearance of particular *behavioural* or *physiological indicators* (such as brainwave patterns as measured by an electroencephalogram/EEG) linked to levels of arousal occurring immediately prior to a report. But more important as indicators of the existence of a distinct mental state are the cognitive correlates of reporting, immediately after waking (such as the detailed description of a dream). These correlates may themselves be correlated, as when eyeball movements (during rapid eye movement/REM sleep) correspond to events that supposedly occurred in the dream. This inference is supported by the fact that an overwhelming majority of people report such experiences under these conditions. But all of these data might only tell us something about the nature of the reports; by themselves they cannot establish the reality/truth of the experiences that the reports supposedly refer to.

2 Once the researchers are satisfied that a particular phenomenon is real, they might turn their attention to the actual contents of the experience, and systematically explore how it can be modified or transformed. For example, this could be done externally through drugs or sensory deprivation, or internally through acts of will or cognition.

How do we know that private experiences are real?

According to Roberts (2001):

> *Although experiences such as dreaming, remembering and consciously experiencing the world are private, we assume their veracity in others, partly through our mutual identification with them as beings like us who have the same kind of conscious experiences that we do. When it comes to claims of more esoteric experiences (e.g. alien abductions), this type of common ground simply does not exist.*

So, in these various ways, science is not opposed in any fundamental way to the study of experience. What makes science distinctive is in its *interpretative stance* towards reported experience:

> *By itself experience cannot be and is not regarded as sufficient evidence for the independent reality of what people observe. The difficulties of interpreting reports of certain experiences [especially paranormal phenomena] . . . are compounded by virtue of their frequently being presented in terms of an interpretation – an explanation of their origins – rather than an account of only the contents (the phenomenology) of the experience . . .*

In other words, reports of OBEs, ESP and other paranormal experiences are usually made in terms that presuppose the causes behind them. For example, 'OBEs are caused by the mind leaving the body,' or 'People share common thoughts, etc., because thought transmission takes place between them.'

We need to disentangle the process by which people arrive at an interpretation of their experience and just what it was they originally experienced. In the case of people claiming to have seen ghosts, for example, closer questioning should lead to a distinction between (i) perceived physical sensations (such as coldness) and psychological sensations (such as fear or anxiety) experienced at the location; and (ii) the subsequent attribution that these are causally linked to someone having died there. Roberts believes that the psychology of attribution can help shed light not just on the 'wild and wonderful' experiences people report, but also on their beliefs about how the world is structured (see Gross, 2005).

Are paranormal experiences a special case?

Roberts (2001) argues that:

> *The correct attitude of the scientists faced with reports of unusual experiences is to seek further evidence for or against the existence of such experiences. It does not mean that such accounts must necessarily be dismissed. Absence of evidence is not of course the same as evidence of absence . . .*

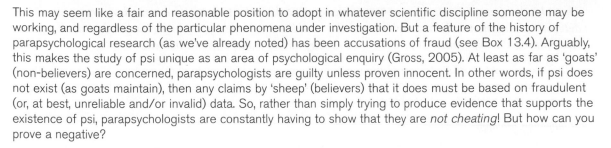

This may seem like a fair and reasonable position to adopt in whatever scientific discipline someone may be working, and regardless of the particular phenomena under investigation. But a feature of the history of parapsychological research (as we've already noted) has been accusations of fraud (see Box 13.4). Arguably, this makes the study of psi unique as an area of psychological enquiry (Gross, 2005). At least as far as 'goats' (non-believers) are concerned, parapsychologists are guilty unless proven innocent. In other words, if psi does not exist (as goats maintain), then any claims by 'sheep' (believers) that it does must be based on fraudulent (or, at best, unreliable and/or invalid) data. So, rather than simply trying to produce evidence that supports the existence of psi, parapsychologists are constantly having to show that they are *not cheating*! But how can you prove a negative?

The history of PP also seems to highlight a number of methodological issues, which, while they recur throughout all areas of psychological research, assume a more exaggerated or extreme form in relation to psi. According to Rao and Palmer (1987), these include:

- the question of the '*conclusive experiment*'
- the *replication problem*
- *publication bias* (or the '*file-drawer*' *problem*)
- the *inadequacy of controls*
- *experimenter* and *participant effects*.

The question of the 'conclusive experiment'

According to Abelson (1978, in Rao and Palmer), the editor of *Science*, 'extraordinary claims require extraordinary evidence'. This implies that the strength of evidence needed to establish a new phenomenon is directly proportional to how incompatible the phenomenon is with our current beliefs about the world. If we reject the possibility of this new phenomenon (its *subjective probability* is zero), then no amount of empirical evidence will be sufficient to establish the claim. However, as Rao and Palmer point out:

> . . . *In serious scientific discourse . . . few would be expected to take a zero-probability stance because such a stance could be seen to be sheer dogmatism, and the very antithesis of the basic assumption of science's open-endedness.*

Abelson's 'extraordinary evidence' sometimes means, in practice, demands for a 'foolproof' experiment that would control for all conceivable kinds of error, including experimenter fraud. This assumes that at any given time, one can identify all possible sources of error and how to control for them. According to Rao and Palmer:

> . . . *The concept of a 'conclusive' experiment, totally free of any possible error or fraud and immune to all sceptical doubt, is a practical impossibility for empirical phenomena. In reality, evidence in science is a matter of degree . . . a 'conclusive' experiment [should] be defined more modestly as one in which it is highly improbable that the result is artifactual . . .*

In other words, there are *no absolutes* in science (no certainty, no once-and-for-all 'proof'), only *probabilities*; in *this* latter sense, Rao and Palmer believe that a case can be made for 'conclusive' experiments in PP. What might such an experiment be?

In a typical PK study, a computer might be connected to a micro-electronic random-event generator (REG) (e.g. Schmidt, 1969, in Rao and Palmer) or random-number generator (RNG) that by chance alone would produce two different outcomes equally often. The equipment is arranged so that each of the two outcomes is associated with a different event that the participant witnesses. For example, one outcome might lead to a light bulb getting brighter, the other to it becoming dimmer. The participant's task might be to try mentally to make the light bulb become brighter; his/her performance would be measured in terms of how often this happened above the 50 per cent chance baseline. According to Henry (2005b):

These kinds of experiment offer an automated protocol, as the targets . . . are random and determined automatically by machine and the results are recorded without human intervention . . . Automating the experimental protocol in this way makes fraud difficult indeed.

The REG experiment represents one of the major experimental paradigms in contemporary PP, it is regarded by most researchers as providing good evidence for psi, and it has been closely scrutinized by critics. Despite this – and almost inevitably – it *has* been criticized.

The replication problem

This has been addressed above in relation to the use of MAs as a way of assessing the validity of PP research (see Box 13. 5). Rao and Palmer argue that science is concerned with establishing general laws, not unique events. (This relates to the *idiographic-nomothetic* debate: see Chapter 3). The ability to repeat an experiment would seem to be a reasonable thing to demand of a field aiming to achieve scientific respectability (*New Scientist*, 2004).

However, many sceptics argue that only 'replication on demand' (*absolute* replication) can produce conclusive proof of psi. According to Rao and Palmer, an experiment isn't either replicable or not replicable, but rather it is on a continuum:

In this sense of statistical replication, an experiment or an effect may be considered replicated if a series of replication attempts provides statistically significant evidence for the original effect when analyzed as a series.

In other words, does the evidence *overall/as a whole* support the existence of the effect being investigated? *On balance,* does the accumulated evidence based on a large number of replication attempts point towards the existence of psi, or not?

However, while this is fine in principle, in practice it's proved impossible to reach any kind of consensus. As we have seen, different MAs can reach different conclusions, despite them (supposedly) following the same 'rules'. But there are times when different MAs are clearly following different rules. For example, four different MAs were conducted of the 30 Ganzfeld experiments reported between 1995 and 1999. Two of these MAs concluded that the findings were significant, while the other two concluded that they weren't. The biggest discrepancy between them was the inclusion (or not) of a hugely successful study by Dalton (1997) carried out at Edinburgh University. It was omitted from two of the MAs on the grounds that it was an 'outlier': because its results were so much better than any others, it should be discounted (an accepted practice in MA). However, another accepted practice is that MAs must use all available data. So, Dalton's study was included in the other two MAs (*New Scientist*, 2004). So much for scientific objectivity!

Rao and Palmer argue that, once we abandon the idea of 'replication on demand', parapsychological phenomena have been replicated in a statistically significant sense. Also, many parapsychologists claim that any failure to replicate should be taken as a positive result: it confirms what they knew all along, namely, that paranormal phenomena are inherently elusive. You cannot expect to pin them down in the laboratory (*New Scientist*, 2004).

Publication bias (or the 'file-drawer' problem)

This too was discussed in Box 13.5 in relation to MA. Consistent with the discussion of individual MAs above, Rao and Palmer claim that the 'file-drawer' problem cannot explain away the significant number of replications in PP. But isn't it impossible ever to establish how many studies have been 'binned'? Some answers are provided in Box 13.7.

BOX 13.7 SOLVING THE 'FILE-DRAWER' PROBLEM

- Parapsychologists are more sensitive to the possible impact of unreported negative results than most other scientists. In the USA, the Parapsychological Association (PA) has advocated publishing *all* methodologically sound experiments, regardless of the outcome. Since 1976, this policy has been reflected in publications of all affiliated journals (such as the *Journal of Parapsychology*) and in papers presented at annual PA conventions.
- There are relatively few parapsychologists, and most are aware of ongoing work in the various laboratories around the world. When conducting an MA, they actively seek out unpublished negative studies at conventions and through personal networks.
- There are also some areas where we can be reasonably certain we have access to *all* the experiments conducted; for example, research into the relationship between ESP performance and ratings obtained on the Defence Mechanism Test (DMT: Kragh and Smith, 1979, in Rao and Palmer, 1987). Because the administration and scoring of the test require specialized training available to only a few individuals, it is relatively easy to keep track of the relevant experiments.

(Based on Atkinson et al., *1990; Rao and Palmer, 1987)*

The inadequacy of controls

According to Alcock (1981), replication of an experimental result by other experimenters:

. . . does not assure that experimental artifacts were not responsible for the results in the replication as well as in the original experiment.

This is perhaps like saying that 'two wrongs don't make a right'. While it is true that replicating an effect implies nothing directly about its cause, it is also a basic premise of experimental science that replication reduces the plausibility of *some* causal explanations, especially those related to the honesty or competence of individual experimenters (Rao and Palmer, 1987). As Alcock himself says in another context:

It is not enough for a researcher to report his observations with respect to a phenomenon; he could be mistaken, or even dishonest. But if other people, using his methodology, can independently produce the same results, it is much more likely that error and dishonesty are not responsible for them.

Experimenter effects

The experimental system in PP research is a particularly 'open' one. Whenever human participants are involved, they will try to make sense of the experimental situation, which includes trying to work out the aims of the experiment and their role in relation to the aims – they look for the *demand characteristics* in the experimental situation (Orne, 1962; see Chapter 10). The usual 'blind' methods used to prevent or limit the experimenter's unintentional influence on the participants' behaviour do not apply here. If ESP really exists, can the participant read the experimenter's mind? Can the experimenter use PK to directly influence delicate physical instruments? If this is possible, the experimental environment is even more open than was previously thought. Watt (2001) states that:

If psi is a genuine effect, this has the startling implication that all research is vulnerable to unintended exchange of information and influence.

It might be impossible to use completely blind methods, because these could be penetrated by ESP.

While this does not invalidate all experimental research, it means that researchers have to learn more about its limiting conditions. In general, researchers must become more sophisticated in developing strategies to deal with the study of complex open systems. Parapsychologists are particularly well placed to develop this expertise, as the question of experimenter influence has a particularly high profile. It is already well established that certain experimenters consistently obtain positive results (*psi-permissive* experimenters), while others consistently obtain non-significant results (*psi-inhibitory* experimenters). While this could be just a chance pattern, some critics have suggested that the former are either fraudulent or sloppy. However, there's no consistent evidence to support this claim. Another possibility is that PP's experimenter effects are due to experimenter psi, with some particularly psychic experimenters able to influence a study's outcome according to their desires and expectations (Watt, 2001).

The experimenter effect (EE) is one of PP's longest-standing controversies. This is largely due to the 'Heads I win, tails you lose' interpretation that many 'sheep' place on the findings regarding experimenter differences described above. The fact that positive results are obtained by experimenters with psi abilities – but not by those without – 'proves' that psi exists. Rather than being a confounding variable as 'goats' would claim, believers argue that EEs in the context of parapsychological research actually *demonstrates* the phenomenon under investigation.

According to Palmer, of the Rhine Research Centre (in McCrone, 2004), 'the strongest predictor of ESP results generally is the identity of the experimenter'. The EE is now the object of intense research, with new explanations emerging. For example, some parapsychologists claim that it arises not through experimenters' influence over mind or matter, but because they use their extra-sensory powers to pick the right moments to sample a fluctuating process and catch any 'fluky', but natural, departures from randomness (McCrone, 2004).

CONCLUSIONS: PARANORMAL PHENOMENA, THE MIND–BRAIN RELATIONSHIP AND THE LIMITS OF SCIENCE

Underlying accounts of psi is the notion of minds affecting other minds (as in ESP) or matter (as in PK), which is exactly what our common-sense beliefs about free will (see Chapter 11) and consciousness (see Chapter 12) maintain. If it could be shown that psi exists:

> Not only would strictly mechanistic models of psychology – such as Skinnerian behaviourism – have to be scrapped, but many of the assumptions and theories of physical science would need at least to be thoroughly overhauled . . .
>
> *(Evans, 1987b)*

The popular view is that if ESP exists, it proves that mental phenomena are *non-local* (independent of space and time). If PK exists, it proves that mind can reach out beyond brain to affect things at a distance (Blackmore, 1996). However, not all parapsychologists are necessarily *dualists*, believing in the mind-matter distinction, just as they are not necessarily 'believers' (Beloff, 1987). Blackmore is a parapsychologist who regards psi as a function of the brain (see Gross, 2008; Gross and Rolls, in press).

If you equate mind with consciousness, then, hey presto, ESP and PK prove the 'power of consciousness' (a view that Blackmore strongly rejects: see Chapter 12). She argues that it is a wish to demonstrate this power that fuels much of the enthusiasm for the paranormal.

Whether or not you agree with Blackmore, it seems difficult to disagree with Matthews (2004), who claims that science alone cannot give us what we seek – an objective view of reality. As he says:

> More than any other scientific discipline, parapsychology pushes the scientific process to its limits and reveals where its faults lie. In particular, it has highlighted that, contrary to the insistence of many scientists, data alone can never settle this or any other issue.

SUMMARY

○ Paranormal or anomalous phenomena are those that defy explanation in terms of currently available scientific knowledge. Parapsychology (PP) is the scientific study of these phenomena, collectively called psi.

○ Extra-sensory perception (ESP) refers to telepathy, clairvoyance and precognition. Other examples of paranormal phenomena include psychokinesis (PK), apparitions and anomalous/exceptional experience (such as near-death experiences (NDEs)).

○ PP grew out of spiritualism, which stimulated 'psychical research' and which was popular among many Victorian scientists. The Rhines wanted to put this research on a respectable scientific footing.

○ Throughout PP's history, parapsychologists have been accused of fraud, which makes the study of psi unique as an area of psychological investigation.

○ Anomalistic psychology (AP) attempts to understand paranormal/bizarre experiences in terms of known psychological and physical factors, without assuming there is anything paranormal involved. But it allows for the possibility that paranormal forces do exist.

○ Most psychologists are goats, believing that paranormal phenomena do not merit serious study. But this narrow-minded view is being challenged as PP and AP research expands.

○ Early studies of ESP involved the use of Zener cards. Despite experiments using these cards becoming more tightly controlled, the results have always been disputed and their interpretation controversial. An alternative method is free-response ESP, such as remote viewing.

○ The most successful free-response method has been the Ganzfeld. This involves reduced sensory input combined with increased internal attention.

○ The Ganzfeld represents a standardized experimental procedure, which has generated many studies since 1974, resulting in the famous 'Ganzfeld debate' in 1985. The outcome was a fully automated Ganzfeld. But the debate continues.

○ In the physical/natural sciences, the doctrine of scientific realism must be valid, otherwise technological applications of scientific theories could not work. But scientific activity is driven by many factors other than the phenomenon under investigation, and is essentially creative.

○ Science only works because of an article of faith regarding the laws of nature, plus a self-correcting tendency that helps to distinguish science from other attempts to discover the truth.

○ Trying to apply scientific realism to psychology is problematical and controversial, especially when the subject matter consists of people's self-reports of paranormal experiences. Looking for correlations between self-reports and more objective, observable phenomena (behavioural/physiological/cognitive) is one solution, although this cannot by itself establish the reality of the reported experiences.

○ A problem with establishing the reality of paranormal experiences is that they are often described in terms of an interpretation which presupposes their causes. We need to disentangle the process by which people interpret their experience from the original experience.

○ The history of PP highlights certain methodological issues that recur throughout psychological research as a whole, in particular the 'conclusive experiment' question, the replication problem, publication bias/the file-drawer problem, the inadequacy of controls, and experimenter/participant effects.

275

○ Meta-analysis (MA) is a widely used statistical technique which allows the synthesis of large numbers of different studies. Some of its advantages over traditional research reviews include its ability to provide a file-drawer estimate and calculation of the percentage of experiments and experimenters obtaining significant results (the replicability of psi).

USEFUL WEBSITES

www.skeptic.org.uk
www.parapsychology.org/
www.rhine.org/
www.psiresearch.org/para1.html
www.goldsmiths.ac.uk/apru
http://moebius.psy.ed.ac.uk
www.spr.ac.uk
www.iands.org

RECOMMENDED READING

Blackmore, S. (1993) *Dying to Live: Science and the Near-Death Experience.* London: Grafton.

Gross, R. (2008) *Key Studies in Psychology* (5th edn). London: Hodder Education. (Chapter 21.)

Henry, J. (ed.) (2005) *Parapsychology: Research on Exceptional Experiences.* London: Routledge.

Rao, K.R. and Palmer, J. (1987) The anomaly called psi: recent research and criticism. *Behavioral and Brain Sciences, 10*, 539–643.

Roberts, R. and Groome, D. (eds) (2001) *Parapsychology: The Science of Unusual Experience.* London: Arnold. (Especially Chapters 1, 3, 4, 6, 10 and 12.)

CHAPTER 14

THEORETICAL APPROACHES TO PSYCHOLOGY

Different psychologists make different assumptions about the particular aspects of a person that are worthy of study, reflecting an underlying model or image of what people are like. In turn, this model or image determines a view of the nature of development, preferred methods of study, the nature of psychological normality, the major cause(s) of abnormality, and the preferred methods and goals of treatment. However, not all of these apply to all theoretical approaches.

An approach is a perspective that is not as clearly outlined as a theory and that:

> . . . provides a general orientation to a view of humankind. It says, in effect, 'we see people as operating according to these basic principles and we therefore see explanations of human behaviour as needing to be set within these limits and with these or those principles understood'.
>
> (Coolican et al., 1996)

As we shall see, most of the major approaches include two or more distinguishable theories or strands but, within an approach, they share certain basic principles and assumptions that give them a distinct 'flavour' or identity. The focus here is on the behaviourist, psychodynamic, humanistic, cognitive, social constructionist and evolutionary psychological approaches.

While particular approaches have dominated psychology at different times in its history (see Chapter 11), and although some appear to be complementary, Coolican et al., 2007 warn us against regarding them as all equally 'valid':

> Many uncomplimentary words have been uttered, and even careers lost, in the frequently bitter battles between the different 'schools' of psychology.

THE BEHAVIOURIST APPROACH

Basic principles and assumptions

Watson's methodological behaviourism

According to Skinner (1974):

> The first explicit behaviourist was John B. Watson, who in 1913 issued a kind of manifesto called Psychology as the Behaviourist Views It. As the title shows, he was not proposing a new science but arguing that psychology should be redefined as the study of behaviour . . . Most of the psychologists at the time believed they were studying mental processes in a mental world of consciousness, and

they were naturally not inclined to agree with Watson. Early behaviourists wasted a good deal of time, and confused an important issue, by attacking the introspective study of mental life.

Watson (1913) claimed that only by modelling itself on the natural sciences could psychology legitimately call itself a science. He argued for a certain type of behaviourism, namely *methodological behaviourism*: only events/phenomena that can be *intersubjectively verified* (that is, agreed upon by two or more people) are suitable for scientific investigation. Cognition, thinking, believing, feeling, pain and so on are private events and so are not accessible to anyone else. Therefore, they should be excluded from a science of psychology.

In this sense, what was revolutionary about Watson's behaviourist manifesto has become almost taken-for-granted, 'orthodox' psychology. It could be argued that all psychologists are methodological behaviourists (Blackman, 1980). Belief in the importance of empirical methods, especially the experiment, as a way of collecting data about humans (and non-humans), which can be quantified and statistically analysed, is a major feature of mainstream psychology (see Chapter 10).

Skinner's radical behaviourism

Skinner, generally regarded as the arch-behaviourist, rejected Watson's insistence on 'truth by agreement'. According to his *radical behaviourism*, cognitions are covert behaviours ('within the skin') that should be studied by psychologists along with overt behaviours (capable of being observed by two/more people). He *was not* 'against cognitions' but said that:

so-called mental activities are metaphors or explanatory fictions and . . . behaviour attributed to them can be more effectively explained in other ways.

For Skinner, these more effective explanations of behaviour come in the form of the principles of reinforcement derived from his experimental work with rats and pigeons. What is 'radical' about Skinner's radical behaviourism is the claim that feelings, sensations and other private events cannot be used to explain behaviour but are to *be explained* in an analysis of behaviour (*behaviour analysis*). Since private events cannot be manipulated, they cannot serve as independent variables, but they can serve as dependent variables. Some recent studies of consciousness seem to support Skinner's claim that our common-sense belief that we will our actions is an illusion (see Chapter 11).

Leslie (2002) argues that cognitive psychological theories are doomed to fail, a distraction or blind alley, arising from a mistaken assumption about the necessary features of psychological explanation:

The mistake is to assume that behaviour (what someone does) is necessarily caused by cognition (what the person thinks). Behaviour analysis instead states that both overt (visible) behaviour and the other apparently 'private' aspects of human psychology arise from interaction with the environment . . .

While methodological behaviourism proposes to ignore such inner states (they are *inaccessible*), Skinner ignores them only as variables used for explaining behaviour (they are *irrelevant*) and argues that they can be translated into the language of reinforcement theory (Garrett, 1996). According to Nye (2000), Skinner's ideas are also radical because he applied the same type of analysis to both covert (thoughts and feelings) behaviour occurring 'within the skin' and overt, publicly observable behaviours.

Skinner stressed the importance of identifying *functional relations* between environmental conditions and behaviours. According to Leslie (2002):

. . . the psychology of an individual consists primarily of an account of those functionally defined behavioural characteristics that occur in the environments typically encountered by that individual.

A person, if you like, is primarily to be understood as 'what he or she does' and that account of their behaviour cannot . . . be described without also describing the location or occasion of those behaviours and the important consequences of those behaviours . . .

From the perspective of behaviour analysis, the key process of psychological change is *operant conditioning*:

. . . whereby those behaviours that are functionally effective for the individual become more frequent (in the corresponding environment) while other behaviours decline in frequency . . .

(Leslie, 2002)

The behaviour is not caused by either the individual or the environment. Rather:

. . . it is the history of interaction between the behavioural repertoire of the individual (that is, the whole range of behaviours shown by the person) and the environment that selects, and in a sense causes, the behaviour . . .

(Leslie, 2002)

Skinner also saw his brand of behaviourism as a thorough-going, 'deep' behaviourism (O'Donohue and Ferguson, 2001):

Behaviourism is not the science of human behaviour; it is the philosophy of that science. Some of the questions it asks are these: Is such a science really possible? Can it account for every aspect of human behaviour? What methods can it use? Are its laws as valid as those of physics and biology? Will it lead to a technology, and if so, what role will it play in human affairs?

(Skinner, 1974)

So, radical behaviourism *is not* a scientific law or set of empirical findings. It is *meta-scientific* – that is, it attempts to define what a science of behaviour should look like. The questions that Skinner asks are essentially philosophical. According to O'Donohue and Ferguson (2001):

radical behaviourism is a philosophy of science, or more exactly, a philosophy of psychology. Skinner calls the science based on this philosophy the experimental analysis of behaviour or behaviour analysis.

Given this important distinction between methodological and radical behaviourism, we need to consider some principles and assumptions that apply to behaviourism *in general*. These are described in Box 14.1 (page 280).

Theoretical contributions

Behaviourism made a massive contribution to psychology, at least up to the 1950s, and explanations of behaviour in conditioning terms recur throughout psychology. For example, apart from learning and conditioning, imagery as a form of organization in memory and as a memory aid is based on the principle of association, and the interference theory of forgetting is largely couched in S–R terms. Language, moral and gender development have all been explained in terms of conditioning, and some influential theories of the formation and maintenance of relationships focus on the concept of reinforcement. The behaviourist approach also offers one of the major models of abnormal behaviour. (Skinner's notorious views on free will are discussed in detail in Chapter 11.)

As with Freud's psychoanalytic theory (see below), theorists and researchers critical of the original, 'orthodox' theories have modified and built on them, making a huge contribution in the process. Noteworthy examples are Tolman's (1948) *cognitive behaviourism* and *social learning theory* (mainly associated with Bandura and

BOX 14.1 BASIC PRINCIPLES AND ASSUMPTIONS MADE BY THE BEHAVIOURIST APPROACH

- Behaviourists emphasize the role of *environmental factors* in influencing behaviour, often to the (apparent) exclusion of innate or inherited factors (see Chapter 5). Ironically, however, Skinner saw psychology as a branch of *biology* and was heavily influenced by Darwin's theory of evolution. The environment selects certain behaviours over others, and this determines their frequency in future generations. *Operant conditioning* is itself an evolutionary adaptation: the ability to learn from the consequences of behaviour is an evolutionary development that proved advantageous. *Classical conditioning* is another learning mechanism that evolution has produced (O'Donohue and Ferguson, 2001).

- Behaviourism is often referred to as 'S–R' (stimulus–response) psychology. However, the stimulus and response relationship can be defined in fundamentally different ways. Only in classical conditioning is the stimulus seen as triggering a response in a predictable, automatic way, and this is what's conveyed by 'S–R' psychology. Therefore, it is a mistake to describe operant conditioning as an 'S–R' approach. However, the two forms of conditioning, together, are referred to as '(classical) learning theory'.

- Part of Watson's rejection of introspectionism was his belief that it invoked too many vague concepts that are difficult, if not impossible, to define and measure. According to the *law of parsimony* (or 'Occam's razor'), the fewer assumptions a theory makes, the better (more 'economical' explanations are superior).

- The mechanisms proposed by a theory should be as simple as possible. Behaviourists stress the use of *operational definitions* (defining concepts in terms of observable, measurable, events).

- The aim of a science of behaviour is to *predict* and *control* behaviour. This raises both conceptual questions (about the nature of science – in particular, the role of theory: see Chapter 10) and ethical questions (for example, about power and the role of psychologists as agents of change: see Chapter 9).

Mischel). O'Donohue and Ferguson (2001) state that 'behaviourism is not an unequivocal term but rather describes a family of different philosophies'. They claim that, given the variety of forms of behaviourism, Watson's and Skinner's influence is less than you would think.

Practical contributions

Methodological behaviourism's emphasis on experimentation, operational definitions and the measurement of observable events (see Box 14.1) has had a major influence on the practice of scientific psychology in general, quite unrelated to any views about the nature and role of mental events. Other, more 'tangible' contributions include the following:

- *Behaviour therapy* and *behaviour modification* (based on classical and operant conditioning respectively) are major approaches to the treatment of abnormal behaviour (see Chapter 10) and one of the main tools in the clinical psychologist's 'kit bag'. The ethics of some forms of behaviour modification (such as the *token economy*), and certain aspects of *applied behaviour analysis* (especially the use of punishment with vulnerable individuals), have been seriously questioned (see Chapter 9).

- *Behavioural neuroscience* is an interdisciplinary field of study, using behavioural techniques to understand brain function and neuroscientific techniques to elucidate behavioural processes. While many believe that behaviour can be reduced to/explained by brain processes, the evidence shows that each is dependent on the other (Leslie, 2002: see Chapter 12).

- *Behavioural pharmacology* involves the use of *schedules of reinforcement* to assess the behavioural effects of new drugs that modify brain activity. Most importantly, the research has illustrated how many behavioural effects of drugs are determined as much by the current behaviour and reinforcement contingencies as by the effects of the drug on the brain (Leslie, 2002).

- *Environmental enrichment studies* have produced evidence for *neuronal plasticity* – the brain's capacity for change and adapting to changing environmental conditions. These findings have exciting implications for the treatment of strokes and other conditions involving brain damage. According to Leslie:

> *The life-long interaction between the behaviour of the individual and the environment produces changes in the brain. This in turn changes behaviour, and so the interaction goes on. Any attempt to deal with a human behavioural problem can involve changes to the nervous system, behaviour or the environment.*

- *Biofeedback* as a non-medical treatment for stress-related symptoms, derived from attempts to change rats' autonomic physiological functions through operant conditioning.
- *Teaching machines and programmed learning*, which now commonly take the form of *computer-assisted learning* (CAL).

An evaluation of behaviourism

Central to Skinner's experimental analysis of behaviour is the famous 'Skinner box', the 'auto-environmental chamber' in which rats' and pigeons' environments can be totally controlled by the experimenter. It has been used with many species, emitting a wide range of operant responses producing a variety of consequences. Yet the same behavioural processes are revealed in all the experiments; many of these can be summarized as operant conditioning (Leslie, 2002). A rat pressing a lever was intended to be equivalent to a cat operating an escape latch in Thorndike's puzzle box (1898), so counting the number of lever presses (the *response rate*) became the standard measure of operant learning.

Despite Skinner's claims to not having a theory, 'the response' in operant conditioning has largely considered only the frequency of behaviour, ignoring intensity, duration and quality. As Glassman (1995) observes:

> *While the focus on frequency was a practical consideration, it eventually became part of the overall conceptual framework as well – a case of research methods directing theory.*

But in everyday life, frequency is not always the most meaningful aspect of behaviour. For example, should we judge an author's worth by how many books s/he publishes, rather than their content?

Skinner's claim that human behaviour can be predicted and controlled in the same way as the behaviour of non-humans is usually only accepted by other behaviour analysts. Possessing language allows us to communicate with each other and to think about 'things' that have never been observed (and may not even exist), including rules, laws and principles (Garrett, 1996). While these can only be expressed in words, or thought about through words, much of people's behaviour is governed by them. According to Garrett, when this happens, 'behaviour is now shaped by what goes on inside their [people's] heads . . . and not simply by what goes on in the external environment'.

So, what people think is among the important variables determining what they do and say, the very opposite of what Skinner's radical behaviourism claims. However, behaviour analysts recognize the limitations of their approach. For example, Leslie (2002) admits that 'operant conditioning cannot provide a complete account of psychology from a behavioural perspective, even in principle'. Leslie argues that classical conditioning, modelling and verbal instruction all help produce variation of behaviour, which is vital if selection is to occur.

O'Donohue and Ferguson (2001) acknowledge that the science of behaviour cannot account for creative behaviour, as in music, literature and science. Environmental selection as identified by Skinner merely sets parameters on the range of responding – it does not tell us where the novel behaviour comes from in the first place. However, they contend that his psychology is solidly based on hard facts and that 'the science of behaviour has more empirical evidence supporting its claims than any other area in psychology'.

The impact of behaviourism

According to Richards (2002), it was for a long time believed that behaviourism represented the most advanced 'paradigm' for experimental psychology. But while it certainly pervaded the intellectual atmosphere of American psychology, 'it never in fact dominated psychological practice to the extent which is often claimed'.

Most American researchers between 1918 and 1939 were what Richards calls 'eclectic functionalists', still inclined to include 'experience' alongside 'behaviour' as part of psychology's subject matter. But its impact went beyond theory to influence the whole way of conducting and reporting research (i.e. methodological behaviourism). However, by the 1950s, the tide was turning against behaviourism in favour of cognitive psychology (see below). Richards claims that:

> . . . behaviourism should be considered not so much as a theory in itself but as a conceptual framework in which theorizing could be undertaken; a 'unified discourse' and set of methodological practices within which propositions could be formulated and theoretical debates conducted and, hopefully, settled.

This echoes Skinner's own view of radical behaviourism as a philosophy of psychology (see above).

Richards sees behaviourism as leaving behind one of two main images of the psychologist in popular culture, namely the white-coated scientist running rats round mazes, discovering cunning ways to control behaviour ('human beings are maze-bound rats'), and the expert in behavioural control who is subtly affecting our lives using scientific techniques that we're unaware of. He concludes by saying:

> . . . as with all psychological doctrines, behaviourism's impact is a psychological fact in its own right and the concepts and images of human nature which it yielded have, for better or worse, irreversibly entered our culture.

> (Richards, 2002)

THE PSYCHODYNAMIC APPROACH

The term 'psychodynamic' denotes the active forces within the personality that motivate behaviour, and the inner causes of behaviour (in particular the *unconscious conflict* between the different structures that compose the whole personality). While Freud's was the original psychodynamic theory, the approach includes all those theories based on his ideas, such as those of Jung (1964), Adler (1927) and Erikson (1950). Freud's *psychoanalytic theory* (sometimes called 'psychoanalysis') is psychodynamic, but the psychodynamic theories of Jung and others aren't psychoanalytic. So the two terms *are not* synonymous. However, because of their enormous influence, Freud's ideas will be emphasized in the rest of this section.

Basic principles and assumptions

Freud's concepts are closely interwoven, making it difficult to know where their description should begin (Jacobs, 1992). Fortunately, Freud himself stressed acceptance of certain key theories as essential to the practice of psychoanalysis, the form of psychotherapy he pioneered and from which most others are derived (see Box 14.2).

Theoretical contributions

As with behaviourist accounts of conditioning, many of Freud's ideas and concepts have become part of mainstream psychology's vocabulary. You do not have to be a 'Freudian' to use concepts such as 'repression', 'unconscious', and so on, and many of the vast number of studies of different aspects of the theory have been

> **BOX 14.2** THE MAJOR PRINCIPLES AND ASSUMPTIONS OF PSYCHOANALYTIC THEORY

- Much of our behaviour is determined by *unconscious* thoughts, wishes, memories and so on. What we are consciously aware of at any one time represents the tip of an iceberg: most of our thoughts and feelings are either not accessible at that moment (*pre-conscious*) or are totally inaccessible (*unconscious*). These unconscious thoughts and feelings can become conscious through the use of special techniques, such as *free association*, *dream interpretation* and *transference*, the cornerstones of psychoanalysis.
- Much of what is unconscious has been made so through *repression*, whereby threatening or unpleasant experiences are 'forgotten'. They become inaccessible, locked away from our conscious awareness. This is a major form of *ego defence*. Freud singled it out as a special cornerstone 'on which the whole structure of psychoanalysis rests. It is the most essential part of it' (Freud, 1914). Repression is closely related to *resistance*, interpretation of which is another key technique used in psychoanalysis.
- According to the *theory of infantile sexuality*, the sexual instinct, or drive, is active from birth and develops through a series of five *psychosexual stages*. The most important of these is the *phallic stage* (spanning the ages three to five/six), during which all children experience the Oedipus complex. In fact, Freud used the German word *Trieb*, which translates as 'drive', rather than *Instinkt*, which was meant to imply that experience played a crucial role in determining the 'fate' of sexual (and aggressive) energy.
- Related to infantile sexuality is the general *impact of early experience* on later personality (see Gross, 2005). According to Freud (1949):

> *It seems that the neuroses are only acquired during early childhood (up to the age of six), even though their symptoms may not make their appearance until much later . . . the child is psychologically father of the man and . . . the events of its first years are of paramount importance for its whole subsequent life.*

conducted by critics hoping to discredit it (such as Eysenck and Wilson, 1973, and Eysenck, 1985: see Gross, 2005, 2008).

Also like behaviourist theories, Freud's can be found throughout psychology as a whole. His contribution is extremely rich and diverse, offering theories of motivation, dreams, forgetting, attachment and the effects of early experience (see Chapter 9), moral and gender development, aggression and abnormality (Chapter 7). Psychoanalytic theory has also influenced Gould's (1978) theory of the evolution of adult consciousness, and Adorno *et al.*'s (1950) authoritarian personality theory (a major account of prejudice).

Finally, and as noted earlier, Freud's theories have stimulated the development of alternative theories, often resulting from the rejection of some of his fundamental principles and assumptions, but reflecting his influence enough for them to be described as psychodynamic.

Some major alternative psychodynamic theories

- *Ego psychology*, promoted by Freud's daughter, Anna, focused on the mechanisms used by the ego to deal with the world, especially the ego defence mechanisms. Freud, by contrast, stressed the influence of the id's innate drives (especially sexuality and aggression) and is often described as an instinct theorist (but see the third point in Box 14.2). The ego, as well as the id, originates in basic human inheritance and has its own developmental course. It uses *neutralized* (non-sexual) energy, which makes possible an interest in objects and activities that aren't necessarily related to underlying sexual and aggressive drives.

According to Nye (2000), the increased attention given to an independent ego has probably resulted partly from a change in the types of patient psychoanalysts are treating. In recent years, patients have tended more often to be troubled by the problems of an increasingly complex society (vague anxieties, insecurities and dissatisfaction), and are seeking ways to find meaning and value in work, family and social roles:

> *Since the ego is the part of the personality that must deal with the external world in some rational, decision-making way, it seems natural that more emphasis should be given to it. Perhaps for the contemporary patient it is important to focus more attention on conscious thought processes and coping mechanisms; he or she is less likely to be plagued by unconscious guilt and repressed sexuality than by the uncertainties and rootlessness of modern society that requires the ego to grapple with existential problems.*

> *(Nye, 2000)*

- Erik Erikson, trained by Anna Freud as a child psychoanalyst, also stressed the importance of the ego, as well as the influence of social and cultural factors on individual development. He pioneered the *lifespan approach* to development, proposing eight *psychosocial stages*, in contrast with Freud's five *psychosexual stages* that end with physical maturity.
- Two of Freud's original 'disciples', Carl Jung and Alfred Adler, broke ranks with Freud and formed their own 'schools' (*analytical psychology* and *individual psychology* respectively). Jung attached relatively little importance to childhood experiences (and the associated *personal unconscious*) but considerable importance to the *collective* (or *racial*) *unconscious*, which stems from the evolutionary history of the human species.
- Like Jung, Adler rejected Freud's emphasis on sexuality, stressing instead the *will to power* or *striving for superiority*, which he saw as an attempt to overcome feelings of inferiority faced by all children as they grow up. He also shared Jung's view of the person as an indivisible unity or whole, and Erikson's emphasis on the social nature of human beings.
- Melanie Klein (1932) is often seen as a key transitional figure between Freud's instinct theory and the *object relations school* (see Box 14.3). Like Anna Freud, she adapted Freud's techniques (such as pioneering *play therapy*) in order to tap a young child's unconscious, and maintained that the superego and Oedipus complex appear as early as the first and second years of life.

Practical contributions

The current psychotherapy scene is highly diverse, with only a minority using Freudian techniques, but, as Fancher (1996) points out:

> *Most modern therapists use techniques that were developed either by Freud and his followers or by dissidents in explicit reaction against his theories. Freud remains a dominating figure, for or against whom virtually all therapists feel compelled to take a stand.*

Both Rogers, the major humanistic therapist, and Wolpe, who developed *systematic desensitization* (a major form of behaviour therapy), were originally trained in Freudian techniques. Perls, the founder of *Gestalt therapy*, Ellis, the founder of *rational emotive therapy* (RET) (see below) and Berne, who devised *transactional analysis* (TA), were also trained psychoanalysts.

Even Freud's fiercest critics concede his influence, not just within world psychiatry but in philosophy, literary criticism, history, theology, sociology, and art and literature generally. Freudian terminology is commonly used in conversations between therapists well beyond Freudian circles, and his influence is brought daily to therapy sessions as part of the cultural background and experience of nearly every client (Jacobs, 1992).

BOX 14.3 OBJECT RELATIONS THEORY

- The *object relations school* (the 'British school') was greatly influenced by Klein's emphasis on the infant's earliest (pre-Oedipal) relationships with its mother. It places far less emphasis on the role of instincts and more on the relationship with particular love objects (especially the mother), seeing *early relationships* as crucial for later patterns of relationships with others. Fairbairn (1952), for example, saw the aim of the libido as *object-seeking* (as opposed to pleasure-seeking), and this was extended by Bowlby (1969) in his *attachment theory* (see Gross, 2005). According to Nye (2000):

  Although both object relations theory and Freudian theory are concerned with childhood experiences and the inner world of the person, the former puts more emphasis on discrepancies between inner-world and real-world persons and situations. The latter puts more emphasis on the role of factors such as instinctual drives and unresolved Oedipus conflicts . . .

- Object relations theory refers to a number of separate ideas proposed by different theorists. However, they all stress that internal images ('representations') of one's self and of 'objects' (a technical term usually denoting another person toward whom we direct emotion and action: significant others) can have powerful effects on our relationships with others.
- Mahler (1975) and Winnicott (1958) stress the movement from the newborn's absolute dependence to the independence and autonomy of adults as the primary and lifelong developmental task. Development proceeds from symbiotic fusion with the mother, through various stages of partial differentiation of the self and other, to a state of increased individuation and independence. The internalized images of others (objects) in the infant (and the psychotic adult: see Chapter 7) are primitive, engulfing, devouring and otherwise menacing. Only when separation from the mother has been successfully achieved are we capable of empathizing with others and seeing them as they really are (rather than as projections of our primitive fantasies).

  (Based on Holmes, 1993; Nye, 2000; Zeldow, 1995)

Many mental health practitioners (including psychotherapists, counsellors and social workers), although not formally trained as psychoanalysts, have incorporated elements of Freudian thought and technique into their approaches to helping their patients (Nye, 2000).

An evaluation of the psychodynamic approach

Falsifiability and testability

A criticism repeatedly made of Freudian (and other psychodynamic) theories is that they are *unscientific* because they are *unfalsifiable* (incapable of being disproved). For example, if the Freudian prediction that 'dependent' men will prefer big-breasted women is confirmed, then the theory is supported. However, if such men actually prefer *small*-breasted women (Scodel, 1957), Freudians can use the concept of *reaction formation* (an ego defence mechanism) to argue that an unconscious fixation with big breasts may manifest itself as a conscious preference for the opposite, a clear case of 'Heads I win, tails you lose' (Eysenck, 1985; Popper, 1959). However, it is probably a mistake to see reaction formation as typical of Freudian theory as a whole.

According to Zeldow (1995), the history of science reveals that those theories that are the richest in explanatory power have proved the most difficult to test empirically. For example, Newton's Second Law could not be demonstrated in a reliable, quantitative way for 100 years, and Einstein's general theory of relativity is still untestable. Eysenck, Popper and others have criticized psychoanalytic theory for being untestable. But even if this were true:

> . . . the same thing could . . . (and should) be said about any psychological hypotheses involving complex phenomena and worthy of being tested . . . psychoanalytic theories have inspired more empirical research in the social and behavioural sciences than any other group of theories . . .
>
> (Zeldow, 1995)

Fisher and Greenberg (1996) conducted an extensive reappraisal of studies of psychoanalytic theory carried out up to the early 1990s. Agreeing with Kline (1989), they argue that Freud's theory should be evaluated in terms of a series of specific hypotheses (or mini-theories), rather than as a whole. They also believe that what should be considered are *overall trends* across studies.

While their review is extremely broad, it is not comprehensive (for example, it does not cover repression and other defence mechanisms, or transference). The strength of the evidence presented is variable and sometimes indirect, and where it is supportive it rests on Fisher and Greenberg's interpretation of the results (Andrews and Brewin, 2000). However, for Zeldow (1995) the mere existence of such reviews 'gives the lie to the notion that all psychoanalytic ideas are too vague or abstruse to be tested scientifically'.

Freud's theory provides methods and concepts that enable us to interpret and 'unpack' underlying meanings (it has great *hermeneutic strength*). Popper's and Eysenck's criticism above helps to underline the fact that these meanings (both conscious and unconscious) cannot be measured in any precise way. Freud offers a way of understanding which differs from theories that are easily testable, and it may actually be more appropriate for capturing the nature of human experience and action (Stevens, 1995). Jones and Elcock (2001) make a similar point when they say:

> Much more than most approaches in Psychology the approaches in psychoanalysis are explicitly attempting to create a framework of understanding for human experience. In common with other theories of human nature there is a degree of self-fulfilling prophecy about psychoanalysis, as terms, concepts and ideas have become integrated into our cultural common sense. Our awareness of Psychology has to some extent changed at a fundamental level our psychology, and in this psychoanalysis has been much more successful than any approach within Psychology to date.

In other words, Freud's theories are not merely *about* human behaviour and the mind, they actually help to *change* behaviour and minds. This relates to the broader issue of the nature of psychological constructs, which is discussed further in Chapter 10. (See also Box 14.4.)

Despite mainstream psychology's dismissal of much of psychoanalytic theory as unscientific (see above), Reason (2000), among others, believes that it is time to re-acknowledge Freud's greatness as a psychologist. According to Kline (1998):

> After 100 years, Freudian theory cannot be uncritically accepted just as it cannot be totally rejected. However . . . Freudian theory contains some profound observations and understanding of human behaviour. These must be incorporated into any adequate human psychology, not only its theory but also its methods . . .

How can we account for Freud's greatness?

Grayling (2002) and Richards (2002) identify several reasons for the power of Freudian ideas.

1 Freud's genius as an author and generator of ideas. He had an extraordinary ability to weave together medical knowledge, some genuine insights into the human condition and a powerful imagination. He had

BOX 14.4 IS THE UNCONSCIOUS A VALID CONCEPT?

According to Ogden (1989, in Mollon, 2000):

> *The unconscious is by definition unknowable . . . The psychoanalyst is therefore in the unfortunate position of being a student of that which cannot be known.*

But is Ogden right? Mollon sees the idea of unconscious motivation as an inference that provides an explanation for the gaps and distortions in our conscious awareness. It brings coherence to behavioural and mental data that would otherwise appear incoherent, such as slips of the tongue and other *parapraxes* ('Freudian slips') to which we are all prone. While Freud did not invent the concept of the unconscious, he was the first to investigate it systematically. Mollon says that:

> *His genius was to see that such seemingly trivial phenomena were worth studying, and moreover to recognize the link between these and other mental creations like dreams, jokes and neurotic symptoms.*

One of Freud's great 'discoveries' is that the unconscious operates according to completely different principles or 'logic' from the conscious mind. For example: (i) mutually incompatible ideas or impulses can exist without these appearing contradictory; love and hate could both be expressed at the same time unconsciously, whereas the conscious mind would experience these as conflicting; (ii) meaning may be *displaced* easily from one image to another; (iii) many different meanings may converge in one image (*condensation*); (iv) unconscious ideas and feelings are timeless; (v) the unconscious does not take account of external reality but represents internal psychic reality. Thus, dreams are perceived as real.

An exciting recent development is the convergence of psychoanalysis and neuroscience (as Freud had always hoped), forming the new discipline of *neuropsychoanalysis*. This is providing many insights into unconscious emotional processing. Basically, the right hemisphere of the brain, which specializes in visual perception, imagery and emotion, is the basis of the unconscious mind. The left hemisphere, which specializes more in linguistic and sequential/logical processing, is the basis of the conscious mind and matures slightly later than the right (see Mollon, 2000).

According to Reason (2000), Freud was probably wrong to assert that (nearly) all slips (of the tongue) are in some way intended. But he was certainly correct in claiming that 'Freudian slips' represent minor eruptions of unconscious processing. Instead of taking a strictly psychoanalytic interpretation of 'unconscious', Reason prefers one that relates to processes that are not directly accessible to consciousness, i.e. automatic processing or habitual performance (see Chapter 11).

Similarly, much of modern cognitive psychology and neuropsychology is consistent with the Freudian view that behaviour is not dependent on conscious experience (Power, 2000). One example is *blindsight* (Weiskrantz, 1986: see Chapter 12). According to Power (2000):

> *Whereas cognitive psychology has emphasised the co-operation between conscious and automatic processes (essential, for example, whilst driving), psychoanalysis has always emphasised conflict instead. The most recent models in psychology have come to consider both co-operation and conflict between conscious and unconscious processes.*

the narrative skills of a first-rate novelist, and a knack for devising striking ways to describe psychological phenomena. These included metaphors, often drawn from the science of the day.

2 The immense appeal of any theory that offers to each individual an explanation of his/her own hidden secrets. People spend far more on psychoanalysis than astrology, because it has the 'respectability' of science (but see above).

3 Psychoanalysis seemed to have finally delivered what science had failed to deliver before, namely a proper theory of human nature. Richards considers Freud's to have been the 'first thoroughly modern image of human nature'. It coincided with cultural revolutions in painting, music and literature, a common feature of which was the turning away from 'reason' to emotion. But it was the First World War that was perhaps the historically most crucial factor. This had a profound and traumatic effect on Europeans, making all previous accounts of human nature seem totally inadequate. Only after the war ended in 1918 did psychoanalysis begin to make huge inroads into popular culture and consciousness.

4 Sex was at the centre of his package, 'the most delicious, anxious and titillating of all taboos' (Grayling, 2002). Although it is a myth that sex was not discussed before Freud, 'what was distinctive was that sexual discourse (other than the frankly pornographic) was seemingly impossible unless infused with official morality or packaged as something else' (Richards, 2002), such as for medical or scientific male professionals, or in the context of seemingly scientific anthropological studies. According to Richards:

> The Freudian move was unique not only in openly discussing sex but in identifying it as the motivational force underlying all human behaviour from infancy onwards. In effect it sought to enable people to admit and confront their sexuality, identifying the primary aetiological factor in psychopathology as failure to do this . . .

5 Freud's ideas offered both lay people and professional therapists alike a path towards self-re-evaluation and exploration.

THE HUMANISTIC APPROACH

Basic principles and assumptions

As we noted earlier, Carl Rogers, one of the leading humanistic psychologists (and therapists) was trained as a psychoanalyst. Although the term 'humanistic psychology' was coined by Cohen (1958), a British psychologist, this approach emerged in the U.S. during the 1950s. Abraham Maslow (1968), in particular, gave wide currency to the term 'humanistic' in America, calling it a 'third force' (the other two being behaviourism and Freudianism). However, Maslow did not reject these approaches but hoped to unify them, thereby integrating both subjective and objective, private and public, aspects of the person, and providing a complete, holistic psychology. (See Box 14.5.)

Theoretical contributions

Maslow's *hierarchy of needs* (1954) (see Gross, 2005) distinguishes between motives shared by both humans and non-humans (*deficiency* or *D-motives*) and those that are uniquely human (*growth, being* or *B-motives*); this can be seen as an extension of the psychodynamic approach. Freud's id would represent physiological needs (at the base of the hierarchy), Horney (a major critic of the male bias in psychoanalytic theory: see Chapter 6) focused on the need for safety and love (corresponding to the next two levels), and Adler (see above) stressed esteem needs (at the fourth level). Maslow added self-actualization to the peak of the hierarchy (Glassman, 1995).

According to Rogers (1951), while awareness of being alive is the most basic of human experiences, we each fundamentally live in a world of our own creation and have a unique perception of the world (the *phenomenal field*). It is our *perception* of external reality that shapes our lives – not external reality itself. Within our phenomenal field, the most significant element is our sense of *self*, 'an organized consistent gestalt, constantly in the process of forming and reforming' (Rogers, 1959). This view contrasts with those of many other self theorists, who see it as a central, unchanging core of personality (see Chapter 4).

Rogers's contribution to the freedom versus determinism debate is discussed in Chapter 11 (pages 228–9).

BOX 14.5 SOME BASIC PRINCIPLES AND ASSUMPTIONS OF THE HUMANISTIC APPROACH

Both the behaviourist and psychoanalytic approaches are *deterministic*. People are seen as driven by forces beyond their control, either unconscious forces from within (Freud) or reinforcements from outside (Skinner). Humanistic psychologists, by contrast, believe in free will and individuals' ability to choose how they act (see Chapter 11).

A truly scientific psychology must treat its subject matter as fully human, which means acknowledging individuals as interpreters of themselves and their world. Behaviour, therefore, must be understood in terms of the individual's *subjective experience*, from the perspective of the actor. This describes a *phenomenological approach*, which explains why this is sometimes called the 'humanistic-phenomenological approach'. According to Rogers, knowledge of an individual's immediate conscious experiences/perceptions of reality is essential for understanding human behaviour. Each of us acts in accordance with our subjective awareness of ourselves and of the world around us. As Nye (2000) says:

> *The implication is that objective reality (whatever that might be) is not the important determinant of our actions; rather, we react on the basis of how we view that reality . . .*

The phenomenological approach (which Rogers used in both his therapy and research: see text below) contrasts with the positivist approach of the natural sciences, which tries to study people from the position of a detached observer. Only the individual can explain the meaning of a particular act and is the 'expert' – not the investigator or therapist.

Maslow argued that Freud supplied the 'sick half' of psychology, through his belief in the inevitability of conflict, neurosis, innate self-destructiveness and so on, while Maslow (and Rogers) stressed the 'healthy half'. Maslow saw *self-actualization* as the peak of a hierarchy of needs (see text below), while Rogers talked of the *actualizing tendency*, an intrinsic property of life, reflecting the desire to grow, develop and enhance our capacities. Although 'actualization' is not identical in Maslow's and Rogers's theories, in both cases it included the growth and fulfilment of basic potentialities. Humans are viewed as essentially growth-oriented, forward-moving and concerned with existing choices.

Rogers assumed that basic human nature is positive – there is nothing inherently negative or evil about us; personality development is positive and naturally moves towards healthy growth. He suggested that, if we are not forced into socially-constructed moulds but are accepted for what we are, we will live in ways that enhance both ourselves and society. Humans basically need and want both personal fulfilment and close, intimate relationships with others. A *fully functioning* person is the ideal of growth.

Maslow's contacts with Wertheimer and other Gestalt psychologists led him to stress the importance of understanding the *whole person*, rather than separate 'bits' of behaviour.

(Based on Glassman, 1995; Nye, 2000)

Practical contributions

By far the most significant practical influence of any humanistic psychologist is Rogers's *client-* (or *person-*) *centred therapy*. It was originally (in the 1950s) called 'client-centred' (CCT), but since the mid-1970s it has been known as 'person-centred' therapy (PCT):

> *. . . psychotherapy is the releasing of an already existing capacity in a potentially competent individual.*

> *(Rogers, 1959)*

The change in name was meant to reflect more strongly that the person, in his/her full complexity, is the centre of focus. Also, Rogers wanted to convey that his assumptions were meant to apply broadly to almost all aspects of human behaviour – not just to therapeutic settings. For example, he saw many parallels between therapists and teachers: they are both 'facilitators' of an atmosphere of freedom and support for individual pursuits (Nye, 2000). For Nye:

> *At the level at which Rogers' ideas were developed originally, in therapy, and counselling situations, his impact certainly has been significant and far-reaching. A wide range of individuals – psychotherapists, counsellors, social workers, clergy and others – have been influenced by Rogers' assumptions that, if one can be a careful and accurate listener, while showing acceptance and honesty, one can be of help to troubled persons.*

Less well known is the prolific research that Rogers undertook during the 1940s, 1950s and 1960s into this form of therapy. According to Thorne (1992):

> *This body of research constituted the most intensive investigation of psychotherapy attempted anywhere in the world up to that time . . . The major achievement of these studies was to establish beyond all question that psychotherapy could and should be subjected to the rigours of scientific enquiry.*

Rogers helped develop research designs (such as Q-sorts) which enable objective measurement of the self-concept, ideal self and their relationship over the course of therapy, as well as methodologies (such as rating scales and the use of external 'consultants') for exploring the importance of therapist qualities. These innovations continue to influence therapeutic practice, and many therapists are now concerned that their work should be subjected to research scrutiny. Research findings are now more likely than ever before to affect training procedures and clinical practice across many different therapeutic orientations (Thorne, 1992: see Gross, 2005). Rogers has been called the 'father of psychotherapy research' and his research tradition continues, with several of the most important current psychotherapy researchers affiliated with the PCT tradition (Bohart, 2003).

By emphasizing the therapist's personal qualities (*genuineness/authenticity/congruence*, *unconditional positive regard* and *empathic understanding*), Rogers opened up psychotherapy to psychologists and contributed to the development of therapy provided by non-medically qualified therapists (lay therapy). This is especially significant in the USA, where (until recently) psychoanalysts had to be psychiatrists (medically qualified). Rogers originally used the term 'counselling' as a strategy for silencing psychiatrists who objected to psychologists practising 'psychotherapy'. In the UK, the outcome of Rogers's campaign has been the evolution of a counselling profession whose practitioners are drawn from a wide variety of disciplines, with neither psychiatrists nor psychologists dominating. Counselling skills are used in a variety of settings throughout education, the health professions, social work, industry and commerce, the armed services and international organizations (Thorne, 1992).

An evaluation of the humanistic approach

According to Wilson *et al.* (1996), the humanistic approach is not an elaborate or comprehensive theory of personality, but should be seen as a set of uniquely personal theories of living created by humane people optimistic about human potential. It has wide appeal to those who seek an alternative to the more mechanistic, deterministic theories.

Like Freud's psychoanalytic theory, many of its concepts are difficult to test empirically (such as self-actualization), and it cannot account for the origins of personality. Since it describes but does not explain personality, humanistic psychology is subject to the *nominal fallacy* (Carlson and Buskist, 1997).

However, in its defence, Rowan (2001) contends that humanistic psychology is more than just psychology. While it is indebted to Eastern thought, it is also interested in science:

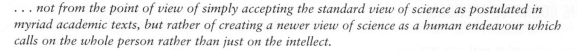

. . . not from the point of view of simply accepting the standard view of science as postulated in myriad academic texts, but rather of creating a newer view of science as a human endeavour which calls on the whole person rather than just on the intellect.

Rowan states that humanistic psychology has some claim to be the only *true* psychology. Most psychology, using 'empiric–analytic inquiry', makes the classic mistake of trying to study people by using the '*eye of flesh*', that is, how we perceive the external world of space, time, and objects:

This then isolates their behaviour – the observable actions they pursue in the world – and ignores most of what is actually relevant – their intentions, their meanings, their visions.

By contrast, humanistic psychology is the classic way of using the '*eye of the mind/reason*', by which we obtain knowledge of philosophy, logic and the mind itself. While positivist science (including behaviourist and cognitive psychology) involves a *monologue* ('a symbolizing inquirer looks at nonsymbolizing occasion'), humanistic psychology involves a *dialogue* ('a symbolizing inquirer looks at other symbolizing occasions'). As Rowan says:

Empiric-analytic inquiry can proceed without talking to the object of its investigation – no empirical scientist talks to electrons, plastic, molecules, protozoa, ferns, or whatever, because he or she is studying preverbal entities. But the very field of humanistic inquiry is communicative exchange or intersubjective or intersymbolic relationships (language and logic), and this approach depends in large measure on talking to and with the subject of investigation . . . any science that talks to its subject of investigation is not empirical but humanistic, not monologic but dialogic.

In other words, humanistic psychology is 'real psychology, proper psychology, the type of psychology that is genuinely applicable to human beings'. (This is consistent with what we said above about the *hermeneutic strength* of Freud's theory, an approach that Maslow, for example, did not reject but saw as presenting the negative face of human beings as opposed to humanist psychology's positive face.)

More specifically, criticisms have been made of Maslow's definition and investigation of self-actualization. In attempting to identify the core components, he began by identifying people he regarded as high self-actualizers (such as Albert Einstein and Eleanor Roosevelt), then used interviews, biographical and autobiographical accounts to distil the core characteristics. The problem with this approach is that, by deciding in advance who is and isn't a self-actualizer, the whole theory is based on Maslow's personal opinion (Sheehy, 2008). This involves circularity: the core components of self-actualization are derived from people identified as having those components.

Furthermore, Maslow estimated that only 2 per cent of human beings achieve self-actualization; he produced a list in 1970 which consisted of just nine living and nine historical figures. In contrast with Rogers's view of the actualizing tendency as an ongoing process, Maslow's conclusion that most of us will never attain the peak of his hierarchy can be regarded, ironically, as a rather negative view of human personality.

According to Sheehy (2008), Maslow's humanistic psychology stimulated the development of new kinds of therapies that focused on realizing personal resources for growth and healing. For all its shortcomings, the humanistic approach as a whole represents a counterbalance to the behaviourist and psychodynamic approaches and has helped to bring the 'person' back into psychology. Crucially, it recognizes that people help determine their own behaviour and are not simply slaves to environmental contingencies or to their past.

THE COGNITIVE APPROACH

Basic principles and assumptions

Despite its undoubted influence within psychology as a whole (see below and Chapter 10), it is more difficult to define the boundaries of cognitive psychology compared with the other major approaches. Its identity is not as clearly established, and it cannot be considered as a specific, integrated set of assumptions and concepts. It has several contemporary forms, with many theories, research programmes and forms of psychotherapy having a 'cognitive tilt' (Nye, 2000).

Also, there is no specific figure who can be identified as central to its development in the same way as Watson, Skinner, Freud and Rogers can with their respective approaches. As Wade and Tavris (1990) say:

> Cognitive psychology does not yet have a unifying theory, and unlike other 'brands' of psychology . . . it lacks an acknowledged spokesperson.

However, there are certain key figures in the developmental history of cognitive psychology. Many of these were not psychologists but electrical engineers (e.g. Shannon), mathematicians (e.g. von Neumann), and logicians (e.g. Turing), who were at the centre of technological developments in radio, television and aero-engineering in the 1930s. The Second World War intensified the need for increasingly versatile calculating machines, as used in radar, and from these developments emerged the concepts that would form the basis of the 'cognitive revolution' (Richards, 2002).

Richards identifies three central ideas that were to transform how cognition would be conceptualized.

1 *Information*: in 1948, Shannon used 'binary logic' to give information a precise technical meaning, allowing it to be measured. The key question is: 'How many yes/no decisions are required to specify the information ('bit' = 'binary digit')?' This is easily converted into hardware: yes/no (1/0 in binary) is equivalent to on/off states of electrical switches. Shannon's *information theory* allowed 'channel capacity', 'storage capacity', 'noisy signals' and 'redundancy' (surplus information) to be discussed. This idea of measuring information first entered psychology through psychophysics and reaction-time studies. It was then applied to memory, attention and other processes: 'The upshot was to recast the study of cognition as the study of human information processing.'

2 *Feedback*: in his *cognitive behaviourism* (1948), Tolman tried to incorporate the concept of 'purpose'. But this was seen as incompatible with that of scientific determinism: how could something later in time (a goal) cause something earlier in time (behaviour)? Causes were supposed to *precede* effects, not follow them. But then Weiner (who founded *cybernetics*) and Craik introduced the concept of *negative feedback*: a system's output is 'fed back' in such a way as to return it to some desired (goal) state (as in a room thermostat maintaining a constant temperature, or the body's homeostatic mechanisms doing the same). The *negative feedback loop* was a way of explaining purposive behaviour in informational terms.

3 *Program*: with the advent of electronic computers (originally in the mid-1940s), 'programming' acquired major significance. For psychologists, the concept of 'program' seemed equivalent to 'plan', which made it possible to handle complex, higher-order behaviour. So:

> By the 1950s humans could thus be viewed as information-processing systems operating according to complex sets of programs derived from a variety of sources from genetic to social, and sustained in this way by sophisticated self-monitoring 'feedback' capacities . . .
>
> *(Richards, 2002)*

> **BOX 14.6 SOME BASIC PRINCIPLES AND ASSUMPTIONS OF THE COGNITIVE APPROACH**
>
> According to Parkin (2000), psychologists in general, and cognitive psychologists in particular, face a problem not faced by other scientists:
>
> *The human brain is not like other organs of the body in that looking at its structure does not reveal anything about how it functions. We can see that . . . the heart [acts] as a pump, and the kidney as a filter. The brain, however, is a large mass of cells and fibres which, no matter how clearly we look at it, gives no indication of how we think, speak and remember . . .*
>
> For these reasons, cognitive psychologists are forced to seek *analogies* and *metaphors* when trying to describe a construct within the brain – that is, how the brain works is compared with the operation of something we already understand. Many different analogies have been used in cognitive psychology. By far the most dominant is that internal mental abilities are *information-processing systems* (the *computer analogy*: see Richards's account above). Included within this overall analogy are several central ideas or concepts, such as *coding*, *channel capacity* and *serial/parallel processing*.
>
> Von Eckardt (1993, in Braisby and Gellatly, 2005) identifies several assumptions commonly made in the cognitive approach. These include:
>
> 1 Cognitive capacities can be partitioned such that individual capacities can be studied separately (for example, language can be studied in isolation from memory).
> 2 Cognitive psychology tends to focus on individuals and their natural environment (de-emphasizing the influence of culture and society).
> 3 Cognitive capacities are relatively autonomous from non-cognitive capacities (such as emotion and motivation).
> 4 It is useful – and meaningful – to distinguish 'normal' from 'abnormal' cognition.
> 5 Adults are sufficiently alike that we can talk about the 'typical' cognizer and generalize across cognizers, ignoring individual differences.

Theoretical contributions

Cognitive behaviourism and *social learning theory* (see above) both stress the central role of cognitive processes in learning. The influence of the information-processing approach is obvious in relation to attention, pattern recognition and memory (see Box 14.6), but it has permeated many other areas of psychology. *Social cognition* is now a commonly used term to refer to many aspects of the perception of people (see Chapter 1), attribution, attitudes and attitude change (including prejudice), and other areas of social psychology (see Gross, 2005). The information-processing approach also represents an increasingly influential view of cognitive development and of the nature of intelligence.

Practical contributions

In relation to counselling and psychotherapy, Ellis's *rational emotive behaviour therapy* (REBT – previously called just rational emotive therapy, or RET) deserves special attention (Nye, 2000). According to Rorer (1998), 'the cognitive revolution in psychotherapy began with the publication of [Ellis's 1962 book] *Reason and Emotion in Psychotherapy*'. REBT is the predecessor of the current cognitive and cognitive-behaviour therapies and continues to evolve and gain in popularity. Ellis's emphasis on the primacy of cognition in psychopathology is at the forefront of practice and research in clinical psychology (Nye, 2000).

REBT attempts directly or actively to get clients to dispute their irrational and unscientific beliefs, and replace them with rational beliefs, which are less likely to be associated with extremely negative emotional states or maladaptive behaviours. The key concept underlying REBT (and other cognitive approaches) is that people are disturbed not by events but by their perception of them. (This is similar to Rogers's phenomenal field: see above.)

Although Ellis (1987) believes that people have a biological tendency to think irrationally, REBT is an optimistic approach. It emphasizes that:

> . . . people have enormous power to think about their thinking, to use rationality and the scientific method, and to radically control and change their emotional destiny – providing they really work at doing so.
>
> (Ellis, 1987)

An evaluation of the cognitive approach

The parallels between human beings and computers are compelling (Parkin, 2000) (see Box 14.7). According to Lachman et al. (1979):

> Computers take a symbolic input, recode it, make decisions about the recoded input, make new expressions from it, store some or all of the input, and give back a symbolic output. By analogy that is what most cognitive psychology is about. It is about how people take in information . . . recode and remember it, how they make decisions, how they transform their internal knowledge states, and how they translate these states into behavioural outputs.

BOX 14.7 SOME OTHER SIMILARITIES BETWEEN COMPUTERS AND HUMANS AS INFORMATION PROCESSORS

- Computers operate in terms of *information streams*, which flow between different components of the system. This is conceptually similar to how we assume symbolic information flows through human information channels (for example, see Atkinson and Shiffrin's (1971) *multi-store model of memory/MSM*).
- All computers have a *central processing unit*, which carries out the manipulation of information. At the simplest level, a central processor might take a sequence of numbers and combine them according to a particular rule in order to compute an average. This was seen by many as analogous to how a person would perform the same type of mental operation.
- Computers have *databases* and *information stores*, which are permanent representations of knowledge the computer has acquired. In many ways this is comparable to our permanent (long-term) memory.
- Information sometimes needs to be held for a period of time while some other operation is performed. This is the job of the *information buffer*, which is a feature of computers and information-processing models of human attention and memory (again, see Atkinson and Shiffrin's MSM).

(Based on Parkin, 2000)

Can computers ever be like brains?

According to Rose (2003), the neuronal system of brains – unlike computers – is *radically indeterminate*:

> . . . brains and the organisms they inhabit, above all human brains and human beings, are not closed systems, like the molecules of a gas inside a sealed jar. Instead they are open systems, formed

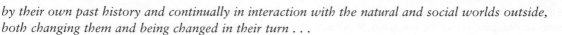

by their own past history and continually in interaction with the natural and social worlds outside, both changing them and being changed in their turn . . .

This openness creates a further level of indeterminacy to the functioning of both brain and behaviour. Unlike computers, brains aren't error-free machines. Yet brains are capable of modifying their structural, chemical and physical output in response to environmental events (they are highly *plastic*). They are also extraordinarily resilient in the face of injury, with damaged parts taking over the function of damaged areas (they are highly *redundant*).

Rose argues that brains process and remember information based on its *meaning*, which is not equivalent to information in a computer sense. An essential difference between human and computer memory is that:

. . . each time we remember, we in some sense do work on and transform our memories, they are not simply being called up from store and, once consulted, replaced unmodified. Our memories are re-created each time we remember . . .

(Rose, 2003)

At least for the foreseeable future, it seems that brains will continue to outperform computers when doing the kinds of things they were *naturally* designed to do. One of these might be *consciousness* (see Chapter 12).

Cognitive psychologists implicitly adopted, at least initially, a strong nomothetic view of human mental processes – that is, they assumed that any information-processing model would apply equally to everyone (see Box 14.6 and Chapter 3). But the influence of *individual differences* soon became apparent. The general rule is that the more complex the cognitive process, the more likely there are to be individual differences (Parkin, 2000).

Until the mid-1980s, mainstream cognitive psychologists took little interest in the study of how *brain damage* affects subsequent cognitive and behavioural functioning. *Cognitive neuropsychologists* now study people with acquired cognitive deficits in order to learn about the nature and organization of cognitive functioning in normal people (the *cognitive architecture* of mental processes).

Richards (2002) believes that:

Cognitive Psychology represents a very major example of how novel technologies and scientific discoveries can change how we think about ourselves . . . Some recent writers have also seen its US origins . . . as rooted in a distinctly militaristic view of human nature in which humans are reduced to the status of expendable pieces of equipment . . .

Since the late 1980s there has been a growing criticism of cognitive psychology, both from traditional critics (such as humanistic psychologists and behaviourists) and from various philosophers. phenomenologists and social constructionists.

THE SOCIAL CONSTRUCTIONIST APPROACH

Basic principles and assumptions

Social constructionism (SC) has played a central role in the various challenges that have been made to mainstream, academic psychology during the last 30 years or so, and we have discussed some of these at various points in earlier chapters.

The emergence of SC is usually dated from Gergen's (1973) paper 'Social psychology as history' in which he argued that all knowledge, including psychological knowledge, is historically and culturally specific, and that

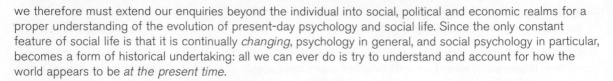

we therefore must extend our enquiries beyond the individual into social, political and economic realms for a proper understanding of the evolution of present-day psychology and social life. Since the only constant feature of social life is that it is continually *changing*, psychology in general, and social psychology in particular, becomes a form of historical undertaking: all we can ever do is try to understand and account for how the world appears to be *at the present time*.

The paper was written at the time of 'the crisis in social psychology'. Starting in the late 1960s and early 1970s, some social psychologists were becoming increasingly concerned that the 'voice' of ordinary people was being omitted from social psychological research: by concentrating on *decontextualized* laboratory behaviour, it was ignoring the real-world contexts that give human action its meaning. Several books were published, each proposing an alternative to positivist science and focusing on the accounts of ordinary people (e.g. Harré and Secord, 1972). These concerns are clearly seen today in SC.

While there is no single definition of SC that would be accepted by all those who might be included under its umbrella, we could categorize as social constructionist any approach based on one or more of the following key attitudes/assumptions (as proposed by Gergen, 1985). Burr (2003) suggests we might think of these assumptions as 'things you would absolutely have to believe in order to be a social constructionist'.

1 A critical stance towards taken-for-granted knowledge

Our observations of the world do not reveal in any simple way the true nature of the world, and conventional knowledge is not based on objective, unbiased 'sampling' of the world (see Chapter 10). The categories with which we understand the world do not necessarily correspond to natural or 'real' categories/distinctions. Belief in such natural categories is called *essentialism*, so social constructionists are *anti-essentialism*.

Essentialism, in turn, is related to *correspondence theory*, an important element of the positivist view of truth. According to correspondence theory, a description is true if it corresponds to the object or event in the world that it describes. But social constructionists argue that it is an illusion to believe that we can establish secure and determinate relationships between words and what the words refer to, that knowledge mirrors nature, and that scientific theory merely reflects or maps reality in any direct or decontextualized way (Bem and Looren de Jong, 1997). In fact, language, and thus our theories, do not refer to the world at all: they have no truth-value. The basic function of language 'is not the representation of things in the world . . . It works to create, sustain and transform various patterns of social relations' (Shotter, 1991).

2 Historical and cultural specificity

How we commonly understand the world, and the categories and concepts we use, are historically and culturally *relative*. Not only are they specific to particular cultures and historical periods, they are products of that culture and history, and this must include the knowledge generated by the social sciences. The theories and explanations of psychology thus become time- and culture-bound, and cannot be taken as once-and-for-all descriptions of human nature:

> The disciplines of psychology and social psychology can therefore no longer be aimed at discovering the 'true' nature of people and social life . . .
>
> *(Burr, 2003)*

As Bem and Looren de Jong (1997) observe:

> Social constructionists challenge the supposedly objective and universal basis of . . . knowledge; they are sensitive to cross-cultural psychological or ethnographic studies which reveal that such psychological concepts differ among wide-ranging cultures because they are produced by and sustain the social, moral, political and economic institutions . . .

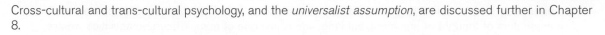

Cross-cultural and trans-cultural psychology, and the *universalist assumption*, are discussed further in Chapter 8.

3 Knowledge is sustained by social processes

Our current accepted way of understanding the world ('truth') does not reflect the world as it really is (*objective reality*), but is constructed by people through their everyday interactions. Social interaction of all kinds, and particularly language, is of central importance for social constructionists – other people, both past and present, are the sources of knowledge:

> *We are born into a world where the conceptual frameworks and categories used by the people in our culture already exist . . . Concepts and categories are acquired by each person as they develop the use of language and are thus reproduced every day by everyone who shares a culture and language. This means that the way a person thinks, the very categories and concepts that provide a framework of meaning for them, are provided by the language that they use. Language therefore is a necessary pre-condition for thought as we know it . . .*
>
> *(Burr, 2003)*

By giving a central role to *social interactions* and seeing these as actively producing taken-for-granted knowledge of the world, it follows that language itself is more than simply a way of expressing our thoughts and feelings (as typically assumed by mainstream psychology). When people talk to each other, they (help to) *construct* the world, such that language use is a form of *action* (it has a *performative* role). Topics and concepts such as gender, aggression, person, self, emotion, schizophrenia, child and mother's love are social constructions, products of historically specific interactions between people.

4 Knowledge and social action go together

These 'negotiated' understandings could take a wide variety of forms, so there are many possible 'social constructions' of the world. But each different construction also brings with it, or invites, a different kind of action: how we account for a particular behaviour (what caused it) will dictate how we react to and treat the person whose behaviour it is (see Gross, 2005).

Mainstream psychology looks for explanations of social phenomena *inside* the person, by, for example, hypothesizing the existence of attitudes, motives, cognitions and so on (*individualism*: see Chapter 6). This can also be seen as *reductionist* (see Chapters 5 and 13). Social constructionists reject this view: explanations are to be found neither inside the individual psyche, nor in social structures or institutions (as advocated by sociologists), but in the *interactive processes* that take place routinely between people. For Burr (2003):

> *Knowledge is therefore seen not as something that a person has or doesn't have, but as something that people do together . . .*

Who are social constructionists?

Burr (2003) and Jones and Elcock (2001) use the label 'social constructionist' to refer to psychologists who may otherwise be referred to as discursive psychologists or critical psychologists. These represent two quite distinct strands of constructionist theorizing in psychology.

(i) *Discursive psychology* (DP) has been described as the 'second cognitive revolution' (Harré, 1995). According to this approach, the mind is not a mental machine processing information. Rather, 'mind' denotes certain activities – that is, skilled use of symbols, performed both publicly and privately. Since discourse is primarily public and only secondarily private, so cognition (the use of various devices for mental tasks) is also primarily public and only secondarily private. Discourse usually implies verbal presentation of thought or argument, but language is just one of many discursive activities we are capable of (see Burr's third point above).

   For Potter (1996), the central idea of DP is that the main business of social life is found in interaction, stressing the practical dimension of social life. For example, how does a husband produce a particular narrative (account) of relationship breakdown to show that it is his wife's problem rather than his own? Or how is a rape victim presented as subtly responsible for the attack and how might she resist such a presentation? Through analysis of tape-recordings, transcripts of conversations, videos (and other records of interaction), discursive psychologists have found that they need to rework notions such as attitudes, violence and aggression, and memory (see Gross *et al.* 1997).

(iii) *Critical psychology* (CP) looks more broadly at the structure of the discourse in its cultural context, asks where discourses come from, and how they constrain people's lives. It also focuses on how selfhood, subjectivity and power are reflected in specific discursive practices. While positivist, mainstream psychology sees 'single parent', 'woman', 'individual', 'self' and so on as 'natural' categories (see Chapter 10), existing objectively, CP sees them as 'subjective positions' constructed through discourse, providing us with ways of thinking and communicating about ourselves.

CP has been most heavily influenced by Foucault (1926–84), the French philosopher, and Lacan (1901–81), the French psychoanalyst. It has also been more influenced than DP by Marxism and contemporary feminism. Not surprisingly, then, CP is the more explicitly political, advocating empowerment and emancipation of those who are oppressed by psychological and other discourses (McGhee, 2001).

When defining and measuring 'internal' entities, such as 'personality', 'attitude', 'motivation' and 'intelligence', and comparing different groups on these dimensions, psychology paints a rather simplistic, static and de-socialized picture of the phenomenon. In contrast, critical social psychology shows them to be complex, contradictory and constructed, thereby disrupting social psychological narratives of 'objectivity' and 'progress'. Wetherell (1996) advocates:

> . . . a critical 'social psychology' which takes the term 'social' very seriously indeed. We are not isolated individuals but social beings. Our dreams, hopes, fears and expectations may be the products of solitary reflection but they also tell us a great deal about the ways in which we are inserted into society. Social psychology should be a social science, not an imitation natural science. We belong with disciplines such as sociology, politics and cultural studies rather than physics, chemistry and astronomy. Our methods, research aims and theories should reflect the particular nature of social action . . . We should work with and study the ambiguities, fluidity and openness of social life rather than try to repress these in a fruitless chase for experimental control and scientific respectability.

Theoretical contributions

According to *social representation theory* (SRT), people come to understand their social world by way of images and social representations (SRs) shared by members of a social group. These representations act like a map that makes a baffling or novel terrain familiar and passable, thereby providing evaluations of good and bad areas. Attitudes are secondary phenomena, underpinned by SRs. SRT tries to provide a historical account of people's understanding of the world (Potter, 1996).

SRT is a *constructionist* theory: instead of portraying people as simply perceiving (or misperceiving) their social worlds, it regards these worlds as constructed, and an SR is a device for doing this construction. It allows someone to make sense of something potentially unfamiliar and to evaluate it. For the French psychologist Serge Moscovici (e.g. 1984), all thought and understanding are based on the working of SRs, each of which consists of a mixture of concepts, ideas and images; these are both in people's minds and circulating in society.

Moscovici originally conducted his research into the layperson's understanding of psychoanalytic theory in the 1950s, but SRT was not published in English until the early 1980s; since then research has snowballed, especially in Europe, Australia and South America (though it has been largely ignored by mainstream North American social psychologists in the experimental cognitive tradition). Potter (1996) suggests that one reason for this may be that the latter's pursuit of general laws and processes is directly challenged by SRT's emphasis on the specific content of a culture's or group's SR as the main object of analysis.

Another important theoretical contribution of SC is in the form of the relationship between it and feminist psychology. This link is discussed in Chapter 6.

An evaluation of SC

A recurring problem with SC concerns its *relativism* (see Burr's second point above). Relativism here refers to the belief that there is no absolute, ultimate, objective truth (as claimed by mainstream psychology and positivist science in general) or universal values. There are only truths – different accounts or versions of the truth as judged from different perspectives and viewpoints, or *different values*, reflecting different group memberships and experiences (i.e. *pluralism*).

But this seems to deny the 'reality' of the world as we experience it: our common-sense understanding of the world seems to correspond to scientific realism and the related correspondence theory (see above). Is SC claiming, in effect, that the world as we know it doesn't exist at all? One relevant example is emotion. According to Gergen (1997):

> . . . *there are only certain actions that warrant anger as an intelligible response (for example insult, expressions of hostility). And once anger has been performed, the other is not free to act in any way; convention requires that one react, for example, with an apology, with an exonerating explanation, or with anger.*

In other words, any inner feelings of anger seem to be irrelevant to the *meaning* of anger. Emotion is being characterized as a feature of social interaction, *not* an inner and private experience (McGhee, 2001).

But perhaps we do not have to abandon belief in a real (physical) world altogether. For example, Wetherell and Still (1996), pointing out that social constructionists share the common-sense belief that people will be killed if their plane crashes into a hill, consider the idea of 'New Zealand' and 'hills' as constructed objects. There really is some land in the southern hemisphere of that name, but that should not blind us to how our understanding and knowledge of it are relative. They argue that:

> . . . *the real world is no less constructed for being able to get in the way of planes. How those deaths are understood and what is seen as causing them will still be constituted through our system of social constructions.*

Mainstream, positivist psychologists also criticize SC for not being scientific enough. But this is irrelevant as far as SC itself is concerned, because there is little or no attempt at hypothesis testing or generalizing from one study to another. So, issues of comprehensiveness, testability, empirical support and so on are not at stake as they are in experimental psychology. Social constructionist analyses are often subtle, novel and imaginative, but their value is apparent only to other social constructionists.

However, just as in experimental psychology, there is good and bad SC research – although it is more difficult to say what criteria are being used to make this judgement (McGhee, 2001). But according to Salmon (2003), the issue as to how we recognize good research, whether it is qualitative (as in most SC research) or quantitative (as in experimental research), is far from straightforward. He uses the term 'methodologism' to mean judging research to be good if it has been conducted according to certain methods, and argues that 'it's a forlorn belief that quality can be guaranteed simply by following procedures'.

THE EVOLUTIONARY PSYCHOLOGICAL APPROACH

Basic principles and assumptions

Sociobiology (Wilson, 1975) grew out of the work of evolutionary biologists in the 1960s. Wilson set out to explain all non-human and human social behaviour in terms of evolution and other biological principles. It concentrated on the evolutionary origins of behaviour, and tended to imply rigid genetic control (Archer, 1996). Since then, many of these principles have been used to study topics covered by the social sciences – including psychology.

Evolutionary psychology (Buss, 1995) is a development of sociobiology (and is often referred to as 'neo- or modern Darwinism'). According to Archer (2001):

> *Just as the evolutionary approach led ethologists away from concentrating on the immediate causal mechanisms controlling animal behaviour, so evolutionary psychology seeks to lead conventional psychologists away from explanations that concentrate only on immediate mechanisms and mental events. Instead, it offers a single unifying starting point for understanding why we think and behave as we do today: natural selection has made us this way.*

Campbell (2001) makes a similar distinction between (i) the *how* question (relating to proximal mechanisms) with which mainstream psychology is preoccupied, and (ii) the *why* question, which distinguishes 'evolutionary hypotheses about adaptations from alternative explanations that view the origins of human behaviour as culturally acquired and nearly infinitely malleable'.

However, contrary to what some critics claim, evolutionary psychologists don't deny the role of cultural factors. But fitness-relevant aspects of culture are seen as being constrained by genetic evolution ('genes hold culture on a leash'). Culture acts as a selecting environment for genotypes (Campbell, 2001). (See the evaluation section below.)

According to Rose (2000):

> *The declared aim of evolutionary psychology is to provide explanations for the patterns of human activity and the forms of organization of human society which take into account the fact that humans are animals, and like all other currently living organisms, are the present-day products of some four billion years of evolution . . .*

Theoretical contributions

As indicated in Box 14.8, evolutionary psychological (and sociobiological) explanations can be found throughout psychology. For example, the harmful effects of stress have been explained in evolutionary terms. While the body's stress response evolved to help us cope with life-threatening situations ('emergencies'), most 'modern-day' stressors are not like this. Consequently, our bodies react in an inappropriate and potentially life-threatening way to 'chronic' stress. This would be accepted by most (bio-)psychologists as a useful and uncontroversial insight into why stress can be harmful.

Rather more controversially, Buss (1994) claims that men, because they can in principle father a virtually infinite number of children, are much more inclined towards promiscuity than are women. Women, because

> ## BOX 14.8 SOME BASIC PRINCIPLES AND ASSUMPTIONS OF EVOLUTIONARY PSYCHOLOGY (EP)
>
> - EP rejects the *Standard Social Science Model* (SSSM; Tooby and Cosmides, 1992), which makes two broad assumptions about human beings: (i) there is no such thing as human nature or, if there is, it has so little effect on people's social lives that it can be ignored; (ii) explanations of social behaviour can be derived from considering only social roles, socialization and culture.
> - Human social behaviour, like that of non-humans, can be understood in terms of its past contribution to survival and reproduction. For example, instead of regarding young males' proneness to violence in terms of social learning (modelling) or frustration (Berkowitz, 1993), EP views it as the result of its past contributions to obtaining resources, status and access to women (Daly and Wilson, 1988; see text below).
> - While acknowledging their debt to sociobiology, evolutionary psychologists contend that sociobiologists often ignored the role of *mind* in mediating links between genes and behaviour. According to Barkow, Cosmides and Tooby (1992), the mind consists of a collection of specialized, independent mechanisms, or *modules*, designed by natural selection to solve problems that faced our hunter-gatherer ancestors, such as acquiring a mate, raising children and dealing with rivals. The solutions often involve such emotions as lust, fear, affection, jealousy and anger. Together, these modules and the related emotions constitute *human nature*.
> - Drawing heavily on the jargon and conceptual framework of computer science and artificial intelligence, evolutionary psychologists see the mind as a *cognitive machine*, an information-processing device 'run' by the brain. It is not a general-purpose computer but (as we have seen) comprises several specific modules.
> - EP, as a whole, is, about *universal* features of the mind. In so far as individual differences exist, the default assumption is that they are expressions of the same universal human nature as it encounters different environments. *Gender* is the crucial exception to this rule. Natural selection has constructed the mental modules of men and women in very different ways as a result of their divergent reproductive roles (*sexual dimorphism*: see text below).
> - EP *is not* a form of *genetic determinism* (or *nativism*: see Chapter 5). Like most modern biologists and social scientists, evolutionary psychologists argue that 'nature or nurture' is a false dichotomy, and they distinguish themselves from behaviour geneticists (see text below and Chapter 5).
>
> *(Based on Horgan, 1995; Rose, 2000)*

they can average only one child per year, are choosier in selecting a mate. Men, in all cultures, place greater emphasis on youth and physical attractiveness, while women look to men's 'resources'. Similarly, because men can never be sure that a child is theirs, their jealousy tends to be triggered by fears of a mate's sexual infidelity. Women, on the other hand, become more upset at the thought of losing a mate's emotional commitment – and thus his resources. In turn, women make greater 'parental investment' in their children than do men. According to Buss: 'Women's current mate preferences provide a window for viewing our mating past.' Evolution has favoured women who prefer men who possess 'attributes that confer benefits and who dislike men who possess attributes that impose costs'. This female preference is ancient and unlikely to change.

An evaluation of EP

Is language an instinct?

According to Pinker (1994), a linguist 'converted' to EP, language is far too complex to be learned: it must stem from an innate programme hardwired into our brains. Language almost certainly arose, he claims, because it was adaptive – that is, it conferred benefits on our hunter-gatherer ancestors. It would have allowed early hominids to share learned tool-making, hunting and other skills, and those especially adept at

language could manipulate others and form alliances that would increase their chances of producing offspring.

Ironically, these claims are denied by Chomsky, a fellow linguist and colleague of Pinker's. Chomsky first argued in the 1950s that language represents a distinct mental module (or 'language organ') unique to human beings and independent of general cognitive ability, and that we all possess an innate language acquisition device (LAD: see Chapter 5). In this way, he laid the foundation for EP, and evolutionary psychologists are, in a sense, his heirs (Horgan, 1995; Kohn, 1998).

However, Chomsky disputes the assumption that language is a 'selected trait': just because language is adaptive now does not mean that it arose in response to selection pressures. Given the enormous gap between human language and the relatively simple communication systems of other species, and given our fragmentary knowledge of our evolutionary past, science can tell us little about how language evolved. It may have been an incidental/accidental by-product of a spurt in intelligence or of the human brain's large size (Horgan, 1995; Kohn, 1998). The same may be true of other properties of the human mind.

Are we really sexually dimorphic?

According to Fausto-Sterling (2000), the claim that humans display sexual dimorphism (see Box 14.8) has been largely based on studies of primate societies, such as African baboons. Females were seen as meekly following after the males, who competed with one another for mates and leadership. But over the last 20 years or so, ideas about animal sexual behaviour, and the evolution of sex differences, have undergone a revolution.

During the 1970s, women flooded into the field of animal behaviour, especially the study of primates, and they began, almost for the first time, to watch the behaviour of females. Based on studies of a wide range of species, the message is clear: 'female behaviour can determine the pattern of evolution and their activities are every bit as varied, dynamic and complicated as [those] of males'.

Patient observations over many years and several generations, noting which individuals mated, with whom, and which initiated sexual contact, 'refuted the dogmatic assertions that females don't really want sex, females don't gain from exuberant sexual behaviour, and that females do best by choosing their mates prudently and with discrimination'.

The essential point is that:

> ... in animals and humans alike, male–female interactions around sex and the rearing of offspring are variable matters. Depending on their environments, both sexes can exhibit a wide range of behaviours ...
>
> (Fausto-Sterling, 2000)

EP's hardwired view of the inflexibility of human social arrangements flies in the face of the evidence of the *plasticity* of behaviour. Plasticity itself, rather than specific behaviour, may be under genetic control and may have evolved through natural selection (Fausto-Sterling, 2000). Consistent with this view, Karmiloff-Smith (2000) claims that developmental psychologists see plasticity during brain growth as the rule, rather than the exception or a response to brain injury.

Our hunter-gatherer past

EP is based on the belief that the human mind is adapted to cope with life as a Pleistocene hunter-gatherer – which we were for about two million years before the ancient Chinese, Indian, Egyptian and Sumerian civilizations (Abdulla, 1996). Forms of behaviour and social organization that evolved adaptively over many generations in human hunter-gatherer society may or may not be adaptive in modern industrialized society, but have become to a degree fixed by humanity's evolutionary experience in the Palaeolithic *Environment of Evolutionary Adaptation* (EEA), thought to be the African savannah (Rose, 2000).

However, just as Chomsky's argument with Pinker concerned how language evolved (rather than whether or not it evolved), so the story of our human hunter-gatherer ancestors is, inevitably, partly a work of fiction (Turney, 1999). According to Rose (2000), the descriptions offered by EP of what hunter-gatherer societies were like read little better than 'just so' accounts:

> *There is a circularity about reading this version of the present into the past, and then claiming that this imagined past explains the present.*

Figure 14.1 Can we use 'images' like these of our hunter-gatherer ancestors to explain how our current human abilities evolved?

In other words, based on what human beings are capable of *now*, evolutionary psychologists imagine how these abilities may have evolved, then put forward this *constructed past* as the cause of these current abilities.

Evolutionary psychologists also claim that the timescale of human history has been too short for evolutionary selection pressures to have produced significant change. But we know very little about just how quickly such change can occur (Rose, 2000). Evolutionarily modern humans appeared 100,000 years ago. Allowing 15–20 years per generation, there have been 5000–6600 generations between human origins and modern times. We really have no idea whether these generations are 'time enough' for substantial evolutionary change:

> *However, granted the very rapid changes in human environment, social organisation, technology, and mode of production that have clearly occurred over that period, one must assume significant selection pressures operating . . . the automatic assumption that the palaeolithic was an EEA in which fundamental human traits were fixed, and that there has not been time since to alter them, does not bear serious inspection.*

> *(Rose, 2000)*

Nature versus nurture, biological versus cultural evolution

According to Dunbar (2008), the rise of EP in the last decade has produced a surprisingly negative reaction from more traditional cognitive and developmental psychologists and a very heated debate. He argues that this debate is based on a misunderstanding of the role of an evolutionary perspective, seeing it as a competing paradigm that would show these more mainstream theories to be either redundant or wrong. However, as we noted in Box 14.8, it is a mistake to interpret an evolutionary approach in terms of the nature/nurture debate (see Chapter 5). As Dunbar says:

> *. . . Since the environmentalists gained the upper hand in developmental psychology during the 1980s, a 'naturist' view (which is firmly equated with the genetic determination of cognition and behaviour) has been viewed with deep suspicion by most psychologists. An evolutionary approach emphasizing the adaptiveness of the human mind has seemed rather like a return to the Dark Ages*

that most had assumed were now firmly closed off behind us – the imputation of genetic differences between races, genders or even social classes.

According to Dunbar, another false dichotomy is that between *biological* and *cultural evolution*:

> *... cultural evolution is as natural a component of the Darwinian world as something like eye colour that is more obviously under direct genetic control. Culture is not something that is somehow opposed to, or contrasted with, biology – culture is biology ...*

Dunbar believes that an evolutionary framework allows us to integrate a wide range of different sub-disciplines (including neuropsychology, sociology and ecology) when accounting for any example of behaviour (such as 'Dunbar's number' – the apparently universal typical size of social circles at around 150 individuals).

> *... our understanding of the phenomena we study is the richer and the more complete for this breadth of explanation. But more than that, our real appreciation of what is involved is only possible by integrating all these disciplines into a single seamless framework. And the only framework we have that can do this job is evolutionary theory.*

(Dunbar, 2008)

CONCLUSIONS

The focus of this discussion of various theoretical approaches within psychology has been on how each conceptualizes human beings. Freud's 'tension-reducing person', Skinner's 'environmentally controlled person', and Rogers's 'growth-motivated person' really are quite different from each other (Nye, 2000). The person-as-information-processor and the person-as-shaped-by-our-evolutionary-past are different again – both from each other and from the first three approaches. Social constructionism's image of the person is rather less concrete and more elusive: what people are like and what they do are *relative* to their culture, historical period and so on.

However, we have also noted some important similarities between different approaches, such as the deterministic nature of Freud's and Skinner's theories, and the influence of the information-processing approach on evolutionary psychology. Each approach has something of value to contribute to our understanding of ourselves – even if it is only to reject the particular explanation it offers. The diversity of approaches reflects the complexity of the subject matter, so, usually, there is room for a diversity of explanations.

SUMMARY

○ Different theoretical approaches/perspectives are based on different models/images of the nature of human beings.

○ Watson's methodological behaviourism removes mental processes from the science of psychology and focuses on what can be quantified and observed by different researchers. Skinner's radical behaviourism regards mental processes as both inaccessible and irrelevant for explaining behaviour.

○ The behaviourist approach stresses the role of environmental influences (learning), especially classical and operant conditioning. Psychology's aim is to predict and control behaviour.

○ Tolman's cognitive behaviourism and social learning theory represent modifications of 'orthodox' learning (conditioning) theory.

○ Methodological behaviourism has influenced the practice of scientific psychology in general. Other practical contributions include behaviour therapy and modification, behavioural neuroscience and behavioural pharmacology.

○ The psychodynamic approach is based on Freud's psychoanalytic theory. Central aspects are the unconscious (especially repression), infantile sexuality and the impact of early experience.

○ Freud's ideas have become part of mainstream psychology, contributing to our understanding of motivation, sleep and dreams, forgetting, attachment, aggression and abnormality.

○ Major modifications/alternatives to Freudian theory include ego psychology, Erikson's psychosocial theory and the object relations school.

○ All forms of psychotherapy stem directly or indirectly from psychoanalysis. Many trained psychoanalysts have been responsible for developing radically different therapeutic approaches, including Rogers, Perls and Wolpe.

○ Maslow called the humanistic approach the 'third' force' in psychology. It believes in free will, adopts a phenomenological perspective, and stresses the positive aspects of human personality.

○ Rogers was a prolific researcher into the effectiveness of his client-person-centred therapy (PCT), opened up psychotherapy to psychologists and other non-psychiatrists, and created a counselling profession that operates within a wide diversity of settings.

○ Compared with other approaches, the cognitive approach lacks both a central figure and a unifying theory. It uses analogies and metaphors when trying to describe what is going on inside the brain, in particular the computer analogy and the view of people as information processors.

○ Modern cognitive psychology emerged from a re-conceptualization of cognition in terms of information, feedback and programs. These concepts derive from electrical engineering, logic, mathematics and telecommunications.

○ Other important features include the concepts of coding, channel capacity and serial/parallel processing.

○ A major application of the cognitive approach has been cognitive behaviour therapy, as in Ellis's rational emotive behaviour therapy (REBT).

○ While the computer analogy is a useful way of understanding cognitive processes, there are also some important differences between how computers and people process information.

○ One of the goals of social constructionism (SC) is to correct the tendency of mainstream psychology to decontextualize behaviour. Related to this is the universalist assumption, which is challenged by (trans) cultural psychology.

○ SC is also anti-essentialism, which involves a rejection of the correspondence theory of truth. Other key concepts are relativism and a rejection of individualism. Two distinct strands within SC are discursive psychology (DP) and critical psychology (CP).

○ Social representation theory (SRT) is a social constructionist theory, according to which all thought and understanding are based on the working of SRs; these exist in people's minds and circulate within society.

○ Evolutionary psychology (EP) grew out of sociobiology. Unlike the latter, EP puts the mind centre stage, identifying several independent mental mechanisms or modules. These form the core of human nature.

305

○ A major assumption of EP is that these mental modules have become fixed by our hunter-gatherer ancestors' experience in the Palaeolithic Environment of Evolutionary Adaptation (EEA). But knowledge of the EEA is largely speculative, and there is good reason to believe that human traits have changed since that time.

○ Objections to EP are rooted in false dichotomies between nature/nurture and biological (Darwinian)/cultural evolution.

USEFUL WEBSITES

http://www.freud.org.uk/
www.psychoanalysis.org.uk
http://plato.stanford.edu/entries/behaviorism/
www.furman.edu/~einstein/watson/watson1.htm
www.emory.edu/LIVING_LINKS
www.ahpweb.org/aboutahp/whatis.html
www.ahpweb.org/rowan_bibliography/
www.en.wikipedia.org/wiki/Evolutionary_psychology
http://www.psych.ucsb.edu/research/cep/
www.en.wikipedia.org/wiki/Cognitive_revolution
www3.niu.edu/acad/psych/Millis/History/2003/cogrev.htm
www.en.wikipedia.org/wiki/Social_constructionism
http://openlearn.open.ac.uk/mod/resource/view.php?id=211063

RECOMMENDED READING

Burr, V. (2003) *Social Constructionism* (2nd edn). London: Routledge.

Edwards, D. and Jacobs, M. (2003) *Conscious and Unconscious*. Maidenhead: Open University Press.

Gay, P. (1988) *Freud: A life for our time*. London: Papermac.

Glassman, W.E. (2006) *Approaches to Psychology* (4th edn). Maidenhead: Open University Press.

Nye, D. (2000) *Three Psychologies: Perspectives from Freud, Skinner and Rogers* (6th edn). Belmont, CA: Wadsworth/Thomson Learning.

O'Donohue, W. and Ferguson, K.E. (2001) *The Psychology of B.F. Skinner*. Thousand Oaks, CA: Sage Publications.

Pinker, S. (1994) *The Language Instinct: How the mind creates language*. New York: Morrow.

Rose, H. and Rose, S. (eds) (2000) *Alas, Poor Darwin: Arguments Against Evolutionary Psychology*. London: Jonathan Cape.

Rowan, J. (2001) *Ordinary Ecstasy* (3rd edn). Hove: Brunner-Routledge.

REFERENCES

Abdulla, S. (1996) Illuminating the hardware. *The Times Higher*, 1 November, 18.

Abramson, L.Y., Seligman, M.E.P. and Teasdale, J.D. (1978) Learned helplessness in humans: critique and reformulation. *Journal of Abnormal Psychology, 87*, 49–74.

Adler, A. (1927) *The Practice and Theory of Individual Psychology*. New York: Harcourt Brace Jovanovich.

Adorno, T.W., Frenkel-Brunswick, E., Levinson, J.D. and Sanford, R.N. (1950) *The Authoritarian Personality*. New York: Harper & Row.

Agassi, J. (1996) Prescriptions for Responsible Psychiatry. In W. O'Donohue and R.F. Kitchener (eds) *The Philosophy of Psychology*. London: Sage.

Alcock, J.E. (1981) *Parapsychology: Science or Magic?* Oxford: Pergamon.

Allport, D.A. (1980) Attention and performance. In G. Claxton (ed.) *Cognitive Psychology: New Directions*. London: RKP.

Allport, G.W. (1937) *Personality: A Psychological Interpretation*. New York: Holt.

Allport, G.W. (1960) *Personality and Social Encounter*. Boston: Beacon Press.

Allport, G.W. (1961) *Pattern and Growth in Personality*. New York: Holt, Rinehart & Winston.

American Psychiatric Association (1952) *Diagnostic and Statistical Manual of Mental Disorders*. Washington, DC: American Psychiatric Association.

American Psychiatric Association (1968) *Diagnostic and Statistical Manual of Mental Disorders* (2nd edn). Washington, DC: American Psychiatric Association.

American Psychiatric Association (1980) *Diagnostic and Statistical Manual of Mental Disorders* (3rd edn). Washington, DC: American Psychiatric Association.

American Psychological Association (1985) *Guidelines for Ethical Conduct in the Care and Use of Animals*. Washington, DC: American Psychological Association.

American Psychiatric Association (1987) *Diagnostic and Statistical Manual of Mental Disorders* (3rd edn, revised). Washington, DC: American Psychiatric Association.

American Psychiatric Association (1994) *Diagnostic and Statistical Manual of Mental Disorders* (4th edn). Washington, DC: American Psychiatric Association.

American Psychiatric Association (2000) *Diagnostic and Statistical Manual of Mental Disorders* (4th edn, Text Revision). Washington, DC: American Psychiatric Association.

American Psychological Association (2002) *Ethical Principles of Psychologists and Code of Conduct*. Washington, DC: American Psychological Association.

Anastasi, A. (1958) Heredity, environment and the question 'How?'. *Psychological Review, 65*, 197–208.

Andrews, B. and Brewin, C.R. (2000) What did Freud get right? *The Psychologist, 13*(12), 605–7.

Antaki, C. (1984) Core concepts in attribution theory. In J. Nicholson and H. Beloff (eds) *Psychology Survey, 5*. Leicester: British Psychological Society.

Appignanesi, L. (2008) *Mad, Bad and Sad: A History of Women & the Mind Doctors from 1800 to the Present*. London: Virago.

Archer, J. (1996) Evolutionary social psychology. In M. Hewstone, W. Stroebe and G.M. Stephenson (eds) *Introduction to Social Psychology* (2nd edn). Oxford: Blackwell.

Archer, J. (2001) Evolving theories of behaviour. *The Psychologist, 14*(8), 414–18.

Argyle, M. (1983) *The Psychology of Interpersonal Behaviour* (4th edn). Harmondsworth: Penguin.

Argyle, M. (2002) *The Psychology of Happiness* (3rd edn). London: Methuen.

Armstrong, D.M. (1987) Mind–body problem: philosophical theories. In R.L. Gregory (ed.) *The Oxford Companion to the Mind*. Oxford: Oxford University Press.

Aronson, E. (1992) *The Social Animal* (6th edn). New York: W.H. Freeman & Co.

Asch, S.E. (1951) Effect of group pressure upon the modification and distortion of judgements. In H. Guetzkow (ed.) *Groups, Leadership and Men*. Pittsburgh, PA: Carnegie Press.

Asch, S.E. (1952) *Social Psychology*. Englewood Cliffs, NJ: Prentice-Hall.

Ashworth, P. (2003) The origins of qualitative psychology. In J.A. Smith (ed.) *Qualitative Psychology: A Practical Guide to Research Methods*. London: Sage Publications.

Association for the Teaching of Psychology (1992) Ethics in psychological research: guidelines for students at pre-degree level. *Psychology Teaching*, New Series, No. 1, 4–10.

Atkinson, R.C. and Shiffrin, R.M. (1971) The control of short-term memory. *Scientific American, 224*, 82–90.

Atkinson, R.L., Atkinson, R.C., Smith, E.E. and Bem, D.J. (1990) *Introduction to Psychology* (10th edn). New York: Harcourt Brace Jovanovich.

Ayer, A.J. (1936) *Language, Truth and Logic*. London: Victor Gollancz Ltd.

Bailey, C.L. (1979) Mental illness: a logical misrepresentation? *Nursing Times*, May, 761–2.

Baltes, P.B. and Kunzmann, U. (2003) Wisdom. *The Psychologist, 16*(3), 131–3.

Bandura, A. (1971) *Social Learning Theory*. New York: General Learning Press.

Banks, W.P. and Pockett, S. (2007) Benjamin Libet's Work on the Neuroscience of Free Will. In M. Velmans and S. Schneider (eds) *The Blackwell Companion to Consciousness*. Oxford: Blackwell Publishing.

Bannister, D. and Fransella, F. (1966) A grid test of schizophrenic thought disorder. *British Journal of Social & Clinical Psychology, 5*, 95–102.

Bannister, D. and Fransella, F. (1967) *A Grid Test of Schizophrenic Thought Disorder*. Barnstaple: Psychological Test Publications.

Bannister, D. and Fransella, F. (1980) *Inquiring Man: The Psychology of Personal Constructs* (2nd edn). Harmondsworth: Penguin.

Barker, P. (2003) Assessment – The Foundation of Practice. In P. Barker (ed.) *Psychiatric and Mental Health Nursing*. London: Arnold.

Barkow, J.H., Cosmides, L. and Tooby, J. (1992) Introduction. In J.H. Barkow, L. Cosmides and J. Tooby (eds) *The Adapted Mind: Evolutionary Psychology and the Evolution of Culture*. New York: Oxford University Press.

Barlow, H. (1987) The biological role of consciousness. In C. Blakemore and S. Greenfield (eds) *Mindwaves*. Oxford: Blackwell.

Baron, R.A. and Byrne, D. (1991) *Social Psychology* (6th edn). Boston, MA: Allyn & Bacon.

Baron, R.A. and Byrne, D. (1994) *Social Psychology: Understanding Human Interaction* (7th edn). Boston, MA: Allyn & Bacon.

Bassett, C. (2002) Nurses' and students' perceptions of care: A phenomenological study. *Nursing Times, 98*(34), 32–5.

Bateson, G., Jackson, D., Haley, J. and Weakland, J. (1956) Toward a theory of schizophrenia. *Behavioral Science, 1*, 251–64.

Bateson, P. (1986) When to experiment on animals. *New Scientist, 109*(1496), 30–2.

Bateson, P. (1992) Do animals feel pain? *New Scientist, 134*(1818), 30–3.

Batson, C.D. (1991) *The altrusim question: Toward a social-psychological answer.* Hillsdale, NJ: Erlbaum.

Baumrind, D. (1993) The average expectable environment is not good enough: A response to Scarr. *Child Development, 64*, 1299–317.

Becker, H.S. (1963) *Outsiders: Studies in the Sociology of Deviance.* New York: Free Press.

Bee, H. (1989) *The Developing Child* (5th edn). New York: Harper & Row.

Bee, H. (1994) *Lifespan Development.* New York: HarperCollins.

Beloff, J. (1987) Parapsychology and the mind–body problem. In R.L. Gregory (ed.) *The Oxford Companion to the Mind.* Oxford: Oxford University Press.

Bem, D.J. (1983) Constructing a theory of the triple typology: some (second) thoughts on nomothetic and idiographic approaches to personality. *Journal of Personality, 51*, 566–77.

Bem, D.J. and Allen, A. (1974) On predicting some of the people some of the time: a search for cross-situational consistencies in behavior. *Psychological Review, 81*, 506–20.

Bem, D.J. and Honorton, C. (1994) Does psi exist? Replicable evidence for an anomalous process of information transfer. *Psychological Bulletin, 115*, 4–18.

Bem, S. and Looren de Jong, H. (1997) *Theoretical Issues in Psychology: An Introduction.* London: Sage Publications.

Bem, S.L. (1984) Androgyny and gender schema theory: a conceptual and empirical integration. In R.A. Dienstbier (ed.) *Nebraska Symposium on Motivation.* Lincoln, Nebraska: University of Nebraska Press.

Bem, S.L. (1993a) Is there a place in psychology for a feminist analysis of the social context? *Feminism & Psychology, 3*(2), 230–4.

Bem, S.L. (1993b) The Lenses of Gender: Transforming the debate on sexual inequality. New Haven, CT: Yale University Press.

Bennett, M. (1993) Introduction. In M. Bennett (ed.) *The Child as Psychologist: An Introduction to the Development of Social Cognition.* Hemel Hempstead: Harvester Wheatsheaf.

Bentall, R.P. (1993) Personality traits may be alive, they may even be well, but are they really useful? *The Psychologist, 6*(7), 307.

Bentall, R.P. (2003) *Madness Explained: Psychosis and Human Nature.* London: Penguin.

Bentall, R.P. (2007) Researching psychotic complaints. *The Psychologist, 20*(5), 293–5.

Berger, P.L. and Luckmann, T. (1966) *The Social Construction of Reality.* Harmondsworth: Penguin.

THEMES, ISSUES AND DEBATES IN PSYCHOLOGY

Berkowitz, L. (1993) *Aggression: Its Causes, Consequences and Control*. New York: McGraw-Hill.

Bernstein, M.D. and Russo, N.F. (1974) The history of psychology revised: or, up with our foremothers. *American Psychologist, 29*, 130–4.

Berry, J.W. (1969) On cross-cultural comparability. *International Journal of Psychology, 4*, 119–28.

Berry, J.W., Poortinga, Y.H., Segall, M.H. and Dasen, P.R. (1992) *Cross-Cultural Psychology*. Cambridge: Cambridge University Press.

Berscheid, E. (1985) Interpersonal attraction. In G. Lindzey and E. Aronson (eds) *Handbook of Social Psychology* (3rd edn). New York: Random House.

Bettelheim, B. (1965) The problem of generations. In E. Erikson (ed.) *The Challenge of Youth*. New York: Doubleday.

Bhugra, D. and Bhui, K. (2001) *Cross-Cultural Psychiatry: A Practical Guide*. London: Arnold.

Bieber, I., Dain, H.J., Dince, P.R., Drellich, M.G., Grand, H.G., Bundlach, R.H., Dremer, M.W., Rifkin, A.H., Wilbur, C.B. and Bieber, T.B. (1962) *Homosexuality*. New York: Vintage Books.

Blackman, D.E. (1980) Image of man in contemporary behaviourism. In A.J. Chapman and D.M. Jones (eds) *Models of Man*. Leicester: British Psychological Society.

Blackmore, S. (1984) A postal survey of OBEs and other experiences. *Journal of the Society for Psychical Research*, 52, 225–44.

Blackmore, S. (1995) Parapsychology. In A.M. Colman (ed.) *Controversies in Psychology*. London: Longman.

Blackmore, S. (1996) Do you believe in psychic phenomena? Are they likely to be able to explain consciousness? *The Times Higher*, April 5, v.

Blackmore, S. (1997a) Probability misjudgement and belief in the paranormal: a newspaper survey. *British Journal of Psychology, 88*, 683–9.

Blackmore, S. (1997b) In search of the paranormal. *Psychology Review, 3*(3), 2–6.

Blackmore, S. (2001) Consciousness. *The Psychologist, 14*(10), 522–5.

Blackmore, S. (2003) *Consciousness: An Introduction*. London: Hodder & Stoughton.

Blackmore, S. (2005) *Consciousness: A Very Short Introduction*. Oxford: Oxford University Press.

Blakemore, C. (1988) *The Mind Machine*. London: BBC Books.

Blakemore, C. and Cooper, G.F. (1970) Development of the brain depends on the visual environment. *Nature, 228*, 477–8.

Block, N. (1995) On a confusion about a function of consciousness. *Behavioral & Brain Sciences, 18*, 227–87.

Boas, F. (1911) *The Mind of Primitive Man*. New York: Macmillan.

Boden, M. (1993) The impact on philosophy. In D. Broadbent (ed.) *The Simulation of Human Intelligence*. Oxford: Blackwell.

Bohart, A.C. (2003) Person-Centred Psychotherapy and Related Experiential Approaches. In A.S. Gurman and S.B. Messer (eds) *Essential Psychotherapies: Theory and Practice* (2nd edn). New York: The Guilford Press.

Boniwell, I. and Zimbardo, P. (2003) Time to find the right balance. *The Psychologist, 16*(3), 129–31.

Boring, E. (1966) Introduction. In C.E.M. Hansel (ed.) *ESP: A Scientific Evaluation*. New York: Scribners.

Bowers, K.S. (1973) Situationism in psychology: an analysis and critique. *Psychological Review, 80*, 307–36.

Bowlby, J. (1953) *Child Care and the Growth of Love*. Harmondsworth: Penguin.

Bowlby, J. (1958) The nature of the child's tie to his mother. *International Journal of Psycho-Analysis*, 39, 350–73.

Bowlby, J. (1969) *Attachment and Loss. Volume 1: Attachment*. Harmondsworth: Penguin.

Boyle, M. (2007) The problem with diagnosis. *The Psychologist, 20*(5), 290–2.

Brady, J.V. (1958) Ulcers in 'executive monkeys'. *Scientific American, 199*, 95–100.

Braisby, N. and Gellatly, A. (2005) Foundations of cognitive psychology. In N. Braisby and A. Gellatly (eds) *Cognitive Psychology*. Oxford: Oxford University Press in association with the Open University.

Braud, W.G. (1975) Psi-conducive states. *Journal of Communication, 25*, 142–52.

Brehm, J.W. (1966) *A Theory of Psychological Reactance*. New York: Academic Press.

Brehm, S.S. (1992) *Intimate Relationships* (2nd edn). New York: McGraw-Hill.

Brehm, S.S. and Brehm, J.W. (1981) *Psychological Reactance: A Theory of Freedom and Control*. New York: Academic Press.

Bretherton, R. and Orner, R. (2003) Positive psychotherapy in disguise. *The Psychologist, 16*(3), 136–7.

Brislin, R. (1993) *Understanding Culture's Influence on Behavior*. Orlando, FL: Harcourt Brace Jovanovich.

British Association for Counselling and Psychotherapy (2002) *Ethical Principles of counselling and psychotherapy*. Lutterworth: BACP (http://www.bacp.co.uk/ethical_framework/ethics.php)

British Psychological Society (1978a) Ethical principles for research with human subjects. *Bulletin of the British Psychological Society, 31*, 48–9.

British Psychological Society (1978b) Report of Working Party on Behaviour Modification. Leicester: BPS.

British Psychological Society (1981) *Principles Governing the Employment of Psychological Tests*. Leicester: BPS.

British Psychological Society (1985a) A code of conduct for psychologists. *Bulletin of the British Psychological Society, 38*, 41–3.

British Psychological Society (1985b) Guidelines for the Use of Animals in Research. Leicester: BPS.

British Psychological Society (1990) Ethical principles for conducting research with human participants. *The Psychologist, 3*(6), 269–72.

British Psychological Society (1993) Ethical principles for conducting research with human participants (revised). *The Psychologist, 6*(1), 33–5.

British Psychological Society (1995) *Division of Clinical Psychology Professional Practice Guidelines*. Leicester: BPS.

British Psychological Society (2000) *Code of Conduct, Ethical Principles and Guidelines*. Leicester: BPS.

British Psychological Society (2006) *Code of Ethics and Conduct*. Leicester: BPS.

British Psychological Society (2007a) *Guidelines for Psychologists Working with Animals*. Leicester: BPS.

British Psychological Society (2007b) *Guidelines for Ethical Practice in Psychological Research Online*. Leicester: BPS.

British Psychological Society Scientific Affairs Board (1985) Guidelines for the use of animals in research. *Bulletin of the British Psychological Society, 38*, 289–91.

Broad, W. and Wade, N. (1982) *Betrayers of the Truth: Fraud and Deceit in the Halls of Science*. London: Century Books.

Bronfenbrenner, U. (1979) *The Ecology of Human Development: Experiments by Nature and Design*. Cambridge, MS: Harvard University Press.

Bronfenbrenner, U. (1989) Ecological systems theory. *Annals of Child Development, 6*, 187–249.

Brown, J.A.C. (1961) *Freud and the Post-Freudians*. Harmondsworth: Penguin.

Brown, L.S. (1997) Ethics in psychology: cui bono? In D. Fox and I. Prilleltensky (eds) *Critical Psychology: An Introduction*. London: Sage.

Bruce, V. and Young, A.W. (1986) Understanding face recognition. *British Journal of Psychology, 77*, 305–27.

Bruner, J.S. (1990) *Acts of Meaning*. Cambridge, MA: Harvard University Press.

Burr, V. (1995) *An Introduction to Social Constructionism*. London: Routledge.

Burr, V. (2003) *Social Constructionism* (2nd edn) Hove: Routledge.

Burt, C. (1949) The structure of the mind: a review of the results of factor analysis. *British Journal of Educational Psychology*, *19*, 110–11, 176–99.

Burt, C. (1955) The evidence for the concept of intelligence. *British Journal of Educational Psychology*, *25*, 158–77.

Buss, D.M. (1994) Mate preference in 37 cultures. In W.J. Lonner and R.S. Malpass (eds) *Psychology and Culture*. Boston: Allyn & Bacon.

Buss, D.M. (1995) Evolutionary psychology: a new paradigm for psychological science. *Psychological Enquiry*, *6*(1), 1–30.

Buss, D.M. (2000) Quality of life: An evolutionary psychological perspective. *American Psychologist*, *55*, 15–23.

Butler, J.M. and Haigh, G.V. (1954) Changes in the relation between self-concepts and ideal concepts consequent upon client-centred counselling. In C.R. Rogers and R.F. Dymond (eds) *Psychotherapy and Personality Change: Coordinated Research Studies in the Client-Centred Approach*. Chicago: Chicago University Press.

Byrne, W. (1994) The biological evidence challenged. *Scientific American*, May, 26–31.

Caldwell, R. (1997) Dan Dennett and the conscious robot. *Philosophy Now*, 18, Summer, 16–18.

Calhoun, L.G. and Tedeschi, R.G. (1999) *Facilitating posttraumatic growth: A clinician's guide*. Mahwah, NJ: Lawrence Erlbaum.

Campbell, A. (2001) Behaviour – Adapted? Adaptive? Useful? *The Psychologist*, *14*(8), 426–7.

Caplan, P. (1991) Delusional dominating personality disorder (DDPD). *Feminism & Psychology*, *1*(1), 171–4.

Carlson, N.R. and Buskist, W. (1997) *Psychology: The Science of Behavior* (5th edn). Needham Heights, MA: Allyn & Bacon.

Carver, C.S. and Scheier, M.F. (1992) *Perspectives on Personality* (2nd edn). Boston: Allyn & Bacon.

Cattell, R.B. (1944) Psychological measurement: normative, ipsative, interactive. *Psychological Review*, *51*, 292–303.

Cattell, R.B. (1965) *The Scientific Analysis of Behaviour*. Harmondsworth: Penguin.

Chalmers, D. (1996) *The Conscious Mind: In Search of a Fundamental Theory*. Oxford: Oxford University Press.

Chalmers, D. (2007) The hard problem of consciousness. In M. Velmans and S. Schneider (eds) *The Blackwell Companion to Consciousness*. Oxford: Blackwell Publishing.

Child, A.L. (1954) Socialization. In G. Lindzey (ed.) *Handbook of Social Psychology, Vol. 2*. Cambridge, MA: Addison-Wesley.

Chomsky, N. (1965) *Aspects of the Theory of Syntax*. Cambridge, MA: MIT Press.

Chomsky, N. (1968) *Language and Mind*. New York: Harcourt Brace Jovanovich.

Claridge, G. and Davis, C. (2003) *Personality and Psychological Disorders*. London: Arnold.

Clarke, V. (2002) Resistance and normalization in the construction of lesbian and gay families: a discursive analysis. In A. Coyle and C. Kitzinger (eds) *Lesbian and Gay Psychology: New Perspectives*. BPS/Blackwell.

Clift, S.M. (1984) Should we still teach Freud? *Psychology Teaching*, December, 8–14.

Cohen, J. (1958) *Humanistic Psychology*. London: Allen & Unwin.

Cole, M. (1985) The zone of proximal development: where culture and cognition create each other. In J. Wertsch (ed.) *Culture, Communication and Cognition*. New York: Cambridge University Press.

Cole, M. (1990) Cultural psychology: a once and future discipline? In J.J. Berman (ed.) *Nebraska Symposium on Motivation: Cross-Cultural Perspectives*. Lincoln, NA: University of Nebraska Press.

Cole, M. (1993) Mind as a cultural achievement: implications for IQ testing. In M. Gauvin and M. Cole (eds) *Readings on the Development of Children*. New York: Scientific American Books, W.H. Freeman & Co.

Cole, M. (1996) *Cultural Psychology: A Once and Future Discipline*. Cambridge, MA: Harvard University Press.

Colman, A. M. (1987) *Facts, Fallacies and Frauds in Psychology*. London: Unwin Hyman.

Coolican, H. (1994) *Research Methods and Statistics in Psychology* (2nd edn). London: Hodder & Stoughton.

Coolican, H., Cassidy, T., Chercher, A., Harrower, J., Penny, G., Sharp, R., Walley, M. and Westbury, T. (1996) *Applied Psychology*. London: Hodder & Stoughton.

Coolican, H., Cassidy, T., Dunn, O., Harrower, J., Sharp, R., Simons, K., Tudway, J. and Westbury, T. (2007) *Applied Psychology* (2nd edn). London: Hodder Arnold.

Costa, P.T. and McCrae, R.R. (1993) Bullish on personality psychology. *The Psychologist, 6*(7), 302–3.

Coyle, A. and Kitzinger, C. (eds) (2002) *Lesbian and Gay Psychology: New Perspectives*. BPS/Blackwell.

Crick, F. (1994) *The Astonishing Hypothesis: The Scientific Search for the Soul*. London: Simon & Schuster.

Cullberg, J. (2006) *Psychoses: An Integrative Perspective*. London: Routledge.

Dalton, K. (1997) Exploring the links: creativity and psi in the Ganzfeld. In *The Parapsychological Association 40th Annual Convention: Proceedings of Presented Papers*. Durham, NC: Parapsychological Association.

Daly, M. and Wilson, M. (1988) Evolutionary social psychology and family homicide. *Science, 28*, October, 519–24.

Damasio, A.R. (1994) *Descartes' error: Emotion, reason, and the human brain*. New York: Putnam.

Danziger, K. (1990) *Constructing the Subject: Historical Origins of Psychological Research*. New York: Cambridge University Press.

Danziger, K. (1997) *Naming the Mind: How Psychology Found Its Language*. London: Sage.

Darley, J.M. and Latané, B. (1968) Bystander intervention in emergencies: diffusion of responsibility. *Journal of Personality & Social Psychology, 8*, 377–83.

Darwin, C.R. (1859) *The Origin of Species by Means of Natural Selection*. London: John Murray.

Darwin, C.R. (1872) *The Expression of Emotion in Man and Animals*. Chicago: University of Chicago Press.

Davis, S.N. and Gergen, M. (1997) Toward a New Psychology of Gender: Opening Conversations. In M. Gergen and S.N. Davis (eds) *Toward a New Psychology of Gender: A Reader*. New York: Routledge.

Davison, G.C. and Neale, J.M. (1994) *Abnormal Psychology* (6th edn). New York: John Wiley & Sons.

Davison, G.C. and Neale, J.M. (2001) *Abnormal Psychology* (8th edn). New York: John Wiley & Sons.

Davison, G.C., Neale, J.M. and Kring, A.M. (2004) *Abnormal Psychology* (9th edn). New York: John Wiley & Sons Inc.

Dawkins, R. (1976) *The Selfish Gene*. Oxford: Oxford University Press.

Dawkins, R. (2006) *The God Delusion*. London: Transworld Publishers.

Deary, I.J. and Matthews, G. (1993) Personality traits are alive and well. *The Psychologist, 6*(7), 299–311.

Deci, E.L. (1980) *The Psychology of Self-determination*. Lexington, MA: D.C. Heath.

Deci, E.L. and Ryan, R.M. (1987) The support of autonomy and the control of behavior. *Journal of Personality & Social Psychology, 53*, 1024–37.

Deese, J. (1972) *Psychology as Science and Art*. New York: Harcourt Brace Jovanovich.

Delle Fave, A. and Massimini, F. (2003) *The Psychologist, 16*(3), 133–4.

Denmark, F., Russo, N.F., Frieze, I.H. and Sechzer, J.A. (1988) Guidelines for avoiding sexism in psychological research: a report of the ad hoc committee on nonsexist research. *American Psychologist, 43*(7), 582–5.

Dennett, D. (1987) Consciousness. In R.L. Gregory (ed.) *The Oxford Companion to the Mind*. Oxford: Oxford University Press.

Dennett, D. (1991) *Consciousness Explained*. London: Little, Brown & Co.

Dennett, D.C. (2003) *Freedom Evolves*. London: Allen Lane.

Dewey, J. (1896) The reflex arc concept in psychology. *Psychological Review, 3*, 357–70.

Diener, E. (1999) Subjective well-being: Three decades of progress. *Psychological Bulletin, 125*, 276–301.

Diener, E. (2000) Subjective well-being: The science of happiness and a proposal for a national index. *American Psychologist, 55*, 56–67.

Diller, A. (1999/2000) Detecting androids. *Philosophy Now, 25*, Winter, 26–8.

Doyle, J.A. (1983) *The Male Experience*. Dubuque, Iowa: Wm C. Brown Co.

Draguns, J. (1980) Psychological disorders of clinical severity. In H.C. Triandis and J. Draguns (eds) *Handbook of Cross-Cultural Psychology, Vol. 6: Psychopathology*. Boston: Allyn & Bacon.

Draguns, J. (1990) Applications of cross-cultural psychology in the field of mental health. In R. Brislin (ed.) *Applied Cross-Cultural Psychology*. Newbury Park, CA: Sage.

Dunbar, R. (2008) Taking evolutionary psychology seriously. *The Psychologist, 21*(4), 304–6.

Duncker, K. (1945) *On Problem Solving*. Washington, DC: American Psychological Association.

Dunn, J. and Plomin, R. (1990) *Separate Lives: Why Siblings are so Different*. New York: Basic Books.

Eagly, A.H. (1987) *Sex Differences in Social Behavior: A social-role interpretation*. Hillsdale, NJ: Lawrence Erlbaum.

Edelman, G. (1992) *Bright Air, Brilliant Fire: On the Matter of the Mind*. Harmondsworth: Penguin.

Edwards, D. (1997) *Discourse and Cognition*. London: Sage.

Edwards, D. and Potter, J. (1992) *Discursive Psychology*. London: Sage.

Eiser, J.R. (1994) *Attitudes, Chaos and the Connectionist Mind*. Oxford: Blackwell.

Ellis, A. (1962) *Reason and Emotion in Psychotherapy*. Secaucus, NJ: Lyle Stuart (Citadel Press).

Ellis, A. (1987) The impossibility of achieving consistently good mental health. *American Psychologist, 42*, 364–75.

Endler, N.S. and Magnusson, D. (1976) Toward an interactional psychology of personality. *Psychological Bulletin, 83*, 956–74.

Epstein, S. (1979) The stability of behavior: On predicting most of the people much of the time. *Journal of Personality & Social Psychology, 37*, 1097–126.

Ericsson, K.A. and Simon, H. (1984) *Protocol Analysis: Verbal Reports as Data*. Cambridge, MA: MIT Press.

Erikson, E.H. (1950) *Childhood and Society*. New York: Norton.

Erikson, E.H. (1963) *Childhood and Society* (2nd edn). New York: Norton.

Erikson, E.H. (1968) *Identity: Youth and Crisis*. New York: Norton.

Evans, C. (1987a) Parapsychology: A History of Research. In R.L. Gregory (ed.) *The Oxford Companion to the Mind*. Oxford: Oxford University Press.

Evans, C. (1987b) Extra-sensory perception. In R.L. Gregory (ed.) *The Oxford Companion to the Mind*. Oxford: Oxford University Press.

Ewen, R.E. (1988) *An Introduction to Theories of Personality* (3rd edn). Hillsdale, NJ: Lawrence Erlbaum.

Eysenck, H.J. (1953) *The Structure of Human Personality*. London: Methuen.

Eysenck, H.J. (1960) Classification and the problem of diagnosis. In H.J. Eysenck (ed.) *Handbook of Abnormal Psychology*. London: Pitman.

Eysenck, H.J. (1965) *Fact and Fiction in Psychology*. Harmondsworth: Penguin.

Eysenck, H.J. (1967) The Biological Basis of Personality. Springfield, IL: C.C. Thomas.

Eysenck, H.J. (1970) *Crime and Personality* (revised edn). London: Paladin.

Eysenck, H.J. (1985) *Decline and Fall of the Freudian Empire*. Harmondsworth: Penguin.

Eysenck, H.J. and Wilson, G.D. (eds) (1973) *The Experimental Study of Freudian Theories*. London: Methuen.

Eysenck, M.W. (1994) *Perspectives on Psychology*. Hove: Lawrence Erlbaum.

Fairbairn, G. (1987) Responsibility, respect for persons and psychological change. In S. Fairbairn and G. Fairbairn (eds) *Psychology, Ethics and Change*. London: RKP.

Fairbairn, R. (1952) *Psychoanalytical Studies of the Personality*. London: Tavistock.

Fancher, R.E. (1979) *Pioneers of Psychology*. New York: Norton.

Fancher, R.E. (1996) *Pioneers of Psychology* (3rd edn). New York: Norton.

Fausto-Sterling, A. (2000) Beyond difference: feminism and evolutionary psychology. In H. Rose and S. Rose (eds) *Alas, Poor Darwin: Arguments Against Evolutionary Psychology*. London: Jonathan Cape.

Fechner, G. (1966) *Elements of Psychophysics, Vol. 1* (trans. H.E. Adler). New York: Holt, Rinehart & Winston (originally published 1860).

Ferguson, M.J. and Bargh, J.A. (2004) How social perception can automatically influence behavior. *Trends in Cognitive Sciences, 8*(1), 33–9.

Fernando, S. (1991) *Mental Health, Race and Culture*. London: Macmillan, in association with MIND Publications.

Festinger, L. (1957) *A Theory of Cognitive Dissonance*. New York: Harper & Row.

Festinger, L. and Carlsmith, J.M. (1959) Cognitive consequences of forced compliance. *Journal of Abnormal & Social Psychology, 58*, 203–10.

Feyerabend, P.K. (1965) Problems of empiricism. In R. Colodny (ed.) *Beyond the Edge of Certainty*. Englewood Cliffs, NJ: Prentice-Hall.

Feyerabend, P.K. (1978) *Science in a Free Society*. London: NLB.

Fisher, S. and Greenberg, R.P. (1996) *Freud Scientifically Reappraised: Testing the Theories and the Therapy*. New York: Wiley.

Fiske, S. and Taylor, S. (1991) *Social Cognition* (2nd edn). New York: McGraw-Hill.

Flanagan, O. (1984) *The Science of the Mind*. Cambridge, MA: MIT Press.

Flanagan, O. (1992) *Consciousness Reconsidered.* Cambridge, MA: MIT Press.

Frankl, V.E. (1969) *The Will to Meaning: Foundations and applications of logotherapy* (Expanded edn). New York: Meridian.

Fransella, F. (1970) And there was one. In D. Bannister (ed.) *Perspectives in Personal Construct Theory.* London: Academic Press.

Fransella, F. (1972) *Personal Change and Reconstruction: Research on a Treatment of Stuttering.* London: Academic Press.

Fransella, F. (1980) Man-as-scientist. In A.J. Chapman and D.M. Jones (eds) *Models of Man.* Leicester: British Psychological Society.

French, C. (2001) Why I study . . . anomalistic psychology. *The Psychologist, 14*(7), 356–7.

Freud, S. (1900/1976a) *The Interpretation of Dreams.* Pelican Freud Library (4). Harmondsworth: Penguin.

Freud, S. (1901/1976b) *The Psychopathology of Everyday Life.* Pelican Freud Library (5). Harmondsworth: Penguin.

Freud, S. (1914) Remembering, Repeating and Working Through. *The Standard Edition of Complete Psychological Works of Sigmund Freud, Vol. XII.* London: Hogarth Press.

Freud, S. (1930) *Civilization and its Discontents.* London: Hogarth Press.

Freud, S. (1949) *An Outline of Psychoanalysis.* London: Hogarth Press.

Frijda, N. (1988) The laws of emotion. *American Psychologist, 43,* 349–58.

Frith, C. and Rees, G. (2007) A brief history of the scientific approach to the study of consciousness. In M. Velmans and S. Schneider (eds) *The Blackwell Companion to Consciousness.* Oxford: Blackwell Publishing.

Fromm, E. (1942) *The Fear of Freedom.* London: RKP.

Fromm, E. (1964) *The Heart of Man.* London: RKP.

Gable, S.L. and Haidt, J. (2005) What (and why) is positive psychology? *Review of General Psychology, 9,* 103–10.

Gahagan, J. (1984) *Social Interaction and its Management.* London: Methuen.

Gahagan, J. (1991) Understanding other people: understanding self. In J. Radford and E. Govier (eds) *A Textbook of Psychology* (2nd edn). London: Routledge.

Gale, A. (1995) Ethical issues in psychological research. In A.M. Colman (ed.) *Psychological Research Methods and Statistics.* London: Methuen.

Gardner, R.A. and Gardner, B.T. (1969) Teaching sign language to a chimpanzee. *Science, 165* (3894), 664–72.

Garfinkel, H. (1967) *Studies in Ethnomethodology.* Englewood Cliffs, NJ: Prentice-Hall.

Garnham, A. (1991) *The Mind in Action.* London: Routledge.

Garrett, R. (1996) Skinner's case for radical behaviourism. In W. O'Donohue and R.F. Kitchener (eds) *The Philosophy of Psychology.* London: Sage.

Gazzaniga, M.S. (1997) Why can't I control my brain? Aspects of conscious experience. In Masao Ito, Yasushi Miyashita *et al.* (eds) *Cognition, Computation, and Consciousness.* Washington, DC: American Psychological Association.

Gazzaniga, M.S. (1998) *The Mind's Past.* Berkeley, CA; University of California Press.

Gay, P. (1988) *Freud: A Life for our Time.* London: J.M. Dent & Sons.

Gelder, M., Gath, D. and Mayon, R. (1989) *Oxford Textbook of Psychiatry* (2nd edn). Oxford: Oxford University Press.

Gergen, K.J. (1973) Social psychology as history. *Journal of Personality & Social Psychology, 26,* 309–20.

Gergen, K.J. (1985) The social constructionist movement in modern psychology. *American Psychologist, 40,* 266–75.

Gergen, K.J. (1997) Social psychology as social construction: the emerging vision. In C. McGarty and A. Haslam (eds) *The Message of Social Psychology: Perspectives on Mind in Society*. Oxford: Blackwell.

Gesell, A. (1925) *The Mental Growth of the Preschool Child*. New York: Macmillan.

Gilligan, C. (1982) *In a Different Voice: Psychological Theory and Women's Development*. Cambridge, MA: Harvard University Press.

Gilligan, C. (1993) Letter to readers (Preface). *In a Different Voice* (2nd impression; see entry above).

Glassman, W.E. (1995) *Approaches to Psychology* (2nd edn). Buckingham: Open University Press.

Goffman, E. (1963) *Stigma: Notes on the Management of Spoiled Identity*. Englewood Cliffs, NJ: Prentice-Hall.

Goffman, E. (1971) *The Presentation of Self in Everyday Life*. Harmondsworth: Penguin.

Golombok, S. (2002) Why I study lesbian mothers. *The Psychologist, 15*(11), 562–3.

Gottesman, I. (1991) *Schizophrenia Genesis*. New York: W.H. Freeman.

Gough, B. and McFadden, M. (2001) *Critical Social Psychology: An Introduction*. Basingstoke: Palgrave.

Gould, R.L. (1978) *Transformations: Growth and Change in Adult Life*. New York: Simon & Schuster.

Gould, S.J. (1981) *The Mismeasure of Man*. New York: Norton.

Gould, S.J. (1987) *An Urchin in the Storm*. Harmondsworth: Penguin.

Graham, H. (1986) *The Human Face of Psychology: Humanistic Psychology in Historical, Social and Cultural Context*. Milton Keynes: Open University Press.

Gray, J. (1987) The mind–brain identity as a scientific hypothesis: a second look. In C. Blakemore and S. Greenfield (eds) *Mindwaves*. Oxford: Blackwell.

Gray, J.A. (1991) On the morality of speciesism. *The Psychologist, 4*(5), 196–8.

Grayling, A.C. (2002) Scientist or storyteller? *Guardian Review*, 22 June, 4–6.

Greenfield, P.M. (1997) Culture as process: empirical methods for cultural psychology. In J.W. Berry, Y.H. Poortinga and J. Pandey (eds) *Handbook of Cross-cultural Research, Vol. 1, Theory and Method*. Boston, MA: Allyn & Bacon.

Greenfield, S.A. (1995) *Journey to the Centres of the Mind*. New York: W.H. Freeman & Co.

Gregory, R.L. (1981) *Mind in Science*. Hove: Lawrence Erlbaum.

Gregory, R.L. (1987) Paranormal. In R.L. Gregory (ed.) *The Oxford Companion to the Mind*. Oxford: Oxford University Press.

Gross, R. (2001) *Psychology: The Science of Mind and Behaviour* (4th edn). London: Hodder & Stoughton.

Gross, R. (2003) *Key Studies in Psychology* (4th edn). London: Hodder & Stoughton.

Gross, R. (2005) *Psychology: The Science of Mind and Behaviour* (5th edn). London: Hodder Arnold.

Gross, R. (2008) *Key Studies in Psychology* (5th edn). London: Hodder Education.

Gross, R., Humphreys, P. and Petkova, B. (1997) *Challenges in Psychology*. London: Hodder & Stoughton.

Gross, R. and Rolls, G. (in press) *AQA(A) Psychology for A2*. London: Hodder Education.

Guilford, J.P. (1959) Three faces of intellect. *American Psychologist, 14*, 469–79.

Haggard, P. and Eimer, M. (1999) On the relation between brain potentials and awareness of voluntary movements. *Experimental BRAIN Research, 126*, 128–33.

Hall, E.T. (1959) *The Silent Language*. New York: Doubleday.

Hall, E.T. (1966) *The Hidden Dimension*. Garden City, NY: Doubleday & Company.

Hampson, S.E. (1988) *The Construction of Personality: An Introduction* (2nd edn). London: Routledge.

Haney, C., Banks, C. and Zimbardo, P. (1973) A study of prisoners and guards in a simulated prison. *Naval Research Reviews, 30*(9), 4–17.

Harding, S. (1986) *The science question in feminism*. Milton Keynes: Open University Press.

Harlow, H.F. and Zimmerman, R.R. (1959) Affectional responses in the infant monkey. *Science, 130*, 421–32.

Harper, D., Cromby, J., Reavey, P., Cooke, A. and Anderson, J. (2007) Don't jump ship! New approaches in teaching mental health to undergraduates. *The Psychologist, 20*(5), 302–4.

Harré, R. (1993) Rules, roles and rhetoric. *The Psychologist, 6*(1), 24–8.

Harré, R. (1995) Discursive psychology. In J.A. Smith, R. Harré and L. Van Langenhove (eds) *Rethinking Psychology*. London: Sage.

Harré, R. and Secord, P.F. (1972) *The Explanation of Social Behaviour*. Oxford: Blackwell.

Harré, R., Clarke, D. and De Carlo, N. (1985) *Motives and Mechanisms: An Introduction to the Psychology of Action*. London: Methuen.

Harris, P. (1989) *Children and Emotion*. Oxford: Blackwell.

Hartshorne, H. and May, M. (1930) Studies in the Nature of Character. New York: Macmillan.

Haworth, G. (1992) The use of non-human animals in psychological research: the current status of the debate. *Psychology Teaching, New Series No. 1*, 46–54.

Heather, N. (1976) *Radical Perspectives in Psychology*. London: Methuen.

Heider, F. (1958) *The Psychology of Interpersonal Relations*. New York: Wiley.

Henry, J. (2005a) Parapsychology. In J. Henry (ed.) *Parapsychology: Research on Exceptional Experiences*. London: Routledge.

Henry, J. (2005b) Psychokinesis. In J. Henry (ed.) *Parapsychology: Research on Exceptional Experience*. London: Routledge.

Herrnstein, R.J. (1971) IQ. *Atlantic Monthly*, September, 43–64.

Herrnstein, R.J. and Murray, C. (1994) The Bell Curve: Intelligence and Class Structure in American Life. New York: Free Press.

Herskovits, M.J. (1948) *Man and His Works: The Science of Cultural Anthropology*. New York: Alfred A. Knopf.

Hewstone, M. and Antaki, C. (1988) Attribution Theory and Social Explanations. In M. Hewstone, W. Stroebe, J.-P. Codol and G.M. Stephenson (eds) *Introduction to Social Psychology*. Oxford: Basil Blackwell.

Hewstone, M., Stroebe, W. and Stephenson, G.M. (1996) *Introduction to Social Psychology* (2nd edn). Oxford: Blackwell.

Hilliard, A.G. (1995) The nonscience and nonsense of the bell curve. Focus: *Notes from the Society for the Psychological Study of Ethnic Minority Issues*, 10–12.

Hilliard, R.B. (1993) Single-case methodology in psychotherapy process and outcome research. *Journal of Consulting & Clinical Psychology, 61*(3), 373–80.

Hofstede, G. (1980) *Culture's Consequences: International Differences in Work-related Values*. Beverly Hills, CA: Sage.

Hogg, M.A. and Vaughan, G.M. (1995) *Social Psychology: An Introduction*. Hemel Hempstead: Prentice Hall.

Holmes, D.S. (1994) *Abnormal Psychology* (2nd edn). New York: HarperCollins.

Holmes, J. (1992) Response [to Masson's 'The tyranny of psychotherapy']. In W. Dryden and C. Feltham (eds) *Psychotherapy and Its Discontents*. Buckingham: Open University Press.

Holmes, J. (1993) *John Bowlby and Attachment Theory*. London: Routledge.

Holt, R.R. (1967) Individuality and generalization in the psychology of personality. In R.S. Lazarus and E.M. Opton (eds) *Personality*. Harmondsworth: Penguin.

Honderich, T. (1987) Mind, brain and self-conscious mind. In C. Blakemore and S. Greenfield (eds) *Mindwaves*. Oxford: Blackwell.

Honorton, C. (1985) Meta-analysis of psi Ganzfeld research: a response to Hyman. *Journal of Parapsychology, 49*, 51–91.

Honorton, C. and Ferrari, D.C. (1989) Meta-analysis of forced-choice precognition experiments. *Journal of Parapsychology, 53*, 281–308.

Honorton, C. and Harper, S. (1974) Psi-mediated imagery and ideation in an experimental procedure for regulating perceptual input. *Journal of the American Society for Psychical Research, 68*, 156–68.

Honorton, C. and Krippner, S. (1969) Hypnosis and ESP: a review of the experimental literature. *Journal of the American Society for Psychical Research, 63*, 214–52.

Horgan, J. (1993) Eugenics Revisited. *Scientific American*, June, 92–100.

Horgan, J. (1995) The new social Darwinists. *Scientific American*, October, 150–7.

Horowitz, F.D. (1987) *Exploring Developmental Theories: Towards a Structural/Behavioral Model of Development*. Hillsdale, NJ: Erlbaum.

Horowitz, F.D. (1990) Developmental models of individual differences. In J. Colombo and J. Fagan (eds) *Individual Differences in Infancy: Reliability, Stability, Predictability*. Hillsdale, NJ: Erlbaum.

Howe, M. (1997) *IQ in Question: The Truth about Intelligence*. London: Sage.

Humphrey, N. (1986) *The Inner Eye*. London: Faber and Faber.

Humphrey, N. (1992) *A History of the Mind*. London: Vintage.

Humphrey, N. (1993) Introduction. In N. Humphrey, *The Inner Eye* (new edn). London: Faber and Faber.

Hyman, R. (1985) The Ganzfeld psi experiment: a critical appraisal. *Journal of Parapsychology, 49*, 3–49.

Hyman, R. and Honorton, C. (1986) A joint communiqué: the psi Ganzfeld controversy. *Journal of Parapsychology, 50*, 351–64.

International Molecular Genetic Study of Autism Consortium (1998) A full genome screen for autism with evidence for linkage to a region of chromosome 7q. *Human Molecular Genetics, 7*, 571–8.

Jackson, G. (1992) *Women and Psychology – What Might that Mean?* Paper given at Association for the Teaching of Psychology Conference, July.

Jacobs, M. (1992) *Freud*. London: Sage Publications.

Jacobsen, B., Joergensen, S.D. and Joergensen, E. (2000) The world of the cancer patient from an existential perspective. *Journal of the Society for Existential Analysis, 11*, 122–35.

Jahoda, G. (1978) Cross-cultural perspectives. In H. Tajfel and C. Fraser (eds) *Introducing Social Psychology*. Harmondsworth: Penguin.

James, O. (1997) *Britain on the Couch*. London: Arrow Books.

James, O. (2007) *Affluenza*. London: Vermilion.

James, O. (2008) *The Selfish Capitalist*. London: Vermilion.

James, W. (1890) *The Principles of Psychology*. New York: Holt.

Jensen, A.R. (1969) How much can we boost IQ and scholastic achievement? *Harvard Educational Review, 39*, 1–123.

Johnson-Laird, P.N. (1983) *Mental Models*. Cambridge: Cambridge University Press.

Johnson-Laird, P.N. (1987) How could consciousness arise from the computations of the brain? In C. Blakemore and S. Greenfield (eds) *Mindwaves*. Oxford: Blackwell.

Johnson-Laird, P.N. (1988) *The Computer and the Mind*. London: Fontana.

Jones, D. and Elcock, J. (2001) *History and Theories of Psychology: A Critical Perspective*. London: Arnold.

Jones, E.E. and Nisbett, R.E. (1971) *The Actor and the Observer: Divergent perceptions of the causes of behavior*. Morristown, NJ: General Learning Press.

Jones, S. (1993) *The Language of the Genes*. London: Flamingo.

Joscelyne, T. (2002) Time for a change? *The Psychologist, 15*(4), 176–7.

Joseph, S. and Linley, P.A. (2006) Positive Psychology versus the Medical Model? *American Psychologist*, May–June, 332–3.

Joynson, R.B. (1974) *Psychology and Common Sense*. London: RKP.

Jung, C.G. (ed.) (1964) *Man and his Symbols*. London: Aldus-Jupiter Books.

Kahneman, D. (1999) Objective happiness. In D. Kahneman, E. Diener and N. Schwarz (eds) *Well-being: The foundations of hedonic psychology*. New York: Russell Sage Foundation.

Karmiloff-Smith, A. (2000) Why babies' brains are not Swiss army knives. In H. Rose and S. Rose (eds) *Alas, Poor Darwin: Arguments Against Evolutionary Psychology*. London: Jonathan Cape.

Kashdan, T.B., Biswas-Diner, R. and King, L.A. (in press) Reconsidering Happiness: The costs of distinguishing between hedonics and eudaimonia. *Journal of Positive Psychology*.

Kay, H. (1972) Psychology today and tomorrow. *Bulletin of the British Psychological Society, 25*, 177–88.

Keller, I. and Heckhausen, H. (1990) Readiness potentials preceding spontaneous motor acts: voluntary vs involuntary control. *Electroencephalography and Clinical Neurophysiology, 76*, 351–61.

Kelly, G. (1955) *A Theory of Personality: The Psychology of Personal Constructs*. New York: Norton.

Kelly, L. (1988) *Surviving Sexual Violence*. Cambridge: Polity Press.

King, L.A. and Napa, C.K. (1998) What makes a life good? *Journal of Personality & Social Psychology, 75*, 156–65.

Kirby, R. and Radford, J. (1976) *Individual Differences*. London: Methuen.

Kitchener, R.F. (1996) Skinner's Theory of Theories. In W. O'Donohue and R.F. Kitchener (eds) *The Philosophy of Psychology*. London: Sage.

Kitzinger, C. (1987) *The Social Construction of Lesbianism*. London: Sage.

Kitzinger, C. (1990) Heterosexism in psychology. *The Psychologist, 3*(9), 391–2.

Kitzinger, C. and Coyle, A. (2002) Introducing lesbian and gay psychology. In C. Kitzinger and A. Coyle (eds) *Lesbian & Gay Psychology: New Perspectives*. BPS/Blackwell.

Klein, M. (1932) *The Psycho-Analysis of Children*. London: Hogarth.

Kline, P. (1989) Objective tests of Freud's theories. In A.M. Colman and J.G. Beaumont (eds) *Psychology Survey No. 7*. Leicester: British Psychological Society.

Kline, P. (1993) Comments on 'Personality traits are alive and well'. *The Psychologist, 6*(7), 304.

Kline, P. (1998) Psychoanalytic perspectives. *Psychology Review*, 5(1), 10–13.

Kluckhohn, C. and Murray, H.A. (1953) Personality formation: the determinants. In C. Kluckhohn, H.A. Murray and D.M. Schneider (eds) *Personality in Nature, Society, and Culture* (2nd edn). New York: Knopf.

Koestler, A. (1967) *The Ghost in the Machine*. London: Pan.

Kohlberg, L. (1969) Stage and sequence: the cognitive-developmental approach to socialization. In D.A. Goslin (ed.) *Handbook of Socialization: Theory and Research*. Chicago: Rand McNally.

Kohn, M. (1998) Survival of the chattiest. *The Independent on Sunday*, 5 April, 44–5.

Kraepelin, E. (1913) *Psychiatry* (8th edn). Leipzig: Thieme.

Krahé, B. (1992) *Personality and Social Psychology: Towards a Synthesis*. London: Sage.

Krupat, E. and Garonzik, R. (1994) Subjects' expectations and the search for alternatives to deception in social psychology. *British Journal of Social Psychology, 32*, 211–22.

Kuhn, T.S. (1962) *The Structure of Scientific Revolutions*. Chicago: University of Chicago Press.

Kuhn, T.S. (1970) *The Structure of Scientific Revolutions* (2nd edn). Chicago: University of Chicago Press.

Lachman, R., Lachman, J.L. and Butterfield, E.C. (1979) *Cognitive Psychology and Information Processing*. Hillsdale, NJ: Lawrence Erlbaum Associates.

Laing, R.D. (1961) *The Self and Others*. London: Tavistock Publications.

Laing, R.D. (1967) *The Politics of Experience and the Bird of Paradise*. Harmondsworth: Penguin.

Lakatos, I. (1970) Falsification and the methodology of scientific research programmes. In I. Lakatos and A. Musgrave (eds) *Criticism and the Growth of Knowledge*. Cambridge: Cambridge University Press.

Lalljee, M. and Widdicombe, S. (1989) Discourse analysis. In A.M. Colman and J.C. Beaumont (eds) *Psychology Survey, 7*. Leicester: British Psychological Society.

Lamiell, J.T. (1981) Toward an idiothetic psychology of personality. *American Psychologist, 36*, 276–89.

Lamiell, J.T. (1982) The case for an idiothetic psychology of personality: a conceptual and empirical foundation. In B.A. Maher and W.B. Maher (eds) *Progress in Experimental Personality Research, Vol. 11*. New York: Academic Press.

Lamiell, J.T. (1987) *The Psychology of Personality: An Epistemological Inquiry*. New York: Columbia University Press.

Latané, B. and Darley, J.M. (1968) Group inhibitions of bystander intervention in emergencies. *Journal of Personality & Social Psychology, 10*, 215–21.

Leahey, T.H. (2000) *A History of Psychology: Main Currents in Psychological Thought* (4th edn). Englewood Cliffs, NJ: Prentice-Hall.

Lerner, G. (1979) *The Majority Finds Its Past: Placing Women in History*. New York: Oxford University Press.

Leslie, J.C. (2002) *Essential Behaviour Analysis*. London: Arnold.

LeVay, S. and Hamer, D.H. (1994) Evidence for a biological influence in male homosexuality. *Scientific American*, May, 20–5.

Leyens, J.P. and Codol, J.P. (1988) Social cognition. In M. Hewstone, W. Stroebe, J.P. Codol and G. M. Stephenson (eds) *Introduction to Social Psychology*. Oxford: Blackwell.

Libet, B. (1981) The experimental evidence of subjective referral of a sensory experience backwards in time. *Philosophy of Science, 48*, 182–97.

Libet, B. (1985) Unconscious cerebral initiative and the role of conscious will in voluntary action. *Behavioral & Brain Sciences, 8*, 29–539.

Libet, B. (1999) Do we have free will? *Journal of Consciousness Studies, 6*, 47–57.

Libet, B. (2003) Can conscious experience affect brain activity? *Journal of Consciousness Studies, 10*(12), 24–8.

Libet, B. (2004) *Mind Time: The Temporal Factor in Consciousness*. Cambridge, MA: Harvard University Press.

Libet, B., Freeman, A. and Sutherland, K. (1999) *The Volitional Brain: Towards a Neuroscience of Free Will*. Thorverton, Devon: Imprint Academic.

Libet, B., Gleason, C.A., Wright, E.W. and Pearl, D.K. (1983) Time of conscious intention to act in relation to onset of cerebral activity (readiness potential): the unconscious initiation of a freely voluntary act. *Brain, 106*, 623–42.

Libet. B., Wright, E.W., Feinstein, B. and Pearl, D.K. (1979) Subjective referral of the timing for a conscious sensory experience: a functional role for the somatosensory specific projection system in man. *Brain, 102*, 193–224.

Lilienfeld, S.O. (1995) *Seeing Both Sides: Classic Controversies in Abnormal Psychology*. Pacific Grove, CA: Brooks/Cole Publishing Co.

Lilienfeld, S.O. (1998) *Looking into Abnormal Psychology: Contemporary Readings*. Pacific Grove, CA: Brooks/Cole Publishing Co.

Linley, P.A. (2008a) Positive psychology (history). In S.J. Lopez (ed.) *The Encyclopaedia of Positive Psychology*. Oxford: Blackwell.

Linley, P.A. (2008b) Strengths perspective (positive psychology). In S.J. Lopez (ed.) *The Encyclopaedia of Positive Psychology*. Oxford: Blackwell.

Linley, P.A. and Joseph, S. (2003) Trauma and personal growth. *The Psychologist, 16*(3), 135.

Linley, P.A., Joseph, S., Harrington, S. and Wood, A.M. (2006) Positive psychology: Past, present and (possible) future. *The Journal of Positive Psychology, 1*, 3–16.

Littlewood, R. and Lipsedge, M. (1989) *Aliens and Alienists: Ethnic Minorities and Psychiatry* (2nd edn). London: Routledge.

Locke, J. (1690) *An Essay Concerning Human Understanding*. Oxford: P.H. Nidditch.

Lodge, D. (2002) Sense and sensibility. *Guardian Review*, 2 November, 4–6.

Lumsden, W. and Wilson, E.O. (1981) *Genes, Mind and Culture*. Cambridge, MA: Harvard University Press.

Lyubomirski, S., King, L. and Diener, E. (2005) The Benefits of Frequent Positive Affect: Does Happiness Lead to Success? *Psychological Bulletin, 131*(6), 803–55.

McCrae, R.R. and Costa, P.T. (1989) More reasons to adopt the five-factor model. *American Psychologist, 44*, 451–2.

McCrone, J. (2004) The power of belief. *New Scientist, 181*(2438), 34–7.

McCullough, M.E., Kilpatrick, S., Emmons, R.A. and Larson, D. (2001) Is gratitude a moral affect? *Psychological Bulletin, 127*, 249–66.

McCullough, M.E., Tsang, J. and Emmons, R.A. (2004) Gratitude in intermediate terrain: Links of grateful moods with individual differences and daily emotional experience. *Journal of Personality and Social Psychology, 86*, 295–309.

McDougall, W. (1908) *An Introduction to Social Psychology*. London: Methuen.

McGhee, P. (2001) *Thinking Psychologically*. Basingstoke: Palgrave.

McGinn, C. (1999) *The Mysterious Flame: Conscious Minds in a Material World*. New York: Basic Books.

McGurk, H. (1975) *Growing and Changing*. London: Methuen.

Maddux, J.E. (2002) Stopping the madness: Positive psychology and the deconstruction of the illness ideology and the DSM. In C.R. Snyder and S.J. Lopez (eds) *Handbook of Positive Psychology*. New York: Oxford University Press.

Maddux, J.E., Snyder, C.R. and Lopez, S.J. (2004) Toward a positive clinical psychology: Deconstructing the illness ideology and constructing an ideology of human strengths and potential. In P. A. Linley and S. Joseph (eds) *Positive Psychology in Practice*. Hoboken, NJ: Wiley.

Maher, B.A. (1966) *Principles of Psychopathology: An Experimental Approach*. New York: McGraw-Hill.

Mahler, M. (1975) *The Psychological Birth of the Human Infant*. London: Hutchinson.

Mahoney, J. (1998) Mates past their prime. *Times Higher Educational Supplement*, 25 September, 18.

Malinowski, B. (1929) *The Sexual Life of Savages*. New York: Harcourt Brace Jovanovich.

Markus, H.R. and Kitayama, S. (1991) Culture and the self: implications for cognition, emotion and motivation. *Psychological Review, 98*, 224–53.

Marzillier, J. (2004) The myth of evidence-based psychotherapy. *The Psychologist, 17*(7), 392–5.

Maslow, A.H. (1954) *Motivation and Personality*. New York: Harper & Row.

Maslow, A.H. (1968) *Toward a Psychology of Being* (2nd edn). New York: Van Nostrand Reinhold.

Massimini, F. and Delle Fave, A. (2000) Individual development in a biocultural perspective. *American Psychologist, 55*, 24–33.

Masson, J. (1988) *Against Therapy: Emotional Tyranny and the Myth of Psychological Healing*. New York: Atheneum.

Masson, J. (1992) The tyranny of psychotherapy. In W. Dryden and C. Feltham (eds) *Psychotherapy and its Discontents*. Buckingham: Open University Press.

Matsumoto, D., Kudoh, T. and Takeuchi, S. (1996) Changing patterns of individualism and collectivism in the United States and Japan. *Culture & Psychology, 2*, 77–107.

Matthews, R. (2004) Opposites detract. *New Scientist, 181*(2438), 38–41.

May, R. (1967) *Psychology and the Human Dilemma*. New York: Van Nostrand.

Mee, B. (2000) We'll see you in court. *The Independent on Sunday*, 21 May, 9–12.

Merleau-Ponty, M. (1962) *The Phenomenology of Perception*. London: RKP.

Merleau-Ponty, M. (1968) *The Visible and the Invisible*. Evanston, Ill.: Northwestern University Press.

Midgley, M. (2003) Fate by fluke. *Guardian Review*, 1 March, 12.

Midgley, M. (2004) Do we ever really act? In D. Ress and S. Rose (eds) *The New Brain Sciences: Perils and Prospects*. Cambridge: Cambridge University Press.

Milgram, S. (1963) Behavioral study of obedience. *Journal of Abnormal & Social Psychology, 67*, 371–8.

Milgram, S. (1974) *Obedience to Authority*. New York: Harper Torchbooks.

Milgram, S. (1977) Subject reaction: the neglected factor in the ethics of experimentation. The Hastings Centre Report, October, 19–23. (Reprinted in S. Milgram (1992) *The Individual in a Social World* (2nd edn). New York: McGraw-Hill.)

Miller, D.T. and Ross, M. (1975) Self-serving biases in the attribution of causality: fact or fiction? *Psychological Bulletin, 82*, 213–25.

Miller, E. and Morley, S. (1986) *Investigating Abnormal Behavior*. London: Weidenfeld & Nicolson/Lawrence Erlbaum.

Miller, G.A. (1956) The magical number seven, plus or minus two: some limits on our capacity for processing information. *Psychological Review, 63*, 81–97.

Miller, G.A. (1969) Psychology as a means of promoting human welfare. *American Psychologist, 24*, 1063–975.

Miller, J. (1997) Theoretical issues in cultural psychology. In J.W. Berry, Y.H. Poortinga and J. Pandey (eds) *Handbook of Cross-cultural Research, Vol. 1, Theory and Method*. Boston, MA: Allyn & Bacon.

Milton, J. (2005) Methodology. In J. Henry (ed.) *Parapsychology: Research on Exceptional Experience*. London: Routledge.

Milton, J. and Wiseman, R. (1999) Does psi exist? Lack of replication of an anomalous process of information transfer. *Psychological Bulletin, 125*, 387–91.

Milton, M. (1997) Roberto: Living with HIV. In S. du Plock (ed.) *Case Studies in existential psychotherapy and counselling*. Chichester: Wiley.

Mischel, W. (1968) *Personality and Assessment*. New York: Wiley.

Mischel, W. (1977) The interaction of person and situation. In D. Magnusson and N.S. Endler (eds) *Personality at the Crossroads: Current Issues in Interactional Psychology*. Hillsdale, NJ: Lawrence Erlbaum.

Mischel, W. (1983) Alternatives in the pursuit of the predictability and consistency of persons: stable data that yield unstable interpretations. *Journal of Personality, 51*, 578–604.

Moghaddam, F.M. (1998) *Social Psychology: Exploring Universals Across Cultures*. New York: W.H. Freeman & Co.

Moghaddam, F.M. (2005) *Great Ideas in Psychology*. Oxford: Oneworld Publications.

Moghaddam, F.M., Taylor, D.M. and Wright, S.C. (1993) *Social Psychology in Cross-Cultural Perspective*. New York: W.H. Freeman & Co.

Mohamed, C. (2000) Race, culture and ethnicity. In C. Feltham and I. Horton (eds) *Handbook of Counselling and Psychotherapy*. London: Sage.

Mollon, P. (2000) *Freud and False Memory Syndrome*. Cambridge: Icon Books.

Morea, P. (1990) *Personality: An Introduction to the Theories of Psychology*. Harmondsworth: Penguin.

Morris, R.L. (1989) Parapsychology. In A.M. Colman and J.G. Beaumont (eds) *Psychology Survey, 7*. Leicester: British Psychological Society.

Morris, R.L., Cunningham, S., McAlpine, S. and Taylor, R. (1993) Towards replication and extension of Ganzfeld results. In *The Parapsychological Association 36th Annual Convention: Proceedings of Presented Papers*. Durham, NC: Parapsychological Association.

Morris, R.L., Dalton, K., Delanoy, D.L. and Watt, C. (1995) Comparison of the sender/no sender condition in the Ganzfeld. In *The Parapsychological Association 38th Annual Convention: Proceedings of Presented Papers*. Durham, NC: Parapsychological Association.

Moscovici, S. (1985) Social influence and conformity. In G. Lindzey and E. Aronson (eds) *Handbook of Social Psychology* (3rd edn). New York: Random House.

Much (1995) Cultural psychology. In J.A. Smith, R. Harré and L. Van Langenhove (eds) *Rethinking Psychology*. London: Sage.

Murphy, J., John, M. and Brown, H. (1984) *Dialogues and Debates in Social Psychology*. London: Lawrence Erlbaum/Open University.

Murray, H.A. (1938) *Explorations in Personality*. New York: Oxford University Press.

Myers, D. (1994) *Exploring Social Psychology*. New York: McGraw-Hill.

Myers, D. (2000) *The American Paradox: Spiritual hunger in an age of plenty*. New Haven, CT: Yale University Press.

Nagel, T. (1974) What is it like to be a bat? *Philosophical Review, 83*, 435–50.

Naito, T., Wangwan, J. and Tani, M. (2005) *Journal of Cross-Cultural Psychology, 36*, 247–63.

New Scientist (2004) On the edge of the known world. *New Scientist, 181*(2438), 32–3.

Nicolson, P. (1995) Feminism and psychology. In J.A. Smith, R. Harré and L. Van Langenhove (eds) *Rethinking Psychology*. London: Sage.

Nisbett, R.E. and Ross, L. (1980) *Human Inference: Strategies and Shortcomings of Social Judgement*. Englewood Cliffs, NJ: Prentice Hall.

Nisbett, R.E. and Wilson, T.D. (1977) Telling more than we can know: verbal reports on mental processes. *Psychological Review, 84*, 231–59.

Norman, D. and Shallice, T. (1986) Attention to action: willed and automatic control of behavior. In R.J. Davidson, G.E. Schwartz and D. Shapiro (eds) *Consciousness and Self-regulation: Advances in Research and Theory*. New York: Plenum.

Nozick, R. (1974) *Anarchy, State, and Utopia*. New York: Basic Books.

Nye, D. (2000) *Three Psychologies: Perspectives from Freud, Skinner and Rogers* (6th edn). Belmont, CA: Wadsworth/Thomson Learning.

O'Donohue, W. and Ferguson, K.E. (2001) *The Psychology of B.F. Skinner*. Thousand Oaks, CA: Sage Publications.

Oakes, P.J., Haslam, S.A. and Turner, J.C. (1994) *Stereotyping and Social Reality*. Oxford: Blackwell.

Ochert, A. (1998) Madness becomes normal. *Psychology Review, 4*(4), back page.

Oishi, S., Dieiner, E. and Lucas, R.E. (2007) The Optimum Level of Well-Being: Can People be Too Happy? *Perspectives on Psychological Science, 2*, 346–60.

Olds, J. and Milner, P. (1954) Positive reinforcement produced by electrical stimulation of septal area and other regions of the rat brain. *Journal of Comparative & Physiological Psychology, 47*, 419–27.

Orne, M.T. (1962) On the social psychology of the psychological experiment – with particular reference to demand characteristics and their implications. *American Psychologist, 17*(11), 776–83.

Ornstein, R.E. (1975) *The Psychology of Consciousness*. Harmondsworth: Penguin.

Paludi, M.A. (1992) *The Psychology of Women*. Dubuque, Iowa: Wm C. Brown.

Park, N., Peterson, C. and Seligman, M. (2004) Strengths of character and well-being. *Journal of Social and Clinical Psychology, 23*, 603–19.

Parkin, A.J. (2000) *Essential Cognitive Psychology*. Hove: Psychology Press.

Parlee, M.B. (1991) Happy Birth-day to Feminism & Psychology. *Feminism & Psychology, 1*(1), 39–48.

Penfield, W. (1958) *The Excitable Cortex in Conscious Man*. Liverpool: Liverpool University Press.

Pennington, D. (2003) *Essential Personality*. London: Arnold.

Pervin, L.A. (1985) Personality: current controversies, issues and directions. *Annual Review of Psychology, 36*, 83–114.

Peterson, C. (2000) The future of optimism. *American Psychologist, 55*, 44–55.

Peterson C. and Seligman, M. (2003) Character strengths before and after September 11. *Psychological Science 14*(4), 381–4.

Peterson, C. and Seligman, M.E.P. (2004) *Character Strengths and Virtues: A handbook and classification*. Washington, DC: American Psychological Association.

Piaget, J. (1950) *The Psychology of Intelligence*. London: Routledge and Kegan Paul.

Pike, A. and Plomin, R. (1999) Genetics and development. In D. Messer and S. Millar (eds) *Exploring Developmental Psychology: From Infancy to Adolescence*. London: Arnold.

Pike, K.L. (1954) Emic and etic standpoints for the description of behavior. In K.L. Pike (ed.) *Language in Relation to a Unified Theory of the Structure of Human Behavior, Pt 1*. Glendale, CA: Summer Institute of Linguistics.

Pilgrim, D. (2000) Psychiatric diagnosis: More questions than answers. *The Psychologist, 13*(6), 302–5.

Pinel, J.P.J. (1993) Biopsychology (2nd edn). Boston: Allyn & Bacon.

Pinker, S. (1994) *The Language Instinct: How the Mind Creates Language*. New York: Morrow.

Pinker, S. (1997) Why they kill their newborns. *New York Times Magazine*, 2 November, 52–4.

Place, U.T. (1956) Is consciousness a brain process? *British Journal of Psychology, 47*, 44–51.

Plomin, R. (1994) *Genetics and Experience: The Interplay Between Nature and Nurture*. Thousand Oaks, CA: Sage.

Plomin, R. (1996) Nature and nurture. In M.R. Merrens and G.C. Brannigan (eds) *The Developmental Psychologists: Research Adventures across the Life Span*. New York: McGraw-Hill.

Plomin, R. (2001) Genetics and behavior. *The Psychologist, 14*(3), 134–9.

Plomin, R. and Rutter, M. (1998) Child development, molecular genetics and what to do with genes once they are found. *Child Development, 69*, 1221–40.

Plomin, R. and Thompson, R. (1987) Life-span developmental behavioral genetics. In P.B. Baltes, D.L. Featherman and R.M. Lerner (eds) *Life-Span Development and Behavior, Vol. 8*. Hillsdale, NJ: Erlbaum.

Plomin, R., DeFries, J.C. and Loehlin, J.C. (1977) Genotype-environment interaction and correlation in the analysis of human behavior. *Psychological Bulletin, 84*, 309–22.

Popper, K. (1959) *The Logic of Scientific Discovery*. London: Hutchinson.

Popper, K. (1972) *Objective Knowledge: An Evolutionary Approach*. Oxford: Oxford University Press.

Potter, J. (1996) Attitudes, social representations and discursive psychology. In M. Wetherell (ed.) *Identities, Groups and Social Issues*. London: Sage, in association with the Open University.

Power, M. (2000) Freud and the unconscious. *The Psychologist, 13*(12), 612–14.

Pressman, S.D. and Cohen, S. (2005) Does Positive Affect Influence Health? *Psychological Bulletin, 131*(6), 925–71.

Prince, J. and Hartnett, O. (1993) From 'psychology constructs the female' to 'females construct psychology'. *Feminism & Psychology, 3*(2), 219–24.

Rao, K.R. and Palmer, J. (1987) The anomaly called psi: recent research and criticism. *Behavioral & Brain Sciences, 10*, 539–643.

Rappaport, J. and Stewart, E. (1997) A Critical Look at Critical Psychology: Elaborating the Questions. In D. Fox and I. Prilleltensky (eds) *Critical Psychology: An Introduction*. London: Sage.

Reason, J. (2000) The Freudian slip revisited. *The Psychologist, 13*(12), 610–11.

Reason., P. and Rowan, J. (eds) (1981) *Human Inquiry: A Sourcebook of New Paradigm* Research. Chichester: Wiley.

Rhine, L.E. (1969) Case study review. *Journal of Parapsychology, 33*, 228–66.

Richards, G. (1996) Arsenic and old race. *Observer Review*, 5 May, 4.

Richards, G. (2002) *Putting Psychology in its Place: A Critical Historical Overview* (2nd edn). Hove: Routledge.

Riesen, A.H. (1947) The development of visual perception in man and chimpanzee. *Science, 106*, 107–8.

Roberts, R. (2001) Science and experience. In R. Roberts and D. Groome (eds) *Parapsychology: The Science of Unusual Experience*. London: Arnold.

Roberts, R. and Groome, D. (2001) Preamble. In R. Roberts and D. Groome (eds) *Parapsychology: The Science of Unusual Experience*. London: Arnold.

Rogers, C.R. (1951) *Client-centred Therapy: Its Current Practice, Implications and Theory*. Boston: Houghton-Mifflin.

Rogers, C.R. (1959) A theory of therapy, personality and interpersonal relationships as developed in the client-centred framework. In S. Koch (ed.) *Psychology: A Study of a Science, Vol. 3, Formulations of the Person and the Social Context*. New York: McGraw-Hill.

Rogers, C.R. (1961) *On Becoming a Person: A Therapist's View of Psychotherapy*. Boston: Houghton-Mifflin.

Rogers, C.R. (1983) *Freedom to Learn in the '80s*. Columbus, OH: Charles Merrill.

Rogers, C.R. and Dymond, R.F. (eds) (1954) *Psychotherapy and Personality Change: Co-ordinated Research Studies in the Client-Centred Approach*. Chicago: University of Chicago Press.

Rogoff, B. and Morelli, G. (1989) Perspectives on children's development from cultural psychology. *American Psychologist, 44*, 343–8.

Rorer, L.G. (1998) Attacking arrant nonsense forthrightly. *Contemporary Psychology, 43*, 597–600.

Rose, D. (2006) *Consciousness: Philosophical, Psychological and Neural Theories*. Oxford: Oxford University Press.

Rose, H. (2000) Colonising the social sciences? In H. Rose and S. Rose (eds) *Alas, Poor Darwin: Arguments Against Evolutionary Psychology*. London: Jonathan Cape.

Rose, H. and Rose, S. (eds) (2000) *Alas, Poor Darwin: Arguments Against Evolutionary Psychology*. London: Jonathan Cape.

Rose, H. and Rose, S. (2001) Much ado about very little. *The Psychologist, 14*(8), 428–9.

Rose, S. (1992) *The Making of Memory: From Molecules to Mind*. London: Bantam Books.

Rose, S. (1997) *Lifelines: Biology, Freedom, Determinism*. Harmondsworth: Penguin.

Rose, S. (2000) Escaping evolutionary psychology. In H. Rose and S. Rose (eds) *Alas, Poor Darwin: Arguments Against Evolutionary Psychology*. London: Jonathan Cape.

Rose, S. (2001) DNA is important – but only in its proper place. *The Psychologist, 14*(3), 144-5.

Rose, S. (2003) *The Making of Memory: From Molecules to Mind* (revised edn). London: Vintage.

Rose, S. (2005) *The 21st Century Brain: Explaining, Mending and Manipulating the Mind*. London: Vintage Books.

Rose, S., Lewontin, R.C. and Kamin, L.J. (1984) *Not in Our Genes: Biology, Ideology and Human Nature*. Harmondsworth: Penguin.

Rosenhan, D.L. and Seligman, M.E.P. (1989) *Abnormal Psychology* (2nd edn). New York: Norton.

Rosenthal, D. (1966) *Experimenter Effects in Behavioral Research*. New York: Appleton-Century-Crofts.

Rosenthal, D. and Jacobson, L. (1968) *Pygmalion in the Classroom: Teacher Expectation and Pupils' Intellectual Development*. New York: Holt, Rinehart & Winston.

Ross, L. (1977) The intuitive psychologist and his shortcomings. In L. Berkowitz (ed.) *Advances in Experimental Social Psychology, Vol. 10*. New York: Academic Press.

Ross, L. and Nisbett, R.E. (1991) *The Person and the Situation: Perspectives of Social Psychology*. New York: McGraw-Hill.

Rotter, J. (1966) Generalized expectancies for internal versus external control of reinforcements. *Psychological Monographs, 30*(1), 1–26.

Rowan, J. (2001) *Ordinary Ecstasy: The dialectics of humanistic psychology* (3rd edn). Hove: Brunner-Routledge.

Rubin, Z. and McNeil, E.B. (1983) *The Psychology of Being Human* (3rd edn). London: Harper & Row.

Ruch, J.C. (1984) *Psychology: The Personal Science*. Belmont, CA: Wadsworth Publishing Co.

Rumelhart, D.E., Hinton, G.E. and McClelland, J.L. (1986) A general framework for parallel distributed processing. In D. Rumelhart, J.L. McClelland and the PDP Research Group (eds) *Parallel Distributed Processing: Vol. 1 Foundations*. Cambridge, MA: MIT Press.

Rushton, J.P. (1995) *Race, Evolution and Behavior*. New Brunswick, NJ: Transaction Publishers.

Rutter, M. and Rutter, M. (1992) *Developing Minds: Challenge and Continuity across the Life Span*. Harmondsworth: Penguin.

Ryan, R.M. and Deci, E.L. (2000) Self-determination theory and the facilitation of intrinsic motivation, social development, and well-being. *American Psychologist, 55*, 68–78.

Ryan, R.M. and Deci, E.L. (2001) On happiness and human potentials: A review of research on hedonic and eudaimonic well-being. *Annual Review of Psychology, 52*, 141–66.

Rycroft, C. (1966) Introduction: causes and meaning. In C. Rycroft (ed.) *Psychoanalysis Observed*. London: Constable.

Ryder, R. (1990) Open reply to Jeffrey Gray. *The Psychologist, 3*, 403.

Ryle, G. (1949) *The Concept of Mind*. London: Hutchinson.

Salmon, P. (2003) How do we recognize good research? *The Psychologist, 16*(1), 24–7.

Salovey, P., Rothman, A.J., Detweiler, J.B. and Stewart, W.T. (2000) Emotional states and physical health. *American Psychologist, 55*, 110–21.

Sarbin, T.R. (1986) The narrative as a root metaphor for psychology. In T.R. Sarbin (ed.) *Narrative Psychology: The Storied Nature of Human Conduct*. New York: Praeger.

Scarr, S. (1992) Developmental theories for the 1990s: development and individual differences. *Child Development, 63*, 1–19.

Schank, R.C. and Abelson, R.P. (1977) *Scripts, Plans, Goals, and Understanding*. Hillsdale, NJ: Lawrence Erlbaum.

Scheff, T.J. (1966) *Being Mentally Ill: A Sociological Theory*. Chicago: Aldine Press.

Schlitz, M.J. and Honorton, C. (1992) Ganzfeld psi performance within an artistically gifted population. *Journal of the American Society for Psychical Research, 86*, 83–98.

Schneider, K. (1959) *Clinical Psychopathology*. New York: Grune & Stratton.

Schneider, S. and Velmans, M. (2007) Introduction. In M. Velmans and S. Schneider (eds) *The Blackwell Companion to Consciousness*. Oxford: Blackwell Publishing.

Schwartz, D. (2000) Self-determination: The tyranny of freedom. *American Psychologist, 55*, 79–88.

Scodel, A. (1957) Heterosexual somatic preference and fantasy dependence. *Journal of Consulting Psychology, 21*, 371–4.

Searle, J.R. (1980) Minds, brains and programs. *Behavioral & Brain Sciences, 3*, 417–24.

Searle, J.R. (1992) *The Rediscovery of the Mind*. Cambridge, MA: MIT Press.

Searle, J.R. (1997) *The Mystery of Consciousness*. NYREV, Inc.

Searle, J.R. (2007) Biological Naturalism. In M. Velmans and S. Schneider (eds) *The Blackwell Companion to Consciousness*. Oxford: Blackwell Publishing.

Segall, M.H., Dasen, P.R., Berry, J.W. and Poortinga, Y.H. (1990) *Human Behavior in Global Perspective: An Introduction to Cross-Cultural Psychology*. New York: Pergamon.

Segall, M.H., Dasen, P.R., Berry, J.W. and Poortinga, Y.H. (1999) *Human Behavior in Global Perspective: An Introduction to Cross-Cultural Psychology* (2nd edn). Needham Heights, MA: Allyn & Bacon.

Seligman, M.E.P. (1974) Depression and learned helplessness. In R.J. Friedman and M.M. Katz (eds) *The Psychology of Depression: Contemporary Theory and Research*. Washington, DC: Winston-Wiley.

Seligman, M.E.P. (1999) The President's Address. *American Psychologist, 54,* 559–62.

Seligman, M.E.P. (2003) Positive psychology: Fundamental assumptions. *The Psychologist, 16*(3), 126–7.

Seligman, M.E.P., Abramson, L.Y., Semmel, A. and Von Beyer, C. (1979) Depressive attributional style. *Journal of Abnormal Psychology*, 88, 242–7.

Seligman, M.E.P. and Csikszentmihalyi, M. (2000) Positive Psychology: an introduction. *American Psychologist, 55,* 5–14.

Seligman, M.E.P., Steen, T.A., Park, N. and Peterson, C. (2005) Positive psychology progress: Empirical validation of interventions. *American Psychologist, 60,* 410–21.

Serpell, R. (1982) Measures of perception, skills and intelligence: the growth of a new perspective on children in a Third World country. In W. Hartrup (ed.) *Review of Child Development Research, Vol. 6*. Chicago: University of Chicago Press.

Shannon, C.E. and Weaver, W. (1949) *The Mathematical Theory of Communication*. Urbana, Ill.: University of Illinois Press.

Shaver, K.G. (1987) *Principles of Social Psychology* (3rd edn). Hillsdale, NJ: Lawrence Erlbaum.

Sheehy, N. (2008) Abraham Harold Maslow. *Psychology Review, 13* (4), 14–15.

Sheldon, , K.M. and King, L. (2001) Why positive psychology is necessary. *American Psychologist, 56,* 216–17.

Sherif, M., Harvey, O.J., White, B.J., Hood, W.R. and Sherif, C.W. (1961) *Intergroup Conflict and Co-operation: The Robber's Cave Experiment*. Norman, OK: University of Oklahoma Press.

Shiffrin, R.M. and Schneider, W. (1977) Controlled and automatic human information processing: II – perceptual learning, automatic attending and a general theory. *Psychological Review, 84,* 127–90.

Shotter, J. (1975) *Images of Man in Psychological Research*. London: Methuen.

Shotter, J. (1991) The rhetorical-responsive nature of mind. A social constructionist account. In A. Still and A. Costall (eds) *Against Cognitivism: Alternative Foundations for Cognitive Psychology*. Hemel Hempstead: Harvester Wheatsheaf.

Shotter, J. (1992) 'Getting in touch': the meta-methodology of a postmodern science of mental life. In S. Kvale (ed.) *Psychology and Postmodernism*. London: Sage.

Shotter, J. and Gergen, K.G. (eds) (1989) *Texts of Identity*. London: Sage.

Shweder, R.A. (1990) Cultural psychology – what is it? In J.W. Stigler, R.A. Shweder and G. Herdt (eds) *Cultural Psychology*. New York: Cambridge University Press.

Singer, P. (1993) The rights of ape. *BBC Wildlife Magazine, 11*(6), 28–32.

Singer, P. and Cavalieri, P. (eds) (1993) *The Great Ape Project: Equality beyond Humanity*. London: Fourth Estate.

Skinner, B.F. (1948) *Walden Two*. New York: Macmillan.

Skinner, B.F. (1971) *Beyond Freedom and Dignity*. New York: Knopf.

Skinner, B.F. (1974) *About Behaviorism*. New York: Knopf.

Skinner, B.F. (1986) Is it behaviorism? *Behavioral & Brain Sciences, 9*, 716.

Slee, P. and Shute, R. (2003) *Child Development: Thinking About Theories*. London: Arnold.

Smart, J.J.C. (1959) Sensations and brain processes. *The Philosophical Review, 68*, 141–56.

Smith, C.U.M. (1994) You are a group of neurons. *The Times Higher Educational Supplement*, 27 May, 20–1.

Smith, J.A. and Osborn, N. (2003) Interpretative phenomenological analysis. In J.A. Smith (ed.) *Qualitative Psychology: A Practical Guide to Research Methods*. London: Sage Publications.

Smith, P.B. and Bond, M.H. (1993) *Social Psychology across Cultures: Analysis and Perspectives*. Hemel Hempstead: Harvester Wheatsheaf.

Smith, P.B. and Bond, M.H. (1998) *Social Psychology across Cultures* (2nd edn). Hemel Hempstead: Prentice Hall Europe.

Smith, P.K. and Cowie, H. (1991) *Understanding Children's Development* (2nd edn). Oxford: Blackwell.

Snyder, M. (1987) *Public Appearances/Private Realities: The Psychology of Self-monitoring*. New York: W.H. Freeman.

Snyder, M. and Ickes, W. (1985) Personality and social behavior. In G. Lindzey and E. Aronson (eds) *Handbook of Social Psychology, Vol. 2* (3rd edn). New York: Random House.

Soal, S.G. and Bateman, F. (1954) *Modern Experiments in Telepathy*. London: Faber & Faber.

Soyland, A.J. (1994) *Psychology as Metaphor*. London: Sage.

Spearman, C. (1904) General intelligence objectively determined and measured. *American Journal of Psychology, 15*, 210–93.

Spearman, C. (1927) The doctrine of two factors. Reprinted in S. Wiseman (ed.) *Intelligence and Ability*. Harmondsworth: Penguin.

Stephenson, W. (1953) *The Study of Behavior: Q-technique and its Methodology*. Chicago: Chicago University Press.

Stern, W. (1921) *Die differentielle Psychologie in ihren methodologischen Grundlagen* (3rd edn). Leipzig: Barth.

Stevens, R. (1995) Freudian theories of personality. In S.E. Hampson and A.M. Colman (eds) *Individual Differences and Personality*. London: Longman.

Strachey, J. (1962–1977) Sigmund Freud: a sketch of his life and ideas. (This appears in each volume of the Pelican Freud Library; originally written for the *Standard Edition of the Complete Psychological Works of Sigmund Freud*. London: Hogarth Press.)

Sue, S. (1995) Implications of the bell curve: whites are genetically inferior in intelligence? *Focus: Notes from the Society for the Psychological Study of Ethnic Minority Issues*, 16–17.

Sulloway, F.J. (1979) *Freud, Biologist of the Mind: Beyond the Psychoanalytic Legend*. New York: Basic Books.

Sumner, L.W. (1996) *Welfare, happiness and ethics*. New York: Oxford University Press.

Targ, R. and Puthoff, H. (1974) Information transmission under conditions of sensory shielding. *Nature, 251*, 602–7.

Targ, R. and Puthoff, H. (1977) *Mind-reach*. New York: Delacorte.

Tasker, F. (2002) Lesbian and gay parenting. In A. Coyle and C. Kitzinger (eds) *Lesbian and Gay Psychology: New Perspectives*. BPS/Blackwell.

Tavris, C. (1993) The mismeasure of woman. *Feminism & Psychology, 3*(2), 149–68.

Taylor, G. (2002) Psychopathology and the social and historical construction of gay male identities. In A. Coyle and C. Kitzinger (eds) *Lesbian and Gay Psychology: New Perspectives*. BPS/Blackwell.

Taylor, R. (1963) *Metaphysics*. Englewood Cliffs, NJ: Prentice Hall.

Taylor, R. (2000) The Singer revolution. *Philosophy Now*, 28, August/September, 10–13.

Taylor, S.E., Kemeny, M.E., Reed, G.M., Bower, J.E. and Gruenwald, T.L. (2000) Psychological resources, positive illusions, and health. *American Psychologist, 55*, 99–109.

Tedeschi, R.G., Park, C.L. and Calhoun, L.G. (eds) (1998) *Posttraumatic growth: Positive changes in the aftermath of crisis*. Mahwah, NJ: Lawrence Erlbaum.

Teichman, J. (1988) *Philosophy and the Mind*. Oxford: Blackwell.

Thibaut, J.W. and Kelley, H.H. (1959) *The Social Psychology of Groups*. New York: Wiley.

Thomas, K. (1990) Psychodynamics: the Freudian approach. In I. Roth (ed.) *Introduction to Psychology, Vol. 1*. Hove, East Sussex/Milton Keynes: Open University/Lawrence Erlbaum.

Thomas, G.V. and Blackman, D. (1991) Are animal experiments on the way out? *The Psychologist, 4*(5), 208–12.

Thomas, R.M. (1985) *Comparing Theories of Child Development* (2nd edn). Belmont, CA: Wadsworth Publishing Co.

Thorndike, E.L. (1898) Animal intelligence: an experimental study of the associative processes in animals. *Psychological Review Monograph Supplement 2* (whole No. 8).

Thorne, B. (1992) *Carl Rogers*. London: Sage.

Thurstone, L.L. (1938) Primary mental abilities. *Psychometric Monographs, 1*.

Tolman, E.C. (1948) Cognitive maps in rats and man. *Psychological Review, 55*, 189–208.

Tooby, J. and Cosmides, L. (1992) The psychological foundations of culture. In J.H. Barkow, L. Cosmides and J. Tooby (eds) *The Adapted Mind: Evolutionary Psychology and the Evolution of Culture*. New York: Oxford University Press.

Torrance, S. (1986) Breaking out of the Chinese room. In M. Yazdani (ed.) *Artificial Intelligence: Principles and Applications*. London: Chapman & Hall.

Trevena, J.A. and Miller, J. (2002) Cortical movement preparation before and after a conscious decision to move. *Consciousness and Cognition, 11*, 162–90.

Triandis, H.C. (1972) *The Analysis of Subjective Culture*. New York: Wiley.

Triandis, H.C. (1980) Introduction. In H.C. Triandis and W.E. Lambert (eds) *Handbook of Cross-Cultural Psychology: Vol. 1. Perspectives*. Boston: Allyn & Bacon.

Triandis, H.C. (1990) Theoretical concepts that are applicable to the analysis of ethnocentrism. In R.W. Brislin (ed.) *Applied Cross-Cultural Psychology*. Newbury Park, CA: Sage.

Triandis, H.C., Kashima, Y., Shimada, E. and Villareal, M. (1986) Acculturation indices as a means of conforming cultural differences. *International Journal of Psychology, 21*, 43–70.

Triandis, H.C., Leung, K., Villareal, M. and Clack, F.L. (1985) Allocentric vs idiocentric tendencies: convergent and discriminant validation. *Journal of Research in Personality, 19*, 395–415.

Turner, J.C. (1991) *Social Influence*. Milton Keynes: Open University Press.

Turney, J. (1999) Human nature totally explained. *The Times Higher*, 12 March, 18.

Tyerman, A. and Spencer, C. (1983) A critical test of the Sherifs' Robber's Cave experiment: intergroup competition and cooperation between groups of well-acquainted individuals. *Small Group Behavior*, *14*(4), 515–31.

Ullman, M., Krippner, S. and Vaughan, A. (1973) *Dream Telepathy*. New York: Macmillan.

Unger, R.K. (1979) *Female and Male: Psychological Perspectives*. New York: Harper & Row.

Unger, R.K. (1984) Sex in psychological paradigms – from behavior to cognition. *Imagination, Cognition & Personality, 3*, 227–34.

Unger, R.K. (1993) The personal is paradoxical: feminists construct psychology. *Feminism & Psychology, 3*(2), 211–18.

Utts, J. (1991) Replication and meta-analysis in parapsychology. *Statistical Science, 6*, 363–403.

Utts, J. and Josephson, B.D. (1996) Do you believe in psychic phenomena? Are they likely to be able to explain consciousness? *The Times Higher*, 5 April, v.

Vaillant, G. (2000) The mature defences: Antecedents of joy. *American Psychologist, 55*, 89–98.

Valentine, E.R. (1992) *Conceptual Issues in Psychology* (2nd edn). London: Routledge.

Veenhoven, R. (2003) Happiness. *The Psychologist, 16*(3), 128–9.

Velmans, M. (1991) Intersubjective science. *Journal of Consciousness Studies, 6*(2/3), 299–306.

Velmans, M. (2000) *Understanding Consciousness*. Florence, KY: Taylor and Francis/Routledge.

Velmans, M. (2002) How could conscious experiences affect brains? *Journal of Consciousness Studies, 9*, 3–29.

Velmans, M. (2003) Preconscious free will. *Journal of Consciousness Studies, 10*(12), 42–61.

Vernon, P.E. (1950) *The Structure of Human Abilities*. London: Methuen.

Wachtel, P. (1977) *Psychoanalysis and Behavior Therapy: Toward an Integration*. New York: Basic Books.

Wachtel, P. (1997) *Psychoanalysis, behavior therapy, and the relational world*. Washington, DC: American Psychological Association.

Wade, C. and Tavris, C. (1990) *Psychology* (2nd edn). New York: Harper & Row.

Watson, J.B. (1913) Psychology as the behaviorist views it. *Psychological Review, 20*, 158–77.

Watson, J.B. (1928) *Behaviorism*. Chicago: University of Chicago Press.

Watt, C. (2001) Paranormal Cognition. In R. Roberts and D. Groome (eds) *Parapsychology: The Science of Unusual Experience*. London: Arnold.

Weiner, B. (1972) *Theories of Motivation: From Mechanism to Cognition*. Chicago: Rand McNally.

Weiner, B. (1992) *Human Motivation: Metaphors, Theories and Research*. Newbury Park, CA: Sage.

Weiskrantz, L. (1986) *Blindsight: A Case Study and Implications*. Oxford: Clarendon Press.

Weiskrantz, L. (2007) The case of blindsight. In M. Velmans and S. Schneider (eds) *The Blackwell Companion to Consciousness*. Oxford: Blackwell Publishing.

Weiskrantz, L., Warrington, M.D., Sanders, M.D. and Marshall, J. (1974) Visual capacity in the hemianopic field following a restricted occipital ablation. *Brain, 97*, 709–28.

Weisstein, N. (1993a) Psychology constructs the female, or, The fantasy life of the male psychologist (with some attention to the fantasies of his friends, the male biologist and the male anthropologist [this is a revised/expanded version of 'Kinder, Kuche, Kirche as scientific law: psychology constructs the female', 1971]. *Feminism & Psychology*, *3*(2), 195–210.

Weisstein, N. (1993b) Power, resistance and science: a call for a revitalized feminist psychology. *Feminism & Psychology*, *3*(2), 239–45.

Wellman, H.M. (1990) *The Child's Theory of Mind*. Cambridge, MA: MIT Press.

Werner, E.E. (1989) Children of the Garden Island. *Scientific American*, April, 106 11.

Wetherell, M. (1996) Group conflict and the social psychology of racism. In M. Wetherell (ed.) *Identities, Groups and Social Issues*. London: Sage, in association with the Open University.

Wetherell, M. and Maybin, J. (1996) The distributed self. In R. Stevens (ed.) *Understanding the Self*. London: Sage.

Wetherell, M. and Still, A. (1996) Realism and relativism. In R. Sapsford (ed.) *Issues for Social Psychology*. Milton Keynes: Open University Press.

Wilkinson, S. (1989) The impact of feminist research: issues of legitimacy. *Philosophical Psychology*, *2*(3), 261–9.

Wilson, E.O. (1975) *Sociobiology: The New Synthesis*. Cambridge, MA: Harvard University Press.

Wilson, E.O. (1978) *On Human Nature*. Cambridge, MA: Harvard University Press.

Wilson, G.T., O'Leary, K.D., Nathan, P.E. and Clark, L.A. (1996) *Abnormal Psychology: Integrating Perspectives*. Needham Heights, MA: Alyn & Bacon.

Winnicott, D.W. (1958) *Through Paediatrics to Psychoanalysis*. London: Hogarth Press.

Wise, R. (2000) *Rattling the Cage: Towards Legal Rights for Animals*. London: Profile Books.

Wiseman, R. (2001) The psychology of psychic fraud. In R. Roberts and D. Groome (eds) *Parapsychology: The Science of Unusual Experience*. London: Arnold.

Wober, M. (1974) Towards an understanding of the Kiganda concept of intelligence. In J.W. Berry and P.R. Dasen (eds) *Culture and Cognition*. London: Methuen.

Wood, A., Joseph. S. and Linley, A. (2007) Gratitude – Parent of all virtues. *The Psychologist*, *20*(1), 18–21.

World Health Organization (1973) *Report of the International Pilot Study of Schizophrenia, Vol. 1*. Geneva: WHO.

World Health Organization (1979) *Schizophrenia: An International Follow-up Study*. London: Wiley.

Wright, J.C. and Mischel, W. (1988) Conditions of hedges and the intuitive psychology of traits. *Journal of Personality & Social Psychology*, *55*, 454–69.

Wundt, W. (1974 [1874]) *Grundzuge der physiologischen Psychologie*. Leipzig: Engelmann.

Zebrowitz, L.A. (1990) *Social Perception*. Milton Keynes: Open University Press.

Zeldow, P.B. (1995) Psychodynamic formulations of human behavior. In D. Wedding (ed.) *Behavior and Medicine* (2nd edn). St Louis, MO: Mosby Year Book.

Zimbardo, P. (1973) On the ethics of intervention in human psychological research with special reference to the 'Stanford Prison Experiment'. *Cognition*, *2*(2, Pt 1), 243–55.

Zimbardo, P. (1992) *Psychology and Life* (13th edn). New York: HarperCollins.

INDEX

Note: page numbers in **bold** refer to figures and information contained in tables.

THEMES, ISSUES AND DEBATES IN PSYCHOLOGY